FREEDOM BY A THREAD

FREEDOM BY A THREAD

THE HISTORY OF QUILOMBOS IN BRAZIL

Edited by

JOÃO JOSÉ REIS AND FLÁVIO DOS SANTOS GOMES

DIASPORIC AFRICA PRESS, INC.
NEW YORK

This book is a publication of

DIASPORIC AFRICA PRESS

NEW YORK | WWW.DAFRICAPRESS.COM

Liberdade por um fio: História dos Quilombos no Brasil © Companhia das Letras 1996

English translation © Diasporic Africa Press 2016

All rights reserved. No part of this publication may be reproduced or distributed in any form or by any means, or stored in a database or retrieval system, without the prior written permission of the publisher.

Library of Congress Control Number: 2014938292

ISBN-13 978-1-937306-31-1 (pbk.: alk paper)

Obra publicada com o apoio do Ministério da Cultura do Brasil / Fundação Biblioteca Nacional

Work published with the support of the Brazilian Ministry of Culture / National Library Foundation

CONTENTS

Acknowledgments 1

1. Introduction: A History of Freedom 3
2. Palmares: A Rebel Polity through Archaeological Lenses / *Pedro Paulo A Funari and Aline Vieira de Carvalho* 19
3. Refiguring Palmares / *Richard Price* 43
4. God against Palmares: Lordly Representations and Jesuitical Ideas / *Ronaldo Vainfas* 51
5. From Singular To Plural: Palmares, Capitães-Do-Mato, and the Slave Government / *Silvia Hunold Lara* 72
6. St. Anthony, the Divine Capitão-Do-Mato / *Luiz Mott* 94
7. Mining, Quilombos, and Palmares: Minas Gerais in the Eighteenth Century / *Carlos Magno Guimarães* 121
8. The Quilombo and the Slave System in Eighteenth Century Minas Gerais / *Donald Ramos* 144
9. Violence in Frontier Lands / *Laura de Mello e Souza* 169
10. Quilombos in Mato Grosso: Black Resistance in a Border Area / *Luiza Rios Ricci Volpato* 179
11. The Quilombos of Gold in the Captaincy of Goiás / *Mary Karasch* 203
12. Quilombos of Rio De Janeiro in the Nineteenth Century / *Flávio dos Santos Gomes* 223
13. Black Plains: Quilombos in Rio Grande do Sul / *Mário Maestri* 248
14. Slaves and the Coiteiros in the Quilombo of Oitizeiro, Bahia, 1806 / *João José Reis* 288
15. Cantos and Quilombos in a Hausa Rebellion in Bahia, 1814 / *Stuart B. Schwartz* 326
16. The Quilombo of Malunguinho, the King of the Forest of Pernambuco / *Marcus Joaquim M. Carvalho* 344

17. Quilombos in the Province of Maranhão, Brazil / *Matthias Röhrig Assunção* 367

18. "I was Born in the Forest; I've Never Had an Owner": History and Memory of the Mocambo Communities in the Low Amazon Rainforest / *Eurípedes A. Funes* 399

    Appendix: The Map of Buraco do Tatu (The Armadillo Hole) 428

    Notes 432

ACKNOWLEDGMENTS

João Reis and Flávio Gomes would like to thank the History departments of the Federal University of Bahia (UFBA) and Pará (UFPA), the Masters program in History of UFBA and the National Council for Scientific and Technological Development (CNPq), for having supported this project in various ways. We are also grateful for the openness with which authors of the chapters published here received the commentaries and for the promptness with which they addressed the solicited revisions. Our thanks also go to the managers and employees of the Geographic and Historic Institute of Bahia, the Public Archive of the State of Bahia, and the UFBA Center for Bahian Studies, for having allowed and facilitated photographic reproductions of rare books and documents that are part of their collections. The photographer Bauer Sá is responsible for these reproductions.

João Reis would like to express his gratitude to Princeton University's History Department, which, during the months of March and April of 1995, provided him with ideal working conditions for the preparation of this book.

The editors thank each other for the mutual and conflict-free intellectual collaboration that has strengthened their bond of friendship. We would also like to thank the following individuals who helped with this English translation of the original Portuguese: Carla Beatriz Melo, Isis Costa McElroy, Laurelann Porter, Jonathan Michael Square, and Kristy Johnson. Finally, we thank the publisher, Diasporic Africa Press, for making this important volume available to an English-speaking audience.

—*João José Reis*
Flávio dos Santos Gomes

The period texts cited in this work, originating from the most diverse sources, presented inconsistencies and inaccuracies in ways of writing. Based on the understanding that keeping the original format would not have contributed to the substance of the work, and given the goal of facilitating reading, the editors of this book have updated the language in accordance to the following orientation: vocabulary, construction and capitalization were kept as in the original; punctuation and spelling were corrected according to current standards. As for Portuguese currency used in Brazil, readers can easily use this example: 530$380 *réis*, for instance, can be read as five hundred and thirty thousand, three hundred and eighty *réis*. The editors have also allowed the contributors to this volume to pursue their own style of writing and documentation, though most have used standards well known in the historical profession.

I

INTRODUCTION

A HISTORY OF FREEDOM

João José Reis and Flávio dos Santos Gomes

The enslavement of Africans in the Americas consumed the lives of around fifteen million or more men and women who were ripped away from their land. The slave trade through the Atlantic was one of the greatest commercial and cultural enterprises marking the foundation of the modern world and the establishment of a global economic system. Brazil's participation in the tragic venture was enormous. It is estimated that close to 40 percent of the African slaves came to Brazil. Here, in spite of the intensive use of indigenous work force,[1] it was the Africans and their descendants who constituted the main labor force for over three hundred years of slavery. Slavery penetrated every aspect of Brazilian life. In addition to setting sugar mills, farms, mines, plantations, factories, kitchens and large halls into motion, the slaves from Africa and their descendants made their mark upon various other aspects of material and spiritual life in this country, its agriculture, culinary, religion, language, music, arts, architecture, etc. The list is long and we are already tired of hearing it.

Where there was slavery there was resistance—a struggle that took on many forms. Even under the threat of the whip, slaves either negotiated spaces of autonomy with the slave masters or played lazy at work, broke tools, set fire to plantations, attacked slave masters and overseers, or rebelled individually and collectively. Here too, the list is long and well known. There was, however, a type of resistance that could be characterized as most typical of slavery and of other forms of forced labor: the escape and formation of communities of runaway slaves. Yet, it is important to remember that escape not always led to the establishment of such groups. Escape could be executed both individually and in groups, but slaves eventually would seek to disappear behind the anonymity of the mass of enslaved and freed black people. In these cases, their destiny could be the cities, where the circulation of men and women of various skin tones was not unfamiliar. In fact, they came to constitute considerable portions of the free population and even became a majority in some regions.

Escapes that led to the formation of runaway slave groups, often joined by other social characters, took place in the Americas where slavery thrived. These groups had different names: in Spanish America: *Palenques, cumbes,* etc.; in the English: *Maroons*; in the French: *Grand maroonage* (to differentiate from the *petit maroonage*, the individual escape, generally temporary). In Brazil, these groups were mainly called *quilombos* and *mocambos* and its members, *quilombolas, calhambolas* or *mocambeiros*.

The phenomenon of quilombo-formation has been heavily studied across the American continent, yet the quality and quantity of the studies vary from place to place. For instance, some of the most studied are the quilombos of Jamaica and Suriname, which were able to celebrate peace treaties with the colonial powers, acquiring a dose of autonomy, allowing them to survive to the present day. Because they were able to constitute themselves as relatively independent communities, it was possible to study these quilombos "from the inside," that is, through oral sources and the surviving memory of its descendants.[2] We can assert that this memory has not been totally erased in Brazil, once we consider the communities called "remnant *quilombos*" which are actually able to trace their past to the groupings constituted prior to the abolition of slavery in 1888.[3] In this volume, this is the case of the chapter written by Eurípedes Funes, which is largely based upon memories of remnant quilombolas from the state of Pará. Yet, unfortunately, the study of the majority of quilombos in the Americas and in Brazil, in particular, depends exclusively upon reports written by foreigners, and often by members of repressive forces. Nonetheless, even though the history told by these sources is problematic—as Richard Price has demonstrated so well while comparing and examining divergences and agreements between documents from the Dutch colonizers and the oral tradition of the *Saramaka*—the researcher should not give up investigating the history of quilombos. For the historian, the most sensitive approach is to follow basic guidelines to read documents critically, identify circumstances and intentions of scribes and what can be read between the lines, and to explore small evidences, as one attempts to hear the silences. At last, it is advisable not to be misled by documents that articulate the voices of repression, but rather to use them as weapons that may open the path towards a history of runaway slaves.

Nonetheless, the problems regarding sources are only one of the obstacles. There are theoretical and methodological issues that may be even more crucial—issues related to themes, which we could call "classical" in the approach towards the given phenomena. Among these themes we could list: The conditions that stimulate escape and the constitution of quilombos, such as the nature of relations within the slavery system and a geography that facilitates the installation and defense of fugitive communities; the defense tactics and repression of quilombos; the demography, economy, society and the structures of power inside quilombos; the relations of the quilombos with the society around them (combining various previous aspects); the type of society and culture created by quilombos and the continuities and ruptures with experiences brought from Africa. When we say that this last aspect synthesizes the issue discussed as a whole, we place ourselves at the heart of a discussion that has permeated every study about quilombos in the Americas and particularly in Brazil.

The list of authors that have studied Brazilian *quilombos*, especially that of Palmares, is quite long.[4] As shown by Silvia Lara in this volume, colonial essayists had foregrounded the quilombola resistance and the difficulties in eradicating them as early as the end of the seventeenth century. Even so, this mode of slave struggle was emphasized in their writings mainly in order to extol the colonial authorities that repressed it. Palmares and other quilombos would become brief chapters in Brazil's military history. In spite of some important contributions, this treatment barely changed until the nineteenth century.[5]

More systematic reflections related to quilombos would appear in Afro-Brazilian studies in the 1930s. Generally speaking, following the foundational studies of Nina Rodriguez at the turn of the century, Arthur Ramos and Edison Carneiro furthered its interpretations through a cultural studies lens. At a later time, Roger Bastide took on this task. According to this current of thought, the social organization of quilombolas was identified with a counter-acculturation effort and as a resistance to the European acculturation of those living in the slave quarters. R. K. Kent, a North American Africanist, followed some clear clues left by Nina Rodrigues and Edison Carneiro, as he sought to redefine Palmares as a true African state in Brazil. This is the vision of quilombo as a restoration project, in the sense that the fugitives sought to restore Africa on this other side of the Atlantic. An interpretation that holds a restoration perspective can also be found in Eugene Genovese's important study on slave rebellions in the Americas. Many times, inadvertently, these authors have inspired a popular conception of quilombos as isolated and isolationist communities whose intention was to recreate a pure Africa in the Americas. They would be a type of alternative society to the slavery-based one, where everyone would be free and possibly equal, just as they would have been in a considerably romanticized Africa.[6]

In spite of the effort of some authors to document the social and cultural syncretism developed in quilombos since Palmares, there remains in these readings a basic impulse to locate Africanism or African survivals—a method that became internationally successful as a result of Melville Herskovits'[7] studies of Afro-American cultures. To balance this out, we suggest that it would be more productive to investigate how quilombolas kept on living in their havens with rhythm and means that were rather distinct from the formation of an Afro-Brazilian society that had begun in the slave quarters. Institutions and, above all, worldviews brought by Africans (who were not simply a blank slate upon which slave master, government and colonial church inscribed their desires for domination), performed a fundamental contribution to the creation of this new society. Cultural exchange and social alliances were intensely forged among Africans themselves, originating from diverse African regions, in addition to, of course, those born from the relations that were developed with the local black, white, indigenous and mixed race inhabitants. This process took place all around, following rhythms and generating combinations that varied across the territorial immensity of an enslaving Brazil. And above all, it is towards this process of building new institutions, cultures and social relations that the scholar should turn, so that s/he may discover why quilombolas and slaves in general chose to keep certain aspects of their African origins over others while Africanizing their new world and renewing whatever they could carry from the old Africa.[8] And to better understand this process, we believe that it is important that the slavery historian, and in particular, those focusing on slave rebellions, investigate the history of Africans prior to the Atlantic crossing.

Since the end of the 1950s, studies on slave rebellion have gained popularity, first in parallel to the expansion of left movements and, in a following moment, to the rise of black movements. We are not saying that left and black militants had neither reflected upon nor been inspired by slave rebellions prior to that date. Palmares itself had been memorialized during the formation of black organizations in the 1920s and 1930s, one of which, the Palmares Civic Center, founded in 1927, provided leaders and ideas to the Brazilian Black Front (Frente Negra Brasileira) in the following decade. At the same time, Marxist intellectuals of that period, such as Aderbal Jurema, wrote about slave rebellions as episodes of Brazil's class struggle. And we should not forget the connection of Edison Carneiro, an expert on Palmares, with the Brazilian Communist Party—which led to his persecution. He found refuge in the *candomblé* spiritual center *Axé Opô Afonjá,* presided by his friend, the famous high priestess, *dona* Aninha. In fact, we can assert that the mixed-race socialist Edison Carneiro practiced a double militancy, in the left and in the black movement, as his engagement against racism and the persecution of *candomblé* spiritual centers attest.[9]

In Clóvis Moura's *Rebeliões da senzala* (*Slave Quarters' Rebellions*), originally published in 1959 by Zumbi Press, *quilombos* were revisited from a more strictly Marxist perspective. Rich in empirical material gathered from printed sources, the book came out during a moment in which various scholars—the most well known of them being those connected to the University of São Paulo—placed great effort on combating an old idea systematized by Gilberto Freyre in the early 1930s: the conception that Brazil's slavery relations had been generally harmonious. But if in the revisionist analyses of the so-called "Paulista School"—formed by Florestan Fernandes, Fernando Henrique Cardoso, Octavio Ianni—the slave resistance was placed as second priority in order to highlight the objectification of slaves, Clóvis Moura and later Luís Luna, José Alípio e Décio Freitas, among others, would favor addressing resistance. Thus, quilombos and rebellions began to figure among issues in focus, even though their study was overburdened by a tendency to discuss guerilla tactics and the interaction between quilombos and other political movements. The predominant inclination of this historiography was to define black resistance in the quilombos as a negation of the captive system through the creation of an alternative free society. There was, in this sense, a return—though through other means—to the thesis centered on the marginalization and isolation of quilombos, generally defined based on the Palmares model. At the same time, this historiography figured quilombolas as incapable of proposing the destruction of the slavery regime as a whole. The rebels had not reached the "level" of class consciousness necessary to take this definitive step in the struggle, as they were incapable of deciphering the "laws" that supposedly rule social transformation. A political behavior and logic of power specific to the rebel slave, upon which his actions could be analyzed, was simply not conceivable. Generally guided by a more or less disguised evolutionism, these authors substituted the investigation of meanings that slaves themselves lent to their actions with a lamentation over their inability to grasp the meaning of a history mastered by the historian. In this regard, there is indeed a convergence of these authors with the theses from the "Paulista School."[10]

A few more recent studies on quilombos and slave rebellions, written in the 1980s and 1990s, have neither abandoned the cultural problematic nor the Marxist influence. In fact, in many cases, they are inheritors of these paradigms, since we find as much continuity and rupture in these as we do in those that preceded them. Nevertheless, they have generally renewed the discussion of the phenomena as they have given up both the desperate search for African traces and the teleological rigidity of conventional Marxism, updating the debate based on new perspectives of recent historiography—particularly in regards to elements that have been innovating slavery studies both inside and outside of the country. These are studies that also owe a lot to the renewal of Marxist historiography, which has sought to incorporate into its concerns, through social anthropology, the symbolic aspects and rituals of life in society, while contextualizing them historically. Yet, above all, it must be emphasized that these studies reflect a concern for archival research as well as the discovery and analyses of manuscripts and oral sources that considerably expand our knowledge about quilombos in various Brazilian regions, indicating a complex relation between fugitives and diverse societal groups around them.

This collected volume presents a sample of the ways in which quilombos are being studied in Brazil. The authors of the chapters are fortunately not part of a specific historiographical "school." The intention that guided the organizers was to provide a broad picture of the various interpretative possibilities. The readers will have the opportunity to detect theoretical and methodological differences among the authors, who, in some cases "dive" into the same data and even into the same archive, only to emerge with divergent interpretations. Another preoccupation was to cover various periods and regions of Brazil, although, for reasons beyond our control, there were certainly important slavery zones that were omitted, such as São Paulo.

The collected volume begins with a classical theme of the studies on Brazilian *quilombos*: Palmares. This community of runaway slaves, the largest and perhaps the one that survived the longest, is revisited under various perspectives. Pedro Paulo Funari's essay, which opens the debate, provides a historical and historiographical contextualization of the great quilombo and then presents the first results of his archeological research in the Barriga mountain range, where, the Macaco Mocambo, capital of Palmares, was supposedly located. Among us, archeology represents a new approach to the study of quilombos and promises to reveal aspects that are impossible to approach based on conventional documentation, often found in archived manuscripts.[11] Unfortunately, the current stage of excavations has not yet provided us with many definitive answers. One of the most interesting hypotheses presented in Funari's essay, which was based on the type of ceramics found, is that the indigenous presence would have been denser than it considered up until then. It is well known that not only African and Brazilian-born blacks inhabited quilombos, but whites and various kinds of mixed race and indigenous people as well. But would indigenous and mixed race indigenous people have represented a substantial portion (say thirty or forty or more percent) of the Palmarian population? Or would the revelations drawn from ceramics found reveal only influences of the indigenous culture upon the material culture of the Palmarian blacks? Are the ceramics Palmarian or post-Palmarian? The historical implications dependent upon this answer could be crucial in reassessing the Afrocentric interpretation of the famous quilombo. Finer analyses of the excavated material, including more precise dating methods, could reveal a lot more in regards to a quilombo, about which, in fact, little is known.

This ignorance was the central factor that led the anthropologist and historian Richard Price to imagine what would have become of Palmares had it survived until these days. Some would call it an irrelevant question. Not this author, who has dedicated a great part of his life to studying the Saramakas, a quilombolas community in the forests of Suriname that has been able to celebrate peace with whites and to survive to this day along with their language and kinship system, that is, with culture and identities of their own. The author's exercise of the imagination incites us to formulate other questions in regards to known documents about Palmares, such as questions concerning the process of formation of an Afro-Brazilian culture in the quilombo or the implications of Ganga Zumba's attempt to legitimize the famous 1678 peace treaty. It was through a treaty of this kind that the Saramakas secured their freedom and survived to develop their peculiar Creole culture, primarily based on a pan-African syncretism, with focus on their new language and new gods.

In Brazil, God was set against Palmares—the all-powerful Catholic God, we must specify. Ronaldo Vanigas discusses this divine theory entertained by some literary clergy in colonial Brazil, which was dedicated to reflecting on that quilombolas' community. The Jesuits, the priests that wrote more about slavery, did not reflect directly upon Palmares, except for Antonio Vieira, whose famous statement disposed of the possibility of a pacifying mission to the Barriga mountain range since he deemed its inhabitants unyielding. He, along with other Jesuits, reflected upon slavery, affirming, defending, and even practicing it, though they recommended a reform in order to diminish the possibilities of slave revolts as large as those of Palmares.

However, the colonial authorities began to develop more practical measures to avoid a replication of the Palmarian haven. Silvia Lara produced a detailed analysis of repression strategies applied to this quilombo and those posteriorly developed to secure peace in the slave quarters. It was in this context of reflection and sometimes panic about what had occurred in Palmares that the idea of a specialized force to persecute runaway slaves and destroy quilombos came about. Thus, the disastrous figure of the slave catcher was created—an institution that matured and expanded itself with variations and regional denominations along the eighteenth century. Product of slave masters' fear of slave rebellions, the slave catcher became inseparable from slavery and survived until its end. The class of slave masters and the colonial authorities had learned the lesson of Palmares, whose singular repression had inspired the dissemination and pluralization of repression measures deployed by thousands of slave catchers spread across Brazil.

And as if these men made of flesh and bone were not enough, the slave masters and the colonial authorities had to deploy divine forces as well. This is the theme of Luiz Mott's essay on the figure of santo Antônio as discoverer of runaway slaves and spiritual ally of quilombo destroyers. The saint would even have participated in the campaign against Palmares, to the point of even gaining military status for this and other services paid to the colonial enslaving order. Santo Antônio, in fact, was an ambiguous figure in terms of his relations with slaves, since he both persecuted and protected them. Eurípedes Funes' chapter describes how quilombolas from the state of Pará used to consult the image of the saint in order to learn about approaching assault troupes.

With or without human or divine slave catchers, *quilombos* continued to people the nightmares of colonial masters. This is largely because slaves continued to escape and gather in large and small groups, some of which reached hundreds of members. Quilombos and mocambos flourished with particular vitality in the Minas Gerais captaincy during the eighteenth century, the so-called Golden Century. Carlos Magno Guimarães counted 160 mocambos, although, given that the colonial definition of quilombo was that of a community of five or more runaway slaves,[12] he included some very small ones as well. A mountainous topography and more loose slavery relations certainly counted as factors that facilitated escapes in Minas, particularly once the character of mining activity obliged slaves to circulate through uninhabited areas in the prospecting and search of gold. However, mining would go on as an activity of the runaway slaves themselves, who exchanged metals and precious stones for what they needed to survive in freedom, in both Minas and other areas of Brazil.[13] In this manner, the quilombola miners appear in various essays in this volume that deal not only with the region of Minas Gerais, but also Goiás, Mato Grosso and Maranhão.

Minas Gerais is highlighted in Silvia Lara's chapter on the evolution of the legal and military repression of the runaway slaves—a chapter largely based upon the correspondence of the local authorities, who, embarrassed with the proliferation of *quilombos*, were always consulting the metropolis regarding how best combat them. The region of Minas resurfaces as a focus in three other essays by Carlos Magno Guimarães, Donald Ramos and Laura de Mello e Souza, while marginally appearing in Mary Karasch's article on Goiás, since the two *capitanias* disputed jurisdiction about some areas of its borders during the eighteenth century. The great quilombo of Ambrosio, for instance, seems to have been established in one of these legally disputed areas.

Carlos Magno views the quilombo phenomenon, for various reasons, as a "structural contradiction of the reality of slavery." In another work he refers to the phenomenon as a "negation of the enslaving order"[14]—thus the preoccupation of the authorities with combating it systematically. This chapter enforces the hypothesis by Silvia Lara that a great fear of Palmares repeating itself in Minas Gerais was circulating among the governing body in Minas. As in other regions of Brazil, in addition to mining, the quilombolas dedicated themselves to robbery, recruitment and kidnapping of slaves, as well as agriculture, hunting and collection. These activities varied in intensity depending on the period and area in which fugitives established themselves. All these activities threatened the stability of slavery. The greatest danger came from the fact that quilombos were politically structured, supported by a renowned leadership and a network of alliances with diverse social sectors. The author emphasizes that quilombolas engaged in politics and had their own political projects, a thesis that opposes those that highlight the reification of enslaved peoples and their incapacity to think and act politically. Most quilombola leaders gained either the title or self-entitled themselves "king" or "queen," or, less frequently, "captain." The same naming system existed between rebel leaders and quilombolas from other regions. Thus, it is unclear whether the system pertains to a reconstitution of leaderships established in Africa or was entirely invented in Brazil. It is possible that both things occurred, depending on each case.[15] The important issue, we insist, is that we are able to identify quilombolas' organizational and political model—a model that is reinforced by the alliances they celebrated with slaves in the quarters, former slaves and even with free white people, and by the way in which they received information from these people about the movement of troupes while keeping barter relations and sometimes even affective exchanges with these informants. Nonetheless, individuals originating from these groups also actively participated in the repression of quilombos, including slaves themselves, some of which even attained the position of slave catcher, a little known angle of this institution. Most common in all of Brazil was the presence of freed slaves in these posts, which reached, for instance, up to 15 percent in Minas Gerais.

Donald Ramos treats similar questions, but under a rather different perspective. For him, instead of a pure threat to the system, quilombos from Minas became part of the colonial society, given the "symbiotic relationship" they had developed with various sectors of the population. His central focus of analysis is Vila Rica, capital of colonial Minas, where a politics of repression was generated towards the numerous quilombos that surrounded it, as well as towards other areas of the captaincy. For the government, the task was difficult primarily due to the support many slaves, freed slaves and free man gave to *calhambolas*.[16] Among these supporters, it was mainly the merchants who gave these slaves shelter, while selling to and buying from them various products. These relations fueled the proliferation of quilombos, which, in spite of causing damages and wearing out Minas society, at the same time served as a kind of escape valve to the tensions caused by slavery, and kept them from exploding into a major revolt. The authorities, however, feared that quilombolas would contribute to this explosion, providing a model and leadership to the numerous slave populations in the region. In fact, in Minas, quilombolas seemed to have contributed to some slaves' conspiracies that were never concretely manifested. It was under this fear that repression was developed—and Ramos provides a detailed examination of its various modalities, which were often brutal—including not only the mobilization of slave catchers, but also of local militia, or even of expeditions of greater volume.

The day-to-day of these expeditions is discussed by Laura de Mello e Souza. In 1769, under the command of *mestre-de-campo* Inácio Correia Pamplona, a troupe whose objective was to hunt quilombolas, find gold and settle, departed to the arid backlands of Minas.[17] An anonymous diary about the whereabouts of this troupe allowed for the reconstitution of its members' unusual behaviors, such as the quotidian dedication to devotional prayer and mass, and the appreciation of soft music and banquets, which culminated with crude poetry delivered by the table. At the same time that they chased runaway slaves and destroyed their quilombos, these rude and violent men tried to bring civilized manners characteristic of urban centers in Minas Gerais to the countryside. Similar to others times in history, civilization went hand in hand with violence, in combat with what its perpetrators defined as barbarism.

The expansion to the west took gold mining and slavery to Mato Grosso and Goiás. Luiza Volpato dedicates herself to the study of quilombos from Mato Grosso and analyzes them as part of a broader phenomenon of a border society in a territory disputed between the Portuguese and the Spanish, as well as between them and the indigenous peoples of the region. The latter tried to block the advances of the colonizers and their slaves, who were in search of new alluvial deposits, but, as it occurred in other regions, these indigenous peoples also allied themselves to quilombolas, ethnically mixing themselves and living with them in mocambos. In some cases, if both indigenous peoples and *caboclos* were taken into account, "Indians" even reached leadership and majority in the quilombos.[18] The combat strategy towards border quilombos was similar to the armed conflict with the Spanish—a combination of military force and settlement. At least on one occasion, the authorities, impressed with the productive capabilities of defeated and captured quilombolas, sent them back to the border as free settlers, a rare occurrence in the history of Brazilian slavery. Quilombos continued to grow when the slavery economy diversified itself during the mining crisis of the eighteenth century. During the second half of the nineteenth century, this diversity of quilombo populations' origins expanded with the presence of criminals and deserters amongst the runaways, particularly after the Paraguay War. There was even a quilombo led by an officer of the National Guard—a usual border practice. These facts have problematized the image of quilombos as refuge for runaway black slaves.

The relation between gold, frontier and quilombo continues in the essay by Mary Karasch about Goiás in the eighteenth century, which presents a well-structured discussion of the factors that facilitated the escape, the reasons for the escape, the geographic distribution of quilombos, as well as the protagonists in the repression against quilombolas, among other topics. Amid the factors that led slaves to escape was the search for gold to buy their freedom, which turned quilombolas from Goiás in pioneer trailblazers and discoverers of new gold lodes. The escape was facilitated by the low vigilance upon the slaves in mines, by the presence of a sparse, free population, a dense African slave population, and by ecosystems—rivers, forests, mountain ranges and mountains—that constituted ideal escape routes and hiding places for runaway slaves. From Goiás one could reach the Spanish colonies, crossing the tangled rivers and swamps that reached down to Mato Grosso and the Paraguayan border. It is true, however, that the same waters that led to freedom also presented extraordinary dangers to those who were escaping, such as insurmountable floods, pestilent insects and lethal fevers. And there were also human obstacles. The indigenous of the region could ally themselves to the quilombolas, yet they found themselves more frequently on the side of repression, which they supported in order to gain rewards and to revenge themselves in response to quilombolas' constant assaults upon their villages. In these offensives, they also took indigenous women from the villages. The fact is that the "heathen," generally speaking, did not treat the runaway blacks that ended up on their territory with politeness. According to Karasch, the colonial authorities counted upon other free and freed blacks to combat quilombolas in the capacity of militia or slave catchers because the stability of slavery was of interest to them, who themselves were either slave owners or desired to become one.

Without a doubt, the opposition with quilombos constituted a complex interweaving of interests and relations but no less complex was the web of factors that promoted the quilombos and their maintenance. This is the core of Flávio Gomes' perspective on quilombos in Rio de Janeiro, in particular on those situated in the region of Iguaçu, in the valleys of the rivers Sarapuí and Iguaçu and next to sugar cane farms, sugar and sugar-cane rum mills, brickworks, and subsistence farms—all of them moved by slave labor. The author emphatically asserts that the relation of quilombos with society, and not its isolation, explains its formation and survival. As in other regions, in Brazil, quilombolas built "a subterranean world" constituted by slaves, freed blacks, landowners, and innkeepers. All of them populated what the author calls the "black field," a social, economic and geographic territory, in which diverse social groups circulated. These groups were not necessarily composed of blacks or solely of slaves.[19] Quilombolas, for instance, disputed or negotiated with boatmen the control of fluvial pathways of the area, which were fundamental to the outflow of products to the court and other markets. Through boatmen that served as intermediaries or employers, the fugitive extracted wood from the mangroves that served to heat the ovens of the capital. There, they also kept in contact with slaves and black urban workers, the so-called "winners," and probably with the small quilombos that surrounded the city.[20]

Suburban quilombos were quite common, as in the case of Vila Rica and those that depended upon the relations with free and enslaved populations living in neighboring cities and villages. The same applies to quilombos neighboring Pelotas and Porto Alegre, studied by Mário Maestri. In Rio Grande do Sul, in fact, many aspects of the quilombolas' history will repeat themselves elsewhere, such as the fluidity of the international border, the instability and smallness of mocambos, its alliances with manumitted blacks and *pardos*,²¹ as well as with slaves in slave-quarters—in addition to former soldiers and deserters that got to join them. Other aspects included the hiring of runaway slaves by dried meat farmers, and, finally, the diversity of economic activities the quilombolas engaged in, such as extracting wood, planting foods, stealing cattle, recruiting slaves and kidnapping female slaves. In spite of the foreign incentive to escape towards neighboring countries, the rebel slaves preferred to find freedom in quilombos located in territory belonging to Rio Grande do Sul, sometimes in small islands in lakes, other times in the mountain range of Tapes, close to the dried meat farms of Pelotas. Such strategy reflected the option of keeping close to known sources of supply, but also of not breaking formed bonds among them and the slaves of the farms and villages from which they had fled.

Hundreds of kilometers north, in Bahia and in Pernambuco, quilombolas also settled next to urban centers or settlement areas. João Reis studied a quilombo situated in Barra do Rio de Contas, in the region of Ilhéus, south of Bahia, where runaway slaves installed themselves in 1806 in a small community of yucca farmers. This chapter provides a detailed discussion on the relations between quilombolas and *coiteiros*,²² including coiteiro slaves that employed runaway slaves in their own granges. The Oitizeiro was a quilombo where there were both slave masters and slaves, in addition to quilombolas, who were all participants in complex relations of production that would transform the place in a prosperous yucca cellar, as yucca was transformed into flour there to be sold in the regional market. Having received complaints about what was going on, the Count of Ponte, who had recently taken office as governor of Bahia and who was famous for the hard line he adopted towards the control of slaves, sent a troupe entirely formed by indigenous people to the site. They dispersed the inhabitants of Oitizeiro and settled there for a few months while conducting raids against blacks in the region.

Eight years later, in Salvador, the indigenous would find themselves on the side of the rebels, according to the investigation that revealed an extensive conspiring network directed by Hausa slaves, in 1814. Stuart Schwartz studies this conspiracy that united urban slaves to slaves in quilombos in the vicinities of the Bahian capital. In this sense, the conspirators tried to repeat what had occurred two months earlier, when fishermen slaves from the whaling stations received support and leadership from a nearby quilombo during an uprising that took place in the areas surrounding Itapoá, causing great damage and many victims on both sides. Other Bahian rebellions also sought to combine the action of urban and rural quilombola rebels. But the conspiracy of May 1814 brought an important novelty: Among the rebel allies, which included Africans of various nations commanded by the Hausa, were also indigenous people to whom the lands stolen by whites would be given back, once the slave rebellion had been victorious. This study is accompanied by a transcription of the investigation against this unknown episode, which broadens what is known about the cycle of Bahian rebellions.

Also close to the capital of Pernambuco, in a sugar plantation zone, another quilombo was formed —or a group of mocambos—studied here by Marcus Joaquim de Carvalho. Known as Catucá or Malunguinho, it survived for various years, growing with the periodic revolts that devastated the region and getting smaller when the elite was united and the province pacified. The author presumes that the mocambo might have been formed around the revolution of 1817 by African slaves that had crossed the Atlantic together, being therefore called *malungos*—thus the *malunguinho* denomination. This mocambo dissipated around 1853, when it was led by a slave born in Brazil, the Creole João Batista.[23] Although this mocambo located in the woods of Caducá was initially formed by runaway slaves, indigenous, pardos and even whites (among them deserters and other outlaws) joined on different dates, thus representing another example of the ethnic multiplicity found in quilombos. Members of these groups found themselves on the side of repression, once again beside indigenous people whose action had been, according to the author, "fundamental" for the final destruction of the quilombo. Politically well-structured, with "a hierarchy of power more or less solid," malunguinhos depended, however (as almost all quilombos mentioned in this collection), on the support of various sectors of the population that protected them, who would keep them informed on the movement of the troupes and trade with them.

Further north, in Maranhão, we find ourselves once again in a border region, not in the political, but rather in the agricultural sense. The government and the slave masters had little control beyond this border. Mathias Assunção divides quilombos in Maranhão among those that were close to small farms, in isolation, dedicated to predatory activity, which possessed their own economy and traded some surplus, and those that combined subsistence agriculture with mining. The quilombos existed in the region since the end of the eighteenth century, but the best known are those that flourished in the following century. And they were many; some gathered hundreds of slaves, who got involved in the turmoil that shook the province after independence, particularly in the uprising known as Balaiada (1838–1841). In this episode, under the leadership of the exceptional freed black, the Cearense Bento das Chagas,[24] it is estimated that the quilombola forces may have reached two thousand men, who were defeated with great difficulty and under a high blood price by the legal forces led by the future Duke of Caxias. Similar to Bahia, quilombolas descended the mountain to cause agitation in the slave quarters located in the state of Maranhão, as it occurred in 1867 in Viana, in a movement distinguished by its demand for abolition of slavery. Other mocambos or "late *quilombos*," as the author calls them, continued to develop in the following decade, in a moment slavery was undergoing a growing crisis. In this period, provincial authorities went as far as implementing an original negotiation politics with the fugitives, not always with success. Like other authors, Assunção discusses the economy of mocambeiros, which also involved other sectors of the population, and informs us about their political hierarchy and political culture, although these two aspects, as in other cases, only fragmentarily appear in the archives.

Closing this volume is the study of Eurípedes Funes on the west of the state of Pará, a region known as Low Amazon. This chapter is suited to close the volume not only for ending our journey through Brazil at the extreme north, but also because it discusses quilombolas communities that developed under slavery and projected themselves towards the future, reaching our own times. A substantial part of the history of the quilombolas in the Amazon forest arrives to us through the voice of its descendants: "A memory that functions simultaneously as a referent of ancestrality and identity," as Funes writes. Besides oral sources, the author also uses written sources, some of which support and at times correct the other. The quilombos of this region distinguish themselves by being located in remote areas, above rapids and waterfalls of the Amazon River effluents, in the valley of Curuá and Trombetas, a few leagues from the border with Suriname, in a thick forest, away from urban centers. Developing an economy centered on extractivism, mocambeiros sought to cohabit with the forest, to which they adapted thanks to the frequent assistance received from its original inhabitants, the local indigenous peoples, who, as in most places, could be divided into those who were friendly and those we were hostile. "Our mother forest is life itself," declared a survivor from these quilombos. The green protection indeed favored the formation of lasting communities, within which Funes was able to identify familiar groups, a growing population and established power structures. And in spite of the long distances, quilombolas sold what they extracted and the surplus from the little they planted. Their products reached the urban centers of the coast, or even the independent quilombos in Suriname, through the assistance of indigenous groups. And, in spite of the isolation of the forest, they received both national and international news. During the War of Paraguay, they asked for peace and liberty, otherwise they threatened to immigrate to the Dutch Guiana, where they knew slavery no longer existed. And in 1876, one of their groups protested to the government when, after agreeing to enter into negotiations for peace, was then betrayed and re-enslaved. And even though justice had been partially submerged by the abolitionist tide, it was enacted against its masters. Once freed, the mocambeiros returned to their old mocambo, reencountered the forest and lived in a state of abundance that is today remembered with nostalgia by their descendants who are drowning in poverty.

Brazilian slaves from Palmares and the other quilombos that survived up to the last years of slavery built an exciting history of freedom. Yet, it is a history filled with traps and surprises, advances and setbacks, conflict and commitments, without a linear sense—a history that makes the perspective of our past more expanded and complex. "Freedom," wrote the historian Barbara Fields, "is not a fixed condition, but a target in constant movement"—these words were written for another context, yet has an almost universal value.[25] The Brazilian quilombolas occupied deserts and forests, surrounded and penetrated cities, villages, mines, mills and farms; they were attacked and used by groups of enslavers, whom they also attacked and deployed for their own interests; they ran away from enslavement and committed themselves to slavery; they struggled with and allied themselves with other blacks, indigenous and poor whites; they created their own, often prosperous economies; they formed small, agile, mobile and temporary groups, or larger groups that were sedentary, a generation older, and politically structured; they got involved with political movements of other social sectors, developed their own movements, some of abolitionist character; they took advantage of the conflictive national, regional, even international political conjuncture to grow and amplify alliances, as well as to advance their immediate interests and more ambitious projects of liberty. These events and many others are part of the history told in this book. To say that quilombolas were heroes does no justice to the richness of their experience. They may be celebrated as heroes of freedom, but what we celebrate in this volume is the struggle of men and women whom, in order to live in freedom, could not always count with the certainties and coherences normally attributed to heroes.

2

PALMARES: A REBEL POLITY THROUGH ARCHAEOLOGICAL LENSES[1]

PEDRO PAULO A FUNARI AND ALINE VIEIRA DE CARVALHO

Introduction

The aim of this chapter is to deal with the political context of maroon development in colonial Brazil, turning then to the contributions of historiography and archaeological literature on the discussion of the political organization of the free polity. The most enduring free African polity in the Americas, Ngola Janga or Palmares lasted for almost the entire seventeenth century, in South America, as an innovative political subject in a colonial context. Out of their African experience, former enslaved people forged a new society open to other outcasts and rebels. This was a unique contribution for the development of a political structure independent and opposed to the oppressing colonial states. This chapter tells this story through the lens of the archaeological contribution.

Palmares in context

In order to understand the constitution of the Palmares Quilombo it is necessary to return to the fifteenth century, the period of maritime expansion during which Portugal sought new routes to the Indies. In 1415, the Portuguese overtook Ceuta in North Africa and started the process of expansion across coastal Africa. In the following decades, they conquered the Southern Atlantic and arrived at the land that is today the country of Brazil. From the second half of the sixteenth century through the beginning of the seventeenth century, when commerce with the Indies proved to be unprofitable to the Europeans, the Portuguese implemented a new type of production in their newly discovered territories: sugar cane.

Many sugar mills were set up in the Brazilian coast of Bahia and Pernambuco. The sugar yielded profit not only for Portugal but also Holland, responsible for the refinement of the product. Production depended on the labor of enslaved Africans and local Indians, known as *negros da terra*, blacks of the land. While the Portuguese dedicated themselves to the implementation of the sugar mills, they also faced the escapes of Blacks and Indians. Together these slaves started a maroon polity, which later came to be known as Palmares Quilombo.

During the period of the Iberian Union (1508–1640), when Portugal was incorporated to the Spanish Crown under the power of Philip II, Palmares received new immigrants while located approximately 60 km inland from the Brazilian coast. According to quilombo historiography there were not only Indians and blacks in the Quilombo but also Jews and Muslims. In 1612 the polity had already been acknowledged by the Portuguese as a powerful and dangerous refuge for the slaves. The religious disputes that existed in Europe in the seventeenth century had repercussions in the daily life of the Brazilian Colony as a whole and Palmares in particular. Philip II, king of Catholic Spain, forbade Holland to trade with Brazil (which belonged to Spain due to the Iberian Union). This was motivated by the loss of Spanish territories in the Netherlands. The Dutch, mostly Protestants, invaded Brazil in 1630 to search for sugar and as a response to the actions by Philip II. The Dutch authorities who then dominated the region of Pernambuco also acknowledged the danger of the polity of Palmares but despite all military efforts were unable to destroy it.

Following the end of the Iberian Union in 1640, and after the expulsion of the Dutch from Brazil in 1654, the colonial authorities and mill owners concentrated military forces to destroy Palmares. As a response, maroon people started to attack farms along the coast in order to get weapons, free slaves, and get revenge against the mill owners and overseers. In one of the many conflicts, the captain of the infantry, Fernão Carrilho, imprisoned about two hundred members of the free polity in 1676. Due to this increasingly hostile political climate, Ganga-Zumba, military chief of the Palmares Quilombo, tried to negotiate a deal. He proposed to the governor of Pernambuco, Aires de Souza e Castro, that the inhabitants of Palmares would be disarmed if, in exchange, they could claim ownership over the lands of Palmares, and if those born in the maroon polity would be guaranteed their freedom.

Discord arose inside Palmares because of Ganga-Zumba's attempt to strike a deal in 1678. Another military leader, Zumbi, allegedly led the opposition against Ganga-Zumba and organized Palmares's resistance to the colonial forces. In 1687, the governor of Pernambuco decided to summon Domings Jorge Velho, a *bandeirante*, to command the expeditions against Palmares. After seven years of attempts, Domingos Jorge Velho, leading an army of colonists, Indians, and *mamelucos* (mix of the indigenous population and the Portuguese), finally destroyed the settlement. Zumbi was not captured until the 21 November 1695.

Atlantic connections

Africans in the Old World controlled the sheer volume and ethnic origin of captives offered to Europeans, selling slaves at prices they determined. The most comprehensive study of the role of Africans in the early modern period concluded that:

> we must accept that African participation in the slave trade was voluntary and under the control of African decision makers [...] the willingness of Africa's commercial and political elite to supply slaves should be sought in their own internal dynamics and history.[2]

Thus, Africans involved in the slave trade were equal and un-coerced partners of metropolitan merchants and officials, and that the development of the slave trade enhanced African control.

Africans in the New World, however, were submitted to inhuman hardships. There is no need here to recall the details of the oppression suffered by slaves in the Americas, even though we should acknowledge their suffering and realize that the oblivion of past exploitation usually resulted in the manipulation of history in favor of eurocentric paradigms. If we remain aware of the unbearable levels of barbarism associated with slavery in the New World, it is easy to understand the importance of runaway settlements to both the descendants of slaves and to scholarship. African resistance to slavery was a major feature of the experience of Africans in the American colonies. Slaves responded to exploitation by intentionally carrying out their tasks poorly, by revolting, and by escaping to runaway settlements. Considering that the scholarly lingua franca of the period was Latin, it was very natural that they were called in the contemporary documents *res publicae* (polities), which have been translated into modern languages as republics, repúblicas, and republiques. The use of such a concept, applied usually to European colonial powers and to the ancient and most noble Roman republic, reveals the importance the colonial authorities attached to the maroons. They were considered as a political entity, as true polities.

The terms *Maroons, palenques, mocambos, quilombos* were introduced somewhat later, usually with derogatory connotations. The English term maroon comes from the Spanish *cimarrón*, initially applied to escaped feral livestock. In documents specifically referring to Palmares, fugitive slave settlements are known as mocambo, from the Kimbundu *mu-kambo* or hideout. The word was quickly adopted by the Portuguese colonists, and is still a most common word today: mocambo refers to a common dwelling, usually inhabited by poor people. Originally, though, it referred to a settlement out of sight, hidden in the forest (this is the meaning of the root of the word in Bantu). Furthermore, runaway settlements became ubiquitous features of colonial life in the Americas, the most effective way of opposing slavery. In Latin America, toponyms referring to maroons are very common. There has never been slavery in the New World without maroon settlements nearby.

Africa

Most of the inhabitants in Palmares came from Africa, particularly from the Congo and Angola Bantu areas. The history of Portuguese intervention in Africa is a long one. In 1491, a Portuguese mission arrived at the court of King Nzinga Kuwu, head of a confederation of local states in the area around today's Congo and Angola. The monarch, called *manikongo*, and many of his companions became Christians. The Christian King Afonso succeeded to the throne in 1506 but by this time, the Portuguese were more interested in slaving than evangelizing the locals. Kongo had a social and political environment that would be very familiar to a Portuguese arriving there in the early sixteenth century, encouraging cooperation between the African kingdom and the Portuguese.[3] Within a few years, his own people considered Afonso a Portuguese puppet, because of his links with the Portuguese, and the King's authority began to erode. Following Afonso's death in 1545, the traffic in slaves encouraged rivalry among local rulers, further undermining the authority of the manikongo. The arrival of the eastern Jaga finally put an end to the kingdom.

Slaving, therefore, fragmented the kingdom and the Portuguese shifted their interests southwards to Angola, resulting in a formal alliance between the Imbangala and the Portuguese around 1612.[4] The Portuguese Atlantic trade drew slaves mostly from the Angolan coast, south of the Zaire River, especially from Luanda, from the 1570s, and from Benguela, since the 1610s.[5] Most African societies enslaved war prisoners, but the victors seldom kept them as servants and most of them were sold to traders.[6] It is true, however, that since the late sixteenth century kings in Angola drew substantial revenues from villages of their slaves planted throughout the country.[7] In 1571, Angola became a Portuguese colony and until the twentieth century production of slave labour for plantations in Brazil and elsewhere was condemned.

A formal alliance between the Imbangala or Jaga and the Portuguese became effective around 1612. The Imbangala state of the Kulashingo formed mercenary camps on the fringes of the Portuguese in Angola. The same happened to other related Imabangala chiefdoms among the Mbundu. Skilled warriors who captured local farmers for sale as slaves and who joined Portuguese expeditions to fight in the backlands ruled these states. South of the Kwanza River, warriors of the *kilombo* were engaged in ongoing conflict with the Europeans. The kilombo was an Ovimbundu warrior society with well-defined initiation procedures and strict military discipline. The strong magic associated with their rulers and their military skills enabled these bands of Imbangala warriors to overrun the Mbundu later in the seventeenth century. Warriors of the kilombo would supply captives in exchange for European trade goods.[8] The degree of cultural interaction between Africans and Portuguese can be judged by the fact that a new art of war developed in Angola that combined European and African aims and strategies.[9] The Portuguese army in Angola was largely an African force under its own command structure, with the Portuguese simply serving as leading generals.[10]

Slavery and plantations

On the other side of the Atlantic Ocean, the Portuguese were soon to develop sugar plantation in Brazil. By 1570, there were already more than fifty mills, or *engenhos*, in the colony and by 1584 there were already some fifteen thousand African slaves working in plantations. The indigenous populations were also enslaved and some authors consider that the bandeirantes, or pioneers from São Paulo, in the South of the Portuguese colony, brought about some 350,000 slaves during the sixteenth and seventeenth centuries, one third of all slaves entering the Brazilian economy in these two centuries.[11] It is thus probable that these sugar plantations combined African and indigenous slaves with some free wage labor. Even though rife with conflicts, the Portuguese sugar interests were supported by firms engaged in processing and financing in the Low Countries. In 1629, the Dutch managed to occupy Pernambuco and to stay at Recife until 1654. By 1600 there were already some 20,000 African slaves in the Dutch colonies and by the mid-seventeenth century the number rose to between 33,000 and 50,000. Thanks to the Dutch invasion and to low sugar prices from the mid century onwards, a steady decline in the sugar industry ensued, in particular from the 1670s onwards.

Just after the restoration of independence of Portugal, King John IV established the Conselho Ultramarino or Overseas Office, whose constitution was published on 14 July 1642. As a result of the emergence in Portugal of centralized administrative control over its colonies, the Companhia Geral do Comércio para o Estado do Brasil, or Brazilian Company, was established in 1647. From 1661 onwards foreign ships were no longer allowed to trade in the colony and from 1684 ships sailing from Brazil were not permitted to anchor in non-Portuguese ports. Within the colony, armed slave-raiders from São Paulo played an important role in the maintenance of the slaveholding society. They traveled long distances, and from the 1620s their main hunting ground was on the borders of Paraguay. They were also used, however, to chase runaway slaves in the Northeast of Brazil. It is in this context that we must consider the history of runaway settlements in seventeenth century Pernambuco, their spread, and their final destruction.

Rebel polities

Runaway slaves settled in the hilly forest areas, some fifty miles from the coast in the beginning of the seventeenth century (Map 1.1). The first Portuguese expedition to Palmares, in 1612, attested to the importance of the polity early in the century. The polity continued to grow up to the 1640s, when the Dutch consider Palmares as a "serious danger." Bartholomeus Lintz describes the polity as formed by two main polity areas: a capital village at Serra da Barriga and a smaller hamlet at the left bank of the Gurungumba River (Fig. 1.1). Bartholomeus Lintz "lived among them [and] after staying with them [knew] their places and mode of life."[12]

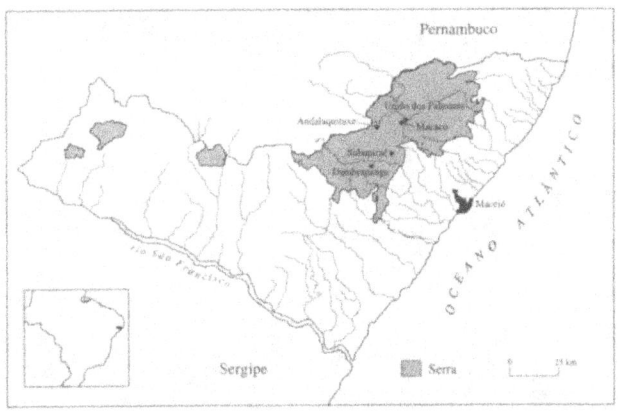

Map of sites in the state of Alagoas.

PALMARES: A REBEL POLITY THROUGH ARCHAEOLOGICAL LENSES

A unique contemporary image of Palmares, provided by Barleus in 1647.

Some information about the nature of the main polity can be gleaned from period accounts. Baro led a Dutch attack on the polity in 1644 and claimed to have killed one hundred people and captured thirty-one out of the six thousand people living in the main settlement. During this campaign, the polity was described by Baro as a half a mile long village, surrounded by a double-stake fence with two entranced and agricultural fields nearby. Out of the thirty-one captives, seven were Amerindians and some mulatto children, suggesting that a significant portion of the population could be considered of native origin.[13] The next year Blaer Reijmbach led a second Dutch expedition to Palmares. We learn from Reijmbach's account that at this time Palmares was a polity comprising nine separate villages. He made mention of a New Palmares as well as Old Palmares, which he described as a village containing some fifteen hundred people living in two hundred and twenty dwellings. He probably referred to the early settlements as Old Palmares and recent ones as New Palmares.

From 1654 to 1667, following the Dutch expulsion by the Portuguese, the Portuguese were able to carry out several expeditions against Palmares as well. Starting in 1670 the authorities initiated a systematic campaign to destroy Palmares, involving almost yearly assaults on its villages. Between 1670 and 1687, historical accounts indicate that a "Great Lord" or Ganga Zumba ruled the polity. He lived at the capital, in a hill, called Macaco, possibly founded by 1642, if we believe the documents by the Dutch assailants.[14] The name of this town could be related to Bantu languages (e.g., *mokoko*, "cock"), although Portuguese-speaking colonists interpreted it as a reference to monkeys (*macaco*).[15] It was also known as the Royal Stockade, because it was the fortress town of the king (as interpreted by the Portuguese). The inhabitants of the rebel polity called it *Ngola Janga*, using thus an African definition for their own polity. The name can be interpreted as Little Angola or The Little Red Polity (if so, it could refer to the cock's crest, if we accept *mokoko* as "cock"). Whatever the meaning, still unclear, it is rather evident that the rebels preferred to refer to themselves using African terms, not European ones.

Several expeditions were launched from 1667 onwards and the nephew of King Ganga Zumba, Zumbi, first distinguishes himself in a battle in 1674. His own name, Zumbi, suggests that he may have played an important spiritual role in the community. Indeed, *nzumbi* is associated with a Bantu priestly and military title in Angola.[16] Fernão Carrilho led an expedition against Palmares in 1676, discovering a fortified village at Subupira, burned and abandoned before he was able to assault it. In 1678, Carrilho claimed to have destroyed the maroon, bringing with him two sons of King Ganga Zumba. The Portuguese and representatives of Palmares met at Recife and a peace treaty was struck. Some maroon leaders did not accept this outcome, King Ganga Zumba was killed and his nephew Zumbi was proclaimed King of Palmares.

The next fifteen years witnessed the most violent period in the history of the polity. From 1679 up to 1692, different local captains tried to destroy Palmares with very limited effect. By this time it had become clear that local expeditionary forces would not be able to cope with the rebel kingdom. The Brazilian sugar industry entered a period of stagnation and decline, resulting from declining prices for sugar, as well as from the steadily rising prices for slaves.[17] From 1670 onwards, as a consequence of the Brazilian economy, the sugar industry was in tatters.

In 1685 Domingos Jorge Velho, a mercenary bandeirante, asked for license to conquer the native Brazilians in the Pernambuco captaincy. The Portuguese called their provinces in Brazil captaincies. Two years later the authorities decided to use him against Palmares. An agreement relating to the use of captives and land was drawn up between the mercenary and the governor for the destruction of the maroon polity. As commander in chief of the expeditions, Velho claimed ownership of most of the booty. In February 1694, after a 42 day siege, Macaco fell, two hundred maroon settlers died, another two hundred perished falling from high precipices, five hundred were captured and sold out of the captaincy. Several rebels, among them Zumbi, managed to flee, but on 20 November 1695, the King was captured, executed and his head put on public display as a frightful memento: slaves must obey, not defy the slave system. Today, Zumbi and Palmares are considered important symbols for African-Brazilians and indeed for all those people fighting against oppression and for freedom.

The polity itself can be better understood as a frontier society. The archaeological evidence calls into question our entire notion of colonial settlement systems, with sharp boundaries between inside and outside the colonial polity. Palmares seems to have successfully negotiated an interstitial position between multiple frontiers in this region. Several historians may use the concept of *Frontier History*—as F. J. Turner developed it and as it was used to explain the progressive conquest of American continent's territory.[18] The first aspect to be stressed, though, is the definition of a frontier that is not an imaginary and fixed line separating two states, like the nineteenth century European sense of the word, but on the contrary, the frontier is the zone of contact between two areas.[19] It is understood that marginality can be politically constituted and so there is no reason to expect marginal groups, such as maroons, would necessarily be minority groups.[20] Palmares, or Ngola Janga, proved marginality could shape a unique landscape, in constant and porous contact with the coast, the backlands and beyond.

The marginality of the settlement started with the status of outsiders in African polities. Outsiders were kept as slaves in Africa and they did not belong to the local social system, but neither were they chattel. Usually, the acquired outsider, or domestic slave, moves from total marginality toward progressive incorporation into the institutions of the host society. Status mobility was enacted by affective mobility, so that rehumanization of the slave in a new social setting was the key element in traditional African societies. African institutions, such as households, kin groups, offices, have always been highly absorptive of outsiders.[21] It is evident that all those African features were essential for Palmares, as a society constantly absorbing new members. A related African feature is diversity, particularly considering that most Africans came from Bantu-speaking areas. The ethnographic evidence has shown that, despite linguistic similarities amongst Bantu speakers, there is a plethora of cultural differences.[22] This diversity is also at the root of maroons in the Americas, and of Palmares, in particular.

Several features must be stressed. First, new members of the polity went through a process of incorporation and dehumanization. Chattel slaves, though non-persons, they step by step acquired new social roles in a new society. The transatlantic connection lies less in the wholesale transfer of an integral set of African practices than in ad hoc strategies of assembling new communities out of refugees from a wide variety of African origins. People in West Central Africa were used to the techniques of assembling refugees in new communities under tight discipline aiming at self-defense. The military, strategic features of maroons were rooted in the African experience, and the inclusion of indigenous people in the new community building process was thus not that different from what was common in Africa itself.[23]

Then again, another ad hoc institution was responsible for innovative gender relations. Polyandry was possibly a new, creative way of establishing social relations and incorporating people. The reversal of social roles, enbling women to mate with several males, points to empowerment mechanisms within the African polities in the New World. The empowerment of former chattel slaves opened the way for other empowerments, not least a sexual one. This applies to women and probably to other sexual minorities, such as gays, as proposed.[24] Another feature of the polity relates to the adoption by maroon people of colonial material culture, particularly common glazed wares. This is also the result of the marginal character of the rebel polity.[25] The use of colonial material items by maroons constitutes a conscious act of resistance by oppressed, marginalized people against the colonial power.[26] It also reveals how complex and well articulated was the political organization of the polity, able to interact with the indigenous people, colonists and other social groups, aiming at strengthening the polity in face of aggression and attack.

Interpreting Palmares and the role of historiography

Since the end of the seventeenth century, Palmares has been described in documents in political, military, and religious terms. The interpretation of this historical evidence by chroniclers, archivists, historians, sociologists, anthropologists, lawyers, and playwrights has resulted in the creation of two opposing images of Palmares. The first gives us the touching example, "worthy of pity," of the slave movement against the colonial authorities, while the second exalts the free polity as an example of the heroic resistance of the black people. The former stresses oppression, the later resistance. However, both features necessarily do shape daily life of the maroon.

Palmares historiography, therefore, has been marked by dualistic categories: good versus evil, black against slave catcher, black people against colonial authority, among others. Six authors are worth mentioning, in chronological order, as important figures of this historiography until the 1980s and, because of this, are essential to the understanding of the interpretative changes about the political organization of Palmares: Ernesto Ennes, Arthur Ramos, Edison Carneiro, Clóvis Moura, Décio Freitas and Abdias do Nascimento.

Ernesto Ennes, a librarian and archivist who wrote during the 1930s and 1940s used official sources about Palmares to demonstrate heroic qualities of the bandeirantes from São Paulo in opposition to barbaric characteristics of the quilombolas. Associated with the Paulista Museum his book *The Wars against Palmares*, published in 1938, was dedicated to Afonso E. Taunay, director of the institution—and to the elites of southeast Brazil. Ennes organized countless documents in an epic narrative with a clear intention to reconstruct the so-called the true history of Palmares and to elevate Domingos Jorge Velho, the bandeirante who commanded the last attack expedition against Palmares, to heroic status. The hero, in this history, was described as a brave paulista (man from São Paulo).

Ennes argued that the advent of Palmares resulted because black slaves were unable to initiate a revolution within the colony, because of presumed incapacity to do so against their white masters. Since they could not revolt, these black slaves escaped and formed the maroon at a place far from the sugar mills. Initially, these runaway slaves lived off pillage and thefts from the plantations. As the polity attracted a greater number of slaves, the practice of pillage and theft was slowly replaced by hunting, fishing, and harvesting. The maroon thus began to reproduce a way of life that had existed in Africa.

According to Ennes, the maroon organized itself as a political confederation: the Palmares Confederation. The polity was divided into many villages with autonomous capacity for production and decision-making. Furthermore, each of these units had its own military and political commander. Despite the relative autonomy of the villages, the Palmares Confederation had a capital—Macaco—and a chief military leader. For Ennes, the Palmares Confederation could have become the foundation for a Black State in Brazil, an outcome that never became a reality thanks to the brave bandeirante from São Paulo, Domingos Jorge Velho.

Responding to Ennes's position, anthropologist Arthur Ramos and historian Edison Carneiro defended the notion that Palmares was a lasting example of the persistence of African culture in Brazil.[27] In their works, Ramos and Carneiro collectively argued that the African slaves escaped to the maroon polity in order to preserve the culture they had brought from Africa, thus maintaining its independence from the threats of white culture (such as the Catholic religion, the clothes, food, among others). In this way, the maroon became a viable alternative to culturally contaminating effects of proximity to European culture within plantation society. It is interesting to note the idea of cultural purity in this work: the white men would be always and essentially white and the black man inevitably black. One could also argue that Carneiro and Ramos were spousing a nationalist approach, considering that black culture could only remain black with dramatic intervention and the creation of a new polity. If so, this would clearly be a nationalist cry for an independent nation state to guard the interests of a particular ethnic group: the oppressed Africans.

Carneiro and Ramos describe the political structure of Palmares in a similar way to Ennes. Indeed, they emphasize the existence of small settlements with some autonomy and local military leaders. In contrast to Ennes, however, these small villages did not unite under one leader to form a confederation. They argued, rather, that these villages form the Palmares Republic. The difference lay in the fact that the central military leader had greater power of decision and more influence, as was the case with Zumbi, the last king. The emphasis was put on the military role in political organization in each village and in the polity as a republic. Each settlement was independent, united though for military purposes.

The studies about Palmares from the 1930s and 1940s that emphasized the incapacity of the black people in rebelling or slave docility in trying to maintain African culture in America were broadly criticized by the historians of the 1960s. Clóvis Moura and Décio Freitas are good examples of this criticism.[28] Drawing inspiration from Marxist thought, Clóvis Moura and Décio Freitas later focused attention on the role of rebellion in the emergence of Palmares. Centering their argument on the notion of class struggle, Moura and Freitas suggested that Palmares was the inevitable product of slavery. In other words, for Moura and Freitas, Palmares existed precisely because of the fact that class exploitation was present. On the other hand, the mere presence of runaway settlements was perceived as responsible for making the slave system itself more dynamic and especially for driving it to extinction, reflecting an ambivalent stance on the causative role of slavery in stimulating the emergence of Palamares. The authors engaged the broader public with description of punishments suffered by slaves in Colonial Brazil, the difficulties faced by the quilombolas in escaping captivity, and the potential for a free life beyond the limits of colonial polity inside the maroon polity. They also focused attention on heroes worthy of admiration, such as Zumbi, the warrior. In this light, slave revolts and maroon attacks can be considered as ways through which Africans in the colony could recover their human dignity (lost in the process of slavery).

For Moura, in particular, many additional factors contributed to the growth of Palmares: its isolation, crucial for the protection of the maroon people, the fertility of the soil, and the possibility of recruiting new members, among others. Initially they practiced hunting, fishing and harvesting. In the economic field, there was a predominance of mixed farming based on corn, beans, manioc, sweet potatoes, banana and sugar cane. The lands were probably held communally. Indeed, Moura states that there is little information about land property in Palmares, and the surplus production was distributed throughout the polity.

In the political sphere, each mocambo, or small village, had a leader who is interpreted as its absolute lord. Only in war situations would the leaders unite themselves to deliberate about the future of the Republic. Moura stresses that, in this situation, the leaders of the various villages submitted themselves to the command of the supreme leader of the Republic, such as Zumbi. Perhaps the most original interpretive contribution by Moura is the suggestion that polyandry existed in Palmares along side polygamy.[29] Moura did not consider polyandry a regression to matriarchy, as others proposed, but as a new, maroon-born social relation, empowering women and thus showing the innovative political organization of runaway settlements. This move can be interpreted as a social response to limited access to female reproductive partners, a rather innovative social structure.

Following a similar logic to that of Moura, Freitas suggests that life in Palmares, marked by fishing and harvesting, represented a historical regression for its inhabitants since in Africa "they had been farmers, shepherds, craftsmen, merchants and artists."[30] Running away was the only method for gaining freedom and, in consequence, recovering their dignity. According to Freitas, each polity that formed the Palmares quilombo had a leader chosen on the merits of "strength, intelligence, and dexterity."[31] However, these leaders were led by a council whose goal was to manage the polity as a whole. The inhabitants of the polity participated actively in the political life of the polity through assemblies gathered to discuss crucial matters. Palmares legislation, based in traditions and customs, punished theft, adultery, homicide, and desertion with death, guaranteeing the functioning of the independent polity. In this way, Freitas argued that the quilombolas had near total political and civil freedom.

According to Freitas, slavery could therefore not exist in Palmares, for it was anathema to its very nature.[32] A low number of adult males drove members of the maroon to abduct slaves from the plantations and thus strengthen the polity. These were considered prisoners of Palmares until they participated in a mission to capture other slaves. From this incursion onwards, prisoners became free and participated in the political organization of Palmares. The lack of women in the free polity also encouraged raids to abduct indigenous women, mulattas, and even colonial women to supply wives for the polity. Some women undoubtedly would not consider this as an abduction, but as liberation from oppression.

In the same period, Abdias do Nascimento glorified Palmares as a heroic example of the power of black people in the New World.[33] A self-proclaimed African-Brazilian intellectual, he preached the immediate Pan-Africanism (the union of all the "Children of Africa"—descendants of Africans born in other continents), whose inspiring model should be Palmares. Nascimento describes Palmares as "the first government of free Africans in the lands of the New World."[34] Comprising approximately thirty thousand rebellious Africans, Palmares formed a Black Republic that lived in a traditional African manner through mixed farming and a centralized government in the figure of a military leader. These Africans traded products with indigenous people and farmers, agents that were external to the maroon itself; they did not mingle with them. Zumbi thus becomes the first hero of Pan-Africanism and Palmares an icon to be followed, a society that the black people of Brazil and the world could visualize and champion.[35]

According to historian Célia Marinho Azevedo, the six scholars discussed above longed to recover "through exhaustive and empirical research" the Palmares as it "really" was.[36] However, they portray a polity full of expectations, doubts, and answers that are dated by the period lived by each scholar. The colonial maroon no longer represented just a historical event but symbolized the struggles of their own times; symbol of "black weakness and inferiority," at first, the political organization images evolve to become a clear example "of African richness and power." After the 1980s, studies about Palmares enlarged their scope to include economics, as well as families, women, eating habits, Zumbi's sexuality, and discursive analysis, among other possibilities. The repercussions for those debates on the political organization of Palmares are mixed in the wake of the attention towards so-called postmodern issues and micro-power relations.

Archaeology of Palmares

The archaeological study of this large maroon polity has been carried out in relation to a single archaeological site, Serra da Barriga or Potbelly Hill, known in seventeenth century documents as "Oiteiro da Barriga' or "Hill like an altar in the shape of a belly." The site itself, declared a National Heritage Monument in 1985, is located within the rural area of União dos Palmares and was identified, by both local people and scholars alike, as the historical capital of Palmares, Macaco.

Measuring approximately 4,000 meters east to west and 500 to 1,000 meters north to south, Serra da Barriga is sited from 150 to 560 meters above sea level, in primary forest. Two field seasons (1992–3) were undertaken in order to confirm that this hill was indeed a maroon settlement. Archaeological evidence recovered by pedestrian survey and trial excavations, however, resulted in the location of several additional sites. Pottery found ubiquitously on these sites has been interpreted to be of Native South American, European or mixed styles. A second phase of archaeological research has been carried out by a postgraduate student, Scott Allen, resulting in a master's thesis on the pottery recovered on this project, and continued survey on the hill since 1996.[37] As a direct result of this research, Palmares is now the best-known Brazilian historical site outside of South America, and has produced theoretical insights into African rebel polities in the New World. Indeed, Orser has integrated this research on Palmares into an overall global perspective on historical archaeology.

Map of the sites of Palmares.

Archaeological research at Palmares revealed a significant amount of pottery, including indigenous, European, and mixed style pottery. Indigenous potteries are hand-made using the coil technique with a sand temper. The pottery may be undecorated and, if decorated, carving, brushing and incisizing are the techniques most often used. The most frequently used colors for painted vessels were brown and red. Allen identified four ceramic wares as Tupiguarani. European style pottery consists of four varieties of lead-glazed earthenware. These glazed ceramics have a distinctive kind of opaque glaze containing tin oxide. This kind of maiolica was commonly used in the Iberian Peninsula since the reconquest (Reconquista) of southern areas of the Peninsula from the Moors. The Moors had originally introduced glazed ceramics and the conquering Christians adopted this glazed earthenware. Maiolica is found in most sites in the Iberian colonial world. However, at Palmares there were not fine maiolica, but utilitarian, ordinary glazed wares. Perhaps they were produced in the coast of Brazil, or even in Europe, but they were not intended for elite use, considering they are crudely made.

The third kind of pottery was locally made, Palmares ware. It is not a known European type, and it is quite different from indigneous wares. In 1645, Jürgens Reijembach recorded that Palmares inhabitants manufactured pots. The ware is wheel-thrown and low-fired and the vessels are small, shallow bowls, flat based. Palmarino pottery does not show signs of temper and it appears to be finger-smoothed on the inside, resembling some Colono wares fount at slave quarters in the Old South of the United States. Some large storage vessels found at the Serra da Barriga are similar to Tupinambá indigenous pottery, but it could also equally be related to storing jars used by the Ovimbundu in Angola.[38]

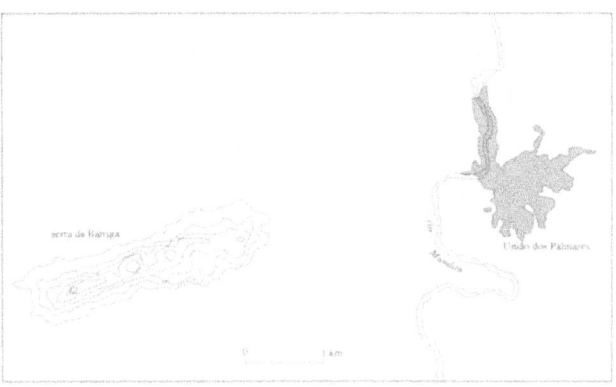

Serra da Barriga and the Union of Palmares.

There is a prevalence of African, indigenous, colonial and imported wares at Palmares. If fluidity is ubiquitous, as recent anthropological and archaeological literature implies, then instead of searching for Tupinambá, Ovimbundu, or tout court "African" traits in pottery, it is more reasonable to discuss "Palmares pottery." Glazed and unglazed Maiolica and wheel-turned wares were found throughout Palmares. They were not Portuguese or Dutch imports, but rather locally made wares used by ordinary people in the Portuguese colony. Hierarchy within the maroon community could also be seen in the differences within the settlement, as common pottery has been found in several sites, while a much less restricted distribution of glazed maiolica could indicate maroon elite areas. At one site in Potbelly

Hill, imported wares appear with indigenous and slave ceramics, suggesting that one section of the polity may have been associated with an elite group. Judging from the ceramic evidence, the elite at Potbelly Hill was not homogeneous. They were pluralistic elite maintaining consistent and long-term trading or barter links with ordinary colonists on the coast. Rowlands interprets the evidence as indicating that Palmares was neither a multi-ethnic society of fusion and assimilation, nor one of ethnic difference. It could have a more pluralist structure with relatively little differentiation in the material culture, but increasing elite distinction in a specific area of the settlement.

This evidence does not deny identity building at Palmares. Rather, the people of Palmares had a positive sense of their community. They had a common consciousness of themselves as a rebel group. Their common enemy provided them with enough solidarity to resist several onslaughts, over the seventeenth century. Solidarity however does not imply the absence of friction, divisions and even inner contradictions. In any case, the archaeological evidence strengthens the perception that Palmares was far from being homogeneous, having social hierarchies and inner conflicts, as well as conflicts with the outside world.

The mutualist approach proposed by Orser integrates archaeological and documentary evidence to explain the importance of both large scale and small-scale economic and power relationships, de-emphasizing the notion of a "culture" and stressing the connection between the communities in the modern world, so that Africans, indigenous South Americans and Europeans cannot be disentangled. Palmares can only be properly understood within the context of global colonialism, Eurocentrism, capitalism, and modernity, each one being central to historical archaeology in general and to the understanding of Palmares in particular.[39]

Still, Palmares was itself an ethnicaly diverse polity, reflecting the broad ethnic diversity of the colonial experience in Brazil. Indeed a variety of different ethnic groups settled the backlands of the Portuguese colony, most of them speaking Tupian languages. On the coastal plantations, the slave-owners used enslaved Africans, indigenous people and those of mixed descent. Considering the presence of pottery of indigenous South American style at the site, the references in documents to indigenous people maintaining friendly ties with the maroon and living there, and the fact that three villages of Angola Janga bore indigenous names (Arotirene, Tabocas, and Subupira), it is natural to suppose that some groups allied themselves with the rebels. They shared common concerns with the African polity.

Others, however, were used by the Portuguese to attack the freedom fighters.

Additionally, references in the colonial documents both to the presence at Palmares of Jews, Muslims, heretics, witches and other outcasts persecuted within the colony make it difficult to overestimate the contacts between rebels and settlers. However, most people living in the maroon were presumably of African birth or descent.

The study of the pottery at the site by Allen established the presence of three main wares: indigenous South American, European, and Palmarino wares. Rejecting the notion African, indigenous American or European traits' can be identified in the archeological record, Allen emphasized that Palmares people forged a new syncretic culture within their specific cultural and historical context. Using an ethno-genetic approach, Allen proposes that the observed process in which the Palmarino emerged as a new cultural group, challenges the culture historical search for ethnic markers and should contribute to the development of new focusing on the construction of cultural identity and ethnic group formation. Contextual interpretation facilitates an understanding of the role of pottery as it relates to networks of exchange, social organization, polity patterns, the creation of identity, and so on. The presence of indigenous and European wares underscores the integration of Palmares into a larger, regional system, a society not isolated, but whose escaped slaves were fully cognizant of the colonial situation and constructed a culture and identity which could be used in their interactions with colonists and indigenous South Americans.

Rowlands goes further to suggest that the site was already occupied by indigenous people with whom the first runaway found refuge and that archaeologically the picture indicates neither a multi-ethnic society of fusion and assimilation nor one of ethnic difference. There is thus a possibility of a more pluralist structure with relatively little differentiation in the material culture of much of the site but increasing elite distinction in specific areas of the settlement. Palmares was not a refuge site but owed its growth, survival and final destruction to the role it played in coast/inland trade, as mercantile interests and Palmares opposed those of the nobility and plantation slave owners, which were able to triumph in the end, due to the strength of pre-capitalist groups in both Portugal and in the colony. Furthermore, the ideal of racial mixing, which would be dominant from the end of the seventeenth century, as it was cheaper to locally reproduce than to buy new Africans, was a side effect of this crushing of a tendency towards pluralism in the early history of Brazil.

As Rowlands' interpretive framework suggests, Palmares can also be approached emphasizing continuity rather than change, as colonialism and Eurocentrism are practices whose origins can be traced back to the Roman world. Furthermore, the colonial society, especially in the Iberian world, was actively recreating feudal institutions and worldviews, like the town councils, the cult of the Virgin, the medieval social structure, church presence, administrative and commercial rules, scholasticism, and so on.[40] Palmarino society was not only enmeshed with other contemporary groups, like the settlers, the indigenous South Americans or the Africans, but also with the past. We cannot understand why Muslims are quoted in documents referring to Palmares if we do not pay due attention to the Catholic, crusader outlook of colonial authorities, who were persecuting infidels, as defined within medieval thought. The same applies to other continuities, like the use of African titles of nganga and nzumbi to refer to the rebel leaders, for these "kings," as described by the European sources, were considered as sacred rulers in tune with African religious traditions. It is true that nganga was in Africa the translation of "catholic priest," but it was the church father that was being reinterpreted within African frameworks, so that even Catholicism, acknowledged in Africa and at Palmares, was very much embedded in an African Weltanschauung. Indigenous South Americans, whose pottery and place names are common features of Palmares, established continuities with the human fashioning of the landscape in the backlands of the North East, as pots, hills, rivers, and the other environmental contexts, were interpreted within their own traditions, rather than African or European.

Material culture, conflict and diversity

Iberians, Portuguese and Spanish were keen to Christianize the souls of new subjects and enforce compliance with the Roman Catholic philosophy.[41] Despite the efforts of the colonists to homogenize society, several European cultures coexisted in Brazil with different cultural mores. The most creative interpretive framework, born in Latin America itself, but also rooted in African studies, is trans-culturation, hybrid mix, pluralism, and proliferation, as stresses Jean-Godefroy Bidima:

> Plurality is rooted in African history, as it not linked to one place (as African values are also in Europe and the Americas), nor to one time. Black African thinking is not a state (stasis), but a process, an act, and, as a consequence, there is no single definition, but a proliferation process.[42]

Several Latin American thinkers have interpreted this fluidity as a unique mix of cultures, trans-culturation, as proposed Gilberto Freire and Fernando Ortiz early on.[43] The archaeological study of maroons in Latin America has developed fast in the last decades and is now common currency in several countries, from Brazil to Cuba, through Colombia and Argentina.[44] Mestizaje is now a keyword in the archaeology in Latin America.[45] Palmares has contributed particularly to the discussion of the mixed features of maroon life and political organization.

In Africa, diversity was prevalent and because Africans themselves were active participants in the slave trade, and because slavery was widespread in Africa, African societies were not without conflict themselves. These tensions carried over to the New World, as some Brazilian freedmen were slave owners in their own right, just as there was a slave-owning elite in Angola. In this context, at least one historian believes that there was a ruling elite in Palmares that had many privileges.[46]

Palmares in modern narratives

Perceptions of Palmares need to be examined within the context of Brazilian society.[47] From its inception, Brazil has been authoritarian and patriarchal, dominated by patronage, a "hierarchizable society," in the words of anthropologist Roberto DaMatta.[48] The social exclusion of indigenous peoples, homosexuals, landless peasants and street children goes hand in hand with discrimination against several minorities and Brazilians of African descent, who, despite accounting for roughly half the population, are conspicuously absent from positions of power and influence. This is due to several causes, not least a colonial heritage of patronage and patriarchal social relations. An aristocratic setting prevailed for the first centuries of the country's development, and when capitalism and modernity were introduced in the mid nineteenth century, subaltern groups were absorbed by the dominating hierarchical ideology and habits. The country was ruled by the military from 1964 to 1985, and the end of the dictatorship led to formal expresson of freedom. From the 1960s, Palmares has been a potent focus of attention by academics, activists and ordinary people in their struggle for re-interpreting the past.[49]

Serra da Barriga was declared a National Heritage Site in the mid 1980s, after a mobilization by the Black Civil Movement. Since the 1970s, activists used Palmares as a model for a modern day state. Abdias do Nascimento spearheaded the movement for the establishment of a National Maroon State, inspired by the seventeenth century Palmares "Republic," as the rebel state was called in the historical documents of the period. A communist interpretation of Palmares, following a Soviet Proletkult style, interpreted it as a People's Republic and Zumbi (the last leader of Palmares) as a people's guide, a Black Iron Man, or Stalin (Iron Man being the translation of the nickname "Stalin").[50] Zumbi has also been presented as a learned Catholic novice, well acquainted with classical Latin war literature, hailed as a mythic hero.[51] All these popular perceptions were grounded in a search for struggling for a less conservative understanding of the past, an interpretation that recognized diversity and African roots.

Archaeology has played an important role for a better understanding of the maroon as a mighty African polity in the Americas. Africans and people of African descent are often subjected to harsh and discriminatory censure by traditionalists. Some leading intellectuals, such as historian Evaldo Cabral de Mello declared Palmares an enemy to destroy, in the wake of the commemoration of the third century of Zumbi's death in 1995. Even less conservative observers continue to refer to people of African descent as gregarious, artistic and pleasant, but with little attention to their political skills. The archaeological study of Palmares, in association with other scholarly research and the social movements, were able to highlight the originality of the maroon polity. Its strength was in its capacity of absorbing people of different ethnic and cultural backgrounds, fostering freedom in several ways. Gender relations are just one innovative aspect of maroon life, as were the social mechanisms of inclusion and incorporation of new members.

These political moves were not originated by the Europeans: they were first the result of African experiences, re-created and re-enacted in the American context, with an important contribution of indigenous political mores. Several oppressing features marred colonial society, not least the subjection of everybody to inequity. Inequity refers to the exploitation of slaves, primarily, but also of women, and religious minorities. Colonial politics could not inspire the rebels in their quest for freedom. They turned to the experiences in Africa, where there was no chattel slavery. The impacts of colonialism in Africa were sometimes more muted and new forms of practice often emerged to subvert colonial ideology. They turned also to Amerindian societies, where women sometimes played unique social roles and could have contributed to polyandry as a political strategy.[52]

In the end, Ngola Janga, or Palmares, represented a most successful political challenge to the oppression of European colonialism. It was an inspiring polity, grounded on Africa, but open to all those fighting for political freedom. Archaeology contributes to a less biased, less-dependent account of the polity, overcoming the prejudices of the elite documents.

Ngola Janga was a powerful polity, inspiring us today in the twenty-first century.

3

REFIGURING PALMARES

RICHARD PRICE

As part of the 1995 tri-centennial commemoration of the fall of Palmares, the largest and most famous of Brazilian *quilombos* (runaway slave communities), I prepared a paper in an attempt to raise questions about our historiographic knowledge. This article revisits and expands those ideas.[1] I spent some time reminding myself what is known—and how it is known—about this iconic site of black resistance in the Americas. Toward this end, I reread the rich work of scholars such as Raymundo Nina Rodrigues,[2] Arthur Ramos,[3] Ernesto Ennis,[4] Edison Carneiro,[5] M. M. de Freitas,[6] R. K. Kent,[7] Clóvis Moura,[8] and Décio Freitas.[9] In addition, I thought back on the two Palmares films of Carlos Diegues (*Ganga-Zumba* and *Quilombo*), which I had seen years earlier. I also had the opportunity to read a preliminary report of the ongoing archaeological investigations by Pedro Funari and his team.[10]

What strikes me most forcefully from this perusal of the literature is *how little we actually know about Palmares* relative to what might be available to know, in more depth. I wish to be precise in explaining what I mean, since I write from a special, unashamedly comparative perspective, one that despite its necessarily superficial and tentative nature I hope may foster further scholarship and reflection, especially by scholars in Brazil.[11]

Palmares was one of a class of "Maroon societies" (sometimes single communities, in other cases confederations, republics or quasi-nations) that developed and flourished throughout the colonial Americas, wherever African slavery was established. While such Maroon communities were, from one perspective, the antithesis of all that slavery stood for, they were at the same time an embarrassingly visible and widespread part of these systems. Just as the very nature of plantation slavery implied violence and resistance, the wilderness setting of early New World plantations made marronage and the existence of maroon communities a ubiquitous reality. Throughout Afro-America—from what became the United States down through the Caribbean and onto Brazil—such communities stood as an heroic challenge to colonial authority, and as living proof of the existence of a slave consciousness that refused to be limited by the whites' conception or manipulation of it.[12]

My own expertise concerns a Maroon society some 2,500 kilometers northwest of Palmares, in what is now the Republic of Suriname. At first blush, it appears to have many historical similarities to Palmares but it also has one major difference—the Saamaka Maroons continue to exist as a proud and semi-independent people today.[13] I have had the privilege to work with Saamakas as ethnographer and historian for nearly fifty years and I want, here, to try to tease out some possible lessons from that work, as they might be applicable to our understanding of Palmares.

It strikes me that if we had only written documents to rely on—and the contemporary Dutch documents about the wars against the Saamakas are remarkably similar to the Dutch and Portuguese documents about the wars against Palmares—we might envision Saamaka society, during its first century of existence, very much the way we visualize Palmares during its own splendid century. Yet, based on other kinds of evidence—not available for Palmares—we now know that such a picture of Saamaka would not only be incomplete but, in important respects, false. I have published an anthology of contemporary documents related to the colonial wars against the Saamakas—the field diaries of expedition commanders, the official interrogation of a slave spy sent in to learn about the Saamakas and then escape back to the whites, the journals of "peacemaking" expeditions, and detailed treaties between colonists and Maroons.[14] There is much here of interest and a useful exercise might be to try to "read through" these documents with the objective of gaining an insider's perspective to understand what these very marginalized outsider observers were experiencing. Yet such an effort falls dramatically short, as I will suggest, when put in the context of information originating with Saamakas themselves. It is important to underscore that the great bulk of our knowledge of Palmares comes from the very similar writings of military men, or administrators, all of whom were seeking to destroy the great quilombo—so these writings are strong in describing Palmarino military fortifications, weaponry, and the like. We should never forget that almost all of what we know about Palmares derives from the written words of its mortal enemies.

What is different for Saamaka is that it has been possible for me to work with the descendants of the very people who fought in the colonial wars of liberation, who, today, preserve precious and precise memories of that period and its continuing meaning in their lives, and to record their views of events and society during the years they refer to as "First-Time." The picture of Saamaka life and society that emerges differs in important ways from that contained in the outsider documents.[15] And by considering some of these differences we can, perhaps, begin to imagine some of what might be missing in our picture of Palmares, which is derived from very similar outsider sources.

The half century of persistent, organized *entradas* into Palmares produced what scholars have assumed to be a clear picture of the quilombo's political organization: a quasi-monarchical system that made sense to the Dutch and Portuguese (who were thinking of European models), and to mid- and late twentieth-century historians (who envisioned African models)—Ganga-Zumba with his high council, followed by the redoubtable Zumbi. What emerges from twentieth-century Saamaka accounts of their own early political history is, first, that the presumed centralization of authority was vastly exaggerated by the whites, and second that the identities of many of the Saamakas' foremost political leaders were absolutely unknown to the colonists.

Colonial Saamaka population and territory was roughly comparable in scale to that of Palmares—many different communities spread over a vast landscape. But we now know that actual political authority was far more dispersed than the whites believed, with rival leaders from different, geographically dispersed communities (or groups of communities) constantly jockeying for power. The oral accounts make clear that one of the cardinal principles of Saamakan survival strategy was not to reveal to the whites the identity of their leaders. During the wars, however, some of the names of leaders did indeed filter out—during the torture of Saamaka captives, during the interrogations of slave spies sent in to get information, and during the abortive attempts at peacemaking. But the identity of the bulk of political leaders—and certainly of the key ritual/spiritual leaders, who often wielded similar authority—was successfully hidden from the whites. Without twentieth-century historical ethnography in Saamaka, we would have only a very dim view of the actual nature of Saamaka political and military organization during the wars of liberation, and we would not even know the names of some of their greatest leaders. Incidentally, the same goes for the names of many of the wartime Maroon communities themselves. How many of the names of the eleven population centers of Palmares—Macaco, Subupira, Acotirene, and so forth—were the names used by the *quilombolas* themselves? If we judge by the Suriname experience, only some of the whitefolks' names for Saamaka strongholds were substituted in the documents for the names used by Saamakas (which were often deliberately protected from the colonists' knowledge). Even as late as the 1960s, some of the names for Saamaka villages on the official maps of Suriname were the names of nearby cemeteries or were obscenities spoken by Saamakas to the urban map-makers who had asked them (and who didn't understand their language).

Based on its Suriname analogs, our understanding of the 1678 treaty signed by Ganga-Zumba in Recife deserves further interpretation. The agreement, on the part of the Palmarinos, to turn back to the colonists those community members who were not born in Palmares, has often been assumed by scholars to be the measure of Ganga-Zumba's weakness and the cause of his ultimate downfall. From a Suriname perspective, I would make several alternative speculations. First, by this time, the proportion of locally-born people in Palmares would have been quite high (though, as has been pointed out, perhaps not as high in Zumbi's mocambo as in Macaco itself). But more importantly, it was common for a similar clause to be part of Maroon treaties throughout the Americas but for Maroons, over time, to quietly but effectively subvert that part of the treaty.

Over the course of fifty years, we have very detailed information about the outcome of the Saamaka treaty—which they "signed" with the whites by ritually drinking each other's blood—agreeing to return to the colonists all of their fellows who were not members of their communities prior to the treaty. The story gleaned from the whitefolks' documents (which claim general success with the process) and that from Saamaka oral accounts show radical contrast. In fact, the Saamakas effectively hid from the whites—despite there being white administrators present much of the time in their villages after the treaties—very large parts of their population who were, according to the treaty, "illegal." How they managed this feat is too complex to go into here.[16] However, there seems little reason to assume that a promise by Maroons to their colonial enemies to betray, say, their own sisters or their own brothers-in-law (and such would have been the effects of the Saamaka treaty—or that in Palmares—had they been honored) would have been kept by the Maroons. While the emphasis in thinking about Palmares has been on war and military strategies of force, in part because of the nature of the available documents, more attention ought to be paid to strategies of dissimulation, to the ways Palmarinos interacted with surrounding populations, to the ways in which they undoubtedly knew far more about whitefolks and their intentions than did the colonists.

Another example can be seen in the nature of domestic organization. Outsider documents depict Palmares as severely lacking women (one slave spy reported common polyandry) and quilombolas, like their Saamaka counterparts, frequently participated in raids on plantations to capture and carry off their women. Moreover, among the colonists, the specificities of

Brazilian psycho-sexual realities seem to have created a peculiar fixation on Rape-of-the-Sabines stories involving *white* women—fueled by fears of their wives and sisters being carried away by marauding Maroons—which do little to help us understand what was going on within these Maroon communities themselves. Though sex ratios were undoubtedly skewed in Palmares at the outset (as they were on contemporary slave plantations), within two or three decades fairly even sex ratios most likely became the norm, as each new generation of children grew into adulthood, women married soon after menarche, and adult males were lost in raids and battles. In Saamaka, at least, a quite normal way of domestic life, including polygyny for powerful men, developed rapidly and contributed to the stability of social life throughout the war years. And there seems no hard evidence to suggest that it was otherwise for Palmares.[17]

The presence, in Macaco, of a "chapel" and scatterings of outsider observations have led scholars such as Edison Carneiro to conclude that "Los negros tenían una religión más o menos semejante a la católica" and even to "explain" this by the alleged "pobreza mística de los pueblos bántus."[18] Of course, in the 1940s, scholars had not yet learned of the genuine richness of Bantu religious thought and practice. But even so, the presence of that *capilla*—like the similar reports of shrines in Suriname Maroon villages devastated by colonial armies—does not begin to tell us of the enormously complex ritual life enjoyed by early Maroons. In the Saamaka case, oral testimony reveals an arsenal of ritual protection used in one form or another by every man before entering battle—to protect against gunshot and bayonets, to send the enemy in the wrong direction, or to render oneself invisible. Likewise, agriculture, from a Maroon perspective, depended on countless rites for its success– which the colonists describe in their documents in some detail from an outside, purely utilitarian perspective. Again, in the Suriname case, after their escape, the completely unfamiliar forest area that the Maroons occupied had to be, from their perspective, "domesticated"—they had to become friendly co-habitants with the as-yet-unknown-to-them spirits and other supernatural beings who already lived there. So, through divination that is remembered in considerable detail today, early Saamaka Maroons consulted with the Mother of Waters by diving to the bottom of the river; they learned of the class of deities known as *apúku* who inhabit forest trees and boulders and how to deal with them; they discovered and learned to placate the various kinds of gods that live in boa constrictors and anacondas; and they met and tried to befriend a host of other similar beings who lived in the surrounding forest. We also know, from oral testimony, that early Saamaka funerals, healing, birth rites, and many others "marked" occasions involved spectacularly elaborated beliefs and practices. Indeed, the lives of early Saamakas—as we know it from the kinds of "documents" we do not have for Palmares—was shot-through with ritual concerns, much as is the lives of their descendants today. And I would suggest that the lives of Palmarinos, despite our lack of strong confirming evidence, would have been similarly inflected by their own African American religion.

We know from the documents that the Africans who made up the original population of Palmares—like that of Saamaka—were highly mixed in terms of ethnicity. The central cultural process that would have characterized their initial years was inter-African syncretism, the creation of new cultural forms based on the diverse beliefs and ideas and practices of the Africans who composed the original population. Rather than interpreting the history of Palmares simply in terms of our current ideological needs (à la Carlos Diegues, who says he made the film *Ganga-Zumba* to emphasize the theme of "liberty" and *Quilombo* to emphasize that of "utopia") with very much the same sort of political sensibility Alex Haley used in conceptualizing *Roots*—might there be something to be learned by trying to "read Palmares" from the ideological perspective of Suriname Maroon societies?[19] The shared and unusual process that we might call "creolization-while-in-a-state-of-war" certainly lends tremendous similarity to the two cases. And it might provide a window from which to try to discern more of what went on within Palmares during its tumultuous hundred years.

I cannot read the documents and interpretations of Palmares without imagining a different outcome from that which occurred 300 years ago. In colonial Suriname, during nearly a century of hostilities, the Saamakas (and their Ndyuka brothers and sisters) posed a sufficient threat to the plantation system so that the Dutch crown had to sue them for peace and grant them their freedom. The men and women of Palmares came tantalizingly close to such an outcome; that is in posing a similarly serious threat, in defeating for decades the successive waves of entradas mounted against them, and in creating what must have been a vibrant and unique African American culture. But it was not to be.

I would be shirking my responsibility not to report here that all is not well with the Saamakas and other descendants of First-Time Maroons who live in Suriname. The period of national independence, which began in 1975, has not been kind in general to the Republic of Suriname, which was racked by civil war between 1986 and 1992 and has yet to recover. For the Saamakas and the other Maroon populations who constitute more than 18 percent of the national population, the past decade has been truly disastrous. The civil war pitted the Maroons against the national army, and during its course hundreds of Maroon civilians—women and children as well as men—were brutally murdered. Whole villages were razed by government troops and some 25 percent of the Maroon population was forced to seek refuge across the border in French Guiana.[20] To these effects of war can now be added a more sinister and perhaps more devastating specter. In its efforts to unite the nation by "development," the government has set out on a plan of unification or normalization designed to end what it sees as the ethnic autonomy and separate rights of such population groups as Maroons and Amerindians. During the 1990s and early 2000s, much of the forest for which the ancestors of the Maroons spilled their blood was auctioned off by the national government to Chinese, Indonesian, Malaysian, Australian, Canadian, American, and Brazilian timber and mining corporations. From our own perspective, the government's unilateral program to abrogate the Maroons' eighteenth-century treaties, in the alleged interest of national unity, is tantamount to ethnocide. In twenty-first-century Brazil, I hardly need spell out the implications of the ongoing struggle between indigenous groups or quilombolas and the State over rights to land, over rights to decide what kinds of family law prevails within communities, and so forth.[21] But I do want to emphasize that the descendants of Suriname Maroons, who have carried on traditions very much like those of the heroic Palmarinos during the past three centuries, find themselves today under severe threat—threats to their human rights, threats to the land rights they fought so hard for centuries ago, and, ultimately, threats to their continued existence as separate peoples within the modern world.

In 2007, the landmark Saamaka victory before the Inter-American Court of Human Rights in the case of "Saramaka People *v* Suriname" set important precedents in international law and laid out major protections for Saamakas and other "tribal peoples" in the Americas.[22] However, the State has been very slow in carrying out the mandate of the Court to grant the Saamaka People considerable sovereignty over their 9,000 square kilometer territory within Suriname.[23]

The language Palmarinos spoke, according to what I have read, was a kind of Portuguese mixed with African forms, but sufficiently different so that other Brazilians could not understand it—there were always special interpreters accompanying the entradas in order to interrogate captives.[24] The Saamaka language was described by colonial sources in identical terms. It is, in fact, a Portuguese-based creole—the slave-owners from whom most Saamakas marooned were Sephardic Jews who came to Suriname from Brazil– a New World linguistic invention incorporating deep-level African grammatical principles. So my dream goes like this: I walk into Palmares today, with its surrounding fields of manioc and sweet potatoes and plantains, and address the first person I see in the Saamaka language. And she, or he, replies and there is understanding—one Maroon language and another, across the forests, through time. Are there ways that we, as historians and anthropologists, might build on this dream in seeking greater understanding of the Palmares experience and its meaning for Brazil, and for us all?

4

GOD AGAINST PALMARES: LORDLY REPRESENTATIONS AND JESUITICAL IDEAS

RONALDO VAINFAS

Oh if only the Black folk removed From the thickets of their Ethiopia And passed on to Brazil, Had known well how much they owe to God, And to His Holy Mother For this that might appear to be Exile, bondage and misfortune Is nothing but a miracle And a great miracle!

—Antonio Vieira, *1633*

God is word
—Pedro Rates Hanequim, *1700s*

Colonization and Rebellion: Centuries of Fear

In one of his most famous books, Jean Delumeau declares that fear of sedition was certainly the one that most afflicted the governing European classes of the Old Regime. Kings and princes, nobility and clergy, the holders of power and the guardians of the old Christian consciousness, both catholic and protestant, were all terrified with the virtual emergence of rebellions and mutinies. They feared rebellions of hungry peasants, such as that of the Muntzer sectarians in fifteenth century Germany, an uprising of the urban poor, troubled by extreme scarcity that oppressed them daily. All of them felt a particular dread of beggars, vagabonds and bandits, the offspring of a Europe in transformation, whose repression occupied a great part of the "social legislation" in modern Europe. "It is necessary to fear the rage, fury, and rebellions of the people," wrote one of the authors of the popular French *prédictions*, in 1602, predictions that spiced up the vision of the apocalypse with popular uprisings.[1]

In the colonial world, the picture would not be different; the dominant classes of the European enclaves abroad lived in panic vis-à-vis the imminent revolts of the subjugated peoples. And maybe, if we excluded the numerous regional variations, we could say that there, in the Americas,

"Asias" and "Africas," the elites' fear was greater than that felt in the metropolis. For the world overseas, the dangers seemed to be concretely greater since the restless masses of thousands or millions outnumbered the settlers. Besides, the forces of repression were weak, and the resentment of entire societies subjugated to exploitation and destruction of their traditions was fervent. A large number of Africans of various origins found themselves in extreme circumstances, as they had been uprooted from their environments and boarded into filthy ships in order to become slaves in the American continent. It was not by chance that the enslaved that made the Atlantic crossing used to call each other *malungos*, which meant, at least in the case of the peoples of the Bantu language group: A travel partner in the journey towards *calunga*, the land of the dead from where the White people came.[2]

The history of Portuguese America, our colonial Brazil, provided the most eloquent examples of this climate of insurrection, the "ire of the people," and the consequent fear, or rather, panic, of those that ruled and enslaved bodies and souls whenever possible. This reality dates back to the sixteenth century, when the Portuguese had barely "scratched the sand like crabs"—to use the well-known phrase of Friar Vicente. Constrained to the coast, the Portuguese people built *engenhos* (sugar production facilities) mainly in the more developed captaincies of the Northeast, Pernambuco and Bahia, generating an economy initially powered by indigenous labor. Certainly, the reaction to the savagery of the captors came from them—a resistance animated by traditional beliefs and rites.

The Portuguese people and *mamelucos*[3] serving them frequently found themselves objects of cannibalistic rituals to be devoured in ceremonies dedicated to replacing members of the tribes swallowed by colonial conquest and enslavement. It is in a similar resistance context that the so-called indigenous *santidades*—the communities of runaway natives that had escaped slavery and religious conversion—could be seen as the true ancestors of the *quilombos* on Brazilian soil.[4]

The lordly panic in face of these indigenous santidades[5] *was* quite extraordinary as Africans also took part in them, joining the indigenous peoples in ceremonies and wars that were markedly anti-colonialist. The primary manifestation of these santidades occurred in Bahia, in the early part of the 1580s, lead by a certain "Indian" in the village of Tinharé, who had encountered the Jesuits and escaped. He was undoubtedly a special indigenous person, since he was considered *Pajé-açu* or *Caraíba Tupinambá*, a shaman who was said to incarnate the great ancestor of the *Tupinambá* peoples (Tamandaré), at the same time was also considered the "pope of the true church." The santidade of Bahia was quite rebellious; it was a movement that shook up the entire bay area of Bahia de Todos os Santos, setting fire to sugar mills and Jesuit villages, and promising to its adepts legal freedom in a "land bereft of evil," a *Tupi* paradise, as well as the future death and enslavement of the Portuguese by the very indigenous people they had attempted to colonize.

Even after the destruction of the indigenous temple in 1585, under the orders of Governor Manuel Teles Barreto, and the consequent punishment and re-enslavement of the rebels, the Bahian santidade was responsible for a true frenzy among the lords of the captaincies, Jesuits and governors. The archive of the First Visitation of the Holy Office of the Portuguese Inquisition to Brazil, located in Bahia and in Pernambuco between 1591 and 1595, shows evidence of that. This Visitation, for reasons that go beyond the scope of this article, would end up bringing to light the details of the great indigenous insurrection of sixteenth century Brazil. It was mainly constituted by indigenous people, particularly from the Tupinambá ethnic group, some of which were Christians, others pagans. Yet, it had an active participation of male and female "Blacks from Guinea" (as slaves from Africa were called then), who were attracted by the "promise of freedom" announced during the rebellious indigenous ritual.[6]

For all these reasons, the Bahian santidade was a kind of predecessor, in indigenous style, to what Palmares would become in the seventeenth century that great African rebellion of colonial Brazil, located in the Barriga mountain range of the Pernambuco captaincy, region of Alagoas. In the Bahian santidade there were African rebels, just as there would be indigenous in Palmares; both were radical rebellions fighting against colonial slavery. But perhaps Palmares is, with proper cause, the greatest symbol of resistance. It lasted for almost a hundred years, and lead to humiliating defeats of the Portuguese and their defenders on numerous occasions. Palmares refused to negotiate with the colonial rulers (unlike the Tupinambá santidade), in spite of the "Recife agreement," signed by Ganga Zumba, the leader of Palmares, with Governor Aires de Souza e Castro in 1678.

Palmares was a greater resistance, at least due to its very name. The rebels themselves called it "*Angola Janga*," "Little Angola," and, unlike the santidade of the rebel *Tupis*, the refuge was registered in history not with a Portuguese and Christian name, but rather as a quilombo, a term of Bantu origin (*Kilombo*) allusive to encampment or fortress. Quilombo or *mocambo*—this last term derived from the Kimbundu term *mukambu*—were words that the Portuguese would use to designate the African towns built in the Brazilian forests by Africans in the diaspora.[7]

The Fear of Palmares: The Hesitations of Colonialism

The first signs of rebellion that would come out of the Palmares quilombo, a conglomeration of mocambos that would gather, in its apogee, thousands of *quilombolas* (residents of a quilombo), seems to date from the end of the sixteenth century. This is what Décio Freitas, author of one of the most popular books on the subject, tells us, as he mentions an insurrection of Blacks who were slaves in a sugar mill in the extreme south of the Pernambuco captaincy.[8]

The end of the sixteenth century and the beginnings of the seventeenth century were times in which the enslavement of Africans grew substantially, replacing indigenous labor in the agro-manufacturing of sugar. Slave insurrections would not take long in spreading across the American Portuguese coast, especially in the northeastern region. The Black rebellions induced panic and played on the fear that colonizers, Jesuits and monarchical authorities felt toward the indigenous—a panic of very long duration that, far from being restricted to the colonial period, would reach its pinnacle in the nineteenth century.

As it is known, Palmares was, in fact, the greatest and most emblematic manifestation of the colonial quilombo. It resisted repressive expeditions for about one hundred years; it promoted attacks on sugar mills and colonial towns and it gave stimulus to massive escapes of slaves in the captaincy. Palmares provoked such unrest among the colonials, priests, and royal officials that the Portuguese crown, under pressure from a variety of sources, attempted at various moments to negotiate with the rebels, similarly to the way other colonial governments had done or would do in other parts of Afro-America. The agents of Portuguese colonialism, for various reasons, really did not know what to do, terrified of the daily Palmarian rebellion and frustrated with the successive defeats that the calhambolas imposed upon their infantry battalions. For this reason, they would end up as prisoners of their own dilemmas and hesitations.

The unrest and uncertainties would begin at the threshold of the seventeenth century, when the groupings at the Barriga mountain range were still recent and fragile. The lateness of Governor Diogo Botelho in making his trip to Bahia after landing in Recife (in 1602) attests to that. He ended up having to stay an extra year in Pernambuco in order to contain the Palmarian attacks. To explain his delay to King Felipe II of Spain, a testimonial letter was written in his favor by more than twenty residents, who unanimously declared that it was the need to combat "the insurgent Blacks of Palmares" that was the motive for the governor's permanence in Pernambuco.

Diogo Botelho had sent, in fact, an expedition led by a certain Bartolemeu Bezerra, which was mainly constituted by mamelucos, following the practices of their fifteenth century antecessors in the combat against indigenous santidades and rebellions. And, just like the others, the expedition would take on a triumphant tone, assuring the king that it had managed to destroy the *quilombo*, an innocuous flattery that our early governors used to toot their own proverbial horns. Time proved otherwise for Diogo Botelho, the governor that dreamt of turning Brazil into "another Peru."

Neither Diego Botelho nor his successors, in spite of decades of attempts, had been able to defeat the Palmarian refuge. Following the clues of Décio Freitas, we find that the scenario only got worse, particularly as demonstrated by the correspondence of the Governor Diogo Menezes, successor of Botelho. Writing from Pernambuco to Paço, a little after arriving in Brazil in 1608, the governor would go so far as to radically propose the end of African slavery in the captaincy, by substituting Blacks completely with indigenous people. "Blacks were always rebelling," and no one could defeat them. "They may grow in a manner that in order to defeat them we will have to pay a high price," wrote Diogo Menezes in the heat of that moment.[9]

Décio Freitas mentions another document, possibly from the same governor, in 1612, in which the description of the scenario is clearly much tenser. He mentions that the indigenous from the Ignatian villages themselves—the same whom the naive governor had judged to be conciliatory—were joining and expanding the groups of "Blacks from Guinea," all of them engaged in "abominable behavior and rites" and perpetrating "scandalous and violent thefts." It was impossible not to remember that, only a year later, Bahia's residents would complain to the king about a certain "*santidade* of fugitive indigenous peoples, settled in the same region of Jaguaribe, formerly a site for the explosion of the greatest *Tupi* insurrection, which I have already mentioned. In the same Jaguaribe, the indigenous precursor to Palmares, rebellion was still pulsating, and the presence of Blacks from Guinea there generated wide spread despair."[10]

Once the proportions were inverted, with a majority of indigenous people in Bahia and a predominance of Africans in Pernambuco, the colonized peoples continued to turn the lives of slave masters and colonial settlers in Brazil into a living hell. In the case of Bahia, the indigenous santidade had already passed into its final phase, but in the Pernambuco captaincy, Palmares was clearly ascending. In both cases, however, indigenous people and Africans appeared together, setting fire on sugar cane plantations, encouraging escapes and promoting rituals in their homes, topics that are unfortunately little known by historians.

Everything seems to indicate that the turn in Palmarian history occurred in the decades of 1630 to 1650, a period in which the Dutch occupied Pernambuco, where they remained from 1630 to 1654, after having failed at conquering Bahia in 1624. It was in such a context of Luso-Dutch wars and very high growth of slave trafficking to Pernambuco —since Angola was under Dutch dominion for some time— that Palmares consolidated its position as a "Black State" embedded in Brazil's slavery system.

It is certain that many Africans or their descendants fought in the infantries of both colonizing armies, attracted by the promise of manumission with which the Europeans teased them. It is also certain that some even gained notoriety in these combats, such as the renowned Henrique Dias, Black commandant of the Luso-Pernambucan insurrection against the Dutch, who was also a "patron" of the famous Black infantry of the Henriques, traditional in northeastern colonial history. But it is equally certain that, as a whole, the growing enslaved African population in the captaincy knew how to take advantage of the intercolonial wars in order to escape in mass to the Palmarian refuge, turning it into a permanent headquarters of contestation towards the colonial slavery system.

The period in Pernambuco that followed the Dutch domination, witnessed Palmares as a political-military reality that no longer could be ignored, despite the arrogant claims of the first governors of the seventeenth century. Due to the successive defeats suffered by official expeditions in the vicinities of Palmares and to the continuation of the quilombola raids upon the captaincy, a project to establish armistice with the Black state began to take shape. Perhaps the first to consider sincerely the idea had been Francisco de Brito Freyre, successor to the famous André Vidal de Negreiros in the governing post of the captaincy, which he occupied from 1661 to 1664.

Despite the pressure against it, which came from Pernambuco's noble classes, who insisted in waging war on quilombolas without taking into account military failure, Brito Freyre considered granting manumission to Palmarians "in the same fashion as that of all other Blacks enrolled in the Henrique Dias regiment." The governor proposed an incredible paradox, as it reveals hesitation and fear of agents of the Lusitanian colonialism: grant manumission to quilombolas, equaling them at discursive and legal levels to those who fought for Portugal and its slave colonization.

Aside from hesitations and fears, the granting of manumission to quilombolas and the political recognition of quilombos was not exclusive of the Portuguese. This proceeded and continued among colonial powers in other parts of Afro-America, above all in the Caribbean, a region under permanent warfare between masters and slaves from the seventeenth through nineteenth centuries. One cannot deny that there was something of a strategy behind this apparent seigniorial retreat before the organized uprising. By granting manumission to quilombolas in exchange for suspending the guerilla warfare and returning new fugitives implied a rupture of the nexus between mocambos and slaves on the plantations. In the end the quilombos would decline, repression would be facilitated, which happened many times, or at least the colony was quieted while peace lasted. To quilombolas who, in truth, almost never fought slavery, those treaties were a way to get freedom for mutineers and guarantee, at least *pro tempore*, autonomy for Black villages.

It is not necessary to repeat how precarious such treaties were, perhaps even more precarious than those tacit agreements between masters and slaves in everyday slavery. As a rule there was often mistrust on both sides: for fear of re-enslavement, in the case of quilombolas; for fear of continuing Black havocs and assaults, in the case of settlers and their agents. Brito Freyre himself suggested the agreement with Palmarians, although he did not hide an extreme distrust he felt with regard to "those barbarian people." But he insisted reaching peace with Palmares was needed, for out of the supposed Portuguese victories over Blacks in Pernambuco what remained were "memories more than the effect."

In any case, the confrontational option prevailed until the late 1670s, notwithstanding the failure of the colonial military, which, among numerous expeditions always retreated without defeating the quilombolas, despite the notorious boasting of expeditionary commanders. Palmares' fame would spread beyond the captaincy boundaries, as well as the fear of quilombo resistance it instilled. It is worth remembering that around 1675 the *paulistas* (São Paulo factions) refused to combat Palmares—at that time they were in Bahia under the leadership of Estevão Baião Ribeiro Parente, the famed "decimator and capturer of indians." According to Décio Freitas, the paulistas argued that it was one thing to confront the suicidal tactics of the indigenous who recklessly dashed themselves against the enemy making it easy for mamelucos, as few as they were, to win. It was another thing entirely to confront the stealthy guerrilla tactics of the Blacks who camouflaged themselves in the bushes, a kind of warfare for which they had no experience.

During the government of Pedro de Almeida, the old armistice project gained new breath in the wake of defeats or false victories by the experienced Fernão Carrilho. The government sent an official ensign to offer a peace proposal to Ganga-Zumba, head chief of Palmarians. The government spoke of having captured children and relatives of the "king of Palmares," but the proposal was far broader than simply releasing them: the guarantee of manumission and the right to land for those who surrender. Not until the government of Aires de Souza e Castro, in 1678, was the armistice effectively sanctioned, though former Governor Pedro de Almeida was there in person, and in the presence of Ganga Zumba's grandiose entourage. In exchange for peace, which the Black king accepted, he was offered manumission for those born in Palmares, the granting of land in Cucaú, and the guarantee to be able to trade with surrounding residents and the Crown's court of vassals.

The rest of the story I will not detail here, as it doesn't fit into this essay's goals, but its great events are well known: dissidence by Palmarian leaders who, under the leadership of Zumbi, insisted on insurgency; conspiracy against Ganga Zumba; assassination of the ex-leader by poisoning; war between Palmarian factions; breakdown of "official" grouping of Cucaú. At the end of the events, a good part of the Cucaú population, which some call "anti-Palmares," ended up re-enslaved and distributed among the lords of the region. The main leaders of the anti-Ganga Zumba defection were summarily beheaded. The Palmarian insurgency did not stop, as we know, and perhaps continued more vigorously after such episodes. It was an ultimate war effort on the part of the colonizers, with no room for negotiation. *Bandeirante* Domingos Jorge Velho was called up to lead an expedition, perhaps because he was a more fearless man than was Estevão Baião and more renowned than him in the struggle to raid and detain captives. Palmares' final defeat and the death of legendary Zumbi in 1695.

Christianization versus Enslavement

What really matters at this point of our reflection concerns episodes in Cucaú, particularly with the re-enslavement, as "perpetual servitude," of those who had followed Ganga Zumba in his, as it were, exile. It gave rise to what perhaps had been the first major Jesuit intervention regarding Palmares. It was done from Lisbon, in 1680, by priest Manuel Fernandes, a professor of rhetoric, philosophy and theology, and private confessor of none other than King Pedro II. Our dear Jesuit stated, quite clearly, that the people of Cucaú were free and could never have been captured, claiming so on four reasons that I summarize as follows.[11]

The residents of Cucaú had gained manumission by warranty from Governor Aires de Souza e Castro on behalf of His Royal Highness. They became Christians, were baptized and confirmed, and instructed in the holy Catholic faith. They could not fall into (religious) bondage again, for that was against the laws of the State. Besides, and this is a curious argument to say the least, they could only fall into captivity by way of legal sentence because "slavery equals death, and death does not take place without hearing the defendant." Many inhabitants of Cucaú were children of a young age, others were ill, and many neither had conspired against Ganga Zumba nor were allied to the Palmarian faction. Therefore, there was no argument to punish everyone when only some betrayed the 1678 agreement. The 1678 agreement guaranteed freedom to all those who observed what was agreed upon in the armistice; however, re-enslavement was inevitable for those who broke the agreement, which effectively insured a return to the rebellion. Consequently, the Jesuit insisted that several apprehensions carried out in 1680 were exceedingly *unjust* and flatly violated the armistice law. The crime attributed to the majority of the inhabitants of Cucaú had been based on "extra-judicial investigations, each one giving or relying on ill-gotten news."

The eminent Jesuit, the confessor of the king, therefore rebelled against bondage of those who had abjured the rebellion. If those Blacks had abjured it, by embracing the "true Christian faith," how could they be slaves? He hinted, thus, at an idea dear to Ignatians—that being slave and being Christian were mutually exclusive situations. This was a cherished conception and *widely trumpeted regarding the indigenous,* since Nóbrega and Anchieta, but *never in relation to Africans.* It seems that, in this case, the Jesuit had clung to legal formalities, to the legitimacy of the "just war"—which for him was absent in the case of Cucaú—and to the fact that many re-enslaved Blacks were children, ill and, most times, faithful to God and the king.

There remains, however, a major inconsistency or imprecision. More than anything this was a historical inconsistency, since, Jesuits *had always justified and defended slavery of Blacks,* even when they were Christians, although they fought against captivity of indigenous people. In the case of the indigenous, it's worth remembering, catechesis and slavery were in opposition to one another—as can be seen in Nóbrega's and Anchieta's sixteenth century writings, and in Antônio Vieira's sermons in the following century. On the contrary, in the case of Africans, the more that Blacks became Christians the better slaves they would be—so thought Ignatians in Brazil, especially by the Vieira, in the seventeenth century. On the other hand, writing from Lisbon and with no colonizing experience, priest Manoel Fernandes would even *compare slavery to death,* admitting that rebel

Blacks could enjoy the status of freedmen reserved for the indigenous of Brazil.

Christianization versus enslavement was the dilemma in which the Jesuit confessor of the king of Portugal struggled with in condemning the enslavement of Blacks in Cucaú. This was a completely singular dilemma concerning a Jesuit arguing, in the middle of the seventeenth century, about the captivity of Africans. Jesuits spoke little on Palmares—a taboo subject—and the first one to face the theme did it with great hesitation of principles, taking into account the attitude of the Society of Jesus towards slavery. After all, in the seventeenth and eighteenth centuries, it never hurts to remember that the very Jesuits, renowned as missionaries, educators and literati in colonial Brazil, managed to gather valuable assets, including sugar mills and slaves. Priest Manoel Fernandes discussed, however, the situation of Blacks who, as ex-rebels, had embraced peace and Christianity. He touched a highly sensitive issue that for decades had tormented the Church, particularly the Ignatians. How does one reconcile slavery and catechesis of Blacks? Here is the problem; here is the equation to solve. Jesuits in Brazil had already provided the solution, *ad majorem Dei gloriam*, or were about to provide it, and at the most difficult time.

Writing from Lisbon, Manoel Fernandes seemed to have penetrated the dilemma of the very noble class of Pernambuco who were scared and did not know how to handle the Palmarians. There was a pressing need to put things back on track, to seek doctrinal consistency that would substantiate the Christianization of all, as demanded by the Council of Trent, and the enslavement of some, for the glory of the king and appeasing of divine wrath. In short, before Palmares could be established, reconciling the universality of the Catholic faith and the maintenance of class privilege, along with those in Africa, was what occupied the minds of Jesuits in Brazil. African slavery, and indirectly Palmares, was actually a subject of paramount importance to Jesuit reflection. Although, talking about such Jesuit thought is not a simple thing as Ignatians were the flower of the flock among Portuguese intelligentsia, the drivers of education, the apologists of Christian humanism in Trent, heirs of Saint Thomas' scholasticism, masters of Baroque preaching, doctors in the art of transfiguration made of allegories and metaphors designed to edify their moral example.

Indeed few Jesuits spoke about Palmares explicitly. But they spoke a lot about African slavery and, I believe, they did so mainly because of Palmares. In this case, the silence of Ignatians was more apparent than real—suitable for Baroque times. They seemed to follow Calderón de la Barca's saying: "if we have to see power, majesty and pomp falling into obscurity let us make the most of the bit that has to do with us for we only live that which delights us in our dreams." Jesuits dreamed of reconciling slavery and Catholicism of Blacks. A utopia befitting of the verses by Álvaro de Brito in the old *Cancioneiro geral*:

> We should not be common, If not to love God and to serve. Neither can we all be one, in richly dressed shoes and clothes.

Avoiding another Palmares: The Slavery-Christian Project

It was precisely in the seventeenth century when Jesuits started to worry more closely about African slavery. From this concern, the traces that have endured come from what was published in the seventeenth and early eighteenth century, such as the *Sermões* (Sermons) by Vieira, the sermons by Jorge Benci organized in *Economia cristã dos senhores no governo dos escravos* (1705), or the celebrated work by Andreoni or Antonil, *Cultura e opulência do Brasil por suas drogas e minas* (1711). Just traces of evidence, I repeat, that can, however, cast light on a more general Ignatian concern with the issue of the enslavement of Black people.

What is well known is only what was published. But it is presumed that this genre of sermons preached in Black brotherhoods or in churches attended by settlers were actually more widespread. The message that such sermons or prescriptions sought to internalize in the audience obviously varied according to the possible recipient of the speech. The message to slaves called for conformism to their situation as slaves and the hope for a better life after death. To masters, the tone was usually that of the threat of punishments in Heaven and on Earth if they did not take care of Blacks' spiritual and human salvation or denied them the possibility of catechesis or abused their right in exploiting and punishing them. The content of these speeches indicated, in clear ways, a *new* concern, because up until then the Society of Jesus, regarding the issue of slavery, had limited itself to fighting the enslavement of indigenous people, and by clearly confronting the "mercantile purpose of colonization," siding in favor of catechesis and missionary work. As for Africans, in the sixteenth century, there is no apparent concern about catechesis, or any evidence of indignation against unjust captures or exaggerated punishments. The novelty of the seventeenth century resides precisely in the "awareness" on the part of the Jesuits. They realized it was necessary to take care of Blacks' souls and ease slavery's misfortune. But, unlike what they did with regards to the indigenous, they never fought African slavery, despite the struggle they fought with masters in Brazil.

I think that behind this concern, overall, was the growth of African slavery itself on the coast and, consequently, the escapes and rebellions. While in the sixteenth century the slaves in the sugar mills were indigenous, although there were enslaved Africans as well. At the turn to the seventeenth century, Blacks would be the basic workforce of the costal colonial economy.[12] But there is no doubt that the growing Blacks' riots and escapes—attested, among other sources, by the General Government documentation already in the sixteenth century—had considerable influence in this awareness of the "soldiers of Christ."

Palmares, as a topic, has always been omitted by the Jesuits both in sermons and in the manuals on how to treat and rule slaves well. When preaching to masters they alluded, at most, to the dangers of Blacks' mocambos, riots, escapes and vengeance. They had great pleasure in using metaphors to warn masters and call their attention by telling them about the sad fate of kings and people who strayed from God and thus perished. Nevertheless, they remained silent about Palmares. But I am convinced that quilombolas led by Ganga Zumba, and later by Zumbi, featured within the folds of these speeches and all the more so as Palmarian resistance revealed itself to be tenacious and famous. If Palmares was not the *leitmotiv* of the new Jesuit discourse about the enslavement of Blacks, it was like a ghost haunting both the speech of the preachers and what the listeners heard as well.

> Gentlemen (lords), so you call yourselves today, remember that to move from freedom to bondage it is not necessary to pass through Babylon, as this change can happen on your own land…[13]

Antônio Vieira, in 1633, preaching to Blacks on a sugar production facility in Bahia recited the inaugural speech that may have served as the founding speech of Ignatians' new missionary crusade. That is when Vieira, then a young man of 26 years old, developed the idea that Africans and Blacks, whom he called "Ethiopians," were God's elected ones and created in Christ's image to save humankind through sacrifice. Vieira preached to slaves in the sugar production facility, "you are imitators of Christ crucified […], because you suffer in much the same fashion that the Lord himself suffered on his cross and in his whole passion." The outstanding Ignatian would go on with his sermon and detail the evidences for the comparison:

> Christ was naked and you are naked; Christ ate nothing and you are hungry;
> Christ was mistreated in all things and you are mistreated in everything.
> Irons, prisons, whippings, wounds, offensive names, of all these is your im-

itation made up, and if accompanied by patience it will also achieve the worthiness of martyrdom.[14]

To Blacks, Vieira preached patience and the promise for the glorious salvation God owed martyrs. When preaching in a Black brotherhood for Catholic slaves, as a rule, he advised they accept bondage, punishment, and affronts. The catechesis of Blacks, in that it was possible to do it, reinforced slavery and sought to curb uprising impulses. The two ideas were then combined, that of mission, perfectly suited to Counter-Reformation dictates, and the concerns with slave order—an order that would increasingly be threatened by the expansion of Palmares in the neighboring captaincy of Pernambuco.

The socially conservative aim of Counter-Reformation overseas would not be, however, restricted to the colony nor solely encouraged by slaves' revolts. It is possible to see it in the middle of Lisbon and in the very voice of the tireless Vieira. Preaching to the poor of the metropolis, he would tell them not to complain about the hunger that tortured them, because the more emaciated they were, the less devoured their bodies would be in the grave. The rich, instead, for being thus so full and fleshy, what a banquet they would give the worms! A sad fate the rich would have, ended the priest: "eat to be eaten."[15] Jean Delumeau captured very well the conservative aspect of this essentially Tridentine logic that associated Christianization, with the apparent contempt for worldly things and with the "refusal of any sedition and, all the more so, of every revolution."[16]

In colonial Brazil, Vieira would preach to slaves and masters till the end of his life, by appealing to the slaves to bow to the "sweet hell" of the sugar mills, and threatening the lords with the worst punishments in heaven and earth, if they did not reduce the mistreatments they imposed upon the slaves. Punishments from heaven included banishment from Paradise and eternal damnation, and punishments from earth included rebellion and sedition, of which Palmares would be the best example, although Jesuits did not talk about them in their preaching. Jorge Benci, an Italian Jesuit, was the author of the best and thorough prescription book addressed to masters on how to treat slaves in the Christian fashion. Benci was in Brazil between 1683 and 1700. He took on several posts in the Jesuit College of Bahia, and was a visitor and secretary to the provincial government. During his stay in the colony he, therefore, followed the most acute and ultimate stage of Palmarian history, from the Recife Agreement (1678) and Zumbi's death (1695), to the assassination of Ganga Zumba, the Cacaú massacre and upsurge of quilombola resistance.

Priest Antonio Vieira.

His book—*Economia cristã dos senhores no governo dos escravos*—was published in 1705 in Rome but had been written in 1700 based on various sermons preached by the Jesuit in Brazil. Sermons preached in the heat of Palmarian fights or a little after the quilombo's destruction. Sermons committed to give colonial slavery Christian features so that Blacks would also be instructed in the "true faith" and certainly to prevent them from uprising and ruining the whole colony. "Avoiding another Palmares": the title I gave this section fits the Italian Jesuit's speech like a glove. It can be summarized by the very formula used by Benci in advising masters on how to treat slaves: *panis, disciplinae et opus servo*—bread, discipline or punishment, and work, a formula extracted from Ecclesiastes combined with Aristotle.[17] What Benci explicitly intended was to provide "rule, standard and model" by which Christian masters should guide themselves in order "to fulfill their obligations as true masters."[18] According to Benci, therefore, masters should first of all conduct themselves in the light of the divine precepts of Catholicism so as to be worthy of seigniorial status. The true masters were the Christian ones and only by taking on this role could they well govern slaves.

This very rich manual sought to Christianize masters and slaves, whites and Blacks in Brazil, by promoting in the tropic an authentic *Christian republic,* inspired by the Council of Trent Tridentine and yet, at the same time, to strengthen slave hierarchy and slave order. I have mentioned it elsewhere, explaining what I then called the Christian slave project, a Jesuit project committed to combining Tridentine Catholicism and slavery. A project, hence, opposed to excessive punishments, over exploitation of Black labor, and the sexual permissiveness allegedly existing in *casas-grandes* and *senzalas*. A project radically against Blacks' *batuques* (drumming) and *calundus* (trance dancing rituals) that were allowed by masters and that prevented them from entering the path of God. A project which opposed the idea that slaves worked for themselves on Sundays and holy days, days of God, days of mass. A project committed to fostering the sacrament of matrimony among Africans so they ceased licentiousness and increased servile progeny in the laws of Christ, to forge a God-fearing captive community, totally adapted to a Christian style of bondage. A moderate, just, rational, profitable, and balanced bondage. A bondage that is perfectly compliant with the Council of Trent's rules and dogmas and completely immune to rebellions, to another Palmares.[19]

Hence the famous formula that structures Benci's work and sermons: *bread* understood as physical and spiritual food, including the sacraments; *punishment* so that, applied sparingly (only whips and chains), slaves obeyed and feared the master as they feared God; *work* so that everyone's sustenance would be achieved and, for being free from idleness, the captive would not throw himself into all sorts of disobedience, sexual depravations and false devotions they were used to with the acquiescence of their masters.

A formula somewhat simplified, and a bit sarcastic, was the one used by the famous Antonil, who had been secretary to Vieira when the latter returned to Brazil in 1681. As simple as PPP: *pão, pau* and *pano*, (bread, stick, and materials). Antonil would not stress the "spiritual bread" so dear to the Jesuit project, and would go so far as to allow slaves to have "their entertainments" and "Epiphany," dances and chants, as long as they were done innocently, and, on some days of the year, and only "after having done their morning celebration of Our Lady of the Rosary."[20] Overall, however, Antonil would line up with the bulk of the slave-Christian project ideals: in favor of marriage among slaves; opposed to rampant libertinage; an advocate of moderate punishments; opposed to abuse. He was also explicitly concerned with slaves' escapes and with quilombos, although he did not mention Palmares:

> You [masters] better be aware that this is of help because they [slaves] will sometimes escape, anyway, to some *mocambo* in the bushes, and if they are caught it is possible they may kill themselves...[21]

Antonil wrote these lines between 1693 and 1698, a time when the Palmares war reached its peak and lived its last chapter. It is impossible to see a mere coincidence between Ignatian concerns with Black bondage and contemporary insurgency led by Zumbi.

Although avoiding another Palmares is one of the deep motivations of this speech, the true project called for completely Christianizing colonial slavery, turning sugar mills into missions, masters into watchful missionaries, and slaves into obedient sons of God. In the end, a conservative and proslavery utopia that admitted Blacks into heaven, if they remained slaves, and relentlessly condemned them to hell if they committed the mortal sin of rebellion.

Slavery God: Vieira and the Destruction of Palmares

Jesuit opinion would end up being truly decisive in the destruction of Palmares and this thanks to none other than Antônio Vieira. The famous Jesuit, author of what I called the founding sermon of the slave-Christian project in year 1633, was now an old and sick man in 1691. He was 83 years old and his prestige was just a shadow of what it was in the society and even among monarchy decades before. Vieira went through clashes in Maranhão where he had been a missionary and visitor. He wrote the greatest Sebastianist libels that turned Bandarra, the shoemaker from Trancoso, into the prophet of Portuguese Restoration in 1640. He served as a politician and diplomat during the reign of D. João IV, the first of the Braganças, a period when he gained the highest prestige and political importance in the Kingdom. He also endured some time in prison and inquisitional proceedings for the accusation of preaching the resurrection of D. João IV in his writings. It is true he was later rehabilitated but he would never again be the Sebastianist Vieira, the caustic accuser of captors of indigenous peoples, the audacious critic of the Inquisition and of the persecution of New Christians for which he became famous.

D. Pedro II regarded as "treacherous" and "scheming" the once prestigious Vieira, who, when returning to Brazil in 1681, would closely monitor the growing prestige of Italian and German Jesuits to the detriment of the Portuguese ones. This resulted in disputes caused in part by the ascension of Antonil in the Society of Jesus—he, the one who was taken to Brazil by Vieira himself as secretary. Despite everything, it was Vieira whom Roque Monteiro Paim, president of *Junta das Missões*, addressed, in 1691, according to João Lúcio de Azevedo, Palace High Court judge and secretary of the king. The consultation dealt, among other topics, with the case of Palmares. Unfortunately, the content of this consultation is not known (at least to date) in full, but it is certain that most of it dealt with Palmares. It was a time of great hesitation then. Quilombolas, from Palmares, led by the bold Zumbi increased the number of attacks on sugar mills and farms in Pernambuco. The colonial government did not know what else to do after a failed armistice signed by Ganga Zumba and a destroyed "official refuge" in Cucaú. The Monarchy itself and the Overseas Council seemed perplexed.

The main subject in the letter sent from Lisbon to Vieira asked that the Jesuit consider the suggestion given by an Italian monk, apparently a Jesuit one, "to reach out to Palmares." To go and catechize them, to go and convince them to surrender or to make a new attempt for an agreement, one does not know exactly what, for sure, suggested the Italian monk. One can assert, however, that the idea was to go and meet the Palmarians and propose some kind of agreement to them, and Jesuits would be the ones in charge of this important mission. Vieira's reply, published in full by João Lúcio de Azevedo in *História de Antônio Vieira*, and the document were deposited in the Évora Library under the title "letter from Antônio Vieira to a certain nobleman," dated 2 July 1691.[22] Besides being strange that superiors of the Jesuit Province in Brazil did not learn about such a proposal, in the long passage relating to Palmares Vieira begins by discrediting the Italian monk, the author of the proposal. Vieira wrote that Jorge Benci, a Jesuit engaged in the slavery issue, was a priest that had "not many years of age," with "little or no experience in these matters," even though "of good spirits and fervent." Having discredited the Italian monk, Vieira moved on to belittle the proposal, adding that the matter had been put in consultation and all priests judged it impossible to go to Palmares. He then listed five reasons, which appear below:

> Because if it were possible, it should be through the native-born Angolan priests that we have, whom they believe and trust and understand for they share a common homeland and language; but everyone agrees that this is a baseless and hopeless matter.
>
> Because even they [priests], in this case, will not be trusted in any way, for they [slaves] are always suspicious and believe that they [priests] are spies of the governors to whom they [priests] secretly tell how they [slaves] can be conquered.
>
> Because any of these suspicions, either in whole or in part, even the slightest one, will be enough to kill them [priests] with poison, as they [slaves] have done to each other in hidden and secret ways.
>
> Because even if they ceased the attacks they carry out on the Portuguese villages, they will never stop embracing the ones from their nation that flee to them.
>
> Most importantly and completely, for being rebels and captives, they are committing and persevering in continuous and current sin, from which they will not be absolved, nor will they be granted God's grace, if they do not resume their service and obedience to their masters, which they in no way will do. There is only one efficient and effective way to truly limit them, which is His Majesty and all their masters granting them spontaneous, liberal and safe freedom to live in those places like other free Indians and gentiles do, so that their parish priests may become their clergy and indoctrinate them like all the others.

The five assertions made by Vieira, especially the last two, are extraordinarily rich not only to track down what was, after all, the content of the proposal made by the "Italian monk" but also to clarify for the last time where Jesuits stood concerning Black slavery and rebellion. For the first time, apparently, Jesuits gave their opinion on Palmares in writing on Brazil soil. The first reason is, so to speak, of a "technical" nature that rather belongs to the domains of communication: only priests from Angola or, those priests who know the "languages," would be able to discuss with quilombolas, since the ones from Bantu culture were predominant among Palmarians. The following two reasons, however, overthrow the initial hypothesis when Vieira claims that, even if such priests went to Palmares, there was great danger of being taken for spies and killed "with poison." In regards to the Palmarian poison mentioned in his third reason, Vieira shows an awareness of what had been happening in the refuge of Cucaú, of the assassination of Ganga Zumba and the fratricidal struggle that followed it.

Jesuit church and college in Salvador, c. 1858 ("Ancient collège des jésuits à Bahia, Brazil pitoresco. Album of views, landscapes, monuments, costumes, etc. [Paris: Lemercier, 1861]).

The fourth reason suggests, first, that the Jesuit embassy's aim was to attempt some sort of agreement: to get the promise out of Palmarians that they would no longer attack Portuguese villages and sugar mills nor admit new runaways into their mocambos. There is nothing original in it, as we can see, neither in the history of Palmares nor in the history of Afro-American *marronage*. But in exchange for what, one might ask, would Jesuits make such a demand? So far the document does not explain what Jesuits would offer in return. It clarifies, however, Vieira's completely skeptical position concerning Palmarians' predisposition to negotiate with Jesuits. Vieira did not believe in rebels. In the fifth reason, "most importantly and completely," lies the crux of the matter. Vieira insists that, while being rebellious and thus remaining in mortal sin, they could not receive the "grace of God" nor could they be subjugated. What does this "grace" indicate? Would Vieira be referring to the sacraments, to the doctrine, to the catechesis? And when he speculates about the way "to truly limit them," living in their settlements like free gentiles and indoctrinated by the priests, would Vieira be alluding only to military agreements?

It seems to me, indeed, that the plan Vieira looked into included turning Palmares into something similar to Jesuits settlements: mocambos comparable to missions. Following this line of interpretation, limiting Palmarians would imply, firstly, granting them manumission and then submit them to the missions through which priests who would "indoctrinate them like all the others." Should the raised hypothesis be correct, we are faced with a disconcerting paradox. Palmares, the greatest focus of resistance to colonial slavery, would end up converted into a kind of Black settlement of the Society of Jesus. It would be like going directly from rebellion to mission, by transforming a massive quilombo into an exemplary scenery of the Christian-slavery project. In this case, similar to what happened to the indigenous people, Christianization and freedom would walk together, and evangelization implying, at least, widespread manumission to rebels.

In any case, Vieira did not fall into this trap, but rather stated, quite clearly, that complete incompatibility between Christianization and freedom in the case of Blacks:

> Yet, this very freedom would be the total destruction of Brazil, because knowing how all the other Blacks who through this means had managed to be free, each town, each village, each place, each sugar mill would soon become many other Palmares, as they would escape and hide in the bushes carrying all their wealth, which is no more than their own body.

The triumph of colonialism, sugar mills, and slavery. For being rebels, quilombolas were in mortal sin and, hence, did not deserve the grace of God. They owned no more than their own body—a body enslaved to the masters—since the soul was enslaved to the devil. No sacraments or doctrine for rebels is what Vieira seems to suggest. When it comes to Blacks, catechesis would only make sense if they were slaves. There was nothing the Jesuits could do in the quilombo of Palmares.

On 6 February 1692, the king himself would personally write to Vieira agreeing with his position and confirming the suspension of any compromise policy. It would not take long for the quilombo to be finally destroyed and Zumbi killed. A triumph of colonialism and, at least in theory, of the slave-Christian project? The Jesuits may not have been successful in catechizing Black slaves—prevented by masters, by "customs in Brazil," to impose their model of a patriarchal, family and Christian slavery—but at least they remained consistent with not catechizing the seditious, by keeping associated with, in the case of Blacks, the ideas of bondage and Christianization. It is true Palmares was destroyed. But the Jesuits also would not achieve success in the "holy purpose" of establishing a Christian slavery in Brazil. In the end, the clash between God and Palmares would have no winner.

5

FROM SINGULAR TO PLURAL

PALMARES, CAPITÃES-DO-MATO$_1$, AND THE SLAVE GOVERNMENT

Silvia Hunold Lara

Paradoxically, the great *quilombo* of Palmares became part of history at the hands of a highborn *baiano,* a sugar cane plantation owner, on the banks of the Paraguaçu River. This entrance into history happened with the *História da América portuguesa,* written by Sebastião da Rocha Pita in 1724.[2] The book is divided into ten "books" which tell the main events in this part of the Portuguese Empire from its discovery until the beginning of the eighteenth century. Somewhere around the eighth book, apparently worth less space than the common maladies of the time, which are mentioned several times at the summaries at the ending of each part, we can find 26 paragraphs mentioning the "war […] with the blacks of Palmares."[3]

The report is quite objective, giving "news about the conditions and principles of these enemies, the origins of the village or republic they had established, the laws by which they ruled themselves, the damages they did to our villages during sixty years […] and the harm they caused to their inhabitants."[4] The majority of the text is dedicated to the initiatives and "hard endeavors" which led to "a glorious and useful end of the war we had with the Palmares blacks."[5]

As usual, the quilombos became known by their destruction: the history of Palmares was long, and many reports about repressive expeditions served as the basis for the construction of its "history," as highlighted in *Diário de Viagem do Capitão João Blaer aos Palmares em 1645* and *Relação das guerras feitas aos Palmares de Pernambuco no tempo do governador Dom Pedro de Almeida de 1675 a 1678.*[6] But the quilombo's final destruction does not have a direct testimonial narrative: its historical reconstitution relies on the governor's communications, queries, opinions, resolutions of the Overseas Council, royal letters and other documentary sources. Despite all the investment on historiography produced in this century, there is large-scale confusion concerning data, dates, places, etc., and there are still controversies about the largest and longest-lasting Brazilian quilombo.

Nevertheless, the narrative presented by Rocha Pita in 1724 has elements that have been maintained and reiterated for a long time by previous historiography, and even by authors whose writings were widely favorable to the *quilombolas* (descendants of quilombos) and not to their destroyers. His text became a paradigm of "historical interpretation" about Palmares. Therein lies the motives that led to the formation of the *mocambos* (a word used interchangeably with quilombos) at Serra da Barriga, the main aspects of life and the Palmarian organization, and, above all, its colossal resistance from the attacks commanded by Domingos Jorge Velho and the suicide of Zumbi.[7] This was all done in an epic and pompous style, in which there was no shortage of praises to the then governor of Pernambuco, Caetano de Melo de Castro, and frequent comparisons with heroes of classical history and literature.[8] The most impressive fact yet is that this baiano scholar also set a "tone" for subsequent historical narratives. Even in works composed from within a strong critical effort and that undertake a "leftist" view about Palmares, we can find the same metaphors and comparisons (the slave war started by enslaved gladiators in ancient Rome, the abduction of the Sabine women) or sometimes characterizations with misguided meanings, like calling Palmares "a rustic republic and orderly in its own way."[9]

Putting aside these historiographical aspects, it is important to ask why Rocha Pita needed to include this episode in his *História da América portuguesa*.[10] Once they had ruined the mocambos of Serra da Barriga, sold and disbanded the survivors, made the solemnities, masses and the *Te Deum* (Latin: "God, we praise you"), would it not have been better to adopt the customary practice of silence, erasing Palmares from memory, ignoring the episode when writing their history?

Rocha Pita himself provides us with some clues for a preliminary answer to this question. The object of his report was not Palmares itself, but the "very difficult" enterprise of destroying them, undertaken "with valor" and achieved "with fortune" by Caetano de Melo e Castro.[11] As "from the most arduous endeavors reap the greatest applauses," the author used the comparison with the slave war in Rome to accentuate the "damages" caused by the quilombolas, "the calamity which Pernambuco suffered by this oppression from Palmares." To face an enemy so formidable they had to raise an army with sufficient training, valor and command carefully described to the point that they could face Palmares "with military pomp, festive attitude, and all the resources of a long campaign." The difficulty of the war makes a better victory, and the valor of the enemy—whose "prince" with his "most valiant warriors [...] disdaining death by our swords, elevated themselves to the highest esteem and voluntarily ran headlong into battle with us"— emphasizes the "glory of battle."[12]

In other words, Palmares needed to enter into the *História da América portuguesa* because it was difficult to overcome. The glory of this victory became therefore significant to the colonial and metropolitan public opinion. As Governor Fernão da Costa Coutinho stated in 1671, Pernambuco "wasn't less dangerous [...] with the boldness of those negros than with the Dutch," and this episode offered a good opportunity to demonstrate the efficiency of metropolitan and colonial powers over their *internal* enemies.[13] In this context, Palmares was also important because of the questions raised against the traditional policy of preventing escapes and gathering fugitives. Finding solutions to these problems (in an irregular and inconstant way) and the impact of policies of control over slave movement inside the colony resulted in significant changes, which had spread secularly into the metropolitan and colonial legislation, and regulated relations between the slave and master. This essay intends to follow some clues, and analyze some steps in the interpretation of this process.

If "escape is inherent to slavery," as Perdigão Malheiro argued, so too is the association between fugitives and the supportive aid received in a direct or indirect way from third parties.[14] The existence of fugitive slaves was always acknowledged by slave owners, although it was never seen as a crime. It is evident that there were measures to prevent them, and that recaptured escapees were arrested, brought back to their masters and punished. It was a punishment that was punitive as well as preventive of new escapes; the punishment made examples of recaptured slaves and focused on the future, aiming to avoid new runaways.[15] The ones considered criminals were those who helped the slave on his escape and this became law very early.[16]

However, while taking into account the masters' actions and legislation, their assembling of a systematic repressive apparatus to prevent escapes was a rather slow process. At least until 1603, the hunt for fugitives was a sporadic and temporary activity: if someone "came across" a runaway slave, they were supposed to turn him back to his master or the local magistrate within a fortnight. In exchange, he could get twenty *réis* per day that the slave was kept and three hundred *réis* as a "finder's fee."[17] The *ordenações filipinas* determined that each town or city should have its *quadrilheiros* (agents of the police). Nominated by the Town Council for a three year mandate, one for every twenty neighbors, their objective was to control a determined area and its residents, avoiding disorder, loitering, gambling, prostitution, and the provision of shelter or protection to criminals.[18] However, nothing in this text or in subsequent statutes said anything related to the task of hunting slaves.

Maybe because of it, the institution of the quadrilheiros faced difficulties when attempts were made to implement it in colonial areas. The general magistrate of Rio de Janeiro, for example, acknowledged the necessity of its creation in a document published in 1626, but, a hundred years later, there was still pressure on the council to fill these positions and to elect people to the quadrilhas that did not exist yet in the city. The documents indicate the difficulties were related to the status of the position in the colony and the form of payment. In 1730, responding to this appeal, the town council of Rio de Janeiro informed the magistrate that the necessary arrangements had already been made, but using the name *capitão-do-mato* (captain of the forest), considering that "maybe this name would facilitate the acceptance of the profession." When the magistrate answered insisting on the appointment of a quadrilheiro member to each parish in the city, he also gave him the power to arrest runaway slaves, being paid to do so with the same amount as for the capitães-do-mato.[19]

FROM SINGULAR TO PLURAL

*Capitão-do-mato, c. 1825 ("Capitão do mato," M. Rugendas,
Malerische Reise in Brasilien [Paris: Engelmann & Cie., 1835]).*

In little more than a hundred years, the principal focus changed from controlling the population to capturing runaway slaves—from the metropolitan approach to the colonial approach—and a central figure of the capitão-do-mato emerges. Although frequently associated with African slavery in Brazil, little is known about the origins and the functioning of this figure.[20] The term capitão-do-mato appears in several different colonial documents as early as the mid-seventeenth century; this is seen in the practice of paying them for "services rendered," that is, he is paid a fee per slave seized and delivered to his master. However, the position, the appointment of regular posts, and the determination of amounts to be paid were established little by little, becoming systematically regulated only beginning in the first decades of the eighteenth century.

What might have happened in the period from the middle of the seventeenth century to the early decades of the eighteenth for this profession to be established so firmly in colonial life? I think that Palmares—or rather, the fear of the emergence of many new places like Palmares—could have played an important role in the minds of slaveholders and, especially, in the heads of some colonial officials, in the development of this new "machinery." There was no planning, neither was this the case of a single person's creation, but the profession may have resulted from a long, erratic and contradictory process that had its epicenter in the impact caused by the resistive force of Palmares' inhabitants to subsequent and increasingly repressive expeditions.

I do not intend to recover here the long trajectory of the attacks against Palmares. For the purposes of this essay of historical interpretation, it suffices for us to remember that various expeditions, the failures and even contracts with experienced frontiersmen exemplify the more traditional forms employed in the repression of runaway slaves and the gathering of fugitives.

Against the inevitable slave escapes, the masters took their measures, each taking care of themselves and of their own. If the escapees did join forces and began to put the roads in danger or "influence" other slaves to escape, groups of repressive special forces were formed, with participation of militias or interested parties, using permanent troops when necessary. The costs were shared among residents, either directly or through the always complicated and difficult financing granted by the Town Councils. For those who achieved victory, especially in the more severe cases, the awards included the profit from the sale of the prisoners, with the requisite payment of the "one fifths," and even land or the granting of titles and patents.[21] In each failure, official efforts were increased, in an attempt to achieve greater effectiveness, including more armed men, more supplies, and better tactics.

We have to remember to stay in the final decades of the seventeenth century in the expeditions of Manuel Lopes Galvão (1675) and Fernão Carrilho (1676–1678) against Palmares. The first one, commanded by a sargeant-major, had 280 men and took a month to get from Porto Calvo to get to the first attack against one of the mocambos, returning after a five month campaign with approximately a hundred prisoners but without destroying the mocambos. In the next year, the governor sought aid from an experienced captain, a veteran from combats in the hinterlands; with the help from several town councils, he mustered a large amount of money to arm more than four hundred men. In fact they were just 185 "whites and António Filipe Camarão's Indians," who left Porto Calvo on September of 1677 and built a makeshift fort in place of one of the destroyed mocambos. Many armed recruits with more supplies joined them in the following months; they engaged in several battles, expeditions, sieges and arrests until January 1678, when Fernão Carrilho retired "destroying Palmares and vanquishing the Blacks."[22]

The 1694 army that vanquished Palmares in less than a month was composed of more than six thousand men: one-third commanded by Domingos Jorge Velho, plus three thousand recruited between the inhabitants of Olinda, Recife and neighboring villages, another 1500 from Alagoas, in addition to volunteers and others from several neighboring villages close to Palmares.[23] In order to destroy the communities at Serra da Barriga that kept being rebuilt after being declared vanquished, they once again mustered local troops that were supported by veterans from the hinterlands. With efforts from the slaveholders, the city council and governor, they launched an annihilation expedition.[24]

In all three cases, there were long discussions that preceded and followed the battles, particularly discussions about sharing the booty of prisoners and securing His Majesty's one-fifth share. The contract with Domingos Jorge Velho was negotiated in 1687 and finally ratified in 1693. Caetano de Melo e Castro, when reporting to the king "the news of the glorious restoration of Palmares," mentioned the first steps already taken to enforce that contract. A few months later, however, he backed out, thinking that it should not be entirely enforced.[25]

That was the way the slaveholder's fear worked in relation to the quilombos. Most of the time, the slaveholder's policy was to weaken the escapees with a good flogging and close scrutiny to prevent the runaways from assembling in a dangerous way. When the mocambos, a community or a quilombo gather enough strength to pose a threat to the roads and farmlands, they mustered a small army to "bring back the peace." Not by chance, several writers comment that the formation of Palmares, initially no more than a small group of escaped slaves from a sugar mill, would have taken advantage of the weakening of the manorial control caused by the Dutch presence. After expelling the invaders, the colonists initiated more intense attempts to destroy the "internal enemy," as described by the memoirist hired by Dom Pedro de Almeida.[26]

It is quite true that the colonial and metropolitan authorities did not always agree with each other on the measures to be taken. After the victories of Fernão Carrilho, the Governor Dom Pedro de Almeida even made a peace treaty with the people of Palmares. His successor, however, in the following year, sent a bloody but unsuccessful expedition.[27] The peace, again designed by João da Cunha Sotomaior in 1685, was clearly repudiated by the Overseas Council in 1686.[28] In 1682, the king resorted to more drastic measures. With all the pomp of a royal charter, he determined that besides the continuity of the armed campaign against the rebels of Palmares, residents of the province of Pernambuco had to give up "the rights that they may have in the domain" of those blacks that were distributed to soldiers after they were captured. Generously, the king approved that slaveholders that are more reluctant should get 12 thousand *réis* per slave lost, passing regulations on "freedom [and on] the captivity of those Blacks": those who were free before they went to the Palmares would remain free, opening a period of five years for the litigation. None of them, free or enslaved, could remain in the State of Brazil, for the captives who escaped again would be "sent to the galley." More important, however, was the opening of a "crime of wanton treachery" by the breach of the peace agreement with the Governor of Pernambuco. The culprits would be condemned to death, and their heads raised on "high public posts," in the place of the offense and to be consumed by time.[29] In the eyes of the metropolis, there is nothing better than the old practices of exemplar punishment to extinguish feelings of rebellion and treason, like the ones occurring in Pernambuco.

I believe that Palmares managed to let the slaveholder's fear of slave flights reach its maximum point and that it marked the high point of the great annihilation armies. In the official correspondence between the metropolis and the governors from the late seventeenth-century, the comparison of Palmares with the Dutch invasion of Brazil is relatively frequent, because of all the damages, dangers and war difficulties involved.[30] Possibly it was the favorable conjuncture that helped the formation of such a powerful and immense quilombo, powerful enough to jeopardize the colonial and slaveholder's might in a large piece of land in the Pernambuco province. Never before had a Brazilian quilombo reached this size and power; the reasons why it did so are important to consider.

The reasons, in my opinion, should be found less in the movement of the slaves and more in the alterations in the slaveholder's policies about the control of slaves. Some authors link the impact of Palmares to the royal measures of 1688 which tried to curtail the cruelty of slave punishments.[31] This was a metropolitan initiative that combined the content of the recommendations of Italian Jesuit Jorge Benci, whose sermons delivered in Bahia were published in 1705. For this Jesuit priest, a punishment ruled and measured was the best way "to bring out well tamed and disciplined slaves."[32]

Others claim that, after Palmares, the concentration of slaves of the same ethnic group was always to be avoided in order to make it more difficult for captives to form unions or alliances.[33] In the absence of any documentary evidence for this possibility, which should be further investigated, we can only point out that such measures came to be the object of discussion between the colonial authorities, as evidenced by the correspondence between the Overseas Council and the Governor of Rio de Janeiro regarding the slave conspiracy in Minas Gerais at the beginning of the eighteenth century. In 1726, for example, Luís Vaía Monteiro reasoned that experience had shown that "to avoid the uprisings that cause fear," "the differences between the nations" were "the most effective means" because "the division was always the biggest antidote." His suggestion that "blacks from all nations should be introduced in Minas" was approved by the Overseas Council in 1728.[34]

However, more than a possible greater "benevolence" in the treatment of slaves or any attempt to promote the mixing of ethnicities, I believe that the key to this question seems to be the slow validation of the position of capitão-do-mato and their assignments.[35] The first documentary reference to a certain specialization in the capture of fugitives is from the middle of the seventeenth century. Some suggest there were people named specifically for this task; others refer to cash rewards posted by the Town Councils per captive apprehended.[36] In most cases, the solutions were sporadic, almost right on top of the expeditions that would repress certain quilombos, and not always the term capitão-do-mato was employed. The expressions that were interchangeably used were "field captains," "entry captains," or "assault captains," which may also appear in the merged forms of "forest-entry captains" or "entry and assault captains."[37] There is evident confusion in terminology, but "assault captains" seem to have received a specific mention in a statute of January 1676, which, unfortunately, remains lost.[38] Maybe this was the first legal document of metropolitan or colonial origin for regulating the activity. The variety in nomenclatures, assignments, attributions and jurisdictions reinforces the fluid character of the post, which seems to be unlinked to the Ordinance Service, although they share some similarities with company captains.[39]

In February 1680, for example, the Governor of Pernambuco granted the rank of "Captain-Major of the field of the province of Alagoas" to André Dias, an experienced man who had previously fought against Palmares. His assignment was to patrol the fields and other places where they had news of runaway slaves "to arrest them, and even enter the homes and farms or kill those who resist." The charter stipulated that Dias would enjoy all the privileges and had authority over the other field captains of the region and its districts and should be helped by the officers of ordinances and by the councils if necessary.[40] Royal letters dated from 1696 suspend the nomination of two persons to the post of "captain-major of *mocambo* entries and fugitive slaves," one in Ilhéus and another in Bahia under the allegation that "for this post to be created again," the governor of the State of Brazil is to be prevented from making new appointments in these cases.[41] Nevertheless, in 1714, the king gave permission to the marquis of Angeja, at the time the viceroy of the State of Brazil, the creation of the posts of "captain-major of *mocambo* entries and fugitive slaves."[42]

Part of the bibliography used situates the creation of the post of capitão-do-mato in Minas Gerais, as from the granting of the statute in 1724.[43] Alípio Goulart contests this date, calling attention to the statute of 1676, the one of 1722 and an order dated from 1741.[44] The period between the end of the seventeenth century and the beginning of the eighteenth seems crucial, but we to need look at the nuances and follow up more closely the relations and intentions of the metropolitan and colonial authorities. In this sense, we can follow some small clues indicated by the sources, evident from Pernambuco to Minas Gerais.[45]

In 1715, after consulting the Magistrates of Vila Rica and Vila Real, the governor of the independent province of São Paulo and Minas de Ouro, Dom Brás Baltasar da Silveira, signed a statute in which he established the amounts to be paid for captured slaves to the capitães-do-mato.[46] The capitães-do-mato would be paid four eighths of gold for those captured within a league radius of a village, a little more for those captured from a greater distance, and an even larger amount for the ones captured deeper into the woods, and so on.[47] Also the document stipulated that the captured prisoners should immediately be delivered to their masters, in exchange for a "finder's fee" payment; any delay in delivery could result in a penalty for theft.

I know nothing about the motives that may have given rise to such measures, but everything indicates that this was an attempt to regulate activity in this region. The text, worked out between the governor and the magistrates on February 4, 1715, is fairly simple and straightforward. The councils would choose people to be appointed and the governor would publish the respective licenses; if someone else held a fugitive, he would get "half of what a *capitão-do-mato* would get." Little more than a year later, it was stipulated that any person who caught a slave on the run, even though not being a capitão-do-mato, would get the same payment that they would get, "given the lack of these and the complaint that there were too many slaves fleeing."[48] So despite having a "statute," the presence of the capitão-do-mato was still uneven and seemed insufficient to curb the escapes and quilombos, insomuch that the function could be performed by people who didn't have the appropriate license.

It is probable that the movement of slaves in the Minas de Ouro region, circa 1718–1719, and the anguish of some rulers led to new and significant changes. The correspondence between the Count of Assumar and the King, between 1718 and 1719, was intense regarding the "various settlements of blacks," which threatened to cause a "big downfall to the residents of Minas." Faced with so much danger, the governor tried several repressive measures. In December 1717, Assumar signed an order authorizing attacks on the quilombos, without impediment, to whoever wanted to do it. Besides, it provided penalties and exile to Benguela for those who knew about the existence of quilombos and did not denounce them, in addition to rewards to members of the quilombos who gave information about their quilombos. The following January, he signed an order for the capitães-do-mato to arrest any slave without permission of the owner, who were found in the village or outside it after nine o'clock at night.[49]

Writing to the king in the middle of the year, Assumar went much further in his assessment noting that the issue of gangs of runaway slaves was a matter of much importance "that on it may depend the conservation or destruction of this country [...] because I see a trend in this negro government to act in a form similar to the Palmares of Pernambuco." For that reason, he asked for urgent arrangements, suggesting they adopt similar measures as in Mississippi or Louisiana, cutting the right leg of the fugitives and replacing them with wooden legs. It was a good way to avoid losses. Or, one could still adopt what was practiced in lands under the King of Castile, where there was "an officer called the provincial *alcaide* (governor or commander of a castle or fortress), whose main obligation was to bring people continuously into the woods in case of news of a black uprising or runaway slaves," with jurisdiction to execute the death penalty and be paid by the number of fugitives arrested.[50]

Assumar seemed very engaged in the question and drew on experiences of other slave holding regions of the Americas to find the best path to combat "these thugs and robbers." The king, however, in January 1719, recommended to the Count that, to remedy the existence of quilombos, he should use "the way that is practiced in all the provinces of Bahia, Rio de Janeiro, Pernambuco and Paraíba, and this way meant paying a capitão-do-mato for each slave they could capture."[51] In other words, there was no need to rely on foreign examples; for the metropolitan onlookers, there was a "custom" already practiced in Brazil and was sufficient to follow. Although without mention to a specific statute, the activity of the capitães-do-mato already appeared as effective and sufficiently consolidated.

The Governor of Minas disagreed, as if the king or the overseas advisers didn't know what was going on in Brazil. In April, Assumar would insist on the issue, in a long letter which reiterated the arguments already made clear in the middle of 1718, reminding all of the "importance of this matter for it seems to me, on good grounds, that some blacks could be conducting some operations similar to the one in Palmares of Pernambuco, bound together in their multitude and in their masters' relative trust in them."[52]

Undoubtedly, Assumar was fearful of the movement of slaves in Minas, having managed to abort a general uprising against white people scheduled for the Thursday before Easter that year. He had already taken several measures: enforcing the ban on gun possession by the black and mulatto slaves, and arresting suspects and punishing several others. The letters and hints, addressed both to the king and other colonial rulers succeeded.[53] In November of 1718, the abundance of forest, the lack of repressive forces and the numerical superiority of blacks facilitating escapes and putting "in danger the Government of Minas," Assumar proposed various "remedies," among them the cutting off the Achilles tendon, which would not hinder work but would make escapes impossible. Another order, on the same date, commanded summary executions for "blacks found in the woods and the ones who walk away from the obedience of their masters," with their heads to be left exposed at the entrance of villages, in addition to other measures such as the ban on manumissions without the license of the king and the baptism of slaves with black godparents.[54]

Assumar seems to have actually been a man tormented by the danger represented by the vast slave concentration in Minas Gerais, seeing at every moment the possibility of a new Palmares. His proposals, however, were not always implemented, whether by refusal of the metropolis or by disagreements with the local slaveholders. These proposals reveal that his fear, although sharp, was not always the same and, above all, had not yet found effective answers to avoid or at least control the escapes, mocambos and quilombos, at a tolerable level.

Only with his successor, Dom Lourenço de Almeida, were more general and preventive measures taken, with a detailed statute of procedure published in December 12, 1722, revoking the existing one.[55] The measure was justified as a way of trying to accumulate experience, and resolve questions and problems that the occupation of capitão-do-mato had created. So instead of fixed geographic parameters, he stipulated an amount for "a finder's fee" from the dwelling place of the capitão-do-mato. Still they paid four eighths for fugitives who were caught within a mile of the village, but then everything changed: eight eighths for those caught up to a two days' journey distance, twelve eighths for up to four days of travel, seventeen eighths up to eight days and twenty five for larger distances than that.[56] For each slave arrested "in *quilombos* formed distances from any settlement with more than four blacks," the capitão-do-mato received twenty eighths. Actually, the governor did not wish there to be any doubt, showing (probably for the first time in an official document) a clear definition of what was a quilombo: more than four blacks with ranches and food mills that are far away from the breadth and strength of Palmares, or even the revolt of 1719 aborted by Assumar.

But the detailing of the rules did not stop there. Now, unlike the previous statute, the fugitive arrested should be handed over to a local judge (or other equivalent authority) to verify if this was even a runaway slave and, in this case, be put in jail and the master informed. The slave could only be returned to the master after paying this "finder's fee" (*tomadias*), expenditures made, incarceration—all counted and controlled by the judge.[57] All fugitives seized should necessarily be given to the judge and, if a capitão-do-mato takes more than fifteen days with their catch, he could lose the right to receive the bounty and still be obliged to pay a tax for the days spent with the slave. The eventual death of slaves were only permitted in the case of "resistance" and "natural defense"; otherwise, the capitão-do-mato could be subjected to penalties under the law.[58]

The position of capitão-do-mato also gained certain exclusivity, since the paragraph that authorized individuals to receive the same remuneration was erased.[59] There were still more general rules about the character of the trade. Capitães-do-mato who arrested obedient slaves could be prosecuted and even forbidden to continue in the post. No capitão-do-mato could leave his parish, except with special orders, subjecting themselves to the command of the captains of entries when doing a group survey. The payment, however, remained separate. Finally, to ensure that all went well, the local judges or equivalent authorities would be responsible for preventing the capitães-do-mato from remaining idle in villages and towns, urging them to enter into the forest to arrest runaway slaves, under penalty of themselves being condemned to prison.

Necklace and chains: Punishment for runaway slave's c. 1825 ("Porteursd'eau," M. Rugendas, Malerische Reise in Brasilien, [Paris: Engelmann & Cie., 1835]).

As one can see, this is a detailed regulation, with excessive examination of space, specification of jurisdictions, responsibilities, hierarchies, compensation and penalties, in addition to measures to ensure its effectiveness and continuity. Far from the statesman that fears for the continuity of rule over the colony and for the safety of the empire, the text reveals more pragmatic concerns, aimed at settling quarrels between local authorities, capitães-do-mato and slaveholders, each in his own way, interested in the defense or security of their own domains, interests and powers.

What also draws our attention here is the preventive character of the regulation: a systematic and specialized practice directed against the fugitives, a practice intended to prevent the formation of any settlement of runaway slaves in the woods. No longer is it necessary to form a specific army to deal with one particular quilombo. It is now a general procedure against *all* potential and existing quilombos. From a singular target to a plural one, the habituated activity of hunting fugitives began to be official.[60]

The statute of Lourenço de Almeida tried to solve various problems posed by the role of the capitães-do-mato. Besides the doubts about the value, shape and occasion for the payment of "wages," there was the need to avoid the arrest of slaves who were not on the run and possible deaths of escapees and quilombolas.[61] All recurrent questions that accompanied the routing consolidation of the capitão-do-mato's roles[62] were properly addressed and governed by this document, which could even serve as a "template" for the preparation of other rules, such as the recommendation made by the governor of the Province of São Paulo in 1733.[63]

That year, the councilors of São Paulo drew up the "regulation regarding the captain-majors and the captains of entries of this province," based on the document from Minas of 1722.[64] The names continued to vary, mentioning the "captain-majors, sergeants and captains of entries" and the values of the fees they took, "considering the poverty of the inhabitants of the province." But the details were multiplying. The statute commanded the payment of 1,200 *réis* per escaped slave caught within the distance of a league from the town, but an item said that, if this league were a league from where the owner lived, the arrest could only be made having a written order from him—which was not the case with arrests made shorter than a league of the capitão-do-mato's residence. The amounts were not stipulated by travel days, but only for leagues traveled, calculated by an ordinary judge "or the highest ranking official available in the neighborhood" of the owner's residence. Capitães-do-mato who did not fulfill the statute or arrested slaves that were not escaping could have their licenses revoked. The document also carefully mentions the need to respect the hierarchy between "high ranking officers and lower ranked ones," both in aid during due diligence as well as in the division of "wages." Finally, established mechanisms for the companies of ordinance, the capitães-do-mato and the council had a list of fugitives, updated every three months and sent to the registrar of the capitães-do-mato. Knives and firearms used by them were also regulated.

Comparing the statutes of 1715, 1722 and 1733, we can observe the detailed measures that attempted to achieve the difficult balance between the interests of slaveholders, the quick and efficient recovery of their fugitives, the greed or arrogance of the capitães-do-mato, and the required maintenance of the hierarchical respect towards local authorities, civilian and military. Behind the growing entanglement of finer points, the pragmatism of the slaveholders seemed to increase significantly. On the other hand, it is not until the beginning of the eighteenth century we find appointments made to many different posts or even capitães-do-mato recruited by governors, generals, captains or field officers. From the middle of this century, however, they began to be nominated almost exclusively by the Town Councils, who shared the territory under its jurisdiction in districts that circumscribed the area of operation of each nominated capitão-do-mato and his soldiers.[65]

An examination of the minutes of the Town Council of the São Salvador dos Campos dos Goitacases revealed that there was a certain bureaucratic ritual regarding the election or consent to a petition for the nomination, drafting of a provision, an oath ceremony, and an investment ceremony for the capitão-do-mato throughout the second half of the eighteenth century.[66] The creation of posts, or the nomination of someone, seemed to follow a rhetorical praxis, always beginning with the mention of the existence of runaway slaves, who allegedly robbed and caused disturbances in a given region, as a way to justify and expound the urgency of such appointment. The same characteristics can be found in the licenses issued to the many different "captains" by the Council of Rio de Janeiro in the last decade of the eighteenth century.[67]

Of course, not all allegations of "insult and robbery" committed by the runaways were merely a rhetorical form, and there were many instances where the escapes followed by the formation of quilombos reasonably worried the slaveholders and the colonial and metropolitan authorities. Then, they would return to the old tactic of mobilizing specific troops to get total control over the slaves. Neither of these practices or the regulations relating to capitães-do-mato were enough to take preventive or enforcement actions in fully effective ways. In the colonial world, different instances of dominion crossed each other, made alliances within themselves and clashed with the forms of controlling the slaves. At the same time, different forms of strategies and politics were adopted by the captives, to deal with the condition to which they were submitted.[68]

What I want to emphasize here is the slow process in the creation of the capitão-do-mato position, whose detailed rules and proper bureaucratic and rhetorical rituals implied an adaptation in the control polices for escapees and for the prevention of quilombos. This is, I insist, a non-linear and even rather contradictory process. For example, a 1741 charter made into law ordered the branding with the letter "F" on the shoulder of runaway slaves, and an ear could be cut off in the case of recurrence, so as to remedy and prevent "this disorder" that "makes runaways vulgarly called *calhambolas* (a pejorative term for runaway slaves), become excessive and prompts them to join or form *quilombos*."[69]

On this occasion, however, a royal provision issued by the Overseas Council took more detailed preparation for future eventualities, given the cries of the Town Council of Villa Rica that called for the appointment of capitães-do-mato "in a number provided for the needs of each parish in Minas Gerais." After hearing the complaints from Villa Rica, the opinions of councilors and the governor of Minas Gerais, the provision ordered that Gomes Freire de Andrada, in cases when the Council did not have sufficient resources to respond to runaway slaves, was to collect three hundred eighths of gold from among all residents in a radius of twelve leagues from the area "infested" by "the *calhambolas*" in order to defray costs necessary to reduce the "large and continuous insults, robberies, costs and deaths caused by fugitive slaves." It was also determined that, observing the third paragraph of the statute of 1724,[70] they should be paid twenty eighths of gold per "black from a *quilombo*" apprehended.[71] But what was meant by a quilombo was clarified as "all dwelling runaway slaves gathered in a group bigger than five living on uninhabited land even if the had not yet raised ranches or food mills." Andrada was also ordered to uphold the "practice of giving the *capitães-do-mato* six eighths per head killed for resisting capture at the *quilombos*," paid by the Town Council in these cases, besides the stipends paid by the masters of such slaves. Finally, he reiterated an order of 1699 addressed to the government of Rio de Janeiro exempting from due process or charges the capitães-do-mato and people "who were to kill or injure some blacks in joining the invasion of that *quilombo*."[72]

On 12 June 1741, the band of Gomes Freire de Andrada implemented these measures, including changing the meaning of a quilombo; two days later, they were ordered to observe the law from March 3 about branding with a hot branding iron the letter "F" on the bodies of fugitives.[73] While colonial jurisdiction was calling for the strengthening of the capitães-do-mato system with measures to circumscribe space and allow full exploration and prevention in the woods to inhibit escapes, the Overseas

Council authorized nominations and payments to those who attacked the quilombos, as a supplemental regulation to better encourage people to respond to "disturbances caused by the fugitive blacks and members of *quilombos*." Prizes of "style" offered a significant reinforcement and although the statute of the capitães-do-mato is mentioned, the activity of the capitães-do-mato could now be exercised by others who did not possess the title. In parallel, the Crown resorted to traditional resources for using corporal punishment as an example to other slaves.

These determinations appear to be intended to help a situation particularly dire, to which the practices normally followed would be insufficient. The change in the definition of a quilombo was quite significant in qualitative terms. It no longer emphasized the conditions of survival in the woods (with ranches and food mills) but rather included "all dwellings of runaway slaves [...] in unpopulated areas."[74]

The statute passed in the Council of São Paulo in 1733 defined the concept of quilombo as a gathering of "more than four slaves living in the woods, and committing robberies and homicides," even distinguishing between the ones formed near the city and the most distant ones.[75] In 1757, the officers of the Town Council of São Salvador dos Campos dos Goitacases understood the quilombos to be where slaves "were fortified and well installed and optimistically prepared to defend themselves [so] they will not get caught," clarifying that such ranches were not any but those that will "repair themselves in the time" and stipulated that "the act of finding a gathering of six slaves or more will be understood [as a] *quilombo*."[76]

The definitions are similar, but based on different bases: one considers the distance of the place where they settle, another disposition to resist or the ability to live on for a long time in the woods. In all of them, we can notice the small number of fugitives that define a quilombo. This is an operational definition, directly related to the establishment the salaries of the capitães-do-mato, but and above all a *political* definition. In the situation immediately after the slaveholder's victory over Palmares, the common restrictive character to all translations of the word quilombo in the various statutes appears as a clear sign of the changed posture of the masters in relation to their slaves escaping. More than a purely pragmatic matter, it reveals the master's intention to establish the necessary limits to the continuity of governing the slaves.

Everything indicates that this intention was reaffirmed several times throughout the eighteenth century. In 1769, following a request from the governor of the province of Sao Paulo, the Count of Valadares issued all of "the orders which are in this Secretariat [Minas Gerais] and statutes on the *quilombos*, and pertaining to the captains of entries." Therein, we can find in sequential order, the provision of 12 January 1719 that gave orders to observe the practice of having capitães-do-mato; the statute issued by Dom Lourenço de Almeida in 1722, the provisions of 24 February 1731 and 31 December 1735 granting the governor of Minas and his magistrates the authority to exact the death penalty on slaves who killed their masters; the charter of 3 March 1741 ordering the branding of fugitives with an "F" on their shoulders; and Gomes Freire de Andrade's statute of 12 June 1741 concerning the assaults on the quilombo. This seems, therefore, a legislative series that was available in the colony on the matter.[77]

A policy of controlling slave movement was finally solidified by a decision of the count of Linhares. On 31 May 1809, he ordered the Town Councils to begin "training companies of *capitães-do-mato*" and put "in full compliance with the orders, laws and statutes regarding this matter," issuing "orders to be circulated to the captain-majors and colonels of the militias that the first companies on the front lines should be composed of black and brown men needed to form said companies."[78] The function that had emerged as sporadic and episodic seemed to win, finally, a rough and contradictory movement, with the pride of a permanent and generalized militia to the whole colony.[79]

Palmares was the largest, longest lasting and most numerous quilombo in the history of Brazil. There is already a large number of research and controversies about it.[80] Over the centuries, the historiography has discussed whether the political organization of Palmares corresponded to a republic or a monarchy,[81] if their members owned slaves or not and if slavery in Palmares was a recreation of African forms of captivity or not,[82] a debate on who was responsible for end of the Palmarian mocambos and on what date this happened, and whether or not the death of Zumbi could have been avoided. Some, following the footsteps of Rocha Pita, emphasized the war against Palmares, which Loreto Couto called "a civil war"; others are more concerned with the life and times of residents of the mocambos of Serra da Barriga.

In many aspects, Palmares was constituted as the object of an intense symbolic investment. Since the 1670s the destruction of mocambos of Serra da Barriga became an increasingly constant theme in the correspondence between Council Houses, the government of the province of Pernambuco, the general government of Brazil and the metropolitan jurisdictions.[83] The extinction of Palmares became so vital to slaveholder and metropolitan powers that the commitment of the governor of Pernambuco to give evidence of its efficiency resulted, in addition to masses and solemn processions, a specific chronicle of events of 1676–78.⁸⁴ In 1694, the "glorious restoration of Palmares" was celebrated in that province with "six days of festivals of lights and many other demonstrations of joy."⁸⁵ At the headquarters of the general government, the Town Council of Salvador sent to proclaim the good news on the streets and ordered the population "to make luminarias and give thanks to God for the happy success of our winning weapon against the blacks in Palmares 'with the officers' that serve as a gift to our Lord Governor" and nobility of the city going "incorporated" to the Sé to offer thanks for "such a personal mercy and blessing."⁸⁶ This "happy victory" had now entered the ranks of the public solemnities which moved towards towns and cities on the occasion of births, marriages and deaths of kings and princes, or the arrival of authorities and representatives of the metropolitan power: parties that served to honor and revive the real power in colonial lands, reiterating hierarchies and praxis of the master domain.

These are probably reflections of those lights that were present throughout the eighteenth century, especially in the writings of Rocha Pita and Loreto Couto, illuminating the epic content about Palmares, scoring, as said regarding prisoners taken in Recife, "in their disgrace our triumph." Although qualified as a "terrible *quilombo*," Palmares also was not forgotten by scholars of the Brazilian Historical and Geographical Institute which collected "the largest possible number of documents on the history and geography of Brazil."⁸⁷ The victorious memory permeated the eighteenth and nineteenth centuries and walked hand in hand with the widespread fear of escapes and the formation of quilombos. However, this can still be sensed in the more recent works of a conservative historiography, as in the case of Nina Rodrigues. Comparing Palmares with the revolt of Spartacus or the war of Troy served to accentuate the dangers and problems that were exposed to the great work of Portuguese colonization on American soil.⁸⁸

Similar metaphors were used to accentuate the power of Palmarians and struggles against slavery, making the event become paradigmatic of the black struggle against slavery. The abolitionist literature gave Palmares and to the episode of Zumbi's suicide "the epic importance of freedom, and the sublimation of a race redeemed through sacrifice and refusal to submit."⁸⁹ In his 1870 manuscript, Joaquim Nabucco, despite considering Palmares "one of the legends of Pernambuco" and "an isolated incident in our history," emphasized the heroism of the "only attempt of the Blacks to emancipate themselves from us."⁹⁰ In 1870 Castro Alves wrote a passionate poem, hailing that "nest of daring eagles" that in a "region of the valiant" released a "turbulent flaming banner [...] over the waves of slavery."⁹¹ In this century, we have already seen the political outcome in a historiography devoted to the study of slave resistance and especially the works of Ernesto Ennes, Edison Carneiro and Decio Freitas, Zumbi depicted as the image of the warlike heroic struggle against slavery. More recently, Zumbi has also represented the fight against racial oppression, raised as a symbol of the black movement itself with his spirit of resistance and liberating counciousness.[92]

However, in a "leftist" reading of the history of Palmares, that memory also appears often, only inverted: constructing Palmares militantly as the reverse of racist and stately perspectives, this historiography ends up as just as much a prisoner of the same paradigms, and losing historicity. Despite the huge investment in historiography, which has sought to contextualize the war *against* Palmares, "the war *of* the slaves," it has not yet managed to recover all the meanings of those years and those fights for slaves or for relations between masters and slaves, both during the seventeenth century, when Palmares was a living presence in the southern lands of Pernambuco, and in the eighteenth century, when it became a strong point and relative constant that began to be associated with revolutionary Haiti (or even, in political and symbolic terms, being supplanted by it). The lack of documentation is an obstacle, but the changes in the slaveholders' policy may not have occurred without major changes in the strategies and actions of the captives.

The waves of the impact of Palmares on governing slaves were probably much broader than imagined to the frightened colonial rulers. In the slaveholder and metropolitan eyes of the past, the symbolic strength of Palmares was almost always presented in a laudatory tone, rekindling constantly the superiority of the colonizer and their fear of slave revolts. Palmares served as a foothold for improving the policies of slaveholders who tried to control the escapes and movement of captives in search of freedom, giving new dimension for government policy over slaves. During the eighteenth century, Palmares served as a catalyst for the fears of slaveholders and colonial authorities, dyeing itself sometimes with the strongest colors of the slave uprising that could endanger colonial rule (as in the case of Assumar), sometimes with the nuances of a stubborn quilombo facing the attacks of slaveholders, or the roundup of fugitives who frightened travelers, farmers and miners and served as a bad example for slaves.

With all the colors and nuances, the fear of a new Palmares seems to have been constant throughout the eighteenth century. In the nineteenth century, however, the slaveholder's fear seems to have increased with the revolt of Santo Domingo, seeing the danger of "Haitianism" everywhere. The impact in reshaping the practices of the slave government, however, was much more enduring: the figure of the capitão-do-mato became almost inseparable from slavery in Brazil. An image so strong, to the point that, in a much later period, with the abolitionist campaign in full swing, it caused an impact to such a degree that the official Military Club refused to play the role of capitão-do-mato. In October 1887, they made a formal request to the imperial government that the soldiers would no longer "be tasked with the charge of capturing poor Africans that were fleeing from slavery." They agreed to intervene in the hypothesis of an uprising "that was a menace to the tranquility of families," but, taking an attitude radically different from that assumed by their colonial colleagues, refused to suppress "men fleeing, calm, without noise, with tranquilness more than cattle that disperses the fields, avoiding both slavery and battle and offering themselves as an example of morality as they traversed the city, defenseless."[93]

6

ST. ANTHONY, THE DIVINE CAPITÃO-DO-MATO[1]

LUIZ MOTT

> *If a slave runs away, Saint Anthony!*
> —Father Antônio Vieira, 1663

Introduction

The significance of many famous historical figures, as well as national institutions, often change completely over the course of history. For example, Zumbi's image changed from a dreaded bandit in the seventeenth century to a symbol of the anti-slavery struggle today; Princess Isabel, in 1888, was proclaimed by former slaves as the Redeemer, but a hundred years later had her "historical death" decreed by those who today idolize the hero of Palmares; *quimbanda*, in the sixteenth and seventeenth centuries Angola, was synonymous with "band of sodomites sorcerers"; however, now in Brazil, it is equivalent to "black magic"; *calundu* since the time of Gregório de Matos and throughout the eighteenth century was the generic term to define African-Brazilian religious practice, but in contemporary Bahia means a mere "bad mood."

The same is happening with Saint Anthony: today remembered almost exclusively as the matchmaker saint, in the Christian imagination he has played the most variegated of roles in the eight centuries that separate us from his death. The main litany in the seventeenth century summarizes some of his gifts: "Son of Seraphim, *Gadelha* of Portugal, Light of Italy, Gloria of Padua, Refulgence of France, Admiration of Spain, Arch of the Testament, Hammer of Heretics, Throne of God, Wonder of the Angels, Haunting of Hell, Sun of the entire world."[2] There is no reference to the gift of good marriages for stranded girls.

Not only have St. Anthony's titles changed over generations; the power attributed to the most celebrated of all the children of Portugal has also changed—more renowned and revered than Vasco da Gama, Camões, or D. Sebastião.[3] In a memorable sermon preached in São Luís do Maranhão in 1663, Father Antônio Vieira described the main occasions in which

Brazilian settlers resorted to the thaumaturge ("performer of magic or miracles") for their daily afflictions: "If your child gets sick, St. Anthony! If a slave runs away, St. Anthony! If you need a witchcraft, St. Anthony! If you await the sentence, St. Anthony! If you lost the smallest offal of your home, St. Anthony! and maybe if you wish other people's goods, St. Anthony."[4] As far as we know, this is the oldest explicit reference to the power of *Divinus Antonius* in recovering runaway slaves. So present was the Franciscan factotum in the Christian imagination of that time that he was aptly named by Vieira the "universal saint." Both in the Portuguese kingdom and overseas, our little saint is omnipresent:

> St. Anthony is everywhere: in stone niches and painted in tiles to keep the houses safe; in silk frames at the bed's headboard watching us sleep; in scapulars and medals close to the chest to take care of our steps; carved or painted on the ox's cloths to preserve them from dangers; helping Christ in the *alminhas* along the way to redeem the souls of purgatory; on the prows of the Portuguese ships giving them the name to rid them from the sea fury; patron saint of the flags of the professions; in the riddles embroidery; painted on the alms boxes, amulet in St. Anthony's coins, in sanctuaries and oratories etc. etc...[5]

The objective of this study is to retrieve one of the most intriguing facets of St. Anthony's charisma: his job as capitão-do-mato in the recovery of runaway slaves and the destruction of quilombos. Although one can already see the presence of Africa and of the captives in certain aspects of the medieval thaumaturge's biography even before the introduction of his devotion in slave societies of the New World, it is in slaveholding Brazilian society that St. Anthony became not only the most popular patron saint of all social strata, but also made a metamorphosis into our holy warrior par excellence, defending Portuguese America from the invasions of the French and the Dutch heretics, protecting those in power against the throbbing menace of the indomitable slaves, and applying his divine help in the recovery of blacks who had fled or were living in quilombos.

St. Anthony of Padua, Moreover, of Lisbon

> *God, of all the kingdoms of the world, particularly chose Portugal for his own Empire and home in the Earth. And all that is due to St. Anthony because he is the Sun of the world, and Portugal is the Empire of God.*
> —Friar Agostinho da Conceição, Rio de Janeiro, 1674

The King D. Sancho I reigned in Portugal when, in August 15, 1195, the boy Fernando was born in Lisbon. That was the baptismal name of St. Anthony, the son of two noble Lusitanian strains: Bulhões, from the father's side, and Taveira, from the mother's side. Residing near the patriarchal cathedral, he had his religious initiation as the pious boy at the choir of the main temple in Lisbon. Once he entered puberty, legend has it that on one occasion, he was almost captivated by a very beautiful Jewish girl, but having made the sign of the cross before succumbing to temptation, the fascinating Israeli disappeared. Today, the famous cross through which the saint faced the demon disguised as a Jewish woman remains in the same cathedral. Saint Anthony would preserve himself as pure and chaste until his death.[6] He first joined the Order of the Regular Canons of St. Augustine, where he became Master in Theology. However, in 1220, his monastery of Santa Cruz de Coimbra received the remains of the first Franciscans martyred in Morocco. The young Anthony was deeply in love with the ideal of this novel mendicant order, which from then on gave a new direction to his religious life: he dressed in the habit of the minor friars, boarding soon after as a missionary to Africa.

In the vision of religious people at the turn of this first millennium, especially those from mendicant orders, (northern) Africa, popularly called "barbaric," was synonymous with the land of the infidels, and privileged ground wherein to obtain the so desired palm of martyrdom. Biographers say that it was precisely with the aim to destroy Islamism and bear witness to his faith in Christ with his own blood that the man from Lisbon embarked to Morocco. Divine Providence destined him, however, to other fields: Anthony would become, centuries later, the capturer of the Africans who, besides being Christian properties, became inevitable prey for the Demon. The impetus of the missionary was frustrated: he fell very ill, and was forced to return to Europe. Another unexpected event: a storm diverted his boat to Sicily, and since then he settled in the Franciscan province of Italy. He traveled intensely throughout Italy and France, teaching dogmatic theology, and playing with the Cathars—the inspiration for his epithets of Hammer of Heretics and Arch of the Testament. He quickly acquired fame as a thaumaturge, prophet, and great preacher, gathering more than 30,000 listeners in public squares. He performed over fifty miracles, collected by the Bollandists—among them several resurrections; the control of nature, including obedience of pets and wildlife; healings of all kinds of sickness; he converted a frog into a chicken and then another chicken into a frog in order to confuse a heretic; he made a baby speak to defend the honor of his mother; and he had the gift of bi-location, being at the same time in Milan and Lisbon, where he went to save his own father, sentenced to the gallows.[7]

In June 13, 1231, at only 36 years old, Friar Anthony of Lisbon, born Fernando and popularized as St. Anthony of Pádua, died. He was canonized by Rome less than a year after his death. His devotion expanded throughout Christendom: in 1722, his death was decreed a saint day in Spanish and Portuguese America, and he was declared by Pius XII, in 1946, to be Doctor of the Universal Church. Also, in 1993, the Vatican graced the city of Borba, in Amazonas, with authentic objects that belonged to the saint—it was the first church in Latin America and the fifth in the world to house such precious *ex ossibus* fragments.[8]

St. Anthony of Lisbon with military insignia (Source: José Carlos de Macedo Soares, S.A. de Lisboa militar no Brasil, Rio de Janeiro, 1942, p. 94).

Father Antônio Vieira, despite being a Jesuit, a religious sect that sustained frequent contentions with the Franciscan order, was probably the person who preached and published the most sermons dedicated to his fellow compatriot. Between 1638 and 1657, our defender of indigenous peoples dedicated nine homilies to St. Anthony, preached in Bahia, in São Luís, in the kingdom and in the church of the Portuguese in Rome. Besides proclaiming him the "universal saint," Vieira argued that the Portuguese thaumaturge "being only one, is all the saints together, for in the six celestial hierarchies, in all of them, he has eminent place, having been patriarch, prophet, apostle, martyr, confessor and virgin."[9] The Ignatian preacher, practicing the most creative of the exegetical juggling, proves, by the New and Old Testaments, that our holy matchmaker "was so great that Christ, before him, seems small," equating St. Anthony to the Sun, and the son of God to a simple lamp, using, among other arguments, the fact that the Franciscan saint, during one preaching, converted 22 thieves all at once, while Jesus converted only one.[10]

In fact, few saints recorded in the *Acta* and in the *Flos sanctorum* bear such a miraculous curriculum as rich and diverse as the one of the Evangelic Doctor. The explanation is clear: St. Anthony was privileged by the Almighty with a rather populist mission: to be "the general refuge of tribulations and the lawyer of the lost causes and things."[11] Since all creatures go through daily tribulations and we are always losing our belongings or forgetting where we left them, logically the recalling of the little saint is much more frequent than that of saints with less prosaic attributes.

Some scholars ponder that St. Anthony's support to find or recover lost objects, including fugitives, had its origin in one of the first miracles performed by the blessed man while he was still living in Padua, an occasion in which a novice fled his convent taking a precious psaltery. By intercession of the zealous professor of theology, the Devil himself appeared when the little runaway friar was crossing a bridge, obliging him to return to the religious community. Therefore, not only the precious parchment had been recovered, but also the soul of the repentant and sacrum thief. In his fantastic work, confirm the Bollandists: "God intended that St. Anthony refunded the legitimate owners of the things lost or stolen," so much so that on the very recited "Responso de santo Antônio," whose authorship is attributed to the main Franciscan doctor, St. Bonaventure, one of his highlighted virtues was the one of recovering what had been lost, "*membra resque perditas*":[12]

> *If miracles you desire, refer it to St. Anthony,*
> *You will see the Demon and the infernal temptations run away.*
> *One recovers what is lost, the hard prison breaks up,*
> *And in the height of the hurricane, weakens the brave sea.*
> *By his intercession, the plague flees, the error, the death,*
> *The weak becomes strong, and the sick becomes sane.*

All human evils become moderate, withdraw,
Tell us those who saw it and tell us the ones from Padua.

He is called by Vieira the "facer"; that is, the one who *faces*, who finds what has been lost—an expression until the early eighteenth century, which the lexicographer Morais already considered to be in disuse by the end of the same century. The Ignatian orator pondered that such charisma "is a grace so singular and a privilege so sovereign that it seems like God gave St. Anthony a better job than the one he took upon himself, for God gives, St. Anthony recovers."[13] In *Vida de santo Antonio, sol nascido no Ocidente e posto ao nascer do sol,* Friar Braz Luiz de Abreu (1725) listed some of these miracles: "the saint faces with special offers many lost things, such as the precious ring to the consul of Padua, another ring of the bishop of Cordoba, various papers of the bishop Ambrósio Catharino, another ring in Trento, in Alcacer do Sal another ring, a bill to a lay of Sicily, a needle to a religious from Alcalá, etc."[14] There is no reference in this source, however, of him having found runaway captives.

It was only two centuries after his death that the intercession of *Pavor Infidelium* in the recovering of runaway slaves began, and in the restoration of objects stolen by slaves or Africans. In the *Acta sanctorum* there is a reference that, already in 1429, in the convent of Perpignan, a noble had registered the miraculous recovery of his runaway servant, who returned to his domains thanks to the intercession of the Portuguese saint.[15] In the early seventeenth century, in Naples, it would be St. Anthony's turn to take sides against an African who had stolen large amounts of silver and fled on a ship; in the middle of a violent storm, the Franciscan saint appeared menacing the black man, stating that if he did not return the spoil to his master he would die from drowning. On his knees, repenting, the Ethiop confessed his crime, asked for forgiveness and, thus, got the salvation of his soul.[16] Around 1640, at the convent of Aracoeli, a servant fled the community and a few days later, when he was already in Lombardia, the saint of Padua appeared to him ordering that he return to the convent.[17]

Referring to the list of miracles of the Portuguese-Italian thaumaturge, we notice that in the middle of the seventeenth century, wonders attributed to his mediation would become more frequent and universal. Farmer, in the *Dictionary of Saints*, confirms that the popularization of his support as the finder of lost objects dates from the same time.[18] It was in 1652 that the Basilica of St. Anthony in Padua donated a hefty slice of the relic of his arm to the Republic of Venice, on the same block where the Father Vieira uttered almost a dozen sermons dedicated to him. It is, therefore, especially after the seventeenth century—right at the time when blacks living in the quilombo of Palmares caused larger unrest to the power brokers—that the servant of God would escalate all posts in the military hierarchy, becoming the main holy warrior of Christianity and the capturer of runaway slaves in Brazil.

Catholic hagiography abounds with saints linked to martial arts: among other titles, Yahweh himself had the one of God of the Armies. Saint Michael, the Archangel, always bears the sword in his hand and became the captain of the heavenly militias when he thwarted the rebellion of Lucifer. Saint Sebastian was a Roman soldier, Saint Martin of Vertou was a valiant military, and Saint Ignatius of Loyola fought in the Spanish army.

St. Anthony—as a typical young man of the time of the Crusades and a contemporary of the implementation of the Inquisition—had the same ideals of the apostle Paul when he encouraged the Christians who would uninterruptedly combat the hosts of the Devil's army. In the times of Saint Anthony, Satan was personified especially in two great enemies of Christianity: the infidels and the heretics. The Jews were a kind of familiar demons.[19] Frustrated about his project to convert the infidels in their own territories, the thaumaturge from Padua gave particular attention to the poor Christians living captive in barbarism. Actually, rescuing the Christians from Islamic captivity was a real obsession in Saint Anthony's century, a contemporary of Saint Peter Nolasco and Saint Raymond of Penyafort, founders of the Mercedarian Friars, also known as The Order of the Blessed Virgin Mary of Mercy, which was intended primarily for the rescue of the captives.

Since the thirteenth century, it had been included in the saint's responsory, among his gifts, *to break the hard prison*, including under this aspiration both those who suffered unjust imprisonment and above all, the Christians kept captive by the Moors. That is the origin of his title of *Pavor Infidelium*. One of the constant miracles in the *Acta sanctorum*, "*Captivus apud turcos solvitur a catenis*" refers to the fact that in 1674 Saint Anthony miraculously freed an Albanian prisoner from Dalmatia from being whipped by a Turk.[20]

The other front of Saint Anthony's holy war was against heretics—notably, the Cathars. "The hatred against the heretics was as implacable as was untiring the activity of his fiery zeal," says a biographer of the seventeenth century.[21] Another sacred historian ponders that "Saint Anthony knew how to unite softness and strength: there was something inside him of lamb and of lion. He was bland with the little ones of this world, sweet with the boys he caressed, with the poor people he consoled, and with the sinners he converted. He was, however, terrible with the powerful, he hated heresies." And he concludes: "It was an eminently Christian hate!"[22] Father Antônio Vieira, nationalist, completes:

> To the infidels, he took his spirit because it was a Portuguese spirit. To Catholics, he took the peace, but to the infidels, the perpetual war. To form the Hammer of Heresy, God went to get the iron from the mines of Portugal, because the natural hardness of Portuguese iron can break and convert the infidels, veneer and baptize the losers, and make them become a living part of Christ's mystical body.[23]

In our view, the theological inspiration and the historical substrate of the transformation of Anthony into holy warrior—with numerous military ranks, among them, the one of capitão-do-mato—connects to this facet of his biography forgotten in the contemporary popular imagination, and is overshadowed by his iconography and his mellifluous and effeminate statuary. By incorporating Saint Anthony into the military service, whether through the interests either of the Portuguese Crown in its struggle against the heretic foreigners or the Brazilian settlers in recovering their runaway slaves and destroying quilombos, the devotees were simply updating his original charisma involving fear of infidels and being the Hammer of Heresies. It was through this process of modernization that the matchmaker saint would become in our land "the divine sergeant, leading the armies to looting and killing, defending fortresses and cities."[24]

The public devotion to Saint Anthony in Portuguese America begins with the building of the church and fortress of Saint Anthony of Barra, where the first donor of Bahia established the ownership pattern of the captaincy, the site of Tomé de Sousa's landing on the occasion of the founding of Salvador, as well as where the Dutch invaded Bahia in the following century. Therefore, it was a vulnerable point that needed the presence of a well-armed porter-janitor: Saint Anthony of Barra.

Church of Santo Antonio da Barra, Salvador, c. 1858.

Just a few decades went by until another historical episode related the figure of the Awe of the Unfaithful to the affirmation of the Luso-Brazilian Catholicism in opposition to the heretic foreigner. Here are the words of Afrânio Peixoto in his *Breviário da Bahia*:

> Saint Anthony is the greatest of our saints, particularly honored in Bahia. At the end of the sixteenth century, a fleet rendered in France, of Huguenots, to take Bahia, in reparation to the expulsion of the French in 1567 from Rio de Janeiro. Passing the coast of Africa, it attacked the Castle of Arguin, a Portuguese possession, where they stole an image of Saint Anthony, which was brought for mockery. A terrible storm destroyed the fleet, the saint was thrown to the sea, without thereby the pirates being saved, around Morro de São Paulo. The image arrived to Itapoã (and was miraculously found standing on the beach, without any person to have raised it!), collecting it to the compassion of Francisco Dias d'Ávila, of the Tower House, who honored her, taking her to Church D'Ajuda and then to the convent of Saint Francis in a procession on August 23, 1595 (fourth centenary of his death) where he received an altar and the title of boss and patron of the city Bahia.[25]

Friar Antônio Maria de Jaboatão, the leading chronicler of the colonial Franciscan history, he himself author of a "Saint Anthony's sermon" published in 1751, reported that in the place where the Calvinists struck it with a machete, the image poured true blood. Actually a similar miracle took place with statues of the same saint in the chapels of *engenho Velho do Cabo*, *engenho do Meio* and *freguesia da Vargem* on the occasion of the struggle between people from Pernambuco and the Dutch.²⁶ According to this author, the devotion to the saint repeated also in Brazil the same ardor observed in the Kingdom:

> Being among all the Portuguese very unique, the deeply manifested veneration for our Saint Anthony of Lisbon, it becomes extreme in these parts of Brazil, generally shown by all. Because besides the many parish churches of which he is the holder, there are innumerable chapels and shrines devoted to his name, and out of these there is not one that does not include in its altars one or many images of Saint Anthony. There is no house that does not venerate him in its oratory, and, still not satisfied with this common devotion of the faithful, each one wants to have their Saint Anthony only for themselves.²⁷

It was at the fortress of the Barra of the Bahia de Todos os Santos, in the late sixteenth or early seventeenth century, that its owner, Saint Anthony, was incorporated for the first time in the Portuguese army as the post of private. A devotee initiative involved not only the confident protection of this divine soldier to the fortress and to his colleagues in uniform, but also the interesting payment by the royal treasury corresponding to his post, which amount was intended to cover the costs associated with the cult and the celebrations of the first saint of June. We did not find information in any other source that confirmed the foreseen presence of such devotional innovation in the metropolis, though later Saint Benedict and Saint Francis Xavier have also deserved military rewards.²⁸

Although the saint did not act when the Dutch invaded Bahia in 1624, ruthlessly bombing its fortress in Barra, people did not forget that it was at the fortress of Saint Anthony of Além do Carmo, at the other end of the upper city, where in 1638 the army of Prince Maurice of Nassau was beaten, retreating to Pernambuco.²⁹ It was on this occasion that Father Vieira recited his first "Saint Anthony's sermon, preached at the church and at the day of this saint, having the Dutch raised the site they had put in Bahia, seating their barracks and batteries in front of the same church." Enthusiastic about the victory attributed to the Lisbon-born thaumaturge, the sermon states: "If you ask me how to hath the victory in Bahia between the Lord and his servant, I will say that the city of Bahia is the city of the Redeemer and the defense of Bahia of all saints belongs to Saint Anthony."³⁰

A few years after the restoration of Bahia, in 1645, the city councilors of Salvador made a perpetual vow that if Recife was released from the heretic Batavians, they would annually devote a solemn feast to the saint, covering his image with a mantle made of silver—a decorative fad much in vogue in the seventeenth century, spurred by abundant shipments of the precious metal from the mines of Potosí, in the Viceroyalty of Peru. Only nine years after the promise, in 1654, the Dutch were expelled from Pernambuco. From then, the council members from Bahia accomplished their promise.

It was in the late seventeenth century, after the victory against the quilombo of Palmares in which St. Anthony played an important role, that the saint became the most successful military persona in Brazil, attaining at least fifteen promotions in different captaincies from North to South of Portuguese America.[31] Such promotions, as we will demonstrate later, can be interpreted as a symbolic reinforcement to another important function attributed to the Haunter of Hell: to keep slave owners protected against slave insurrections and runaway slaves.

> Saint Anthony of Lisbon,
> does not want one to call him a saint,
> want one to call him a soldier
> general, mestre de camp.[32]

In 1705, the City Council of Salvador was granted king's authorization to promote the *intertenido* soldier Saint Anthony to the post of captain of the Barra Fortress. At the time, Bahia could boast of having a small but brave Saint Anthony Battalion, for this servant of God was captain of the Barra Fortress, ensign of the military train in his Church at Mouraria, private at Sé, and ensign at the prison of Morro de São Paulo. In 1709 he was appointed private in Paraíba, with a wage of 30$700. In 1717, in Pernambuco, Saint Anthony, who was already patron of the captaincy since 1645, received the post of Lieutenant of Artillery, and was stationed in the fortress of Buraco. In 1750, the king accepted a petition from the people of Goiás, determining that he was settled as a soldier and paid him the corresponding wages.

Also in the south of the colony, the Distinguished Coat of Arms of Portugal was awarded with military insignias and incomes: in Rio de Janeiro, the image of Saint Anthony of the Franciscan convent, which had already received a soldier's stipend since earlier times, was elevated to the post of captain, in appreciation for his intersection when, in 1710, the locals repelled the invasion of the French captained by General Duclerc. In 1750, the king appointed Saint Anthony to the Brotherhood of the Sé of São Paulo as captain of the Troops of captaincy, and he was elevated to colonel in 1771. When justifying his nomination to this rank, the governor of São Paulo, d. Luís Antônio da Lapa, remembered, "the aforesaid saint is admirable in miracles and a singular protector of the Portuguese, very powerful with the Lord of Armies, whom he has in his hand." In Espírito Santo, he is enlisted as a private in 1752. The Friars Minor of Vitoria Monastery benefitted from its corresponding salary. In Minas Gerais, where there were ten brotherhoods related to Saint Anthony, the devotees of the parish of Pilar de Vila Rica call him the Credit of the Nation and the Prototype of Holiness, getting in 1786 the promotion of Saint Antonio to the position of captain, with an annual salary of 480$000.[33]

This is not the end of the nominations and military promotions of our saint. The Prince d. João, particularly devout of the advocate of lost causes, in gratitude for arriving safely to Brazil when the French invaded his Kingdom, gave the post of Staff Sergeant to the images of Saint Anthony at the Franciscan convent of Bahia and Rio de Janeiro, in 1811, renewing such magnanimity in 1814, when they began to receive the wage of a lieutenant colonel.[34] In addition to this picturesque military curriculum, Saint Anthony was sometimes awarded with rich military objects, important not only for how much they were worth in precious stones and metal, but above all for what they symbolized in the collective imagination. His most venerated statue in Rio de Janeiro, at the Franciscan convent of the Largo da Carioca, received in 1705 the baton of the governor of the colony of Sacramento, Sebastião Veiga Cabral, in gratitude for protecting six hundred men of his garrison when besieged during six months by six thousand Spaniard troops backed by warships. In 1814, it would be the turn of d. João VI to, once again, provide him with the Grand Cross of the Christ Order, donating to Staff Sergeant Saint Anthony of Lisbon an opulent cane of authority, for his own use, with 84 rubies, 72 *crisolitas*, and rich fouling in gold.[35]

On several festive occasions, especially in crowded and frequent processions taking place almost monthly, Saint Anthony was dressed in all his military insignias: hat and gallon identifiers of his post in the military, sword at the waist, baton and cane typical of an authority. In the most beautiful book dedicated to him in our country, *santo Antonio de Lisboa, militar no Brasil*, by José Carlos Macedo Soares, the reader is presented with beautiful woodcuts and paintings in which the saint is depicted in great military style. All this militarization of the matchmaker saint had, in our view, two objectives: the most obvious was to adduce to the convents, churches and religious groups extra donations from the Treasury in order to perpetuate and supplement the most Luso-Brazilian of the devotions. Investment was not only with a preternatural return, but with undeniable resonance in the macro-political area, to the extent that the dearest son of Portugal catalyzed, more than any other Lusitanian hero, the Lusitanian feeling, especially when the homeland or its overseas territories were menaced by French Huguenots, Calvinists Dutch, Barbarian Moors, or even by Spaniard invaders, as during the eighty years when the Felipes reigned with the two crowns. This seventeenth-century rhyme sum up the anti-Spain feeling associated with he who was called the Gloria of Portugal and Spain's Admiration:

> Saint Anthony is a good saint, who frees the father from the arcana who also must free us from the power of the Castilians...[36]

This is, therefore, the second explanation underlying the militarization of the worship of Saint Anthony, especially in slaveholding Brazil: as there were no longer heretics to hammer nor captives to rescue from barbarism, the dogmatist Saint Anthony had his firepower now redirected at other sheep set apart from the flock of the Good Shepherd: the black sheep.

While the fugitive mortals depended, above all, on their courage and cunning, a good horse, cold weapons, and fire, Saint Anthony, the divine capitão-do-mato, in addition to his particular prestige with the God of Hosts, boasted graded military titration and powerful military insignias that made him become, in the eyes of slave owners, a lawyer doubly powerful. First, he was viewed as a defender of the Portuguese America from the menace of mobs, especially the slaves, always motivated to rebellions; and second, as separator of fugitive captives, he restituted the owners of their propriety, and the flock of Christ with the lost sheep. To the astonished eyes of the humblest people, especially Africans recently introduced to "civilization," a saint loaded with so many weapons would certainly cause great respect and fear.

As we shall see, to retrieve a runaway slave or a slave from the quilombos, Saint Anthony acted perfectly according to the Aristotelian-Thomistic doctrine, which saw slavery as a lawful and ethical institution, according to which the slave should be submissive and the slave owner should be generous. Insubordination or escape from captivity would be a grievance and would deeply disturb the natural order of life in society. Thus, to recover the escaped slave, Saint Anthony fulfilled two acts of Christian justice: he restituted the owner of his legitimate property, since the slave did not have the right to evade captivity, and also he reconciled the black prodigal son to the bosom of his holy mother, the Church, because, as taught by the dogmatic theology, *extra ecclesiam non est salus*, outside the Church there is no salvation. And since one of the Christian justifications for the slave traffic was that Africans transported to the Christian kingdoms were thus rescued from the empire of the Devil, allowing them to flee or to live in quilombos was the equivalent of sending them back to the power of darkness. That is why returning them to the authority of their legitimate and Catholic owners was perceived as a missionary and charitable action. Vieira epitomized the missionary character of the saint who returned the lost sheep: "Taking them from the realm of idolatry, subjecting them to Christ, converting mosques and pagodas in temples; Gentile in Christians, barbarians in men, beasts in sheep." Could there be a better destination for a fugitive from Christianity?[37]

For slaveholders and for the free population in general, the militarization of Saint Anthony was inspired in a double conviction: the most spiritual certainly believed that by pleasing God's servant with honors and gallons, they would be forcing him to ensure, as a military servant, the tranquility of the inhabitants of such lands as the Hottentots. The most realistic surely realized that by covering the images of the Hammer of Heretics with bellicose insignia and respected military titles, they would inspire more fear in all captives who had the intention of running away from the Catholic flock or from the boss. St. Anthony represented, within the temples and in the imagination of the slaves, a kind of bogeyman, as feared as the mules-without-head or *chibungos* who, rumor had it, were hiding in the forests.

Our hypothesis is confirmed by the petition that the devotees of the Brotherhood of Saint Anthony in Pilar de Vila Rica addressed to the Queen in 1786. Here is how the population from Minas Gerais argued their request to give the Universal Saint the rank of captain: "This capital of Minas has more need for protection of a higher arm to defend it, because its small number of inhabitants [is] much lower than the number of Ethiopian slaves." The *slavephobia* of the population needed a powerful spiritual solace: provided by Captain Saint Anthony. It is not without reason that it was in Minas Gerais that the capitães-do-mato were more numerous than in other parts of the colony.[38]

> Saint Anthony, Capitão-Do-Mato
> Saint Anthony, tie the black very well tied.
> —candomblé song, Mãe Jandira, São Paulo, 1970

Africa has been present in Saint Anthony's biography since the moment he was confronted with the sacred relics of the five Franciscans martyred in Morocco. This encounter redefined the life of the young canon. A terrible disease prevented him from pursuing his new project of becoming a missionary in the continent of Prestes João (Prester John). Especially after the capture of Ceuta's Square (1415), Africans, blacks, and slaves started to be part of the endless list of receivers of his miracles, usually in the position of runaway slaves whom the thaumaturge returned to their legitimate masters.

In Brazil, where the escape of slaves was a constant headache and caused great economic distress for their proprietaries, the institution of the work of capitão-do-mato or *capitão-do-campo* was one of the solutions created to recover the runaway. According to Stuart Schwartz, the first records of the existence of such an institution date probably from 1612, the year in which the donor of Pernambuco, Alexandre Moura, asked the Crown to nominate one capitão-do-mato for each of the eight parishes of the captaincy. In 1625, the City Council of Salvador already had a table of rewards for these slave hunters, which was a formal capture system formalized by law in 1676.[39] José Alípio Goulart demonstrates that in Cachoeira, Bahia, in 1672, there was already a municipal regulation instituting the creation of such a job, and in the city of Rio de Janeiro, in 1676, there was a special regiment of *capitães-das-entradas*. According to the author, it would be especially after the first quarter of the eighteenth century that such institution would receive a major boost, especially in Minas Gerais.[40]

The reader should note the fact that the regulation and institution of capitães-do-mato goes *pari passu* with Saint Anthony's functional progression in the military hierarchy, also coinciding with the consolidation of its work as a defender of Portuguese sovereignty, keeping the slave order and becoming the most effective capitão-do-mato in Brazil. This association between St. Anthony and the security and tranquility of slave ownership can already be detected in the beginnings of the seventeenth century, although it was still a devotional surprise that the most irreverent came to be treated with derision and traditionalists with the suspicion of heresy. In the second visit of the Holy Office to Bahia, in 1618, the cassava farmer Cristóvão Luís de Solazar, fifty years old, confessed to having spoken before its image that "Saint Anthony is my overseer [...] mocking the ideas that the saint had power to guard his farm and doubting of his miracles."[41] Two decades later, Vieira informed the world that it was already part of the colonial devotion to consider the saint fundamental in the recovering of runaway captives, by including such information in one of his sermons as: "If a slave runs away, Saint Anthony!"

In the imagination of the Portuguese-American devotees, the Son of Seraph had power not only to individually recover certain runaway slaves; he was also was credited with the surrender of Ganga Zumba and his quilombo, in the year of 1678. After signing the peace treaty with the governor of Pernambuco, the putative uncle of Zumbi went with a large retinue, alongside the most important authorities from Pernambuco, to the cathedral of Recife on the day of the Infidels Terror's party, and "in the thanksgiving mass thanked to Saint Anthony for the glories that they received."[42] A few decades earlier, the same image of the holy warrior had flickered in Pernambuco's banners when the expulsion of the heretical Dutch took place.

After eight years of this solemnity, when a powerful armed force came from Recife to disrupt the quilombo of Palmares, Governor João da Cunha Souto Maior, by the order of 13 September 1685, determined the enlistment of the glorious Saint Anthony as soldier of the army, and paid the assignee of the Olinda Convent the salary to which he was entitled. According to what Pereira da Costa teaches, "effectively departed St. Anthony to the war in Palmares, his image entrusted to friar André da Anunciação, a Franciscan religious man, who marched as chaplain, and only returned when finished the campaign with the full destruction of the famous republic of Palmares, the black Troy." We owe to the same author the disclosure of such an unusual request, in verse form, in which a soldier asks for rewards for services rendered in the Palmares campaign, citing the testimony of the patron saint as proof of his bravery. In this simple poem, dramatic scenes of the Palmares campaign are pictured. This is the petition of the soldier from Pernambuco:

> To the Overseas Council, which is so just, Zebedeu, standing soldier, son of Braz Victorino, Very young man, almost a boy, marched to Palmares, Over there got hurt, becoming one of the unfortunate Who returned maimed, and in the end nothing gained. There, with a musket in his hands, day and night fighting, Dying of hunger and cold, barefoot, feet in the floor, Besides the tough, Felix José dos Açores, Who only saw the horrors of the unfolding panel, Was trying to remain quiet, with great eagerness. From what I come to narrate, despite being simpleton, Can the Father Saint Anthony, very well corroborate: What one cannot expect, proceed otherwise Pat attention to its fidelity, affection, and valor, For with me night and day, did not desert the trench. He saw, just like me, when the fight started, When the horn sounded, the people who ran away! And that was occurred, as gallant and brave, Land, money, rank, with great injustice and disorders, To those who the vile slaves, did not treat as people. To you, famous Council, that envisions justice, Why don't you befriend the poor cripple? Who in the abandoned world, no having one person to extend his hand, Certainly has the perdition of life, because almost dead, Will only take comfort if you make him captain.[43]

The presence of the Saint from Bologna in the trench, night and day without pause, validates the trust the settlers had in their servant of God, especially in that carnage where the soldier Zebedeu, a teenager, had the sensitivity to perceive and report his musket collaborators who "did not treat as people" the miserable slaves.

At least concerning the religiosity of the blacks from Palmares, Saint Anthony apparently had nothing to complain about, because, according to reports from the Dutch, a chapel with images of the infant Jesus, Our Lady of Immaculate Conception, and Saint Blaise were found in one of the quilombos. Had he found his own image, whose side would the holy warrior have taken?

It is, however, in the Ouvidoria de Sergipe del Rei that we will find the most detailed description of Saint Anthony's performance as a genuine capitão-do-mato and lackey of the ruling classes. We owe this record to Friar Antônio de Santa Maria Jaboatão in his illustrative *Novo orbe seráfico* (1761). Here is the Franciscan chronicler:

> We will not fail to repeat a miracle of our Saint Anthony also on behalf of his devotees. Fled from Colonel Domingos Dias Coelho, a resident in the districts of the city of Sergipe del Rei, a black, his slave, taking with him two black women, also slaves from other masters. With them he went to accommodate in the backlands of Jacoca, where he lived a few years away from the commerce of other people. In the beginning with what gave him the wilderness, the woods, and the rivers of Vazabarris, and then with fields and crops planted by him, dressing himself and his concubines, as well as his children that they gave birth to, with deerskins he grabbed with pitfalls and arrows, and tanned.
>
> The master of the slave relied, after other ineffective attempts, on Saint Anthony. Behold a friar appears to the black man, the hidden place where he had been living, and with a reproachful voice, asked him: 'Black man, what are you doing here?' And he said he was there for not being able to deal with the services ordered by his master, who did not let him rest. 'So be it true or not,' said the friar, 'get out of here!" And while the black man did not leave, the friar kept following him, putting himself always upfront, and always repeating: 'Negro, get out of here!'
>
> Finally, the black man came back, and the friar before him, until arriving to the house of the owner of one of the black women, who was handed back to her owner. And pausing there for some time, was seen by the capitão-do-campo, who arrested him and gave him to his master, as well as the other black woman, who belonged to him, having Saint Anthony done this bene-

fit to his devotee, and also being the reason to rid the souls of these miserable slaves from the continuous guilt they felt.[44]

It is symptomatic that the owner of the runaway slave, Domingos Dias Coelho, was a familiar of the Holy Office of the Inquisition, and one of the most authoritative landowners in Sergipe's history, who, rather than have recourse to Saint Peter the Martyr, the patron of his inquisitorial militia to recover the captive runaway, knelt at the feet of *Divinus Antonius* to obtain the desired grace.[45]

Saint Anthony's performance of providing the Sergipe backlands a brother of habit as his emissary is identical to that observed in other miracles, such as the conquest of Oran square, in Algeria, where the same Franciscan friar was serving as spokesperson of the vigilante of Padua. The dialogue with the slave also reveals the Franciscan spiritual commitment to the defense of slavery in the sense that, even if the complaint of the runaway slave that his master hurt him with excessive work were true, the friar ordered that the captive returned to its owner. Besides sending him back to whom he "belonged," he sent the black man and his concubines to the true fold of Christianity, from which they had lived apart because of their "guilt" (polygamy). The delivery of the runaway blacks by the divine capitão-do-mato to a capitão-do-campo completed the cycle of Saint Anthony's attributions: Heaven and Earth working together to keep the bondage.[46]

Other episodes registered in the Holy Office of Lisbon manuscripts report that the use of St. Anthony as a capturer of captives occupied an important place in popular devotion, sliding into certain religious manifestations considered by the inquisitors as disrespectful, heterodox, or maybe even suspicious of connivance with infernal forces. Therefore, the figure of Saint Anthony was part of a *continuum* of recovering devotions, living side-by-side with witchcraft and alternative sorceries that together or alternately realized the recovering of runaway captives. Already in 1592, in Olinda, Ana Jácome, a native of Granada, was reported to have declared, "if one gave her the name of the long time runaway black, she would make him appear with her art." It was a general piece of gossip among the first settlers of Pernambuco that in fact the Spanish woman had recovered some slave who had fled.[47] Some settlers had their names cited to the visitor Heitor Furtado de Mendonça in Bahia in 1591, for referring to the saint with unacceptable verbal promiscuity: Antonio da Costa, forty years old, a *mameluke*, resident of the Recôncavo Baiano, promised a mass to Saint Anthony in case he retrieved an escaped slave. Already in possession of his black slave, "he said the rogue Saint Anthony was sagacious, that he knew very well that the saint did not want to give the black slave back unless after he promised the mass." Another *mameluke* from Bahia, Lázaro Aranha, resident in Perabuçu, promised one *cruzado* (currency) to the Lawyer of Lost Causes in case he could recover his black slave. But when he found him, he cursed with ingratitude: "The rogue Saint Anthony was mistaken for thinking he would give him a *cruzado!*"[48]

Even more serious was the accusation of witchcraft made against Ana Martins, born in the village of Pouca de Aguiar, who came to be sentenced by the Lisbon Inquisition in 1694 for misuse of divine arts. She was considered guilty of involving Saint Anthony directly in her strong prayers. Among the accusations was the fact that she used to frequently pray the forbidden "Responso of lost things," reciting:

> *Miraculous Saint Anthony, for the cord you girded, for the breviary you have prayed, for the cross you took... I ask you, Saint Anthony, make appear (what has been stolen, lost or fled...)*[49]

It is, however, in rural Pernambuco, in 1762, in the parish of Serinhaém, in a ceremony held by the commissioner of the Holy Office, Antonio Teixeira Lima, where the practice of many kinds of witchcraft with the support of the Attorney for the Lost Causes in the recovering of runaway slaves was proven. The documents suggest that these superstitions have probably been practiced more widely than was assumed. Among the denounced, there were Antonia Mendes, who lived in Sibiro, "the one who says Saint Anthony's prayer to ask for the return of runaway slaves, as indeed they return after a few months." Also mentioned is the *matuta* ("Roman goddess") "Petronila with Saint Anthony's prayer brings up lost things and she prays with a cord [of the saint] with which she measures the door through which the slave had run away." And Joana Carneira, "woman of the slave of the Franciscans from Serinhaem, says Saint Anthony's prayer."[50]

Such witchcraft or unorthodox arrangements aiming at the recovery of fugitive slaves are also found in the subculture of the Roma population who, in the eighteenth century, were banished to Brazil. In the collection of the strong prayers of this ethnicity, the prayers of brokenness, prayers to get what is difficult, and to see who is absent, there was also the "prayer to find fugitive blacks." Devotion is certainly contradictory, for it is known that the Gypsies in Brazil were specialized, in colonial Brazil, in the internal slave trade, being *vox populi* and proven in documents that state that many Gypsies used to steal free blacks and mestizos to turn them into slaves. But from whom would the blacks have fled, the subjects of such prayers: from the Gypsies themselves or from some legitimate owner who believed in the power of Roma mourners? It is clear that the Roma were especially devoted to the saint, mainly in Bahia, where he presided over the temple and village where they settled in: Santo Antônio da Mouraria (Saint Anthony of Mouraria).⁵¹

Actually, it seems to have been in Salvador, in the eighteenth century, that a specific image of the Hammer of Heretics was particularly associated with his role of recovering slaves: it is said that little Saint Anthony is even today venerated in the small chapel in front of the Santa Casa de Misericórdia da Bahia. The devotees make their prayers and throw coins through an iron barred door. This same image was known in the past as Saint Anthony of the Old Bárbara, whose history, briefly, is this: goody Bárbara rescued from the hands of a bunch of irreverent sailors an image of the saint, who was enthroned in his oratory:

> Since then the sacred figure of the Thaumaturge of Lisbon revealed its miraculous effectiveness. Those who had fugitive blacks resorted to old Bárbara, so that she could obtain the return of the fugitive, praying to her saint, and they were immediately satisfied. Breathless, the poor captive returned to the house of his master, saying he had been chased by a Franciscan friar, who beat him with a belt, and the religious man would disappear as if by magic by the residence door. Passing away the old creature, the venerable simulacra went to the Brotherhood of Misericórdia, which then allocated him at the chapel where he is now.⁵²

Other documents attest that Saint Anthony served as an example among men and saints in his function of helping owners recover their runaway slaves. At least two "popular saints" in slaveholding Brazilian society have included in their curricula this very same attribution. The first of these to be recorded in the *Novo orbe seráfico* is the Friar José de Santo Antônio, lay brother, a Portuguese man from Ponte do Lima and resident of the Franciscan convent of São Paulo in the second quarter of the seventeenth century. Very charitable, he distributed clothes for those who did not have them, gave bread to the poor, and helped the afflicted. One desperate farmer from São Paulo once approached him, asking him to bring back his only slave, who had escaped, because the slave was instrumental for him, and he promised to donate five arrobas (125 pounds) of cotton, which the friars asked for "as charity" in case his loss was recovered:

> Go here by the fence of the convent, said the friar who brought Saint Anthony on his onomastic, and when you get there close to the car door, note that

you can find the black man there. The applicant left and thus it happened. And then making it back to the ordinance with the same slave, he thanked for the finding, sending not only the five arrobas of cotton, but as many as the friar wanted.⁵³

Also in Rio de Janeiro, coincidentally in the same convent where Saint Anthony was the owner of the earlier noted cane and the attire of the military commander, another saint friar helped owners to recover their runaway slaves. In the *Instrumento judicial e autentico dos privilegios e maravilhas que Deus tem obrado por intercessao de seu servo de Deus frei Fabiano de Cristo* (1747), it is stated that the chaplain of the church of Our Lady of the Rosary of the Blacks, Father Pedro Nolasco, said under oath that eight days earlier a black slave, Narciso, had ran away. The priest reminded him to beg the holy saint from Rio: "If my black slave, who has disappeared, serves God where he is, do not let him come back. However, if he offends God, make him come back home very soon." Arriving at his residence, he found the slave had voluntarily returned, although in the other frustrated attempts of escaping he only came back handcuffed.⁵⁴

According to Mary Karasch, the connection between the patron saint and the power to recover captives was still strong in the imagination of Catholics in Rio de Janeiro during the first half of the previous century.⁵⁵ The traveler Thomas Ewbank is the person who better corroborates this assertion: visiting the Franciscan Convent of Largo da Carioca, the monk who guided him into the church lingered long in the description of the punitive actions this saint implemented in the fight against the infidels, confirming that Captain Saint Anthony was constantly invoked in cases of runaway slaves. Ewbank said that a so-called Mrs. P. carried his medal on her chest, and, like everyone else, kept an image of him in her house. Not a day went by without her asking for his protection. And to convince the incredulous foreigner that he was a real miraculous saint, she guaranteed that the saint had recovered a slave of her mother after a long absence as well as the same occurring with one of her slaves who was very valuable. She also confirmed that if the devotee tortured the holy image, the fulfillment of the request would be accelerated. This pious informant told details about the steps taught by her mother to retrieve the fled black: one should light a candle in front of the patron saint and ask him to send the fugitive back, taking care of him without, however, giving him rest until the slave returned to its master's home. After a few weeks, if the requirement continued unanswered, the solution was to lay the saint's image on the floor, placing a heavy stone on top. If one continued without news about the black man, one should call for a last resort: to leave the saint hanging from a rope inside a dark well. Once the grace was obtained, his image would be properly cleaned and placed on the table of the house, with two candles, receiving prayers from the entire family. Ewbank, who calls *Divinus Antonius* of "heavenly Negro-catcher," said he heard the same version from a so-called Mr. H., whose runaway slave returned just a few weeks after the image of the patron saint remained languishing in a well in the backyard of his house.[56] This relation, sometimes menacing, sometimes violent, from the devotees *vis-à-vis* the saint's image, was already referred to with some indulgence by Father Vieira, and remained present in the devotion of our ancestors. Richard Burton confirms that in the city of Santo Antonio de Paraibuna de Juiz de Fora, in 1867, he heard the information that when the saint did not answer the request, he was "beaten, submerged in the well, and left in the open for a cold night."[57]

> *Saint Anthony between the Cross of Christ and the Sword of Ogum*
> *Saint Anthony takes the pain, but does not prevent the blow.*
> —*Popular saying, Bogum, Salvador, 1980*

Despite the strong linking of the Divine Capturer to the owners of power, the evidence that Saint Anthony also had countless devotes in the popular strata are numerous, even among the large population of color. We have much evidence of this, since in the first half of the eighteenth century, the miracle worker from Lisbon was worshiped in at least three different Afro-Brazilian rituals: in the *calundus* of Angolan inspiration and in the *acotundá* of Mina tendency, also appearing in cultural areas linked to *umbanda*.

The devotion to the Sun of the World was often suspected of being connected to heresy or blasphemy, as in the case that occurred in 1777 in the village of Itapecerica, in Minas Gerais, where Brígida Maria Roque and her lover, a black man from Angola, were reported to the commissioner of the local Holy Office for practicing *calundu* rituals, "sometimes taking the statue of Saint Anthony and Christ to the forest to do penance." What kind of penance would this couple do? "They danced with many gestures and alternated moves, at the sound of guitar and tambourine while Brígida said that the souls of the dead introduced themselves into the living who remained here...."[58] Also, the black Antônio Barbosa, a resident of the royal town of Queluz, was denounced for "doing his dances that they called *calundu*, with his house full of blacks, Afro-Brazilians, brown and mulattos, using smoker and passing ointment in hands and feet, requiring that others kissed a crucifix to avoid bewitchment, passing the crucifix and the statue of Saint Anthony in the legs of those who would try to *get lucky*."[59]

We found explicit reference to the veneration of the most famous kingdom native to Afro-Brazilian rituals documented at least since 1739. In the *calundu* of Luzia Pinta, a former slave from Angola, head of the most famous house of worship of Sabará, and one of few "witches" to be sent to the secret prisons of the Inquisition in Lisbon, she confessed that

> when it comes to her the disease of Angola, which people call *calunduz,* with which she loses control of herself and goes on to say the remedies that she has to minister to the sick, that in the occasions in which there are cures, it is always asked from the sick two octaves of gold (currency), with which shared Masses are celebrated, and half of that goes to Saint Anthony and the other half goes to Saint Gonçalo, and through the intervention of these saints those cures are made.[60]

Also in houses of worship of Mina inspiration, in the captaincy of Ouro, Saint Anthony already appears in the first half of the eighteenth century. In "Dança de tunda" or *acotundá*—a proto-candomblé existing in the small village of Paracatu in 1747—the head of the religious practice, Josefa Maria, from the *courá* nation, originally from Lagos in the kingdom of Benin, in the middle of the ceremony, already under the effect of trance, "went down to preach in her language, saying that she was the daughter of Our Lady of the Rosary and St. Anthony and that the saint was her godfather and he baptized her and sent her to this Earth that already for a long time was his." A telling detail that reinforces the illation of coeval association of Saint Anthony with orisha Ogum (Ogun) is the presence in this house of worship, at the foot of the holy altar, of a pot of *feijoada,* a dish traditionally served in honor of the warrior god: *Ogunhê!*

Proclaiming herself goddaughter and emissary of the most powerful saint of the heavenly court, in a house of worship frequented only by Africans and their descendants, speaking in a language of the coast of Mina, more than a league from the small village of Paracatu, the presence of Saint Anthony as godfather of the owner of this proto-candomblé made her much more respected than the rest of the mortals, legitimizing even more, thanks to the Catholic syncretism, the strength of her power. But in this specific case, it seems that the witchcraft turned against the witch, because, despite the proclaimed protection by the holy godfather Saint Anthony, a few days after that preaching, five capitães-do-mato invaded the yard of *acotundá,* disrupting the participants and seizing their worship objects.[61]

Saint Anthony did not offer any special treatment either for the other *courana* black, Rosa Egipcíaca, a former prostitute and founder of the religious house of Our Lady of the Milk and Happy Delivery. Arrested by order of the first bishop of Mariana in 1749, accused of being deceitful and suspected of a pact with the devil, she waited for a whipping punishment in the prison. In her confession archived at the Torre do Tombo, Rose Egipcíaca stated that

> being locked in a little house in the prison, waking in the morning she saw a Franciscan monk who seemed to be thirty years old and looked very handsome, with a burning candle in his hand, and told her that he wanted to exorcise her. And since she was guilty and feeling joy in her heart for seeing that figure, he said her again to come near him. And when this same figure was approaching her, she called the people in the house where she was and that vision disappeared, with the closed doors.[62]

Since she was a devotee of the saint from Padua, there is no doubt that the Franciscan friar that comforted her in the prison was the same that appeared a few years before, on the beaches of Oran, in Salvador, at the time of Old Bárbara, and in the backlands of Sergipe—that is, the same Saint Anthony who, in all these episodes, disguised himself as a friar to exercise the mission of the messenger of Divine Providence. These are messages that often sadden the expectations of the afflicted devotees: in these cases, the *vox populi* tried to sublimate the deception through the popular saying: "When God does not want, Saint Anthony cannot!"

In the nineteenth century, Stanley Stein says that Africans and their descendants in Vassouras (Rio de Janeiro) retained in *senzalas* statues of Saint George, Saint Benedict, Saint Sebastian, Saints Cosmas, and Damian, but Saint Anthony was the favorite one, "always present in the table of quimbandeiros." A curious note: these saint icons often held in their arms not the traditional Baby Jesus, but a black baby, who was removed until the devotee could have his or her solicitation granted.[63]

Robert Slenes also found in Vassouras the presence of Saint Anthony as the patron of a secret mystical association, called umbanda, which planned a slave revolt in 1847. This author follows the same inspiration of M. Karasch by outlining certain analogies between the Afro-Brazilian religious syncretism and the mythological imagination of the Central African cultural area (Bantu), including the use of pine knot as material for making popular statues of this saint:[64]

> The fact that at least some groups of slaves involved in the rebellion plan sought the protection of the saint not only reveals the presence of a clear Central African religious consciousness, but perhaps also a subversive inten-

tion in the state level. After all, Saint Anthony was known as a warrior saint [...] a kind of patron saint of the Portuguese state and, after independence, the Brazilian state. In this context, adopting it as standard of a rebellion would not mean the intention of turning Brazilian politics, along with the economic system, upside down?[65]

There are records, however, that show a tense and aggressive relation between people of color and the beatified capitão-do-mato. Would it be a kind of vendetta of the oppressed against the lackey of the oppressive slave masters? The mulatto Ana Jorge, a prostitute, resident in Massus (Minas Gerais, 1777), was charged with putting under the mattress of her bed a holy statue of Saint Anthony, along with the crucifix; images that, besides flogging, she threw on the wall saying, "since they did not do what I requested, they have to be punched and flogged."[66] Rosa Gomes, a forty-year-old Mina black, and the former slave of another Mina black woman, then a freed slave, resident at street of Bananeiras in Sabará in 1762, was even more aggressive and iconoclastic:

> desperate in her home, between four walls, lonely and without fortune, she asked the saints and they did not answer her, and without finding neither stick nor rope to hang herself, so desperate and out of control, irrational, she took off her beads and scapulars and destroyed with a machete the statues of Our Lady and Saint Anthony, plucked their arms and heads. And resting on both knees, raising her hands, she showed that she venerates the same torn statues while she repeated: *good fortune and spells.*[67]

Some songs are intoned in Afro-Brazilian houses of worship and certain popular sayings ratify the perception, by African descendants, that the power of Saint Anthony, at least for blacks, was more limited than it was for whites. We have two versions of a candomblé song. The first one, collected by Maria Lúcia Mott in the candomblé Angola yard of Mãe Jandira (Osasco, São Paulo, early 1970s), says, "Saint Anthony, tie the black there on the way...," and the second one, recorded in the yard of Mãe Calunga, in Rio de Janeiro, in 1994, says, "Saint Anthony, tie the black very well tied." Such verses allow us three different interpretations: they could be simple appropriation by the *candomblezeiros* of the same devotion to the capitão-do-mato saint, begging him to immobilize some unwanted black; or, since "tied" in religious language can mean "state of the individual affected by bad vibrations that harm his or her life, his or her business etc."[68] In asking to keep the black well tied, one is using the saint as a collaborator in the "immobilization" of an enemy; finally, such verses could be a salute to Ogum, the lord of the gates and paths, often syncretized as the Franciscan saint in houses of worship in Northeastern Brazil, begging that Ogum keep Exu (Eshu), the black lord of the streets and crossroads, well tied, in order to not disrupt the normal course of the religious celebration.

I end this approach to Saint Anthony's role as capitão-do-mato in Brazil with another verse I heard in my childhood, almost half a century ago, in the village of Araçariguama, in São Paulo, and which children recited while playing *pegador* (catcher), a form of play in which the person upon whom fell the last syllable of the word *pegador* should go running after the other participants:

> *I went to the woods to cut firewood, Saint Anthony called me*
> *When the saint calls us, it's a sign of pegador!*

Would this mythological pegador that, until the middle of the current century, chased other children, be an allusion to the coeval capitão-do-mato, which in past centuries chased the fugitive slaves, "with eyes on the prize, angry in search of the escaped black, tireless until grabbing them by their waistbands"?[69] If this hypothetical parallel makes sense, then we probably are in the face of the last vestige of a cult that, crucial at the time of our great-grandparents, with the end of slavery, today remains fossilized in the children's folklore, void of any explanatory understanding from the contemporaries. In this sense, the metamorphosis of the Sun of the World from capitão-do-mato to mellifluous and matchmaker saint does not cease to be auspicious: was it not the Apostle of the Gentiles who had taught, "it is better to marry than to get angry?" In other words, is it better *to make love than war*?

7

MINING, QUILOMBOS, AND PALMARES: MINAS GERAIS IN THE EIGHTEENTH CENTURY

CARLOS MAGNO GUIMARÃES

This chapter aims to raise questions about the occurrence of *quilombos* in Minas Gerais in the eighteenth century, from the analysis of documents produced by colonial authorities. The mining company, formed by a process triggered by the discovery of gold in the late eighteenth century, had in slavery one of the dominant forms of work organization. Quilombos manifested themselves as a basic contradiction of modern slavery—taking into account also the situational specifics of this very same slavery— and are one of the expressions of conflict involving all classes. Their starting point lies in the clash between masters and slaves. The discussion is divided into three parts. In the first, the objective is to identify the formation of quilombos, its survival and its destruction in the slave mining social order. The second part deals with both the exercise of power within the quilombos as the positioning of the different classes, and class fractions before the phenomenon formed by them was constituted. Finally, the third part shows how the existence of the Quilombos dos Palmares, destroyed in the late seventeenth century, created in mining colonial authorities the fear that the Palmares phenomenon would be replicated in Minas Gerais.

I

In the late seventeenth century and the first half of the eighteenth century, the discovery of gold, and later diamonds, caused great impact on the process of Portuguese colonization in Brazil. Mining activity had its great moment in the first half of the eighteenth century, but already, in 1750, its crisis was evident, and closer to the end of the century, it became more pronounced. A key indicator was the decline in tax revenues of the Portuguese Crown. Logically, evasion is another variable that influences the decrease in collection. It is important, however, to understand that the crisis was mainly of the mining activity and not of the entire economy. Since the beginning, the diversification of the economy gave elasticity to the economic structure, preventing the mining crisis from turning into a general decline in the mining economy. The fact that that crisis was overcome later is reflected in the data on the slave population. After a sharp drop after 1738, the slave population increased again, reaching its greatest dimension in the nineteenth century, not in the eighteenth century, as would be expected.[1]

Diamonds convoy, 1825 ("Convoi de diamants passant par Caiete," M. Rugendas, Malerische Reise in Brasilien, Paris, Engelman & Cie., 1835)

Among the economic activities, mining clearly stands out, although other activities were developed from the beginning, such as agriculture, livestock production, and some manufacturing activities, such as the production of sugar, brown sugar, *cachaça* (liquor distilled from sugarcane juice), spinning, weaving, etc.[2] The society, which was based on this economic diversity, consisted of a diverse population comprising a varied social structure in which whites, blacks, indigenous and *mestizos* had qualities that were either consistent or conflicting with the conditions expressed in the categories free people, freed slaves, and slaves. The slave class has stood out for its number and its refractoriness since the beginning of the eighteenth century. Although the data does not cover all regions of Minas Gerais, there are indicators that the slave class never comprised less than 30 percent of the total population in every age, and that the free population in some regions was lower than the slave population. In turn, the freed slave class, which in the first half of the seventeenth century amounted to only 1.2

percent of the slave population, 35 percent of the total population in 1786 and reached 41 percent in 1808.³ The slave, African or Afro-Brazilian, was the basic modality of the workforce, but not the only one, and was employed in all regions and activities, both during and after the period covered in this chapter. Wherever slavery was implanted, we find the emergence of communities formed by slaves who escaped from their masters: the quilombos.

Main Quilombos in Eighteenth Century Minas Gerais. The names indicate the locations in the vicinity in which the quilombos were located and destroyed.

Quilombos constituted one of the most complete and complex forms of reactions to slavery in Minas Gerais in the seventeenth century. To get an idea of their participation in social dynamics, just remember that for the period between the years 1710 and 1798, the researched collection of documents confirms the discovery and destruction of at least 160 quilombos in the area of Minas Gerais.⁴ Such given data is enough to reject the common theses of soft slavery; the harmonic relationship between masters and slaves; and the acceptance by the slaves of their condition. The existence of the quilombos created damage not only to slavery as an economic system, but to slave society as a whole. Having been formed mainly by fugitive slaves, quilombos express a structural contradiction of the slavery reality, to the extent that they mean:[5]

- the withdrawal of the slave from the production process and thus the impossibility of creating income for the slave owner;
- the impossibility of return on capital invested in the acquisition of the slave;
- the unproductive consumption generated by the expenditures required for the creation of a repressive skilled system;
- property damage as a result of activities developed by quilombolas (robberies, assaults, fires, etc.);
- decreases in tax revenue that the Crown could receive on slave labor.

Besides the material costs, the existence of the quilombos caused other forms of damage as important as the ones mentioned above:

- the negation of the effectiveness of the legal and ideological apparatus designed to prevent escapes and punish fugitives and recaptured quilombolas;
- the presence of a permanent fear on the part of the authorities and the population in general by the constant threat of attacks by quilombolas or even the "misconduct" of the officials responsible for repression of the quilombos.

As for the number of its members, quilombos could have small populations (less than a dozen inhabitants) or could reach significant numbers of inhabitants (hundreds of quilombolas). There are documents on Quilombo do Ambrósio, destroyed in 1746, which mention more than six hundred and even a thousand inhabitants.[6] The population growth of the quilombos depended on two factors: accession of new fugitive slaves, and the reproduction of quilombolas that could form families depending on opportunities.[7]

The activities developed by quilombolas in order to survive were many: hunting, gathering, agriculture, animal husbandry, mining, smuggling, troops, farm robberies, etc. In each of the different regions of the captaincy of Minas Gerais in the eighteenth century, these various activities were developed by quilombolas. This leads us to affirm that, on the one hand, all quilombos are similar, but on the other hand, they are different. They are similar to the extent that, formed mainly by runaways, they all represent the same mode of expression of slave defiance. They are different, for each of them has its own duration, its own region, and its own survival mechanisms, thus establishing a specific historical and cultural configuration. In the area of gold or diamond extraction, quilombolas were generally devoted to mining (logically illegal) and used the product to trade with smugglers to obtain what they needed, such as gunpowder, weapons and food. In areas where there was no mineral occurrence, as in the captaincy backlands, quilombos had to engage in other activities, such as agriculture and hunting.

The above argument touches on a fundamental point: the various types of links between quilombos and slave society. These connections were manifested primarily by:

- clandestine trade with smugglers, innkeepers, black female street vendors, farmers;
- attacks on travelers, drovers, farms, villages, suburbs, and hamlets;
- effective relations established among slaves, freed slaves and quilombolas, as quilombolas usually frequented the peripheries of urban centers or farms in rural areas.

If the types of bonds mentioned were advantageous for the quilombos, because they constitute mechanisms for their survival, another type of bond, this time negative, includes the attacks carried out by armed oppressors of slave society. By denying the basic principles of the slave system, quilombolas logically provoked against themselves a repression characterized by a preventive and punitive legislation and the formation of specialized troops in the task of recapturing fugitive slaves and destroying quilombos. The escape of slaves and the formation of quilombos established a contradiction to the slave society, and this became the basis for a significant part of its dynamics. In the case of Minas Gerais, the occurrence of quilombos became an issue of such magnitude to the colonial authorities and society in general that the legislation eventually produced a significant amount of proclamations, permits, regulations, and royal orders that intended to limit and extinguish the chances of the quilombos' survival.

Throughout the eighteenth century, there was a sequence of proclamations that brought the same prohibitions, proving their inefficiency on the one hand and the permanence of the quilombos on the other hand. From time to time, a proclamation is fully or partly reissued under the justification that it was not fulfilled by the population, as with the prohibition of the use of arms by the slaves, the attempt to prevent the displacement of slaves without written permission from their masters, and the claim to limit the trade carried out by the female street vendors and by sales of manumission. The reasons for the bans were recurrent and intended to limit the mobility of the captive.[8]

In the captaincy of Minas Gerais, the quilombos' repression led to the creation of a specialized troop whose work was regulated by the Regiment of the Capitães-do-Mato. Although it was not formed by the military, this company was hierarchical along the lines of regular wage-remunerated troops. The positions correspond to the military ranks, although payment for their services only materialized when there were positive results in recapture expeditions and destruction of quilombos: recaptured quilombolas or their heads were used to prove they were killed in attacks.[9]

The payment for the services of the *homens-do-mato*—the *tomadia*—was regulated by the distance between the home of the fugitive slave and the place where he had been recaptured. The greater the distance, the larger the tomadia. A common practice was the use of former slaves in the profession of homens-do-mato. The knowledge that the former slaves behaved like fugitives justified this practice. In the Minas Gerais of the eighteenth century, nearly 15 percent of the homens-do-mato were freed slaves.[10] If the tomadia was an expenditure that the owner of the recaptured slave handled, the destruction of a quilombo demanded the formation of a troop whose costs were larger and distributed between the Crown, the legislative chambers, and owners of slaves from the area affected by the quilombo. In this case, the Crown (or the captaincy government) was responsible for the supply of arms, ammunition, and specialized professionals, besides the troop organization. The legislative chambers were responsible for the supply of money and sometimes equipment, such as canoes, etc. The owners of the area affected by the quilombo(s) were responsible for the supply of food to the troops and sometimes were still required to provide animals or slaves for the transport of food. In some cases, masters even armed their current slaves to participate in shock troops. This last aspect highlights one more contradiction that the slave society produced: slaves used in the fight against fugitive slaves.

Such an analysis of quilombos helps us understand the true character of slavery, and contributes to the perception of some of the contradictions generated in the context of slave society. The study of the importance of the quilombo, through its character of resistance to slavery, allows us to deepen our understanding of slave agency, situating it within a class struggle, and as an integrant part of a society that is based on slavery. The assessment of the quilombo, in terms of social dynamics, must be considered in two aspects: on the one hand, it is necessary to take into account the set of relations established between quilombos and the slave society; on the other hand, one should consider the fact that the slave society developed mechanisms to absorb the shocks caused by the existence of quilombos.

2

As stated, we intend to discuss the exercise of power within the quilombos and how classes and class fractions stood before the existence of the quilombos. As the relationships and conflicts between classes are political in nature, and the quilombos configured political movements, our starting point will be to define, even if briefly, this aspect of the matter. In his *Dicionário de política*, Norberto Bobbio raises some points that are fundamental to our reflection.[11] In developing the classical typology of forms of power, Bobbio states, "the concept of politics, understood as a form of activity or human praxis, is closely linked to power." The nature of power concerns the "dominion over other men," which means an imposition of will and determination of behavior. This relationship of power can be expressed in different ways: as a relationship between rulers and ruled, sovereign and subjects, states and citizens, between authority and obedience, etc. "There are several forms of power of a man over a man; political power is only one of them." Yet for Bobbio, "the political power is, in every society of unequal, the supreme power," to the extent that it is to it, as a coercive power, which "all social groups (the dominant class) resort, ultimately [...], to defend themselves from external attacks or to prevent, with dissolution of the group, that they are eliminated."

To these aspects defined by Bobbio, we judge necessary to add others. In the social totality, the various forms of power are articulated or are intertwined in relationships of determination. The articulation between instances of the social life is reflected in the existence of the power structure prevalent in society. Thus, in the slave society, the domination of the master over the slave constitutes the fundamental axis of power in the economic, political and ideological spheres. This axis will be a central point around which the entire structure of power articulates itself and the conflict that will be the keynote of social dynamic development. This does not mean that we ignore the fact that other classes and conflicts are related to that reality. The concept of social class as defined by Lenin works as a basis of discussion here, although recognizing its limitation as being from a fundamentally economic perspective. According to Lenin, classes are

> large groups of people that are distinguished by their place in a system of social production historically determined, by their relationship (more often fixed and formulated in law) with the production means, by their role in the social organization of work and consequently by the achievement and the dimensions of the part of social wealth at their disposal. Classes are groups of people, one of which can appropriate the work of other for the fact it occupies a different place in a determined system of social economy.[12]

This definition allows us to identify slaves and their owners as members of different classes. We still risk considering the freed slaves as a class whose existence has the peculiarity of being originally from a slave status; however, what seems to be simple in that scheme becomes extremely complicated when we analyze the situational reality. If being a slave represents a clear position in the social structure, being a slave owner is not as clear. Slaveholders could be free, freed slaves, or even other slaves.

As we unfold each category with its own specificities, the complexity of the social fabric and the difficulty of apprehending it become more evident. Our starting point is the realization that quilombos represent (and are the center of) a conflicting reality, which different—if not all—social categories participate in. But this reality is fundamentally a conflict between masters and slaves, allowing us to attribute to it a political character.[13] The great question is to unravel how each of the social categories (slaves, masters, freed slaves, etc.) participates in this great conflict. Before addressing this question, we will see first how the researched documents deal with the exercise of power within the quilombos. At this point, the question is to identify the ways in which quilombos are governed.

There is evidence that the communities of quilombolas had units (or leaderships) to which its members were subordinated; yet, identifying the character of these units can be problematic. The information contained in the documents is very precarious. The first piece of information is found in a letter, dated 9 November 1730, sent to Don Lourenço de Almeida, then governor of Minas Gerais. According to this document, there were in the region

> blacks who invade the road and houses whose tyranny is so big that they set fire to the same houses and the bodies after they killed and robbed them, promising greater ruin with the freedom with which they live and making themselves powerful in quilombos that have forty, fifty, and more *blacks*

ruled by king, others ruled by a captain, being these quilombos like a village of gentiles hidden between bushes.[14]

Although the document distinguishes the rule of a king from the administration of a captain, it does not clarify this difference. Similarly, it does not add any information about the type of "reign."

In 1736, a quilombo near Baependi was destroyed. In chronicling the expedition, Thomé Roiz Nogueira says that he demanded

> the hunt continue to engage in the pursuit of the more persecuted and starving ones who were forced to fetch the homes of their masters, and the only one missing is *the mulatto titled as king* with a concubine, two sons and four slaves and who is wanted so that this district can be reassured.[15]

In December 1738, Governor Gomes Freire de Andrade wrote to captain-general Nicolau Carvalho Azevedo about "two black females" who were captured. He suggests that Azevedo "keeps them safe for perhaps it can be possible that the black males want to come and take *their queen*, and then it is a good occasion to make them wait."[16] In both of these documents, the idea of quilombos governed by a king and/or queen is clear, but the meaning of this is not. On June 14, 1746, in a letter addressed to the various legislative chambers, asking that they contribute to the formation of troops that should attack quilombos located in the region denominated Campo Grande, the governor of Minas argues that

> the parts closer to the mentioned quilombo are already depopulated and the most distant ones still are suffering a very pernicious damage, more than 600 blacks who obey a king and a queen in that quilombo and that we understand that they intend to defend and save themselves with strength precautions and fitting equipment.[17]

On August 8 of the same year, Gomes Freire writes to the king, reporting the measures taken in relation to these quilombos. Although it is inaccurate, the reference surely fits the Quilombo of Ambrósio, whose reputation is of being the largest that existed in Minas Gerais in the eighteenth century.

> Departures of twenty and thirty blacks who carried thefts and very cruel deaths were happening continuously; some were captured and, despite being punished, that was not enough as the number of black quilombolas has increased and it was so big that, according to the best calculations, they were more than a thousand, besides a large number of black females and off-

> spring: with this united power, they *elected a king* and formed a rather strong platform and, determined to appear, they insolently burned homes, killed their owners, oppressed families and took away the slaves who they understood as recruits.[18]

The increase in number of quilombolas from six hundred to one thousand was probably a strategy of Gomes Freire to make a greater impression and give the idea that the "solved problem" was bigger. The reference to the "kings" of the quilombos also appears in the two aforementioned documents, as does the probable "election" of one of them in the second document. Certainly, this information should be considered with extreme caution, since no other comes to us from these sources.

In 1767, after destroying a quilombo located in Pitangui parish, ensign Bento Rebelo sent a petition to the governor of Minas in which he describes the attack:

> Investing against the mentioned quilombo, the supplicant and more people he invited, with the set of twenty two firearms, attacked the mentioned blacks, that were thirty, of which six were arrested, and since they resisted to the conflict, we killed *the so-called king and captain*, destroying fourteen ranches of grass and land where they grew corn, bean, cotton, watermelons and more fruits.[19]

The governor favorably granted the ensign's request that he could "penalize" people, when necessary, in order to destroy quilombos.[20] In the following year, 1768, one quilombo located in the backlands of Pedra Menina was attacked. The commander, João Duarte de Faria, explains in a letter of December 16 that

> two of the chief architects of the killings and robberies they had done were killed, from whom I send the ears, and ten quilombolas and one offspring were tied as one sees from the report that I sent together to Your Exc. Fifteen fled from the same quilombo, among which the *king called Bateeiro* and others who are also responsible for killings and robberies.[21]

In the case of this quilombo, it seems that leadership was divided between the cited Bateeiro and other quilombola known as Beiçudo.[22] In February 1769, Bateeiro was arrested and interrogated in the jail of Vila Rica.[23] In correspondence of 8 January 1777, the judge of Mariana, Ignácio José de Souza Rabelo, writes of an interesting case. After an attack on a quilombo "in the woods of Forquim," the result was the imprisonment of "nine black males and five black females." The quilombo was "strong, because it took a lot of people to do the diligence, and despite of that they did a good defense with firearms shooting many times." Many of the recaptured had been runaways for many years. One of them, in the interrogation, "was said that to have fled ten years ago and that *he was the foreman*, that his master would have given 40 Eighths *(currency)* to who bring his head for he has ruined others, and made great damage and that *he was the king*."[24]

Of particular interest in this case, if we are to believe in the veracity of the document, is the situation where a slave who was a ranch foreman eventually became a "king" in a quilombo. In addition to this, there was the undeniable leadership of this slave, who had not only escaped but could bring other slaves with him, "ruining" his master to the point of there being established a reward that was twice as much as the one stipulated by the Regiment of Capitães-do-Mato. The vengeance of this master had an expensive price: 40 eighths of gold.

Regarding this aspect—the exercise of the internal power in quilombos—the documents do not allow us to progress, but it is possible to verify that the quilombos had one form of power exercised by the authority (leadership) of an individual, sometimes accompanied by his wife. In the case of the quilombo of Pedra Menina, two leaders probably shared that authority. The great question that the documents do not allow us to answer concerns the character of these "reigns." After all, what was the criterion used in the definition of who would be considered king? What was the real (practical) power of these "kings"? And were there any links with "aristocratic" lines from Africa? Another doubt that remains is the following: to what extent did the designation of "king" and "queen" for these leaders reflect the fact that kings and queens governed the slave society? After all, subjects of those kings and queens produced the documents consulted for this research.

As mentioned, the issue to identify here is how different social categories positioned themselves before the conflict that unfolds between masters and slaves. The first point that we will address concerns the heterogeneity of collective categories, mainly regarding their political action. If categories such as "slave" and "freed slave" define clearly a great part of the economic reality experienced by these subjects, this does not happen in the case of those who are free regardless. These may or may not be slaves' owners, or they could also be peasants or urban artisans. Finally, the condition of being free is not sufficiently clear and objective in defining the reality of this category. On the other hand, although the economic reality has a fundamental say in the political action of the categories, it does not determine one homogeneous pattern for all of them. That is why analytical schemes can contribute to the comprehension of social dynamics, but they can also lead to the reductionisms that have been so frequent in the literature that deals with Brazilian slavery. These observations will become clearer later.

Let us start with the slave class: how did slaves position themselves before quilombos, given that the majority of them did not flee? In 1714, Governor Don Braz Balthazar banned the use of weapons in Minas, except for masters during their travel. In this case, they could take armed slaves to defend themselves on the road.[25] One of the threats travelers faced on the roads of Minas was the quilombolas. In 1722, Governor Don Lourenço de Almeida awarded the rank of Ordinance Staff Sergeant to João Roiz Cortes, who participated in campaigns against quilombos using his own slaves as attackers.[26] Ten years later, in 1732, the *capitão dos dragões*, José de Morais Cabral, suggested in a letter to Don Lourenço that the royal department of treasury purchase 24 slaves who, armed, would be used in place of capitães-do-mato in the county of Serro Frio.[27] In 1736 it was the turn of Benedict Ferraz de Lima to be awarded the rank of Captain General of Catas Altas after having executed well the task of destroying quilombos at Caraça hill, "in which he expend considerable goods on taking many armed slaves."[28]

In all of these cases, the situation presented was one in which masters armed their slaves and used them against quilombolas. These were slaves who, in the conflict between masters and slaves, fought alongside their masters. It is clear that an explicit explanation for this may be that their masters forced these slaves to fight. But it is not so easy to understand why, being armed, slaves did not turn against their masters. It is still possible to admit that they could consider the slave condition more advantageous than the *aquilombamento*. If the participation of slaves in the troops commanded by the master is a situation that can explain the behavior of these slaves, such does not happen when the slave acts alone or out of the master's orbit. On January 17, 1731, the "black slave" Amaro de Queiroz, a property of José de Queiroz, was awarded the rank of capitão-do-mato to act in the district of Antônio Pereira, a suburb of the village of Carmo. On 5 November 1760, Domingos Moreira de Azevedo, an "Afro-Brazilian slave" owned by André Álvares de Azevedo, was awarded the rank to act in the area of Piracicaba and Caraça, and, in December 1779, the rank was confirmed to José Ferreira, "brown slave" owned by captain Antonio João Belas.[29] In the last three cases, the autonomy of each one of the slaves was great. There was no presence of their masters in the moment that they acted professionally; and yet they did not run away and still worked as important players in maintaining the system that keeps them as slaves.

Well, if on the one hand, we have slaves fighting to defend slavery—and it seems that their number was large—the contrary position may have been the most common. A constant complaint of the colonial authorities was concerning an information network created by quilombolas that warned the fugitive slaves of the movements of armed troops. This network acted from *senzalas* (black slave residences). In 1759, Bartolomeu Bueno do Prado, in his campaign in Campo Grande, found a large quilombo abandoned because the quilombolas had been informed in advance of the organization and the movements of the troops.[30] In 1769, the Count of Valadares wrote to the auxiliary captain, Manoel Rodrigues da Costa, asking him to make inquiries in the "farm Azevedo and in the other farms as well" where there was the suspicion that slaves harbored or passed on information to quilombolas.[31] On 25 February 1773, Commander Manoel Gouvea wrote to Captain General Liberato José Cordeiro to inform him that

> after reliable reports that there were fugitive blacks in the backlands of Crumatahy, I went to the land of Francisca Antonia and, thinking that her slaves spoke to and communicate with the fugitive ones, I intended to search the senzalas of her slaves, who came up armed and hindered the diligence, having the boldness to provoke us until the ranch that extend more than half a league from Domingos de tal.[32]

An application from Captain Elias Antonio da Silva of 1792, in which he requests an ordinance authorizing him to attack quilombos, presents as argument the fact that the applicant has, at that moment, five slaves who fled and

> despite the diligences and ambushes or decoys that have been made against them, it is not possible to seize them because they take refuge in a few farms that serve as constant harbor for blacks fleeing their masters, and the slaves of the same farms facilitate the mentioned harbor and even some owners of the above-mentioned farms did the same in extremely serious damage to the particular and the common good.[33]

In 1795, the farmer Marcelino Costa Gonçalves sent correspondence to the governor of Minas, saying

> being stolen with contempt of his person by fugitive blacks on January 24, now he has the news that the quilombolas were accompanied with others from neighboring farms who were cultivating beans and managing sickles

> when attacked, perhaps with the project of sharing the theft which was not small, and because, therefore, some things still may appear in the senzalas of the mentioned slaves, those that the petitioner suspects that have an alliance with the quilombolas, with whom they divide the groceries from the storeroom of their masters or in the houses of their mistress who harbor and favor them.[34]

If some of the slaves who do not flee advocate the preservation of the slave system, another portion is clearly, and sometimes blatantly, on the quilombolas' side, providing them with material assistance, information, and even participating in their looting activities. From what has been discussed thus far, we deduce that in its development the conflict between masters and slaves generates, on the one hand, quilombos, and on the other hand, causes a rupture within the slave class, making a part of it fight against the masters and the other part fight on the masters' behalf.

In the case of freed slaves, the first important data is expressed in the number of them who entered the profession of homens-do-mato, whose objectives were to recapture fugitive slaves and to destroy quilombos. Almost 15 percent of the 467 people with the rank of homens-do-mato were awarded to freed slaves.[35] Other scholars perceive the utilization of freed slaves in key positions by the slave system in various circumstances.[36] Besides that, there is the fact that a large number of freed slaves eventually became slave owners, a situation that placed them in the condition to defend their interests fighting for the system's preservation. To cite just two numbers, according to Francisco Vidal Luna, in Serro Frio, in 1738, 387 of 1,744 owners of slaves were freed slaves; and in the parish of Congonhas do Sabará, in 1771, 51 of 235 owners of slaves were freed slaves.[37]

Because of the possibility of the freed slave to become a master, slavery acquired a greater capacity to resist the slave class pressures. Thus, some of the former slaves were co-opted to fight in defense of slavery. But the other slaves went in the opposite direction. The first documentation refers to the Count of Assumar who, in 1719, accused freed slaves of helping quilombos "frequently with gold, provisions, gunpowder and projectile." Continuing, Assumar also protested freed slave women who own grocery stores because, according to him, "in the homes of these depraved women [the quilombolas] make their gatherings and resolutions to insult and disquiet with extreme danger whites in their farms."[38]

In 1732, in a letter addressed to the Count of Galveas, who at that time was the governor of Minas, the king asked for an opinion on certain measures to be taken against these same freed slave women, owners of grocery stores, accused of prostitution and of having in their homes

> provided black robbers from quilombos of whatever they needed, taking note of persons from whom they will steal and of information on where it is more convenient to enter and leave, what they do easily once receiving help and harbor from these black women that work at the grocery stores.[39]

Governor Gomes Freire de Andrade, in turn, expressed an opinion on the issue in 1736. He considered that there should not be the deployment of troops to the rescue of the Navy (in one specific circumstance) because they were necessary against "internal enemies that can be considered in similar occasion not only fugitive blacks that often steal, but the freed mulattos, and mamelucos ['mestiço' or bands of 'slave-hunters'] and even slaves."[40] In July of that same year, "residents of São Sebastião parish" made a request to Governor Martinho de Mendonça to attack a "quilombo of blacks and search the homes of freed slaves and flog the offenders."[41] In January of the following year, this governor, serving the petition of capitão-do-mato Francisco Soares, determined that the supplicant was not prohibited from entering taverns and homes of freed blacks and mulattos when looking for fugitives.[42]

In 1764, Governor Luís Diogo Lobo da Silva tried to put under control the slaves and freed slaves of Minas. In a broad promulgation, in which he resorted to laws created in 1719, he forbade black female street vendors (both freed and slaves) of trading their products in areas where the disappearance of gold and transactions with quilombolas were possible.[43] The evidence is sufficient. Like the slaves, the conflict between master and slave affected freed slaves as a whole. They were lead to the position of being on one side or the other. The positions leave no doubts: either they fought against the rebellious slaves or they made alliances with them.

Gold washing in Minas Gerais, c. 1825 ("Lavage du mineral d'or près de la montagne Itacolomi," M. Rugendas, Malerische Reise in Brasilien, Paris, Engelmann & Cie., 1835)

Now that we have addressed slaves and freed slaves, we cannot fail to mention that some free men and even owners of slaves also had an interest in favoring quilombolas. At least one case deserves a reference, much more for its character of exception than for it being a general trend. Having made a raid in the house of Lieutenant Antonio Muniz de Medeiros in 1781, the existence of a "hidden grocery store where fugitive blacks and miners would get provisions" was discovered. The lieutenant claimed that the products were to be sold to their own slaves, although in the region everyone knew that he sold

> only to the fugitive blacks and to the miners, to the extent that quilombos near his house never fail to exist, and there was so much freedom that even his female slaves visited the quilombo at daylight to talk to fugitive blacks.[44]

What is exceptional in this case is not that a free individual covered up quilombolas, but the fact that this individual was a slave owner. A similar situation can be seen in the document cited above, in which one reads that some farmers whipped quilombolas. It is a contradiction of the slave system. Clearly, these slave masters made alliances with quilombolas to the extent that their slaves had not fled to quilombos, and even they could still earn a profit, as in the case of Lieutenant Antonio Muniz.[45]

The rarity of this behavior leads us to conclude that, on the one hand, the lower classes (including slaves and freed slaves) were divided in the master-versus-slave conflict, and on the other hand, the survival of the system required a minimum of cohesion from the slave owners. The political nature and prominent leader roles of a certain number of slaves in the quilombos is worth addressing. There were slaves designed as leaders and performed a fundamental task: convincing other slaves to flee; acting as guides for new *quilombolas*; and in making connections between various quilombos.

In December 1759, Governor José Antonio Freire de Andrade wrote to the judges and officials of the chamber of São João Del Rei about an arrested quilombola in Campo Grande. To justify the transfer of this quilombola to Rio de Janeiro, the governor argued that

> captain Antonio Francisco França has assured me two or three times that if this black man is released, no other blacks will remain in this captaincy for they will go to the quilombos of Campo Grande.[46]

The quilombo of Cascalho, destroyed in 1760 during the administration of José Antonio Freire de Andrade, received this name from its leader. This quilombola was arrested when "he had gone to recruit people to the quilombo."[47] In 1771, the Count of Valadares recommended that Captain Manoel Furtado Leite Mendonça "avoid terrible damage from the prison of freed black and a group that has been inviting others who have been quiet at the home of their masters."[48] Ten years later, in 1781, Antonio José Dias Coelho wrote from Paracatu to inform the governor of the local residents' unrest over quilombolas, because among other reasons they were

> walking at night in the neighborhood of Arraial, and entering homes cautiously to persuade black women to flee from their masters [...] it's easy to believe that, within Arraial, there will be blacks who has a relation with fugitive slaves to notify the spies about the intentions of capitães-do-mato and, because of that, when they leave the diligence is frustrated for they warned about it.[49]

In the same year, the residents of the district of Ressaca, a suburb of the village of São José, complained of "fugitive slaves that not only mislead their slaves as well as steal their animal raising and provisions."⁵⁰

Finally, the case of Captain Elias Antonio da Silva is noteworthy, cited in an application; he was also resident of the suburb of Vila de São José. It refers to

> one of the slaves of the mentioned farms [who] is experienced and currently gives asylum to fugitive slaves, bailing them out with so much scandal and animosity that everyone agrees that he is aware of and knows about any quilombo existent in the distance of 30 or 40 leagues.⁵¹

There is no doubt that the work of persuasion executed by these slaves would be seen as an activity with a specific goal: to enable the foundation and development of quilombos. If we understand quilombos as a political manifestation, the political character of these activities is also evident. On the other hand, it is necessary to consider that these slaves had an acute awareness of their reality and of how they should face it. It is to that extent that it seems possible to perceive the quilombo as the concretization of a political project.

We can draw some conclusions from the discussion. The first is the need to overcome the theory of the political inability of the slave, because there are no elements that sustain it. The second is the need to perceive quilombos not only in their economic dimension, but also in their political dimension, as a collective agent in the game of contradictions that gave tonic to the social dynamic. The third is the fact that the quilombo, as an expression of class struggle between masters and slaves, is a reality on which slaves and freed slaves were divided. The fourth is the undeniable cohesion among the slave owner class in their position before the aforementioned conflict. The last one is the perception of the quilombos not only as a manifestation of rebellion, but mostly as a political project that shows strategies of autonomy by their members.⁵² Ultimately, thinking of the quilombo in its various nuances may permit us to understand better its dynamic and its insertion in the slave society.

3

In the final part of this chapter, we plan to the address two issues: first, the constant fear, among authorities, of the possibility that what occurred in Palmares could also happen in Minas Gerais; and second, how the contribution of the colonial administration of Minas Gerais is perceived in transforming Palmares as a symbol of the anti-slavery resistance. Palmares' destruction coincided with the discovery of gold in the hinterlands of Brazil (Minas Gerais), and this gave birth to the violent and painful process of instituting the colonial slave society in Minas Gerais. Probably discovered in the year before the destruction of Palmares, gold caused a rampant process of occupation, exploitation, and predation of natural resources in an unprecedented rhythm in the colony's history. The ecological and historical-cultural consequences are still markedly felt.

In 1699, less than one decade after the beginning of colonization in Minas Gerais, Arthur de Sá e Menezes received a letter from the Crown, dated from September 24, in which one of the points raised concerned the fact that the capitães-do-mato were being sued by owners of fugitive slaves that were killed in attacks on quilombos. The slave owners, mindful of their property, wanted the capitães-do-mato to compensate them for the deaths that occurred. The king's order indicates the need for opening an investigation to prove or disprove that it was the capitão-do-mato's fault, and according to the conclusion, he then would be punished.[53] The king himself was dismayed about the case of Captain Roque Fernandes, arrested eleven months before for having killed a quilombola and having been denounced by the owner of the dead slave. The royal concern was founded on the argument that it could be given "with this mode of proceeding, occasion for blacks to do the same that they did in *Palmares de Pernambuco.*"

If, in 1699, there is no evidence that quilombos existed in the region of Minas Gerais, it does not mean that they did not exist. Already in the first years, thousands of slaves had been displaced to the region for mining and, probably, since the beginning they were fleeing and constituting quilombos. Two decades later, after the separation from Rio de Janeiro, Minas Gerais united with São Paulo. At this time, 1719, the administration of the captaincy was exercised by the Count of Assumar, who hated Minas Gerais. He had three good reasons to be disgusted with Minas Gerais and, of course, with the people born there (mineiros). The first was the discovery of the quilombo of Caraça, which was terrorizing the region of the same name. The second was the articulation of the rebel movement, of an anti-taxation character, which passed into history with the name of Sedição de Vila Rica and culminated in the summary judgment and execution of Felipe dos Santos by order of Assumar himself. Finally, the third reason for discontent: a slave rebellion, maneuvered between slaves of several of the main urban centers, in combination with rural slaves and quilombolas, to put an end to slave owners.

On 21 November 1719, Assumar wrote to the general *ouvidor* of Rio das Mortes County, one of the administrative subdivisions of the captaincy.[54] After ordering measures for the destruction of the quilombo of Caraça, he made a series of observations that allow us to perceive not only what he himself thought about slavery, but also what was then the prevalent thinking that determined the state's operation. Inspired by further legislation, Assumar suggested that the punishment for the fugitive slave recaptured was like cutting "an artery of the foot."[55] Aware that the proposed measure would practically make the slave useless for most activities, the count proposed that the "parish" pay compensation to the slave owner

> because I was already concerned about this and I have understood that, without a very straight severity against blacks, it will be possible to happen that one day this administration will be a pitiful theater of their wrongdoings and the same that occurred in *Palmares de Pernambuco*, or worse, since the blacks under this administration have a different freedom [...] given that it is not real slavery the way they live today when one can call it licentious freedom with more property.[56]

If not all these reasons were enough to make Assumar dislike Minas Gerais, there was the enduring fear of a recurrence of the episode of Palmares. All these facts led our count to produce one of the most expressive reflections on the character of Minas Gerais and of mineiros, according to which

> the days never begin serene; the air is perpetually cloudy; all is cold in that country, except the addiction, that is always burning [...] the earth seems to evaporate riots; the water exalts riots; gold executes insults; the air distills freedoms; clouds vomit insolence; disorders influence the stars; the climate is the tomb of peace and the cradle of rebellion; nature is restless with itself and, mutinous inside itself, is like hell.[57]

One decade later, in 1730, Minas Gerais was separated from São Paulo and at that time, the governor was Don Lourenço de Almeida.[58] On May 7, he wrote to the king complaining about "continuous offenses" committed by "bastards, Carijós, mulattos and blacks" in Minas Gerais.[59] For Don Lourenço, the root of this criminality was the lack of the death penalty in the captaincy. According to the reasoning of the governor, if a judicial system with power to impose the death penalty had been established in Minas Gerais, as it was in Rio de Janeiro and Bahia, the increase of criminality may have been prevented. The belief in death penalty as a solution for combating crimes appears here in one of its first legal incursions in the captaincy. Don Lourenço requested "Your Magnanimity to give the general *ouvidor* of counties the same jurisdiction that the ones in Rio de Janeiro have, of sentencing to death, in accordance with the governor and ministers" slaves accused of crimes punishable by death. It was necessary to have "the permission to sentence to death" and "the execution of the sentences" to avoid "the multitude of offenses" that were committed. In the words of Don Lourenço, there was no time when the roads were not

> full of black robbers and killers, and it's necessary for them to be punished with the death penalty, executed in these villages to set an example for the other blacks, because if that there is no punishment, those blacks will become more numerous and will require the same care that *Palmares in Pernambuco* did, besides the many deaths caused by Carijós, mulattos and bastards.

The citation takes us back to at least three aspects. The first is the realization of a constant state of rebellion by the slave population. The second is the practice of public punishment by way of example: the exemplary punishment. The exemplary punishment would serve to terrify the slaves, and such felling would alleviate the slave owners of their constant fear of a slave uprising or an attack by quilombolas. Finally, the quotation refers us to the fear of a new Palmares in Minas Gerais, given the large amount of slaves concentrated in the region.

Less than ten years later, on April 15, 1738, General Gomes Freire de Andrade, the governor of Minas Gerais, demanded that someone get a royal letter at the Secretaria do Rio de Janeiro, sent to Arthur de Sá Menezes (on September 24, 1699), and file it as a valid diploma with Secretaria de Governo das Minas Gerais.[60] The measure adopted by Gomes Freire highlights the fact that quilombos continued their contradictory existence in the colonial mining slave society. This continuity can be seen in numbers. In the years of 1737 and 1738 alone fourteen quilombos were discovered and destroyed in Minas Gerais.[61] It was the same Gomes Freire de Andrade who, eight years later, on June 14, 1746, sent a circular to the city councils of Vila Rica, Mariana, São João del Rey, São José del Rey, Sabará, and Vila Nova da Rainha. In this circular, the governor ordered that each council be prepared to contribute to the organization of the troop that would destroy the quilombos that were installed in Campo Grande. Apparently, this expedition destroyed the quilombo of Ambrósio.[62]

According to Gomes Freire, "parts" of that region closer to the mentioned quilombo were already depopulated and the most remote one suffered constant attacks. For the governor, in the region there were brutally more than 600 blacks that were in quilombos with king and queen, to whom they obey, and I understand that they intent to defend themselves and keep going with strength, precaution and fixtures, which they use to rob and increase their population recruiting willing and unwilling blacks, and that makes me understand that, exhausted our tolerance, we shall undoubtedly see the same successful case that happened in Palmares de Pernambuco.[63]

The quotation allows for some inferences, although superficial, on the population, the form of government, defense techniques, war tactics, and recruitment of new members for the quilombo. After all, the old concern was about the possibility that the same type of destructive phenomenon that had happened in Palmares could occur in Minas Gerais. The systematic repetition of the example of Palmares leads to other reflections, as in the fact that some of the most powerful authorities of the colonial society of Minas Gerais erected Palmares as a symbol of a form of slave rebellion that should be combated at any cost, so that it would not be repeated. This part of the process transformed Palmares into a symbol, although a negative one.

The sentiment expressed throughout the documents indicates clearly a denunciation of the Palmares event, to the extent that it intends to avoid the repetition of such a rebellion. On the other hand, in passing the information through generations of colonial administrators (governors and others), what is reinforced is the permanence of the rebel content of Palmares. Implicitly, the colonial authorities recognized that Palmares functioned as a symbol, and it was, for the slaves, both an example of what must be fought and of what must be followed. In fact, the process is the same, but the class element interferes with the vision one has about Palmares. The important thing to realize is that the state, which was pro-slavery, also participated in the process of constructing Palmares as a symbol. Also, it is important to note that the reality of Minas Gerais, with its great incidence of quilombos, is on the other side of this process. The concern with Palmares manifests itself to the extent that the explosive reality of the slave society in Minas Gerais presents typical elements of the slave rebellion embodied in Palmares. If the reality in Minas was not so full of rebellious attitudes by the slaves, the authorities would probably not have remembered Palmares so often.

In conclusion, we would like to reaffirm the need to study quilombos in order to comprehend the societies in which they developed. Such communities, in constituting themselves as an opposition to the slave society, end up giving specific traces to social dynamics, whose comprehension is indispensable if we intend to reach, in a larger perspective, a global comprehension of the society. This happened in the northeastern society with the secular existence of Palmares, and with the colonial society of Minas Gerais, with the large number of quilombos we identified. As we have attempted to show, a reliable vision of the processes that these two societies faced requires the study of their quilombos.

8

THE QUILOMBO AND THE SLAVE SYSTEM IN EIGHTEENTH CENTURY MINAS GERAIS

DONALD RAMOS

Much of what is known about *quilombos* in Minas Gerais during the Golden Age was aptly summarized in a poem written in 1806 by Joaquim José Lisboa, an *alferes* in Vila Rica. In his long poem, Lisboa wrote, among other things, of the runaways who were still a matter of concern to him and the other residents of the mining district.

> The African slaves there,
> When they have bad Masters,
> Runaway, become highway men
> And are our opponents.
>
> They enter the forests,
> And they procreate and plant
> They entertain themselves, play and sing
> They have no need for anything....
>
> At night they come to the hamlets
> And with entreaties and bunk,
> They seduce some African women
> with promises of marriage.
>
> Immediately they elect Queen
> And King whom they obey
> They forget captivity,
> They laugh, they rob.
>
> Thus the news spreads
> Of the crime, of the contempt,
> The slave catchers fall on them,
> And finally destroy everything[1]

The widespread presence of quilombos and their role in colonial life offers an important insight into the nature of the complexities of colonial Brazilian society. At the same time an examination of these examples of resistance to slavery permits us, from today's vantage point, to explore the intricacies of the relationship between master and slave, between those with power and those who superficially had little.[2] By itself, the prevalence of the quilombo is a tribute to the indomitable spirit of people who rejected the institution of human bondage. But it also serves as a window into a society which felt compelled to come to terms with the *calhambolas*, as the residents of the quilombos were called in eighteenth century Minas Gerais.[3] Finally such an examination permits a more nuanced and realistic view of the system of slavery that evolved in Brazil.

It is within the context of the entire system of slavery that the quilombos can best be examined. Quilombos in Minas Gerais did not exist in isolation: typically, slaves did not run far away from the urbanized mining communities. In the proximity of the mining zones, there were no large quilombos on the scale approaching that of a Palmares. But there were a host of small quilombos, most unnamed or defined only by their location. These were the magnets attracting disgruntled slaves. These quilombos were within a few kilometers of where free people lived and worked. This ensured that the quilombos were not far from the minds of mineiros, who had to think about them regularly. The quilombos therefore played an important role in the complex social fabric that was the Brazilian slave system. The very commonplace existence of quilombos throughout the eighteenth century may well explain the absence of armed rebellion in a society in which slaves constituted a major part of the society and where the fear of rebellion seems to have been a preoccupation of their owners.

The Captaincy of Minas Gerais and details of the Quilombos in Vila Rica.

It is possible to view the quilombo as a rejection of the institution of slavery, and no doubt for many slaves it was.[4] But it is also possible to view the quilombo not as a systemic rejection of slavery but as a vehicle for the escape of the individual slave from bondage. The community created by the escaped slave, the quilombo, however often existed and cooperated with elements of the society left behind. That is, while individual slaves rejected their enslavement, as a group they did not generally work to overturn the institution of slavery. The quilombo in Minas Gerais did not threaten Luso-Brazilian society but often cooperated with it. In a complex fashion, the quilombo complemented the slave system. In order to understand better this view of the quilombo it is necessary to look at the broader issue of the nature of the slave system as it developed in Minas Gerais.

The Quilombo within the Slave System

A central theme of the colonial history of the Americas is slavery. That is no less true for Brazil prior to 1888. The impact of slavery transformed the Luso-Brazilian world both before and after the abolition of slavery. Both the slave system and the presence of Africans left an impact that was felt on so many levels of social and institutional life that it permeated virtually all aspects of Brazilian society and culture.[5]

Slavery, as it evolved in Brazil, functioned within a complicated set of imperatives. It survived because of the combination of the ability to impose on the slaves a set of values and the availability of awesome coercive power to impose these values and to punish transgressions of the defined parameters of behavior and belief. The system thus was a balance of the use of values and violence—potential and, all too often, real violence. The utilization of values was affected largely by the Catholic Church through the doctrine and institutional structure of religion and by the state through the manumission process. Complementing this structure built around control through values was the quilombo. In this essay, I argue that the quilombo was a part of the broader slave system and not simply an escape from it. In the mining zones of Minas Gerais, the quilombos, those both very large and very small, were a part of colonial society. In a real way, they functioned as a safety value, drawing away those slaves unable or unwilling to function within the evolving social fabric. The runaway rejected the social and cultural system but, for the most part, lived as a part of it in economic terms. The quilombo was a common feature of the mineiro landscape and this presence could explain the absence of slave rebellions in the mining zone during the Age of Gold. Rebellion was an effort to destroy the system while the quilombo was, on the surface at least, an individual rejection of the system. The ready accessibility of quilombos in close proximity to the mining centers could well have drawn those slaves most disgruntled with their misery and those slave leaders most prepared to organize rebellions.

In the society of the eighteenth century, the Catholic Church played an essential role in terms of both content and process. The efforts of the Church could be a double-edged sword for the slave. The Church became a key vehicle for the imposition of values that would both acculturate and control the slave but it also served to provide the slave with an invaluable space for cultural survival. The Church became an institution and a set of beliefs valuable both to slave owners and to slaves. However, ultimately and predictably, the greatest advantage accrued to the slave owners. The degree of advantage can be seen, for example, in the By-Laws of the Brotherhood of Our Lady of the Rosary (*Nossa Senhora do Rosário*) of Itaverava: "This Brotherhood must never by subject to the Brotherhood of the whites and thus will have under its control all the vestments that presently exist."[6] In this simple statement of a claim to control the vestments owned by the brotherhood summarizes the dilemma facing Africans and their descendants. The black members were resisting control by a white brotherhood but in the process accepting, at some level, a religion that had been imposed on them by whites. The slave could find space inside the Church but only at the cost of accepting all or parts of the religion that was a vehicle for the transmission of the dominant Luso-Brazilian culture.

Some of the means by which the Church functioned as an instrumentality of slave control are both obvious and clear. At the most elementary level, by functioning in Portuguese and Latin, the Church was able to use language as a means of acculturating the field slaves.[7] The masters of slaves were required to send their slaves to church activities conducted in a language that reflected the paradigm of the day—one that continuously compared the master-slave relationship to the father-child relationship. Just as a father was to ensure the religious education of his children so was the master to do so for his slaves.

The impact of the brotherhoods is well known but their role is so important as to warrant comment even if brief because of the light which is shed on the nature of slave society.[8] The brotherhoods reflect the ability of Catholicism to function as a means of channeling some of the inherent conflicts of a slave-holding society into non-violent activities.[9] This process did not go unnoticed by contemporaries. Fray Agostinho de Santa Maria in 1721 described the festivals of the black brotherhood of Our Lady of the Rosary of the African Blacks, *Nossa Senhora do Rosário dos Pretos*, in the following terms: "The blacks conduct their festival with much grandness; because in no way do they want to show themselves inferior to the others, especially to the whites." Concerning the building of their side altar, Fray Santa Maria noted that they tried "to equal or surpass, if they could, those of the Brotherhood of the parish church."[10] This competition over regalia and the appearance of churches between brotherhoods representing different social groups would continue through the century and demonstrates the social schisms of colonial society and the role of the Church in both reflecting and mediating them.

The brotherhoods also provided both a physical and a political space for slaves and others. Urban slaves, in particular, benefitted from the availability of both forms of space. In the first place, the custom in Minas Gerais whereby churches were built and maintained by brotherhoods meant that those controlled by blacks such as Nossa Senhora do Rosário or Nossa Senhora das Mercês and Santa Efigenia were able to provide a physical space for people of color to gather, talk, reminisce, pray, share and in the process transmit customs and values. But the brotherhoods also provided an institutional structure for the development of leadership. Thus it was not uncommon for slaves to be elected to the governing boards or as male and female judges of brotherhoods which contained whites. In a symbolic sense as well as in practical ways, this was a world turned on its head. Election to a leadership position elevated the individual and was a mark of distinction. It was important enough to be listed in a person's last will. Joana Carvalho de Araújo, in her will, for example, noted that "I already served twice as a judge of the Brotherhood of St. Efigenia and I implore that Brotherhood for the Love of God to accompany me [during her funeral]."[11]

The brotherhoods served to give their members a sense of identity and pride, the antithesis of the objective of slavery which sought to dehumanize those held in bondage. Again, this process was recognized by contemporaries who, in some cases, tried to stop the process. This can be seen in the ongoing conflict between the parish priests and the brotherhoods that occurred throughout the eighteenth century in Minas Gerais. The power of the brotherhoods had come at the expense of the parish priests. Finally, in 1795, well after the decline in gold production had substantially weakened the brotherhoods, the parish priests of Minas Gerais reacted and petitioned Lisbon to remove some of the prerogatives held by the brotherhoods. In their petition, the priests indicated that destitute slaves "considered themselves great personages when they attended their Brotherhood especially when serving in the governing of the Brotherhood, as officers of the board, and seeing themselves thusly in the position of being able to use, deliberate and claim waivers and to contest the jurisdiction of the parish priests and the Prelate….." In the process,

> those spirits, naturally haughty, ungovernable, and bold lose [further] Respect for all the Hierarchy and explode into the greatest excesses as they have repeated times, and as did the two brotherhoods of African and creole blacks winning Provision in an appeal against their parish priest, placing luminaries, … and with explosives and fireworks they ran tumultuously from the cross, making an uproar throughout the parish….[12]

The parish priests' complaint then concluded with a brief description of one of the few recorded examples of racially motivated mass action by brotherhoods who had marched in protest on the governor's palace in Vila Rica.

But beyond providing a context for language and culture to be assimilated and the institution of the brotherhoods, the church functioned in equally important other ways to control the slaves by integrating them into the life of the community. Of these, two are particularly important: the church's insistence on access to religious education and instruction and its insistence on equal access to the sacraments. Both efforts were not, strictly speaking, humanitarian in nature. The church insisted that slavery was a civil institution over which it had no control. But by interfering in the relationship between master and slave, the church was unwittingly helping the slave as well as, from its perspective, fulfilling its evangelical mission. But again the double-edged sword is evident: in obtaining greater protection and more rights, the slave was implicitly acknowledging the slave system which held them in bondage.

The matter of education of slaves was a recurring issue throughout the eighteenth century. The clearest statement of its role can be seen in a 1719 letter by the Conde do Assumar, the official most responsible for imposing effective royal control over the unruly goldminers. Assumar, in 1719, argued that royal sovereignty was based upon the king's promise to evangelize the people. Because the Portuguese brought the slaves to Brazil, they had assumed the responsibility for educating them about religion.[13] The religious education of slaves was an obligation of the king.

Parish priests were the instruments of religious education. In 1749 the inspector of the chapel of São João Bautista in Vila Rica admonished priests, heads of families, and slave masters to ensure that slaves learned Catholic doctrine.[14] This admonition was repeated in 1754, this time the priests were given specific instructions:

> We exhort all the parishioners to send their children and slaves to learn the Doctrine and beyond this, the heads of families and Masters of slaves should know that they have the grave obligation of teaching the Doctrine to all their family....[15]

What Assumar and others clearly saw was that, along with its concern with salvation, the evangelical process served as a means of political acculturation. While slaves were taught the values of Catholicism, they were also being urged to obey the state. When the parish priests petitioned the king in the early 1790s, they complained that the prevalence of brotherhoods had so weakened the parish churches that it weakened

> the obligation which the parish priests have by Divine Law to teach and illustrate to the People with Christian doctrine the loyalty they owe to their King, their natural master; the obedience they owe to his Laws, Respect to his Magistrates from which also results in the People being obligated to hear and respect ... the instructions of their Pastors because otherwise preaching without listeners is to throw wheat on rocks....[16]

The issue of access to sacraments is an important one and too complicated to explore fully here. But in terms of integrating the slave into Luso-Brazilian society obviously this process was crucial. The baptism of slaves was so important that the ever-vigilant Conde do Assumar, for example, in 1719, ordered parish priests to ensure that slaves were catechized, baptized, and further insisted that they notify the royal judges, *ouvidors*, of the identities of those who refused so that punitive action could be taken.[17]

There is evidence that some parish priests took this concern seriously. To date only one confessional roll, *rol de confessados*, from the mining district has been discovered. Dated June 1780, it comes from Catas Altas. Unlike the Portuguese practice, this roll simply listed those individuals who had not confessed or received communion for Easter.[18] Many of the entries are for individuals but there are also entries for entire living units: "João Gonçalves Valadares and his slaves and retainers," "Francisco José Barros, his wife and slaves," and "Quitéria Araújo and her children and slaves." In another case, an individual slave, Antonio, slave of Eusebio Alvares, is identified.[19] The implication of this document is that other slaves had been confessed and had taken communion. In fact, it is significant that the parish priest chose to list slaves at all. It was a recognition that the rules were intended to apply to slave and freeman alike.

Likewise the church sought to ensure equal access to the sacrament of marriage. The *Constituições primeiras da Bahia*, the by-laws for the Church in Brazil, reiterated the right of slaves to marry without the interference of their masters. Masters were ordered not to interfere in the marriage of slaves and not to sell married slaves to remote areas.[20] Again this was not simply an ideal languishing on the aging pages of a seldom-read manuscript. The ecclesiastical inspector to Lavras do Funil in 1773, for example, repeated a commonly held view of the "grande escandulo" caused by consensual unions, or *mancebia*. In expounding on the problem, he saw *amancebaria* as a sin contrary to divine law. But he went further, asserting he saw it as contrary to the interests of the slave owners since "perhaps the shortage of marriages is the reason this captaincy of minas [Gerais] is seen as so desolate, in the absence of gold as in the increase of the said slaves since if they married they could procreate and multiply such they increase the number of slaves owned by the Masters...."[21] The inspector ordered all parish priests to determine whether those slaves who were living in concubinage (*concubinados*) wished to marry. Where possible they were to be married "even against the wishes of their Masters...." This was true even if the slaves belonged to different masters: "Should some slave concubinado with the slave of another Master, wished to marry her, the Reverend Parish priest should proceed in the same fashion with only the difference that after married the slaves should not harm their Masters in their service nor should the Masters impede their marriage in an appropriate time."[22] Occasionally the parish priest interfered to stop sexual exploitation. In 1733, a visitor to Itatiaia discovered that one Francisco Teixeira was amancebado with a slave woman he owned. The parish priest forced Teixeira to marry his slave to another slave. Teixeira openly wept in desperation during the ceremony. While Teixeira formally complied, he still managed to foil the priest's intentions. After the wedding, Teixeira refused to permit the slave couple to have sexual relations.[23]

Certainly, these efforts on the part of the Catholic Church were not the rule. The abuses exceeded the best efforts of some priests. The best of intentions often wilted when faced with the powerful interests of the slaveholders. While there is increasing evidence that slaves married in hitherto for unexpected rates, that does not appear to be consistently true in the mining zone.[24] Pointing out the role of the Catholic Church is not intended to excuse the extraordinary excesses which occurred or in any way to justify the horrors of slavery. It is intended simply to suggest that the Church played a pivotal role in the process of integrating the slave into Luso-Brazilian society in a very large number of ways. In this view of slavery, the slave was able to use this integrative process to carve out a space for the creation of a new culture and a new identity. But this meant accepting some of the values of the dominant culture and it was the Catholic Church which defined, disseminated and then monitored these values.

The ideals of the Church were, in many ways, reinforced by the activities of the Portuguese state. The clearest manifestation of this was the process of manumission. From my perspective, manumission was an important support of the slave system. Essentially, it was a reward for services rendered and for accepting the fundamental values of Luso-Brazilian society. In this regard, who was freed is less important than the recognition of the high level of manumissions, especially in an urban context. It is in the urban context of the mining zone that lower slave/master ratios were encountered. This should have permitted a higher level of acculturation to occur than in rural zones with its high slave/master ratios and lower levels of master-slave contacts.[25]

But the issue ran much deeper than this. One of the major concerns of Portuguese authorities was the development of slave leaders outside of proscribed bounds. Thus the selection of slaves as leaders of brotherhoods was acceptable. But the selection of leaders in less controlled situations was not. In 1719, Governor Assumar, reacting very strongly to the news of a projected broadly based slave rebellion, decreed that "among Negros there should be no subordination of one to others, as until now there has been...."[26] Noting that some slaves had become godfathers to numerous slaves, he expressed concern that these leaders had replaced slave masters as authority figures, often receiving the money earned by slaves, that they "persuaded them and stirred them up to escape, counseling them to the disservice of their Masters," and that they could easily instigate another uprising.[27] Assumar ordered that only whites could serve as godfathers of slaves at either baptisms or marriages. This order had little effect as the priests opposed it because having godparents who came from the "same Nation" facilitated the acculturation and indoctrination of the slave.[28] Assumar's efforts to prohibit non-whites from serving as godparents also stemmed from a fear that the godparents would become leaders, "who formed gangs going into the woods forming quilombos governed by them, all of which is pernicious...."[29]

Assumar was concerned with the total subjugation of the slave to his master. "...Because it is important to make them Recognize Subjugation without a shred of Liberty and not even in their memory should reside this stimulus and incentive of (being) a majority and of Superiority, which they clearly desire...." The governor futilely banned "that in their festivals they acclaim and crown Negro Kings and Queens ...."[30] But the authorities also took other steps. Some were very direct in nature. For example, in 1714, Governor Braz Balthazar de Silveira ordered a resident of Trepui, the opening to the farms and pastures of Cachoeira do Campo and the release from the mountain valley in which Vila Rica was located, to use his slaves to prevent runaways from escaping the area. He was told to employ his own slaves in the effort and was offered a bounty for every slave captured by his slaves.[31]

The combination of the activities of church and state was the evolution of a system by which many slaves could become integrated in a peripheral but clear way to Luso-Brazilian society. This is not to say that they acquiesced in their bondage. No doubt, many slaves fought against the system in many individual ways, many of them recorded in the reports of investigations, *devassas,* opened to look into the actions of slaves against their masters, including their killing. Many, perhaps most, slaves fought from within the system largely created by the dominant culture. In a paradoxical way, they acknowledged the system in order to live and probably fought against it where possible.

For those slaves who could not accept life under these conditions, there were two organized responses—rebellion or escape. In the gold mining zone, there were no substantial rebellions during the eighteenth century. Several plots were exposed to authorities before they could be implemented. The most well-known is that of 1719 but there were others in 1711, 1728, and 1756.[32] From the distance of over two centuries, it is now almost impossible to determine whether these were real plots or one group of slaves getting even with another within the context of a society that had an almost paranoid fear of slave rebellion. What is clear is that no rebellion went into action. While there were many instances of slaves killing their masters, there were no instances of organized rebellion in the mining zone.

But the situation with regard to runaway communities is very different. Quilombos were so common, in both the sense of frequency and of geographical location, throughout the eighteenth century that the researcher is forced to view them as an integral part of Brazilian colonial society. They constituted a way out of the horrors of slavery but, at the same time, the calhambolas became a part of the larger system that developed in the mining zones. Their existence permitted slaves to move into and out of different roles: obedient slaves most of the time, but cooperating and helping the calhambolas some of the time and perhaps joining them permanently or temporarily as well. This created an ambiguity of status that caused no end of frustration to local authorities.

The Quilombo and Vila Rica: The Nature of the Relationship

The remainder of this essay focuses on the issue of quilombos in Vila Rica, the capital of the captaincy of Minas Gerais in order to demonstrate the prevalence of quilombos, their largely symbiotic relationship with the settlers, and their impact on mineiro society.[33] The quilombos are seen as the response of slaves to this horrid system but also as an escape valve that helped prevent a social rebellion. While Vila Rica is the focus of this study, examples will also be drawn from other areas in the captaincy as appropriate.

Vila Rica surrounded by mountains that hide the calhambolas, c. 1825 ("Villa Ricca," M. Rugendas, Malerische Reise in Brasilien, Paris, Engelmann & Cie., 1835)

Slavery was, of course, a central feature of mineiro life. In 1738, there were at least 101,607 slaves in the captaincy, 47,544 of whom resided in the judicial district, *comarca*, of Ouro Preto and 21,012 in the county, *termo*, of Vila Rica.[34] In 1767, the overall population of the captaincy was 335,203 of whom 38 percent were slaves.[35] Slaves constituted an important segment of mineiro society throughout the century. For the community of Vila Rica, reasonable estimates of the total population are not available until the very end of the century, well after the end of the Age of Gold. In 1796, the parish of Ouro Preto, one of the two that comprised Vila Rica, had a total population of 5,639 of whom 38 percent were slaves.[36] Both figures represent the period after the decline in gold production was well under way. There are no good statistics for the period of the gold boom for the free population. But it must be clear that slaves constituted a significant part of the population throughout the eighteenth century.

An important issue that confronts the student of eighteenth century mineiro society is the prevalence of quilombos. For the residents of Vila Rica, the quilombo was a constant feature of life—a societal preoccupation. At no point during the eighteenth and early nineteenth centuries did the quilombo vanish as an issue. These were not the major runaway communities such as that of Palmares or even the Quilombo Grande or the Quilombo do Ambrozio of Minas Gerais. These were the relatively small quilombos which infested the mountains on which Vila Rica was built and those which surround the urban center.[37] These were quilombos which never really threatened the existence of Vila Rica but which were substantial enough to interdict communication between Vila Rica and the farms and pastures of Cachoeira do Campo in one direction and the religious capital of Mariana in the other. On the one hand, they were at times a nuisance, on the other a trading partner of vilarican businessmen. While they may not have threatened the life of the capital, they were a reminder of the potential danger posed by the presence of slaves in great quantity. And they certainly were seen as a threat by the community leaders and royal officials—to these leaders the quilombos represented a constant violation of the natural scheme of things—a violation of the order and hierarchy which formed such an important part of the dominant cultural paradigm. But the real threat posed was the possibility that the calhambolas would unite with slaves and sympathetic freedman and freemen to organize a rebellion. It was the possibility of rebellion that ate at the imagination of the free population.

The central issue was defined early in the century in a letter from the town council of Vila Rica to King João V. In 1719, Portuguese authorities foiled a conspiracy to launch a slave rebellion in the mining zone. While it is not clear if there really had been a plot, local authorities reacted quickly and forcibly to prevent the presumed plot from being implemented. The response of the town council reveals the complexity of these issues and their inter-relationships. The council began noting that Governor Assumar had ordered that any slave found in a quilombo be killed by whoever discovered them. It then went on to criticize the "many whites who to inveigle Respect gave weapons to their slaves and perhaps consented to their haughtiness ...."[38] The council then described its aggressive action when informed of the plot. It sent militia units into the gold fields to keep order. About thirty slaves "generally known as Leaders" were arrested.[39] The people wanted to kill these leaders, but the governor refused, insisting on following judicial due process. The interrogations provided no confessions and no useful evidence since "the Negros were stubborn in guarding Their Secrets."[40] In view of that, the council wanted the slaves, "as well as freed Negros and Negresses who do not fulfill a useful purpose in this Community (República) or to His Majesty be seen as vagrants," sent to Colonia do Sacramento and their owners indemnified for their losses. Here the contradictions that rippled through the century were exposed: the fear of rebellion counterbalanced by the continued arming of slaves and the cooperation of freemen, including whites with slaves; the overreaction of the authorities counterbalanced by the organized opposition of the slaves; and the need to punish presumed threats while being indemnified for the losses.

Within a decade of the official elevation of the mining camps of Antonio Dias, Ouro Preto, and Padre Faria, among others, to the status of a town, the issues that would bedevil the area for more than a century had become clear. The presence of quilombos had been linked both to the arming of slaves and then with the ever-present fear of a slave rebellion. The quilombo was treated as less a threat than the rebellion. Runaways, dangerous slaves, and freedmen were seen by authorities as cooperating to threaten the Luso-Brazilian way of life that had been established at such great cost. The history of Vila Rica could be written around the reports of quilombo activities. Among the earliest references to quilombos in Minas Gerais is that made by Governor Albuquerque in January 1711 concerning "many runaway slaves, Robbing, infesting Farms (*Rossas*), and assaulting travelers on the roads...."[41] By the end of this first decade of the institutional history of the mining zone, Governor Conde do Assumar had come to see the quilombos "of such importance that on them could depend the conservation or ruin of this land...." He described the situation in the following terms:

> Not only infesting the roads and [endangering] those who travel them but those who inhabit in sites and farms in the areas surrounding Towns, taking from houses not only gold, foodstuffs, but also things of lesser importance and of greater volume because everywhere their boldness they join in gangs of twenty-five and forty armed men and provided with weapons they run away from their Masters....[42]

In 1719, Governor Assumar ordered the militia to attack a quilombo in São Bartolomeu which posed a threat to travelers "reaching such excess that the negros not only attack the roads in public but they kill and wound white men...."[43] This tone of incredulousness that whites would be personally threatened is one commonly found during the eighteenth century and again reflects the sense that there was a natural order and a natural way of doing things which were being threatened by the activity of the quilombos. The governor attributed the presence of the quilombo to the failure of slave masters or authorities to administer timely punishment.[44]

Mining in the vicinity of Villa Rica, c. 1825 ("Vila Rica," M. Rugendas, Malerische Reise in Brasilien, Paris, Engelmann & Cie. 1835)

The years 1719 and 1720 were important watersheds in the history of Minas Gerais because of the congruence of the uproar over the alleged 1719 slave plot, the elite-led tax riots in Vila Rica in 1720, and a heightened sense of unease provoked by the activity of quilombos. But the danger posed by the quilombos was apparent even earlier and authorities had been quick to respond to the danger. The very first indications of the presence of quilombos and the response to them had come soon after the founding of Vila Rica. The best understood of these responses is the slave catcher, *capitão do mato*. The capitão do mato probably functioned in the mining district before the incorporation of the towns in 1711, although the first commissions found date from February 1711.[45] For most of the eighteenth century, their activities were governed by the statute, *regimento,* issued on December 17, 1722 by Governor Lourenço de Almeida.[46] The regimento established the schedule of payment and code of behavior for these slave catchers who came from all the colors represented in the mining zone. The capitães do mato generally acted as independent bounty hunters although they could receive specific commissions from the council or the governor.

Throughout the eighteenth century, the capitão do mato would constitute a concern to authorities. Often accused of being lazy and unwilling to risk his life in facing the runaways, preferring to stay in the towns rather than patrolling the countryside, mistreating those slaves captured and using them for personal gain, or presenting for bounty payment the heads of slaves who were not really calhambolas, the capitão do mato was never fully trusted by the authorities. Nonetheless, they were forced to depend on this first line of defense against the quilombos. It is clear that while the capitão do mato could be effective in catching isolated runaways, they were not very effective against quilombos. This failure frequently provoked the ire of local authorities.

Beyond the capitão do mato, another official who was used was the captain-major of the discoveries, *Capitão-mor das Entradas*. The instructions issued to this official, in 1733, contained fifteen articles. Four of these dealt directly with the requirement that slaves away from their masters carry written documents, *escripturas*—although officials were empowered to arrest anyone with a escriptura on suspicion of being a runaway. The captain-major was required to patrol the community and the immediate area around the town looking for violators of the law. Particular attention was drawn to the woods around the town to keep the runaways away. The recurring concern was contact between the runaways and residents, especially freedmen or slaves. Thus, for example, the capitão-mor was to "exercise great caution in learning whether ex-slaves in their houses or captives who are in shops or alone in houses without their Masters allow in negros during the day or night...."[47]

Other authorities were pressed into the effort to alleviate the resident's concerns with the quilombos. The fiscal inspectors, *almotaceis*, whose jurisdiction normally centered on the issue and licensing of weights, measures, and licenses, were instructed in 1733 to look for

> 5. People or shops which customarily invite outside negroes into their houses or shops given them hiding places [and] buying some things from them assuming they be slaves.
>
> 6. Any white or Negro person who aids runaway slaves or helps them with foodstuffs.[48]

Ultimately, the capitão-mor das ordenanças played an important role in the effort to stop the calhambolas. But increasingly over the course of the eighteenth-century it was the militia which would bear the brunt of the sporadic efforts to eradicate the quilombos or, at least, to minimize the dangers posed by the calhambolas.

Typically, the crown was less inclined to exercise draconian solutions than were local residents or even local officials.[49] The Conde do Assumar had proposed cutting the Achilles tendon of runaways. But this had not been accepted by the crown. Finally, under pressure from local officials and residents, Lisbon authorities acquiesced to the insistent pressure of local authorities for some form of retribution:

> I the King hereby make it known to all who see this order (*alvará*), that being made aware of the insults committed in Brazil by runaway slaves, popularly known as calhambolas, including the excess of gathering together in quilombos.... I have decided that all the negroes who are found in quilombos, being there voluntarily, be branded with fire on a shoulder (*espadura*), with the letter -F- which is to be stored in the municipal buildings; and if when preparing to execute this punishment, the same mark is already present then an ear should be cut off...⁵⁰

These efforts failed and the rest of the century is a catalogue of complaints of the dangers posed by the quilombos. The complaints come from residents and from local authorities. The years from 1733 to 1735 seemed to residents particularly dangerous with "the grave and continuous Insults Thefts and deaths that the runaway slaves, commonly called calhambolas commit...."⁵¹ The activities of the calhambolas were so aggressive that "no person enters or leaves this town without risking their life...."⁵² Efforts were made to collect taxes to hire capitães do mato throughout the termo of Vila Rica. For example, the Capitão mor das Entradas de Itaubira Dionizio Marques Pinto was given 400 *oitavas* in August 1734 through a tax, *finta*, on slaves in order to eradicate the quilombos in his parish. However, it appears that the efforts of the capitão do mato while initially successful came to a halt when the people refused to pay the finta. This forced the council to call a meeting of the elite, the good men, *homens bons*. From their deliberations emerged a multilevel plan. The first step was to require that all slaves traveling outside the company of their masters have a written pass valid for no more than one month. Second, the leading citizen of each parish was to convoke the people annually to select and support a capitão do mato and soldiers. Third, they recommended that any captured calhambola was to have a hand cut off. Fourth, all parishes were to cooperate in eradicating quilombos. Fifth and finally, powder and shot, "*polvora e chumbo*," were not to be sold to negros, mulattos or mestizos and "no Negro was to carry any type of weapon except when in the company of their Masters."⁵³

No doubt drawing on this meeting with the homens bons, the council of Vila Rica indeed ordered that a capitão do mato be named for each parish and that residents be apportioned a special tax, finta, to pay the expenses of dealing with the quilombos.⁵⁴ The council also urged that calhambolas be severely punished including death for a second capital offense. Capitão do Mato Francisco de Mattos was given the very substantial sum of 2,100 oitavas and twenty-four soldiers and instructed to "exterminate the Negro calhambolas in the districts of the two parishes until reaching the borders...." Mattos was given very specific instructions to keep on the move. If he stayed more than eight days in one place he was to pay a penalty. He was to work outside of the two parishes of the capital until he had pacified the area and to coordinate his activities with that of the militias in the other parishes of the county.[55] Mattos was ordered to place sentinels on the roads entering Vila Rica "since without doubt the said calhambolas who come here find succor in the homes of free negros and whites with no shame...."[56] Mattos' orders reflect the endemic fear that the capitães do mato were not committed to their task of attacking quilombos and therefore specific and precisely stated instructions had to be provided so that they fulfilled their duties.

But these efforts, despite their intensity, also failed and in 1739 reports surfaced of greater danger to the hamlets around Vila Rica. Among these reports was one made by a group of residents who petitioned the council to help stop the depredations of some calhambolas who "invade the hamlets convoking more blacks for this purpose .... [and] who at night withhold Services from their Masters and with guns threaten whites and kill their slaves who go to collect wood and hay...."[57] The situation got so desperate and the complaints so intense that the royal judge, *ouvidor*, of the comarca of Ouro Preto authorized the council to collect funds to supplement council revenue in order to hire a capitão do mato and fifteen men who would constantly patrol the two parishes of Vila Rica. The ouvidor also issued the guidelines for the capitão do mato. Among the items noted were instructions to arrest anyone who helped the runaways, to enforce the rules on slaves bearing arms when not with their masters, and to prevent "frolics and dances which the negroes customarily make and in gatherings where occur conflicts shameful acts, *pudencias*, and offenses to God...."[58] In the same document, the ouvidor referred to the capacity of quilombos to marshal their "troops and squadrons, *esquadrias*" to attack unsettled areas.

In 1741, the council continued complaining vociferously of the depredations of the calhambolas. The council described people "who do not live securely on their farms in incessant terror due to the crimes of the negroes...."[59] But the reality was that the quilombos did not simply pose a danger to people living in rural areas. At about this same time a large group of residents of Vila Rica, over eighty people, petitioned the council to close shops in the neighborhood of Padre Faria and most alleys in the town because they served as hideouts for calhambolas and runaways.[60] Clearly the danger existed inside the urban confines of Vila Rica as the calhambolas maintained contact with the residents and moved among the residents of the capital of the mining zone.

All efforts failed to control the calhambolas. In 1748, residents of the rural hamlet of Xiqueiro reported that the quilombos were blocking the roads to travelers and merchants and that "right up to their own homes they [the residents] experience the loss of their lives...."[61]

The calhambolas, numbering over a hundred men armed with muskets, pistols and knives, carrying a flag and led by their "king," had been able to interdict transit to such an extent that food prices in Vila Rica were being driven upward.[62] The situation had reached such a level of seriousness that Governor Gomes Freire de Andrada reversed a position he had adopted earlier and permitted the militia, *ordenanças*, to be employed to keep the roads open. From this point on, the ordenanças would play an important role in the efforts to destroy the quilombos. It is as if the authorities had finally realized the inability of the capitães do mato to handle the volatile situation which had developed. In December of 1748, a number of ordenança companies were ordered to join with capitães do mato in their parishes and, in a coordinated campaign, to march to a central point. Their orders were to "beat the woods [and] stands of trees" in order to free the area of quilombos. Again, the effort failed. Six months later, the royal magistrate, *ouvidor*, of Ouro Preto was appealing for help "seeing that this town and its jurisdiction is very infested with calhambolas causing deaths...."[63] Well into the 1780s there were reports of the calhambolas being able to disrupt the movement of foodstuffs into Vila Rica and to threaten the shipments of gold leaving the town.[64]

But not even the introduction of the systematic use of the militia stopped the activity of the quilombos. The council continued to be frustrated by its inability to resolve the problem of the quilombos. In 1762, the council submitted a plan to the king that called for each ordenança company to attack quilombos once or twice a month. A commission, *patente*, for a captain of Ordenanças de Pé dos Homens Pardos included as a specific instruction the order to conduct "continuous expeditions throughout the woods against runaway negroes...."[65] Both of these documents seem to reflect several interrelated concerns. Most probably, they reflect the pervasiveness of small quilombos. It makes clear that there was abundant work for the militia to be used and that quilombos reappeared as quickly as they were attacked. But the request for employing the militia suggests continuing dissatisfaction with the capitães do mato. The town council agreed with residents that they spent too much of their time checking slaves to be sure they carried passes from their masters rather than attacking quilombos.[66] There had also been criticism that capitães do mato killed slaves who were not calhambolas in order to obtain the bounties which were to be paid for calhambolas killed while resisting. These were the types of complaints heard throughout the century.

The decreased reliance on the capitães do mato and the complementary increase in the use of the militia reflects the frustration of local authorities with the intransigence of the problem. The capitães do mato were the front line of defense against the calhambolas and quilombos. But they, and the militia as the authorities would quickly learn, faced insurmountable problems. The calhambolas could move freely amongst a population that was largely composed of people of color. Not only was their mobility relatively easy, they had allies within the slave population and even in the free population. The only functional way of controlling these contacts interfered with the interests of key classes of people. The pass system was a way of monitoring mobility but masters often sent their slaves on errands without notes. Notes, no doubt, also were easily falsified by literate slaves or their accomplices. And of course, most importantly, many businesses thrived on the trade with calhambolas. Thus, while some elements of the population wanted to implement policies to prevent contacts between calhambolas and slaves and free people, some groups refused to accept these rules. This provided important space for the calhambolas and the quilombos to continue to survive. It also provided a level of ambiguity between the calhambolas and the free and slave populations that gave cover to the former. The lines between these groups were fluid—a fluidity that discomforted the authorities.

In 1764, the council organized a major effort to eradicate finally the quilombos from the immediate area of the Vila Rica. This was to be the largest effort made by the council during the eighteenth-century. The plan called for seven ordenança companies to mass at different points inside the town and at a given point to climb the mountain at whose base the town was spread out. At the same time, other militia units from Mariana and three neighboring parishes would surround the mountain to ensure that the calhambolas could not escape. Once the mountain was surrounded, the seven companies, in squads, would crisscross the mountain to root out the quilombos.[67] In a demonstration of either fear or apathy, the order for the members of the militia to join their units met with such little response that another order had to be issued threatening to arrest those who failed to appear to perform their duties. Again, despite the efforts of the militia, the calhambolas simply disappeared, perhaps retreating into the mineshafts that pockmarked the mountain. Thus, this effort, despite the large number of forces convoked, also failed, in great measure because the target was not a major quilombo but numbers of small ones.

After the 1760s, despite the decline in gold production and a complementary decline in the proportion of slaves in the area, the level of quilombo activity seems to have continued unabated. In 1784, the council asked the governor of the captaincy for assistance which would "finally rip out the roots of such pernicious actions" as those committed by the calhambolas. The council complained that they continued to interdict transportation and communication even inside the urban core of Vila Rica.[68] In 1786, the militia of Cachoeira, ordered by Governor Rodrigo José de Menezes, to sweep the woods for calhambolas, arrested 313 people.[69] As late as 1798, there were reports of conflicts between capitães do mato and calhambolas such as the one at Bombaça, near Cachoeira do Campo, which left one capitão do mato and three calhambolas dead.[70] Thus, the quilombos of Vila Rica lasted throughout the century—born during the early boom days of the first two decades of the century they thrived during the period of economic stability between 1726 and 1752 and during the period of economic decline after 1752. This specific form of rejecting bondage was a constant throughout the Golden Century.

While there is no record of large quilombos in the jurisdiction of Vila Rica, the existence of large quilombos elsewhere in Minas Gerais served as a reminder of the scale of the problem that could develop if the small quilombos were not contained. Thus, the town leaders were ever vigilant and willing to provide resources to destroy the large quilombos when they were found. The town participated in the destruction of large quilombos when they were found elsewhere in the captaincy. Perhaps the largest of these was the Quilombo Grande or Quilombo do Ambrozio as it was sometimes known. In the commission appointing Bartolomeu Bueno do Prado as the officer in charge of the efforts to destroy it, it was called a "quasi kingdom."[71] This quilombo, or better said collection of quilombos, was the subject of various destruction efforts during the decade following 1746. Gomes Freire de Andrada explained the situation graphically:

> As in years past little relief was applied to the damages in the comarca of São João del Rei and in parts of this comarca caused by the negroes joined together in Grande Campo and Serras which exist between this captaincy and the comarca of Goiás and the relief was too small[;] instead increasing the damages and the danger, depopulating the areas closest to the said quilombo or quilombos with areas more distant also suffering pernicious damages effected barbarously by more than 600 negroes who are in the quilombos with King and Queen to whom they owe obedience, with fort and traps such that

they plan on defending and protecting themselves which is believable seeing that the attacking parties take entire lots of negroes, some of their own will and others without it[.] This leads me to believe that should our tolerance continue we will see, without doubt, the situation of Palmares of Pernambuco....⁷²

The council responded by sending four hundred men to help destroy Quilombo Grande.⁷³ These efforts were only temporarily successful. One decade later, Luso-Brazilian authorities again renewed their efforts to eradicate the quilombos in this region. The stimulus for this renewed interest appears to have been another planned uprising that had been discovered.

Residents of Vila Rica feared the possibility that calhambolas would join with their own slaves in a rebellion. On 3 April 1756, the council warned its sister institutions in Mariana, São João del Rei and Sabará that "we have news negroes quilombados have joined with those who reside in this town and all the others of this captaincy to effect on the night of the fifteenth of this month a general uprising in all the settlements...."⁷⁴ The paranoid fear of the free population is evident in the letter sent by the council to the bishop of Mariana and dated the same day:

> At different times a general uprising of the slaves of this Captaincy has been justly feared and given that the facts have not confirmed this apprehensiveness due to the actions which were taken, this present year the indications are so vehement that they can become probable in as much as the Negro calhambolas have been working with those in the settlements to kill their masters....⁷⁵

In a petition dated April 28, a group of residents of Vila Rica complained that shop and innkeepers were receiving calhambolas and trading for the material that they had stolen. They contended that these shops had become havens for both calhambolas and dens of iniquity for slaves. They noted having made these charges previously and suggested that the plot may have been organized "perhaps through the industry of the innkeepers to protect their interests."⁷⁶ The council acquiesced to this pressure and issued an edict that sought to limit severely the activities of sellers. The clear message was that shopkeepers had been selling to calhambolas. A second edict prohibited sellers from selling powder and lead "to negroes ... because these have been shown to be calhambolas...."⁷⁷ The danger of cooperation between calhambolas and slaves seems to have been one of the concerns that led to renewed efforts to destroy the Quilombo Grande.

Equally intriguing is the issue of arming slaves. Despite the fear of a slave rebellion, slave owners seemed unwilling to disarm their slaves. The eighteenth-century is punctuated by edicts from various levels of authority concerning the arming of slaves, appearing as early as 1710.[78] The difficulty was that masters seemed incapable of dispensing with armed slave bodyguards. Therefore, most of the edicts exempted those slaves in the company of their masters from the prohibition against arming slaves.[79] The weapons training the slaves received no doubt helped them if they escaped and it is possible that calhambolas also benefitted from this training. Also despite the various edicts limiting the availability of weapons, slaves were able to obtain arms.[80] So were calhambolas. Issued in response to depredations made by calhambolas, a 1748 edict forbade the selling of powder and lead, "fire arms as well as pointed knives" to "negroes or male and female mulattos or even to some suspicious whites...." Clearly, the council believed that such weapons were getting into the hands of the calhambolas. Also forbidden was the repair of such weapons as well as shooting by blacks during celebrations such as baptisms and weddings.[81]

The larger problem for the authorities was the symbiotic relationship that had developed between the quilombos and the residents of the mining zone. Clearly, the calhambolas sought aid in Vila Rica and other communities. As the council noted, aid was obtained not simply from freedmen but also from whites.[82] As part of its campaign to destroy the quilombos in 1735, the council noted that shopkeepers "during the night invite in Negro calhambolas in order to sell them everything necessary...."[83] The calhambolas were trading items that they produced or robbed. The ability of calhambolas to obtain powder and lead from shop owners had been reported as early as 1714 by the council. In an edict issued that year, the council complained of attacks on travelers made by calhambolas using powder and lead purchased in town. The council unsuccessfully sought to limit the sale of powder and lead to only one shop in town. At the same time the repair of weapons in the possession of a "Mulatto, Negro, Mestizo [Bastardo] or Indian [Carijo]" was banned.[84] This practice remained so common that in 1741 the council banned the use of half doors (*balcoens com meyas portas*) "because all those residents who have a shop abuse the prohibition of letting Negroes through the doors..."[85] In 1754, an exasperated group of residents complained,

> The business people have brought into their homes the negroes who go about as runaways whenever they wish, as well as negroes from the woods are brought into their houses one by one and others in others and when they

want, they leave the said shops at daybreak such that each shop is a sort of quilombo [.] The shops of whites are even worst than those of negresses....[86]

Much of the trade seems to have involved gold mined by the slaves. Gomes Freire de Andrada referred at one point to the discovery of the vestiges of runaway communities including the mining pans, *bateas*, used in panning gold.[87]

There is, therefore, considerable evidence of cooperation between calhambolas and residents of Vila Rica. This cooperation points to a fluidity in social relations. There was an idea that the quilombos were seasonable with the implication that slaves moved into and out of these small-scale quilombos. Governor Gomes Freire de Andrada, for example, warned in 1737 that vigilance had to be increased "since now there is corn in the fields, the period when they customarily gather in quilombos."[88] Escape was relatively easy for slaves given the mountainous nature of the mining zone. Captain Nicoláo de Freitas Pacheco reported that he owned four slaves, all of whom escaped when he became seriously ill.[89] Clearly, the price of bondage was eternal vigilance. But these escapes were also helped by the proximity of the quilombos. In the case of Vila Rica, doubtlessly calhambolas could look down on the town and its residents from their hideouts on the mountains. Finally the escapes were aided by the ability to blend into the larger community composed of a majority of people of color and a substantial population of people in bondage.

There was also cooperation with Indians and not merely on the periphery of the mining zones. In 1760, three units left Mariana in search of a young white girl who had been kidnapped. The first unit found a quilombo where the girl was being held. Four calhambolas were killed, four males and seven women captured and twenty-one escaped. The second unit encountered another quilombo, capturing four and killing one. The third unit, led by a capitão do mato, attacked still another quilombo but were repulsed by "a great portion of Indians, *gentio*, who Instantaneously Repulsed them with a great shower of arrows resulting in the wounding of three Capitãos do mato...."[90] The calhambolas thus could count on the support of the wide range of social groups throughout the mining zone.

The attention of historians has generally been drawn to the major quilombos such as that of Palmares or that of Ambrozio. But just as significant for our understanding of the past are the hundreds and thousands of small quilombos which dotted the Brazilian countryside in the eighteenth-century. Most of them never had a name but were simply identified by their location such as the quilombo near Itatiaia, identified in a 1737 entry in the Livro de Devassas.[91] These nameless quilombos were an integral part of eighteenth-century life.

Waldemar Almeida de Barbosa has acknowledged the close working relationship between quilombos and the larger community in the Diamond Zone and has described it as unique.[92] The evidence for Vila Rica points to a broader view of these runaway communities. By and large these communities of runaway slaves lived in peace with the larger communities and played a complementary role in the society. In the Diamond District, this involved prospecting for diamonds and exchanging these for supplies. In the area of Vila Rica and probably of the other goldmining communities of the mining zone, the calhambolas prospected for gold, farmed, and then traded gold and foodstuffs in the shops of the urban core. They also sold items stolen from travelers and from isolated farms. The large quilombos may have formed serious threats to the order of the captaincy but the smaller ones seem to have posed little real threat. However, their constant presence was a reminder to the free population of the possibilities both of the formation of larger quilombos on the order of Palmares or of the ability of the calhambolas to form alliances with slaves and others to ferment rebellion—and it was the possibility of rebellion that frightened the residents of Minas Gerais to their core. It is here that the contradictions inherent in slavery are most glaring. The fear of quilombos and rebellions did not stop the arming of slaves. The fear of quilombos never produced a wholesale effort to eradicate the small quilombos. In fact, the quilombos seem to have found a space for themselves in the life of Minas Gerais during the eighteenth century. Of their internal structure, we know very little beyond the information contained in Joaquim José Lisboa's poem. But we can measure their substantial impact on the life of mineiros and we can use them to better understand the ambiguous nature of Brazilian society during the Golden Century.

9

VIOLENCE IN FRONTIER LANDS

LAURA DE MELLO E SOUZA

In the late 1760s and early 1770s, when the Marquis of Pombal's dominance in Portuguese politics was on the decline, tensions between the foreign enemy and the enemy within were intensifying in the colony. Many years earlier, in a deliberation by Portugal's Conselho Ultramarino, dated 1732, this concern had been articulated quite explicitly: "All states are subject to dangers of two natures, some foreign, others internal." The author, Councilor Antonio Rodrigues da Costa, went on to state: "The force and violence that may be wielded by other nations constitute said foreign dangers, while internal dangers are those that may be caused by the country's inhabitants, mainly Negroes and Indians, and by subjects of the Crown." In closing, the councilor declared the greatest of all dangers to be "when foreign forces unite with the internal will and force of these same subjects and of the Negroes and Indians."[1] Indeed, during the end of Pombal's term as minister, while the war was heating up in the south, under Spanish pressure, the boundaries defined under the 1750 Treaty of Madrid were pushed to new limits. As a result, settlers—and not just settlers of European descent but mulattos, blacks, and those of mixed indigenous and white blood as well—within these shifting boundaries were becoming aware that they constituted a unique population, distinct from the Europeans.

With the colony's internal boundaries changing, administrators were required to enforce more efficacious settlement policies that tailored practices dating from the time of discovery to the new context of expansion, that is, to movement inland. An endeavor to employ the idle—so-called vagrants—consequently gained momentum in the 1760s. A Royal Order to the governor and captain general of the captaincy of Bahia, from 1766; the orders of D. Luís Antonio de Sousa Botelho e Mourão, Morgado of Mateus and governor of São Paulo, who around 1767 put vagrants to work navigating the Tietê River and establishing the Iguatemi *presídio,* or settlement outpost; and an official regulation regarding vagrants which D. José Luis de Menezes Castelo Branco e Noronha, Count of Valladares and governor of Minas Gerais, handed down in 1769 stand as three pieces of evidence of this trend.[2]

There was thus significant official concern with fixing rootless, itinerant individuals in one place, a goal to be accomplished by revising and developing notions contained, for example, in the Ordenações Filipinas. This meant drawing social boundaries between the laboring subjects of the Crown and the idle, between the useful and the burdensome, between the healthy and the ill—identifying the rotten fruit that through contact might spoil the whole basket. Curiously enough, Brazil's geographical frontiers were often the place where these undesirables were sent—not just the borders separating the Luso-Brazilian colony from Spain's territories towards the south but its internal borders as well. Those that gradually defined themselves as Portugal settled the colony and reaped economic advantage from what this new land had to offer.

When the gold mines of Minas Gerais were discovered, in the seventeenth century, Brazil saw its economic hub move from the Northeastern sugar-producing region to the country's central-west area. In 1763, the capital was transferred from Salvador, Bahia, to Rio de Janeiro. After an initial boom, gold-mining hit a decline in the 1750s and fiscal earnings consequently fell. Minas became a stage of muted social tensions that, however veiled, inarguably played a decisive role in the process that was to culminate in the 1789 uprising known as the Inconfidência Mineira.

It should be underscored that in Minas it was the gold crisis that fueled the search for alternative economic solutions. The region's governors headed ventures to open and settle Brazil's barren *sertão* or assigned third parties to the task. As of the 1760s, ever greater emphasis was placed on the benefits to be accrued from establishing settlement outposts: they would push back indigenous groups and widen the boundaries of the territory controlled by the Portuguese crown. The centerpiece of the Portuguese colonial empire in the eighteenth century, the captaincy of Minas Gerais was a microcosm reflecting issues, in varying degrees, common to the entire colony, including a wild, hostile geographical environment quite strange to the new inhabitants; the rejection of a certain portion of humanity—mestizos, indigenous people, and blacks; and the white minority's panic over the ever-present possibility of a slave uprising.

The frontier lands of Minas afford us an opportunity to examine the issue of violence within the process of Brazil's social development. I base the present analysis on a number of unpublished testimonies, all dating from the end of the 1760s and first half of the 1770s, that is:

1. Reports from Inácio Correia Pamplona's 1769–70 expedition to conquer Campo Grande, Piuí, Bambuí, and the Picadas de Goiás (trails of Goiás), in the region lying between this cap-

taincy and the captaincies of São Paulo and Minas. The goal of this venture was to capture and banish "savages" and runaway slaves living in *quilombos* and then set up ranches and villages in these "cleaned-up" backlands.[3]

2. Administrative correspondence exchanged between the rulers of Minas and some of their subordinates, particularly concerning the opening of the captaincy's unsettled backlands.

3. Correspondence and rulings by D. Antonio de Noronha, governor and captain general of Minas from 1775 through 1780, in reference to such newly conquered areas and presídios as Cuieté, Abre Campo, and Peçanha and to the practice of resettling vagrants there. Second, the governor's rulings regarding the recruitment of troops to fight the wars to the south.[4]

4. The petition of an anonymous subject of the Portuguese crown, which although not dated was most certainly written in the mid-1770s. Registering some of the orders issued by D. Antonio de Noronha, the document provides evidence that these conceptions were shared by the captaincy's ruling groups—that is, the owners of mining rights, of lands, and of cattle.[5]

Pamplona's reporting of the dangers of the *sertão*, devoid of civilized men, and of the menace of indigenous and runaway slaves residing in *quilombos*—more like "cruel and horrifying monsters" than "rational men"—illustrates Europe's age-old derogatory attitude towards nature in the Americas and the peoples of this new land.[6] Charts were of no use in these mysterious, threatening lands for "in the sertão, everything is open to doubt."[7] Guides were inefficient as well: "Simão Roiz, who was our guide, was an errant guide, for the more he walked, the more lost he became."[8] Violence was a part of daily routine for the small columns assigned to undertake reconnaissance of the land. A man by the name of Cardoso, leader of one such detachment, returned from the brambles saying: "The sertão showed signs of being good, with a capacity for good ranches, and, further, for good gold formations; however, we nevertheless thanked God many times for delivering us from frights and from our fears that we might not leave there alive, because until a certain point there are many black men, and there are nothing but quilombos, and somewhat further on, nothing but savages." Cardoso and his men did not run into any indigenous people or quilombolas but stumbled instead over things these people left behind, such as "pots and pans." The fear these objects instilled in the white men symbolically marked the boundary between two distinct spaces: that of civilized whites and that of inhuman barbarians.[9] Manuel Jacome Soeiro, Justice of Vila do Príncipe and Pamplona's contemporary, shared the latter's notion that the *sertão* was a dangerous, inhuman place where men could be transformed into animals: "Deaths, and assaults, are so common in the sertão that it seems men forget their rational nature to don the nature of beasts which, more untamed than these, commit all type of offense without the slightest fear that might oblige them to renounce their cruelty." In order to handle this situation—or rather to neutralize it—the justice proposed to the Count of Valladares, then governor, that he assign a detachment of dragoons to the area of Rio das Velhas.

In point of fact, advancing into the *sertão* constituted a veritable war operation. Sent to face off quilombolas, some expeditions would beat war drums when they drew near the dwellings of runaway slaves, for the possibility of encountering blacks made them fear for their lives, and they believed the noise would frighten them off.[10] When Pamplona incited his men to self-control and cold-bloodedness, there were shades of strategy to it: "You cannot allow these [savages] to think we fear them." He went on to point out that might was on their side—yet in doing so he made it apparent how afraid the men were of the indigenous people's fighting tactics: "Do not let yourselves be defeated by what you have not yet seen, neither caltrops nor arrows; nor fear their bows, because our weapons shall silence their impulses, with no need for fiercer attacks, so that they will be forced to give up the land and we shall become masters of it."[11]

Such a dangerous enemy justified war. It was necessary to head into the *sertão* with a sizable military entourage, Pamplona told the Count of Valladares—otherwise "going in would be certain, but escaping from such inhuman people would be quite doubtful; for such fierce cattle who have never known a shepherd" could only be held back by the force of troops and imprisonment.[12] Later in this same document, Pamplona summed the problem up: "To govern these men, compassion, compassion; to teach them fear, two or three jailings; to rear them, much is needed; and to lose them, very little."[13] This formula—an allusion to what it would cost the government—captured the essence of Portugal's colonial policy. Pamplona wanted to found European-style settlements in these inhospitable regions, which, if necessary, could be further developed, reviving traditional settlement methods that saw the colonies as "the dungeon of its delinquents."[14] He advocated arresting "idle, scandalous prostitutes" and sending them to the frontier lands, along with any men who kept concubines and those guilty of misdemeanors; their sentences would be banishment to such parts. There, in order to purge their sensuality, they would have to spin cotton and linen and plant "many fields of wheat." But Pamplona, good Portuguese that he was, had his doubts about whether such "bad people" could ensure the success of this type of undertaking:

> In Minas, idleness—especially among women—is the cause of their poverty and of the perversity of customs. I cannot bear it that a white woman in Portugal—I speak of the peasants—takes care of her home, raises her children, fetches water for her kitchen, makes food and carries it to her husband in the field, spins until midnight, always joyful, while a freed black woman here is hard pressed to wash a plate, wallowing in the most excessive laziness. Certain useful activities, were they made to seem more pleasant, might provoke less repugnance and horror; and because mild medicine failed to work, they should not refrain from employing violent medicine.[15]

When it came to such riffraff, there was no alternative left but force. Vagrants, for example, fled from the commanders that combed the woods with the purpose of arresting them and sending them off to remote frontiers. "The softest sound lends their feet wings faster than Mercury's," complained Pamplona, further adding, "If Your Excellency does not decide to begin sending some of these people to those [parts], they will certainly not be taken there of their own accord, because they would rather live in idleness as indigents than enjoy abundance through labor, and without people I cannot proceed with conquests and much less with settlement."[16]

Around the same time that Pamplona advanced into the *sertão* bordering Goiás, the Count of Valladares was advising Captain Antonio Cardoso de Souza in his forays into the Doce River region, near what is now the border with Espírito Santo state. The captain was after new gold streams and out to conquer "the barbarian savages scattered or settled across that continent." As much as finding gold, said the governor, the goal was to bring the indigenous people into the "Christian fold [...] in a mild and gentle fashion." Should this be impossible because the savages proved rebellious and obstinate despite the colonizers' "friendly treatment," then it would be necessary to "uproot them by the force of irons and guns." The end result would be "either the taming of the savages, by means of persuasion, or their total destruction, so that a peaceful life could be enjoyed by dwellers in those locations, where these savages have carried out numerous acts of hostility."[17]

Valladares' letter is an outstanding example of a reflection on how power is wielded and also on how the social body was perceived in political terms under the Ancien Regime and, specifically, within the complex universe of the colonies. The indigenous population were people, equal to the white man; they could not be enslaved. Yet once they proved bellicose and resistant to conversion to Christianity, they lost their human status, joining the ranks of animals, untamed beasts liable to the law of irons and guns. When these indigenous people regressed to their animal state, society's healthy sectors had to be protected—those residing this side of the frontier, who represented the world of culture and civilization, that is, the Christian settlers living on farms. And yet, fearful of reprisals and leery of inciting further indigenous attacks on frontier settlements, Valladares, after first unconditionally authorizing the use of violence, drove home the need to deal with the indigenous population peacefully: soldiers and others entering *sertão* lands had to be advised as to the "gentle, friendly way the savages should be treated whenever encountered, all with the purpose of taming them, for perhaps a warm welcome [would] conquer better than irons."

War against indigenous people and quilombolas, violence against vagrants and the idle, relocation of prostitutes to settlement outposts—this was the population policy Pamplona defended in his correspondence with the count of Valladares during the time of the expedition. Some five years later, D. Antonio de Noronha, Valladares' successor as governor, would continue to divide himself between war (by then war against foreign enemies as well) and the recruitment of vagrants. Up until then, authorities had been troubled above all by the marginalized life-styles these men led and by the question of how to control them. The intensification of the gold-mining crisis, however, made it necessary to turn the "dead weight of the earth" into elements useful to the public order: the vagabond itinerancy of these rootless elements was less a worry now, replaced by a growing concern with how the idle might be gainfully employed.

D. Antonio saw the so-called presidios as "barriers against the affronts of savages" or as "impediments" that would keep them out of the sertão. Neighboring ranches would in turn serve as a "defense against the tyrannical affronts of that barbarian nation."[18] Always troubled by the small number of white men within his captaincy, the governor voiced fear not only of possible attacks by Botocudos or Puris but also of the large number of slaves: "I have taken the measures which I deem most efficacious for averting an uprising of Negroes, who every day run away and join quilombos, perhaps persuading themselves that this captaincy is being depleted of people able to stand against them," as he wrote to the viceroy, the Marquis of Lavradio, on May 13, 1777.[19] Behaving like a general thrashed by war on various flanks, D. Antonio held out against the recruitment policy imposed by Lavradio and sought to conjugate the foreign and domestic wars. Thus, for example, he pardoned deserting mulattos, *cabras* (mixed-breed blacks and indigenous people), mestizos, and freed slaves and assigned them to groups of skirmishers "to employ them not only in wiping out quilombos and imprisoning runaway slaves but also in venturing into the forest lands to repel the assaults of savages and destroy their villages. In like fashion," he went on, "the same squadrons of skirmishers will be used to defend this captaincy should it be invaded." Lastly, should he be called to defend Rio de Janeiro, he would take these troops with him.[20]

Although indigenous people, quilombolas, and Spaniards all terrified D. Antonio, this did not deter him from the goals of colonization. Six years earlier, Pamplona had believed it infeasible to populate the newly conquered Campo Grande with vagrants—"a caste of people overcome by sloth, consumed by vices, and, in short, supremely poor," who, once relocated to settlement fronts, would be unlikely to remain there.[21] But D. Antonio was an enthusiast of this strategy. "Save a small number of whites, they are all mulattos, mestizos, cabras, and freed slaves: through these bold men we may achieve the settlement of remote areas in Cuieté, Abre Campo, and other places," he declared. While defending the presidio from attacks by the indigenous people, these vagrants would also "ferociously" penetrate "virgin forests in search of these same savages," and pursue *quilombolas*, razing their homes and through it all helping open new paths.[22] These people had earned the "hatred of all civilized nations" and become the target of countless laws aimed at rooting them out, but in Minas they would deserve special consideration. In his 1779 "Secret plan to newly conquer Cuieté," D. Antonio prescribed the following norms: "Since conquest cannot be delayed, nor can it thrive so long as the region's new inhabitants are harassed by bailiffs over debt collection and charges of misdemeanors, and since most settlers must of necessity be guilty men laden with debt, as has always transpired in all new colonies, great care must be taken in this regard, and bailiffs should not be granted passes into [Cuieté]."[23]

Let there be no doubts, however, about the methods the government employed in regimenting vagrants for the presídios. Some of the *pardos* (mixed-breed blacks and whites) assigned to help open routes into Cuieté fled into hiding; D. Antonio ordered them to be diligently pursued and once found put in irons in the Vila Rica jail. Their property was to be expropriated, "be it of greater or lesser value," and a competent depositary appointed, who D. Antonio would "later order to publicly auction the property and ensuing earnings be applied to opening this route." If the men were married, he would arrest their wives.²⁴ Cases of cruel treatment of prisoners waiting to be sent to the presídios were common in subsequent years. In 1781, D. Rodrigo José de Menezes ordered that all vagrants within the diamond-mining region be arrested. He had a double purpose: to keep idlers from engaging in smuggling activities and get people to work in the Cuieté presídio. Inclemency and violence were the rule during arrests. Denouncing the fact that dozens were being held under subhuman conditions, the county judge in fact threatened to keep these men from being sent to the presídio. They nevertheless were—but on their way to Cuieté, on the bridge over the Doce River, the fifty-two prisoners managed to escape, aided by the officer in charge.²⁵ D. Rodrigo continued to enforce a policy of regimenting settlers from among the unemployed not only to neutralize their potential onus but also to "clean up" society. He ordered the arrest of all vagrants within the captaincy so they could be sent to work on construction of the Cuieté presídio, "thus accomplishing this important project at *little cost* while likewise *purging* civil society of its disturbers."²⁶ Once again, social and geographical boundaries were blurred.

Returning to the vexing dilemmas of D. Antonio who, caught as he was between foreign and internal war, was intent upon relieving society of the burden of idlers. Like so many others, fearing a slave uprising or attacks by the indigenous population, the governor was apprehensive about depriving the captaincy of many of its best elements by ordering them off to fight the Spaniards. Urged by Lavradio to send Minas' excellent Cavalry Regiment under the command of D. Antonio to Rio de Janeiro, then under the threat of invasion, the latter replied evasively, explaining that his cavalrymen were busy patrolling far-off regions. After an exchange of harsh letters with the viceroy, D. Antonio ended up sending southward 4,000 men regimented from among the idle, aged, and ill—who proved unfit for combat. As these troops passed from town to town, vehement complaints were heard from local authorities, ranging from the governor of São Paulo, Martim Lopes Lobo de Saldanha, to the commander of southern operations, João Henrique Bohm.²⁷

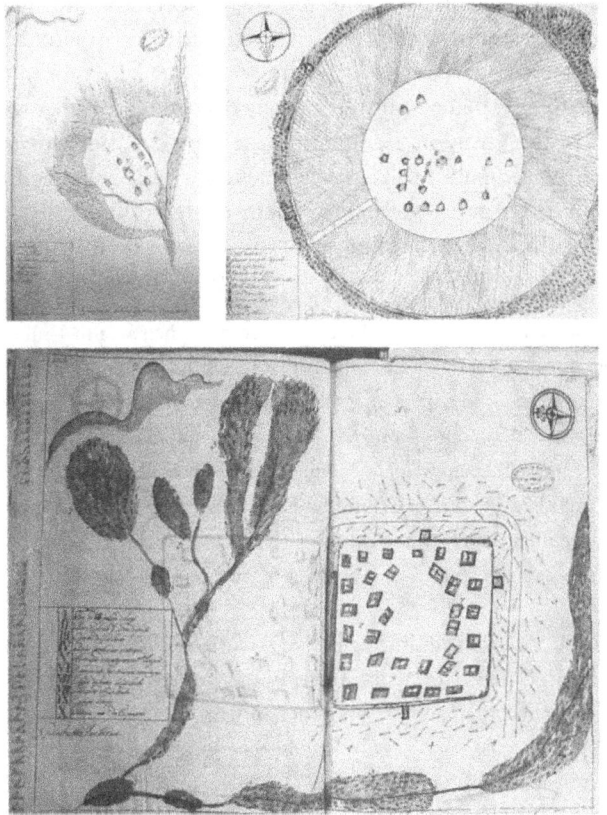

Two blueprints of quilombos in Minas Gerais.

In closing this reflection on the daily practice of violence in colonial society, I would like to call attention to the fact that some ten years before the Inconfidência—an uprising against Portuguese rule which was to occur in Minas in 1789—society there was already divided into antagonistic blocs whose world views clashed, each group engaged in its own particular practices. D. Antonio's ideas on how to make use of vagrants differed from Pamplona's as they were shaped at a time of greater tension, when social issues were demanding urgent solutions. D. Antonio's ideas were embraced by such educated men as Judge Teixeira Coelho, who today is often credited with their authorship since it was he who recorded them in his noteworthy "Instrução para o governo da Capitania de Minas Gerais" (1780). As expressed in his correspondence with Lavradio, D. Antonio's misgivings about recruitment reflected the concerns of "upright men," or found resonance among them. This is what becomes apparent in the "Petition by a subject of the Crown who loves his fatherland," where the anonymous author places himself among the ranks of all other settlers, ready to serve the Crown by defending the territory. But this anonymous writer alerts the king about the risk of leaving wives and daughters behind "in the hands of the most pernicious enemy." He grounded his opinion on the fact that Minas was inhabited solely by

> barbarian black people from Africa and Guinea, which all residents own—some more, some less, in accordance with their wealth—subject to slavery, for they are purchased within that region for money. [...] Since the region of Minas is so replete with such barbarians—albeit tamed by the force of fear and with no other tendency than to harm and kill whites, whom they deem their chief enemies for depriving them of their liberty, and with each white matched by over one hundred Ethiopians, who, like barbarians impelled by their ferocious nature, have often times sought to take our very lives from us and capture our women and daughters.[28]

The captaincy would inevitably be lost were it dispossessed of its white people, recruited for the wars in the south. It was necessary for the monarch to decide promptly what attitude to adopt because, stated the faithful subject in closing, "surely it is better to take more precautions than necessary than not take enough."[29]

In Minas on the eve of the Inconfidência, sectors of the ruling classes might have disagreed on how best to use vagrants on settlement fronts but they agreed when it came to the tactic of propelling socially disqualified elements to its geographic and symbolic frontiers. These sectors were unanimous in vilifying mulattos, indigenous people, and blacks, identifying them as inviable, inhuman people, or negating their status as human beings outright, likening them to the ferocious beasts of the inhospitable *sertão*. Violence in discourse found its counterpart in the real world. If the torture of Tiradentes—the only one of the Inconfidência's rebels to be publicly executed and then drawn and quartered—can be seen as the embodiment of Michel Foucault's "thousand deaths," it was also nothing more than a spectacular and exemplary repetition on the gallows of what, at times, took place in less explicit, more veiled fashion, as part of everyday life.[30]

10

QUILOMBOS IN MATO GROSSO: BLACK RESISTANCE IN A BORDER AREA

LUIZA RIOS RICCI VOLPATO

The Occupation of the Territory

Since the seventeenth century, the region that later came to be the territory of the states of Mato Grosso and Mato Grosso do Sul had already been known by the Trailblazers from São Paulo that trod in search of the indigenous to seize. The setting of the village, however, only took place from 1719 on, when the flag of Pascoal Moreira Cabral struck gold on the banks of Coxipó River, a tributary of the Cuiabá River. Due to the discovery, the pioneers became miners and began prospecting for the gold.[1]

The mines of Coxipó consisted of alluvial gold, and although mining was characterized by easy operation, it was quickly exhausted, so much so that two years after its discovery it was already depleted. In spite of that, in 1722, Miguel Sutil struck gold at the Prainha stream banks, near the hill of the Rosário. These rich deposits produced four kilos of gold within a month, contributing to the creation of numerous fanciful stories on the amount of coveted metal near the Cuiabá River. The disclosure of this news caused an adventurous race by prospectors who, abandoning everything they had, set off for the distant hinterland. The newfound deposits, although very rich, were also quickly exhausted a few years after discovery. The type of gold in Cuiabá region, the alluvial gold, meant that mining was dealt in an itinerant way: the miners were always in search of new mines, wishing they were plentiful and long lasting. The small village continued to send expeditions into the hinterland. Thus, the population of Cuiabá was built in a labile form, depending on the constant travels of its inhabitants.

The land was conquered from the indigenous, who surrendered after much struggle; the distance from the village of São Paulo was very large and communication was made through fluvial navigation, through a route full of rapids and waterfalls, requiring them to carry out numerous deviations to the ground. From 1725, river expeditions came under attacks from Paiaguá indigenes, inhabitants of the banks of the Paraguay River, skilled boatmen and major obstacle to cross the monsoon.[2] Despite all these difficulties, the Portuguese Court was interested in the survival of the population in the region: Cuiabá was the most advanced point of Portuguese western occupation. On January 1, 1727, attended by the Governor of São Paulo captaincy, Rodrigo Cesar de Meneses, the small village was elevated to the category of town. The installation of a formal representation of the Portuguese government did not change people's way of life: many kept their statuses as itinerant miners, coming from and going to the hinterlands in search of new gold deposits. These constant marches increasingly led the village to the west and, in 1731, gold was discovered in the region of river Guaporé, where another nucleus of settlement was created.

The Portuguese occupation progressed considerably on land that belonged to Spain according to the Treaty of Tordesillas. Arriving on the bank of the Guaporé river, the Portuguese settlement, based on the south coast of the colony, entered through the Amazon forest—a dense forest region, named for this reason Mato Grosso ("Thick Forest")—and approached the Spanish settlements, because the distance between the new Lusitanian nucleus and the Spanish missions was only thirty leagues.

Since the beginning of Portuguese occupation, the Mato Grosso region had the burden of being border area, responsible for defending the Portuguese settlement and, if possible, for its expansion. That was the bias that defined the creation of the captaincy of Mato Grosso by a Royal Letter of May 9, 1748, having among its functions to strengthen the Portuguese position in the discussions that resulted in the signing of the Treaty of Madrid. The creation of a Portuguese government representation in the region strengthened the argument that supported all the Portuguese claims: the *uti possidetis* (Latin: "as you possess"). The captaincy of government deployment only occurred from 1751 with the arrival of the first General Captain, Antonio Rolim de Moura, which featured, among the instructions of the Overseas Council, to install the administration headquarters in the Guaporé region, that is, in the furthest west location of the occupation. On March 19, 1752, Governor Rolim de Moura founded Vila Bela da Santíssima, on the banks of the Guaporé River, whose function was to house the headquarters of the captaincy, seeking to attract the inhabitants of the small nuclei therein to the new village.

Throughout the colonial period, Vila Bela and Cuiabá were the main population centers of the captaincy around which revolved its commercial, administrative and military life. The occupation of the border, at a time when the boundaries were fluid and uncertain, and the exploration of mining meant that the Portuguese population in the region had some peculiarities, requiring special attention of the Court. Both conditions put Mato Grosso in specific metropolitan government legislation.

Economy and Black Slavery on a Border Area

Black slaves arrived in Mato Grosso simultaneously to the setting of the village. The first monsoon from São Paulo brought the need for exploration of gold: in addition to grocery and tools, slaves. These were directed to the mining work. If initially slaves arrived in Mato Grosso with monsoons from São Paulo, the navigation of the rivers of the Amazon watershed was released after the installation of the captaincy, allowing the insertion of the region in the operating area of Grão-Pará e Maranhão General Company. Between 1752 and 1778, part of the slaves that arrived in Mato Grosso, particularly those intended to Vila Bela, was sold by that company.

Existing slaves in the region were mainly allocated in the work of mining, agriculture, livestock and public works, and this last activity was intensified after installing the captaincy government. The border zone status, that had the function to contain the possible Spanish advances, demanded its militarization. During the first decades of existence of the colonial government in Mato Grosso, forts, fortresses and fortified population centers were constructed. Both military garrisons and the buildings that now host the various representations of the colonial government were built by slave labor. Even taking place concurrently with other activities, mining was undoubtedly the one that consumed the slave labor. Gold was exploited in quite rudimentary form. The main working tools used by slaves were the lever, miner's pickaxe (*almocafre*), wooden bowl for gold or diamond washing (*bateia*), "conical bowl used in mining" (*carumbé*) and hammer for breaking stones (*marreta*). Some miners came to have plantations with twenty to fifty slaves working a very high numbers for the Mato Grosso conditions. These wealthy miners used their slaves for the construction of tanks, reservoirs and streams to facilitate gold exploration.

The mining works took place in extremely precarious conditions, reducing the useful life of the slaves. The mines were in unhealthy areas facilitating the proliferation of fever and malaria fevers, particularly in the Guaporé region, considered unhealthy even by the colonial authorities.[3] As a mining area, Mato Grosso had its economic output regulated by a rigid colonial legislation concerned to ensure the concentration of the most productive resources in the gold extraction. Thus, agriculture and livestock were developed with restrictions, because the livestock (cattle, horse and mule), as well as the building of mills, was prohibited. For Mato Grosso, these restrictions were intended still to generate a consumer market for the economy of São Paulo, which was in serious trouble in the mid-eighteenth century.[4] Facing restrictions, the cattle was introduced in the region in the 1730s, around the time that the first mills were built.

The growing of supply genres was established in the vicinity of both Cuiabá and Vila Bela. Later, between the villages, other farms emerged, and the most known of them was the Jacobina farm. These properties flourished with an economy based especially in the extensive production of livestock, and its main core consumers were Vila Bela, Cuiabá and the border fortifications.[5] In the first decades of the nineteenth century, Jacobina farm was considered one of the most dynamic properties of the province, having a squad of two hundred slaves busy in various activities, especially agriculture and livestock.[6] The cattle breeding spread throughout the natural grasslands of the upper Mato Grosso wetland region (Pantanal Mato-Grossense).

The planting of sugarcane and sugar production developed particularly near Cuiabá and in the high lands of the Guimarães Plateau (Chapada dos Guimarães). The devices constitute one of the fundamental parts of these properties, and its sugar production was intended for the market of Mato Grosso region, and sub-products—*cachaça* (liquor distilled from sugarcane juice) and brown sugar—were as important as sugar. In the early years of implementation of the mills, the chronicler José Barbosa de Sá found that the distribution of cachaça to the slaves who worked in mining improved their health, increasing their resistance to poor working conditions.[7]

Mid-eighteenth century, the mining in Mato Grosso was in crisis and the captaincy had difficulties in the reorganization of its economy: there was a great distance in relation to coastal ports. The link between Cuiabá and São Paulo, during the first half of the eighteenth century, was made by fluvial navigation through difficult routes. Due to the founding of Vila Bela, navigating through the Amazon basin became legal but also another waterway that was difficult to navigate. In the last quarter of the century, the use of landway through Goiás was intensified because of the extinction of the Grão-Pará and Maranhão General Company in 1778. The increased use of this earthly journey was justified not only by its traffic conditions but also due to the new alignment of political and economic forces of the colony assembly, when groups based in South-Central Brazil began to dispute the hegemony of the Northeast.

The communication with the coast was always one of the obstacles to overcome the mining crisis in Mato Grosso. The solution found in the late eighteenth century was diversification: the same owner allied mining activities with the exploitation of large estates, commercial establishments and exercise of bureaucratic and military positions.⁸

During this period, many miners requested for *sesmarias* (plots of land assigned to settlers by the Portuguese monarchy) for agriculture. Several groups of slaves, some of them numerous for the Mato Grosso parameters, were transferred from mining to agriculture and livestock. The overwhelming economic difficulties of Mato Grosso provoked sharp criticism from the engineer Luis D'Alincourt, when he was there conducting statistical studies at the beginning of the national phase.⁹ An impoverished population expected the provincial authorities to take measures to relieve their condition of destitution. And the authorities were awaiting the action of the central government.

During the 1820s, the cities of Cuiabá and Mato Grosso (formerly Vila Bela) competed for the right to host the provincial government. In 1835, the imperial government chose Cuiabá as its definite center.¹⁰ This measure led to the transfer of Guaporé region's resources to the new seat of government.

In the mid-nineteenth century, the owners were still using the diversification of activities in order to balance an economy in crisis. By that time, however, the cattle export was already the main source of commerce in the province.¹¹ However, Mato Grosso's economy, once established, was self-reliant with only tenuous links with foreign markets. This characteristic, generated in the beginning of the mining crisis, interfered in the volume of importation of slaves, reduced the size of population. In the mid-nineteenth century, the largest groups were in the region of Cuiabá and were composed of two or three dozen of slaves. Despite this drop, compared to groups who worked in mining in the previous century, the slave population in Cuiabá maintained a level of concentration similar to cities like Rio de Janeiro and Salvador. By the 1860s, the provincial capital had 19,543 inhabitants, of which 7,158 were slaves (36.62 percent).¹² Few slaves had some professional training; most of them worked on whichever job they were ordered to perform.¹³

The small size of the enslaved population and the possibility of the farm owner knowing each slave did not diminish the rigors of slavery. Also at the hinterland of Brazil, slavery was characterized by a way of work appropriation based on personal relations, imposed by coercion. Moral constraints and physical punishment were ways to exercise coercion in order to ensure the submission of slaves. But in Mato Grosso, as in the rest of Brazil, subtle mechanisms of domination were also used, minimizing the use of coercive methods and turning slavery into a more feasible productive system. Among these mechanisms, there was concession of a piece of land to the slave where he could take their livelihoods and sometimes a surplus, besides the possibility of gaining his/her freedom in case the master considers him/her devoted, obedient and faithful. In the second half of the nineteenth century, it was possible to identify the acquisition of freedom by means of payment in installments.[14] The existence of this possibility was another spoliation mechanism, which led the slave to extend working hours, making him/her a wage-earning slave (*escravo de ganho*), hoping to get the money needed to purchase his freedom.

But in Mato Grosso, as in any other region where there was slavery, the slaves resisted submission. The resistance took place not only in day-to-day struggles, but also in openly declared resistance. Running away was constant and acquired some peculiar features. The captives living in the Guaporé region, near the border, crossed the demarcation line. During the colonial period, blacks received incentives from the Spanish authorities to cross the border by offering them freedom. In contrast, the Portuguese sought to attract indigenous Hispanic-Americans. On some occasions, the colonial authorities tried to contain these escapes and formulated return agreements.[15] The border, however, presented itself as an alternative both to the escaped slave and for the indebted settler, who also fled because of inability to meet payment obligations.

Slavery also took special configurations in Mato Grosso, during the Paraguayan War: the province was a stage of combat, especially its southern region, occupied by enemy troops. Like the rest of the population, the captives endured the fear of a Paraguayan invasion, but were able to use the loopholes that the war opened in the system of domination. The state of war was skillfully used by the slaves when they considerably expanded the existing quilombos in the province, taking advantage of the difficulties faced by the provincial authorities.

Quilombos in Mato Grosso

To date, the Mato Grosso historiography has given little attention to the study of black slavery, and even less attention to the study of the slave's resistance.[16] Earlier historians, chroniclers and travelers who have written about Mato Grosso did not privilege matters relating to slavery and information about it appears tangentially because of other aspects of regional reality.

In his *Relação das povoações de Cuiabá e Mato Grosso*, José Barbosa de Sá makes reference to the murder of Tomé Anes in 1727—the year the camp was elevated to the category of town—committed by a Black man named

José, whose owner was João Antunes Maciel, in the mines of Ribeirão in Cuiabá.[17] The central axis of the narrative concerns the established dispute between the Captain-General of São Paulo, then living in Cuiabá, Rodrigo Cesar de Meneses, and the *ouvidor* Antonio Alvares Lanha Peixoto, and it was not possible to recover more accurate data about the murder itself. The same chronicler also tells about the escape of a white boy, friend of Miguel Antonio Soberal, accompanied by some slaves of his employer and from another property of João Lopes Zedas, which took place in the year 1731. The escapees wanted to reach the village of São Paulo. The lords of the captives pitched two canoes and set off in pursuit of the fugitives. However, the gentile Paiaguá attacked some and all perished.[18]

The narrative of José Barbosa de Sá gives special emphasis to the confrontation between indigenous people and Portuguese descendents, in the initial stage of the settlement of the village in Mato Grosso. According to the chronicler, the indigenous were a savage people that prevented the consolidation of the Portuguese settlement in the interior of Brazil. Men capable of facing the forestry were valiant, especially Paiaguá, who attacked and decimated the *monções* (fluvial expeditions that explored the interior of Brazil) who crossed their fields, imposing heavy losses navigating the Paraguay watershed. And from this angle that extols the deeds of the mulatto Manuel Rodrigues do Prado, who faced courageously the attack from Paiaguá to the monções, in which came from his native land of Pindamonhangaba to Cuiabá. He made it with great effort. The chronicler adds a reference to the mulatto, which in his point of view was a brave man, saying that for many years he served as capitão-do-mato.[19]

The complimentary way the chronicler refers to *Manuel Rodrigues do Prado* reveals the prestige that the capitão-do-mato activity had in the village at that time. This allows us to estimate a high incidence slaves escaping, and an understanding of the value placed on those who specialized in their capture. The "captains of the forest" (capitães-do-mato) also participated in expeditions organized by the colonial authorities against the Spanish.[20] The presence of such men in these contingents may be explained by the ability they had as trackers, but it is possible to assume that the marches through the hinterlands had as objective a military action against the neighbors and also to identify and destroy villages of runaway slaves.

Elsewhere in his chronicle, Barbosa de Sá reported a new incident involving dispute between the colonial authorities based in Cuiabá. The upheavel that took place at nighttime, made the householders run to the streets armed against their biggest fears, among which included the uprising of slaves:

> The astonished, confused and frightened people stood asking each other what was going on. Some said that we were surrounded by Castilliards, others that it was an invasion of Gentiles, others that it was an uprising of Blacks. Absolutely no one knew what it was and no one knew what to say, amazed, stunned by the darkness of the night and the fright of the novelty.[21]

The chronicles and memories are rich in accounts of the numerous border clashes, when each Iberian metropoli sought to improve their positions in the Guaporé and Paraguay regions. Reports of clashes between whites and Indians in disputes over territory are equally rich but references to clashes between masters and slaves very rarely appear in the same texts. Still, the uprising of slaves was as feared as the Spanish invasion or indigenous attacks. These considerations make room for thinking that small uprisings, or at least violent actions on the part of slaves, were taking place.

As mentioned earlier, the escapes of slaves in Mato Grosso acquired some unique configurations, one of which was the border as an alternative. Another was the density of the indigenous population. The indigenous people often became allies of fugitive slaves, giving them techniques to survive in the forest, the *cerrado* tropical savanna, the wetland. But they could also become a danger to the fugitives, as in the case of the slave Miguel Antônio Soberal. During the eighteenth and nineteenth centuries, several villages of runaway slaves emerged in Mato Grosso territory. Some, of course, had such ephemeral lives that left no records; others, however, were formed in an organized and lasting manner. Among the many villages built in Mato Grosso, information could be obtained about the lives of some of them, including the quilombos Quariterê, Sepotuba and Rio Manso.

Quilombos in Mato Grosso—approximate location.

Quilombos in Mato Grosso—approximate location.

Quariterê Quilombo

One of the most famous quilombos of Mato Grosso was the *Quariterê*. Although widely cited in the historiography, this village has not been studied in-depth.²² Existing information about it originates from a brief comment in the memoirs of Felipe José Nogueira Coelho, the Royal Treasury Superintendent and Quartermaster of Gold, from the eighteenth century.²³ The quilombo Quariterê or Quariteté was situated near river Galera, a tributary on the west bank of the river Guaporé. It was first attacked by a *bandeira* (expedition to chase or capture Africans, indigenous persons, etc) from Vila Bela, the then captaincy government headquarters, commanded by Sergeant-Major João Leme do Prado, in 1770, at the time when Luis Pinto de Sousa Coutinho was governor of Mato Grosso.

Nogueira Coelho states that this village existed since the early days of the mines of the Guaporé region and would have therefore had three decades of existence, at the time it was defeated. At that time, it was inhabited by over a hundred people, 79 blacks (between men and women) and about 30 indigenous persons. Their method of government resorted to the metaphor of "royalty," according to the report of Nogueira Coelho: "They had had a king; then the widow Queen Theresa governed well assisted by indigenous and black women."²⁴ It existed as a Parliament, led by Captain-Major José Cavalo. The Queen, in the exercise of its functions, had the support of an adviser, José Piolho.

As in most studied quilombos, some key concerns were the advocacy efforts that included secrecy about their location. To achieve this goal, the internal discipline was strict and the punishments effectively heavy: when judged necessary, Quariterê authorities ordered the insubordinates to be hung, to have his/her legs broken and to be buried alive. Among the most heavily punished deeds by the quilombo was desertion.

The agriculture of the settlement produced in abundance foodstuffs needed by its inhabitants. Besides these products, they cultivated tobacco and cotton, while maintaining two blacksmith tents, probably for the production of tools and weapons. Once they defeated the quilombo, the owners took the prisoners, destroyed ranches and plantations and returned to Vila Bela. Despite the violent action of the bandeira commanded by Sergeant-Major John Leme do Prado, the blacks who escaped from the attacks hiding in the woods, returned and recomposed the village: the quilombo entered a new stage, which lasted until 1795.

Indigenous persons fight against the advancement of blacks and whites on their territories, c. 1825 ("Guerrillas," M. Rugendas, Malerische Reise in Brasilien, Paris, Engelmann & Cie., 1835).

By that time, the Captain-General João de Albuquerque de Melo Pereira e Caceres decided to organize an expedition with two objectives: conduct prospecting work in order to find new gold deposits, since the mines around Vila Bela were being exhausted, and hunt down runaway slaves, destroying the quilombos.[25] With the funds provided by the Royal Treasury and raised among the population of Vila Bela and neighboring camps, a bandeira of 45 men was organized under the command of the second lieutenant in the Dragões regiment Francisco Pedro de Melo, commander of the Casalvasco fortress. The bandeira left the port of Vila Bela, from the river Guaporé, on May 7, 1795, staying on mission for more than six months.[26] The expedition penetrated the hills of Parecis and, following the guidelines of a freed black that had inhabited the old quilombo Quariterê, reached the Piolho River. From there on, the men began to notice traces and vestiges of the passage of people. On June 19, the "expedition" (bandeira) imprisoned three indigenous, one black and one *caburé* (descendent of indigenous and Blacks), quilombo inhabitants. An indigenous person who belonged to the group managed to escape, and warned the village about the "expedition." The quilombolas tried to escape; however many were imprisoned.

The explorers remained for over a month near Piolho River, searching for fugitives, and managing to imprison others. In exploring the area surrounding the quilombo, members of the expedition were impressed with its natural beauty, the fertility of the land, the bountiful hunting and fishing:

> [...] the present day *quilombo*, located in a beautiful field and far superior in both quality of land as in the high and leafy forests, the excellent and currently grown banks of the rivers Galera, Sararé and Guaporé: abundant hunting, and a lot of fish in the river, which is the same magnitude of the Branco river.[27]

The "expedition" (bandeira) was also impressed by the wealth of the quilombo: large plantations of corn, beans, cassava, peanuts, potatoes, *cará* and other tubercle. They also cultivated fruits such as banana and ananas; planted tobacco and cotton, with which they produced coarse fabric. Furthermore, they raised chickens. During the inquiry that took place in the region, the following were arrested:

Blacks	6
Male indigenous	8
Female indigenous	19
Male Caburés	10
Female Caburés	11
Total	54[28]

Among these people, only six were survivors of the old quilombo, destroyed 25 years ago. The elderly, who had command functions in the village, under whose guidance the economic life of Quariterê was restructured, were equally responsible for the orientation of religious life and patient care. Most of the inhabitants were born in the village itself, descendants of the survivors of the previous settlement.[29]

In his diary, the commander of the expedition claimed that the quilomobolas kept constant conflicts with indigenous Cabixi, attacking them in order to abduct women. After having destroyed the Piolho quilombo, the "expedition" continued attacking other small villages in Parecis Plateau (*Chapada dos Parecis*) and near the rivers Galera, Sararé and Pindaituba.

The fugitives tried to reorganize themselves: they abandoned a quilombo near the Pindaituba River, composed of two villages, fifty paces apart, one of them with eleven houses and the other with ten houses. The quilombo of Mutuca was formed six leagues to the north, with two small camps: one led by the black Antônio Brandão, composed of fourteen blacks, five of them slaves. The other, under the command of the slave Joaquim Feliz, had thirteen black men and seven black women. Interestingly, the expedition diary distinguishes blacks from slaves, implying that some of them were not escaped captives.

The expedition maintained its mission invading those hinterlands, destroying and burning settlements, plantations, persistently pursuing any trace of human passage. The quilombolas fled in a desperate march, abandoning the settlements when they sensed the approach of the expeditions, most of the time leaving behind their provisions. In solidarity, they sought to help each other. On the banks of the river Sararé, for example, a small group was taken prisoner because they had stopped walking to treat a sick woman.

On November 18, 1795, the expedition returned to Vila Bela, leaving behind a trail of destruction, with plantations and settlements turned into ashes. A few quilombolas, who had managed to escape from the numerous attacks, saw their living conditions turned not viable, becoming isolated with their huts, provisions and destroyed possessions. Without any other choice, many walked to the village, and surrendered themselves to their former masters. Such an attitude made the "expedition," which had promoted so much destruction that forced the survivers to surrender, even more successful. The assault on the diverse quilombos in Parecis Plateau, outskirts of rivers Galera, Sararé, Pindaituba and Piolho took place in a very specific time in Mato Grosso's history. By that time, the economic crisis was already quite severe and the turn of the century had been a period of trying to search for new alternatives, with resources transferred from mining to agriculture and livestock. In addition, both the government of the captaincy and their merchants were being pressured by suppliers on the coast, who attempted to be paid for old debts.

These difficulties occurred at the same time that changes were happening in wider spheres, within the framework of colonial policy, strengthening the groups established in the Mid-South, to the detriment of those established in the Northern and Northeastern regions. The support from the south-central group stimulated the dominant segments of Cuiabá village, richer and more populous pole of the captaincy, to question the governor's authority. From Cuiabá, a web of power and interests was formed, including the involvement of border forts in smuggling with the Spanish (who paid for the manufactured products with the silver of Potosi). The metal was drained into the hands of the coastal merchants and played an important role as currency in colonial trade.[30] Thus, the victory over the quilombolas represented political asset to the Captain-General both within the captaincy as well as to the metropolitan authorities.[31] By defeating the quilombos, the governor was victorious over an old and dreaded enemy. In addition, the victory also lifted the spirits of an exhausted population in the struggle for survival in such a distant region of the most dynamic centers of the colony; they were also responsible, with great difficulty, for the costs of the war on the border.

The Carlota Village

Throughout the colonial period, the Mato Grosso captaincy had privileged its boundary condition in the metropolitan projects. As Brazil's rampart, it should block any Spanish advance over the richest areas of the colony, such as Minas Gerais, for example. The defense of territorial boundaries was made especially through settlements. For this reason, several investments were made since the 1750s, aiming to promote the colonization of the western region of Brazil. The opportunities in this direction were not wasted by the colonial authorities. One of these took place when the expedition (bandeira) of Francisco Pedro de Melo shattered the quilombo Piolho in 1795. Commanders of the detachment and later the Captain-General realized the different skills of the imprisoned quilombolas and sought to use them in the interests of the Portuguese crown.

Members of the expedition had been impressed with the organizational and productive capacity of the village: in a time when Vila Bela, Cuiabá and border detachments faced constant outbreaks of production, when famine was raging and ravaging the population, the quilombo had a well-structured and productive agriculture, which kept its inhabitants supplied. Moreover, most of them spoke Portuguese and knew rudiments of Christian doctrine. Given this situation, the colonial authorities were willing to start a settlement with the quilombolas on the border. Thus, the quilombolas were first recruited in order make the former quilombolas see themselves as subjects of the Portugal Crown and defenders of the Christian faith: in a large religious ceremony, the prisoners were baptized in Vila Bela, with the presence of the governor and other colonial authorities.

João de Albuquerque, the governor of Mato Grosso, became the godfather of some former quilombolas, some of them also had people prominent in local society.[32] With this attitude, the governor sought to establish links of identity between him and his prisoners: all became equal "by the grace of baptism," brothers in the same faith and equal again for being vassals of the same woman, the queen of Portugal. In the day after the christening ceremony, the 54 imprisoned people departed to establish the Carlota village (a name chosen in honor of the Princess of Brazil). Quilombolas, reduced by force and metamorphosed into the king's subjects, received what the authorities considered necessary to establish a new settlement:

> Departing all the mentioned 54 people for New Carlota Village on the 7th of October in many canoes taking with them besides groceries for many months, various grains and seeds to plant with corresponding tools, as well as pigs, ducks and chickens for breeding. Establishment from which it is expected prosperous future and public utility.[33]

Despite the investment and the expectation of success, Carlota village did not become a dynamic and productive center as the quilombo. They were no longer free men, responsible for their freedom, but defeated quilombolas, who had received the mercy of acting as free men, but in service to the king.

Referring to the quilombo Quariterê, Nogueira Coelho asserts that its origin is in the exploitation of mines in the Guaporé Valley, during the 1730s. Considering its entire existence, the village survived for about six decades. During this period, its inhabitants learned to establish contacts with the Portuguese settlements, especially São Vicente village, where through exchange some quilombolas could get some products, including tools. The survival of a quilombo depended largely on the ability of its inhabitants to establish a web of relationships that would provide, in addition to the supply of some specific products, information about the actions of their persecutors. The inhabitants of Quariterê also maintained constant relations with those living in the woodlands, characterized at times by alliance and others by confrontation. The quilombolas, however, were able to demonstrate skill in these relations; otherwise, their village would have disappeared prematurely. During the national stage, various other villages emerged in the province. However, they had different characteristics, marked by the new reality.

Quilombos in the Nineteenth Century

The tumultuous period of the National State construction took specific contours in Mato Grosso. One of them refers the dispute for the right to host the provincial capital, established between the cities of Cuiabá and

Mato Grosso, 1820–1835. The final transfer of the seat of government brought to Cuiabá not only the representations of the imperial government, but also much of the resources previously invested in the Guaporé valley. From the decade of 1820 and especially after 1835, the main building and detachments went to Cuiabá. These military forces were composed mostly of soldiers forcibly recruited in various regions of Brazil and brought to Mato Grosso.

In the mid-nineteenth century, the Cuiabá region had a population with a strong presence of poor freemen, mostly descendants of indigenous and freed slaves. The others were former soldiers who had had been dispensed in Cuiaba and did not returned to their original province. Although the army had the function to control the men, the army did not teach a profession to these men, who, after serving for several years, left the military without professional training. As the poor free population grew, a number of concerns emerged because they were not considered suitable for productive and orderly work and were seen as possible allies of the slaves, if an uprising occured. Indeed, the expansion of this social category imprinted specific characteristics on the quilombos that were organized in Mato Grosso, especially at the end of the slave period, by many of these individuals, who fleeing from police or military recruitment, found shelter in the settlements of runaway slaves. The authorities sought to attack and destroy these villages, but the provincial government was in constant lack of resources, and the border patrolling was often presented as a more pressing concern.

In 1839, an expedition (bandeira) was sent against a quilombo located on the bank of the river Piraputanga; quilombolas resisted but were defeated.[34] The village was made up of sixteen houses of two or three levels and two or three of two-storeyed houses. In his annual report, the president of the province, Estévão Resende Ribeiro, expressed his admiration for the quality of the buildings and, even more, the richness found in the storerooms of the village. The quilombo Piraputanga had its houses arranged close to each other, forming a kind of square. Such arrangement, of course, was intended to facilitate its defense. Its inhabitants developed a successful agriculture output and had several small plantations. When the quilombo was defeated, the members of the expedition were not able to load the stored supplies, given their amount. Once again, the quilombolas' organizational capacity and power to produce in plenty the needed goods became evident.

In the second half of the nineteenth century, there were many slave ranches in Mato Grosso, but the provincial authorities did not consider themselves sufficiently armed to face them:

> In addition to the [*quilombo*] Sepotuba, which has existed for over a century, there are still Rio Manso, Roncador, Rafting and Serra Dourada [that] contain large numbers of slaves and perhaps quite a few deserters. Since 1860 for lack of troops it has not been possible to destroy them, which has brought great destruction to crops, that languished for lack of arms.[35]

Referring to the quilombo Sepotuba in 1863, the president of the province, Herculano Ferreira Pena, considered that it already had a secular existence, being seen as one of the oldest in Mato Grosso. It was located near the Sepotuba River, a tributary of the Paraguay River, near Vila Maria, an important point of the border. The news that ran about this quilombo terrified the population of Vila Maria and the farms around it.

The specific situations lived by the Brazilian Empire in the second half of the 1860s, opened up new prospects for the quilombos in Mato Grosso. In November 1864, the Paraguayan war ("Guerra do Paraguai") began with the invasion of Paraguayan troops in Brazil. Early in the conflict, the southern region of Mato Grosso province was invaded, bringing moments of fear and a sense of insecurity to the population. During the war, the effort of recruiting soldiers increased considerably. As the military draft was rejected by the majority of poor men and their families, running away, which was already used as an alternative to get away from recruitment, came to be used more often. Part of the fugitives sought shelter in existing quilombos.

During the Paraguayan war, the quilombolas took advantage of the situation. They knew how to receive and attract the deserters to their villages: former soldiers, who came to the villages carrying guns and possessing instructions, even if rudimentary, about their use. The deserters also brought information on military operations and location of troops. The possession of such data made the quilombolas bolder and less concerned about security, attacking properties even near the capital, intensifying the fear lived by the population. The provincial authorities were aware of the existence of quilombos and the action of its inhabitants, but feared the crumbling of the military forces in wartime. For them, at that time, every effort should be concentrated in the fight against the external enemy.

Among the quilombos that have expanded significantly over the war period is the one of Sepotuba River. During the first moments of conflict, Mato Grosso authorities feared that the Paraguayans would close an alliance treaty with the Republic of Bolivia, which would open a new front of combat to the west. While the imperial diplomacy struggled in that sense, the Mato Grosso population, especially the inhabitants of the border, lived in the aniticipation of an attack.[36]

Domestic punishment, one of the reasons to run away, c. 1825 ("Chatiments domestiques," M. Rugendas, Malerische Reise in Brasilien, Paris, Engelmann & Cie., 1835).

The quilombo Sepotuba stood close to the borderline with Bolivia. It presence alone was one more reason of insecurity for the population. Its inhabitants knew how to take advantage of this situation and attracted to its territory even military officials. Without facing the quilombos ostensibly, the authorities armed escorts that went deep into the woods to hunt deserters. In 1865, one of these escorts, patrolling the vicinity of Vila Maria, imprisoned the criminal Luis Pedroso d'Azevedo, inhabitant of the quilombo Sepotuba.[37] In the next day, the escort was attacked by more than a hundred men armed with guns and knives,

> made up of defectors from several brigades of 1st category National Guards, of criminals and slaves, led by Joaquim José Villas-boas and the Captain of national Guard Antonio Vieira d'Azevedo.[38]

The escort was defeated and humiliated by the quilombolas, who, feeling in superior conditions, made threats to the official forces:

> After being imprisoned and tied up, the very Villas-boas told me that there was more than 200 men to resist any force that was sent from this village [Vila Maria] and could come and take the same headquarter post.³⁹

Some elements can be highlighted in this episode: initially the boldness of the quilombolas, who did not fear provoking the wrath of the escort and, through it, the local authorities. The presence of a National Guard capitan in their troops is also curious: the National Guard was a paramilitary institution set up by the owners to defend their interests. Its rankings were distributed only among the lords of land and slaves and having them was dignifying. These considerations call into question the presence of a captain of this institution between the quilombolas of Sepotuba.

It is interesting to note that this confrontation between the escort and the quilombolas took place in 1865 when a Bolivian invasion was especially feared. Two years later, the provincial police chief informed the president José Vieira Couto Magalhães about the various quilombos in Mato Grosso, which he knew of, among them the Vila Maria (Sepotuba), Diamantino and Rio Manso. He considers that attacking them would not be convenient due to the state of war, but he makes an exception, however, for the quilombo Sepotuba:

> [...] As for the quilombo Vila Maria, I think appropriate to conquer it by its existing force, as it has no way to promply retaliate against the enemy, and it seems to me that its extinction is of great need, to be able to have peace there.⁴⁰

Even this being the opinion of the police chief, the quilombo was not attacked during this period. The president prioritized matters concerning the war, including the opening of other river communication routes to Mato Grosso.⁴¹ Although there are several references to the quilombo Sepotuba, this village has not yet been effectively studied. The data suggests that it was a great and feared quilombo by the authorities and local people. President Herculano Pena himself, when referring to it, contemplated the idea that it was more than a century old. If he were correct, the quilombo would be contemporary to the Portuguese occupation of the region and older than Vila Maria itself.

To survive for so long, with the knowledge of the authorities, it is possible to assume that the quilombolas demonstrated great skill to organize their defense and to structure their economic and political life. They had the ability to build a web of relationships with the inhabitants of the region and that enabled them to obtain information on the actions of the military authorities of the province and, at the same time, to establish forms of exchanges enabling the acquisition of goods that the quilombo did not produce.[42]

Considering a quilombola settlement on the banks of Sepotuba River, near the headwaters of the Paraguay River, at the foot of the plateau of Parecis in the period from the mid eighteenth century and the second half of the nineteenth century, it is also important to point out the relationship with the indigenous population. There are not, to date, data about the exchanges between them and the inhabitants of Sepotuba; however, the indigenous population was dense in the region during this period, leading us to assume such contact took place. The character of these contacts was defined by the life conditions of each group, with the possibility that at some point there may have been alliances and, at others, the clash of interests. Somehow, the quilombolas had the ability to establish these contacts, ensuring the survival of the village.

During the war, the quilombos based near Cuiabá also developed, and among them we should highlight the quilombo of the Manso River. Its existence on the banks of Manso River in the Azul mountain ridge, in the region of fertile land near the capital, close to the parishes of Chapada dos Guimarães and Vila do Rosário, was known to the provincial authorities since 1859.[43] Just as the inhabitants of Sepotuba, the Manso river quilombolas took advantage of the conditions generated by external conflict: assimilated deserters and other fugitives, appropriating themselves of the experiences and weapons that they had. Better armed, they began to take bolder attitudes, attacking people and properties:

> Being recognized that in the Manso River headwaters there is a large *quilombo* where the runaway slaves of this Capital and other neighboring districts continually fled to, and as well as army deserters and criminals, and according to the communication I have just received from the Subdelegate of Rosário's Police relating that these slaves and deserters have the habit of going to this village, from which they guide women to the *quilombo*; I consider necessary to take the necessary steps to conquer it, so as not to have to lament more severe occurences. However, being inconvenient in this situation to distract the service forces from the war, I propose to Your Excellency to increase the detachment of this Vila, raising it to fifty soldiers commanded by an officer [...][44]

As it can be seen, the authorities found themselves in great difficulty: they feared the attacks of the quilombolas and its consequences, but feared also dispersing the military during the term of the external conflict.

In 1868, the quilombolas began to attack the ranches and farms near the parish Chapada dos Guimarães more often, generating insecurity among residents and owners. Because of these attacks, many of them have left their land, moving closer to the capital, assuming they would be better protected.[45] The abandonment of properties meant a heavy burden for the Mato Grosso population: the military occupation of the southern province had interrupted the navigation of the Prata River, jeopardizing importation.[46] A flood of Cuiabá river in 1865 destroyed much of the riverine plantations; two years later the population of the capital and its rural parishes was ravaged by smallpox, hardly recovering themselves from these setbacks. A considerable portion of local resources was committed to the war effort; moreover, the demand for foodstuffs had grown with the expansion of the military detachments. The parish of Chapada dos Guimarães was established in this period as a major producer of provisions, and the escape of part of its population was another difficulty to be faced by the province.

The vicar and some inhabitants of the parish tried in vain to mobilize the authorities to invest against the quilombo. One of these inhabitants, Antônio Bruno Borges, a landowner, managed to co-optate a Black man named Manuel that, upon payment of reasonable amount, pretended to be a quilombola, moving in the quilombo, where he could pass the information to the landowner.[47] Through Manuel, Antonio Bruno Borges learned that the quilombo was composed of four settlements: two close to the shores of the Manso River, a tributary of the Cuiabá River, and two on the river that runs to the north, both close to the ground path to Goiás. The distance between the villages was about fourteen leagues. By that time, the quilombo was inhabited by 293 people:

Men above sixteen years old	260
Women	20
Children	13
Total	293

The command of the quilombo was exercised, for twelve years, by a deserter named Rocha, a native of Pernambuco province. The quilombolas found themselves well armed and took care of their weapons with zeal. In

Cuiabá, they counted with the support of persons responsible for obtaining and passing them information. They also kept some men patrolling the parish of the Guimarães Plateau (*Chapada dos Guimarães*). The quilombolas kept fields of grain, sugarcane and manufactured *rapadura* and coarse fabric. They raised chickens and dogs. They used to get salt in Cuiabá; this activity was suspended during the smallpox epidemic that had ravaged the city last year.[48]

The spy Manuel also informed that one of the favorite amusements of the quilombolas was to meet in the afternoon, when they would tell many stories boasting about themselves. The informant did not know details about the other settlements that made up this quilombo. In his letter to the president of the province, Antonio Bruno Borges revised information about the population, economy, military organization, information system and espionage of the quilombo. He did not explain whether the data Manuel originally gathered was from his own observation or the result of previously formulated questions. Even with accurate data, the then president of the province, Couto Magalhães, considered the attack to the quilombo not feasible.

In 1871, the quilombolas again attacked properties near the town of Rosário, at which they kidnapped two women and murdered Manuel Antonio, who lived with them.[49] The Paraguayan War had ended, and the imperial government sought to deploy its progressive and civilized nation project, therefore making it necessary to eliminate such outbreaks of restlessness. Within this new context, the Provincial Legislature approved a special appropriation to equip a force able to destroy the quilombo. In addition, the Chapada owners participated in the deployment preparation costs, providing the necessary supplies. So, a force consisting of eighty men was assembled, under the command of Captain Luciano Pereira de Sousa, who departed from Cuiabá in August 5, 1871. He had the task of penetrating the area between the headwaters of the Jangada and Roncador rivers, in the shores of Manso River, searching for quilombolas and their settlements.[50]

The expedition roamed the region for three months, in a series of back and forth, without success. They followed some clues derived from information that they subsequently discovered was false, discrediting the detachment before the landowners and the authorities. They always found the settlements abandoned, and did not even have the opportunity to experience a direct confrontation. Very skilled, the quilombolas held a well-assembled information system that allowed them to know in advance the expedition movements, always having the opportunity to anticipate them. On a single occasion, the military force found an opportunity to fight the quilombolas: they surrounded the settlement at night and waited for daybreak to attack. When the day dawned, they saw, with great disappointment, that the quilombo had been evacuated. The quilombolas had retreated hastily, leaving everything behind.

The escape was caused by the firing of a shot made by one of the soldiers that composed the expedition: although explained as an accidental shooting, it was, for the authorities and owners, a suspicion of a deliberate action with the aim of informing the quilombolas about the soldier's presence. Despite the disappointment, the expedition continued its march by the Azul ridge, searching quilombolas on the run. With the time passing by and beginning of the rainy season, the search was becoming increasingly difficult and frustrating. In November, the military could again find the quilombolas: this time, however, the runaway slave André wounded the commander of the expedition, Captain Luciano Pereira de Sousa, killed a soldier from the 21st Infantry Battalion and managed to escape.

After three months of marching, the expedition managed to take to Cuiabá only three free women and four children, and another seven enslaved women with their four children. The enslaved women and their children were arrested in the public jail and, after being recognized, were handed over to their masters by paying the rate of 200$000.[51] Once they got hold of the settlements that made up the quilombo, the expedition members were impressed once again with how bountiful it was:

> [...] the quilombolas fled in haste, their livestock breeding, crops and foodstuffs and even ranches, everything was in perfect condition, and the supply was: corn, rice, beans and cotton, in several storehouses, four fields of manioc and two regular size fields of of corn, four small cane fields, several tobacco plantation (and some portion of this was already being manufactured in the ranches).[52]

Once again, the productive capacity of the quilombolas became evident. This resulted from its form of organization, and its abundance contrasted with the situation in Cuiabá, where the supply was always deficient, causing dissatisfaction and increase in prices, which required the intervention of the authorities, without, however, solving the supply problem of the capital and its neighboring villages.

Not all the effort made was sufficient to eliminate the quilombo Rio Manso. In its annual report, the president of the province considered, however, that the idea that the settlement was invincible was not valid. The story of the quilombo Rio Manso has some interesting aspects that deserve to be emphasized. Here, soldiers acted in solidarity to the quilombolas, against the interests of the military force they represented and a black (perhaps others) was recruited by an owner possibly engaged in an attempt to enforce an individual project. The population of the quilombos of Mato Grosso, during the nineteenth century, had heterogeneious characteristics. Both quilombos of Sepotuba and Rio Manso, besides runaway slaves, housed other marginalized individuals—deserters and criminals. This plurality did not compromise the establishment of solidarity and organization of production. In the case of Sepotuba, it is important to remember the action of the quilombolas to rescue an imprisoned comrade. And, considering Rio Manso, the abundance of its production and the ability to avoid confrontation with the persecutors to attest the integration of the group.

The study of these quilombos also make evident the ability of its inhabitants to take advantage of the difficulties faced by the population of the province and the competence in acquiring information through a network of contacts in the region. This protected them from the punitive expeditions. In the case of the smallpox epidemic, for example, the virus reached Cuiabá and quickly spread throughout the rural districts. In the urban area, half of the population perished. Informed about the spread of disease, the quilombolas suspended its contacts with the capital.

The act of escaping has always been one of the mechanisms used by slaves against oppression. In Mato Grosso, as in other American regions, runaway slaves organized politically and economically structured communities. Communities that at times lasted over time despite the insecurity, since they always lived under the threat of external attacks. These settlements shared some common features, such as organizational capacity, rigidity of the military organization, the abundance of food. They also displayed the ethnic heterogeneity of its members. They were communities of men and women who fought for their freedom. Many died in this fight, succumbing under enemy weapons. Others, even if defeated, did not accept submission.

Quilombos are the result of everyday action of men and women whose names history almost never registered, but that due to their daily action made possible the existence of these communities, small clusters of settlement, where the rigid political and military hierarchy and the rigorous discipline coexisted with group solidarity.

11

THE QUILOMBOS OF GOLD IN THE CAPTAINCY OF GOIÁS

MARY KARASCH

The official history of the *quilombos* of Goiás may begin with a document of 1727 that, according to Gilka Salles, detailed the threat of punishment with whippings for "Africans who in flight took shelter together with other inhabitants and threatened with a fine those who did not denounce their flight."[1] It is unlikely, however, that the 1720s mark the beginning of the quilombo phenomenon in Goiás because indigenous slaves had already fled there in the seventeenth century, and we believe that African fugitives from Maranhão, Bahia, and Pernambuco had also made their way through the *sertão* (backlands) to the north and northeast of Goiás. The quilombos that can be traced through historical documents and local traditions date, in great part, from the eighteenth century, although some continued to exist into the nineteenth century, and a few remained isolated until the twentieth century. This essay, therefore, will largely concern those quilombos that can be identified for the eighteenth century, using these types of records. A definitive history of the quilombos of the captaincy of Goiás remains to be researched through a combination of the disciplines of anthropology, archaeology, and oral history; but what is suggestive from this brief survey is that the quilombo phenomenon was significant to the development of autonomous black communities in Goiás, who supported themselves by mining gold and raising foodstuffs.[2]

Few documents reveal much about the internal structure or economy of the quilombos. What is known is that they were autonomous communities with similarities to other maroon societies in the Americas but with one important difference—i.e., the role of gold mining in the formation and duration of the communities of fugitive slaves in Goiás. Most *quilombolas* of the eighteenth century were fugitive gold miners, and they continued to practice their craft while hiding in remote mountains. We suspect that they exchanged their gold for commodities needed in their hideouts, such as arms, ammunition, *cachaça* (rum), and textiles. Perhaps they also traded with the racially mixed contraband traders, accused by the Portuguese of smuggling gold to Bahia[3] For Goiás, however, we can document that these fugitive miners exchanged the gold they discovered for letters of liberty.[4] Hence, their search for the gold needed to buy their freedom led some of them to discover important mining veins that, afterward, the Luso-Brazilians appropriated for themselves. Thus, the quilombolas contributed to the discovery and exploration of the mineral wealth of the captaincy of Goiás. They also lived by hunting, fishing, and cultivating small plots of land. Although some were involved in raiding, others cared for cattle and processed dried beef. They traded with their neighbors, warred on the local Indian populations—frequently to capture their women—and formed various relationships with the free population of color on the frontier. At this stage in research, we believe that they came to play an important role in the formation of the free black rural communities in the contemporary states of Goiás and Tocantins.

The captaincy of Goiás was an ideal locale for quilombos. Remote from Portuguese administrative centers on the coast, the captaincy was distant from the colonial forces responsible for the destruction of quilombos. The capital of Vila Boa, now the City of Goiás, was months of travel from Salvador or Rio de Janeiro. The Portuguese officers and soldiers who were sent to garrison Vila Boa or the gold checkpoints (*registros*) were few in number for that vast captaincy. In the 1770s and 1780s, the Portuguese employed few of their officers and men in Goiás, and the majority were stationed in the registros in 1772.[5] As the correspondence of the governors reveals, most Portuguese governors were more preoccupied with the Indian wars and gold contraband than with quilombos. In fact, they specifically delegated the duty of quilombo discovery and repression to the militia regiments, including the black regiments, the Henriques. In contrast to the cities of Salvador and Rio de Janeiro, where troop strength and/or other forms of social control were numerous, Goiás was undeveloped. Comparatively speaking, the fugitive slaves of Goiás would not have to confront large, well-trained colonial armies as did the maroon communities of Suriname and Jamaica.

A second advantage the captaincy offered for quilombos in the eighteenth century was that of a sparse population, especially of whites. After all, slave revolts and quilombos usually occur with greater frequency when slaves, especially African slaves, outnumber slaveholders. The census of 1779 for Goiás clarifies that blacks formed, depending on locality, 45 to 80 percent of the population. In the mining towns, such as Crixás, Pilar, Tocantins, and Arraias, where quilombos were especially troublesome to the Portuguese, 70 percent or more of the population would be defined as "black" (see Table 1).

Table 1. The Population of the Captaincy of Goiás in 1779

Julgados	Total	Brancos	Pardos	Pretos	% Pretos
Vila Boa	6954	1460	1003	4491	64,6
Anta	2668	602	689	1377	51,6
Meia Ponte	7885	1809	1581	4495	57,0
Santa Luzia	3384	490	717	2177	64,3
Santa Cruz	1534	562	268	704	45,9
Crixá	2814	219	348	2247	79,9
Pilar	5156	576	930	3650	70,8
Trahiras	5253	679	1398	3176	60,5
Tocantins	4303	276	985	3042	70,7
São Félix	3750	387	682	2681	71,5
Cavalcante	1284	142	168	974	75,9
Natividade	3191	555	656	1980	62,1
Carmo	1171	84	202	885	75,6
Arrayas	1082	156	164	762	70,4
Barra da Palma	1486	530	240	716	48,2
São Domingos	618	118	219	281	45,5
Pontal	890	87	150	653	73,4
Paraná de Cima	1066	198	283	585	54,9

Fonte: IHGB, Arq. 1.2.7, Estatística, "Ofício de Luiz da Cunha Menezes a Martinho de Mello e Castro, remetendo o mapa da população da capitania de Goiáz, com distinção de classes". Vila Boa, 8 de julho de 1780, f. 246.

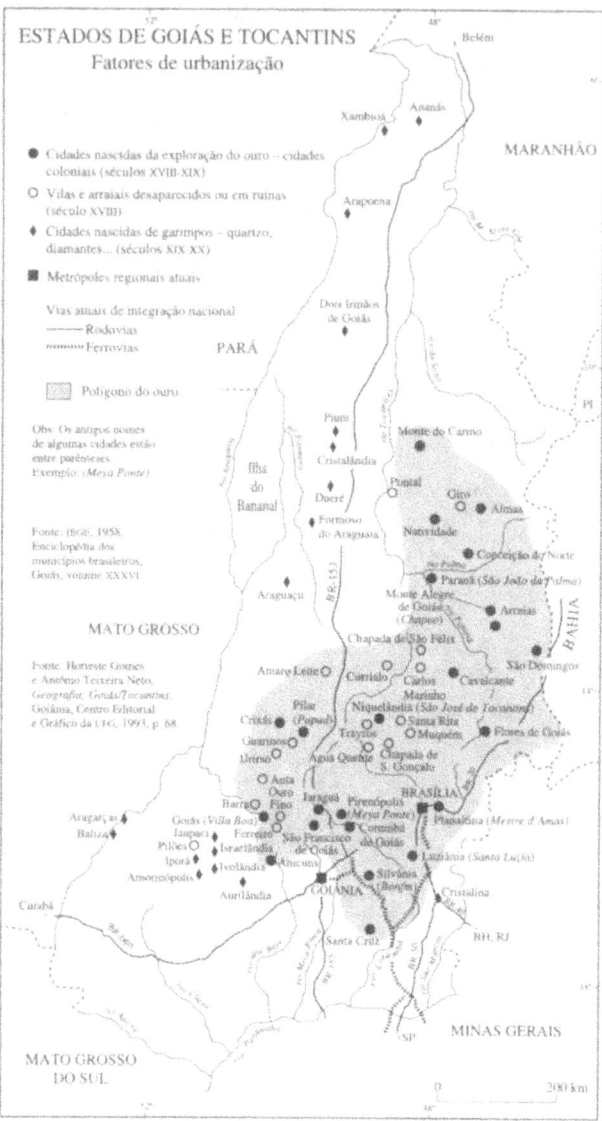

The State of Goiás and Tocantis.

Furthermore, subsequent censuses, which distinguish between enslaved and free blacks, reveal that the majority of blacks were male slaves. In the eighteenth century, male Africans were commonly imported into Goiás to labor on the gold mines of Goiás, traveling there via convoys from Salvador and Rio de Janeiro. By the early nineteenth century, Africans were usually divided into two great "nations," Mina and Angola; but more specific ethnic identities survive in late eighteenth- and early nineteenth-century documents. Hence, the Mina often included the Yoruba (Nagô) and populations from what is now Ghana, such as the Asante. Angolans included the BaKongo and populations of southern Angola, generally termed the Benguelas.[6]

The second major group of fugitives in Goiás were the indigenous nations, who were enslaved as war captives and who escaped at the first opportunity. Among the Indians who fled Paulista bandeiras were the Tupi-speaking Carijós, who sought refuge along the Tocantins River in the 1720s and became implacable enemies of the settlers and their slaves. Known as Canoeiros, they refused to be pacified and settled in villages because of their fear of re-enslavement.[7] Other nations who appear as war captives include the Kayapó, Xavante, and Krahô. When these captives escaped, however, they usually rejoined their own peoples and did not form separate autonomous groups. Except for the Canoeiro Indians, the documents record that the majority of those living in quilombos in Goiás were defined as "blacks."

Black men rather than black women had more opportunity to flee because of the nature of the work that they performed. While women and children were closely supervised in settler households and forced to live with their masters as concubines and domestic servants, or to raise food crops on *fazendas*, the men were led to isolated mining camps and cattle ranches or put to work on large sugar plantations. Only one or two white men were there to control each gang of new Africans at the mines, and some of the latter were permitted to carry weapons to defend the miners from Indian attacks. Given the lack of a great number of armed supervisors in more distant mines, the nature of mining slavery facilitated flight and the formation of quilombos. Every mining town in Goiás, it is said, lived "in the shadow of the quilombos." Still other African men labored on large sugar plantations of 200 to 300 slaves.[8] Maltreatment and brutality in the mines or on the plantations often led the Africans to revolt and, if successful, to form quilombos in the nearby hills and mountains.

The final factor favoring the formation of quilombos is the type of terrain of the states of Goiás and Tocantins.[9] While many regions of provided ideal refuges to fugitives, the captaincy of Goiás must rank among the best for this end due to the inaccessibility of its natural hideouts. The captaincy possessed ecosystems of the same type that protected fugitive slaves throughout the Americas. Flight via canoe or raft was facilitated by three great rivers—the Araguaia in the West, the Tocantins in the east, and the Paranaíba in the south—linked with numerous tributaries. "The first non-Indians to navigate the entire course of the Tocantins" were three fugitive blacks from the mines of Goiás in 1723.[10] Fugitives also found refuge on the islands and swamps formed by the rivers or fled west of the Araguaia River, then the boundary between Goiás and Mato Grosso. Along the Mortes River, which was far from Vila Boa, they found freedom. From Mato Grosso a few fugitives even crossed over into the Spanish colonies.[11]

Other fugitives who were laboring in mining camps fled on foot into the mountains and tablelands. The Pireneus Mountains behind Meia Ponte (now Pirenópolis), the Serra Dourada near Vila Boa, and the *chapadas* (tablelands) near Arraias offered limitless possibilities for hideouts. Although the open *cerrados* (savannas) made escape more difficult, if fugitives could reach the gallery forests and groves of buriti palms along small creeks, they could follow them to escape the persecution of the bush captains. In other areas, vast forests still existed in the eighteenth century, especially in the north between the Araguaia and Tocantins rivers, and quilombolas were frequently located in these forests, particularly those that bordered fazendas or plantations. Thus, various locales were available—dense forests, unexplored mountains, thorny savannas, mosquito-infested swamps, hidden islands, innumerable rivers—at a great distance from whites where quilombos could be raised and provide a life of liberty for slaves.

Although we can understand reasons why the formation of quilombos was possible in Goiás, their exact number is unknown. The common generalization that appears in eighteenth-century sources is that they were "numerous." One reason for their great number is that most were only small groups of runaways from the mines. They were more similar in size to small bands of hunters and gatherers or modern *garimpeiros* (gold prospectors). Rarely did they form large towns headed by a leader or king, where they could live as sedentary agriculturalists. Because of the danger of being discovered, the majority could not remain in a fixed place. Then, when the gold gave out, the fertility of the soil declined, or there were no more animals to hunt, they had to move on to another location for survival. Their dwellings were usually temporary in nature, often similar to those of the Indians of the region. Sometimes the group of slave prospectors did not remain in a quilombo for a long time because they discovered gold, negotiated a return to their owners, and bought their freedom from them. Thus, the quilombos of Goiás were often transitory institutions without permanence in place or time.

Slaves ran away to quilombos for many reasons. Although we do not have the testimony of the quilombolas, the colonial authorities who were responsible for resolving the problem of the constant flights of enslaved Africans and Indians usually accused their masters of maltreatment. In the 1750s, various officials of the Crown blamed the property owners who did not feed or clothe them adequately and subjected them to "barbarous punishments."[12] As in most slave societies, the excessive and unhealthy conditions of work—especially work in fever-ridden rivers—maltreatment and unjust punishments were factors that led the slaves of Goiás to flee their owners. On the other hand, the traditions of the mining town reveal that its mines were discovered by "fugitive blacks who wished to buy their freedom."[13] In other words, enslaved Africans also abandoned their masters with the objective of finding the gold with which they could buy their freedom. They apparently formed small groups of prospectors who applied their mining skills in locating new veins of gold. Once they found the gold—and perhaps freed for their discovery—the Portuguese quickly invaded their settlement and assumed the control of the mines.

The Geography of Quilombos

Two historians of Goiás, Luiz Palacin and Gilka V. F. de Salles, succeeded in identifying the locations of the following eighteenth-century quilombos: Três Barras with 60 blacks, who insulted and caused deaths of passing travelers; and those of Tocantins, Arraias, Meia Ponte, Crixás, and Paracatu (now in Minas Gerais). With reference to the towns of São Félix and Natividade, the Captain-General Dom Marcos de Noronha (1749–1755) complained about the great number of indigenous people who had fled their *aldeias* (villages) and formed quilombos. His fear, and that of other colonial governors, was that the quilombolas would raid the gold convoys or interrupt the production of gold by robbing mule teams and miners. The fear of Noronha may have been due to the presence of quilombos near the capital of Vila Boa. On the hill of São Gonçalo near the city, existed "various huts of quilombolas," who attacked and stole animals from neighboring fazendas and had small farms.[14]

However, besides the quilombos of this basic list there were many others. In order to organize this discussion better, we are going to follow the colonial division of the captaincy of Goiás into two *comarcas* (judicial districts): the comarca of the north (the state of Tocantins) and the comarca of the south (the state of Goiás).[15] A third area for discussion are the quilombos of the disputed borderlands of Minas Gerais and Mato Grosso to the south and west of Goiás, which were then subject to the governor of Goiás, who was responsible for the repression of those quilombos.

The most northern quilombo, with possible links with fugitives from the mining towns of the Tocantins region, was located in Pederneiras, north of Alcobaça and the modern city of Marabá. When the anthropologist Curt Nimuendajú studied the Apinajé in the 1930s, he was informed that they had once raided the quilombolas of Pederneiras in the late eighteenth century with the objective of obtaining iron tools. An eighteenth-century document refers to attacks on fugitive slaves made by the "Gentiles" of the region of the Tocantins River. When the Indians [the Apinajé?] captured them, they cut off their heads, impaling them on sticks and displaying them along the riverbanks. To prevent their attacks, forts were established in Alcobaça, in 1780, and the Arapary rapids, in 1791. Nonetheless, the Apinajé continued to attack Pederneiras, which was then abandoned. Thus ended the history of a settlement that had once been the site of "a large *mocambo* of fugitive slaves ruled by a woman."[16] Other local traditions record the presence of at least one quilombo in the region of the Parrot's Beak between the Araguaia and Tocantins rivers—one can imagine that the slaves hid in the dense forests of that region—and along the Sono River, where the quilombo acquired the name of Mumbuca, an indigenous name for a species of bee.[17]

To the east of the was the former Jesuit mission of Duro. When the Jesuits were forcibly expelled and returned in chains to Rio de Janeiro, the Xacriaba (Sacriaba) and the Akroa (Central Gê populations) rose in revolt. According to José dos Santos Pereira, during the pacification of the Xacriaba and Akroa near São Félix, in 1761, 60 Indians were returned to the garrison, perhaps against their will. These 60 Indians were those that "the [Jesuit] fathers had loaned to a certain man to go give in a quilombo of fugitive blacks, which in reality he did with a political warning." The Indians had fled to the forest because they believed that an expedition led by Lieutenant Colonel Venceslão Gomes da Silva "brought an order to strangle them." Perhaps this brief reference point to the existence of links between the Jesuits, indigenous people, and quilombolas near São Félix or Duro. A later criticism directed at the Jesuits for permitting "four *crioulas*" of the town of Pontal to carry the "Sacrament on a bier" suggests that the rebellious Jesuits (Manoel da Silva and Pedro Tedalde) may have had some positive relations with the blacks of the region—and perhaps with quilombolas.[18]

Vila Boa viewed from the north (1751).

Vila Boa viewed from the south (1751).

To the east of São Félix and south of Duro is one of the richest mining regions of the captaincy, where 10,000 miners once labored between 1731 and 1739. That was the Chapada dos Negros, near the modern town of Arraias. There are now only large stone structures—the last vestiges of "a great settlement." Local tradition refers to "a revolt between whites and blacks." According to Rosolinda Batista de Abreu Cordeiro, "the black gave poof of his vocation for liberty: he rebelled against bad treatments and considered himself free." After the revolt, the whites moved to a new site, which became the town of Arraias in 1739–1740. Elsewhere, she refers to the quilombos of the Chapada dos Negros.[19] Were these quilombos founded by the blacks who revolted? Or, did they pre-exist the 1731 founding of the town of the Chapada dos Negros? Only future archaeology in the Chapada may answer these questions.

In the comarca of the north, possibly the principal site of quilombos was the valley and nearby mountains, such as the Serra do Mocambo. After complaining that quilombos were "one of the principal destructions of this captaincy," Governor Manuel de Mello bragged about the success of one of the bandeiras that he had sent to the Paraná. This bandeira had destroyed a quilombo of "more than 200 fugitive blacks that already had their bananas and fields." The king of the quilombolas had fought "valorously until he had lost his life," but the queen was captured along with other black women. Unlike the other Goiano quilombos, which were composed only of adult men, this quilombo had children living therein.[20] This bandeira, however, did not succeed in eradicating all quilombos of the region. Since the comarca of the north was one of the richest mining areas with thousands of African miners employed there in the eighteenth century,[21] we believe that quilombos continued to flourish in the mountainous areas of the principal mining towns of São Félix, Natividade, Arraias, and Cavalcante. Since the flows through this region, it may have formed a natural highway that facilitated the movement of fleeing slaves. And, as we now know, this inhospitable region continues to shelter 2,000 to 4,000 blacks, the probable descendants of those quilombolas.

Another important region for quilombos was north of the southern comarca near the mining towns of Pilar, São José de Tocantins, and Muquém, today a place of pilgrimage. In Pilar and Muquém bandeiras destroyed quilombos, seized their inhabitants, and began Luso-Brazilian settlements. In 1741, João Godoi Pinto Silveira found the Quilombo do Papuão and "the mines of Papuá, occupied by fugitive blacks." In its place, he established a settlement dedicated to Nossa Senhora do Pilar, which soon became the prosperous mining town of Pilar. About fifteen years later, quilombos must have continued to exist around Pilar since, in 1755, quilombolas conspired with slaves to have a revolt take place there on the occasion of the Feast of the Holy Spirit. The conspirators had obtained gunpowder and lead (*chumbo*) and planned an attack on the local church. Informed of their objectives, the authorities suspended the "feast day and repressed the uprising."[22]

The next mining town, São José do (Niquelândia after 1944), was founded in 1735. While conducting research on the Canoeiro, Dulce Madalena Rios Pedroso collected written and oral traditions on a quilombo near São José. To the southeast, "was found an agglomeration of mountains, preferred locations of the quilombolas and of the autonomous Indians because they were of difficult access." In this region, she reports, exists a locale called "Boca da Mata" (Mouth of the Forest)," where, in 1879, local settlers requested the construction of a small fort to protect travelers from indigenous people and "quilombolas that were established in the forests of the Acaba-vida." Pedroso further confirms the existence of this quilombo in an interview she did with a rancher of Niquelândia, who affirmed that

> The mountains form a space with fertile lands where the river Acaba-vida runs, which has plenty of fish and which drains into the Bagagem River. In its wanderings by the materials of the Acada-vida are found vestiges of neo-Brazilian occuptation: old pillars, stone foundation, furnace, two enormous jatobazeiro trees, etc[23]

Her informant also noted that the forests of the Acaba-vida were formerly "good for hunting." Thus, this region had once sheltered a quilombo that had been abandoned by its inhabitants. Since the quilombolas had lived near the territory of the Avá-Canoeiro, Pedroso suggests that these two persecuted groups might have developed contacts with each other that resulted in miscegenation because "there are strong evidences of occasional crossing among groups of Avá-Canoeiro and blacks in specific localities of the Goiano territory."[24]

One of the best insights we have into the way of life of quilombolas in Goiás in the eighteenth century comes from the local traditions of the pilgrimage town of Muquém, a religious center famous for its pilgrimage, every August 15, of Nossa Senhora da Abadia. According to José Chaves, "there was there in Muquém a quilombo of fugitive slaves, celebrated and feared, that was established some eight leagues to the east of São José de Tocantins, until where the blacks conducted their raids." On 20 December, perhaps in 1740, the day of St. Thomas, a company of free men led by a "captain of assault" reached a mountainous region with "rocks of marble" and "caves." From the height of the rocks, they saw the huts of the blacks at the edge of a forest. Before they attacked the quilombo, they saw the blacks "set fire to some piles of firewood." They then danced and sang around the fire to the "drumbeats of the drums." The attackers waited until the end of the feast, that included food—"meat moqueada, potatoes and manioc"—and aguardente (rum). After everyone had retired to their casebres and gone to sleep, the captain of assault led his men down the mountain and attacked the sleeping quilombolas. Captured, they were all returned to their former masters. In gratitude for the victory—and for the gold they found in abundance there—the captain of assault built a church in honor of St. Thomas, and the settlement was named São Tomé do Muquém. Afterward, an image of Nossa Senhora da Abadia was imported from Portugal and placed in the church. The image soon became the object of veneration to the people of the sertão, including the descendants of quilombolas in northeastern Goiás who have an image of Nossa Senhora da Abadia in one of their chapels.[25]

To the west of Pilar were the two mining towns of Tesouras and Crixás. In 1757, a bush captain located the mines of the town of Tesouras that were under the control of "fugitive captives in the creek of the Quilombo in which area they mined for some time." Apparently, he had been sent to destroy the quilombo because they were causing "as much harm as the Kayapó people in the open country." Crixás was one of the richest mining towns in the eighteenth century, and many slaves worked in its mines. For that reason, it figures prominently in the lists of towns threatened by quilombos.[26] Thus far, little is known about quilombos near that mining town.

Across the Araguaia River in eastern Mato Grosso is the Mortes River, an area reputed to have sheltered quilombolas in the eighteenth century. However, it was often confused with the comarca of Rio das Mortes in Minas Gerais. Governors of Goiás refer to quilombos of the Mortes River, which could indicate locations as much in Mato Grosso, modern Minas Gerais, as in the captaincy of Goiás. According to Gilka V. F. de Salles, "the first great quilombo distinguished [in Goiás] was situated near the in 1746, in the vast open country and mountains that separate Minas from the Goiazes." In that region, more than 600 fugitives lived in a great quilombo. Ruled by a king and a queen, they possessed "small defensive forts and attack platoons." When they attacked fazendas, they captured slaves and took them back to the quilombo. Because of the grave threat this quilombo posed to the mines of Minas Gerais, the Captain-General Gomes Freire de Andrada organized an expedition funded by the inhabitants of Minas Gerais, who raised 3,500 oitavas of gold to cover expenses. This quilombo was "decimated by Bartolomeu Bueno do Prado in 1751."[27] Would this have been the famous quilombo dos Ambrósio that was destroyed by the expedition of 300 men led by Antônio Joáo de Oliveira?[28]

According to legend, the Jesuits had purchased the black Ambrósio in the Valongo slave market in Rio de Janeiro, and brought him to the mission of Tengotengo in the Triângulo Mineiro. There they gave him and his wife Cândida their freedom and left him in charge of Tengotengo, which grew to "more than a thousand" inhabitants. By 1746, Gomes Freire de

Andrada referred to this settlement as a quilombo that sent out "parties of twenty to thirty blacks that executed robberies and very cruel deaths." According to the Goiano historian, José Martins Pereira de Alencastre, "the Africans," who were attacked "by the force that marched against them, after many hours (seven hours) of fire from place to place, with the death of the chief Ambrósio...were dispersed in groups through the sertão, and, afterward reunited to other small quilombos, began to trouble more seriously the convoys and inhabitants of the neighboring vicinity." What that tradition suggests is that the survivors escaped into the sertão of the region between the Grande and Paranaíba rivers, re-grouped in smaller quilombos, and went on the offensive (in revenge raids?) against local settlers. Because of their renewed threat to the mines, José Antônio Freire de Andrade then "ordered many parties of troops to march against them, captained by the frontiersmen Buenos, relatives of Bartolomeu Bueno, who resided in the sertão...between the Parnaíba, Velhas River, and Grande River."[29] Such descriptions place the quilombo do Ambrósio in the region claimed by the governors of Goiás in the eighteenth century.

Another reference to the quilombos of the comarca of the reveals that there was one there about 1767 when the authorities captured "some blacks" and punished them. It was then ruled by a king, "a feared black named the Bateeiro," which was probably an allusion to his work with the *bateia* in mineral prospecting. The king Bateeiro, however, governed "by the mode of a Republic," according to a document of the period that did not clarify much about the political structure of the group. Finally, a quilombo in Mato Grosso, whose location is uncertain, is the quilombo of Carlota, perhaps ruled by a woman, which lasted from at least 1770 to 1795. The quilombolas had survived by raising foodstuffs and raiding the local indigenous groups for women, a subject that we will return to later.[30]

In the south of Goiás to the north of the Paranaíba River were still other quilombos. The inhabitants of the town of the Mesquita, a black community near Santa Luzia, descend from Africans originally from Ghana. Perhaps they were related to the fugitives that "infested the roads of the town of (modern Silvânia), extending their exploits to the roads in the direction of Minas Gerais, in the proximities of Santa Luzia and Santa Cruz."[31] A fugitive black discovered the mines of the hill of Clemente in in 1772. We suspect that the south of the captaincy, extending all the way to the Grande River, was attractive to fugitives because this region was far from both the Portuguese military forces of Vila Boa and those of Vila Rica (Ouro Preto).

Possibly, the first reference to quilombos in the region between Goiás and Minas Gerais occurs with reference to a bandeira of 1733, which was sent with the mission "to repel the aggression of the Indians and to destroy the great number of quilombos which had been formed by fugitive slaves from the mines." The bandeira, "under the command of Urbano do Couto, crossed the São Francisco River and went until the São Marcos River."[32] The São Marcos River is in southeastern Goiás, and part of the river is on the modern border between Goiás and Minas Gerais. In the eighteenth century, the governors of Goiás frequently ordered bandeiras into the region across the Paranaíba River—another celebrated refuge of quilombolas—where they attacked quilombos in the region of the Araguari River or Velhas, which is a tributary of the Paranaíba, and ranged to Paracatu, where quilombos were also numerous.[33] To the east of the Velhas River is the Abaeté River, whose headwaters are not far from the Paranaíba River. Perhaps that was the location of the "quilombo of the cabaceiras of the Abaité."[34] In the far south of the captaincy was the Grande River, the former boundary between Goiás and Minas Gerais until Desemboque and Araxá became part of Minas. On one of its islands, the Kayapó nation discovered:

> A great city of fugitive blacks, and there established since time immemorial. Of this great city there was not until then the most superficial notice, and only it is presumed that those blacks fled from Minas Gerais, and that navigating on the Grande River were established on that island in which they have propagated with peace because of the great distance in which they are...[35]

The Forces of Repression

Additional information on the quilombo phenomenon in Goiás can also be found in a study of the military and indigenous forces that sought to destroy them and the difficulties that the quilombolas faced. The long survival of the quilombos must be weighed against the forces of destruction to appreciate the Afro-Brazilian accomplishment of constructing autonomous communities under such conditions. The quilombolas who preserved their autonomy, escaping detection and destruction, did so in face of great obstacles.

First, the very ecosystems that shielded them from discovery posed their own challenges. In the "time of the waters," it rained "deluges" and flooded the landscape creating great swamps, which led to plagues of mosquitoes. Malaria was a particularly grave problem during the rainy season from about October to March or April. The one advantage that the time of the waters offered quilombolas, however, was that flooded and muddy roads tended to keep the bandeiras in the towns until the rains abated. The coming of the dry season then marked the renewal of the slave-hunting bandeiras who roamed Goiás seeking new captives among the indigenous people and quilombolas. Those who tried to escape the bandeiras in the dry season often lacked water and suffered from thirst. Wherever they found refuge, they also had to deal with an "infinity of insects," such as black bees, *borrachudos* (black flies), large ticks, spiders, and *bichos-de-pé*, who tormented visitors to the rivers, forests, and savannas of Goiás. Jaguars and poisonous snakes also posed special dangers.[36]

It was the human predators, however, who represented the greatest threat to the quilombolas. The bandeiras, bush captains, and indigenous nations frequently attacked them, burning their homes and fields and forcibly returning them to enslavement. The bandeiras were of two types: those organized by the governor of the captaincy of Goiás or a neighboring captaincy and those formed by local masters who tried to re-capture their fugitive slaves or acquire new captives. Since the latter type of bandeira often operated without official sanction, it is more difficult to trace their activities in the documents. Of the many expeditions of both types, the one that may have killed the most quilombolas was that of Bartolomeu Bueno de Prado, who fought against the quilombos on the road between Goiás and São Paulo. He returned to São Paulo with his trophies—allegedly 3,900 pairs of ears, as the sources allege.[37] The majority of bandeiras, however, captured quilombolas who numbered less than a few hundreds. The sources thus far consulted suggest that although the quilombos of Goiás were numerous, the quilombolas were not, or the bandeiras failed to capture all the inhabitants of the larger quilombos. It is evident from the sources consulted that the bandeiras repeatedly attacked the same places over different periods as if the bandeiras attacked whenever they could, but without destroying the quilombos completely.

One of the most detailed histories of a bandeira leader who served over ten years in Goiás comes from the petition for a *mercê*. The inhabitants of the *cabaceiras* of the Rio das Velhas, who wrote on his behalf in 1777, praised José Rodrigues Freire for his charitable acts, such as sending food to feed the indigenous peoples of the mission of Santa Anna and hiring expert women to teach the indigenous girls how to sew and spin. The explanation for the origin of the gold that he used for this is obvious from his other activities as a bandeira leader. While seeking gold and quilombolas, Freire affirmed he had "the felicity of finding gold, and capturing 100 blacks." Further information from his request reveals that he had a long experience as a frontiersman and bandeira leader, since he had fought in the war against the Seven Peoples of the Missions in Uruguay in 1756. By 1765, he was serving in Goiás and participated in the pacification of the Xavante in 1775. His ten years of fighting the indigenous people of Goiás had thus prepared him to lead expeditions against the quilombolas.[38]

In addition to the bandeira leaders who hunted quilombolas, the governors of the captaincy also appointed *capitães do mato* (bush captains). In 1750 the governor of Goiás instructed the sergeant-major of Meia Ponte to form "a company of 18 or 20 bush captains" headed by a corporal. They were to patrol all the roads and sertões to locate "fugitive blacks" and return them to the jail. At this time, the bush captain received a salary of one *vintem* of gold per day and another one for each slave handed over to his owner. In order to combat a quilombo near Arraias, its inhabitants paid four *vintens* for each slave in 1749. If the bush captain killed or wounded "captive blacks," Governor José de Almeida exempted him from criminal prosecution in order to "fight the great increase of quilombos" in 1773.[39] Thus, quilombolas faced bounty-hunters who sought to make their fortunes in gold by capturing as many fugitives, living or dead, as possible. Although we have few specific descriptions of those who served as bush captains, one comes from an early nineteenth-century source. Captain Antônio Moreira da Silva was a "very dark mulatto," who had served as a bush captain since 1807. In robust health but of advanced age, he lived in a state appropriate to a bush captain. He had been the director of numerous war expeditions and had accomplished the reduction of the indigenous people of Puarecamecrã in 1815 with whose Captain Côcrit he had developed "a sincere friendship."[40]

The third group involved in quilombo destruction was the autonomous indigenous people of Goiás. Eighteenth-century sources often suggest that they destroyed more quilombos than the Luso-Brazilian bandeiras. Two nations who frequently attacked and destroyed quilombos were the Xavante and Kayapó. When the Xavante lived to the east of the Tocantins River, they routinely raided local fazendas, killing settlers and their black slaves. Whenever they came across blacks living in quilombos, they also attacked and killed them. In the early eighteenth century, they identified blacks as enemies, whether enslaved or free. This state of war lasted until the 1760s, when the Xavante embarked on a new strategy of encouraging fugitive blacks to take refuge with them and marry Xavante women.[41] This change in tactics worried the Portuguese officials in Vila Boa because they feared that slave miners would revolt and flee to the Xavante for protection, yet in reality few blacks joined them. When the Xavante were pacified and settled in the Christian mission of Carretão in 1788, only fourteen non-Xavante were living among them, including black captives and *libertos* (freed persons).[42] It is uncertain when the Xavante resumed their wars against quilombolas; but after they had migrated west of the Araguaia River, they fought against settlers and slaves in Mato Grosso and possibly against the quilombolas of the Mortes River region where the Xavante eventually settled. The Xavante who remained behind in Carretão, however, intermarried with black slaves, and a racially mixed peasant community that was Afro-Xavante in origin continued to farmlands well into the 1880s.[43]

While the Xavante pursued an ambiguous and shifting policy toward black slaves and quilombolas, the Kayapó of the south and west of Goiás consistently warred against settlers, slaves, and quilombolas. The governors of Goiás regularly reported on their attacks against the quilombos of the captaincy. According to them, they seized "many fugitive blacks that they conducted to the towns of the captaincy." It was the Kayapó who found "a great city of fugitive blacks" on an island in the Grande River. Along the Tocantins River, probably in the 1770s, the work of "many nations of barbarous gentiles" was "to kill and wound whites and blacks." When slaves fled from their masters to indigenous territory, some fell into the hands of the "gentiles," who killed and decapitated them.[44]

Indian success at capturing fugitive blacks is suggested by one well documented case in which the slave Joaquim tried to escape from an expedition led by Thomas de Sousa Villa Real, who was exploring the island in the 1790s. The Karajá quickly captured his runaway slave and held him for Villa Real.[45] One suspects that the Karajá expected to receive typical gifts as a reward for their services to Vila Real, since one of the motivations for Indian raids on quilombos was to acquire captives whom they could trade for tools, textiles, and food in the Portuguese settlements. The Portuguese were more than willing to pay the gifts in order to secure the return of fugitives and for the destruction of quilombos.

Another motivation for attacks on blacks was revenge. Indigenous groups also killed quilombolas because of the long history of quilombola abductions of indigenous women. This motivation is suggested by the history of the quilombo of Carlota across the border in Mato Grosso. Composed of escaped mining slaves (from Goiás?), the quilombolas lived at constant war with the indigenous nations in order to steal their women. They must have been successful, in part due to demographic reproduction, because this quilombo lasted for at least twenty years from 1770 to 1795, when Francisco de Mello Pereira e Carceres "found there plantings of corn, potato and yam, pineapples, squash, tobacco and cotton."[46]

The indigenous hostility to the quilombos may also explain why assimilated indigenous people, who lived in missions under religious control, formed an important part of the *pedestres*, a barefooted frontier force, who engaged in anti-quilombo activity.[47] In the eighteenth century, those Indians who served in the pedestres included the Kayapó, Bororo, and Akroá nations, as well as the racially mixed *pardos* and *mestizos*. Apparently, these were skilled frontiersmen, who carried out a variety of tasks for the governors of Goiás, including the location and repression of quilombos. In 1776, bandeiras returned to Vila Boa with "*calhambolas*," who were apparently captured with the help of the indigenous groups in the quilombo of the Cabeceiras do Abaité. In that year, Antônio Pinto de Castro asked Lieutenant Commander Rodrigues Freire to choose people in the missions, probably including the Kayapó of São José de Mossâmedes, since he refers to this mission elsewhere in the document [?], who could serve in a squad, which was to leave in the next dry season. He was also "to interrogate the blacks that they captured if there is gold in that country."[48] As this document suggests, the Portuguese suspected that whereever calhambolas lived they would discover gold; thus, they enlisted the assistance of mission indigenous groups in destroying their quilombo and at the same time appropriating the gold discovered by the fugitive blacks.

It is more difficult to understand why yet another group, blacks, were involved in hunting fugitive slaves and in the destruction of their quilombos. In 1800 Governor Meneses wrote that a regiment of the Henriques, composed of black soldiers, was "very useful for destroying quilombos of blacks, fugitives in them." In the same letter to the Crown, he requested that Portugal provide 600 firearms and twenty barrels of gunpowder, which were indispensable for the militia forces of Goiás. They were needed to help in the frequent

> expeditions organized against the fugitive blacks in Quilombos, having some [where] they consist of a great multitude of them, so fortified, that they cannot assault them due to lack of firearms and of gunpowder, suffering the people frequent hostilities from them, equally of the Gentiles.

What is of particular interest, however, is that the Governor goes on to explain that the "freed blacks" in the regiment of Henriques possessed an "excellent ability to maneuver with light artillery pieces." By 1800, they had been learning that skill for at least fifteen years. According to a petition of Bento José Marques, he affirmed that he had trained them for the first time in Vila Boa in 1785. Thus, official correspondence confirms that the black regiments, then composed of "crioulos and freed blacks," also fought in the wars against quilombos. Their motivation to do so is partially suggested by the census and militia lists of the 1820s that reveal that the officers of the Henriques were small slave owners. As skilled craftsmen, miners, and small farmers, they too had much to lose if their slaves fled to quilombos, as many must have done. When in 1800 Governor Meneses explained the reasons why he nominated for Colonel José Roiz Ferreira de Santo Antônio and for Lieutenant Colonel Domingos Correia Vila Real, both blacks, he noted that they were "well established in Business, and Slavery."[49]

Given the forces arrayed against them from black ex-slaves in the Henriques to indigenous pedestres and autonomous nations, professional slave hunters (bush captains), and large bandeiras, we can understand why so many quilombos were destroyed and their inhabitants returned to their masters. As in other slave societies in the Americas, as well as in coastal Brazil, the penalties imposed on fugitives and quilombolas were severe. A slave who ran away for the first time was exhibited in the streets of the town before being taken before a judge who sentenced him to be "whipped publicly through the streets." Afterward, he was branded with an "F" on his shoulders and thrown in the jail for "a predetermined time." For the second attempt, an ear was cut off; and for the third flight, he was killed. As late as 1800, quilombolas who resisted capture in the julgado of Natividade were killed and their heads cut off and placed on "a pole in the entrance of the town, conforming [to what] is the use, and custom in these Minas, for an example of the other slaves."[50]

Re-enslaved quilombolas who survived the lashes and mutilations were returned to their owners or sold. More closely supervised and punished, they paid a tragic price for having fled and formed quilombos. We suspect but cannot rigorously document that the majority of attempts to form quilombos ended in tragedy—the defeated died, often at indigenous hands, or were returned to slavery. But we can also establish that a fortunate minority succeeded in avoiding repression and re-capture, forming small black communities that have survived to the present in the modern states of Tocantins and Goiás. It is appropriate, therefore, to end this essay with a mention of the descendants of quilombolas, who now live in the Serra da Cahoeira in the *municípios* of Monte Alegre de Goiás and Cavalcante, and along the banks of the Paraná and Das Almas Rivers. About 2,000 blacks now live in the Vão das Almas, Vão dos Moleques, Contendas, and Calunga. José Sebastião Pinheiro, who visited them, reports that they cultivate "the manioc, corn, and rice and have the activities of hunting and fishing." Each year the men of the communities lead files of donkeys and mules to nearby cities to exchange manioc meal and tapioca for coffee, sugar, salt, and textiles. A resident of the Vão de Almas, of 70 years, was interviewed by Pinheiro. Benicio Deltrude Pereira remembered that "he had already heard the 'oldest' tell that the first blacks went there [having] fled from slavery."[51]

If that tradition is accurate, then future historians may be able to write a more complete history of those quilombolas who succeeded in avoiding re-capture. What is clear from the colonial documentation, however, is that the enslaved Africans of the captaincy of Goiás commonly fled, sometimes revolted, and often created quilombos. Communities of fugitive miners existed wherever mining slavery was significant. Although almost always discovered, attacked, and destroyed, quilombos represent a testament to the desire of enslaved Africans to escape from slavery, no matter the difficulties of the geography and climate, the threat of violent death at the hands of bandeirantes, soldiers, and indigenous people with the reputation of being cannibals, or the danger of re-capture and return to slave labor under conditions worse than those before the flight. Conversely, the Portuguese recognized their very real threat to the slave system, or more specifically their lives and properties and the regular delivery of the king's *quinto* (share of gold) to Salvador and Rio de Janeiro. Therefore, they organized and deployed bandeiras to destroy them. Although often ignored in local official historiography, the numerous quilombos of Central Brazil played an important role in the formation of the mining economy and society of the captaincy of Goiás in the eighteenth century.

QUILOMBOS OF RIO DE JANEIRO IN THE NINETEENTH CENTURY

FLÁVIO DOS SANTOS GOMES

This essay is an analysis of the socioeconomic organizations forged by fugitive communities in the Iguaçu region during the nineteenth century. The study of several battles in which authorities planned several strategies to destroy these villages allows for an understanding of how the escaped slaves constituted their communities, creating complex and unique spaces for their struggles. The *quilombos* that we will analyze were not isolated on the margins of the slave system. These quilombos, as others—and contrary to what the historiography has so far indicated—created an underground world that interacted with slavery. Finally, we intend to scrutinize the worlds created by individuals in the quilombos, showing how they ended up gradually changing the lives of those who remained slaves.

A Hydra and its Marshes

The quilombos from the Guanabara Bay area, more specifically from the Iguaçu lowland, were situated on the banks of the Iguaçu and Sarapuí rivers, in the parishes of Nossa Senhora do Pilar and Santo Antônio de Jacutinga. In 1780, this region was composed, basically—not including the dissolutions and subsequent annexations—by the following parishes: Nossa Senhora do Marapicu, Santo Antônio de Jacutinga, São João de Meriti, Nossa Senhora da Piedade de Iguaçu and Nossa Senhora do Pilar de Iguaçu. In the late eighteenth century, the population of the entire region was 13,054 inhabitants, with 7,122 slaves.[1]

Between 1769 and 1779, the economy of the region, according to the Marquis of Lavradio report, was made up of the following: the parish of Pilar de Iguaçu had, in addition to three distilleries, one additional mill, owned by Captain Luciano Gomes Ribeiro. This parish produced approximately forty cases of sugar and seventeen barrels of sugar cane liquor, and had 74 slaves.[2] In Marapicu parish there were four mills, which produce around 152 cases of sugar and 61 barrels of sugar cane liquor, and had almost three hundred slaves. The Jacutinga parish had seven mills; laborers included about 236 slaves (an average of 39 slaves on each property), producing 163 cases of sugar and 77 barrels of sugar cane liquor. The parish of Nossa Senhora da Piedade de Iguaçu, which had only two distilleries with seventy slaves, produced thirty barrels of sugar cane liquor. Finally, the Meriti parish had nine sugar mills, 307 slaves, an average of 34 slaves per mill and 2 distilleries with 23 slaves. The mills produced about 104 cases of sugar and 46 barrels of sugar cane liquor, while the distilleries manufactured seventeen barrels of sugar cane liquor.[3]

Quilombos from the Guanabara Bay—Rio de Janeiro—Nineteenth Century.

The production of food commodities in the region was also strong. According to statistics provided by the Marquis of Lavradio in the late eighteenth century, this area of the Guanabara Bay had considerable agricultural production, focused on supplying the domestic market (see Table 1).

Table 1: Annual Production of Food in Iguaçu Region—1778 (in bushels)

Parishes	Flour	Corn	Beans	Rice	Total
Marapicu	150	300	800	1500	2750

Parishes	Flour	Corn	Beans	Rice	Total
Jacutinga	25000	1000	1000	10000	37000
Meriti	1000	240	2300	650	4190
Iguaçu	10000	400	400	10000	20800
Pilar	16260	56	177	3470	19963
Total	52410	1996	4677	25620	84703

Source: "Marquez of Lavradio Ratio." In: RIHGB, volume LXXVI (79), pp. 320–4.

Considering the number of slaves in the sugar mills and the total number per parish in the late eighteenth century, it is concluded that only about 20 percent of the slave mass was employed in the cultivation of sugar cane. This sugar production was enough to supply both the external and the internal markets.[4] Most of the slaves were probably involved in harvesting food crops, gathering lumber, and manufacturing bricks and tiles for the supply of the region as well as the Court and neighboring parishes.[5] We can cite, as an example, the Conceição mill, located in the parish of Santo Antônio de Jacutinga (fourteen slaves), which produced only three boxes of sugar and a half barrel of sugar cane liquor, but whose "main crop was cassava, and subsidiary crop was the sugar cane."[6]

Due to its geographical location, crossed by numerous rivers, this region had tremendous ease of distribution for its production. In the São João de Meriti parish, "for its trade and service of farms and mills," there were fourteen ports between the Meriti river, also called São João, and the Sarapuí river. The Nossa Senhora da Piedade de Iguaçu parish distributed its production through two ports, while the Nossa Senhora do Pilar de Iguaçu parish made its trade with eighteen boats and one barge distributed between nine ports. The parish of Santo Antônio de Jacutinga distributed their products through eight ports, four located on the Iguaçu river and the rest on the Sarapuí river.[7]

Most of these ports were controlled by farmers and local traders—by barges and boats operated by slaves—that ran much of the flow of product distribution in the region. Because it extended through other interior parishes, the region was in a privileged position in the local trade, supply and agricultural production. Many ships would travel up and down these many rivers, especially the Iguaçu and the Sarapuí, supplying the entire region and distributing its production out of it. Matoso Maia Forte, who studied the formation of the region, notes that

> its rivers, providing easy access for their products to reach Bahia, and through which they pass by the market of Rio de Janeiro; and its roads, heading straight to the metropolis, assured its agriculture the same place where they could reap the benefits of being at the heart of the colony, within the municipalities of the lowland, on the bay waterfront and beyond.[8]

Undoubtedly, besides its own sugar and food production, the geography of the area, surrounded by rivers and streams, facilitated local economic development. Millet Saint Adolphe, in his *Diccionario geographico* from 1858, wrote that the inhabitants of the Iguaçu area "plow sugar cane, harvest rice, corn, beans, and coffee. These crops are easily transported to Rio de Janeiro, and all the streams and rivers adjacent are as navigable as the big seas."[9] The English traveler John Luccock, who visited Rio de Janeiro in the early years of the nineteenth century, noted that the Guanabara Bay was

> surrounded by a large harbour that is not usable for large plantations because of its shape. Food crops will have plenty of space, as well as on the neighboring islands. The capital of the colony is well stocked, because, those crops are augmented by those of the contiguous areas from the city heading inland, within a radius of more than one league.[10]

Tha fluvial routes of the river in the Iguaçu region also enabled the economic development of surrounding parishes, such as Santo Antônio de Sá, Inhomerim, Magé, Suruí, Campo Grande and Irajá. In addition to the waterway, in the second half of the eighteenth century this area already had roads that led to the Court, as the "Police road" and "Trade road." There were also roads near the parish of Nossa Senhora da Piedade de Iguaçu that interconnected local ports. These roads even transported part of the coffee produced in Piraí, Valência and Vassouras in the first quarter of the century. The municipality of Iguaçu had several shops with large warehouses for storage products.[11]

From the mid-nineteenth century, part of the region also gained rail transportation, most notably, the Maxambomba station, in Santo Antônio de Jacutinga parish. In 1840, given the importance of local trade, there was a project, subsequently shelved, for the construction of a railroad from the Iguaçu village to somewhere near the Guanabara Bay. At the time, one of the defenders of the project pointed out that that village offered greater access not only for the import of a great number of agricultural products, but also for the export of 5,000 kilos of coffee through its ports and roads.[12]

Although there were several favorable conditions for development, the sugar economy of the Iguaçu region was shaken in the mid-nineteenth century. Beginning in the early nineteenth century, this region stagnated due to the sugarcane cultivation expansion in northern areas of the province of Rio de Janeiro (especially the region of Campos) and the increase in coffee production in the Paraíba valley, along with the constant epidemics and floods that took place in the Iguaçu lowland. The gradual process of economic decline occurred even in other areas of the Guanabara Bay.[13]

However, it is known, the economy of some areas of this region, such as the parishes of Itaboraí and São Gonçalo, returned to growth with the introduction of new farming strategies. Most of them adopted agriculture.[14] The transfer of the Portuguese Court to Rio de Janeiro in 1808 had increased the demand for food revitalizing the production of staple food crops in Iguaçu throughout the nineteenth century. However, the region continued to produce sugar until the last quarter of this century and also coffee in the highest elevations.[15]

The cholera epidemic in the years 1855–1856 also impaired the economic vitality, causing a high slave mortality rate both in court and in the interior of Rio de Janeiro province, including Iguaçu. During this period, of the 4,899 victims of cholera in the city of Rio de Janeiro, 2,523 were slaves.[16] In rural areas, the slaves were even more affected. In mid–1856, in just eight days, cholera killed more than thirty slaves on the Rio Seco farm, in the municipality of Rio Bonito. In Barra Mansa, of the 372 dead, 311 were slaves. In the village of São João do Príncipe, in just a month and a half, at the end of 1855 and beginning of 1856, about 498 people were infected, 164 free and 334 captive. Of the 160 deaths, 108 were slaves.[17]

Iguaçu was known to be a "famous area for the devastating epidemic of pernicious fevers."[18] During the outbreak, the region was even more exposed to cholera as a result of its commercial contacts with other regions of the province. Cholera, for example, reached Iguaçu transmitted by an infected captive employee who worked in coastal and shipping services between local rivers and the Governor's island, near the Court.[19] African slaves recently purchased also brought cholera as they were transported to the coffee areas of Vassouras and Valência by way of roads that pass through Iguaçu. In the tables below we can see demographic trends in the region.

Table 2 shows the distribution of the free and slave populations of Iguaçu between the late eighteenth century and early nineteenth. In both periods, the slave population was larger than the free. In 1821, the population of the five parishes reached 18,705 inhabitants, of which 11,155 were slaves, or about 59.7 percent. In Meriti, the least populated of the parishes, this proportion reached close to 70 percent. Between 1779–89 and 1821, the slave population grew 56.6 percent, while the free grew only 27.2 percent.

Table 2: Population of Iguaçu Region; 1779–89 and 1821

Parishes	1779–89						1821					
	Total	Free	percent	Slave	percent		Total	Free	percent	Slave	percent
Marapicu	1821	902	49.5	919	50.5		4202	1708	40.6	2494	50.4
Jacutinga	3540	1404	39.6	2138	60.4		3700	1274	34.4	2426	65.6
Meriti	1616	638	39.5	978	60.5		2264	696	30.7	1568	69.3
Iguaçu	2182	963	44	1219	56		4167	1914	46	2253	54
Pilar	3895	2027	52	1868	48		4372	1958	44.8	2414	55.2
Total	13054	5932	45.4	7122	54.6		18705	7550	40.3	11155	59.7

Source: "Public and economic records of the city of São Sebastião do Rio de Janeiro for use of the Viceroy Luiz de Vasconcellos by his curious observation of the years of 1779 until the 1789." In: RIHGB, volume XLVII (47), p. 17 and RIHGB, volume XXXM (33).

In Table 3, we have the population changes in the region between 1840 and 1872. The data shows a decrease of the slave population. In 1840, the Iguaçu slave population came to be about 62 percent, but in 1872 represented only 32.5 percent. In fact, comparing the 1850 data with 1872 indicates that the number of Iguaçu captives decreased in both absolute and relative terms.

Table 3: Population of Iguaçu Region; 1840, 1850 and 1872

Parishes	Free 1840 Crude n°	Free 1840 percent	Free 1850 Crude n°	Free 1850 percent	Free 1872 Crude n°	Free 1872 percent	Slave 1840 Crude n°	Slave 1840 percent	Slave 1850 Crude n°	Slave 1850 percent	Slave 1872 Crude n°	Slave 1872 percent
Marapicu	2828	43	3322	47	3622	64.4	3758	57	3553	53	2002	35.6
Jacutinga	2148	35.5	2345	42	4458	68	3913	64.5	3290	58	2088	32
Meriti	728	30.3	3536	58	1748	69	1674	69.7	2606	42	776	31
Iguaçu	—	—	973	44	3099	69	—	—	1235	56	1386	31
Pilar	—	—	2122	48	2409	68	—	—	2375	52	1229	32
Total	5704	38	15336	48	15336	67.5	9345	62	13259	52	7381	32.5

Source: "Provincial Presidents Reports of 1841 and 1852"; and "1872 Census."

This situation could stem from a variety of factors. With the end of the slave trade in 1850, it is likely that farmers and farmers in the region failed to renew their herds due to the sudden increase in prices of slaves.[20] In 1850 the population included about 57.5 percent Africans, while in 1872 they were only 16 percent. The Creoles increased from 42.5 percent in 1850 to 84 percent in 1872.[21] That is, in the mid-nineteenth century, the African impact of the slave trade was still present in the slave population of Iguaçu, although the Creole percentage during this period was already considerable.[22]

Considering the age of the slaves in 1850, we have about 50 percent of the captives in the range of fifteen to forty years.[23] Most of the available slave labor was sent to work in the coffee regions of the Paraíba Fluminense valley. Even considering the establishment of small cattle breeding, the rent of slaves and so on, areas not aimed at commercial agriculture probably had difficulty in securing slave labor in the second half of the nineteenth century.[24]

The Guanabara Bay Area and the Quilombo Villages

The quilombos of the Iguaçu region are registered in police documentation with different names. They appear as "Quilombo de Iguassu," and sometimes as "Quilombo do Pillar," or as "Quilombo of Rio Sarapuhi Bar." In the mid-nineteenth century, these quilombos came up with the following names: "Quilombo do Bomba," "Quilombo do Gabriel" and "Quilombo da Estrela."[25]

The Iguaçu region formed a broad plain with streams and wetlands, a location which turned out to contribute decisively to the formation and development of quilombos during the nineteenth century. The slaves found safe haven there to establish their mocambos (quilombo villages). In 1808, the Court police superintendent, Paulo Fernandes Viana, sent official orders to the captain of the local guard of Magé village—an area near Iguaçu—ordering the deployment of troops against the quilombo refugees. The orders were also extended to the captains of Macacu villages, Cabo Frio and Resende.[26]

At the end of the year 1823, an ordinance was issued authorizing the execution of "a general attack on all Quilombos that existed in the parishes of Guia, Inhomirim, Mage and Surui."[27] The decree was executed because the incidence of slaves escaping throughout the region was high. According to prison records for the year 1826, of the total 469 slaves imprisoned for escape in the inland regions, 121 of them were arrested in those five parishes that constituted the Iguaçuana region. Additionally, taking into account some of the surrounding parishes, such as Magé, Suruí, Inhomirim, Guapimirim and Guia, and the suburbs adjacent to the Court, such as Irajá and Campo Grande, that number increases to 207, about 23 percent of all slaves imprisoned that year, both in the Court and throughout the province of Rio de Janeiro.[28]

In 1825, the Chief of Police of the Court informed the Minister of Justice of the existence of "large *quilombos* between Sarapuí, and Iguaçu River, and elsewhere."[29] In April of that year, a farmer near the river Sarapuí, Dr. Jacinto José da Silva Quintão, complained to the court about the presence of quilombos in that place and about the fugitives who constantly raided their boats loaded with tiles, and other vessels carrying products and supplies belonging to many farmers of the surrounding areas. They complained also that the slaves were stealing their cattle. Speaking on behalf of other farmers in the region, Quintão requested immediate action from the authorities, noting even that "this quilombo, sir, has been there for a long time; and always has been attacked yet never extinguished, so that river [Iguaçu] has become impassable."[30]

Quilombos situated on the banks of rivers in the Iguaçu region appear to have been familiar, not only to local residents and farmers, but also to the authorities, possibly as early as the late eighteenth century.[31] The oldest reference we found about quilombos located in Iguaçu is from 1812. In June of that year, the superintendent of the Court's police ordered that the "Commander of the District" of the Parish of Santo Antônio de Jacutinga provide "all the assistance" to the "capitão-do-mato" (sometimes translated as slave-catcher) Claudio Antonio to conduct an expedition to "attack the *quilombos* and arrest all the runaway slaves that you meet." Months earlier, at the end of the year 1811, the police superintendent had also ordered the "Inhomirim Coronel" to take action using "all his activity to rebuke runaway slaves, destroy *quilombos* and contain this band of criminals." Not only the Iguaçu region, but other neighboring areas of Guanabara Bay, were also full of quilombos. In 1812, the Court's authorities solicited farmers' resources to prepare "an entry to the Quilombo" located in São Gonçalo district.[32]

But the Iguaçu lowland seemed to be the area which had the greatest concentration of quilombo refugees. In 1816, quilombo leaders Joaquim Congo, João Mofumbe and José Benguela had all been captured from the "Pilar Quilombo" and imprisoned.[33] Almost ten years later, in 1825, the Court's police prepared one more investigation in order to block the entrances to the streams where—it was reported—the slaves from the Iguaçu quilombos set out to attack the vessels traveling along these streams. These advances, however, did not achieve the desired end, according to the subsequent assessment of the police superintendent.[34]

The products of Iguaçu quilombolas (quilombo inhabitants) arriving in the Court's market, c. 1825 ("Rue Droite a Rio de Janeiro," M. Rugendas, Malerische Reise in Brasilien, Paris, Engelmann & Cie., 1835).

However, on several occasions, many quilombolas were eventually captured. In early 1826, nine were arrested in "Quilombo de Iguaçu," between the middle of that year and early 1827, eight more were captured in the parishes of Iguaçu, Pilar and Meriti and, in 1828, "two recently arrived African slaves" were seized as "slaves from the *quilombos* in Pillar parish." Finally, in 1829 a slave was sent to prison and was described as "Mina, a recently arrived slave from Africa delivered by the freed black man, João Xavier Bazil, having found the slave in the woods near the Iguaçu river."[35]

In the second half of the century, specifically in 1859, the provincial authorities discussed measures for the destruction of those quilombos. Owing to the fruitless investigations of 1825, several others that followed them also failed. Indeed, in 1830, the Justice of the Peace of São João do Meriti parish asked for action regarding the capture of "the escaped slaves who daily increase the *quilombos* and even create new ones."[36] In 1836, five slaves from Ana Rosa da Silva Farms abandoned their farm and eventually took refuge in the quilombo next to the "Sarapuí river sand bar."[37] In 1837, the provincial vice-president would indicate in a report to the imperial government that he had taken, with "the most favorable success," military measures for exterminating "a formidable Quilombo in the city of Iguaçu."[38]

The results of these expeditions seemed indeed ephemeral. In the year 1838, Manuel Joaquim de Souza, a resident of Calundu port, near the Pilar parish, complained to the local Justice of the Peace about the frequent attacks suffered at the hands of the quilombo denizens.[39] In the late 1850s, these attacks were already considered a chronic public security problem in the region, according to provincial authorities.

The constant complaints, not only those published in the Court's papers, but also the number of letters and petitions sent to the Department of Provincial Police, reported that the inhabitants of the quilombos engaged in frequent robberies in the region, especially pirating boats navigating the rivers that were loaded with cargo. According to reports, the slaves from the quilombos were using canoes—which were kept hidden in the marshes of the numerous tributaries of the Iguaçu and Sarapuí—in their assaults, and "to avoid the ill favor of the quilombo robbers some boatswain entered into agreements with them, paying them tributes of meat, flour and other goods."[40] The alleged difficulties the authorities were having in destroying the quilombos were, among others, their location in swampy areas that were difficult to access and the "pacts" between the slaves and the merchants, tavern owners, captives from neighboring plantations, rowers slaves and farmers. In Brazil and other parts of America, such as Jamaica and Suriname, geographical location was an important factor for survival and autonomy of communities of escaped slaves. Despite the difficult access, most of them, whenever possible, were settled in areas that were not totally isolated from arable land (whether they exported their crops or not) or were settled near small trading centers and commercial warehouses. It worked as an economic strategy, since it allowed commercial exchanges between quilombolas, slaves and traders; and those commercial exchanges were very common across America during the slave period.[41]

In choosing a site, protection against constant police interventions also had to be taken into account. In the late 1850s, police authorities of Iguaçu notified the chief of police about the difficulties in accessing those quilombos:

> Recognizing the difficulty, if not impossibility, of extinguishing the existing quilombo in the Iguaçu river marsh, by ordinary means and by organizing an armed siege to capture and arrest the quilombo inhabitants; and being unable to penetrate yet unknown ranches, despite the long-standing efforts constantly employed by the police; and because of the winding nature of the marshy inlets, made more difficult by the presence of poison or poisoned

stakes and barbs, accordingly, trusted officials reported on the topography of the place.[42]

In fact, the geography was a strong ally for the Iguaçu quilombo fighters in their frequent battles against the punitive troops. The occupation of hard to reach places would eventually provide the quilombo inhabitants enough time to abandon their ranches before being surrounded by troops. Thus, they avoided the element of surprise, which was followed frequently by the authorities in repressive actions. In addition, the quilombolas placed poisoned barbs, which could be natural or made with wood or pieces of bamboo and green cane, opened false trails in the woods and made other traps. Thereby, they aimed to delay the advance of the troops inside the forest, often fatiguing them to the point of exhaustion. Some quilombo settlers sought to set up their camps in mountainous, steep locations. They also placed guards at the sites and prepared ambushes against the repressive military expeditions. Thus protected, the quilombo inhabitants could take care of other things besides confrontation with the military.

The available sources on the economic activities of fugitive communities in Brazil are still scarce and scattered. Even considering the large quilombos of the seventeenth and eighteenth centuries, information regarding the economy points to a mere subsistence agriculture accompanied by extraction, hunting and abundant fishing. It is known, however, that many quilombos also produced excess—most notably agricultural crops—on a small scale, favoring commercial exchanges. In many cases, the "pillaging" by means of looting and robbery, could function as a complement to economic activities.[43]

There are reports about the great Palmares quilombos that their inhabitants planted corn, which was "harvested twice a year," beans, sweet potato, cassava, banana and sugar cane. For the captaincy of Minas Gerais in the eighteenth century, there is evidence that the quilombos had a diversified economy. Guimarães points out the existence of three basic economic activities there: agricultural production, theft and mining. Indeed, when the authorities conducted a military campaign against the quilombos of "Paranaíba region" in 1754, they found 76 ranches and "abundant farmimg and supplies collected in the storehouses," although they only arrested eight "blacks." In the year 1766, when a quilombo in Pitangui parish was attacked, the authorities found "fourteen ranches of herbs, corn, beans, cotton, watermelons and other fruit." As for the quilombo of Mariana, attacked in 1733, it was said that the quilombo inhabitants "took refuge and supplied themselves with fresh provisions by having fields in the quilombo, which was necessary to block." After an attack on two mining quilombos in Campo Grande, in 1759, the colonial authorities confirmed that they did have "many groceries and large fields for the future year."[44]

The basis of the agricultural production of the majority of quilombos in Brazil was cassava and corn. The quilombolas obtained other products they needed by trading their agriculture, hunting and fishing surplus, exchanging it with tavern keepers, small farmers and slaves from surrounding farms. These products could be, for example, salt (important in preserving food) spirits, meats, clothes, weapons and ammunition—the last two mainly used for hunting.

From the fragmented information available, it is known that the quilombos in Iguaçu based their economy on subsistence agriculture with "large plantations of pumpkin and legumes" and "insignificant plantation of sugar cane." It was also reported that the villages were set in a "place that was abundant with fish and game." There was also evidence that the quilombo inhabitants robbed the residents of the "neighboring areas, in order to snatch their cattle and other domestic animals to feed themselves."[45] There is also information that the quilombos had an intense trade relations with the local barkeeps. In 1859, police authorities of the province warned about

> the need for all police authorities of Iguaçu, Pilar and Jacutinga to put in place preventive measures for gathering perfect intelligence in this important work, because they are close to the quilombo locations, and it is the location where the barkeepss are most interested in maintaining relations with blacks, with whom they trade on a large scale in mangrove wood, which bring a high price at the Court, giving in exchange, wood canoes and food supplies of small value.[46]

These market relations were not restricted to the Iguaçu region. The "mangrove wood" extracted by the quilombo inhabitants ended up in Court, almost always with the intermediation of the traders. The extraction and wood trade was an economic activity widely known throughout the Iguaçu area.[47] In the late 1870s, the president of the province was still trying to destroy these quilombos and reported to the Minister of Justice that

> In exchange for food and liquor, supplied by the [barkeeps] themselves who went to fill up with firewood, it was there that the quilombolas offered to to cut the firewood in order to load the boats, whose owners, taking advantage of trade so lucrative, prevented any armed movement, so that the police investigations were always unsuccessfully.[48]

In most of the regions where the quilombos were settled in Brazil, such relations between quilombolas and barkeeps were common. In several criminal cases involving quilombolas and runaway slaves, the authorities tried hard to find out how they maintained relations and dealings with local businesses. It was a standard question in inquiries and investigations made against runaway slaves, whether someone helped them to escape, protected them or was maintaining any trade with them. The authorities were fully aware of this practice and, whenever possible, sought to punish people for it. For example, in her study of "black women of tabuleiro e ganho (work in the informal sector)" in the city of São Paulo in the nineteenth century, Maria Odila points out the existence of social networks and frequent "illegal trade" relations involving greengrocers, fugitives slaves hired "for pay" and quilombolas.[49]

The exchange of wood between quilombolas and barkeeps was, according to information from the authorities, "a lucrative trade," at least for the barkeeps, who resold the wood to the Court, where it was sought and for which it was "well paid." In return, the fugitives got "small value food supplies." Quilombolas may have controlled much of this type of wood trade in the region, as they already controlled several river outlets. They could even maintain this domain because the boatmen who did not purchase their firewood from them, or carried it to the Court themselves, or those who did not provide with payoffs that the quilombolas requested, risked having their boats held up. It was known, for example, that the boatswains feared the quilombolas, and so maintained a "pact" with them in the region in order to navigate the rivers freely. This "pact" could involve a "tribute" on goods, because "boatswains from Iguaçu and Pilar who are not in harmony or do not maintain relationships with the inhabitants of this small Palmares, are truly endangered when pass through the vicinity of a quilombo."[50]

The portraits of near horror and panic that often appeared in local newspapers and periodicals and the frequent complaints of residents, farmers and traders from those bordering areas, might not be associated only with the actions of the quilombolas, but may also have been part of an economic and political strategy of some local barkeeps who did not want to lose income or the monopoly of such a "profitable" business. Regarding this fact, the small gazette "Journal of Commerce" reported on one occasion that the barkeeps, merchants, and boat owners that supply wood to the Court

> took advantage of this lucrative trade, always spreading terrifying news about the quilombolas in order to scare off the competition. These individuals seek

any and all means to interest the slaves in the service they are providing, but prevent us from believing there is reason that authorities might resort to all means to arrest them."⁵¹

These trade relations afforded the Iguaçu quilombolas a real safety net, beyond the economic survival. It greatly hindered the action of the repressive troops, whose presence was often warned by barkeeps.

Getting around in the Black Encampments

In the province of Rio de Janeiro, as well as in other Brazilian regions, relations between quilombolas, slaves on plantations and barkeeps were the object of constant concern for the police authorities. Municipal ordinances regulated the operation of taverns, prohibiting their owners to do any kind of business with slaves, escaped or not. Residents of the Court and other inland rural areas complained to the Justices of the Peace about the barkeeps, dealers and peddlers that maintained illicit trade with slaves, many of them escaped from the quilombos. Such relationships included trading cigarrettes and liquor for several products offered by the quilombolas, some of which came from theft.⁵²

In early 1823, the residents of São João de Icaraí sent a petition to a regional magistrate from the royal town of Praia Grande, claiming that in the Sapê parish there was a small market working without a license. The complaint indicated that the "business owners" openly traded with neighborhoods slaves, inducing them to "steal coffee, bananas, cassava, fruits, chickens from their owners," and gave shelter to "vagrant" freedmen and escaped slaves.⁵³ An ordinance issued by the police chief in 1825 regulated the hours of operation for markets and taverns in the Court and its suburbs. This determination was due to the fact that many barkeeps were "opening their markets and taverns long before dawn, based on the lack of an official declaration indicating appropriate business hours."⁵⁴ The concern about the taverns' hours of operation was also related to the constant "madness" of the capoeira practitioners, especially at night. In 1836, the authorities of the Court recommended to the municipal guards that they should patrol the streets, dissolving the possible gatherings of "blacks" in taverns, and "denouncing the barkeeps, who allow these meetings to occur frequently."⁵⁵

The Court and the interior of the province of Rio de Janeiro were marked by great fear at the prospect of slave insurrections. The fear reached a panic dimension in the 1830s, after the episode of the Muslim revolt in Bahia, in January 1835. The constant relationship between traders, slaves, quilombolas and even capoeira practitioners contributed to increased panic. Free persons of mixed race and freed blacks, particularly those of African origin that practiced trade in the Court and in neighboring suburbs, were often accused of inciting slaves to rebellion. Also barkeeps were accused. According to reports, barkeeps were also accused of rousing rebellion and were responsible for supplying weapons and ammunition to captive conspirators.[56] In 1838, the municipal ordinances of the Court (many of which were later followed by other districts of the province) determined prison sentences and fines for the barkeeps accused of trading with slaves.[57] The possibility that quilombolas could enter into these relationship circuits really frightened farmers and authorities who feared mass escapes of slaves and insurrections in support of the quilombolas.[58]

The fear that haunted the Court in the 1830s also reached the Iguaçu lowland. In 1836, complaints were made about the existence of "two central points of insurrection" near the parishes of Santo Antônio de Jacutinga and São João de Meriti, among the slaves of "Nazareth" and "Barbosa" farms.[59] Two years later, in the parish of Inhomirim, there was "some evidence of an insurrection of Africans, freed slaves and slaves." One night, at the end of April of that year, the farmer Miguel Jose Gomes discovered near his home "a riot of 30–40 Africans." Some of these Africans were arrested and interrogated and "they said that the intention of the meeting was to meet each other, make arrangements, and invite more Africans to rise up against the whites, and that this uprising should be on the night of the 2nd to the morning of May 3 of that year."[60] In 1841, the Rio de Janeiro authorities was concerned with "Domingos, the freed black man" of Cabinda origin. He had already been arrested in various parts of the municipality of Magé for being a dangerous, jobless, "recruiter of blacks to insurrection."[61] Quilombolas could become opportune allies of the revolts organized by slaves—especially African-born slaves -, a fact that terrorized the farmers.

The authorities tried to justify their inability to destroy Iguaçu quilombos, citing the existence of commercial relations between fugitives and barkeeps. The president of the province wrote to his police chief in 1859:

> I have reviewed the instructions that Your Honor has to issued for the dispersion and dissolution of the existing quilombo on the banks of the Iguaçu River, it is my duty to inform you that the means Your Honor has indicated to the Delegate to employ in order to promote the capture of quilombolas that are found outside the *quilombos* are the same means that, to date, have been employed with no results; because of this they continue to maintain relations with the owners of nearby markets, who purchase their firewood

and provide them with groceries, and so contribute to the conservation of *quilombos*, as has occurred with one Fuão [male] Penedo of the Tavern located at Sarapuí river bank, in place called—the broom—and with a certain Garcia with a market in Pilar, for as long as these people known for protecting quilombolas and providing shelter for slaves continue to exist, all police inquiries that are based on aid of barkeeps will be deceived and frustrated [...].[62]

Certainly the barkeeps and small businesses involved with those quilombolas, for at least—perhaps—more than fifty years, were not limited to such "Penedo" and "Garcia." Several other barkeeps and dealers were involved, as well as slaves of the region, many of which were oarsmen of the boats that navigated those rivers, and even the paid cargo-loading slaves at the Court, responsible for stowage of products brought from interior ports.[63] Until it reached the city, firewood, of course, went through an extensive network of intermediaries. In 1868, two slaves belonging to "commerce and trading boats from the Court" were accused of maintaining direct relations with the quilombolas of Iguaçu. It is possible that the quilombo firewood reached the Court through some of these boats.[64]

As for this possibility, it is worth remembering that there were paid slaves that worked in court and at ports, unloading the goods that arrived there from the inland regions of the Guanabara Bay. Milk, grass, coal, wood, among others, were products not only transported but also often directly resold by these paid slaves on city streets.

Just as the unloading and transporting of cargo and goods that arrived at the Court, the navigation through Guanabara Bay relied on the participation of slaves. Many of these were also "paid slaves of the Court," and may have had the occupation of rowers in boats and canoes that linked the Court to other areas of the inland bay area, supplying it with products produced by these regions. While some slaves worked in vessels that were property of their masters and/or of third parties, some of them had more autonomy and even may have had their own canoes and boats.[65]

We can see much more than a simple economic relationship in all these connections between quilombolas, slaves on the plantations, barkeeps and rowers; it could also involve traveling salesmen, peddlers, peasants, households, urban slaves, tenants, farmers and even local authorities (many of which owned farms). These contacts eventually formed the basis of a larger web of interests and different social relations, of which the quilombolas knew how to take a crucial advantage to increase the maintenance of their autonomy. And so there emerged a veritable black encampment. This complex network of social relations acquired its own logic, in which interests, solidarity, tensions and conflicts intersected.

What we call "black encampment" is this complex social network. This network could involve numerous social movements and socio-economic practices around various interests in determined Brazilian slavery regions. This black encampment, built slowly, became the scene of struggle and solidarity between the various people who experienced the worlds of slavery. The historical experience of "the black encampment," involving various complex contacts and and relationships with quilombos and by quilombos was by no means restricted to the region of Iguaçu and Sarapuí rivers. In 1832, between the parishes of Guaratiba and Campo Guaratiba, not far from Iguaçu, it was known that the quilombolas had certain "friends and collusions, not only of mixed race people but even whites, who not only sold them gunpowder that will might need, but also gave warnings as well as assistance."[66]

Runaway slave (standing third from left) participates in dance circle, c. 1825 ("Dance batuca," M. Rugendas, Malerische Reise in Brasilien, Paris, Engelmann & Cie., 1835).

Quilombolas captured in Vassouras, city of Rio de Janeiro, in the last quarter of the nineteenth century, declared that they were supplied with goods stolen from nearby farms and from local barkeeps.[67] In 1860, the Iguaçu quilombolas were accused of the murders of the Portuguese man, Luiz Gonçalves Pacheco, employee of a farmer and local merchant, and of the quilombola Cesário. According to information, both were killed "for seizing firewood that belonged to the quilombolas."⁶⁸ Other complaints insisted again on the fact that these quilombolas have had close and frequent relations with the slaves who lived in those areas. The quilombolas of Iguaçu—as previously mentioned—maintained an intense wood trade with barkeeps in the region. Due to an investigation near the banks of the Iguaçu river, in 1876, "a canoe, a packed shotgun, axes, scythes, hoes, fishing net, some carpenter's tools, and 64 cuttings of good firewood" were found in an abandoned camp.⁶⁹

It was among slaves who worked on neighboring farms that the quilombolas of Iguaçu often sought shelter. Also in 1860, many quilombolas sought refuge on the Constante Ferreira Panasco farm because they were cornered by the troops trying to surround the outlets of the tributary streams of the Iguaçu and Sarapuí rivers. It was even known that they ended up sleeping "two nights in the flour mill" of that property. Soon, however, they were discovered, as a neighboring farmer gathered any available people and he managed to arrest at least eight of them.⁷⁰ Also, it is known, the Gonde, Outeiro and Iguaçu farms belonging to the Benedictine Order, were often frequented by the quilombolas of Iguaçu. In the slave quarters, they sought refuge and found solidarity with the slaves. Based on the investigation of local sub-delegates and the complaints of nearby residents, it turned out, for example, that the main camps of the quilombolas were located next to the marshes of the right bank of the Iguaçu River, just within the limits of the Benedictine property.⁷¹

Of the three farms that the Benedictines had in that region, the Iguaçu, with about sixty slaves, produced tile and brick, the Outeiro, with ten slaves, produced cassava, and the Gondê with nine slaves, also produced cassava. To carry what they produced on these properties, in addition to food, especially bricks and tiles, the Benedictines had several boats, operated by their own slaves, linking the ports of their farms to the monastery of São Bento, in the Court, where there was also a pier (including a crane).⁷² However, from the seventeenth century onward, these monks were already leasing lands, especially on the periphery of their properties. In the nineteenth century, with farms in decline, the number of tenants increased.⁷³ In 1864, there were about 65 tenants, many of which were large local farmers, such as the barons of Pilar and Guandu, the Countess of Sarapuí, Commander Francisco Xavier do Amaral and Francisco Xavier de Moura.⁷⁴

Several accusations were made that the quilombolas of Iguaçu traded and maintained frequent communication with the slaves of the Benedictine farms. It was known that a large number of quilombolas of Iguaçu were made up of escaped slaves from the Baron of Iguaçu`s farm, adjoining the monastery property in that region.[75] The slave Querubim, who worked on one of these farms, was denounced in 1860 as one who shelters and protects slaves.[76] The fact is that the quilombolas of Iguaçu were able to set up their quilombos on Benedictine lands. In addition to this refuge, they probably found Benedictine slaves could be opportune partners for trading goods and other exchanges. Incidentally, it is worth commenting on a little life of the Benedictine slaves.

The slaves that worked in the Benedictine farms, both those of Iguaçu as several others scattered throughout Brazil, used to have small plantations and even some cattle. In funds (ordainments) reserved for the canonical visits to the São Bento monastery properties there existed, from the mid-eighteenth century onward, determinations to grant "free days" and "land parcels" to the slaves in order for them to be able to cultivate their own crops for their livelihood.[77] They determined that the slaves should have "Saturday to work in their fields, even if the week had holy day and that they should be given all the land necessary for their crops." Slaves also received payments for time worked for the monks "on their own days," that is, the days designated for the cultivation of their own crops.[78]

In addition to supporting themselves from these crops, slaves used to produce surpluses, which they sought to trade. Trade was probably done with the taverns of the region, held in small local markets, negotiated with other slaves of some neighboring farms or with the quilombolas.[79] There was also the possibility of the monastery itself buying goods produced by slaves. An example of this is when the Benedictine transferred slaves from one farm to another. In 1839, by the time that the slave Severino and his wife were transferred from Maricá farm to Iguaçu, they were compensated at 40$000 réis in compensation for their cassava fields. Two years later, the slave Simian, also sent to the Iguaçu farm, sold the monastery "two sacks of corn." In the Benedictine Iguaçu farms, the slaves, in addition to having fields, manufactured flour for their own consumption and for selling; and they also had "cattle." Between 1839 and 1842, the monastery bought the slaves of the Iguaçu farm a total of nine oxen and three cows "including their offspring."[80]

The silence of the Benedictine documentation about the existence of quilombos in their land, the actions of quilombolas (who robbed boats and stole cattle in the region) and the solidarity of their slaves with them may be an indication that the monastery of São Bento turned a blind eye to it. This may even indicate that the monks did not see imminent "danger" in the actions of local quilombolas, since their properties were probably not plundered and their slaves didn't flee to the quilombos. Perhaps the administrators of the Benedictine farms in the region bought "wood of the mangrove" from the quilombolas to operate the brick and tiles works? And perhaps the quilombolas were able to send their products to the Court through the boats of the Benedictine slaves. It may also be that the quilombolas of Iguaçu transported in their own canoes surplus products from the fields of the monastery captives to the taverns of the region.

Searching for Autonomy

It was around similar webs of social relations that communities of escaped slaves were constituted in Brazil and throughout most of the Americas. In the Iguaçu region, the presence and activities of quilombolas, for nearly a century at least, allowed the creation of a local economy where quilombos turned out to be almost legitimized local communities, at the same time of slavery and as an alternative to it. Although dozens of documents speak about fears most of the time, it is hard to believe that living with the quilombos in that region was always a war without truce. The quilombolas of Iguaçu may have even created a relatively stable peasant community. They negotiated not only the surplus of their crops, but also extracted, stored and controlled part of local trade of firewood.

In several Brazilian slave regions, as well as in other areas of black Americas, the slaves, from their own gardens and economy, and the quilombolas, with their economic activities, eventually formed a black peasantry even during the period of slavery. In order to address this issue, it is important to follow the pioneering analyses of Sidney Mintz. He argues that the definition of the word peasant must be understood as the lived historical experiences and not only in abstract terms of an analytical category. We should bear in mind the varied relationships of certain rural sectors within society as a whole, including their survival strategies, way of life and cultural and economic practices. In this context, it also implies that we need to reconstitute the idea of development and the multifaceted aspects of relations between the various sectors of peasants and non-peasants in any given society.[81]

In other words, Mintz suggests that the formation of a peasantry should be thought of as a historical process, rather than as static typological systems. Analyzing the formation of a black peasantry in the Caribbean in the post-emancipation period, he discusses how this peasantry originated from the development of the economy created by captives during slavery. According to him, slaves of the plantation system and quilombolas organized in communities upon developing various practical and economic relations (including access to local markets), transformed into proto-peasants.[82]

For Brazil, in several areas—save their economic and demographic specificities—slaves and quilombolas developed economic practices that led to surplus production that they sought to sell.[83] In many regions, slaves attended fairs (open-air markets) on Saturdays and Sundays—that is, on their customary "free days"—where they set up "vendor stands" and sold both farm products (tobacco, corn, beans, cassava, etc.) as well as hunting and fishing products. In response to this, in the late 1870s, a journal of the Vassouras region published the following complaint:

> RIO BONITO—I ask you, Mr. Tax Inspector, to go to this place on Sundays, at 3 pm, to see, in a house near the chapel, a gathering of slaves selling their wares; those who pay taxes are footing the bill. This will continue if measures are not taken.[84]

Although in some cases the nobility prohibited it and the population complained about it, slaves in Brazil, the Caribbean, the United States, and in various regions of slavery America, sought to develop, as far as possible, their own economy, winning and thus extending their spaces of autonomy.[85] In the Caribbean, more specifically in Jamaica, Mintz highlights how slaves brought their products to supply the local markets.[86] In Antigua, the "Sunday markets" attended by slaves and freedmen, among others, were places of intense socialization among slaves from different plantations, many of them traveling several kilometers with their products to get to the main market. These markets and the environment around them had important commercial and social roles. In the United States in Georgia, the existence of the informal economy operated by the slaves, who brought their products to be traded in villages and nearby cities, meant, among other things, a major flow of products and information between rural and urban slaves. From the smuggling of goods through boats and rafts, the slave boatmen and boat captains maintained a regular bond of communication and trade with the slaves of urban areas.[87]

We know little of how the slaves developed their own economy in the Iguaçu region throughout the nineteenth century. We saw, however, several indications of the wood trade between quilombolas and traders, the relations of both with the slave rowers and possibly slaves in the Court and with those who possessed their own fields.[88]

In addition to the formation of a black peasantry, from the quilombola communities and communities in slave quarters, we think the creation of a black encampment was as a result of other questions. For most slaveholders, the existence of these networks of solidarity represented a permanent threat. The constant escapes, the possible incitement and communication with the slave revolts, and the raids that could be carried out by the quilombolas were causing fear among farmers. In fact, for these, the mere existence of quilombola groups posed a threat to their authority and control of their farms, since the threat of escapes to the quilombos was constant. Otherwise, the farms attacks, assaults and robberies and murders committed by quilombolas left the gentlemen uneasy.[89] One example is the fact that in 1885 the farmers of the Capivari region complained that

> Besides the scandalous theft we suffer in our coffee plantations, to the point that our crops were reduced to less than half, and nighttime assaults to our properties, we live entirely anxious about the imminent danger of the relationships of these people [the quilombolas] have with our slaves.[90]

As we have highlighted previously, the majority of quilombos, both in Brazil and in other regions of the American continent, was not settled completely isolated from crops or market economy areas. Price draws our attention to this in almost all communities of escaped slaves: the development of a dependent economy.[91]

Contrary to what some authors claim, this phenomenon was more the result of a political choice made by the communities rather than by any structural economic constraints.[92] In an interesting article, Groot, for example, seeks to relativize the character of both economic dependence and independence of fugitive communities from the history of the quilombolas in Suriname. Groot argues also that, in the early formation of these communities, the quilombolas, although distant, were not completely isolated from the plantations, because the subsistence economy in the forest could not always provide them with all their needs. Instead, they sought to supplement their economy effecting purchase and sale of products to traders, farmers and slaves on the plantations. On the other hand, even after the period initiated by the peace pacts, these quilombolas also did not opt for economic isolation. Although established in demarcated lands, they often migrated to other regions in search of better living conditions, such as a market for their products and work in coastal areas of Suriname. This strategy lasted until the mid-twentieth century, with communities of their descendants. In an attempt to remain autonomous, the fugitives from communities across America sought to develop complex economic, cultural and social organizations.[93]

Even the smallest groups of quilombolas must have sought, wherever possible, to adapt to local conditions to remain protected and fed. In Itu, in the province of São Paulo, in the nineteenth century, the quilombolas not only sold stolen coffee to local merchants, but also stole cows and pigs at the behest of leather and wax traders.[94] In Campos, by the end of 1866, there was a group of six quilombolas established in the woods close to the Jacarandá farm, owned by the Baroness of Abadia, who were captured by a stagecoach made up of farmers, foremen and others from neighboring farms. In his testimony, the creole Silla said he had fled about three months prior and "that there were four straw huts and survived by eating banana, cassava, some birds caught in lakes using corn as a trap. This was because they had not made hunting traps yet, since they were there such a short time."[95]

The various economic relations maintained by various quilombo communities, even though most of them had a semi-clandestine character, could have been what led them to prosperity. Looking through a sociopolitical lens, in a slave society, there is no doubt that the escaped slaves formed communities of resistance that were threatening to the farmers and slave owners in general. Indeed, the existence of countless quilombos represented, among other things, a strong pole of attraction, promoting the escape of slaves. The quilombos of Iguaçu, like the immortal hydra with several heads, became the biggest threat to the world of slavery. The immortal heads of the hydra that was Iguaçu, besides the quilombolas themselves, included the barkeeps, the small farmers, the slave boatmen, etc. The swamp where she lived was the black encampment itself.

13

BLACK PLAINS: QUILOMBOS IN RIO GRANDE DO SUL

MÁRIO MAESTRI

The arduous maritime access to the current southern territories of Brazil and the difficulty of engaging them in the production of colonial commodities led the Iberian crowns to neglect these regions. In 1680, when the crisis of the sugar economy hit the fan, Portugal founded the Sacramento Colony, in the unpopulated Banda Oriental next to Buenos Aires, with the aim of joining the lucrative local contraband. In 1686, the Laguna Village (in the state of Santa Catarina) was founded in order to support contact with Sacramento. The crossing between Laguna and the colony was done through the sea. Soon, a terrestrial route connecting the two villages was established—the so-called *caminho do mar*.

Moved by the fear of losing the territories that belonged to them according to the Tordesilhas Treaty, the Spanish crown assigned the protection of these lands to the indigenous Guaranis, colonized by the Jesuits. The first Jesuit-Guarani colonization in the current state of Rio Grande do Sul, initiated in 1626, and retreated in 1637 to the western margins of the Uruguay River, due to offensives by the *Paulistas* (from the São Paulo province). The cattle livestock owned by the Jesuits that were left in the region spread over the immense lands of *Vacaria do Mar*. From 1682 onwards, Jesuits and Guaranis crossed the great river once again, occupied the current *Gaúcho* northwest, founded the so-called Sete Povos and established Vacarias do Pinhais in the northeast of Rio Grande do Sul.[1]

Towards the end of the eighteenth century, the discovery of natural deposits of ores[2] created an important market for cattle, mule, and equine livestock. The existence of large savage herds in the Continente, an area of the so-called *pampa* (grassy plains), located west of the great lakes, created the conditions for the incorporation of these regions into the Portuguese colonial economy. In the early eighteenth century, *Lagunenses* and *Paulistas* occupied the northern coast of Rio Grande do Sul—the grass fields of Viamão—where they established *paradouros* (barns) and *invernadas* (fenced pasture areas)—the *estâncias* (ranches)- in the current regions of Porto Alegre, Imbé, Tramandaí, Morro Grande, São José do Norte, etc. Thus was born the country of Viamão, to the east of the lakes and north of the Jacuí River, under the jurisdiction of the captaincy of São Paulo. Livestock was brought from the Continente to the *minas gerais* (general mines). The waters of the lakes and the Jacuí divided the territories and guaranteed the peace. The Spanish Jesuits controlled the northwestern lands and the Luso-Brazilians, the country of Viamão.

In 1737, Portugal broke with the status quo by founding the Rio Grande village in the southern margins of the Lake Patos' outfall, the only maritime entry to the southern territories. The military command of Rio Grande, dependent upon the royal captaincy of Rio de Janeiro, supported Sacramento—the center of the disputes between the Iberian crowns. Rio Grande had the capacity to dominate the rich grasslands of Continente.[3] In the second half of the eighteenth century, after conquering the Gaúcho coast, the colonizers initiated the occupation of the Jacuí basin, motivated by the Madrid Treaty of 1750, which exchanged Sacramento—until then belonging to the Portuguese—for the missionary regions dominated by the Spanish. Couples were brought from the Island of Azores to colonize the region.

In order to provide support to the demarcation of the new frontier, Tranqueira de Rio Pardo was founded in 1753 between the margins of its homonymous river and the Jacuí River. With the advent of the Guarani War and, above all, after the promulgation of the treaty, Rio Pardo was fortified and thus, it constituted, until 1801, the western limit of the Lusitanian possessions. With the Castilian conquest of the missionary territories, Rio Pardo became the most important mercantile center of the region. Villages emerged along the Jacuí Valley, reinforcing the occupation of the Central Depression. In the decade of 1770, migrants from Sacramento and other villages established themselves in the proximity of the Pelotas Arroyo, a region bordering the grasslands of the Continente and strategically connected to the port of Rio Grande through the Patos Lagoon and the small Lake Mirim. The village of São Francisco de Paula (Pelotas) would become the main southern center of dry meat production. In the beginnings of the nineteenth century, the occupation of Rio Grande do Sul was completed. The Estreito (strait) region of the coastal plains between the sea and the lakes, site of the first occupation, had met an economic and demographic stagnation in face of the development of the *campanha* (cattle plains)—an important center of large-estates' pastoral activities. The village of São Francisco de Paula/Pelotas, favored by dry meat production, had become the most dynamic economic center of Rio Grande do Sul. Porto Alegre, headquarters of the captaincy, had, since 1772, developed into the main political and commercial center. Rio Grande, in contrast, retreated in face of the dynamism of the other two agglomerations. The mountain range region—which reached up to 1,400 meters—was inadequate to cattle farming and remained relatively unpopulated. However, in 1824, the first German couples arrived and established themselves in the Sinos River Valley. New migratory waves of Germans and Italians—the last ones starting in 1875, occupied increasingly more elevated regions of the mountain range and the plateau.

Rio Grande do Sul in the nineteenth century.

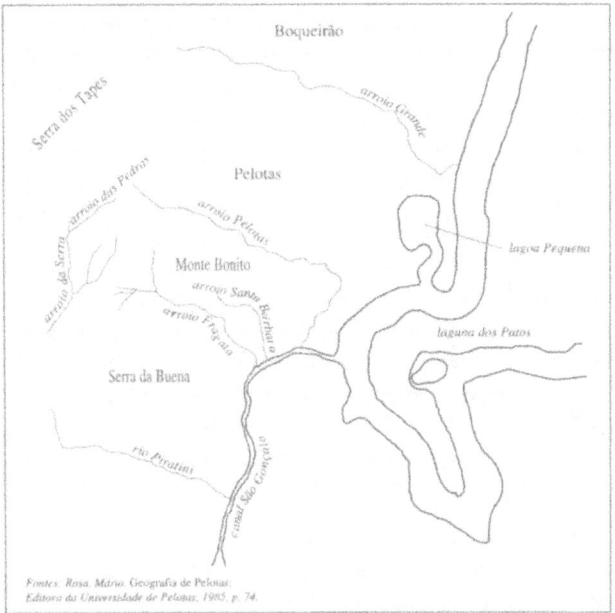

Parishes of the municipalities of the Village São Francisco de Paula located in the Buena and Boqueirão Mountain Range.

I

The enslaved black worker made significant contributions to all stages of settlement and development of the southern society.[4] The captives were one of the main smuggled commodities in Sacramento. Slaves participated in the first official expedition to *Estreito*. The first Gaúcho villages and ranches functioned, in part, as societies settled by the arm of the slave overseer. Following settlement, the dry meat production led to the importation of significant numbers of captives.

Available demographic data attest the importance of the southern slave population. In 1780, the captaincy counted with 9,433 "white" men, 3,388 acculturated "indigenous" and 5,102 (28%) "blacks."[5] In 1814, there were 32,300 "whites," 20,611 "slaves," 8,655 "indigenous" and 5,399 "free" (freed blacks and manumissioned slaves).[6] The absolute and relative importance of the southern captive population only declined in the first decades of the nineteenth century with the European immigration, and, above all, in the early part of the century, when Rio Grande do Sul began to export captives to the south central region. By 1861, the enslaved Gaúcho population was still significant. Rio Grande do Sul would have 344,227 inhabitants—77,588 (23 percent) of which were enslaved.[7]

Until a few years ago, the slave resistance in Gaúcho lands had been largely ignored. Brazilian historiography had simply made no reference to the rebellious character of slaves in Rio Grande do Sul. Almost nothing was known about the Gaúcho *quilombos*. At the most, one would only find brief references to the phenomenon, without much commentary. This historiographical carelessness was supported by a quasi-sophism of historical character. The enslaved Gaúcho worker who ran away to other countries was considered a free man. Thousands of captives crossed the southern border between Uruguay and Argentina. Wouldn't it have been easier and safer to run to the border, instead of forming quilombos?

Multiple causes led the slaves to the formation of quilombos in the South. The distance and difficulty of reaching the border was one of them— slaves had little knowledge of pathways to it, and whites controlled these trails. They had no desire to work as a Castilian laborer. They were afraid of the unknown, and attached to the land. What is known is that a considerable number of southern slaves ran away and formed quilombos in unpopulated mountain ranges, in wild forests, in isolated islands and in the middle of swamps.

The records left by the Gaúcho quilombo societies are abundant. In spite of that, it's possible that there may be not direct or indirect information on a substantial portion of southern quilombos. These concentrations of runaway captives are lost to historiographical endeavor. The written documentation is the richest source for studying quilombos. Other sources can also provide valuable help. We do not have archeological records from quilombos. In the future, archeology may possibly furnish us with rich information on this reality. Toponymy may also contribute to the study of Gaúcho quilombos. It used to be common in Brazil that geographical accidents, above all in regions with a delayed settlements, inhabited by quilombolas, for lack of denomination, were named as the Quilombo's Arroyo, or Mocambo Island, etc. They ended up keeping this denomination, even when the communities no longer existed. However, many of these toponyms fell in disuse and are only registered—when they are—by historical documentation.

In Rio Grande do Sul we have arroyos, localities, island, etc. with the name quilombo in regions with slavery tradition (Porto Alegre, Pelotas, Rio Pardo, Jaguarão, Osório, Viamão, Santa Maria, Santo Antonio).[8] It is unlikely that such a toponym had a different origin. However, the study of toponymy should base itself on archival sources. In the historical record, concentrations of runaways were denominated "Palmares" by association with the great quilombo of the mountainous regions of Barriga, in the current state of Alagoas. The Palmares toponym generally registers the existence of palm trees in the region.

2

In 1738, months after the founding of Rio Grande, the flight of a captive was reported.[9] We have no information in regards the appointment of slave catchers in Rio Grande, in those early times. In June of 1768, the Municipal Council—located in Viamão since the conquest of Rio Grande and the Continente by the *Castellanos*, in 1762—published a public notice to "appoint a slave catcher [...] to take care of runaway slaves and thefts."[10] In June of 1773, the same Council would appoint, as slave catcher, Salvador da Luz Camacho, "for the period of a year." According to city council members, the measure was taken due to the "multitude of runaway slaves hidden in quilombos" that were located in the Continente.[11] The occupation of Rio Grande determined the displacement of Luso-Brazilians from the region. Enslaved workers took this opportunity to escape.

On 2 January 1793, the City Council of Porto Alegre, seat of power of the captaincy, sent payment of 2$560 *réis* for two "little angels."[12] On 31 January 1798, the same Council appointed another slave catcher: "In this Council, Estácio Dutra has been appointed slave catcher of the district of this village's parish and a public notice on the routes he would be making at night was published."[13] On April 18, the following minutes were registered:

> In this council [...] it has been ordered that slaves caught in quilombos be marked with an 'F,' and that one more lynching pole be built in order to tie the slaves that are caught in quilombos, so that the execution of the law can be carried out before they enter the jail.[14]

The runaway slaves were a problem in Porto Alegre. In the mountains surrounding the village and in the nearby islands of the Guaíba River there must have been small concentrations of runaways. The council was referring to those quilombos. It was common for captives to find refuge in the nearby areas and in the river and lagoon islands near the urban centers. Nonetheless, we have no direct references to quilombos in the areas surrounding Porto Alegre. A part of the Ilha das Flores, next to Porto Alegre, is still known as "Quilombo Island."[15]

We also do not possess any information for this period about eventual quilombos in the regions bathed by the Jaguarão River, at the border with Uruguay. However, one of the small tributaries of the Jaguarão River is also known as "*Quilombo.*" The record does not show, under the name of this site, any concentration of runaway slaves originating from *charqueadas* (large cattle ranches centered on dried meat production). The first ranches of this type date from the beginning of the nineteenth century. The Arroyo Quilombo provided protection to runaways in earlier periods. When the Portuguese settled in the region (1801), the name for the site was already in use. There might have been a quilombo in the arroyo—when the Campos Neutrais constituted some kind of no one's land, right in between the possessions of Iberian crowns—and it would have been an ideal safe haven for Spanish and Portuguese captives, at the end of the seventeenth century.[16]

The first known reference to the existence and eventual destruction of a quilombo in Rio Grande do Sul dates from 1813. A correspondence from the *juiz de fora* (external judge)[17] of Porto Alegre, Domingos Francisco Pereira de Andrade, dated April 29, and sent to the governor and general captain of the captaincy, required that the slave catcher Ignácio Franscisco Quintanilha and his companions—responsible for the destruction of a quilombo and the capture of ten quilombolas (seven men and three women) in the Serra Geral possibly in the first days of March—presented themselves in Porto Alegre so that they could proceed with the "devastation according to the law." The quilombolas from Serra Geral were accused of killing "one of their partners" and the slave catcher Antônio. During the assault to the quilombo, an undetermined number of quilombolas ran away.[18]

On the first of September of 1821, the slave Antônio Benguela[19] owned by Manoel Alves dos Reis Louzada, killed a guard with a machete in the vicinities of Porto Alegre, near the Gravataí River, when he was cutting wood with other captives. In the corresponding trial, during which the other captives accused of helping him are found innocent, we find the "the recognition of Antônio Benguela's head, brought by a slave catcher, according to whom the slave was killed in the act of being apprehended in a quilombo." The report refers to a different quilombo.[20]

The records presented so far, which precede the Independence, provide us with a glimpse of what could be called the most explicit barbarism of the Gaúcho and Brazilian slavery system: runaway slaves branded with a burning iron rod; heads cut off as proof of slave capture; lynching poles for public punishment, etc. In addition, after 1822 (date of Brazil's declared independence from Portugal), lawsuits were filed to investigate whether quilombolas killed during capture had reacted to prison. The quilombola belonged to the slave owner. Since he was a valuable commodity to his lord, his death was also a commercial issue.

The decree of 16 March 1849, issued by the president of the province, authorized expenditures with the repression of "several quilombos in the vicinities of the city of Rio Pardo" and recommended that "there should be moderation in the deployment of force, except when quilombolas resist with weapons [...] and there is no other way of capturing them without use of weaponry."[21] On 9 October 1854, a lawsuit was filed to investigate whether the "black" killed in the forests of the mountainous administrative parish of Santa Maria da Boca do Monte, when an attack to the local quilombo was taking place, had been "killed during an act of resistance."[22] We have no knowledge of punishment of excessive violence deployed in the repression of quilombolas.

In September and October of 1829, the newspaper *O Amigo do Homem e da Pátria* reported that a yacht coming from the port of Rio Grande met with "unfavorable winds" near the Barba Negra Island (known today as Itapóa), in the Patos Lake, not very far from Porto Alegre. A small boat sent to the island with a sailor and four slaves in order to catch wood had been attacked by more than thirty sailors, armed with riffles and spears. According to this account, the runaway slaves chased the sailors and tried to board the yacht, which sailed away immediately. An expedition with "One hundred and sixty front line soldiers and another thirty artillery soldiers sent to suppress the attack, sank a small boat with nine quilombolas–six men and three women—who were trying to escape. As they landed on the island, the troops found fields of bean and corn, four completed houses and two in construction."[23]

On 25 January 1829, a slave catcher from Porto Alegre, Antônio Cândido,[24] was notified by Camilo Gonçalves Porto, resident of Itapoã, that "nine negros," among them soldiers armed with "swords, *reiúnas* and pistols," raised a small fortress in the island next to the home of the one who made the complaint.[25] After being notified in early February, the slave catcher resorted to the provincial presidency, requesting "sufficient people" to destroy the quilombo.[26] This was a quilombo in settlement process, which was eventually deemed stable. The quilombolas worked for the dried meat ranchers during the harvest season.

The first urban agglomerations of the Colony and of the Empire possessed great concentrations of enslaved workers. Runaway slaves either tried to pass as freed or free blacks or remained in the vicinities of the agglomerations where they founded small quilombos. They were urban slaves, used to or seduced by urban life. Rural life was either unknown or unattractive. With the help from freed slaves, free poor people, slaves and some slave masters, the suburban quilombos made a living from little thefts, selling of products and services to the urban population. The newspaper *O Observador*, from Rio Grande, reported the repression of a suburban quilombo. The destruction of the Negro Lucas Quilombo, in the Island of Marinheiros, made front-page news in the edition of 9 January 1833. The small paper stated:

> For more than ten years, a black man named Lucas along with many other runaway slaves who found themselves burrowed in the thickets of the Marinheiros Island [...] this savage was always armed, threatening the white residents, to whom he became even more menacing due to the strong protection he received from the blacks and the manumissioned that resided there. He was known to have perpetrated seven assassinations; two of the last victims of his ferocity [...] had been Antônio Vicente, a poor father and a young man, the sheriff's son, of the same island, [...] this one had been shot recently, while he attempted to imprison Lucas.

The Island of Marinheiros, when compared to the lands of the region of Rio Grande, was considered fertile. It was partially covered by major vegetation inhabited by farmers that lived from fruits and vegetables that they sold in the villages. In August 1820, as the French naturalist Auguste de Saint-Hilaire was passing by Rio Grande, he observed:

> I have not been to the Island of Marinheiros but I have heard that it is two and a half leagues long. It is mainly covered in thickets and provides wood to hospitals and military headquarters. It possesses excellent fountain of pure water[...].[27]

An enslaved worker was absolutely prohibited from obtaining a license to bear firearms.[28] Protected by the thickets and by freed and captive slaves who were well armed and fearless, Lucas and his people lived in the island for quite a while, defending themselves with hand-held firearms. A contributing factor to this was the traditional debility of the police force and the military authorities, especially since 1831. The quilombolas' frontal and bloody insubordination to local authorities, epitomized by the death of the Island sheriff's son, would have precipitated an unsustainable situation. According to the newspaper:

> As a result of this last assault, the justice of peace has ordered the sheriff and four national guards to prepare for an ambush in the thicket, with the goal of imprisoning him [Lucas]. The order was executed, and in the end of twelve days of working diligently, there came a light skinned black (who was a runaway hanging in the forest) and warned the national guards that the assassin should be coming in the morning of the fist of the month, to the house of a black slave belonging to Sir Justino José de Oliveira: They took advantage of this occasion and went to the said house, where, at nine in the morning of the assigned day, the barbarian indeed arrived; following his custom, he was armed. With him there came two other blacks armed with spears and a black woman [...].

As we shall see, even the national guards knew where Lucas and his people were hiding; they preferred to organize an ambush with the help of a tattletale. It was certainly the quilombolas' attitude of resistance more than their hideout in the forest that kept them free while so near the repressive forces. The newspaper *O Observador* reported:

> As he [Lucas] got closer to the door, it was opened by the national guards, who were there with the aforementioned sheriff. As soon as they called for his arrest, the black man retreated, kneeled down, and, with great speed, shot with the rifle towards the inside of the house. The shot was so close that it could have killed one of the national guards. He then advanced towards them with a sword, and at the same time, the other two attacked with spears: Finding themselves in imminent danger, one of the national guards shot back at them and hit Lucas, who fell dead on the floor while the other two quickly ran away.

We will possibly never know if Lucas died fighting or if he didn't even know where the bullet that killed him had come from. It was very common to shoot down delinquents who resisted arrest. In spite of their chief's death, the other quilombolas were able to escape.

In the next day, the same sheriff, along with few citizens, came to examine the quilombo, and in it they found a large house with various compartments, some cattle leather pieces (four of which had been branded as belonging to Sir Antônio José Afonso) a lot of meat, animal fat, iron pots, chocolate makers, bottles, containers, jeroboams, a spear and a lot of fire wood, which was cut and tied in bundles, among a number of other provisions. Five black men and four black women that were under Luca's command had escaped from this place—this we learnt through the same mulatto, whom had made the rounds there as a fugitive.

The Island of Marinheiros Quilombo was formed by six men and four women who followed a leader. The quilombolas dedicated themselves to plundering and small commerce with Rio Grande, possibly through the intermediation of captives and freed men from the island. They also prepared leathers, fats, dried meats and sold wood, etc. The quilombo's proximity to the village explained its relative prosperity.

3

The charqueadas (dried meat ranches) at the margins of the Pelotas Creek held great concentrations of enslaved workers. In 1833, the Pelotas municipality had 10,873 inhabitants. Among them, 5,623 were captive, 3,911 free men, 1,137 freed, 5,623 slaves and 180 indigenous people.[29] In 1884, the captive population remained almost the same. Robert Conrad reminds us:

> Out of the five thousands slaves that inhabited the city had, two thousand were domestic servers or port workers and one thousand were deployed in agricultural labor. The other two thousand, according to the president of the province, worked in the charqueadas.[30]

The great concentration of slaves living at the quarters in Pelotas worried the lords. They feared their escape, as well as the formation of quilombos and insurrection. The documentation of the time period registers this anxiety. On 27 February 1835, the city council sent correspondence to the provincial presidency, after having been informed of the great insurrection of the Malê people in Salvador:[31]

> Once the news of the events that took place there in the night of 24th to 25th of the month that has just ended, arrived at the City Council of the São Francisco de Paulo village [...] and though the insurrection was repressed in time, its effects can still cause irreparable damages. Since this province (Rio Grande do Sul) has generally been host to badly behaved slaves, sold from other provinces of the Empire, especially after the Maranhão province has cease to receive them and given that this City Council, according to aforementioned letters, it is known that a good number of Nagôs and Haussás slaves are coming here from Bahia to be sold. We are led to believe that they may be implicated in the insurrection and that their masters in order to save them from the law's revenge, sought to get rid of slaves who [...] at times have committed such horrendous delinquencies. It is also evident that such slaves did come and will be largely sold to charqueadas, [...] which maintain two to three thousand captives nearly in contact with each other given the

> proximity among the aforementioned charqueadas. Therein lies the fear that they may augment the number of these amoral creatures [...] and attempt to wreak havoc [...]

In order to impede the ingress of captive rebels, the City Council asked the provincial authorities that the Nagô and Haussá slaves, recently landed in Bahia, be summoned "to be safely delivered in the Rio Grande village, so that necessary exams could be administered, and, in case those slaves were of the seditious type, these [exams] were to be sent and delivered to the authorities of that province."[32] Insurrection was the greatest preoccupation of the slave lords. The escape from captivity was also feared.

The charqueadas were truly akin to penitentiaries. At the banks of the Pelotas Arroyo there were about forty productive charqueadas with an average of sixty captives each. The production of dry meat was seasonal. Harvest season went from October to May, when slaves were expected to produce the greatest possible quantity of dry meat and other products. The slaughtered animals were prepared by the enslaved worked who labored in specialized, semi-specialized and non-specialized tasks. The captives worked at least sixteen hours, with only brief breaks, moved by the whip of the foreman and a few cups of firewater.[33]

The blacks that worked in the charqueadas were closely monitored. Whenever they rested, they were locked into precarious slave quarters. Yet, escape was common. In the regional newspapers, announcements such as the following were quite common: "On Saturday of Alleluia, the slave Desidério, aged approximately thirty years, escaped from the charqueada of the deceased Joaquim Guillerme da Costa" (*Diário do Rio Grande*, 25 April 1865). After running away from the charqueada the captive could hide away in some of Pelotas' *zungus* (tenements)—a feat neither easy nor common.[34] In order to go unnoticed in the urban environment, the runaway had to rely upon the support of both captive and freed city dwellers. In the vicinities of Pelotas, it was difficult to hide. Its neighboring regions are flat, without notable topographical variety. The runaway had to walk a bit in order to find a hiding place—but not too much.

Up until a few years ago, in the municipality of Pelotas, there were semi-uninhabited territories, of sinuous reliefs and dry vegetation. As we advance towards the northwest of Pelotas, the monotonous and bare coastal relief begins to be transformed into a significant complex of plains filled with small elevations and mountain ranges—the so-called "dorsal spine" of Cangaçu. This region, the Tapes Mountain Range, with local vegetation, arroyos, abundant game and good soil, was the ideal habitat for quilombolas to reconstruct life in freedom. The first rolling hills of the Tapes Mountain Range were found roughly within twenty kilometers from Pelotas. The mountain range possessed a little arroyo known as "Quilombo," affluent from the left margins of the Pelotas Arroyo. The region may have already been, in the late eighteenth century, a site of refuge for runaway captives from São Francisco de Paula and Rio Grande. A small quilombo, on the banks of the arroyo had named the region. Oral tradition describes the site of the quilombo as "an old bridge" or "a wooden bridge."[35]

The documentation on quilombos in Pelotas is rich. In July 1820, the City Council of Rio Grande, then having jurisdiction over Pelotas, protested to the governor and the general captain of the captaincy the recruitment to the Volunteer Legion, of one of the ten members of a "company of slave catchers" formed to capture runaways hiding in the mountain range, especially those coming from the Pelotas charqueadas. According to city counselors, runaway and marooned slaves perpetrated great insults within the parish of São Francisco de Paula and its surrounding areas. The escapes from the charqueadas were so numerous that the captives could run away in groups of four. The soldier of the slave catcher of Pelotas, José Maria de Camargo, had been captured by a "faction of the Legion of the Volunteers," in the very conglomeration, on June 29. This took place just upon his arrival on the Tapes Mountain Range with his men, where he had caught three female slaves. The members of the company feared being recruited to the poorly viewed Legion of Volunteers.[36]

On 19 May 1832, the City Council of Pelotas mandated "the local judges of peace to provide slave catchers for localities within their districts that may find convenient to have them, as well as the number of soldiers they believed their districts should have."[37] On November 14, the same council requested judges of peace from Pelotas and the Buena highland for "their proposals for slave catchers of their respective districts." On 11 January 1833, two judges of peace, Albino Soares da Silveira and Antônio José de Almeida, were named slave catchers of the Pelotas parish,[38] and João Machado dos Santos, slave catcher of the Buena highland parish.[39]

A correspondence from the City Council, dated 11 May 1832, addressed to the president of the province, highlighted the main threats to the order of the slave state: Wrongdoers and slaves.

> The City Council of the São Francisco de Paula village has the honor to bring to the attention of Your Excellency that the location of this village within a crucial site of transit for all the people of the border region, of daily influx of unknown and villainous subjects, in addition to having in its district a great number of slaves [...] leads the Council judges to request [...]

with urgency, twenty to thirty permanent municipal guards for the village –guards whose power allied to the national guards citizens, the council believes to be sufficient in maintaining the good order [....]⁴⁰

In addition to the "wrongdoers" and "slaves," the good men of Pelotas feared that foreigners would "take the blacks down the wrong path." The Council wrote to the presidency on 6 August 1832:

> [...] the march of the national guards from this municipality to the border would be dangerous during the current crisis that the neighboring state [Uruguay] is facing as they are making war among themselves and sending disguised emissaries to rebel against slavery, with which –these are true news—they expect to reinforce their foolish army ranks. The fact is that the district of this village has more than four thousand slaves, almost all united, according to sources from the charqueadas, and the only force capable of containing them is the National Guard [...] ⁴¹

Soon, the foreigners were watched. Two years later, on August 16, the City Council of Jaguarão (a small village near the border with Uruguay) wrote to the council members of Pelotas, who, in turn, sent a copy of the letter to the presidency of the province.

> In today's extraordinary session the City counselors and the City Council of this village has resolved to address to you an announcement that came to our attention through a trustworthy citizen, who asserts that General Rivera has sent emissaries to this province with the goal of inciting the slaves into a rebellion.⁴²

Towards the end of the first five years of the 1830s, references to a strong quilombo activity in the municipality were abundant. A magazine from Pelotas—*Princesa do Sul*—from 1952, cites documents from the City Council from that period that we are yet to find: In the year of 1834, Joaquim José Ribeiro, commandant of a "race to hunt the wrongdoers, received cash for the capture of some and, after this, in the year of 1835, requested aid to support the men that had been, along with him, surveying and protecting the campaign against these dangerous elements."

In fact, on 10 October 1834, the council mandated:

> All judges of peace, especially those of the third district, so that [...] they can extend decisive and immediate provisions to imprison quilombolas who, a few days ago, have committed criminal acts in the Tapes Mountain Range.⁴³

However, the problem was of such magnitude that the Council did not have the means to combat it with efficiency. The minutes of the 3 December 1834 meeting registered the will of city counselors to transfer responsibility to the "justices of peace" and to the "military authorities."

Mister President did not call for a meeting with the Council because he knew that he did not have the means to satisfy such requisition. For this reason, he responded to the aforementioned justice of peace, informing him that the council had already made the due recommendations to all justices of peace of the term, with whom he should discuss the issue, along with the military authorities, when armed forces were needed.[44] Without the means or will to support the expenses, the Council turned to the president of the province. In a session that took place on 30 May 1835, the counselors agreed with the proposal of the "President of the City Council, in regards to the employment of twelve residents of the Tapes Mountain Range as permanent soldiers [...] so that they could be deployed in the imprisonment of quilombolas." However, the Council preferred to present itself as not "authorized" to take such measures and sponsor its costs, so, consequently, it appealed to the presidency of the province. In this occasion, it recommended that the justices of peace of the third, fourth and fifth districts undertake "in common agreement," the "destruction of quilombos" and the "prison of wrongdoers."[45] The correspondence in which the Council asked for assistance from to the highest provincial authority suggests an alliance between urban slaves and quilombolas.

> The City Council [...] must bring to Your Excellency's knowledge that it does not possess the authority to take strong measures towards the destruction of quilombolas that have found refugee in the Tapes Mountain Range (belonging to this village) and that have been stealing and committing murders in these vicinities in a daring and tyrannical manner. As a result, the local residents, terrified with such hostilities, have evacuated their houses and fields, which has caused an agricultural deficit. In spite of the means deployed by the police authorities, they have been unsuccessful; besides, the national guards that have been requested have done nothing since these demands have been made in front of the slaves of these same national guards, whom undoubtedly have established communications with quilombolas, and not having the same authorities available men power to deploy, since the remaining residents of this village, in number of ten, are not apt for campaigns that demand practice, sagacity and confidentiality [...].

In its deliberations on May 30, the Council suggested arming and financing "twelve scheming men, chosen by the justice of peace of the third district, whose immediate orders should be to deploy towards the quilombolas, the same treatment they had given to the residents of the village."⁴⁶ The response of the presidency was immediate. As we've seen, only a few months prior there had been an important insurrection of the Malê from Salvador. Along with the Council's request, there was a dispatch, which was maybe the product of the provincial president's own handwriting:

> We hereby respond, given the article of the provincial budget law, to the order of the Treasurer that the amount of 1600$000 réis be deployed towards the extinction of quilombos in this municipality, and in case this sum is not sufficient, it should be known in time, so that a greater sum can be sent. This order is being sent to the Treasurer today.

The supplications of the citizens of Pelotas were heard. The minutes of the City Council's meeting on 9 July 1835 registered in a provincial official document, dated June 30, stipulated the sum of 1600$000 réis "to be spent on the destruction of quilombolas."⁴⁷ In this occasion, the insatiable City Council wrote to the presidency with a reminder that they had committed a greater sum towards the reward of those who would arrest and eliminate "those ten quilombolas considered responsible for thefts, fires and murders perpetrated within the municipality." The reward was in the sum of four hundred thousand "réis" for the leader of the "Quilombo Manoel Padeiro," and of one hundred thousand for "each of his nine partners." At that time, these amounts were exorbitant. In the 1840s, for instance, one could buy, in Pelotas, "a one-storey home" for five hundred thousand réis.⁴⁸ In the same correspondence, the presidency was informed of the gravity of the facts and the fight against quilombolas:

> [...] the thefts, fires and murders perpetrated by the quilombolas grow day after day. With boldness and craftiness these quilombolas have terrified the pacific residents of the Tapes Mountain Range and made them abandon their homes and tillage. As a result, they've already lost harvests of corn and beans, which will infallibly lead to considerable shortfall of these crops for consumption by the population of this municipality; and in spite of the proceedings of two inspectors of the aforementioned mountain range, under the orders of a certain justice of peace (whom has sent a few armed troupes there to exterminate similar robbers), they were only able to capture a freed female slave that the quilombolas had stolen from her father's house (in the colt farm of São Lourenço), killing him in the process. They also captured three female slaves whom they had stolen from other houses and, as a result, one of the aforementioned quilombolas was killed in this attack. The remainder

of the quilombolas were able to escape, hiding in the forest. Perhaps attesting to the inefficiency of the mission, a few days later, the same quilombolas appeared in other places, committing attacks and daring to come in one given night to this village, where they robbed a tavern and a pottery whose foreman was gravely wounded; and five days ago they've killed a man who was married and had a family and wounded another who was accompanying him—this took place a few leagues away from this village, having the dead been left in the middle of the road with his head severed from his body. For all these reasons, the Council, in order to incite folks in different expeditions, are in the midst of proceedings to imprison or extinguish, under the law, such evil doers, have promised to grant the sum of four hundred thousand *réis*, for the capture or extermination of the leader of aforementioned quilombolas, Manoel Padeiro, and of two hundred thousand *réis* for each of violent man's nine partners [...].[49]

In the following month, on August 17, the Council, in possession of the funds provided by the presidency, issued a decision after having obtained a few victories over the quilombolas:

> [...] the session was opened at 10 am, after consultation with the justice of peace of the third district, Boaventura Inácio Barcellos, in regards to the provisions needed to enact the extinction of Tapes Mountain Range's quilombo. It was decided through unanimous votes that the said justice of peace should send an expedition of seven men and a commandant to, in the name of the Law, imprison or exterminate said quilombo criminals, for the salary of 1,280 réis for the commandant and 640 réis for each soldier, in addition to the gratification they would receive for imprisoning or extinguishing the quilombolas. In turn, for the head of Manoel Padeiro they would pay 400$000 réis and for each of his six partners, 100$000 réis. It was also ruled that the City Council's attorney should deliver the sum of 3000$000 réis to the said justice of peace, for the expenditures of the aforementioned expedition, and make the last responsible for finalizing the payments.[50]

Around September of 1835, in the Tapes Mountain Range, a quilombola named Mariano, after having been separated from his partners due to the persecution of the police troupes, travelled to a meeting point determined by Manoel Padeiro, general of the quilombo. Unarmed and starved, Mariano pleaded Luiz, an enslaved worker of Bernardino Rodrigues Barcellos'[51] farm, for help. Given the cold rain, the comrade in misfortune fed him and invited him to find refuge in the sugar mill's house.

An award of 100 thousand réis weighed over Mariano's head. His supposed protector locked the black man, native of Santa Catarina, who was about 25 years old, in a room of the sugar mill's house. He was immediately sent to Pelotas, and judged in the beginning of December, along with Simão Vergara, an African salesperson that had been granted manumission and had been accused of selling gunpowder to quilombolas. Annexed to the lawsuit pertaining to Mariano and Simão were interrogations of four female captives and a freed adolescent who had been kidnapped by the quilombolas. This documentation provided rich information on the quilombo that provoked great agony for the slave masters of Pelotas.[52]

It's believable that Manoel Padeiro, once recaptured had been able to escape once again, either alone or with someone. Out of the ten runaway slaves that had formed the central nucleus of the quilombo, four were captives of Manoel Padeiro's lord—the rich Boaventura Rodrigues Barcellos.[53] Documentation also reveals that the contact between the quilombolas and that lord's slaves were intimate and constant. It was precisely one of the Commander's captive that Mariano sought for help when he found himself in difficulty.

We do not know exactly when or how the quilombolas got together. What is certain is that during the first days of April 1835, under the unshakable authority of Padeiro, the band began to assault farms in the Tapes Mountain Range. The attacks would only end a month later, towards the end of 1835, with the debilitation of the quilombolas due to deaths and arrests. The documentation registers the first attack as occurring in the house of Jerônimo Lopes Garcia. Twelve quilombolas executed the attack probably in the beginning of April 1835. Members of the group were Manoel Padeiro, quilombo general; Jôao, justice of peace; Alexandre Moçambique, captain; pai[54] Mateus; Mariano Crioulo; Antônio Mulato; Antônio Cabinda or Cabunda; pai Francisco, Congo; Francisco Moçambique; Benedito Moçambique; João, cook and African; and the mulatto Rosa. The African captive Manoel, also property of commander Barcellos, was arrested on the road and had a death order from Mariano, which was denied by Manoel Padeiro. Soon after, he joined the quilombolas. It wasn't possible to elucidate the meanings of the titles "justice of peace" and "captain" (in that context).

In the first assaulted farm, one would find Lindaura, the wife of the owner, Jerônimo Lopes Garcia, which suggests that the mountain range still had not suffered the outbreak of quilombo attacks. In that residence, the quilombolas obtained flour, clothes and three firearms. On that occasion, Alexandre Moçambique proposed the kidnapping of lady Lindaura, but Manoel Padeiro rejected, certainly conscious that the action would lead to a fierce persecution of his group. Nonetheless, Alexandre's desire was not entirely denied. The quilombolas ended up carrying away with them a mulatto woman of twenty-five years of age, named Maria, apparently against her will, who remained with them for a period of two months. Maria was the first of four women—three captives (Maria, Florência and Dorotéia) and a freed one (Senhorinha Alves) who had been kidnapped by the runaways. This would support the thesis that the quilombolas had begun the most aggressive phase of their expeditions across the mountains range with this attack.

The process registered the near obsession of the quilombolas for the "*crioulas*" (mulatto women) and "*pretas*" (black women). After having been discomfited by a police expedition, the first initiative of the group—which was not realized—was to assault a farm in order to get allies and black women. This fact is comprehensible. The sexual repression of slavery has been historically documented. On average, there were two African males to each female arriving from Africa. In 1850–88, in the dry meat farms of Pelotas, the male population rate was determined to be around 87 percent.[55] Quilombos were generally populated by a male majority.

On the event of the first registered attack, eleven men and one woman constituted the quilombo group from the Tapes Mountain Range. Mulatto Rosa, owned by Commander Barcellos, was a strong-minded quilombola. Dressing as a man and carrying two knifes on her belt, she participated actively in the quilombo attacks. It seems that she did not have a fixed partner. She died on 16 April 1835, while resisting the first attack that attempted to re-enslave the group, along with João, "Justice of Peace."

After the assault to the farm of Jerônimo Lopes Garcia, the quilombolas continued their unstoppable voyage along the mountain range. Without ever setting roots in any location, they would alternate stops (for resting, usually in already utilized camping spots) with assaults of residencies in the region. Nine houses and two slave quarters were robbed and set on fire and an undetermined number of houses were sacked. The last assaulted residencies, before the police attack of June 16, brought little profit to the quilombolas. It seems that the terrified residents left the region, taking what they could with them. With the robberies, in addition to precious black and mulatto women, the quilombolas obtained foods (yucca flour, corn, beans, etc.) clothes, tobacco, gunpowder, firearms and valuable objects (stirrup and silver-plated spoons).

The documentation in question provides evidence of a phenomenon common to other Brazilian regions: The promiscuity among quilombolas and the slave population. The followers of Manoel Padeiro gathered information from the slaves of the assaulted houses. Captives participated in the attacks, without following the quilombo afterwards. Blacks were brought to the quilombo encampment, where they would spend the night dancing and eating, and would depart at dawn. However, their support of the quilombos was not always voluntary or without self-interest. Records suggest a more complex reality. Among the quilombolas and the slave workers there was a social and cultural identity, which in fact would lead them towards dialogue of singular ease and frequency, even when a captive would be opposed to escape or to joining the quilombo as a solution to his problems. These profound bonds would also connect, sometimes in contradictory ways, slaves and former slaves.

Possibly at the end of April, Mariano asked Manoel Padeiro for permission to go sell corn and buy tobacco and gunpowder somewhere near the village of Pelotas. The general gave permission and sent Francisco with the black man. Records suggest the precise reason for this choice. After having robbed and bagged the corn, both quilombolas went on a two-way nine-day trip to a store in Boa Vista, in the vicinities of Pelotas, which belonged to the freed African Simão Vergara—known by the quilombolas as *pai* Simão. The African rented part of a house where he lived and other properties to working black men.

Pai Simão's small store was not the best supplied. His wife, Teresa, accompanied pai Francisco so that he could buy fennel, pepper, sugar and cumin, in the other store. At pai Simão's store, the quilombolas bought tobacco and the precious gunpowder. Mariano declared that the negotiations between pai Simão and pai Francisco took place in the "language of the Congo," which he did not speak.[56] The fact that two Africans were called "father" and knew Kikongo suggests that they would be from the same Congo Nation and that, maybe, they were of the same age.

The solidarity among "nations" was not very solid. Pai Simão cheated on his fellow countryman whom, not being well versed in business, exchanged the valuable coin that Padeiro had given him to go shopping—a deed that was punished with whippings when the travellers returned to the quilombo. Mariano, perhaps out of shame, only reported that pai Francisco had been "chastised" by Padeiro. What calls attention here is the fact that the physical punishment, as a form of sentencing for the errors committed, one of the pillars of slavery, had penetrated so deeply into the consciousness of the slave workers that they would adopt it themselves even within the free environment of the quilombo.

The dominance of class upon race and ethnicity in the action of the quilombolas is equally suggested in the documentation. It was the fact of being captive, runaway and persecuted that unified the group formed by slave laborers born either in Brazil or Africa. The action of the quilombolas did not seem to have been guided by a racial consciousness that would be above the contradictions and necessities lived by the group. The mulatto and black women Maria, Florência and Dorotéia were notified by the quilombolas that they were now freed, after having been forced to accompany the attackers. During the time they remained with the group, they were placed under close surveillance.

The Tapes Mountain Range was a zone of medium and small properties dedicated to the production of subsistence items. Large, medium and small lords had farms in the mountain. The nine houses that had been set on fire had straw roofs, which suggests poor resources and investments within a region where brick factories were abundant. Properties that had been broken into, burned down and sacked belonged to free and freed mulattos. Some of them were slave lords themselves. The quilombos seem not to differentiate between white and black lords. They broke into the residency of freed mulatto José Alves and killed the small property owner. After sacking and setting fire to the house, they carried away Alves' daughter, known as mulatto Senhorinha, by force. Israel, Senhorinha's brother, joined the armed group that attacked the quilombos, freed the women, and killed João, "Justice of Peace," along with Rosa.

Records also register the hatred quilombo harbored against the "*capatazes*" —as the Gaúcho foremen were called. The foremen Domingos José Enes, a Portuguese man of fifty-four, and Eufrázio Antônio de Silva, were harshly injured and punished by the quilombolas. During the attack to Tomás Flores's farm, when the quilombolas found out that the foreman was in the house, they broke in through a window with an axe, pulled Domingos Enes out, shot him dead and abandoned his body. Upon that occasion, mulatto Maria, kidnapped by the quilombolas, would have screamed that they should kill the Portuguese man because he was "evil." The conscience of the slave laborers—runaway or kidnapped—joined one another to face the possibility of settling the score with a foreman who had been quite pitiless.

After setting the Tapes Mountain Range in flames and awakening the ire and fear of the lords of Pelotas, on 16 June 1835, as discussed, the quilombolas were attacked by a troupe that came upon the encampment and took hold of the women and the war treasures of the quilombolas. Two runaways died in combat and others were able to escape. However, even if debilitated, the quilombolas regrouped and reinitiated their attacks shortly thereafter.

Two weeks later, in the beginning of July, the followers of Manoel Padeiro, in numbers of six to eight, attacked a brick factory next to Pelotas at night, with the intention of freeing black men and women. During the assault, mulatto Antônio gravely wounded the establishment's foreman. It seems that the runaway did not achieve their intentions. On the same night, they attacked a store on the path of the mountain, where they got bread, flour and tobacco.[57] On July 9, during the march back to the Tapes Mountain Range, they met with Antônio Grande, who was shot, strangled and decapitated for having "said goodbye" to João, the "Justice of Peace."[58]

Nonetheless, the luck of the quilombolas was sealed. On August 12, the justice of peace of the Third District declared that a gang had attacked a group eight quilombolas and that it had managed to kill Manuel Cabunda, who, as we've seen, had joined the quilombolas after having escaped their attempt to kill him.[59] After this or another subsequent attack, Mariano, separated from his partners, sought refugee at the property of Bernardino Rodrigues Barcellos on September 10, where he was, three days later, arrested due to betrayal. Mariano was judged by those he offended when he ran away from work and from the whip and threatened the life and the property of the slave lords. His judicial process was more of a farce than the product of slavery-related justice. Abandoned by his lord, Mariano was "defended" by an appointed lawyer, who did not even take the effort to appeal the death sentence that was unanimously voted by the jury. If his sentence was not later appealed, then Simão Vergar must have paid with fifteen years, six months and twenty days in prison for the act of selling gunpowder to the rebels.

According to a publication of 1928 from Pelotas, at the beginning of the Farroupilha Revolt, in 1835, a sum of "two *contos* and two hundred thousand réis" would have been delivered as "contribution to war" towards the combat of the quilombos of Pelotas. The expedition that counted with a great number of Germans would have been put together under the direction of the justice of peace Boaventura Inácio Barcellos,[60] who appointed Joaquim Luiz da Lima as his interim lieutenant. The two main concentrations of runaway captives would be found "under the margins of two arroyos that were tributaries from the River Pelotas and Arroyo Grande, respectively, and whose course were covered by dense vegetation."[61] We do not know whether those who had remained in Manoel Padeiro's gang formed this quilombo.

With the advent of the Farroupilha Revolution, the number of runaways was multiplied. The revolutionary army assaulted enemy farms and freed the captives that accepted becoming their soldiers. The soldiers of the Empire did the same in the Farroupilha properties. In both fronts, those summoned to war would free their slaves so that these could substitute them in battle. A great number of slaves sought places they deemed safer than the army battalions. Escaping to neighboring countries or seeking shelter in quilombos was an attractive option for an unknown number of runaways. After the peace process, records pointed out that there were various expeditions against quilombos formed during the decade long war. The records on the Farroupilha period were either lost or quite incomplete.

In order to reconstitute the history of quilombos, we count, above all, with the seigneurial archives. Generally, these records pertained to the destruction of quilombo communities. We know very little about the internal life of quilombos or the reasons and means that would lead the runaways to organize them. The judicial report that Pedro Andara issued against the black Antônio, at the Public Archive of Rio Grande do Sul, constitutes a particularly interesting document in regards to the formation of quilombos in Pelotas.[62] The interrogation of the single, forty-year-old African Antônio, accused of inviting slaves to form a quilombo outside of the city, took place on 21 October 1848, in the house of the police sheriff's assistant Antônio Rafael dos Anjos. Pedro Andara had charged Antônio with having attempted to seduce the captive Maria, of the Mina "nation,"[63] who was a slave of his absent brother-in-law.

Everything had started when the young African woman, at the age of twenty, told her master's brother-in-law that the black Antônio, in spite of only knowing her for "two months, had, more or less," invited her "twice" (when she was "selling fabrics on the city streets") to run away with him to a quilombo where she would "gain manumission." The last invite had been made on the day prior to the report. According to an Alcagüete African woman, interrogated on the same occasion, Antônio had not told her where the quilombo was to be formed, but did tell her that he had already made a deal with another three blacks. Maria only knew one of the invitees: Teresa, slave of Nicolas Aleijado.

Antônio Cabinda,[64] slave of commander Boaventura Rodriguez Barcellos, was a salaried captive, like Maria. He had ample freedom of action and had the duty to periodically deliver to his master a certain sum—"the profit." In order to "sell works of [his] trade," he had come to Pelotas to reside on Lavadeiras street—in "house the (manumissioned) black Gegê Fabião,[65] where he had been for four days." In the same home resided "a white man and a white woman."

Since he was a schooled captive, Antônio didn't get confused in his explanations. When inquired whether he had invited Maria "to run away and form a quilombo," he resolutely responded that he had known the African woman for six months and that he had never invited her to such adventure. He had only met with Maria "on the afternoon of the day prior, and she had asked him for two thousand réis needed for her greengrocer." Antônio eventually asserted that he agreed to give her the sum, as long as the young African "would come to his house in the evening of that same day." Thus, he planted the suspicion that due to the indecent proposal, Maria had presented herself in his home accompanied by a man whom he did not know, in addition to six soldiers, who imprisoned him.

4

In the nineteenth century, the Rio Pardo municipality possessed a significant concentration of slaves. A developed agricultural system, and active fluvial port, a rich commercial activity, the dry meat farms of the Jacuí—all these activities employed a great number of servile arms. In 1780, Rio Pardo had 1,317 whites, 438 indigenous people and 619 blacks. At that time, the town was only outnumbered in slave population by the parish of Triunfo (Conceição do Arroio).[66] After 34 years, in 1814, "freed men of all colors" were at the number of 6,900, the indigenous at 818 and the slaves at 2,429.[67]

The indexes, including archival ones and of other types, about quilombos in Rio Pardo are abundant. There was an arroyo named Quilombo in the municipality. The "statistical map," found within a book by José dos Santos Pereira, registers that, in the decade of 1847–57, "newspapers [were] paid to men employed to destroy quilombos in the municipality of Rio Pardo." The "statistical map" informs us of sums but fails to locate the quilombos. According to Guillermino César:

> Between 1847 and 1848, 268$000 were spent. From 1848 to 1849, 240$000. In 1850, 4663$280; in 1853, the expenses went up to their highest yet: 1340$8000. [...] the repression may not have been violent [sic], but, in fact, the diarists were able to cut the evil at its roots to such an extent, that in the years immediately following, not a single cent was spent with this same finality. At least there were no records left in the provincial banks that I have knowledge of. It was only in 1857 that the public power reinstalled

this expense, deploying then 302$420 in daily costs to control Rio Pardo quilombos.[68]

Each registered expense pointed to expeditions against quilombos. It was not a rare occurrence for the gangs to disperse and only partially injure the quilombo strongholds. Some runaways were imprisoned, others killed. The quilombolas that remained burrowed into the forest, regrouping in other sites. In general, it was the colonization of a region that would put an end to the concentrations of runaway captives.

We have information about the operation of 1847. On 4 March 1847, the police sheriff of Rio Pardo, Manoel Alves de Oliveira, wrote to the president of the province in response to the official documents issued on February 2 and 11, in which the highest provincial authority ordained him to ask the commandant of the 9 National Guard Cavalry of the military power to support the destruction of quilombos in the vicinities of Rio Pardo and authorized the hiring of four "cowboys." In this letter, Oliveira informed the presidency that an expedition had already taken place and that he could not calculate the adjustment levels for the salaries of workers: due to the fact that these cowboys have gone from the place where this expedition took place to other points where it is known that other quilombos exist, without having come back to this city. Annexed to this, there was more information:

> My Illustrious lord, as you are already aware, yesterday we saw the return of the cavalry that, according to your orders, had left towards a quilombo located in the mountain range of the Couto District [...]. After marching for three days in the mountains, the above-mentioned cavalry, guided by slave catcher Pedro Rodrigues da Costa, would have managed to attack the quilombo by surprise, at noon, apprehending, as a result, slaves listed in the included document. Due to quilombo resistance to the armed forces, a black man and woman were killed in the first conflict. Common sense dictates that if six to eight black men and two black women escaped it was due to being they were dispersed through the woods, engaged in various activities. We have received news that two large ranches were burned down which had slaves. The fire destroyed if not all, at least great portion of the food stocks gathered. The same slave catcher observed, through the vestiges that in addition to this, there was another 'negro' establishment and assured that he would be victorious over it. As a result, I have put together another gang so that whenever your Excellency judges it convenient, it may go to persecute other quilombos in that area. [...] Military Quarter of the Command

of Our National Guard Cavalry and Munitions of Rio Pardo. March first, one thousand eight hundred and forty even...(1847) [...].[69]

Sergeant Paulino Antônio de Souza, who led the re-enslaving troupe, apprehended and took to Rio Pardo the quilombolas Miguel, slave of lieutenant-colonel Manoel Pedroso de Albuquerque; Duarte, of captain Gaspar Pinto Bandeira; Benedita, of the already deceased widow Edviges do Espírito Santo; Josefa, of Ana de Faria, Porto Alegre resident; Vitória, of Rosaura, also deceased; and Ledórnia, of Francisca Cardoso Andrade Neves. On February 28, the captives were interrogated by the enslaving authorities in Rio Pardo at the residence of the interim municipal judge and police sheriff, the superior guard Manoel Alves de Oliveira. Generally, the testimonies gathered did not greatly deviate from the one provided by the quilombola Miguel:

> The judge asked the slave Miguel what his name was and whether he was manumissioned or captive. He responded that he was called Miguel and that he was a captive of the lieutenant colonel Manoel Pedroso de Albuquerque. The judge asked where he had been imprisoned and the reason for it. Miguel responded that he had been caught in the Geral Mountain Range, deep in the thickets, perhaps as far as fifteen to twenty leagues, since he was running away. The judge also asked him why he went to that quilombo. The slave responded that he went deliberately, and with other mates. The judge then asked for how long ago he had escaped. He answered that it had been a year since he had run away.
>
> The judge asked him whether he knew whom were those that were with him upon his interrogation, on the site of his imprisonment, and whether they were manumissioned or captive. Miguel responded that there were twenty people, out of which seven were women and the remainder of the group were men, all of them slaves. Once again, the judge asked if he knew whether there were, in the vicinities, another gathering of quilombolas. Miguel answered that he did know this due to the smoke upon the mountain range, which he deemed to be another gathering, but that he had not seen anyone. Then the judge urged him to say the truth, since he knew for a fact that close to the place where the accused had been imprisoned, which was about three leagues away, there was another quilombo, which gathered a greater number of people. Miguel responded that it was true that the quilombo existed, with a greater number of people; that it was true that it existed indeed, but that he did not know anyone that lived there.

According to the documentation, the expedition, composed of a slave-catcher, four laborers and national guards, after marching for three days in the mountain range of Couto District, found one old quilombo, of at least sixteen years, which had twenty inhabitants—thirteen men and seven women. The quilombo was formed through aggregation of runaway slaves who escaped alone or in couples at different periods, largely during the Farroupilha War. By 1846, Miguel had been gone for a year; by 1842, Duarte, Ledórnia and Benedita, had been gone for five; by 1841, Josefa, whom had come all the way from Porto Alegre with Ramão, had been gone for six years; Vitória, possibly in her senior years, and perhaps the founder of the quilombo, found herself in the mountain for sixteen years! She escaped in 1831.

Similarly, to the quilombo in the Ilha dos Marinheiros, the quilombolas there lived in a communitarian setting—there were two "large ranches." However, the small group—unlike those of the Tapes Mountain Range—survived primarily through agriculture, hunting, gathering and fishing. The records refer to "gathered provisions" and to dispersed quilombolas "engaged in different labor throughout the forest." The stronghold was assaulted at noon. Part of the runaways—"from six to eight black men and two women"—found themselves away from the quilombo. Those present resisted the attack. Four out of the seven women were captured. Out of the thirteen men, only two were caught. Ten men and only two women escaped the attack. Allegedly, there was a growth in the birthrate of males from a balanced 53.8 percent to a pathetic 80 percent! There was another quilombo in the mountain range. All imprisoned quilombolas confirmed knowing of its existence but asserted that they did not know its location. They could be trying, with their silence, to protect the runaway comrades and other quilombolas. It was difficult to believe that Vitória, having lived there for almost twenty years, did not know the location of the stronghold. Part of the troop was engaged in the search for the second quilombo when the police sheriff wrote his letter on March 4. Two other assaults to the remaining quilombo were attempted, with no results. Two months later, on May 29, as the sheriff was reporting the costs to the president of the province, he declared, "[...] the last two journeys with the same goal, undertaken by these employees [the laborers and the slave-catcher], brought no results, [...] since the quilombolas left to the center of the thickets, which was farther than three leagues from there and we had no time to go after them."[70]

In the following years, captives continued to run away to those regions and the slave master continued to send new expeditions. On 15 November

1848, the provincial presidency was notified of the existence of new quilombos "in the vicinities of the city of Rio Pardo." On 16 March 1849, the police sheriff of Rio Pardo authorized the "hire [of] four or five local cowboys from the place where the quilombos are found in order to command the expedition. The bill for the costs would be sent out to the "competent office." On that occasion, it was required that "all moderation in the deployment of force" be used.[71]

In the following year, in a document dated 28 November 1850, the provincial president recommended that the slave lords of Rio Pardo either keep a closer eye on the recaptured quilombolas or sell them outside of the province. Runaways captured in the municipality had been able to escape once again to the mountain range.[72] On the following month, a new document from the presidency, dated October 31, registered the capture of three captives in "quilombos of the city of Rio Pardo," and determined that the firearms found in them were to be collected and taken to the War Arsenal. A year later, on 27 October 1851, correspondence from the presidency registered the document that arrived from Rio Pardo in the beginning of the month, reminding of "the necessity to destroy a quilombo discovered in the General Mountain Range of the Couto District."[73]

As mentioned earlier, in 1853 the president designated the high sum of 1340$800 réis towards the repression of quilombos in Rio Pardo. Effectively, in January 1853, the provincial government ordered the police sheriff, along with the National Guard Commandant, to organize a group of fifteen "pedestrians" to be lead by a "person of good repute," with the goal of destroying "the quilombos located between the headwaters of the River Pardo and Taquari Mirim." Since this expedition, the presidency utilized a new strategy for the financing of expeditions. The captives would be delivered to their masters "after these had paid for the expenses of the capture." In a public document issued on January 26, the president ordered the provincial treasurer to notify the Collection Agency of Rio Pardo to deliver the funds necessary to "engage the sixteen runaways." On that occasion, it ordered the delivery of "one hundred cartridges" to the troupe.[74] On February 23, the well-armed expedition found and destroyed a quilombo located between the Sampaio and Taquari Mirim Arroyos. The interrogation of the captured revealed that they received arms and other needed objects to live in the forest in exchange for manual labor from the land owner Eleutério Rodrigues de Lima, resident of Pinheiral. It is documented that the presidency of the province demanded that the police sheriff sue Eleutério while "keeping the government updated on the result" of this process.[75]

In letter dated 11 March 1853, the presidency of the province reiterated that the runaways could only be given to the masters if they paid the considerable cost of recapturing them –725$120 réis. From this date forward, and especially in Rio Pardo, the masters were called upon to contribute to the expenses of the expeditions against the quilombos. On April 26, correspondence with the president referred to the repression of two other quilombos in the region and ordered that the "old black woman" found, it appears, in one of them, did not remain in prison due to the fact that the public cost of maintaining her would be an "expense unlikely to be paid back." Since her female master was absent, she should be delivered to Inácio Rodrigues Paes, "uncle of the owner," as long as he signed a "term not to deliver" her to her owner without payment of the "quota that pertains to her, which corresponds to the expense of the capture."[76]

In the same month, April 1853, the president of the province ordered the provincial field marshal and arms-commander to make available to the police sheriff of Pelotas a "military power [...] they deem indispensable to apprehend military deserters," who seemed to "be in a quilombo of blacks made of runaways from the second district of Pelotas."[77] The quilombo activities had been equally intense in 1854. In July, the provincial government notified the Ministry of Justice, in court, that the captain of the police body, Rafael Godinho Valdez, leading a group of "twelve folks," destroyed an important quilombo in the vicinities of Porto Alegre, in the Gravataí Ranch. The quilombolas put up a strong resistance to the attack. One man from the attacking forces was "gravely" injured and two quilombolas were knocked down.[78]

A notification mentions that three captives, two "deserters from the Invalid Company" and seven "*paisanos* [civilians] who were in communication with the referred quilombolas" had been captured in the quilombo. In a correspondence with the police sheriff, dated September 28, the provincial government specified that the prisoners were two "deserters" from the Invalid Company, "six paisanos," one "offender sentenced to hard labor," two "blacks" and a "black woman."[79] On November 18, the provincial presidency reported that it had delivered a letter from the chief of police informing it that the "black men and women (who had escaped from the quilombo that formerly existed there until it was destroyed by a police troupe) had been apprehended by the foreman of the Gravataí Ranch." A month later, on October 10, the president ordered the chief of police of Porto Alegre to decide on a "compensation" for the participants in the operation. The sum should come out of the value of the apprehended slaves, as it has been done in identical circumstances in the municipality of Rio Pardo.[80]

The documentation on this quilombo demands a certain complexity in interpretation and suggests a shift in quality in the southern quilombo phenomenon. It is difficult to define the real input of the "deserters" and "civilians" upon the quilombo. According to the records, they "communicated" [...] "with the referred quilombolas." As early as the first half of the nineteenth century, it was common for "deserters" to live in quilombos. Forced recruitment, negligible and always late salaries, hard work, physical punishment and the despotism of the officials led soldiers to desert with frequency. Freed blacks and mestizos who were obligated to accept such living conditions formed the majority of the imperial and colonial troupes. For obvious reasons, "condemned offenders" commonly hid themselves among the quilombolas. The gallicism "paisano," associated with "deserters," seems to describe free men, of popular and rural origins, rather than those enlisted in the military. The reason for suggesting that this population only had established "communication" with the quilombolas was perhaps born out of a difficulty to incorporate groups of free men with no criminal record with groups of runaway slaves into the quilombo phenomenon. The quilombo in the Gravataí Ranch had been formed by, at least, seventeen members who were either permanent or in close contact with the redoubt: Eight of them were captives and nine were free men. All its members, however, belonged to the social segments that were marginalized by the enslaving society: The blacks, the mestizo peoples and the poor. The group had only three women.

In October 1854, the presidency registered that the quilombo located in the mountain forests of the parish of Santa Maria da Boca do Monte had been assaulted.[81] A black man was caught and taken to Rio Pardo. A second captive was killed due to "having resisted the escorting."[82] A year later, in March 1855, the presidency was informed that there had been robberies in the Costa da Serra, in the district of Cruz Alta.[83] A slave-catcher, accompanied by two men, went to check on the existence of quilombos and found "at the end of four days of search, only farms and smoke" in the forest of the region. The police chief was authorized to "come up with [...] whatever he judged necessary," as long as the expenditures for the captured slaves were reimbursed later by the masters.[84]

On 15 December 1855, the provincial government registered the discovery of a quilombo in the General Mountain Range, close to the Santa Cruz colony, and authorized expenses for its elimination. The maximum provincial authority insisted that the police sheriff made sure that the expenses be moderate, and that he sent out only the necessary troupes and, finally, that he assigned "its command to a prudent person who had no interest in stalling the development of the endeavor."[85] On 25 January 1856, yet again, the provincial presidency authorized expenses to combat "quilombos in the General Mountain Range, close to Santa Cruz and over the Castilhano Arroyo, in the same mountain." On that occasion, the presidency remembered that the expenses of the recapturing were financed, as usual, by the masters of the runaway slaves. "Slaves and deserters" formed the quilombo. Perhaps this was the same quilombo that was mentioned earlier.[86]

The frontal attack of the repressive forces and the capture caused direct losses to the quilombolas. The destruction of residences and, above all, of the harvest, had created a difficult situation for the runaways who had managed to escape. However, it was mainly the occupation of the uninhabited regions that impeded the formation of quilombos. This is the case of the formation of the Germanic colony of Santa Cruz, in 1849, between Rio Pardo and the mountain, which ended up curtailing the development of quilombos in the region, since these were immediately denounced to the authorities.[87]

In January 1857, in a "confidential" letter, the presidency of the province consulted the chief of police about the opportunity to get an advancement of the expenses to use in an attack against two quilombos that were found "in the mountains of Taquari-Mirim and Rio-Pardinho," within the municipality of Rio Pardo. The colonel José Joaquim de Andrade Neves proposed the operation, offered to realize it and accused the authorities of being "omissive."[88] Records from the months of February and April of that same year registered that the operation took place. An official from the provincial police—lieutenant Joaquim Inácio Godinho—went to Rio Pardo and, in agreement with the colonel José Andrade Neves, hired "cowboys and laborers" for the expedition. The operation took place between the months of February and March and did not bear any results. At the moment of report, the presidency tentatively referred to the quilombos "that allegedly existed in the Taquari-Mirim and Rio-Pardinho mountains." The expenditures made with public funds were as high as 303$000 réis.[89]

In June 1863, once again, the provincial government supported the costs of an expedition sent against a "quilombo that should be located between the rivers Pardo and Pardinho." Since "minimal results" were obtained with the operation, the president solicited the chief of police to get "some reduction on the expenses involved in this undertaking." On June

22, the president ordered the provincial government to reduce the daily salary paid to the two "cowboys" from 1$920 réis to 1$500, and those paid to "twenty two laborers" from 1$280 réis to only 1$000.⁹⁰

A little over two years after, in 1859, the then lieutenant Joaquim Inácio Godinho marched to "catch and disperse the deserters and the slaves" that were believed to be gathering in the "vicinities of the Roque Hill." Perhaps afraid of having to pay for the capture themselves, the slave masters caught them and punished them "accordingly." Nonetheless, Godinho marched to the "Cavadeira Peak," where some of the delinquents still remained. After hiding in the thickets, the lieutenant sent a "trusted man" in order to "look with greater certainty for the site where they were. The explorer returned saying that they had removed themselves to the campanha (cattle plains)."⁹¹ According to the 34th edition of the Court's newspaper, *Jornal do Commércio* (possibly based on the news from the province's *Mercantil* newspaper), on 17 July 1866, the Ministry of Justice inquired the provincial government about the destruction of a quilombo that gathered "runaway blacks and deserters" in the vicinities of the Soledade colony.⁹²

5

The series of questions made, in February 1867, to the Paulista soldier of thirty-five years of age, Benedicto Santa Ana de Arruda—deserter of the 3rd Infantry Battalion of the 7th Company (Voluntários da Pátria) who lived in the Quilombo of the Camizão—were truly interesting. According to the soldier, after deserting his battalion during the conflict in "Passo do São Sepé," he walked up the mountain until the nook of Valos, where, during a hunt, he saw "a village or quilombo, from the top of a hill he climbed, composed of "dressed people, children women and men."

The quilombo, at the end of a ravine, "inside a stone wall," had one hundred and fifty people, out of which fifty were able to engage in combat. As Benedicto introduced himself at the entrance of the quilombo, a guard of "six men" told him to stop with a "gun salute." Without giving up his weapons, the deserter met and talked with the chief of the quilombo, "a mulatto by the name of Camizão." Benedicto was accepted into the quilombo, under the condition that he accepted the local customs. In other words, never go out alone, only accompanied—under the penalty of being "persecuted and killed."

According to the deserter, the activities of the quilombo were shared in "stations." One "station" of six men monitored the quilombo's entrance. Another, also of six men, accompanied the chief of the quilombo in long expeditions, from eight to fifteen days, "to the lands of Rincão de Nossa

Senhora," in "the other side of the river," so that they could get salt, gun powder and led, which was melted to make bullets. Other stations took care of hunting and fishing. Benedicto abandoned the quilombo during a hunting expedition because he was sick and feared that the stronghold was going to be attacked. It probably took him, due to his physical conditions, four days of hiking from the quilombo to the house of a "baiano" (someone from Bahia), located at the entrance of the forest. From there, after resting for two weeks, he made a fifteen-day trip to the residence of the "inspector" of the region.

We have no other news about this quilombo—the largest known in Rio Grande do Sul. This obliges us to distrust the veracity of this account. Nonetheless, the details provided by Benedicto correspond to the information we have on the internal organization of other quilombos; utilization of topographical features as protection, incorporation of captives and deserters, control over the new members, division of labor, etc. The militarization of the quilombo do Camizão took place due to the existence of other deserters among the quilombolas. It is also possible that the quilombola-soldier may have exaggerated his account in order to make it more believable and reliable or that he may have been mistaken in regards to the numbers of the quilombo's population.[93]

Another quilombo from this period of the Paraguai War is referred to, in passing, by Aurélio Porto in his *Encyclopedic Dictionary of Rio Grande do Sul*. According to him, "one quilombo of black, with armaments and munitions, with the goal of defending their freedom," was "discovered today in the municipality of Montenegro," "due to the Triple Alliance against Paraguay."[94]

From the 1870s onwards, the incidence of quilombos tended to decrease. Since 1824, German immigrants colonized important regions in the foothills of the Southern Brazilian Plateau. As of 1875, Italians received the highest priced lands in the mountain range. The southern population grew; the unpopulated lands diminished. There was also a dramatic drop in the southern slave population. Captives were freed in order to join the Fatherland Volunteers (infantry battalion). With the end of the international slave traffic, the price of the enslaved worker went up and the South began to export captives to the South-Central region of Brazil.

However, isolated cases were still being documented. On 8 November 1879, the newspaper *Mercantil*, of Porto Alegre, reported that quilombolas had crossed the city streets, before being apprehended in the "savanna capão," located in the Direita Street (current General Canabarro), "on the block between Church Street (current Duque de Caxias) and Arvoredo

(Fernando Machado)." The newspaper called for the "capão" to be "devastated" and highlighted that the nearby residents were "terrified," since the "quilombolas" had hid themselves there at night. Criticizing the responsible authorities, the *Mercantil* made ironic remarks that the runaways should just have "their sleep disturbed by the tigers that assault them." In other words, by the fecal waste of the "tigers" or "potties" that the blacks stubbornly dumped on the empty lots of the city, against city codes. Thus, more than a "quilombo," they were dealing with the repression of runaway captives who were hidden in the city.[95]

It seems that the incidence of quilombos in the last years of slavery increased when the resistance to slavery grew stronger and the enslaving order began to disintegrate. In this moment, the phenomenon took on several meanings. In some of the cases, it became part of the radical abolitionists' struggles, associated with the captive population, as it had occurred in São Paulo and Rio de Janeiro. In 1884, Rio Grande do Sul got acquainted with a large captive emancipation movement, whom were obliged to work for their masters for seven or less years, without any liability, under the "clause of service provision." This law tried to alleviate the abolitionist pressure. In many cases, the revolt grew as this measure did not modify the condition of the servile population.

On 12 January 1885, the abolitionist and republican newspaper *A Federação* reported from Pelotas about the existence of a "new" quilombo, in the proximities of Cerrito, in Jaguarão. The group was composed of a "regular number of runaway blacks," that had slaughtered cattle belonging to Henrique Morais Patacão and robbed "great amount of provisions" from José Campos' farm. The newspaper highlighted that the "residents of that neighborhood" complained about the "police attention." The incident possibly involved some "captives" and manumissioned service force, living off little robberies and cattle-theft.[96]

Two years later, on 11 November 1887, when, in the context of an extremely violent social situation, slavery began to disintegrate in the south central region with the massive flight of captives from the coffee plantations, *A Federação* reported that "the barbaric scenes that slavery had given rise to in the provinces of São Paulo and Rio de Janeiro" were being reproduced there. In other words, the "armed hunting of slaves by slave catchers." This message pertained to the desperate attempt of the dried meat farmers to impede, through terror, that the workers abandoned the productive unities in Pelotas and in the south-central region as well. With "written authorization" from the police authorities, dried meat farmers financed gangs of slave-catchers to hunt workers who found refuge in the

Tapes Mountain Range. The order was to "kill by shooting those" that attempted to "run away" and "flog those that were caught." Some prisoners were flogged in "the establishment of their respective masters." A "black" was killed "by a pistol bullet" and left unburied in the mountain.

A Federação denounced that some of the refugees in the mountain were freed men "under a contract." Thus, they were to be escorted back by force to their work place, but according to the law, they were not to be flogged. The newspaper informed that among the refugees and the recaptured slaves, there were men who were free by law, since they were sexagenarians. On November 23, the republican newspaper referred once again to the events, as it highlighted that the newspaper *O País*, owned by the Court, reported, also on November 11, that "conditionally free men" were hunted down in the Tapes mountains by slave catchers. According to the newspaper, "one man and two women" had already been jailed.[97]

In the records studied those who were proslavery named the quilombolas "negros," "escravos" (slaves), "cativos" (captives), "pretos" (blacks) moleques (brats), "crioulos" (creole). As the southern newspaper reported facts on some of the last quilombos of Rio Grande do Sul, at the moment that slavery lived its terminal phase, the paper referred to those who found shelter in the Tapes mountains simply as "men" and "women." At the level of language, a determined shift towards the abolitionist revolution began a shift at the social, objective level. However, in the dialectical leap, the newspaper explained that the former "negros" and former slaves had been, always and above all, men and women who were socially determined, in other words, enslaved workers.

6

The available records allow for an exploratory systematization of the southern quilombo phenomenon. The first fact to be made evident is that, as in the rest of Brazil, the seigneurial world did not employ the term quilombo univocally. It was used to designate minuscule groupings of runaway captives; mobile groups of robbers; stable rural communities of runaways engaged in subsistence agriculture, etc. Thus, a simple geographic and chronologic identification of a quilombo tell us little about it. We have also established that the three main economic-geographical regions of the South—the coast, the mountains and the campanha—were "acquainted" with quilombos in diverse periods and frequencies. They were frequent in the vicinities of main urban centers—Rio Pardo, Porto Alegre, Rio Grande—and on the mountains and forests next to the mains concentrations of captives—the Tapes and Couto District Mountains. The quilombo's strongholds in the foothills of the Geral Mountains, near the agglomerations of the Central depression—Porto Alegre, Santa Cruz do Sul, Santa Maria, Rio Pardo, etc.—were quite important. The occurrence of quilombos on the fields atop the mountains and high plains were an exceptional phenomena.

The south came to know its first quilombos between the last decades of the nineteenth century and the first of the twentieth: Proof of this was the naming of Arroyo Quilombo, affluent of Jaguarão River; the nomination of slave-catchers in Porto Alegre, in 1798; the records of the destruction of Geral Mountain's Quilombo in 1813. Future studies will certainly bring the settlement date of the first quilombos closer to the very foundation of the captaincy, in 1737. Another reliable data is that Rio Grande never had large quilombos. The reasons are comprehensible.

The first passage of the campanha region—the *pampa*—did not offer geographical accidents that would protect great concentrations of runaways. The southern Coastal Plains were even poorer in potential hideaway sites. The Southern plateau was located relatively far from the slave centers. A good portion of the mountain range, which allowed for sheltering greater concentrations of runaways, was inhabited until very recently by native communities that defended their territories with tenacity. The only known case of a concentration of substantial size is the debatable Camizão Quilombo, with one hundred and fifty members. The population of the southern quilombos rarely went beyond twenty to thirty captives.

Records suggest the dominance of combative groups of quilombos in the vicinities of the cities, living off theft, of an economy of subsistence and small commercial activities. We have abundant information on four of these types of quilombos—the Barba Negra Island one, the one in the Island of Marinheiros, the Manoel Padeiro one and the one at the Gravataí Ranch. However, it is the Preta Vitória Quilombo in the Couto District that would portray the general standard for southern quilombos. It had about twenty residents and had been formed for twenty years through runaway captives, either alone or in couples, into an initial group. The quilombos resided in two large ranches and lived off hunting, fishing, gathering and agriculture.

It is probable that we have less information on semi-stable and stable agricultural quilombos as they passed more easily unnoticeable by the authorities. If they were located by the repressive forces they would easily dispersed. The toponymy suggests, in drier regions, the existence of quilombos that were not registered in the written documentation. We have little elucidative information about diverse rural quilombos that were repressed or never found in the southern lands—Tapes Mountain Range, Couto District, etc. On the contrary, the combative quilombo communities located next to cities, or in contact with them, in permanent confrontation with the police forces, tended to inevitably attract the attention of authorities. Logically, we count with a large documentation about them.

The known records confirmed the great seigneurial violence perpetrated in the repression of quilombos and an equally strong decision on the part of the enslaved laborers to maintain freedom by force. In nine cases in which there was confrontation between the repressive and quilombo forces, in only one—quilombo of Taquara-Mirim—there were captures with no deaths among the quilombos or captors. In eight cases, the quilombolas apposed themselves violently to the enslaving forces—quilombos of Sertão Geral, the Island of Barba Negra, of Marinheiros, of Manoel Padeiro, of Preta Vitória, of the Gravataí Ranch, and of the forests in the mountains of Santa Maria and in the attacks of 1887 in the Tapes Mountains. In five cases, quilombolas either died or were captured—in the quilombos of the Geral Mountains, Manoel Padeiro, Preta Vitória and in the attacks to Tapes. In three of them—quilombos of the Gravataí River, Island of Barba Negra and Island of Marinheiros—even though the quilombolas died resisting, no one had been caught.

In general, the quilombolas were armed with swords, knifes, lances, pistols and rifles. Records of the Manoel Padeiro Quilombo show the importance of firearms and gunpowder supply for the quilombolas. There are no records of either economic or military use of horses on the part of the quilombos, which was transportation and production vehicle extremely common in Rio Grande do Sul. Records suggest that the Gaúcho quilombos never threatened the southern slavery state. They constituted, above all, common cases of discipline in regards to the production and maintenance of the slavery order. The superiority of the slavery forces was non debatable. Records suggest that only in Pelotas, due to the great concentration of captives, were masters concerned with an eventual general rebellion. The quilombos of Manoel Padeiro considered the possibility—and perhaps they tried, in early July of 1835—to assault the dried meat ranches in order to incorporate "soldiers" for the quilombo.

On average, slavery authorities utilized military infantries of fifteen men (generally commanded by a lower rank official, police sheriff, district sheriff, slave catchers, foreman or laborer) in the combating of quilombos. The commandants were followed by line soldiers, national guards, pedestrians, cowboys, comrades, etc. In general, the quilombolas and the slavery agents were in similar numbers. However, the repressors were heavily armed, chosen and trained for the operations. Men and women of all ages and conditions formed the quilombo population, and only a few dangerous combatants. It is comprehensible why the quilombos took on a defensive strategy and ran away from the repressors whenever they could. Quilombos such as Manoel Padeiro and Island of Barba Negra escaped this profile. The first case, as we have seen, was that of a group of slave bandits. For the repression of the second, a true military expedition was organized, not just a policy attack: one hundred and ninety men, between soldiers and marksman.

Records allow us to make some tentative claims about the internal life of Southern quilombos. They possessed about thirty residents, at most. The quilombolas were called "negros," "captives," "slaves." At other times, only by the first name, followed by their profession. They were either creole slaves—born in Brazil—or belonging to a nation uprooted from Africa. Records show Africans of Benguela, Cabinda, Mozambique, Congo and Mina nationalities. We have no records of Nagô or Haussá quilombolas. Subsequent research would provide richer information on this topic. In addition, from the second half of the nineteenth century, we found deserters and poor free man among the quilombos. From the perspective of political organization, the case of Quilombo Manoel Padeiro stands out. In it, a hierarchy of ranks that imitated the police and military organizations of the white world were predominant. Even Manoel had the title of "general"; another was a "captain" and a third, "justice of peace." But the existence of two quilombolas that were referred to as "father" can also indicate that longevity was a source of political prestige, as it occurred in the world of the Africans.

The agricultural quilombos produced foods—beans, corn, pumpkins, etc.—and its residents practiced hunting, gathering, fishing and theft. Even the most distant quilombos obtained salt, gunpowder, lead, tobacco, spices and other products in the farms, stores and villages through barter and theft. In some cases, quilombos would perform clandestine periodic jobs in seigneurial productive units. We possess precise information from the masters who kept some form of understanding with the quilombos. It's the case of Eleutério R. de Lima, from Rio Pardo, in 1853. In the case of Manoel Padeiro Quilombo, the Argentinian Manoel and his employee, the widow Joaquina, were appointed as suppliers of information, gunpowder, and subsistence goods for the quilombos. The records do not make clear whether they did it out of economic interest or in order to escape the attacks of the gang.

Many quilombos did not cut the bonds with the seigneurial world, because they couldn't be absolutely independent of the slavery production. If they did, they would be excluded from the division of labor and could compromise their living conditions. The contacts with the slavery world took place through theft, barter, commerce and, in more rare cases, provision of services. Many communities dedicated themselves to barter, commerce and theft. This is suggested by records from the Island of Marinheiros.

In the south, due to security problems, the symmetry of the quilombo economy—as the quilombo production was identical and not interchangeable—and to the geographical dispersion of the quilombos, contact among the diverse communities was not common. However, this assertion rests only upon conjecture. As with the rest of Brazil, the quilombo population was unbalanced in terms of gender. At the quilombos of Gravataí Ranch and Manoel Padeiro, before the capture of the women, the rate of males surpassed eighty percent. Thus, we can comprehend why, in this case, black men desperately kidnapped young women. Only at the Island of Marinheiros Quilombo do we find a group more balanced in terms of their sex—six men to four women. However, we have no information on the age of the quilombo population. This can invalidate some of our data.

The scarcity of females and the restrictive character of the groups suggest that familial and sexual relations were established according to circumstance. At the quilombo of Manoel Padeiro, four quilombolas are presented in the records as "partners"; João "Justice of Peace" is cited as being partner of African João. Both belonged to the same master Joaquim Ribeiro Lopes da Silva. Alexandre "Capitão," from Mozambique was "partners" with Francisco, of the same nationality. The Gaúcho historian Euzébio Assumpção, the first to refer to these archives, hypothesized in his research the existence of an eventual homosexual relationship between these two couples. The records do not refer to contact among the four quilombolas and Rosa, Senhorinha, Florência, Maria and Dorotéia. Yet, it was Alexandre "Capitão" who proposed the kidnaping of Lady Lindaura.

We have information on the residences and shelters of the quilombos. The Island of Marinheiros Quilombo, with ten inhabitants, possessed only one only collective building with diverse compartments. The house served as residence, storage and work place. At the populous Island of Barba Negra Quilombo, with more than thirty quilombolas, four completed houses and two in construction were found. The quilombo formed at the beginning of the year, with a bit more than ten people. At the Preta Vitória Quilombo, two ranches sheltered ten people. The quilombolas of Manoel

Padeiro built or inhabited occasional shelters. A few times they found shelter in two ranches, and in other times, in three. In a given opportune moment, they built three large ranches and four small ones. The three large ranches were built by Manoel Padeiro, pai Francisco and Francisco of Mozambique.

This data suggests that, with the exception of the mobile quilombo of Padeiro, there were no individual or single-family residences. Yet, it is difficult to know whether, in the quilombos of Island of Barba Negra and Preta Vitória, the ranches served the function of mixed residence or if any of them functioned as storage for goods and work place. In the first case, there were eleven to twenty residents per house. In our archives, with the exception of the Camizão Quilombo, we have no reference to children in these societies. Nonetheless, there were a considerable –and certainly desired—female population. All over Brazil, this lack of reference to children and newborns in the reports of attacks to quilombos is common. It was also common for attackers to divide the children born in quilombos among themselves, or, to kill them whenever they disturbed the returning march. The newborns possessed low commercial value. For obvious reasons, in either case, the records were silent in regards to this segment of the population.

14

SLAVES AND THE COITEIROS IN THE QUILOMBO OF OITIZEIRO, BAHIA, 1806[1]

JOÃO JOSÉ REIS

The formation of *quilombos* is an aspect of slavery that has few studies in Brazil. Even lesser was the relationship between quilombos and the society surrounding them. Although experts on the subject have already highlighted this error, there is a predominant vision of the quilombo that isolates it in the mountains, composed of hundreds of runaway slaves who were united to rebuild an African lifestyle in freedom, meaning one that privileges the "palmarina" conception of the quilombo as an alternative society. A large number of quilombos, perhaps most of them, were not so described. There were a few quilombos, established close to populations, farms, mills, mines, sometimes nearby important urban centers, and kept relationships that were sometimes conflicting, while at other times friendly, with different members of the surrounding society. Quilombos were surrounding and absorbing societies, in the sense that quilombolas moved frequently between their quilombos and the "legitimate" slavery spaces.

This was the case of the quilombo of Oitizeiro. But, this quilombo had even more peculiar features, which oblige me to discuss, during this essay, the conception of quilombo by its contemporaries. In the quilombo, the runaways lived with and worked for free men and their slaves, who assumed the role of protectors and employers of the quilombos. The character of the *coiteiro,* their relationship with the runaways and other free men, will be carefully discussed, since they provide the main aspect in the available documentation.[2] Which quilombo was this? A quilombo managed by free men. A quilombo with slavery. An agricultural quilombo, whose production was integrated into the regional market. This discussion involves the history –or one of the possible histories– of the Quilombo of Oitizeiro, in Bahia in 1806.

I

In 1806, Bahia was ruled by João de Saldanha da Gama Mello e Torres Guedes de Brito, the sixth Count of Ponte. Born and raised in Portugal, where he had his military formation, he was the primogeniture of the House of Ponte, which beside the House of Torre, formed the two wealthiest dynasties in Bahia. When he stepped on Brazilian soil for the first time, in December 1805, with the exact purpose to rule, he had just turned 32 years old of age and owned thousands of cattle heads, hundreds of slaves, mills in Recôncavo, dozens of farms and leased small ranches, covering a vast territory in the backlands of Bahia, in addition to properties in Portugal.[3] He was a formidable opponent for the slaves in Bahia.

Since the beginning of his government, the Count would devote careful repression of all forms of resistance and slave rebellion, policies that brought him a fame which was still alive two decades later.[4] He suppressed drumming, parties, African rituals, customs that he perceived as the prelude of rebellion; he chased runaway slaves, choked the slaves' conspiracies and, above all, put into motion a destructive campaign of Bahia's quilombos. For this, he would frequently send official letters to the local authorities for them to put on alert the slave catchers (or assault-captains) and other officials who served in Salvador, and other counties of Bahia's captaincy.

The severity of the governor served a greater control policy in the colonies. Always insisting that he was just strictly following the "Royal Orders," and avoiding, according to him, what was observed in other captaincies—in an 1807 letter, he explicitly referred to Rio de Janeiro, Pará and Maranhão, as relaxed in the control of slaves. Unlike their leaders, he would not relax "the surveillance and rigorous subordination in which the immense slavery in Bahia should be kept."[5] This is also what the Portuguese government wanted, including a scorched-earth policy for the quilombos, recommending "assaulting them suddenly, to extinguish such gatherings, without leaving a shadow of them;"[6] This order, written in Lisbon in 1799, was certainly still in force in 1805, when the Count of Ponte became Governor and Bahia's Captain-General.

The Count was not at ease with what he considered the meager firmness with which the Bahia masters treated their slaves. A white man from such high lineage, accustomed to living in Portugal with only white people, was nervous in the midst of such an "immense" population of contemptuous slaves who in the years of intense traffic with Africa, kept on growing. Salvador was one of the most important terminals for trafficking in that region, therefore, as picturesquely written by an observer, "The whole city and its mainland have a passion for this trading from Costa da Mina." The Count himself would write in a letter to the Royal Court: over 8,000 captives from the African warrior nations, have landed in Bahia in 1806.[7] His worries were not unfounded, because it was under his rule that the African slaves opened the long cycle of uprisings and conspiracies that would culminate with the Malê Revolt, in 1835. An aristocrat who loved hierarchy, the Count would easily smell the odor of revolt in the air and adopted preventive measures, committed to pursue the runaway slaves, who, according to him, were plenty in Bahia. Therefore, he did not need to go far to fight the quilombolas. By the end of March, in 1807, he had several mocambos scorched, invaded houses of African cults and arrested many enslaved African devotees and runaways in the outskirts of Salvador, especially in districts of Cabula and Mares. In the same year, in response to his orders, he received letters from various authorities reporting the imprisonment of conspiracy suspects, quilombolas, African "sorcerers" who were sheltered in the villages' houses and scattered among several ranches within the sparse forest, that remained dispersed among the sugarcane plantations of the region, the Recôncavo Baiano.[8]

However, one of the first actions in this campaign was directed far from the government's palace in Salvador. In May 1806, the Count of Ponte decided to send an expedition to destroy the quilombo of Oitizeiro, nearby Barra do Rio de Contas.[9] The village of São José da Barra do Rio de Contas, nowadays Itacaré, was in the county of Ilhéus, south of Bahia. Founded in 1732, it was situated on the south side of the mouth of the river Contas, protected on top of a hill against the currents of this river, "that when scorned, when flooding, seems wanting to conquer all barriers that nature will present," wrote in 1802, Balthasar da Silva Lisboa, the ombudsman of the region of Ilhéus. "The land," the same author continues, "is pleasant for its views of the sea and plains of its fields, surrounded by hills from behind." Besides the hills situated on both banks of the river Contas, the area was covered by extensive mangroves, therefore the ideal grounds to protect the quilombolas who would settle there. The county was bordered on the south by Ilhéus, head of the district, and to the north with the county of Maraú.[10] (See maps 1 and 2).

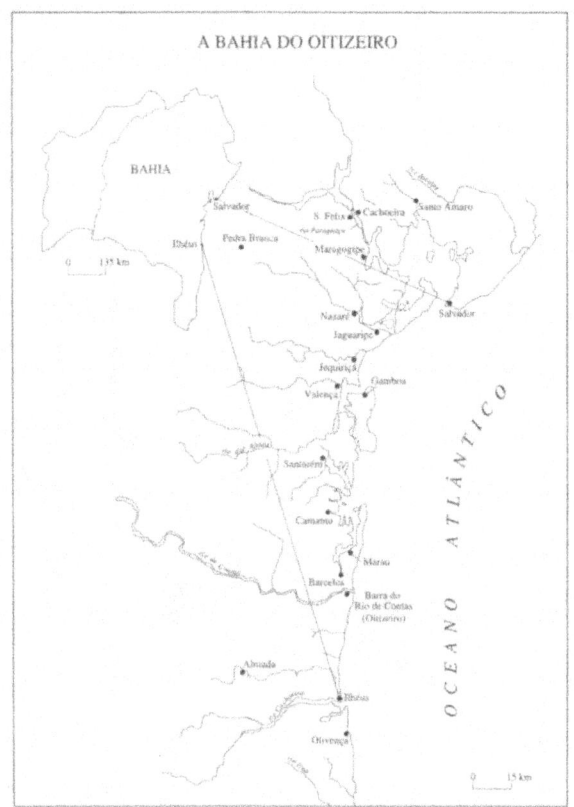

The bay of Oitizeiro.

The region of Oitizeiro.

The population in this place was one of the lowest among the villages of the region. It was smaller than Camamu, with its 5,148 inhabitants, than Cairu, with 3,850, but larger than Maraú, which had 1,498. In Barra do Rio de Contas and its boundaries, lived 1,741 inhabitants in the year of 1780 and about 2,000 in the beginning of the nineteenth century, which, according to Vilhena, were employed "only in farming of cassava, and some rice," which were grown on leased lands.[11] This information was confirmed by the judge Balthasar in 1802, who added that their inhabitants had already deforested between five and ten leagues of virgin forest to plant cassava, "main crop of its investments." The "investors" were mostly small farmers, but there were some owners with fifty to eighty thousand holes for the tubercle, figures presented by the memoirist as being large. In 1799, the village shipped to Salvador 30 thousand bushels of flour and only 150 bushels of rice, and 16 of gum. With a three times greater population, Camamu exported only one–third more (40 thousand bushels) of flour. Barra do Rio de Contas appears to have been the population most intensely dedicated to cassava in the region, as already suggested in 1781 by José da Silva Lisboa, future Viscount of Cairu.[12]

The monoculture in Barra and some surrounding areas was largely due to periodic impositions by the colonial government, which required its farmers to produce cassava in order to correct the chronic supply problem of the growing population, especially in Salvador and Recôncavo. The flour was the "bread of the earth," the most used staple food in Bahia's homes, but also fed the many fleets of ships that were trading between Portugal and Africa. The Recôncavo produced little cassava, and was specialized in far more profitable crops for exportation, tobacco and mainly sugarcane. There is a famous phrase from the plantation owner Manoel Ferreira da Câmara who would not plant "one single cassava, so that he would fall into the absurdity of renouncing to the country's best crop for the worse that it has." In 1806, the sugarcane businesses were prospering, favored by the exit from the market of the world's largest exporter of the product, Saint Domingue, which with its independence in 1804 became Haiti. There, a slave revolution, the only successful one in the Americas, destroyed in the decade starting on 1790, the agro–export economy. With the vacancy in the international market, Bahia grew its number of plantations by large, the area dedicated to planting sugarcane and the number of slaves imported from Africa, which resulted in less land for planting food and more mouths to eat. The expansion of cassava plantations in Barra do Rio de Contas helped to fuel the expansion of the sugarcane croplands in Recôncavo. The sugarcane monoculture in a region caused the monoculture of cassava in others.[13]

Carrying cassava, c. 1858 ("Négresse de la roça," Brazil pitoresco, Álbum de visitas, paisagens, monumentos, costumes, etc., Paris, Lemercier, 1861).

The flour from Barra do Rio de Contas and its surroundings was exported on boat, mainly motorboats, smacks and schooners. The seamanship was an important activity among its inhabitants. In 1819, German travelers Johan von Spix and Carl von Martius, besides praising the fertility of its soil, observed in the village of Barra "a great harbor, with a draft for schooners, smacks and other small vessels."[14] Within the region itself, the transportation of people and crops was made in canoes, which went up and down the coast and penetrated its many rivers, a lesson learned from the numerous indigenous groups who were still living there at the dawn of the nineteenth century. Besides handling the whole agricultural production, the sea, mangroves and the river provided the village and its surroundings with shellfish, crustaceans and fish. On the opposite side, the forest was a source of hunting animals and fruits in abundance.[15]

Peeling cassava, c. 1858 (Éplucheuses de mandioca, Brazil pitoresco. Álbum de visitas, paisagens, monumentos, costumes, etc., Paris, Lemercier, 1861).

Mangrove in the banks of river Contas (Photo: J. Reis).

This is the environment where it was settled, precisely on the banks of river Contas, the quilombo of Oitizeiro, apparently in the early years of the nineteenth century. The County of Ilhéus was aware of what was happening. Taking advantage of a region that was uninhabited and without much surveillance, the slaves would build there, since at least the eighteenth century in Camamu, Cairu and Ilhéus. Around 1696, in the village of São Jorge dos Ilhéus, was created the rank of "Chief Captain of Incursions on Runaway Slaves," indicating that there was a quilombo in the area. In 1699, the Sergeant Major of Cairu lends firearms and recruits indigenous service men for an incursions official to storm a mocambo. In the same village, in 1722, another stronghold with more than four hundred people was attacked, which the government from Lisbon ordered to be destroyed immediately, as to avoid a new Palmares: "destroy this negroes *mocambo* which can be very harmful to us, as our experience shown us in Pernambuco, where they did so much damage." In Barra do Rio de Contas, there was news of a mocambo in 1736, four years after the village foundation. From 1806, the same year of Oitizeiro, there is information that the paths in the county of Ilhéus were not safe for lone travelers due to the presence of highwaymen runaway slaves.[16]

The manufacture of cassava flour, c. 1825 ("Preparation de la racine de la mandioca," M. Rugendas, Malerische Reise in Brasilien, Paris, Engelmann & Cie., 1835).

Therefore, the Oitizeiro was not an extraordinary phenomenon in the region. I do not know when the Count of Ponte exactly took notice of its existence, but certainly received complaints from residents or local authorities who were unable to act on their own. Regarding the military situation in the Ilhéus region at that time, Silva Campos seems to be right when he wrote, "The corps, tercios or regiments existed in name only, in drafts; without a shadow of discipline, some soldiers could be found in the headquarters of villages. These were only a pretext for the nomination of officers."[17] The former were generally local potentates who occupied the captain–major stations and sergeant–major in ordenanzas, an auxiliary militia that had, among other functions, to fight the quilombos and recover runaway slaves.[18] In Barra do Rio de Contas, in 1806, there were these officers, as we shall further see, but apparently they couldn't or didn't even bothered to recruit militiamen against Oitizeiro. The government of the captaincy had to intervene, sending an expedition commanded by a captain of incursions and assaults. The captain's name was Antônio de Andrade e Conceição and the expedition was formed by Cariris Indians (term used at the time) or Kiriri (term used by modern anthropology) gathered as the "Troop for the Conquest of Pedra Barbara's Barbarian Gentiles"—this is the battalion's official title. Earlier, in the beginning of May 1806, the Count ordered the commanding sergeant–major of the troop to send to Salvador the Captain Antônio—that one who was "lame in one leg and resident in the village of Nossa Senhora de Nazaré da Pedra Branca," clarified the Count. Knowing of the fear that his subordinates had, the governor asked the sergeant–major to warn the captain to not be afraid of the order, because he only summoned him "because he is needed for a certain diligence by the Royal Service." We know now what the diligence was, which was kept a secret in the summons. On May 22, he returned the official to Pedra Branca with a load of 25 firearms, half bushel of gunpowder, two of lead, flints and axes, with orders to form two companies with fifty Cariris warriors who, besides these weapons, recommended the Count, should not forget to carry with them their own traditional bows and arrows. He would personally take care of the police details for his government. And like that, started the execution of the attack plan on the Oitizeiro.[19]

Sailboat loaded with cassava flour, c. 1825 ("Ilia Itaparica," M. Rugendas, Malerische Reise in Brasilien, Paris, Engelmann & Cie., 1835).

The ability to use indigenous people against the quilombolas was very common in several regions in Brazilian slavery, in different periods. Palmares was destroyed by an expedition that included numerous indigenous groups among his soldiers. In Bahia, this expedient was also used several times before Oitizeiro and, as we have seen in the passage above, in the very region of Ilhéus.[20] Now, in 1806, would be the time of Pedra Branca's Cariris, a village located on the southwest border of the Recôncavo with the wild forest, about two hundred kilometers of Barra do Rio de Contas (See Map 1). Why these indigenous groups? Would not it have been better suggestion to send the blacks who, led by white officers, formed the two corps of slave catchers based in Salvador?[21] The governor, however, had many services for this troop in the capital, surrounded by many Candomblé *terreiros* ("temples") and suburban quilombos, which he would soon crack down hard. He didn't even sent a graduate assault officer, a captain–major or a staff sergeant, to direct the operation in southern Bahia, sending only one slave catcher, Antônio Conceição, perhaps an experienced slave catcher, nonetheless a smaller captain. Besides that, the captain–general and Count of Ponte were not satisfied with the forces at their disposal to fight against runaway slaves in the interior. In a letter dated 1806 to the Royal Court, he asked for permission to form a cavalry corps. There were many complaints received from "remote districts," among which

> Farmers, whom were robbed or encouraged their slaves to flee, to congregate in bands of evildoers, who banded up in the vast deserts of this inscrutable

continent, stand out in small bodies who perpetrate robberies, abduction of children and women, not sparing to commit the most detestable crimes in favor of its premeditated projects.

Of course, the governor was heavy on the ink pen, in order to make the Royal Crown understand that to preserve its continental colony, they had to invest in that cavalry, ending the "tolerance of the existence of such *Quilombos.*" His plan contemplated the organization of four companies of 255 mounting men.[22]

But, in such emergency, all that remained was to use indigenous troops. An alternative would be to mobilize the indigenous population from the region of Ilhéus. We do not know why this alternative was not used. Because there was, as we have seen—and we shall see further—local indigenous people willing to pursue runaway slaves. But it is possible that those were more integrated in the world of the whites, not organized and trained as regular troops, and others remained at war against the whites. In the latter case were the Pataxós. Several letters written between 1804 and 1808 to the Count of Ponte by a plantation owner in the region, José de Sá Bittencourt, reported attacks by these indigenous groups—referred to as "catachós"—to the people, farms and local villages. In there, it is said that they stole supplies and clothing, they always attacked by surprise, used poisoned arrows against settlers, who therefore gave up from occupying the empty spaces within the county. Bittencourt, who in 1804 hoped to "tame the catachós," in 1808 already wanted to decimate them and considered them as "barbarian cannibals."[23] In this climate, it did not seem a good policy to arm many indigenous groups in the region, even the so-called "tamed" ones, to fight because once invested with some power, it was believed they could always switch sides. As for the Cariris, who came from far away, they had long served the whites in the incursions against rebellious indigenous groups and, more recently—perhaps since the mid–eighteenth century—patrolled roads and watched the gold reserves for the government. They were, as I tried to make clear, a regular battalion, with a commander and all. A letter from Count of Ponte to the Royal Court suggests that the expedition to Barra do Rio de Contas may have represented the initiation of Cariris in the office of assaulting quilombos.[24]

Unfortunately, my frequent expeditions to archives did not result in any detailed information on this troop's expedition against Oitizeiro. There are important data missing, such as a more precise description of their activities and specifically the operation against the quilombo. But we know that the troops, all or part of it, was in the region from June 24, 1806 and

March 7, 1807. It was probably near to the first date that the Barra's village was reached.

The available documents, in particular several detailed expense accounts of the campaign, allow us to have some memory flashes of the troop's day-to-day existence.[25] As for the food, for example, Cariris enjoyed a varied diet. Besides cassava flour, they also consumed fruits, dried and fresh corn, and beans of various species, grounded and whole rice, beef and cow's meat (fresh and from the backlands), pork, lamb, sheep and hunting meat. From the quantities purchased, however, the main core of the diet was flour and beef, both fresh and dried. Confirmed in the case of the purchase of "a chicken for the Captain in his disease," poultry was consumed in smaller amounts, as it was reserved for the sick, which was the custom at the time. The captain had many food and etiquette privileges; for example, recorded among the war expenses he ate using one of the "two couples of fine dining plates" and savored fresh fish bought especially for him. To eat fresh fish, his subordinates had to use the 23 hooks distributed on St. John's day, June 24. What is sure—as is registered—they ate dried fish and cod, the poor man's fish.

Perhaps to keep the troops in good spirits, the captain periodically distributed tobacco and *cachaça* (alcoholic drink distilled from sugar cane). He himself was not deprived of such, and was even favored, because one of the receipts referred to "brandy that was shipped for spending by the said captain." Approximately two liters of wine and one of "the kingdom's *cachaça*" possibly were also used for the officer. Various receipts registered portions of soap, for the body's hygiene and clothing. The Cariris were not ragged soldiers, but were apt for waging war. Seven indigenous warriors received needles, thread and ordinary cotton fabric (waste), with which they sewed themselves their pants and shirts. The same group sewed four shirts and two pants for other soldiers, receiving payment in kind—more fabric: four sticks and a half of waste cotton. But the captain didn't trust the needle of his subordinates, because he hired the tailor Francisco da Cruz to tailor him with two Britain shirts, one fine cloth of cotton, and perhaps other works. There are records for the purchase of fustian, linen, fine scratched British cloth, thin calico and muslin handkerchiefs, but without any mention of the garments that would be made with them, or who would use them.

I suspect that the slave catcher took advantage of the campaign to improve his wardrobe, besides eating and drinking well, at the expense of the government. It really seems that he had a lot of undue expenses, according to the opinion of the ombudsman of the County of Ilhéus, Domingos

Ferreira Maciel, the highest authority of the region, in charge by the governor to oversee the progress of diligence and maintain the troops supplied. According to him, the costs could have been lower if the captain "wouldn't have stretched himself from the beginning." Having reached the village of Barra only two months after the battalion from Pedra Branca—he lived in Ilhéus—the ombudsman was startled by the size of the accumulated account and called for a personal talk with the commander of the Cariris: "Reaching an understanding with the Captain, I made him realize that I would not allow this to happen; and that spending from now on should be more regular, on which he agreed."[26]

There were apparently warlike expenses, lead and gunpowder, purchase and repairs of rifles, as demonstrated by the receipts of the campaign. But it seems that not a single shot was fired on a runaway slave. The assault on Oitizeiro was only a partial success, because the settlers were warned in advance and fled. No one was arrested at the time of the occupation. According to a village innkeeper, "they all abandoned their dwellings when the Cariris arrived here to pound on that *quilombo*." Even so, the event was eloquently defined by other locals as the "destruction of the *quilombo*."[27]

The troop of Cariris set quarters in Oitizeiro for several months and made incursions to arrest the runaways and their coiteiros. Many of the quilombolas simply decided to return to the homes of their masters, others were arrested in the outskirts of the villages of Camamu and Santarém. I do not know exactly when or how many. In December, six months after the dispersion of the quilombo was arrested near the village of Almada, the *pardo* Joaquim, a slave of whom the ombudsman Domingos Maciel said to be "guilty of providing asylum for runaway slaves," among which, his partner, a black quilombola who was arrested with him. She was soon returned to her master, while Joaquim would be taken to the hill fortress of São Paulo, because there was no secure prison throughout the region of Ilhéus for him. The slave would be whipped, for being a coiteiro; and then to be sold and its value would revert to the public coffers, for being a slave coiteiro. None of the free farmers who provided shelter for the slaves in Oitizeiro were arrested, at least until March of 1807, when the ombudsman of Ilhéus made his final report to the Count and sent him the inquiry over which he presided.[28]

Before discussing this inquiry, we will follow other moves in the activities by the anti-quilombo troop. A serious incident, in mid–November, proved that the Cariris did not form the most disciplined troops. In those days, having heard of news that there were escaped slaves in the vicinity of Ilhéus, twelve leagues from the Rio de Contas, especially near Almada, the ombudsman Domingos Maciel agreed with the Captain Antônio de Andrade to send his troops to arrest them. The ombudsman tells us:

> but this diligence can't be executed because last night the Captain appeared here to me, and informed me that by choosing some soldiers for him, they were not pleased, saying that they wouldn't leave from that place unless to Pedra Branca, where they wanted to spend their Christmas Holidays; and, those who were named on the joint list retreated, the reasons with which the Captain wanted to convince them to change their opinions was not of much worth.[29]

The list featured 36 names, to which must be added the names of eight others, who were absent at the time for being hunting, who were also convinced on the way by the others to desert. Of the 50 men on the troop, 43 left. It looked like the deserters had learned well the lessons from the whites, following the Christian tradition to spend Christmas with the family. This is one of those cases in which the subordinate uses the culture imposed on him to challenge the subordination. The attitude from the Cariris demonstrates that their commitment to the rule of the whites had limits. Christmas aside, they also "complained of lack of assistance," which was strongly contested by the ombudsman before the Count. According to Maciel, while they were in Oitizeiro, they ate all the flour they could grind from the cassava found there, besides the meat that was bought for them and local fruits, including, probably, the *oiti*. The flour and the meat would be so much, said the ombudsman, that they took a good amount home with them when they deserted. The governor believed this version of the facts and ordered the commanding sergeant–major of the village of Pedra Branca who, when the head of the deserters, quartermaster Francisco Álvares, arrived there, gave him a sick leave and arrested him and sent him to Salvador "with all safety." It is possible that the quartermaster spent the Christmas of 1806 in jail and not in his home.[30]

There were in Oitizeiro only seven Cariris. The diligence made in Almada was executed about a month later by these soldiers, aided by a few indigenous people from the villages of Olivença and Almada, all led by Captain Andrade. There were in fact four incursions made to Ilhéus. The first, in the beginning of December, coincided with the visit of the ombudsman Maciel to Ilhéus, who travelled there by sea, ordering that "the Captain on the same day of my exit would travel by land, not through the Royal Road, but through the woods, and in such way that the journey would pass by the village of Almada, in which surroundings I heard there were runaway slaves." It was on this occasion that the arrest of pardo

Joaquim and his partner occurred. Other incursions into the woods followed, one against the remaining slaves from Santana, due to a conflict that occurred there three years before. They were five quilombolas who roamed the woods, but that under pressure of the slave hunters, decided to seek a master to negotiate a dignified return to the tutelage of their master, Manoel da Silva Ferreira. And they "were well received by the said master," wrote the ombudsman Maciel. Considering a report to the ombudsman made by one Ferreira three years before, the escapees were probably part of a group of slaves, which included a mestre-de-açúcar, accused by other slaves to be sorcerers. There was a huge fight between each other parties, resulting in the escape of some. This was in 1803. Now, in 1806, the case was finally closed with the help of Captain Antônio and his men.[31]

And these were the eventful journeys of the punitive expedition to the quilombo of Oitizeiro. What remained of the Cariris troops returned home from March 7 to 9, of 1807, more than eight months after reaching Barra do Rio de Contas. A document records the expenses made by the ombudsman of the region "with the support of Pedra Branca Troop Indians returning from Village of Ilhéus to this, from Camamu through the villages of Barra do Rio de Contas and Maraú."[32] In Camamu, a boat was chartered, a master and two sailors hired to bring the captain and his men up to the village of Jaguaripe, at the entrance to the Recôncavo. From there, the Cariris probably followed on foot to their village, after having fulfilled their mission. In that same boat travelled the slave Joaquim, disembarking halfway on the hill of São Paulo, and a bailiff who would proceed to Salvador with copies of the inquiry to the governor.[33]

2

Soon after the invasion of Oitizeiro, the Captain Antônio wrote to the Count of Ponte reporting the facts. I did not find that letter to read it, but the governor and captain–general, who read it, was not entirely satisfied with the news.[34] He did not like the mediocre result of the assault on the quilombo, which was supposed to "catch rapidly the runaways." The count wanted prisoners, evidence, guilty parties, something concrete to offer to the palace in Queluz. What is apparent from reading his letter, dated August 12, 1806, to the ombudsman Domingos Ferreira Maciel, in which he also complained of not having complied with the "Royal Orders recommending the Ombudsmans [...] to take Inquiry of the *quilombos* [...] and against the people who give shelter, help and support for its existence." The count urged the Ombudsman, more than once, on the inquiry's goal: "knowledge of the existence of such *quilombo*, but [also] to punish their protectors and set an example in your county in order to restrain similar protections that are so harmful to the service of His Royal Highness, as well to the Peace among the Peoples." The ombudsman tried to find the quilombo, identify and punish any of the guilty.[35]

The documentation produced by the investigation that the Count of Ponte sent, clarifies various aspects of the assault. The inquiry concluded that several quilombos existed on site, but to have that result, he used a loose definition of quilombo. We normally think of a quilombo as a reasonable number of runaway slaves (at least dozens, if not hundreds), meeting in a place of difficult access, organized politically, occupied with the defense of their refuge, in the best of scenarios by surviving with the production of food, hunting, fishing, gathering, but also by robbing travelers, looting the plantations and animals, at war with the masters and colonial authorities. That is the picture of a classic quilombo, a model inspired by Palmares. Most of the quilombos had a more modest profile. Actually, there was an official definition, almost technical, of a quilombo in the colonial period, covering much simpler groupings: "all runaway blacks dwellings with over five, on uninhabited part, although not having raised any ranches or finding pestles within them," according to a query from the king to the Overseas Council in 1740.[36] The inquiry of Oitizeiro in 1806 followed this narrow concept and therefore did not find only one, but several quilombos.

Accompanied by the chief captain and sergeant major of Ordenanzas in the village of Barra do Rio de Contas, both "experienced farmers of the woods," the ombudsman Maciel traveled to the place of the Oitizeiro. According to the report of the investigation, they found "the following *quilombos* which by their construction and places were clearly used as addresses of runaway slaves":

> A *quilombo* in the place where Pedro José da Rocha worked, was covered and walled all around with straw, with three beds inside, sticks lengthwise with strings of timbó of tourniquets to hang three rifles, on each of the beds, and is behind Pedro José's house in the woods with small trails, and well hidden.
>
> Another *quilombo*, already old, so there was only the place, straw and sticks from its construction were already rotten.
>
> Another in the place of Balthasar da Rocha, who has a house perched on a slope, and going down through it searching for a stream, entering by a hidden path, on the left side hand, a *quilombo* was covered with straw with clay walls and mud that on the side of the hidden path had a small window and four holes as taps on the side of the same path, which were to be used when

> they would shoot their rifles at any time they felt an attack, inside there was a large bed of long sticks, where they could fit four people, and another bed where only one person could sleep, and going up through the same path by another hidden slope, we would end near the house of the said Balthasar through the dense forest was a another *quilombo* made of straw with two beds already on the ground and where there could live another five blacks, in addition to other older [*quilombos*] of which there were only traces.[37]

Here, the definition quilombo is restricted to each house individually, and since they found more than one, then they had several "*quilombos*." The houses became suspicious because they are hidden in the woods, by traces of sheltering people with firearms and, of course, that these people were runaway slaves. The hidden word appears several times in that excerpt of the inquiry, to highlight the illegal aspect of the place. In the first "quilombo" were found chains for hanging rifles; in another were holes supposedly prepared to shoot through them. The authorities try also to calculate the number of runaways who occupied the various hidden houses, finding a bed for "four," they could not go very far in their guessing. It stands out in this passage the name that is the most called among the suspects in the process, Balthasar da Rocha, in whose lands, full of "hidden paths," there were several other hideouts for blacks.

These "*quilombos*" were actually located in a small village inhabited by two dozens of cassava farmers, their families, aggregates and slaves. The alleged hideouts of runaway slaves were practically planted in the backyards of these farmers, as one sees in the passages reproduced above. In fact, what we have is the involvement of farmers in the sheltering of quilombolas, not by a disinterested solidarity, but in the interest of using their labor. It is possible that many quilombolas worked but did not live on Oitizeiro, but in the hills and existing wetlands around the site; however, for the inhabitants of Barra do Rio de Contas, there "was a *mocambos* of runaway blacks," as a witness to the inquiry defined it. Or, said another, "it had many *aquilombados*." The Oitizeiro would be a quilombo hidden as a village of farmers. The land of the quilombo, or at least most of it, had an owner, Balthasar da Rocha, who had acquired them about ten years before.

In the same letter bearing the order of opening the inquiry, the Count of Ponte had already solved the problem when he specified that he wanted to see punished the protectors of the quilombolas from Oitizeiro. The governor would give the name of two of the main accused men: Balthasar da Rocha and his brother, Pedro José Rocha. In the corpus delicti, the first document produced by the inquiry, they would be named separately. At the opening of the inquiry, the "inhabitants of Oitizeiro" were collectively accused of inducing the escape, hiding other slaves and aiding them. Those listed as witnesses during the investigation reveal the details of an operation that certainly was deeply undermining the good government of slaves in the region and, it seems, already lasted for some years.

Occupation	White	Color Pardo	Total
Farmer	5	2	7
Farm Owner	2	—	2
Seafarer	5	2	7
Trader	3	—	3
Innkeeper	2	1	3
Shoemaker	—	1	1
Blacksmith	1	—	1
Carpenter	—	1	1
Jailer	1	—	1
Scribe/Notary	1	—	1
Farmer/Seafarer	—	1	1
Trader/Seafarer	—	1	1
Not Declared	1	—	1
Total	21	9	30

Thirty witnesses were called to testify. Most were married (77 percent) and literate (70 percent), 21 lived in the very village of Barra do Rio de Contas, the others in places and farms in the surroundings. One of the farmers lived on a farm ironically named Mocambo. The witnesses were divided into white and pardo, with the first being two times more numerous than the latter. None of the blacks or indigenous people testified, confirming that they belonged to the lesser classes of the colonial society. To give legitimacy to an inquiry, it was important to call the most prestigious men, white and, in the background, pardos. I said men because the word of women did not have any value in legal proceedings.

Most witnesses were part of occupational groups that would engage all the time with the inhabitants of Oitizeiro, lived from the farming of cassava, or were employed in the trade and transport of flour, and therefore visited frequently the location of the quilombo. Some of them had slaves who found shelter in Oitizeiro, and many recognized, in their passing through it, slaves who belonged to masters who they knew. They were, therefore, people who have had first–hand experience with what happened in Oitizeiro. Few answered the questions of the ombudsman only with an uncompromising "I know by hearsay" or "I know because it is public and well known."

A good number of interviewees even had kinship relationships, symbolic or of blood, with the main parties accused of protecting the runaway slaves. The place was small, sparsely inhabited, so it was not difficult to have many people akin. But the kindred were at war. Anselmo Gomes da Fonseca said to be "a relative in remote degree of Balthasar da Rocha and his brothers," didn't even remotely defend them, declaring himself an eyewitness to the crimes from which they were accused. Another relative "in remote degree" of the Rochas, Martinho da Silva Freire, kept in prison a runaway slave from the Oitizeiro. The seafarer Francisco Xavier Nogueira was the son-in-law of Pedro and José and, therefore, his wife was the niece of Balthasar, but, though he had been one of the few to adopt the formula "I only know by hearsay in public," he narrates a private conversation that incriminated the locals.

Members of the Rocha family showed their local prestige through a wide network of cronyism, now under the menace to be broken. The farmer Joaquim José de Souza was a compadre of Pedro José, whom he accused nominally, and his brother Balthasar, of being the coiteiros in Oitizeiro. He reported, "there was a mocambo of runaway blacks." The trader Januário José dos Reis was a *compadre* of both Balthasar as his brother Pedro, and made detailed accusations against them. The behavior of the coiteiros seems to have broken the web of solidarity that in small communities unites men and women through kinship bonds. Or, more crudely, the competition for labor would have been the corrupter of that solidarity.

The first witness to be named was fifty year old Bernardo José Gomes, a pardo who lived as a farmer and stevedore, a married man who was also a compadre of Balthasar and his other brother, Agustinho Ramires da Rocha. He gave one of the most detailed and illustrative testimonies of the inquiry. When having heard that one of his slaves, the seasoned slave Luiz, had taken refuge in Oitizeiro, Gomes decided to investigate. He secretly went to the place "in disguise, hiding by day in the woods and during the night getting closer to the road." The disguise and the evening protection were justified because he was not unknown to the people who lived there. He didn't see his slave Luiz, but claimed to have seen "many other runaway slaves [...] all armed and always passing at hours for coming and going to service," according to him in the farms of Balthasar da Rocha.

The farmer spent nine days in his investigation and saw groups ranging between fourteen and over thirty slaves and recognized among them several belonging to masters from the region who he personally knew. Other witnesses said to have seen fourteen, fifteen slaves, always armed. One saw fifteen "who were loaded with hunting game, they were twelve male and three female." As it was common in groups of quilombolas, the number of women was much lower than that of men. One of them lived in an abandoned indigenous village of Agostinho Ramires, which was inhabited by few women, but not many men. The Oitizeiro was far from a "big *Quilombo*"—with an uppercase "Q" and with an emphasis in the original—as described by Count of Ponte in a letter that sought to impress the authorities in Lisbon with his efficiency. There, he claimed to have "destroyed" the stronghold of runaway slaves—and the Minister of Overseas Territories must have imagined flames rising, people running, shots, screams, and the smell of death in the air.[38]

The witness Bernardo Gomes would provide a long list of coiteiros and employers of runaway slaves. Where the Rocha family was already mentioned: Balthasar, José Pedro, Agostinho, and the son–in–law of the first, Antônio José da Soledade, and the son–in–law of the last, José Teixeira. The boat sailor Antônio Mendes Soares summed up the role of the Rocha family: "they are plantation lords, if they didn't whip the said runaway slaves they wouldn't be there [...] amocambados." Adding slaves of various members of the family also mentioned as coiteiros and cassava farmers. This list would be confirmed, corrected and sometimes amplified by different witnesses. It consisted of free men and women, slaves and free blacks, whites, pardos and blacks. Besides the Rocha family, these were also part of the group: Valentim Álvares, freed black; the blacksmith Ignácio Félix Santa Rita; his brother Antônio Florêncio and his slave, the black Gonçalo; Francisco Teixeira de Araújo, his slave Benedicto, his brother Felipe Vieira and his slave, Maria; Valentim Correia; Paula, free black, mistress of Balthasar da Rocha; Maria, his former slave. Virtually all residents of Oitizeiro were involved. A former resident, Félix Fragoso, would have moved to Maraú because, as told by a witness during the inquiry, "he couldn't see the robbery that existed there with the services of runaway slaves who were aquilombados in the said Oitizeiro, and that were served by the inhabitants of Oitizeiro."

The operation was not small. In the opinion of the witnesses, everyone was an accomplice, and pointed to decisive evidence: "it was impossible not to serve and have knowledge of these runaway slaves because the place was small and they all lived and worked together with each other, the farms within short distance." A better evidence would be pointed by Antonio dos Reis de Figueiredo, a pardo who, as a farmer, knew what he talked about: "for the crops that today are found in such Oitizeiro, is impossible that for these residents with the few slaves that they have, to be farming such a great plantation of cassava." In Barra do Rio de Contas, cassava was the measure of all things, measuring also the size of a quilombo. Another witness, Januário José dos Reis, was a trader who bought flour in Oitizeiro, spoke of the prosperity of the place and the plenty and developed activity from the runaway quilombolas: "heard many slaves whistling and exiting and entering in canoes"; and more: that it would be impossible for the few slaves owned by the Rochas and other residents "to do the large farms and plantations of cassava that he, as witnesses, had seen."[39]

Most mocambo slaves in Oitizeiro came from places within the county of Ilhéus. According to the registrar Agostinho José de Magalhães, residents of Oitizeiro "provided help to many runaway slaves both from this village [Barra do Rio de Contas] as well as from most of the region's counties and even from outside." Anselmo Gomes da Fonseca saw working in the flourmill of Pedro José Rocha three runaway slaves from Cairu, possession of Bento Correa Magalhães, besides two other slaves and a slave whose masters he couldn't identify. Agostingo Ramires lashed several runaways, including "a slave from Camamu, from the Acarahy farm, Colonel José de Sá Bittencourt, who for such a long time had her hidden that she even gave birth in his home, and then he bought her with the child to her master." Not even the local potentate slaves, the Sá Bittencourt who lived in war with the Pataxós indians, escaped the Oitizeiro network. The history of this slave Colonel was well known because it was repeated by several people in the inquiry. In his escape, the slave had traveled nine leagues between Camamu and Rio de Contas, probably by sea.

To reach the Oitizeiro, the most widely used means of transportation were canoes. This was, at least, the only means mentioned in the inquiry by witnesses who came to the local for different purposes, but mainly to buy flour. The troop of Cariris made use of boats to reach the place, according to receipts for expenses from the campaign. The captain farmer José Bento da Silva—who had a runaway slave in Oitizeiro with the blacksmith Ignácio Félix de Santa Rita—also testified that three armed quilombolas stole a canoe from him and another from his neighbor, possibly to go to the quilombo, because they found them there. At least two of them were slaves of Bento Correa, who lived in Cairu, and are mentioned in various other statements.

The statements describe as coiteiros of runaway slaves men who were themselves slaves. In another deviation from the established model of a quilombo, the Oitizeiro would be a quilombo with slavery, although slavery that allowed some liberties.[40] For example, access to the land that they worked on and the work of runaways, a surprising autonomy regarding the masters. According to Anselmo Gomes da Fonseca, besides the free black Valentine Álvares, "the black Benedicto and Maria were fiery, slaves of Felippe Vieira." Another witness, the scribe Agostinho José de Magalhães, would confirm: "a seasoned slave named Benedicto, slave of Felippe Vieira, and another pardo, belonging to Agostinho Ramires, named Joaquim, sought refuge and served of escaped slaves from others." Very uninhibited in his role as coiteiro was the slave Gonçalo, from Ignacio Félix, who asked the boatman of Manuel dos Reis to supply tobacco and brandy on credit to two slaves protected by him, Gonçalo would pay with flour the next day—which he really did. When Manuel asked him who were the two slaves, Gonçalo said one, a black, was his brother, while the other—cabra or mestizo, the witness was not able to classify him—his nephew. After that, he learned that they were two runaway slaves, one from Cairu and the other from Camamu. But because they were runaway slaves, it doesn't mean that they couldn't also be relatives with the slave Gonçalo. The frequent escape was done to promote the meeting of families of slaves and friends who were separated by their sale, change of residency, master and other circumstances. As in the case of a slave boy who went after his forra's mother, a former slave of Balthasar, who lived in Oitizeiro. As to the slave of Colonel Sá Bittencourt, mentioned a while ago, she may have fled to meet with his partner Joaquim, slave of Agostinho da Rocha.

Besides kinship, the recruitment of quilombolas by the slaves from Oitizeiro depended on other networks of relationships. It is likely that, for example, the slaves of Oitizeiro used their contacts in the region's senzalas to, as they said at the time, "seduce" other runaway slaves. As slaves, they were in a better position than their masters to reach, win the trust and convince potential recruits of the advantages of living in the quilombo. In this scenario, they would act in accordance with their masters, the farmers from Oitizeiro, who took advantage of the work of runaway slaves, as well as allowed their slaves to do the same. The latter, as part of the agreement, perhaps had a considerably lesser workload for their masters. But, what was the advantage for the quilombolas? They were not being forced to work, like they had been under their masters?

The recruitment by force of slaves, especially female slaves, was very common in Brazilian *quilombos*, including Palmares. This was not the case in Oitizeiro. No evidence is given that their free farmers or slaves had used any force to recruit or make quilombolas work. As several testimonies attested, the runaways carried weapons to defend themselves from possible trackers and slave catchers, weapons that could also be turned against their coiteiros. Everything suggests that the slaves were not there against their will, that is, the coiteiros did not force them to be there and to work with them. There was an agreement: shelter, protection, food and maybe some payment—or, more likely, access to a lot of land—for work. We already saw that the runaways worked in the small cassava farms, but witnesses also revealed that the farmers "protected" them. One said that they "gave all support to many runaway slaves," another one "gave them all refuge and help." According to seafarer Antônio Mendes Soares, the coiteiros "kept [the slaves] themselves against the will of their masters" not against the will of the slaves.

Several passages from the inquiry indicate that the members of the quilombo in Oitizeiro were trying to defend themselves against external adversaries. An episode told by the trader Felippe Manoel Lima shows that the runaways were not very kind to whoever came snooping. Passing by a straw house of Pedro do Ló, which was abandoned for some time, and "listening to many people talking inside, he wanted to enter but a mulato, which proved to be a runaway, because he was not a slave to any of the residents there, opened his arms blocked the door in such a way that the witness couldn't see who else was in there." And he pointed with malice: "the house was near the one from Agostinho Ramires." Quilombolas also seemed willing to engage in confrontations that are more direct. They moved around armed, as we have seen in several testimonials. The slave

Joaquim, whose fragments of his life are gathered in the box below, defended violently his partner against a slave catcher who had tried to capture her.

> A SLAVE FAMILY IN OITIZEIRO. The *pardo* Joaquim, slave of Agostinho Ramires da Rocha, was accused of being one of the main coiteiros in Oitizeiro. One day he rescued "violently from the hands" of a slave catcher, a female black from colonel José de Sá Bitencourt, plantation lord of Acarai in Camamu. This incident suggests that Joaquim and this slave were more than just a coiteiro and a *quilombola*. The affective relationship between the two may have started before her flight, and the flight from Camamu to Oitizeiro may have been motivated by his desire to meet his partner. There, they would have a son or daughter. They were already a family when, perhaps by pressure of the slave, his master bought her along with his son. In Oitizeiro, the family were still slaves, but they were together, slave but with the prospect of emancipation. Joaquim was an enterprising man. He had 7,000 covas for cassava in Oitizeiro that was turned into flour and sold in Salvador, he would receive 220$920 réis in 1808's prices. His wife and child had been bought for 180 thousand réis and for the same price they could be emancipated. Before that, the *quilombo* was invaded. Joaquim and his family apparently fled together; he and his wife were captured in Almada, almost six months later. Finally separated, he was imprisoned at the fort in the hill of São Paulo, where he would be whipped and then sold to help pay the costs of the expedition against Oitizeiro; she would be returned to her old master. The documents do not mention the fate of the child.

There was no news of physical violence on the part of the coiteiros against intruders, but there were plenty of reports of threats given, most of all by Balthasar da Rocha. The registrar Agostinho Magalhães complained that he "would challenge" the owners of the refugee slaves in Oitizeiro to come and get them to find out "who Balthasar is." The farmer José Caetano Simplício was more emphatic: "nobody dared to get their slaves with fear of the violence and bravery of Balthasar da Rocha, who being a criminal, walks around this village vomiting bravery and making himself fearsome." Balthasar ran the quilombo and still moved around Barra challenging the authorities and slave owners. Many were personally known to him and confirmed this behavior. The farmer Francisco Travassos claimed to have heard from Balthasar and his son–in–law, Antônio José, "sometimes they said [...] if Justice authorities would go there to contend with them, that they would receive a proper answer," saying this with "a menacing look." The white trader Januário José dos Reis, 36 years old, said that the residents of Oitizeiro "pose as fearsome," in such a way that the masters of the slaves in the mocambos among them "didn't dare talking about it." He told the judge that one of his kids fled to his mother, Maria, an ex-slave of Balthasar who lived in Oitizeiro. He did not seek out after the kid "with fear of the bravery and despotisms of the said Balthasar," but threatened to denounce it. This time, the strong man of Oitizeiro relented and after twenty days returned the slave, perhaps under protest of the mother.

Generally, Balthasar and the whole group from Oitizeiro, acted more or less openly, especially with their flour customers. One of them, the dealer and seafarer José Soares, reported on the blacks protected by Balthasar that he "didn't hide them from him [...] while he asked that when he would go there with someone else, he should shout before reaching his house."

The audacity of Balthasar worked for a long time. There are no records of any local initiative taken against his quilombo. The only incidents known about a slave recapture involved 27 year old blacksmith Félix Gomes de Oliveira who saw several quilombolas when gathering firewood and arrested Caetano, an elder slave who fled from a pardo resident lord in Maraú. The old slave, surprised while breaking into a flour granary in Oitizeiro, would die soon after in prison, in the village of Barra. It is not known under what circumstances his death occurred. Perhaps Caetano had been taken into custody with permission from the coiteiros themselves and other runaways, because of his transgression. It may not have been a coincidence that it happened with a slave of advanced age, who may have been stealing because he could not produce enough for his needs and those of the local townsfolk, and therefore they allowed him to be arrested. That old man and the boy, mentioned a while ago, according to the witnesses of the inquiry, were the only cases of runaway slaves recovered in Oitizeiro before the assault by the troops. Both were left without someone to protect them.

At least some of the refugee slaves in Oitizeiro were not fleeing from slavery, but looking for a change of masters. It was not an uncommon behavior among slaves in many regions within and outside Brazil. This is another one of those behaviors that discredit rigid schemes of analysis of slavery. Studying the captaincy of Rio de Janeiro at the turn of the nineteenth century, Silvia Lara provides some examples of slaves fleeing to find out someone who would buy them or, who wanted to participate in the choice of the buyer. In the same year that the Oitizeiro was attacked, in

1806, hundreds of miles from Bahia, in Campos dos Goitacases, the runaway slave Antônio searched for Inácio José Furtado, according to him "to buy him." According to some colonial laws, mistreated slaves could legally request to switch masters or other freedom actions, and to do so they had to flee to avoid reprisals. It is possible that these Brazilian customs had been brought by other refugees from Africa. Martin Klein writes that among the Wolof and Sereer a slave could choose a new master, creating situations in which he himself would serve as the compensation to the chosen, for example by cutting his ear, or from his horse; if the choice would fall on a chief, the would–be slave could destroy certain poles loaded with protective amulets solemnly planted in the patio or backyard of the chief's house.[41]

The slaves' theft camouflaged such transient escape or, as Eduardo Silva called it, "vindicating escape."[42] Four witnesses took the occasion to denounce a resident of in Rio de Contas who brought a slave in his luggage from a journey made to Jequiriça in the extreme north part of the region, saying that he bought it. The runaway, a cabra (person of "black and mulatto" derivation) called Antônio—turned Joaquim in another statement—sought refuge with Joaquim José Duarte, in whose house he was eventually arrested by the local jailer, after receiving a complaint from the rightful owner. In his testimony, the jailer said that Joaquim had "stolen" Antônio, but it was clear that Antônio allowed himself to be stolen by Joaquim. He lived so relaxed with the new owner that he used the "title of forro" (free). Another informant stated that Joaquim had actually two slaves with him, who were not his, a seasoned slave and a cabra, and when this was arrested, the other "soon disappeared and no longer appeared in this village"[43] The seasoned slave perhaps had undertaken a real escape.

The slaves in Brazil who allow themselves to be stolen, were not doing anything else other than just trying to exchange their masters. In fact, slaves could both be refused to be sold—to avoid your separation from places, friends and family, besides not wanting to risk the unknown –, as well as to promote their own sale, or change their master. In both cases, they sought to overcome situations of tension that could easily evolve into personal violence from both parties.[44] Many lords ended giving in to the refusal of the slaves to serve them, selling them to prevent the escape with no return and reward. A Bahia newspaper reported in 1839, against their will, that a slave wanted to stop serving a family that had grown too much, leading him to work much more. The master allowed the slave to look for a buyer, which he found, and the transaction was made. Soon, however, he discovered that the family of the new master was even bigger than that of the previous master and decided to return, and was accepted back. This happened in Salvador. Hundreds of miles in the backlands of Caetité, a slave of twenty years of age, fled in 1851 to the house of a woman, demanding to be sold to her, and threatened whoever tried to reclaim her that "the head would come home to her lady, but not the body." Her lady was an orphan, and the administrator of her goods was a colonel from the National Guard, who gave into the will of the slave. Amazing and dramatic stories as these certainly did not happen every day, but fleeing in search of a new master was a very common style of escape.[45]

This was the case of some refugee slaves in Oitizeiro. The trader Januário José dos Reis believed to have seen three of them working in the flourmill of Balthasar da Rocha, in an occasion that he went out there to buy flour. The slaves who came carrying cassava baskets, with fear of being recognized, quickly dropped their baskets and hid when they saw Januário. They belonged to a certain Theodoro Álvares Landim, from Camamu, who had already been approached by Balthasar da Rocha to sell them for 100 thousand réis each. But Landim proposed 130 thousand réis, according to the son–in–law of Balthasar, Antônio Soledade, who had traveled nine leagues up to Camamu to propose the deal. Apparently, these were the same slaves, João and Joaquim, who had been seen in the small farm of Balthasar by José Caetano de Saavedra. The slaves told the latter that they were there for a few days looking for someone to buy them, but Saavedra later discovered that they had already lived in Oitizeiro for over a year. Why did they lie? The response of the slaves suggests that looking for someone to buy them was not necessarily strange or criminal behavior, but a part of the opportunities offered in the local slave relationship. That is, a master could allow the slave to look for a new owner, but to be engaged in this task for more than a year without returning home, was already considered as an escape.[46]

In another episode, a pardo slave from Jerônimo Francisco sought refuge in the house of Pedro José da Rocha, where he spent a year. Only after he was sold to a certain Francisco Manuel, did the slave returned to his slavery, already under a new master. The story that slave refugees in Oitizeiro went looking for a change of masters is confirmed by Francisco Xavier Nogueira, who made his "living shipped." He reported that, as he loaded the boat of Felippe Lima, he said to him that he "found a runaway slave who asked him to buy him." Felippe Lima confirmed this information in his own testimony. He went to Oitizeiro to collect a debt, around the time of the last Lent, and he was approached by a "black armed with a rifle, a knife and a sharpened stick, who asked him [...] to buy him from his master Bento Correa in Cairu." Apparently the same slave, with arms and all, also asked Francisco Antônio Dias, another witness in the investigation, who bought him. A fully armed slave, the spitting image of a heroic quilombola who fought for freedom, wanting nothing more than another master who would treat him better.

Another runaway slave of Cairu was called Théo and belonged to Francisco José Torres. Théo approached the farmer José Caetano Saavedra to be bought by him. João Rodrigues de Souza, a white innkeeper, told a similar history about a runaway slave from José Caetano Simplício whom he found in Oitizeiro and who asked him "why he wouldn't go back to the house of his master, and the black told him that he was looking for someone to buy him." So, after the attack by the Cariris troop, with the end of the quilombo, the slave returned to his rightful owner. Considering the risks of fleeing, he preferred to be punished at home. Another case involved the free black Paula, the Paulinha from Oitizeiro, mistress of Balthasar, who protected a pardo slave who fled from Camamu. Twice she tried to buy him, but his owner refused the 80 thousand réis offered because he thought the slave was worth "hundred–odd thousand réis." This and other cases that we have seen already, confirmed that one of the advantages received by the coiteiros was to increase their bargaining power when negotiating the purchase of a runaway slave. To avoid the total loss of the slave, many masters conformed to sell them at a discount—discounted for the escape, may we say. While the trade was not yet done, the coiteiro used the services of the slave. Paulinha, for example, for a few months kept the mulato at her side, working in her small farm and paddling her canoe on the trips that she made to the region. Besides that, the white farmer José Caetano Saavedra, former master of Paula, was the one who reported the story, and, who, seeing the scene, should have thought of how much the seasoned slave had accomplished.

As we can see from these cases, the quilombolas were not undertaking an escape without return to slavery, but trying to negotiate better terms within slavery. They had their own visions of slavery, as much as of freedom.[47] In this case, the freedom to choose their own slavery. The situation of the runaways did not seem to them ideal and, accordingly, the passage through the Oitizeiro represented just part of the adventure, a waiting position, with the home to make contacts that were to resolve his master problem. The quilombo would then be a temporary shelter, not the destination, the place to build a free community, an alternative society.

3

The result of the inquiry was the indictment of almost all the inhabitants of Oitizeiro, ten white, three free blacks (including a woman, Paula) and four slaves (including another woman, Maria). The authorities did not even have the slight thought to condemn the quilombolas. This was the time to punish the coiteiros.

In October 1806, along with the inquiry, the ombudsman Maciel ordered an inventory of the property abandoned by the residents when they escaped from the Oitizeiro and arrested by the troopers over three months before.[48] This inventory sheds more light on the relationships of production and power in the quilombo. The indicted men and women had, as a whole, modest properties, valued at 530$380 réis. Excluding the slaves from Oitizeiro residents who, themselves guilty, naturally fled with their masters. That sum of accumulated goods by the quilombo residents amounted to no more than about five slaves, from the cheapest ones.[49] For a group of seventeen people (here including the slaves, because they were properties who had properties, as we shall see) results in 31$198 per capita. A non–negligible amount, but a small sign of wealth. With this value, what could be bought back in 1806? Based on the items listed in the accounts of the punitive expedition, they could buy four rifles; or sixteen cassava flour bags; or three cows; or five average sheep; or two oxen. The money would not be enough for one year.

As a smaller portrait of the region, the cassava ruled the Oitizeiro. The inquiry did not find another crop worthy of notice, although it is possible that there were others, only for subsistence, with no commercial value. In addition, hunting, fishing and gathering fruits were listed as subsidiary activities that the residents, including the quilombolas, were engaged in. For this, they had rifles, hunting traps (or "mondés") and fishing nets. But the wealth from the place was undoubtedly measured in cassava, which was planted, grounded into flour and sold—or exchanged for other products—there, to traders who came seeking it in boats and canoes. Out of the 530$380 réis evaluation of the confiscated goods, 63.3 percent was equivalent to 217,500 *covas* ("pits") of cassava and practically everything else is distributed between equipment from the mills for flour processing, agricultural tools, bins to deposit flour, two horses, fishing nets, doors, windows and floors from the houses, and a canoe. There were other canoes on the site, in addition to those used for the escape of the residents of Oitizeiro.

In his report, the ombudsman of the county mentioned two more canoes, a large one that sold for 30$000 by the captain Antônio soon after the occupation of the site, perhaps for expenses with the troops' maintenance;

another one was broken, with a hole in the bow, the ombudsman ordered to fix it, so that it could be better sold in Camamu, but which was not yet ready at the time of the inventory. In the inventory, goods worth more than 100 thousand réis were not considered, among which some furniture, which the captain had given to the Oitizeiro residents before opening the inquiry, perhaps even unaware of the extension of their involvement with the runaway slaves. But, we shouldn't rule out that the slave catcher may have had some kind of advantageous agreement with the coiteiros, though strange that none of them were arrested. Anyway, there were those arrested, but were not considered at the time of the inquiry, the land of the Oitizeiro belonging to Balthasar da Rocha. The sale of the homes of the residents was not considered because, besides the doors, windows and floors of wood, they were not worth much since these were constructions of mud, covered with straw. The near absence of furniture of the houses are indications of the modest lifestyle of those farmers, with the exception of Balthasar da Rocha.[50]

Not all the existing cassava was inventoried by the troops who entered the quilombo. The fifty Cariris who occupied the site, according to the ombudsman, grinded and ate flour at will for about four months, until the collective desertion mid–November. And, as we have seen, they even brought flour to fatten their families during Christmas in Pedra Branca. To the confiscated cassava, in October, was given the value of 335$800 réis, which would be enough to produce about 6,525 acres (236,662 liters) of flour. Sold at the lowest price in the local market—where the prices ranged between 320 and 640,000 réis per bushel, probably depending on the quality—the farmers would receive a minimum of 2,888$000 réis. In this case, we would have to redo the previous accounting and increase the real value/cassava per capita for the active population in the quilombo to at least 122$823 réis. Now each farmer could buy, with the arrested roots, four times more than the value given by the authorities: not four, but sixteen rifles; not two, but eight oxen, etc. That is, the cassava from the defendants was evaluated at a very low price, perhaps so that they could sell it quickly or perhaps to benefit the buyers of the arrested goods.[51]

Six people bought all the arrested goods on a public auction, from which only two did not attend the inquiry as witnesses. We can surmise that the accussers had an eye on this future deal. The bulk of goods were sold to Joaquim José de Souza, a married forty year old white man, resident in the town of Barra do Rio de Contas and a cassava farmer. In his testimony, he was one of the few to say that he knew of the facts in Oitizeiro only because they were indeed "public and notorious," but repeated in vivid details what was "public and notorious"—that residents whipped slaves and served them, and that "there was a *mocambo* of runaway negroes." Except for the 23,000 *covas*, Joaquim scooped up all the confiscated cassava, including those from his compadre Pedro José Rocha. He also took two bins, a canoe (also belonging to Pedro José), equipment for the flourmills, wooden floors and other wooden handles and hardware, all worth 373$200 réis. The total value received from the assets managed by the coiteiros was 458$000, 14 percent less than the value at which they were evaluated. The money was not enough to cover the 911$360 réis spent by the battalion of Cariris, but it helped. In addition, there were still to be sold the slave Joaquim, imprisoned on the hill of São Paulo, from Agostinho da Rocha; the lands of Balthasar; and the canoe with a hole. And beyond that, the ombudsman asked for and received the permission from the Count to charge a *tomadia* (fee paid for the apprehension and incarceration of runaway slaves) from the masters of those quilombolas who returned home as a result of the activities of the troop of Cariris. It is possible that, in the end, and despite the spending by the slave catcher, the expedition yielded a small profit for the government.[52]

To whom did the arrested goods belong? The largest single owner of cassava in Oitizeiro was Felippe Vieira, owner of 30,000 *covas* evaluated at 58$800 réis. The smaller ones were a group of three proprietaries, each the owner of a thousand covas, including the free black Valentim Correa and a certain "Victorino so and so" who does not appear indicted in the inquiry, but had its cassava arrested in the same way. The free black Paula, or Paulinha, had between five and 6.5 thousand *covas*—but the documentation is not very clear.

And what of the Rocha family, main target of the inquiry? One of the largest individual proprietaries of the quilombo's cassava was Agostinho Ramires da Rocha, who had 19,000 *covas* evaluated at 19$200 réis. The famous Balthasar had only 12,000 *covas*, but from a more valuable root which reached 20$500 réis. Furthermore, he had containers and a flourmill together with his son–in–law, valued at 19$000 réis. The other Rocha brother, Pedro José, cultivated with an indigenous man, his total of 8,000 *covas*, valued at 12$000 réis, but also had an estimated flourmill of 14$640 réis and a sick horse worth 15$000 réis. Finally, the son–in–law of Balthasar, Antonio José Soledade, was the owner of 4,000 *covas*, estimated at 6$200 réis, and he was a partner with his father–in–law in the flour mill. Other members of the family were José Teixeira, son of Agostinho Ramires, and his brother Francisco Teixeira. These were known as the Teixeirinhas, who appear as large proprietaries compared to the standards of Oitizeiro, with 21,000 *covas* evaluated at 41$000 réis. Yet, we can add the freed black Paula, Balthasar's mistress, with her 5 to 6.5 thousand *covas*. In fact, the members of the Rocha family stand out when considered collectively, owning about 70 thousand *covas*, or 32 percent of the production from the quilombo. A proportion that rises to 40 percent if we add the *covas* controlled by their slaves.[53]

Why they were not arrested (except for Joaquim, who was arrested later), the slaves of the residents were not entered as property in the inventory of goods seized, but as proprietaries. The fact that the slaves' small farms were widely known by the witnesses of the inquiry—many of them accustomed to go buy flour in Oitizeiro, including slaves—confirms the degree of economic autonomy they had, and they were not small proprietaries, they had more than free blacks, for example. To them belonged more than 10 percent of covas—equivalent to 690 bushels of flour—enrolled among the assets arrested from the coiteiros. In detail: 7,000 covas belonged to pardo Joaquim and 6,000 the seasoned slave Pedro, both slaves of Agostinho Ramires da Rocha; the two slaves from Pedro José da Rocha had 4 thousand covas; Gonçalo, slave of Ignácio Félix, had 6,000 covas, besides a flourmill. (His master had 21,000 *covas*, only three and a half times more than his slave.) The cassava slaves were evaluated in 39$000 réis, about 12 percent of the plants seized. Not included here are the other slaves who had cassava inventoried along with their masters. The inventory records "thirty thousand *covas* of cassava, which were said to belong to Antonio Florencio, his slaves, and other aggregates, most of it forever, and another still green," all worth 45$000 réis.

The Oitizeiro slaves not only produced for their own consumption; however, estimates from that time state that each slave needed between nine and ten acres per year for their own subsistence.[54] The six aforementioned slaves would require, at most, sixty from the 690 bushels produced. They seem to have been active market suppliers of the region, which re-exported to the Recôncavo and Salvador, flour that would also supply ships engaged in the slave trade. Although the documentation is not clear on this, they certainly also worked on their masters small farms, or in a regime of sharecropping. But the same documentation makes it clear that they had their own small farms and, like their masters, protected and used the work of runaway slaves that ended up in Oitizeiro. Although paradoxical, their lives as planters reminds us of the historiographical controversy surrounding the so–called "peasant gap," i.e. the small farms from slaves, which control was part of the rights acquired by the slaves. This is the type of arrangement that happened during periods of slavery in several regions in America, but it was very common especially in the Caribbean, where not only the slaves planted and fed themselves with the products from the small farms, but they were also important food suppliers for local and regional markets, much like proto–farmers. In Jamaica, at the end of the eighteenth century, it is estimated that the slaves controlled about 20 percent of the internal circulating medium. Although in the Caribbean it is known as the Brazil system, or Brazilian custom, in Brazil the system was apparently not so widespread, although was found in several regions and in several periods, in various agricultural activities. Regarding the mills in Bahia, José da Silva Lisboa wrote: "It is worth warning that the slaves sustenance is ordinarily not in charge of the masters, because, it is an almost universal custom, that on Saturday and Sunday they can plant for themselves whatever they are good at, assigning to them the land."[55] This was written in 1781, just before the big sugar boom, when there was land available and perhaps the custom could be "almost universal." But, not later. A recent study of B. Barickman concludes that, between 1780 and 1860, in the mills the slave food was mainly their responsibility. The mills were major consumers of meat and flour produced out of them, including the flour manufactured in the Quilombo of Oitizeiro. Yet, in spite a certain ambiguity, in the end Barickman concedes: "in the Recôncavo, as well as in many other agricultural areas which were dependent on slave labor, the small farms allowed the slaves of the mills to create their own restricted 'economy,' but nevertheless significant."[56]

In flour producing regions, as there were many areas of the region of Ilhéus, the institution of small farms seems to have been more significant. Maybe even within the few mills of the region, which however was a cause for a dispute between masters and slaves. One of the documents discussed in more recent studies on Brazilian slavery, the subject of slaves from Ilhéus, in a not too distant date from the episodes of Oitizeiro. In 1789, the slaves of Santana's mill—that same mill that in 1806 recovered quilombolas under pressure from the Cariris troops—killed the overseer, stopped working, formed a quilombo on the grounds of the mill and wrote a famous "peace treaty" in which, among other things, demanded more time and more land to dedicate to their small farms, the restoration of concessions which had recently been removed from them, besides requiring a boat to transport their products to the market in Salvador.[57]

The travelers Spix and Martius, touring the region in 1819, raised questions that can help us understand why the system of small farms run by slaves would be more developed in the region, and discuss its phenomenon of protecting slaves. They wrote about the hardships that a foreign owner would find:

> slaves are for him a constant cause for worries, since the lowest discontent can be a reason to flee to the vast surrounding woods or to hide in the homes of distant farmers. The laws actually determine a severe punishment for the Brazilians who hold others slaves, but it is rare that this will happen; the farmer in the beginning of his enterprise, whose capital is thus partly unproductive, then suffers the lack of arms, being harder when you need them the most.[58]

The coiteiros in Oitizeiro made, in 1806, exactly what thirteen years later the travelers still denounced as a current practice. The situation can be explained because the region was sparsely populated, far from the capital, poorly policed, had a favorable ecology for the formation of quilombos, it also had plenty of woods and indomitable indigenous parts, and the proprietaries were small in size.[59] All different from what happened in the Recôncavo. But there was more.

The southern farmers found it difficult to both find slaves and to keep them obedient. Spix and Martius heard complaints from the Registrar of Barra do Rio de Contas, about the price of slaves, prohibitive for local farmers. The widespread protection perceived by the travelers was probably developed from the competitive environment for the scarce labor.[60] What the Germans did not realize was that the protected slave did not stop from being productive, continuing to work for the coiteiro and for themselves. From this point of view, the agriculture production was not impaired, and perhaps was even better, in the interest of the slaves involved in the plot.

Trusting the travelers evaluation—which is confirmed by the events in Oitizeiro—in southern Bahia, the farmers were weak and the slaves demanding, "the lowest discontent was a reason to flee." In 1806, the masters needed the military intervention from Count of Ponte to free them from the quilombolas and coiteiros. Whoever wanted to keep their slaves at home, needed to grant something that would make the experience of slavery minimally bearable. Slaves of recalcitrant masters would certainly see these relationships happening around them. Many aquilombados in Oitizeiro, more than settling the quilombo, just wanted to change their master; they wanted masters as those from the quilombo, which allowed their slaves to cultivate their own small farms, sell their products, accumulate property and even shelter runaway slaves to help them in this. This reminds me of a document written, fifty years later, by Fluminense masters, from Vassouras, where it can be read: "the slave who has [small farms] never flees nor does he brew disorder."[61] Perfect as an ideology of control, but as we are seeing, the slaves were imperfect. Many thought of going beyond. Those slaves may have invested in small farms with some expectation of emancipation. Remember that one of the farmers indicted in 1806 was the free black Rosa Maria, who had been a slave of Balthasar da Rocha, the strong man of Oitizeiro. How did she obtain her freedom? And, if she bought it, where did she get the money? Most likely from planting cassava, since it was like this that they earned money in the region. The same can be suggested for other *forros* in Oitizeiro. The prospect of emancipation could be in slaves' plans as well as in the quilombolas, who lived there.[62]

There was, without a doubt, a dark side to the small farms, when they were granted only to release the master from the responsibility to sustain their slaves, thus lowering costs for the master with the reproduction of labor. That theme, besides being suggested by current historians, was raised in the region of Ilhéus on the occasion of an ecclesiastical inquiry carried out in 1813 and involving, among other places, the town of Barra do Rio de Contas. Several masters were charged with two sins, which usually came combined: "not giving rations" to their slaves and "allowing" them to work on Sundays and holy days. Others were accused of giving slaves only "the Saturday for them to support and clothe themselves with the fruits of the day."[63] Seen from this angle, the small farms system increased the slave exploitation and may have promoted their dissatisfaction and encourage to escape. In other words, the granting of small farms itself didn't represent a better treatment, did not guarantee peace, because it was also very important the time allowed to cultivate in them—a point raised by Santana's mill rebels, whom I referred to earlier. They needed land and time to work it. But, even when working on Sundays and holy days, in addition to a few hours on other days of the week, the small farm, for allowing slaves self-sustenance, promoted a spirit of autonomy between them and encouraged them in their daily skirmishes with the masters. As it was very well summarized by Dale Tomich, for the slave, the small farm "was a means to develop a style of autonomous life."[64] But, I repeat: the small farm and other concessions from the masters—or slave achievements—were not a guarantee of peace and harmony, a purpose which was incompatible with slavery. Regardless of its function to control, the slaves' access to the small farm would not necessarily prevent their escape. Because, if they did not depend on the master to survive, slaves could think it was better to live without the master.[65]

As discussed, slaves' small farms in Brazil were probably more common in areas with the same features as the south of Bahia, formed by small proprietaries dedicated to domestic supply and not to agriculture for exportation. I suggest it occurred more there than in the Recôncavo or analogous regions, for example, so that historians would have a better chance of finding these small farms. It was what Flávio Gomes found in the region of the Iguaçu county, Rio de Janeiro, where, despite the presence of many mills, most of slaves was dedicated to the production of food.[66] And just like in there, in Oitizeiro, the farming economy was broad, because of the participation of not only the slaves of free residents but also the quilombolas seeking with the coiteiros better survival conditions.[67]

The Oitizeiro is then best understood in terms of how a quilombo was viewed at that time, but not as we are accustomed to imagining what a quilombo was like. It was formed by free men (black, white and even the indigenous population), their own slaves and other protected slaves that formed an important part of the adult population. The coiteiros, remember, were seventeen people; the runaway slaves could reach at least three dozen, and were the majority. We cannot say that the latter were stolen slaves—moreover, they were not described as such in the inquiry—which would mean that they were there against their will. They were so at ease that they walked around freely with arms, working, hunting and whistling. There is strong evidence that they occupied a position of strength, escaping the axiom that "once a slave, always a slave."[68]

But Oitizeiro was a peculiar quilombo, so much that we can ask ourselves if there wasn't a juridical construction of a quilombo, by the ombudsman Domingos Maciel, to meet the expectations from the Count of Ponte, which in turn wanted to impress the regent Prince. Although there is imprecision in accounts of the quilombo, this is due to the nature of where their history was culled. Among other things, history is made of speeches, practices and relationships, which are often ambivalent. Defining the Oitizeiro as a quilombo was not only a politically convenient resource. While some features were unusual, the Oitizeiro had features like any other quilombo from that time of slavery: gathering in one place of a growing number of runaway slaves, who resisted returning to their houses, managed an agricultural production and developed other subsistence activities, occasionally committing robberies, and subjected to and alternative "government" to the surrounding society. The relationships of production and power within the Oitizeiro threatened the slave subordination in the region; about this, there is no doubt. The relationships were dangerous.

However, Balthasar da Rocha and other coiteiros cannot be considered as liberators of slaves, abolitionists' prototypes. It is possible that they were just opportunistic. But, if they used the slaves for their own benefit, the reversal benefits were also true. There was an agreement, negotiation. In the Oitizeiro, the runaway slaves who gathered to create a quilombo found a safe nest, work, food, probably small farms and even tobacco and brandy, away from their masters. For them, the Oitizeiro was a quilombo.

15

CANTOS AND QUILOMBOS IN A HAUSA REBELLION IN BAHIA, 1814

STUART B. SCHWARTZ

Slave resistance in Brazil has usually been divided by historians into two parallel but somewhat distinct categories. The first is *marronage*, or running away, and by extension, the formation of runway communities, or *quilombos*. This process was almost continual throughout the history of Brazilian slavery. The second category is rebellion and the far less frequent large slave revolts, usually urban in nature, and especially those that occurred in Bahia in the early nineteenth century. While other aspects of resistance have received some attention as well, these two phenomena, *quilombos* and revolts, have dominated discussions of slave resistance but usually as distinct activities, as two different strategies for confronting the slave regime. In this chapter, I want to reexamine those two aspects of slave resistance at the moment of the Atlantic Revolutions of the late eighteenth and nineteenth centuries, and to examine a case in which they were not simply two variant responses to the oppression of slavery but mutually supporting tactics in the slaves' war against slavery. My emphasis here will be not on what masters thought or did, but what moved the slaves and what may have lay behind their actions.

In this study, I wish to begin that reexamination by analyzing a previously unknown judicial investigation of a revolt planned by Hausa slaves in 1814 but betrayed to the authorities and thus stillborn (see appendix).[1] The organization and plans of this revolt revealed by the judicial inquiry underline a number of themes common to these Bahian slave risings: the ways in which urban and rural slaves cooperated and coordinated their actions, the role of "ethnic identities" and their meaning in a colonial context, the adherence and participation of non-slaves in these movements, and finally the role that marronage and *quilombos* could play in linking and mobilizing the potential sources of slave rebellion.

In the long history of resistance against Brazilian slavery there was, in fact, nothing quite like the series of revolts and conspiracies that rocked the city of Salvador and its surrounding agricultural zones between 1806 and 1835. This was a turbulent period, characterized in Brazil by barrack revolts, the end of colonial rule, independence, a royal abdication, and general political unrest and instability, intensified by the slave rebellions, which were themselves a product of those general conditions. The Bahian slave revolts were usually organized and carried out along ethnic lines, but sometimes participation and leadership crossed these somewhat artificial cultural boundaries. They occasionally united in common action slaves and freedmen and -women. The slave revolts of nineteenth-century Bahia constituted a series of campaigns or battles in a long war against slavery or, as one slave called it, a Blacks' War (*uma guerra dos pretos*). The relationship between this war and the tradition of marronage and *quilombos* needs to be explored. The Hausa risings of 1814 provide an opportunity to begin that process.

The Bahian slave rebellions have been explained by a variety of interpretations: religious, structural, political, conjunctural, and ethnic. The fact that some of the rebellions, like the largest of them, the Male rebellion of 1835, had a strong Islamic orientation led to a religious explanation, but other authors have pointed out that not all the rebels were Muslims nor were their goals particularly religious. Some authors have argued that the timing of the rebellions in terms of the broad "Atlantic Revolutions" (1776–1840) and in relation to the political unrest associated with Brazilian independence (1822) was in no way accidental and that the rebellions must be seen in that light.[2] At the same time, the strongly ethnic character of many of the revolts, organized as they were by various African peoples, the lack of large-scale participation in them by Brazilian-born blacks (*crioulos*) and mulattos, and the divisions of color, status, and origin within the Afro-Brazilian communities argue against a unifying theme of ideological Jacobinism among the slaves. That kind of more inclusive political thinking and the example of France seems to have been more important in the republican political movements of the period that involved the free people of color, and even the Haitian example had more impact on them and on the slave owners than it did as a motive for the slaves themselves.

Contexts

The captaincy of Bahia had long been a major terminus of the slave trade, but changes in the Atlantic economy, especially the Haitian revolution of 1792, had created new conditions for the expansion of slavery. In the early nineteenth century about eight thousand to ten thousand Africans a year were arriving at the docks of Salvador. Between two-thirds and three-fourths of these Africans came from the Bight of Benin or what the Portuguese called the Mina Coast. In 1806, for example, 8,037 Minas disembarked in Bahia compared to 2,588 slaves from Angola and Benguela.[3] Bahia had a long tradition of direct trade with that part of the African coast, and many slave owners had developed a preference for workers from this region.[4]

Figure 1. *Vista de Salvador, c. 1858* ("Vue de Bahia," *Brazil pitoresco. Álbum de vistas, paisagens, monumentos, costumes etc.*, Paris, Lemercier, 1861. Reprod. Bauer Sá).

The elimination of Haiti as a sugar producer after the rebellion of 1791 had stimulated the expansion of sugar production in Brazil, and traditional plantation areas like Bahia boomed with the creation of new market opportunities. This expansion was accompanied by an increase in slave imports to meet the needs of plantation labor, and it also resulted in a swelling of the urban slave population in Salvador, the port city, the capital of the captaincy, and the administrative hub of Portuguese government in the region.

By the first decade of the nineteenth century, the captaincy as a whole had a population of over four hundred thousand, of which about one-third were slaves. The city of Salvador had a population of over fifty thousand, about half of them black, another 22 percent *pardos*, and only about a quarter of the population were whites. Slaves made up perhaps 40 percent of the city's population.[5] What distinguished the slave population of Salvador and of the captaincy in general (and most of Brazil as well) and often provoked the comments of foreign observers was the African origins of the majority of the slaves. In this period in Bahia, Africans probably made up 60 percent of the slave population. As the population became increasingly African, it became more imbalanced in terms of sex and age as well because of the imbalanced sex ratio in the trade. By the early nineteenth century, the African-born probably made up about two-thirds of Salvador's slaves. The chances for Bahian male slaves to find a mate and form a family were probably worse in this period than they had been since the sixteenth century. Finally, the age structure of the slave population favored young adults, who made up about 60 percent of the city's slave force.[6] Here was a slave population that was predominantly composed of young, African males, and in the early nineteenth century, increasingly so. Little wonder the growing preoccupation of the slave owners, surrounded by a rising sea of foreign, African-born slaves whose gatherings, drumming, and dances had turned parts of the city into something similar to the "backlands of the Mina Coast."[7] Little wonder, too, the rising tide of slave restiveness and ethnic solidarities within the complex structure of Bahian slave society and the context of traditional resistance.[8]

The normal insecurity of slave society had intensified by the turn of the century. Runaways and bandits made the roads insecure. Manoel de Araújo e Góes, who lived at Engenho Camorogi, some fifteen miles from the town of Santo Amaro in the heart of the sugar country, complained that in the woods on his daily trips to his *engenho* (sugar mill plantation) Santa Anna de Pojuca he was in constant danger from brigands or "even from his own slaves."[9] He petitioned for the right to bear a brace of pistols. Going about unarmed in the countryside had become dangerous.

These concerns were not unfounded. Maroons were a common problem. Sometimes newly arrived Africans took the first opportunity to flee, joining others who were fed up with what the French consul called the "intolerable despotism" of the slave owners.[10] Fugitive communities dotted the countryside and served as a beacon and refuge for plantation slaves. The interrelationship of the plantations and *quilombos* and the nature of the threat is made clear in the career profile of Severino Pereira, "captain major of expeditions and assaults of the district of San José de Itapororocas, chief of the effective militia for the control [*reducção*] of escaped slaves and those fortified in *quilombos* or hideouts"—in other words, a slave catcher. Pereira listed among his services to the "internal security of the people and the dominion of masters over slaves and wrongdoers" various activities revealing of the nature of slave resistance.[11] In 1789 he had attacked a fugitive community made up of slaves who had fled the plantation of Bento Simões de Brito and joined a *quilombo* in the Matas de Águas Verdes. In 1791, he had been wounded twice in an attack on a *quilombo* near Matas do Concavo on the Jacuipe River. His main service had been to lead an expedition of two hundred men against the *quilombos* of Orobó and Andrahy, which had been, in his words, "committing robbery, murder, sacking houses, stealing cattle, devastating farms, holding up travelers on the roads, inducing other slaves [to escape] and taking them by force for their reproachable purposes."[12] He was particularly proud of his actions against these "enemies of the State of Your Majesty," who had built a strongly fortified position protected by a network of subterranean pits, traps, and stakes—in other words, a strongly fortified permanent settlement.[13] These "services" were typical of the slave hunters of the period.[14] Each district maintained these bush captains (*capitães do mato*), who not only pursued individual runaways but also mobilized posses or militia units to attack fugitive settlements.

While such *quilombo* activity had been endemic in Bahia since the beginnings of African slavery, governmental concern with them had intensified in the late eighteenth century, especially with the growing number of Africans brought in the post-Haitian revolt agricultural expansion in the captaincy. After 1807, with the tide of revolts, the problem—or at least the fear—became more acute. Many of these *quilombos* were not far from the centers of population, the towns and plantations, and their members lived by raiding or trading with the nearby populations. By the early nineteenth century, these suburban *quilombos* in Cabula, Matatu, or Itapoam on the outskirts of Salvador were increasingly integrated into the life of urban slavery, perhaps even serving at times as places of temporary escape for *petite marronage*, centers for the relief and rest for urban slaves.[15] Fugitives from *quilombos* sometimes entered the city to "fence" their goods, and the relative isolation of the *quilombos* offered opportunities for Africans to maintain a certain cultural autonomy away from the civil and religious constraints of the dominant society, which suppressed the practice of African religions.[16] The *quilombo* of Urubu, destroyed in 1826, housed a *candomblé* (African religious organization).[17] The turnover of residents in these suburban *quilombos* may have been high, but while the settlements themselves were subject to police raids or military attacks, some were able to last for years. Almost invariably after a *quilombo*'s destruction, some of the fugitives would avoid capture and set up a new *quilombo*, soon joined by new runaways in a dialectic of slave resistance. The formation of *quilombos* was a chronic problem for Bahian slave owners and a constant tactic of Bahian slaves.

THE HAUSAS AMONG THE "NATIONS"

By the beginning of the nineteenth century, the slave population of the captaincy and the city had swelled. Large numbers of Mina slaves were arriving, particularly those groups or "nations" that were called in Bahia Nagô (Yoruba), Gege (Aja-Fon), and Ussá or Aussá (Hausa).[18] To some extent, these ethnic designations were colonial creations because they did not recognize African political or religious divisions. Thus, Nagôs might all speak Yoruba, but they came from different and often hostile polities. The same could be said of the Dahomeans, called in Bahia Geges.[19] The formation of new identities and "imagined communities" according to these colonial labels was a complex and incomplete process.[20]

The Hausas were also divided by regional origins and by religious differences. The process of Islamization in Hausaland had been violent, incomplete, and continued in Bahia as converts continued to be made.[21] Hausas were not the most numerous group in Bahia, and in the city of Salvador itself they constituted only about 6 percent of the slave population, but they had begun to enter the captaincy in some numbers with the other peoples from the Bight of Benin after 1780, and increasingly after the Torodbe Fulani Shehu Usumanu Dan Fodio initiated a jihad in Hausaland in 1804 that resulted in the creation of large areas under Fulani control, and eventually the formation of the Sokoto caliphate. The fighting lasted six years and produced large numbers of defeated captives, Muslims and non- Muslims from the Central Sudan who were sold into the Atlantic trade, mostly through the port of Lagos.[22] Eventually, the Islamic expansion also set off a series of wars within the Yoruba area as some of the Yoruba city-states were Islamicized and new states also appeared.[23] These wars generated thousands of prisoners sold into the Atlantic slave trade. In the early decades of the nineteenth century, however, most of the Muslim slaves arriving at Bahia were Hausas. The German scientists Spix and Martius saw them in Salvador and called them "very black, tall, muscular, and very daring," opinions shared to some extent by the French consul in Bahia, who thought the Hausas to be physically strong and less willing to resign themselves to their captivity than other groups. He also noted that most of them were fighting men who had been enslaved as prisoners of war and that it was rare to see Hausa women in Bahia.[24] His personal observations have been confirmed by modern research.[25]

The Hausas had begun to cause trouble in Bahia as early as 1806 or 1807. A supposed plot of Hausas had been discovered by the governor, the Count of Ponte (Conde da Ponte), in which Hausas in the city had elected a "governor" who with the aid of a freedman as his secretary had begun to establish contacts with other Hausas on the Recôncavo plantations. Another account noted that "captains" had been appointed in each of the city's districts.[26] Arms had been gathered and the rising, coordinated between slaves in the city and on the plantations, set to take place on Corpus Christi, when vigilance would probably be lax. The Count of Ponte had acted quickly, suppressing the movement, arresting the leaders, and throwing a guard around the public fountains out of fear of the threat of poison.[27] This conspiracy was noted m a royal order and sentence of October 1807 that pointed out that the plot would have violated "not only the rights of their respective masters, but would also disturb the security and public order on which the conservation of states depended."[28] The leaders were executed and ten other slaves publicly flogged. A curfew was imposed on all slaves in the city, and even the movement of freed persons was curtailed.

Neither these early Hausa rebels nor the Count of Ponte were fools. Both realized that while the origins of slave action and organization might be most favored in the fluid, urban world of the port of Salvador, where slaves and freed people mixed freely, the majority of the captaincy's slaves lived in the countryside on the sugar *engenhos* and cane farms, in the tobacco-growing and food-producing regions, and therefore any hope of success would lie in linking urban plans to a general uprising in the countryside. Thus, from the slaves' point of view, contact with the mass of rural workers was essential, and from the government's perspective, this was the thing to be most feared. The governor's report of the incident specifically noted that the projected uprising had included not only city slaves but also those of the Recôncavo plantations.[29] The Count of Ponte also realized that a real potential danger of possible linkage lay in the fugitive communities, the *quilombos*, which often housed runaways from both the city and the countryside. In April 1807, the Count of Ponte had projected the destruction of suburban *quilombos* in the woods that surrounded the capital, and the Portuguese crown approved this measure to assure the "peace and tranquility of the people."[30] He took a hard-line position on the destruction of *quilombos* as a potential source of revolt and on any manifestations of African culture like the *batuques* (reunions for drumming and dancing), which might serve to agitate rebellion or further unify slaves along ethnic or religious lines.

An example of the potential danger of the *quilombos* was not long in coming. During this period, a group of Hausa runaways who had fled from Salvador and from the rural estates of the Recôncavo had formed a *quilombo* on the Rio da Prata, not far from the rural town of Nazaré das Farinhas. In early January 1809 about three hundred fugitives, Hausas and apparently some Nagôs, attacked Nazaré but were repelled and then badly mauled by militia troops two days later, suffering numerous casualties. Hundreds of rebels from Salvador who tried to join the rising were intercepted on the road. Some ninety-five rebels were captured, but many fugitives continued to roam the countryside in small groups, throwing the towns and plantations of the region into alarm, perhaps as far away as Sergipe d'El Rey. Exemplary punishment was meted out once again, and local officials imposed strict curfews, complaining that slaves circulated in the taverns and at batuques without proper supervision by their masters, but despite such measures, in 1810 the government had to suppress yet another revolt.[31] By 1814, the patterns of the early revolts were already well established: ethnic organization, attempts to link city and plantation countryside, contact with *quilombos*, and government repression.

In February 1814, a new and potentially major revolt erupted just north of the city limits of Salvador at the whaling and fishing stations of Itapoã. A group of perhaps 250 slaves from a nearby *quilombo* attacked the stations and raised the slaves employed there in revolt. With shouts of "Freedom," and "Death to whites and mulattos," the rebels burned the stations and killed between fifty and one hundred people. Led apparently by a Hausa *malam*, or Muslim preacher, the rebels killed a number of whites and mulattos, attacked Itapoam, burned over a hundred houses, and tried to enlist other slaves to join them. Hoping to spread the revolt, the rebels began to march toward the Recôncavo, the heartland of the sugar plantations. They burned two *engenhos* on the line of march, seized arms and horses, and killed anyone who opposed their progress. Intercepted by a cavalry contingent at Santo Amaro de Ipitanga, some fifty rebels were killed in the battle itself while others hanged themselves in despair. The usual repression followed: public whippings, execution of four (leaders?), and the deportation of twenty-three men to Angola. Many others were arrested and subjected to brutal and exemplary punishment. Apparently, others escaped into the woods and reformed again a new *quilombo* in the forests north of the city.[32]

Even while the judicial process proceeded against the rebels of the Itapoã rebellion, word arrived in Salvador in March 1814 of a rising on some of the *engenhos* of the Iguape region near Cachoeira.[33] Slaves had gathered at Engenho da Ponta with the intention of taking the provincial town of Margogipe, but three Hausa freedmen who had been in contact with them were arrested and the revolt dissipated. It was Hausas again across the Bay of All Saints in the sugar and tobacco region of Iguape and its nearby port town of Cachoeira who seem to have organized this revolt. The city council of Cachoeira had already expressed fears in 1813 of such a rising and had warned the government that Hausa dockworkers were planning something, but the new governor, the Count of Arcos, no particular friend of the slave owners or slavery, had thought their premonitions exaggerated and probably due to their own guilty consciences. The government had done little when the revolt erupted on March 20, 1814. The rebels had planned to gather at the large Engenho da Ponta and then march on the town of Maragogipe. They were intercepted and the revolt suppressed, but the planters were now on their guard and disgusted with what they considered to be the vacillating and permissive attitude of the new governor, so different from that of his predecessor.[34]

The War Continues: May 1814

It is in this context that only two months later, on May 26, 1814, a Portuguese named Joaquim José Correa Passos appeared at the office of the lawyer, Elias Baptista Pereira de Araujo Lasso, to declare that he had learned from a woman from the Mina coast with whom he had illicit relations that Hausa slaves and freedmen were planning another great uprising. Lasso was a lawyer at the regional High Court (Relação da Bahia) and he had been involved in the denunciation of the slave revolt of 1807.[35] On revealing this new plot to the senior criminal prosecutor (*ouvidor geral do crime*), Desembargador Antonio Garces Pinto de Madureira, Lasso was ordered by the governor to continue an investigation in all secrecy and to attempt to discover the meeting place of the plotters, their arms, and their plans.[36] One day later (May 27) another slave owner, José Ferreira da Silva, reported that his Hausa slave Germano and a Guruman slave named Jeronimo had overheard a conversation between other Hausas at the docks in which they spoke of a "war against the whites."[37] In fact, what was said in the exchange was that anyone who joined was a man, and those who refused were women. Ferreira was well informed. He had been involved in the slave trade and could speak a number of the languages of the Mina Coast and had been called upon to read some of the documents (*cartéis da guerra*) associated with the rising in February. Lasso convinced Ferreira to have his slave pretend to join the rebels in order to learn of their plans, leadership, and preparations for the rebellion. The lawyer later confirmed the report with another of Ferreira's slaves, promising rewards or even freedom to both slaves for their cooperation. This was done, and Ferreira even provided money to his slave that had been demanded by the plotters to help in the preparations. Ferreira was able to report that his slave had seen two hundred arrowheads (*ferrõens*) wrapped in cloth bundles that had been taken to the woods to prepare arrows. Others had been prepared in the home of a blacksmith. Hausa plotters had also told the informant that five barrels fall of arrowheads were ready and another barrel was held by the slave of a baker. Ferreira and his slave had witnessed the purchase of two bundles of pipe reeds (*canudos*) that could serve as arrows. The slaves were taking the risk of making such purchases because the revolt was planned for St. John's Day (São João), June 24, and the plotters simply had no time to cut arrow shafts in the woods.

Ferreira and his slave reported that the conspiracy involved "all the Hausa blacks, freed and slave, of this city as well as the Recôncavo." Also, supposedly involved were some mulattos and crioulos from outside the city as well as Indians who "wanted the land that the Portuguese had taken from them." Indigenous "ambassadors" to the plotters who arrived in the city on June 12 and 13 were quickly hustled out of town again to avoid provoking attention. Indians were not that common a sight in nineteenth-century Salvador, and their contact with slaves in the city might have produced unwanted attention.[38]

To this point, the plans of the rising seem to fit the patterns of the period. The rebellion was to be initiated at a moment in the secular or religious calendar when the levels of control might be slack: Christmas, Easter, Nossa Senhora da Guia, or St. John's Day being particularly favored. The Eve of St. John was usually celebrated with bonfires, celebration, and fireworks that could disguise the first hostile actions of the plotters. St. John's Day also fell in June, after the *sajra*, or harvest, had been completed and a time when slaves may have been less subject to daily supervision. The collaboration here between Hausas both slave and freed indicates that linguistic or ethnic identities seem to have been more important than the juridical distinctions between slave and freed people, but the rebels' plans to incorporate some Brazilian-born crioulos and pardos and even to mobilize Indians was a curious and somewhat distinctive aspect of the plot. While such cooperation was not common, it was always a possibility. Brazilian-born blacks and pardos might have differences with each other and with the Africans, but cooperation could be forged in times of crisis. Such collaboration was greatly feared by the slave owners. Later Joao Maciel da Costa wrote, "it is an enormous mass of black slaves and freedmen who ordinarily make common cause."[39]

Figure 2. View of slave and freedmen porters and stevedores who formed the cantos. *From Jean Baptiste Debret,* Voyage pittoresque et historique au Brésil, *vol. 2 (Paris, 1834–39).*

The investigation revealed that the leadership of the rebellion was centered in the *negros ganhadores*. A large number of urban slaves and freedmen worked in the city as porters, stevedores, and occasional laborers who hired out their services as *negros de ganho*, or *ganhadores*. They gathered at various points throughout the city in organized working groups, or *cantos*. By the warehouses and docks of the lower city, at strategic points on major streets, and near the fountains and plazas, these cantos were established so that anyone needing laborers to move goods or for occasional jobs knew where to look and could negotiate directly with the workers. So cheap and available was this labor that whites, even servants, rarely carried anything. Foreign observers were greatly impressed by the gangs of porters in the Brazilian cities and the call and response songs that accompanied their labor. They gave the city its character. John Luccock saw the street workers in Rio in 1820 and he gave this account:

> Among the people of the lower classes of Rio, the men that carry things in the streets get the attention of visitors not only because of their numbers but because of their habits. They are not really stevedores because those who are paid for their work for themselves are rare; most of them are slaves sent out to work in the streets with an empty basket and some long poles for the service of their masters. They carry heavy objects, hanging them from a chain suspended from the poles supported by a couple of the men. If it's very heavy four, six, or more will form a work group, captained by the most intelligent of them. To give rhythm to their work and coordinate their steps, the leader will sing a short, simple African song, at the end of which the group will respond in a loud chorus. The song will go on so long as the work lasts and with this they make their burden less and cheer up their spirits. I have at times the impression that these people are not insensitive to the pleasures of their memories of the homes they have lost and will never see again. What is certain is that these songs give to the streets a joy that in other ways they are missing.[40]

The message was not always so nostalgic. The Benguela *carregadores* in Alagoas sang:

> The snake has no arms,
> No legs, no hands, no feet
> How does he rise, and we do not
> We who have arms, and legs, and hands, and feet?[41]

Sometimes the foreign observers recognized that the singing was misleading. The German travelers Spix and Martius wrote: "In the city the condition of those who work for a daily wage (240 *reis*) for their masters is very sad. They are considered living capital in action and since their masters hope to recoup their capital and interest payments as quickly as possible, the slaves are not spared."[42] The seeming freedom of the negros de ganho was also deceptive. Many lived with their masters and were under their vigilance.

The cantos were organized ethnically, that is, membership was usually controlled by a particular African group or by the colonial equivalent of ethnicity since some of the categories were regionally or linguistically defined and did not necessarily imply shared identities. There were cantos of Nagôs (Yoruba), Aussá (Hausas), Gege (Dahomey), Angolas (Ovimbundu,

Congo, Benguela, and so on), and others. In the cantos, slaves and freedmen cooperated.[43]

The negros de ganho could move freely within the city without causing suspicion. Their work on or near the waterfront also brought them into contact with the slaves bringing in goods from the surrounding agricultural areas. Moreover, the cantos were organized, usually choosing or electing their own "captains," sometimes in a ceremony held on the streets, the elections being confirmed by the other cantos.[44] This mobility and organization made them ideal centers for plotting rebellion and for active resistance. They seemed to control the streets. In December 1813, when customshouse officials had arrested a black man for theft, members of the canto of the Alfandega had intercepted them on the way to prison and had set the prisoner free, threatening the accompanying officers at knifepoint.[45] The police did nothing to punish them.

The 1814 investigation revealed that the cantos in the lower city at the Cais (docks) de Cachoeira, the Cais Dourado, and Corpo Santo had taken a leading role in the plot, while the cantos of Trapiche Novo, Trapiche Grande, Pezo do Fumo, Terreiro, Paço de Saldanha, and other locales were also involved. African divisions and rivalries were not forgotten, but witnesses questioned were unsure about the level of collaboration. Some testimony claimed that with the exception of the Tapas (Nupe), the other African "nations," the Angolans, Gege, and Nagôs, had not been brought into the conspiracy.[46] João, a later Hausa witness who had been invited to join the conspiracy by his *malungos*, claimed that Antonio, captain of a canto and the leader of the conspiracy, had told him that all the cantos were involved except the Geges.[47] Perhaps Antonio had exaggerated the level of collaboration in order to impress a possible recruit. Whatever the truth, it was clear to everyone that the ethnic divisions or levels of cooperation were crucial in the plans of the rebels and for their hope of success.

Although the enterprise was led from the docks, slaves throughout the city were involved. A Hausa slave of Antonio Coelho da Fonseca who sold tobacco at the canto of the Cais de Cachoeira revealed that other major figures in the plot were José, the slave of a baker in the Baixa dos Sapateiros who had stored or hidden much of the arms, and a Hausa blacksmith, slave of an old black freedman, who forged most of the arrowheads. The informant Germano reported to his master that he had attended a meeting in a shack near the Pilar Church in which ten conspirators, including two freedmen and two of the leading plotters, had met. Apparently, it was at that gathering he had learned the plan of action.

The key element in the plan was a coordination of action between *quilombo* fugitives and urban slaves. The main point of contact was the Sangradouro woods on the outskirts of Salvador. This scrub forest was extensive and bordered on the smallholdings (*roças*) on the Brotas road, Matatu, the Quinta dos Lázaros, and the Cabula road. This had long been a site of suburban *quilombos*, one having been destroyed at Cabula in 1807. Apparently, after the uprising at Itapoam in February 1814, a number of the rebels had escaped to the safety of the bush. The plan called for a diversionary tactic. Those fugitives hidden in the woods of Sangradouro would mount an attack on the Powder House at Matatú, and when the troops mobilized to meet that threat, the rising would begin in the city. Coordination between the two groups had been maintained by a crioulo who circulated in the woods, in contact with the fugitives and keeping them apprised of recent developments in the city. Actions were to be coordinated by means of conch shell trumpets, which were widely distributed among the plotters.[48] Plans for the rebellion had spread into the countryside. The slaves at the *engenho* of Antonio Vaz de Carvalho were enlisted, as were the Hausas at the farm of Manoel da Silva. The plot was well planned and preparations were extensive. Ferreira Silva's slave Germano reported that on June 16 he had been taken to the Sangradouro woods and shown a large pit filled with arms and several bundles filled with gunpowder. There was, however, little mention of firearms. Most of the preparations had been of bows, arrows, and here, as in most of the other rebellions, bows, arrows, and edged weapons made up the arsenal of the rebels.

The government had acted on June 23, dispatching a small unit of soldiers to the Sangradouro woods to seize the arms. They found over two hundred arrowheads, wood for bows, and bundles of shafts for arrows. João, the Hausa slave of Manoel José Teixeira de Souza, who had informed his master that he had been contacted by Antonio, the captain of a canto who lived at the Fonte de Xixi, to enter the plot, reported that to enlist him, he had been taken to a farm of a widow in Cabeça, on the road to Matatu, near Boa Vista. He claimed to have seen firearms hidden in a sugar crate, African arms (*armas da sua terra*), supplies (*carne de sertão, carne do sol*), and some cattle belonging to the farm owner that would also be used for the rebels. He encountered fifteen blacks, five from the farm and ten strangers, and he learned that there was a great *quilombo* nearby in Matatú where many of the rebels from the rising in February had gathered along with some country folk (*caboclos*). They had money taken in the February rising and were apparently well supplied if not entirely unified in their plans. Some wanted the revolt to begin on the Eve of St. John's Day when the noise of the traditional celebrations would cover their first movements. Others like Antonio, the capitão do canto, wanted to wait until July 10, when the numbers of adherents would be greater. Anyone seen on the road to the *quilombo* would be killed to prevent leaks before the plan could be put into motion. The rebels hoped to seize the Powder House at Matatu, taking what powder they needed and wetting down the rest in order to make it useless to the government's forces. João learned from Antonio that the arms and supplies had been moved from the farm into the woods, and he had worked for much of a day preparing arrows along with other plotters. He claimed to have counted some thirty-seven blacks in the woods. He revealed all this to his master and was dispatched to lead troops to the cache the following morning, but by the time of their arrival, everything had been moved. Whether the plotters had become suspicious of João or he had simply led the troops on a wild goose chase was unclear. Nothing could be found.

The government was not through. Manoel, a twenty-six-year-old apprentice blacksmith, slave of Caetano Soares, was questioned on June 27. Shown two types of arrowheads, he was asked if had made any like them and who had commissioned them and provided the iron. He answered that a Hausa who lived in the lower city, called Jatao in his own language, had asked for them and that he had made ten of them, four of one type, six of the other, from old nails. Manoel claimed he did not know Jatao's Portuguese name, his master's name, or his residence. He was either protecting his accomplice or reflecting the reality that an African world existed in Bahia in which the labels and categories of colonial society did not necessarily apply.

The plot of May 1814 was in some ways a continuation or extension of the rising of February and even involved some of the rebels from the earlier movement. Some slaves invited to join the conspiracy were told that many refugees from the February battle as well as new recruits were hidden in the woods, including "the Muslim priest that they said had been killed in the attack at Itapoã" (*o sacerdote Malamim que sedezia morto no combate da entrada da Itapoam*). To what extent this was a rumor designed to mobilize further cooperation, especially from Muslims, is unclear, but a desire by the rebels of February to continue their struggle from the suburban *quilombos* is obvious. Whatever the truth of the claim, the plot of May 1814 had gone beyond ethnic and religious limitations and had sought to draw crioulos, pardos, and even Indians into the movement.

In the process of resistance, Africans sought to draw on institutions or cultural features that might serve as bases of organization. These might be

African in origin, such as the batuques, or dance meetings, or Candomblés destroyed by police authorities, or they might be colonial institutions like religious brotherhoods or the black and mulatto militia units, adapted and transformed or simply mobilized by slaves and freedmen.[49] As the number of Africans in Bahia swelled, and especially as the tide of rebellion rose, colonial authorities and slave owners increasingly sought to restrict, control, or eliminate those cultural features that brought slaves together or were African in nature. Candomblés became a major police concern, with cult centers raided in Cachoeira in 1785 and Assu in 1829. The control of batuques became a topic of heated controversy between those who saw them as a breeding ground for rebellion and slave autonomy and those, like the more lenient governor, the Count of Arcos, who felt that such gatherings or the election of "kings" by slaves and freed persons during certain festivals made slavery more bearable and kept the "nations" divided.[50] In general, however, the trend was to crush these seeming manifestations of African culture or autonomy. Quilombos also fell into that category, but by their very nature, it was impossible to stamp them out. Institutions that were not so overtly African or that were constitutive of colonial culture and society and served to integrate slaves and freed persons into that society were less likely to be targeted for repression. It was hard to do so. Black brotherhoods, colored militia troops, and cantos were too much a part of colonial reality. A later municipal attempt to impose municipal control over the cantos in 1857 met with stiff resistance and a strike by the slave workers.[51] Despite the role the cantos had played in the 1814 planned revolt, there is no evidence that their activities were more controlled or that their ethnic basis was challenged.

The abortive rising of May 1814 shows clearly that Africans had found in the cantos and the *quilombos* two potential bases for the mobilization of resistance. For different reasons, both offered a certain freedom of operation and a potential to focus resistance. The plotters of May 1814, like their predecessors and those who followed in the next two decades, realized that linking urban and rural risings was the best hope of success, and the *quilombos* seemed to provide points of contact that could facilitate this cooperation. Like a tree scattering its seeds, many of the revolts produced new *quilombos* as rebels avoided capture and sought new spaces for life and action. After the 1814 revolts in Bahia a slave rising in Alagoas in 1815 was forestalled when the government raided a nearby *quilombo* and seized a cache of arms.[52] A worried battalion commander in Sergipe in 1827 noted the marauding fugitives increased their numbers and contaminated those still in slavery. His response was to terrify plantation slaves, but he warned of terrible consequences.⁵³ Slave owners had always recognized the threat that *quilombos* presented to the slave system, but in a period of political agitation and rebellion both they and the slaves came to see *quilombos* as the keys to the success or failure of rebellion.

APPENDIX

*Declaration of Manoel José Teixeira*⁵⁴
Act of Ratification Made by Manoel José Teixeira to the Declaration He Made.

On the 25 th of June 1814 in this city of Salvador of the Bay of All Saints in the residence of the desembargador, ouvidor geral do crime Dr. Antonio Pinto de Madureira, professed knight in the Order of Christ where I, the scribe, came called by his order; Manuel José Teixeira, resident in São Miguel, appeared....

The said judge said that having declared verbally on the 20th of the present month certain facts in respect to the continuation or new convulsion of the slaves of this city with information acquired from his Hausa slave named João, of whose participation the judge has made appropriate use, it is now necessary that he [Manoel José Teixeira] declare and ratify these statements in a legal document, to which end he has been called to the judge's presence so that he can do so under oath to the Holy Evangels. Having been sworn under oath, he said he well remembers what he declared because of his zeal and not as an act of passion or hate, and he ratifies this in the following manner. That being the owner of a slave named João Hausa, this slave without any coercion whatsoever reported that some of his buddies[*malungos*] and particularly the black, Antonio, captain of the canto, resident at the Xixi Fountain, invited him to enter a seditious conspiracy with others who tried to sway him to their opinion; they took him to a small farm [*roça*] of a widow near the beginning of the small road that goes to Matatu near Boa Vista where he was shown firearms in a sugar crate in a room, arms from his land, dried meat [*carne do sertão e carne de sol*], some cows that belonged to the owner of the farms that he was told would also serve as supplies; and finding there fifteen blacks, five of the farm and ten who were not, he also certified that there was a great *quilombo* above Matatu where there were many from the past revolt and some *caboclos* [indigenes or *mestiços*]. They had money stolen in the last revolt and their plan was to break out on the eve or day of Saint John under cover of the usual noise of such days; the first step was to kill the guard of the armory [Casa da Pólvora] of Matatu, take there what they needed and ruin the rest with water; others wished the war to begin on the 10th of July so they could gather together the largest number of blacks; the captain of the canto said that the blacks of Trapiche Novo, Trapiche Grande, or the Tobacco Scale, some of the merchant Cunha, of Friandes, and almost all the cantos of all the nations except the Geges were all ready. They were ready to kill everyone encountered on the road all the way to the *quilombo* in order that no one in the city became aware. Given this statement, he learning of such a grave situation, he told his slave to go with them in order to learn as much as he could, so that he, the witness, might be given proper warning and make a statement to the judge as a loyal vassal. The slave continued in contact with the captain of the canto, who told him on Wednesday the 22nd of the present month that there was news and that everything had been taken from the farmhouse and taken to the Sangradouro woods because there had been some searches made; some weapons were hidden, but those from the house had been carried further away and the slave was taken there where he saw everything that had been in the farmhouse and in addition, four bearded blacks attaching arrowheads to reeds that would be used as arrows in whose service the said slave of the witness worked almost the whole day, having brought a basket of meat manioc flour so that going in the morning, he returned only after five in the afternoon, promising to steal something from the witness and some weapons to return once and for all on Thursday the 23rd of the present month. The judge, learning of this, then required the slave to reveal the place on Thursday in the company of the adjunct scribe of this court, Honorio Fidelis Barreto, who accompanied a senior military official responsible for the investigation and arrest. The party left at eight in the morning in the company of the slave who served as a guide, nothing was found, and he the witness does not know why, being certain of what he had discovered and in the truthfulness of his slave who had reported well and loyally because he believed it his responsibility, as the witness said and declared. The said judge ordered this act made, to which I the scribe attest.

Signed by the witness and the judge. I, Germano Fereira Barreto, Scribe, recorded and signed.

16

THE QUILOMBO OF MALUNGUINHO, THE KING OF THE FOREST OF PERNAMBUCO

MARCUS JOAQUIM M. CARVALHO

> In the wilderness, there is only one King.
> The King of the wilderness is Malunguinho.
> I made my mark, yes
> In the middle of the wilderness, yes
> Protect the crown, yes
> King Malunguinho.[1]

These two verses are sung in present day Pernambuco at the tables of Jurema to call and honor Malunguinho, a figure of great significance to the *catimbo* of Pernambuco.[2] In January 1827, the Government Council of that province placed a price on the head of the black man, Malunguinho, the main leader of the Catucá quilombo. This article will tell the story of this quilombo.

As historical phenomena, quilombos comprised part of a broader spectrum of strategies for survival and resistance among the enslaved. For this reason, they were dynamic, changing across time and space. By the nineteenth century, the quilombo located in the forest of Catucá was very different from the Palmares quilombo of the old Pernambuco captaincy. We must also mention that the older quilombo was located in the new province of Alagoas, which was formed because of the 1817 Confederation of the Equator, just before Brazilian national independence. In the more than one hundred years that separated Palmares from Catucá, the backlands were populated, cotton production began, sugar plantations grew in size and number, and the local population grew to almost 500,000, of which 60,000 resided in the urban areas of Recife and Olinda. At this time, the social hierarchy had solidified, creating a more closed society in which repression of the enslaved was more efficient. Flight into the wilderness had become more difficult, as agriculture crept into the ecological zones best suited as hiding places. The Palmares quilombo had occupied a frontier that lay beyond the sugarcane zones. The Catucá quilombo, on the other hand, bordered the northern portion of the Zona da Mata region, beginning in what was practically a suburb of the Recife-Olinda urban area, and was divided into various groups scattered throughout the wilderness that would act in concert or separately as the necessities of the moment dictated.

Nineteenth century maps of the northern Zona da Mata allow us to pinpoint the location of the Catucá wilderness.[3] It began in the thickets and hills at the edge of the sister cities of Recife and Olinda extending into the interior, between the dams of Apicucos and Dois Irmãos, over the Morno River, all the way to the Beberibe River. Interestingly, a road charted on a mid nineteenth century map of Recife's hydraulic projects was given the suggestive name of "road of the man of the wilderness." From there, the forest extended into the interior, curving northwards at the peak of Macacos, Cova de Onça, and Paratibe. Hence, the path of escape began in an area that is, today, entirely urbanized, part of the Recife-Olinda metropolitan area. It is worth noting that the area remains a lower class district, comprised of lowlands that are framed by hills—"this" and "that" hill in local parlance. These places, once the site of public and private territorial incursions, are now, again, in the hands of the people.

It has already been stated that Catucá is one of the African-named topographical locations in Pernambuco, but it is perhaps misleading to identify the Catucá woods as a single, well-defined forest in the nineteenth century.[4] The soldiers that fought against the *quilombolas* traversed distances that would be unthinkable in our more sedentary times, and ended up using the name as an almost sociological concept—as if Catucá encompassed all of the forests in which black quilombolas lived, from Recife to Goiana, which was, in that period, the province's second largest city, right near the border with Paraiba. These forests were interrupted here and there by some of the largest and oldest sugar plantations in the province, such as Mussupinho, Monjope, Utinga, Araripe, Pau Amarelo, and many others—in total, over one hundred—that bordered the rivers and streams aptly referred to as "rivers of sugar."[5] Therefore, the use of the name Catucá in the documents greatly surpasses the location indicated in maps. Most likely, in an even earlier period, this was the name of the entire Atlantic forest between Recife and the border with Paraíba.

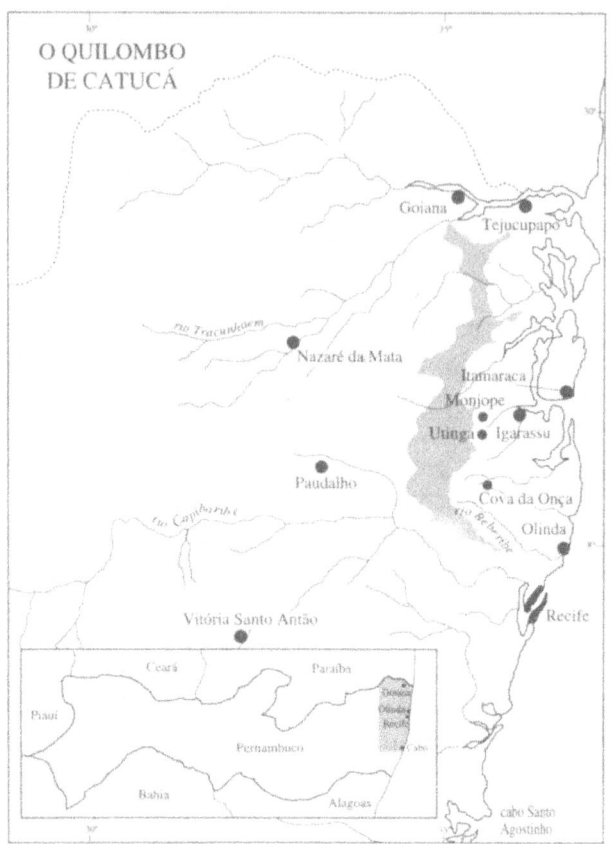

The Quilombo of Catucá.

This wooded area, which extended in a northerly direction through the province's most populous region, the dry Zona da Mata, separating the coastal plantations from the mountains west of Recife, contained the hiding places of the quilombolas. In the area adjacent to the port of Recife, the best lands were already occupied by sugar crops. Nevertheless, there were always leftover patches of wilderness on the plantations that were not suited for sugarcane. The Catucá presented in maps was comprised only of the forests on top of the foothills on the fringe of Recife, bordered by the Dois Irmãos dam to the south, and, to the north, by the Guabiraba heights towards Pau-Ferro, continuing onwards through an extensive area up to the Paratibe river. The center of the forest closest to Recife would have been a spot known as Cova da Onça—a valley surrounded by a group of hills which are to this day sparsely populated. In spite of the damaging use of the soil, this area still possesses ponds and streams.

Roads used to transfer cattle and cotton from the districts of Bom Jardim, Limoeiro, and Nazaré to Recife or to Goiana, an important commercial depot in the Zona da Mata, would cut through this area. These cattle roads would open up, in the wilderness, into clearings that with time transformed into even larger pathways of broken terrain. From the sugarcane zone surrounding Goiana, Igarassu and Itamaraca would send sugar to Recife, mostly by sea. Yet, many smaller roads connected the capital to the towns of this rural region with the highest population density in the province, through which moved a highly diverse free population. Thus, any communication between Recife and the dry Zona da Mata would pass extremely close to the quilombo—an ideal situation for the quilombolas in their attack plans. On the other hand, this proximity to the roads would also facilitate the maneuvers of planters' security forces, and the later destruction of Catucá.

One can assume that the area had been a site of concealment for runaway slaves from time immemorial. Nevertheless, the sources only refer specifically to the existence of a quilombo in Catucá in a later period. Henry Koster, during a visit to the plantation Timbó, mentioned that the woods on the plantation property served as a hiding spot for bandits and slaves. That said, he traveled from Recife to Goiana, offering a detailed description of the route, and even staying for a time in Itamaracá, but did not mention the quilombolas in the area.[6] It seems, therefore, that even assuming that the forests were always a hiding place for fugitives, the quilombo of Catucá only came into existence on the eve of Independence.

It may be difficult to pinpoint exactly when it started, yet we can assume that many slaves must have fled to the wilderness during the revolt of 1817, whose participants were principally planters of sugarcane and cotton from the area surrounding Catucá. Later, in October 1821, it was in this same region between Goiana and Recife that the planters' forces mobilized to overthrow the Portuguese governor Luis do Rego. Additionally, many of the planters involved in the 1824 Confederacy of the Equator came from this region. It is worth underscoring that many of the liberal rebels also lived in Recife, Olinda, and Goiana, and were often repressive slave-owners in their own right. The history of the quilombo of Catucá is thus intrinsically linked to the social and political history of the province. While none of these political conflicts brought any benefits to the enslaved, as they were mostly struggles between whites, they did manage to divide elites that, in turn, led to the disintegration of the apparatus put in place to control and repress the enslaved, facilitating their flight and the creation of quilombos.

Slave masters handled individual cases of escape as private disciplinary matters. Cases of group escape were much more difficult to combat, and the costs of doing so were more extensive. Actions taken against quilombos would frequently require more effort than individual masters would or even several masters could undertake without assistance. For this reason, unity among elites was a necessary precondition for large-scale campaigns. Only when it was not occupied as the arbiter of elite infighting could the State's apparatus of repression effectively support the planters. Therefore, the quilombo would always emerge in times of division among elites, and would suffer its greatest setbacks when the elites were united. The quilombo grew during the independence struggles and the Confederation of the Equator, only to face staunch persecution in the second half of the 1820s. It once again flourished between the late 1820s and the first half of the 1830s, when a variety of political developments rocked Recife and the provincial interior, including the Cabanada (1832–1835) on the other side of the province. Having completed their struggle against the cabano rebels, the forces of repression turned their attention once again to the dry Zona da Mata. Catucá would continue to serve as a refuge for those fleeing state and planter repression, but the quilombo itself had been destroyed by the late 1830s.

While the provincial elites, in their efforts to take advantage of the Liberal Revolution in Porto, formed a government of their own, the quilombo was already beginning to cause problems. In 1822, expeditions were launched against the quilombolas in the complex of forests between Recife, Olinda and Igarassu. One of these expeditions against the fugitives involved up to two hundred men.[7] Nevertheless, the escapes would continue. According to the sources, in 1823, a group of 24 or 25 slaves fled the Abreos plantation in Tracunhaém and sought refuge in the forest. Area planters joined forces on Mussupinho plantation in Igarassu and from there headed for the woods. The planters and their men attacked the Cova da Onça for six days. According to an observer, the fugitives did not have time to form an alliance with quilombolas living in the forest, all of whom fled as soon as the operation commenced. In spite of this, they were still only able to imprison thirteen of the fugitives, who were hidden near the Monjope plantation, and spent no less than 352$925 réis on the expedition.[8]

As Pereira da Costa has observed, by 1824 the quilombo of Catucá was already so well known that even Friar Caneca pejoratively referred to the royalist troops that would attack the Confederation of the Equator as

Catucá, even though they were stationed on the border of Alagoas and Pernambuco, a great distance from the quilombo.[9] That said, the inhabitants of the Catucá quilombo did indeed benefit from the intra-elite war of 1824. In April of that year, Commandant Taylor, under orders from Pedro I, had already blockaded Recife, cutting off exports. The rebel President Manoel de Carvalho Pães de Andrade required all available troops in order to contain the opposing army that was gathering along the Alagoas-Pernambuco border. For this reason, the quilombolas acted more forcefully on the opposite end of the province, with killings and robberies becoming a "daily" occurrence in the words of one source. Accordingly, the highways of the northern Zona da Mata were no longer traversable and plantations were constantly threatened. Not even seigneurial protection prevented attacks from the quilombolas, exemplified by the case of a resident on the Guruguza plantation who was robbed in his own home.[10]

It was only after the fall of the Confederation of the Equator, in April 1825, that the seigneurial class was able to begin a more effective campaign against the quilombo. General Lima e Silva, provisional president of the province sent by Pedro I to topple the Confederacy of the Equator, used the same army that defeated the confederate government to battle the quilombolas.[11] The quilombo survived despite this attempt. In January 1826, the militia commander of Igarassu, head of the plantation next to Catucá, attacked the quilombolas and requested a resupply of ammunition and provisions from the government.[12]

The quilombo's proximity to Recife troubled authorities. At times, the city's police would catch quilombolas in the parishes bordering the forest.[13] The issue took on new seriousness in 1826 when it was raised in a meeting of the Government Council, at the behest of concerned planters. In this meeting, consensus was reached regarding the necessity of combating "the runaway blacks amocambados in the forests next to this city." To that end, the Government Council placed itself at the disposal of the landowners of the area in their efforts to exterminate the quilombo.[14] It was becoming clear that more extensive operations—initiated between 1826 and 1837—would be possible only with the support of State resources. These resources were, primarily, military weaponry, infantry regulars, and funds to pay militiamen (later, the national guard).

A significant problem facing the apparatus of repression was the level of organization achieved by the quilombolas, who utilized highly complex informal channels of communication. According to the documentation, the quilombolas were preparing to attack Recife in early 1827. One official claimed that they were plotting "formal resistance" against the established order, inspired by a recent slave rebellion in Salvador.[15] This consciousness of antislavery struggle in other provinces was a result of existing informal channels of communication among the enslaved; without a doubt, a very dangerous weapon in the view of the master class.[16]

The threat against Recife led authorities to launch another substantial expedition, with the help of the slave masters and their militias. The operation followed the pattern of earlier ones: as the troops attacked the woods, pickets were placed in strategic points in order to stop the fleeing quilombolas, even if only temporarily. The quilombolas fought bravely. An unknown number died in combat and 63 were taken prisoner. Nonetheless, the commander of the operation observed that, "the majority fled," and they would return as soon as the troops left the forest. The commanding official found many "mocambos" and even "houses" beside plots of cultivated land that he endeavored to destroy and burn before withdrawing from the woods.[17]

The explicit mention of houses in the forest indicates that there was opportunity for some of the rebels to construct a sedentary life, with the formation of families, a basic conceptualization of freedom among the enslaved. The tumultuous years between the 1817 Revolt and the 1824 Confederation of the Equator certainly provided the inhabitants of Catucá with the chance to form, if not an alternative society, at least a space of liberty, right in the shadows of the sugar plantations and the province's major urban centers. The continuous repression after 1826 would make this sedentary lifestyle and cultivation of diverse crops aside from omnipresent cassava increasingly difficult to maintain. Thus, the quilombolas began to move more, traveling in smaller groups comprised of both men and women. The participation of women is evidenced in an 1830 attack against the baron of Cimbres by a quilombola "gang" that included four women. When the quilombo was destroyed in 1835, authorities believed that only four men and six women managed to escape the dragnet.[18]

Despite these attacks, in certain periods the quilombo developed a more or less solid hierarchy, yet another indication of the complexity of the Catucá community. In some reports there was mention of a leader being captured. There were also frequent comparisons (with some exaggeration, of course) to the quilombo of Palmares, "a rustic republic [...] but still an example that those from Catucá intended on imitating, electing Chiefs [...]."[19] The most revealing document regarding attempts to form a stable hierarchy, however, is an 1835 report, which deals with one of the most destructive operations against the quilombo. Two leaders were captured, including one who was the son of the former chief who had been killed in combat. Therefore, the authority had passed from father to son, confirming the relative stability of the quilombo, despite constant incursions from the slave masters' militias.[20]

The best known of the quilombola leaders was Malanguinho. He was so famous that many of the sources refer to the entire phenomenon of resistance in this area as the quilombo of Malanguinho. He was the suspected leader of the plot to invade Recife. The provincial government feared him enough to place a 100 mil réis price on his head. For almost twenty years, until Vicente de Paula, the old leader of the Cabanada, continued to agitate in the interior incurring the wrath of the government and a 1 million réis price on his head, Malanguinho was the most sought after fugitive—dead or alive—in Pernambuco's history.[21] The other Catucá leaders, such as Valentim and Manuel Gabão, each drew a fifty thousand réis bounty, and the capture of any other quilombola, a 20 thousand reis bounty.[22]

An analysis of the name Malunguinho provides some clues for better understanding Catucá. The term *malungo* denoted partners or shipmates, those who came to Brazil on the same ship. Two travelers, Koster and Tollenare, indicate that in the mid-1810s, this was an informal bond of great importance between African slaves in Brazil.[23] Curiously, despite all of the reports about the quilombo, there is no concrete documentation on Malanguinho's escape, capture or death. All that we know of him is that he was hunted mercilessly and that a price was put on his head in January 1827.

The documents of a punitive expedition in 1829 explicitly mention the names of five supposed leaders of the Catucá quilombo, and Malunguinho is not among them.[24] In the late nineteenth century, Pereira da Costa characterized Malunguinho as the most feared of the quilombolas, while also affirming that the quilombolas were collectively known as *malunguinhos*. We find confirmation in the extant documentation, which frequently refers to them in this fashion. This fact allows us to speculate that, perhaps, the quilombo originated in the flight of slaves brought on the same ship. Later, perhaps, all of the new members of the quilombo were thus considered malunguinhos, representing a new identity forged in the struggle for survival in the Americas.

Considering that Malunguinho was the chief and Manuel Gabão[25] his right-hand, one can infer that Africans predominated in Catucá in 1827, as was generally the norm at this point in the history of quilombos. This is hardly surprising given that the peak of Pernambuco's involvement in the transatlantic slave trade occurred between the outset of the nineteenth century and Independence. In that period, the province was at the height of its production of cotton, and this white gold expanded with such rapidity that for some time it surpassed sugar as the province's main export. Although it was perpetually subject to highs and lows, sugar production, fed by the agricultural renaissance of the late colonial period, also contributed to the increase in slave trafficking. Pernambuco was such an important redistributor of enslaved people to other provinces that in particular years prior to Independence it received more Africans than Bahia or even Rio.[26] Many of these recent arrivals would take advantage of the instability of 1817, of the divisions between the parties that struggled for power between 1821 and 1823, and of the civil war of 1824 to flee into the wilderness. Even after intra elite order was restored, some recent African arrivals continued to seek refuge in Catucá.[27]

Nevertheless, the use of the diminutive form of the term "malungo" is an indication of a dynamic process of cultural transformation. As Sergio Buarque de Holanda pointed out long ago, "inho" is a trademark of the rural Brazilian vernacular. While "Malungo" is a Bantu term, "Malunguinho" is clearly a creolized derivation.[28] Therefore, though the leader of Catucá may have been African, he had clearly struggled in the Brazilian wilderness long enough to have a Brazilian-influenced name, which symbolically projects the construction of new American identities represented by the quilombo, whose inhabitants were no longer considered just malungos but malunguinhos.

On the other hand, if Malunguinho was never one person but identified any chief of the quilombo, in the perception of those that wrote the documents, the last Malunguinho was João Batista, possibly killed in combat in 1835.[29] The sources do not reveal if he was African or crioulo (his Christian name could have been given to him by a master), but we can assume that his son and heir must have been born in Brazil. Because of its location, it was impossible for the quilombo to focus exclusively on living in peace, constructing an alternative society in the wilderness. As long as it existed, the quilombo would carry out attacks on the area plantations and the houses bordering the wilderness, and low-level merchants and cowboys that traveled on the highways connecting Recife to the northern Zona da Mata and the backlands.

Some of the quilombos' expeditions were large-scale. In 1828, they not only attacked the Guruguza plantation, but also went on to burn the Utinga plantation, which led authorities to organize yet another punitive mission. The documentation does not reveal how many quilombolas were captured or killed, but on the side of the law, there is precise data: at least five soldiers were killed and fifty were injured in combat or by traps that the quilombolas placed on the pathways cutting through the forest. Many of these soldiers were crippled by the fighting according to the commander of the operation, who asserted that he had successfully extinguished the quilombolas in the forests near Goiana but lamented being unable to replicate that success against those closer to Recife.[30]

Plantation: place from which the malunguinhos fled, c. 1825 ("Moulin à sucre," M. Rugendas, Malerische Reise in Brasilien, Paris, Engelmann & Cie., 1835).

Sources suggest that the quilombolas were not isolated. It is, in fact, difficult to imagine how the quilombo could have survived—in an area so close to Recife, and marked by so many roads—without the support of a network of contacts outside of the forest who could alert the quilombolas about the maneuvers of the militias. This is was a constant concern among the slave masters in the area who would regularly underscore the importance of secrecy in the execution of expeditions, because the local population would always tip the quilombo off about the movements of its enemies.[31] In this region, the most populous of the province's rural areas, contact between rebels and freed slaves, and even the enslaved on the plantations, was fundamental to the survival of the quilombo. This cooperation was even evidenced in the quilombolas' attacks. Catucá, therefore, can be accounted among those nineteenth century quilombos that depended on complicity between plantation slaves, quilombolas, and the free and freed population—in sum, non-whites and excluded social segments, more generally. As Suely Robles de Queiroz has observed, the reconstitution of African identities in a quilombo did not segregate necessarily quilombolas from the free poor area population. Following this logic, Catucá had transformed into a mobile quilombo, divided into various groups in the middle of the wilderness, that survived not solely based on hunting and agriculture but through highway robbery and the pillage of plantations, and even some contraband commerce. As early studies have shown, a precondition of this latter activity was cooperation with those residing outside of the quilombo.[32]

According to the authorities, this occurred because the entire population between Paratibe and Cruz de Rebouças consisted of "negros" and "cabras," "associates" of the quilombolas who would purchase gunpowder for them, as well as provide "asylum."[33] In this sense, whites recognized a certain racial solidarity among non-whites in the region.

It is worth mentioning that even the enslaved that remained in the slave quarters would provide assistance to the quilombo. The slaves of the Monjope plantation, for instance, supplied the quilombolas with cassava on at least one occasion.[34]

The freed population would go even further in its support of the quilombo. The fragility of this population's condition helps explain the lack of distance between it and the rebels.[35] In 1829, a military expedition of one hundred men confronted, near Monjope, a Catucá guerrilla contingent of at least twenty people. According to the sources, the leaders of this contingent were two free men, Cosme da Ora and Manoel da Ora, "who often live with Malunguinho." Their father and at least one brother had already been detained in the past for helping the quilombolas.[36]

Furthermore, even some white men were entangled in the web of communication projecting outward from the quilombo. It is widely understood that since the early colonial period in the Americas, planters living in proximity to quilombos would sometimes be obligated to negotiate with their racial and class enemies. In extreme cases, such as the maroon communities of Jamaica and Suriname, treaties were signed establishing a modus vivendi. In Brazil, this strategy was unsuccessfully pursued with the Palmares quilombo. Fear of attack was the principal motivator of these contradictory and contingent pacts with rebels. For Catucá, this dynamic is exemplified in the case of Manoel and Cosme da Ora, allies of Malunguinho, who, to the surprise of a military commander, were freed by local authorities shortly after being imprisoned, because they feared the reaction of the quilombolas.[37]

Nevertheless, we must not forget that the sale of arms and the purchase of stolen goods may have also been a source of income for relatively powerful whites operating on the margins of illegality. The official who sent the aforementioned February 1828 report was deeply disappointed with the region's whites. Not only the residents of plantations but also even some of their owners refused to assist the State, and not only out of fear of the quilombolas' reprisals. According to this source, they also had dealings with the quilombolas, to whom they sold gunpowder and bullets.[38]

Even the most prosperous of the region's planters feared the daring of the inhabitants of Catucá. In 1828, it was known that many quilombolas hid along the edge of the woods surrounding the Monjope and Saquin plantations. The owner of the Saquin plantation, in response to an accusation leveled against him, wrote to a local gazette denying that he ever cooperated with the quilombolas, who he considered his "enemies," as they had set fire to Utinga, one of his family's plantations in the past.[39] Thus, there would be no way to consider the owner of the Saquin plantation as anything other than an "enemy" of the malunguinhos. This part of the planter's argument is very convincing. Nonetheless, it is also evident that the threat of an attack, such as that on Utinga, could have pressured the quilombos' adversaries, at times, to relent in order to avoid further attacks.

In some cases, friendship with the quilombolas guaranteed the safety of a planter and his property. There is at least one well-documented case that demonstrates this. In 1829, there were at least two quilombo "gangs" in the forest. The gang that João Pataca commanded had spent the night before Saint Anthony's Day reveling undisturbed in the slave quarters of the Macaco plantation.[40] A short time later, a group of quilombolas attacked the home of the plantation's owner in the town of Tejucupapo. The master was absent, but the mistress, dona Helena, was present, and the quilombolas attempted to remove the rings from her fingers. One of the slaves of the house went to João Pataca to complain, and in response, he detained two of the attackers and broke them on the wheel. One of them died from the injuries sustained from his punishment.[41]

In the case of the property-less of different racial origins, poverty was the bond that ultimately tied them together. In an aforementioned 1830 attack on a local landowner, sources indicate that aside from four black women and twelve black men, two pardos and at least one white man participated in the group.[42] The literature has already noted the presence of whites in quilombos, especially kidnapped white women. But in this specific case, in which a white man was incorporated into a group that committed highway robbery, it is more appropriate to discuss the transition from slave resistance to outright banditry. Crucially, there was no way for a quilombola to be anything other than an expropriator of the master class' possessions—this is a form of banditry that is not included among

Hobsbawm's classic models but is, nonetheless, important from a social perspective. In the era of Malunguinho, gangs that included people "of all colors" were active throughout Pernambuco's interior.[43] In addition, in 1830, an authority asserted that deserters and criminals frequently found their companions among fugitive female slaves.[44]

Use of the term "white" in the sources must be considered with some caution, as many *mestiço* masters preferred to be considered white. This was typified in Recife's urban riots of 1823, when the throng that occupied the streets sang songs that remarked on the difference between Portuguese "sailors" who were truly white, and the "whitewashed" Brazilians who considered themselves white without actually being white.[45] In this way, reference to the presence of "whites" among the quilombolas could indicate the participation of Brazilian *mulatos*, enslaved or free, in armed resistance. As time passed, the presence of "whites" in the quilombo appeared to have increased, resulting in extensive miscegenation among these marginal groups, making dreams of reconstructing an African society in the wilderness increasingly impracticable while confirming that there were few opportunities for ascension among the free poor. In one report on the "palmar" found in Catucá in 1835, a commander of the militia confirmed that there were people of all colors among the community, going as far as to claim that there were few blacks among the quilombolas.[46] A few months and punitive expeditions later, another authority again confirmed that the quilombo "is not only composed of blacks."[47]

Following the 1827 threat of a quilombola invasion of Recife, the repression became more constant, and the late 1820s would become a terrible time for the quilombolas. In 1829, they were still strong enough to act on the offensive in guerrilla warfare. Twice, they carried out surprise attacks on the soldiers sent to the wilderness. Consequently, the government resolved to station a force of eighty men permanently in the area around Catucá. This was not, however, enough to contain the malunguinhos.[48] They continued their attacks on plantations and highways, frequently with the help of free and freed people. According to the province's Commander of Arms in a report from March 1829, the local justices of peace were impotent against the quilombolas and their allies. As a result, four battalions of approximately sixty men each were sent to the wilderness. This included 45 regulars, 84 militiamen, and 114 auxiliaries. To support them, an additional 237 militiamen and auxiliaries were split into small groups and charged with conducting patrols in the forest. The quilombolas responded by killing at least three soldiers and wounding another three.[49]

Despite the significant number of soldiers involved in combating the quilombo beginning that March, the provincial Commander of Arms still believed that there were between two and three hundred people, divided into four separate quilombos, still hiding in the wilderness. Achieving a resolution would clearly require a change of strategy. The black guerrillas knew the terrain and were frequently aware of their enemies' maneuvers in advance. When attacked, they would hide not just within the wilderness but also in caves, mangroves near the coast, and the area's riverine islets. At some points they went as far as to temporarily leave the wilderness altogether. Some would flee to Recife, where they could hide amongst the urban slaves until the soldiers left the wilderness. This level of mobility explained the consideration given by the authorities to encircling the entire forest during the more serious expeditions against the quilombo. In the rainy season, from June to August, however, the quilombolas would grow confident to form "pure Palmares."[50]

The 1829 documentation allows us to better understand the strategies of resistance and survival employed by the rebels, which included not only an attempt to construct an alternative space, but to insert themselves into breaches in white-dominated society, aiming at the integration of quilombolas as equals, even if this integration was fleeting and fragile. In the documentation, a great deal of attention is directed at João Pataca, the man who punished the quilombolas who attacked the Macaco plantation. According to one source, there were two "gangs" in the part of Catucá near the city of Goiana, comprised of "a hundred and something" rebels. Pataca commanded one of these "gangs." While the other "gang" commanded by João Bamba was "thieving and bellicose," the one that Pataca controlled was more "more mild." Notwithstanding these differences, the two groups always acted in concert. The sources suggest that within Pataca's group, there were people that João Bamba had captured in his attacks. The two groups complemented one another. Pataca negotiated with the outside world, winning the hearts and minds of those still in captivity, leading religious cults and festivals. It is possible to imagine that perhaps time spent with his more "peaceful" group served as a transitional period of training for the life of a guerrilla.

Pataca and his men would appear in the area villages where they made purchases and sold fish. The leader traveled with an "honor guard of black women" conducting *batuques* in the wilderness, on certain area plantations and even within private homes in the village of Tejucupapo.[51] According to one source, they would enter Tejucupapo only as raiders, but "these days [July 1829] they are peaceful village residents, eating, celebrating, traveling armed and coercing people into selling them weapons and gunpowder."[52] The situation in neighboring localities was not much different, insofar as between June 24 and 28 of 1829, Pataca and his followers—all of them well armed—would peacefully lodge in the town of Ponta de Pedras, celebrating there, and leaving to journey to the town of Tabatinga, where they bought gunpowder and drank *aguardente*.[53]

This attitude reveals, on the part of the quilombolas, an attempt to combat not only slavery but also to integrate into society, but as free men. Alliances with the region's poor population, but also with some masters, including Dona Helena of the Macaco plantation, formed part of this larger strategy for survival. Pataca was aware of the respect he commanded in the area. Upon capturing the two men who attacked the Macaco plantation, Pataca brought them to the home of the local militia commander to be imprisoned. The commander told Pataca that there was no jail in which he could place the two men, and that he should take the issue up with the justice of the peace. According to sources written by whites, Pataca retorted that he too was a justice of the peace and resolved to punish the two independently.[54]

Pataca's evolution—perhaps into a king, a spiritual leader, or even both—led the government to step up the repression once again. It decided to encircle the forest, and even utilized boats to access points along the coast, as well as the mangroves and rivers. The commander planned to use five hundred men, spread out in various locations, including canoes with eight men each to hunt for the fugitives in mangroves and rivers, as well as various barricades, each staffed by twenty soldiers, dispersed throughout the margins of the forest to prevent quilombolas from leaving the forest during the operation.[55] Pataca was one of the first to be captured. Using promises of manumission and, later, undoubtedly, threats of punishment, authorities were able to force him and another leader, Antonio Cabunda, to help defeat the remaining fugitives. At the end of the operation, the commander found that their help had been of little use, as the expedition would have played out "in the same way without them." Many rebels were killed, including warrior leader João Bamba and another important chief, José Brabo. But Manoel Galo, another main leader, managed to escape.[56]

The devastation was enormous. Surrounded by various barricades, the guerrillas of Catucá were severely restricted in their mobility. Nevertheless, they resisted bravely. At the end of the operation, authorities claimed, although Catucá had been reduced "to a small number of blacks," it was still "threatening because they are very familiar with these woods, battled-tested and have been fugitives for many years."[57]

The quilombo suffered many losses in these expeditions of the second half of the 1820s, and might have been terminated in that era were it not for, once again, the help of the political context of the late 1820s and early 1830s, which provoked new schisms between the masters of land, cattle, and humans. In this period, the provincial government preferred concentrating the bulk of its forces in Recife, where the Society of Carpenters of São Jose or Jardineira, a radical liberal organization, and the Column of the Throne and Altar, an absolutist group, struggled fiercely. The objective of both organizations was to draw factions of the army, which, as was the case throughout Brazil in this period, divided between Brazilians and Portuguese, to their cause. In this climate of instability, the Commander of Arms felt threatened enough to increase the size of his own security contingent. In October 1829, thirty soldiers guarded his home.

This situation was aggravated in November 1829 by the outbreak of a revolt led by Pinto Madeira in the backlands of Cariri. The nomination of a new provincial president and new commander of arms for Pernambuco did not reduce the agitation, which was already reaching the security forces stationed in Recife. Much to the contrary, as one new commander observed in July 1830, there were liberal constitutionalists and even Republicans resisting authority within the barracks. All of this was taking place at a time in which the army was undergoing a demobilization process following the end of the Cisplatine War, dispatching a large contingent of unemployed ex-soldiers to the streets. In the interior, elites were once again at odds with each other in the wake of elections in February 1829, and they reinitiated the traditional practice of assassination as political strategy. Worsening the situation, documents emanating from authorities in the interior are filled with cases of conflict over jurisdiction between recently elected justices of the peace, older captain majors, and the commanders of local militias. In January 1830, Araujo Lima, the future marquis of Olinda, visited his family's plantation in the Zona da Mata and lamented the state of violence and anarchy in the region. No fewer than thirteen murders of a political nature had been committed in a short stretch of time.[58]

At the end of the first reign, elites were once again divided. As a result, the army and state resources would be occupied with regulating intra-elite conflict. The repression of slaves was left, once again, in the hands of slave masters, allowing the quilombo to flourish once again. In 1830, the revitalized quilombolas attacked three armed men who were hunting in the woods of the Monjope plantation, one of whom was killed. As a result, an important regional landowner wrote to the government requesting assistance with the payment of wages to the contingent that had mobilized against the quilombolas. In his investigations, he uncovered a key contact of the quilombolas, the gypsy Genoíno Dantas. Dantas had been accused of smuggling weapons from the army to the quilombolas, and the accusation was confirmed when a justice of the peace apprehended another gypsy in possession of one of the weapons. Afterwards, this gypsy wrote to the justice of peace requesting the return of the weapon. In his letter, he alleged that he had purchased it from Genoíno Dantas, and that he had others available for sale at the price of five "pesetas." Dantas was also accused of not returning the slaves he captured, having sold ten of them.[59]

In the following months, expeditions against the quilombolas were limited to those executed by the owner of the Timbó plantation, one of the justices of the peace for the region. These expeditions were not always very successful. It was common for contingents to return from the forests not having found anyone. At other times, the quilombolas would attack in small groups with firearms, fleeing shortly thereafter. Six cowboys searching for a cow that had disappeared from an enclosure on the Monjope plantation stumbled upon one such group. A shootout ensued. The malunguinhos fled, leaving behind cassava that, as was already mentioned, a justice of the peace believed slaves from the plantation had provided the malunguinhos. As a result, another patrol of twenty men entered the wilderness. To the surprise of authorities, the quilombolas deceived this patrol and took advantage of the situation to steal even more cassava from the Monjope plantation.[60]

Three months later, a "crioulo" told authorities that he encountered seventeen slaves on the highway who asked him how to find Catucá. This incident illustrates the informality with which information about slave escapes was transmitted. Twenty men were sent to intercept these fugitives before they reached the forest. The slaves did not surrender. Four were killed in combat, and another eight were recaptured, but five managed to escape.[61] Two months later, quilombolas returned to attack plantations. They had no respect for the wealth and power of men such as Domingos de Aguiar Malaquias Pires Ferreira, baron of Cimbres and future provincial president, who, as was already mentioned, was attacked by group of quilombolas that included women and at least one "white man."[62]

The complicated political situation of the early 1830s made it difficult to take action against the quilombolas in the same fashion that authorities had in mid–1829. Furthermore, the brazenness of the quilombolas had reached the point that upon recapture, and under the duress of physical punishment, recaptured quilombolas would refuse to provide the names of their masters.[63] The constant rebirth of a quilombo proved that force alone would not be enough to destroy it. This led to a new approach from the government. Since at least 1826, the master class knew that it would be necessary to clear the forest to prevent it from continuing to serve as a place of refuge.[64] In the late 1820s, many suggestions were made along these lines. One suggestion envisioned the formation of settlements around the forest and the creation of more roads passing through it.[65] A significant step towards this was taken with the creation of the Amélia colony between the end of 1829 and the start of 1831.

The Amélia colony began with 103 immigrants of German origin who had attempted to reach the south of Brazil but had ended up stranded in Recife. The Pernambucan government offered them land in Catucá. Thereafter, more Germans would arrive, among them, dozens of soldiers who had been demobilized after fighting for Pedro I in the Cisplatine War. By the end of 1831, these colonists and their families totaled around 750 people.[66] In order to assist with the establishment of the colony, the provincial government committed to paying a daily subsidy of 160 réis per adult and 120 per child. A German military engineer based in Pernambuco was charged with supervising the colony. The authorities believed that the quilombolas would be unable to withstand this new force of German colonists. Despite some rhetoric in favor of importing free workers for agriculture, the sources make clear that extinguishing the quilombo was the principal goal in the foundation of the Amélia colony. It is no exaggeration to state that the colonists were deceived by the local government that gave them lands that had to be wrested from the quilombolas.[67]

The immigrants did not lead an easy life. In September 1830, they requested the continuation of the subsidy payments in light of the difficulties they had encountered.[68] At least one of the families, the Cristianis, lost members in attacks by the black rebels. The colonists made the sale of coal their principal income. As a result, a large portion of the forest disappeared, complicating the formation of quilombos in Catucá. But the colony was not successful. Its gradual disappearance coincided with the decline of the quilombo.[69] The German colonists were fundamental in the destruction of the quilombo, but suffered to such an extent that they ended up departing from Pernambuco.

The presence of German colonists in Catucá explains the diminution of the quilombolas over the course of the first half of the 1830s in relation to the prior five-year period. The Cabanada (1832–1835), however, forced the state to concentrate its resources on the other side of the province. A lack of confidence in the soldiers stationed in Recife pushed the government into bringing some of the German soldiers of the Amélia colony to occupy an important fortress next to the port during the disturbances of 1831 and 1832.[70] The quilombo revived in the early 1830s, although more tentatively than in the past.

In 1831, fourteen slaves from the plantation of João Vieira da Cunha (a future leader of the Praieira Revolution) fled to Catucá. Robberies and murders began to occur again.[71] In the following year, in the justice of the peace of Goiana's jurisdiction, they continued to "burglarize, depredate, and even seduce and mislead the enslaved from the estates of this region."[72] Beside Igarassu the "*quilombo* blacks" continued to commit highway robberies.[73] The same thing happened on the border between the forest and Recife, in the parish (present day neighborhood) of Beberibe, where the quilombolas even attacked residences.[74]

But the seigneurial repression reemerged before long. Although during the first half of the 1830s there was a lack of great punitive expeditions like those of the 1820s, the measures taken against the quilombolas were constant. In the reorganization of the judicial code in 1830, the justice of the peace was entrusted with repressing quilombos. The expansion of the masters' roles in the National Guard and as justices of the peace was crucial for the purposes of repression insofar as the State distributed arms to masters and empowered them with positions of newfound authority, facilitating efforts against Catucá.[75]

Even with more efficient organization of local justice, around 1835 quilombolas were once again one of the major challenges facing the province's master class. At the outset of that year, they attacked the Mussupinho plantation, one of the province's largest, and committed a variety of robberies.[76] One justice of the peace organized 39 men and began attacking the forest. He found many wells and traps, and after much marching, he stumbled upon a "palmar," "strong because of where it is situated." As they were preparing to attack, they were caught by surprise by the quilombolas' gunfire. Five of the men were injured and "many were shaken." The quilombolas once again had a leader who was recognized as such, the aforementioned João Batista, who had been injured during one of the battles in which he had participated.[77]

At least three more small-scale attacks were launched against the malunguinhos in the first half of 1835.[78] These actions, however, were not enough to vanquish the quilombo. Before long, the region's masters began increasing their requests for assistance from the provincial government. In May, the rebels almost apprehended one of the shipments of weapons sent by the provincial government to assist in the destruction of the quilombo.[79] A force of one hundred men entered the woods to capture Batista and his followers. According to the testimony of a freedman who had been among the quilombolas, there were few of them but they were heavily armed.[80]

Batista continued his activities in July and August. Their mobility in the wilderness saved the quilombolas on various occasions. They would attack near Recife as well as in the area around Igarassu and Goiana, further to the north. According to authorities, the white population in the area moved in fear with the mounting activity of the quilombolas.[81] João Batista's fate was sealed with the end of the Cabanada. In September 1835 the provincial government was bolstered by a large contingent of national guardsmen and infantry regulars who were battle-tested from their participation in the conflicts in the south of the province. They were even supported by a group of Indians from Barreiros that collaborated in repressing the cabanos. They were veterans accustomed to combat against the cabano guerrillas in the dense forests of Água Preta County between Pernambuco and Alagoas.

A large operation was organized. The presence of indigenous people, expert hunters, was crucial to its success. The death of João Batista and his son and successor marked the end of the Catucá quilombo. According to the provincial police chief, only ten people escaped.[82] In late 1836 and early 1837, two more large-scaled attacks were launched against the blacks of Catucá.[83] One can say that, for many years, the woods would still serve as refuge for fugitives from the law or slavery, and landowners would continue to hunt down escapees in the area. However, the quilombo as such seems to have disappeared with the death of its last great leader, João Batista.

What more can be said of the internal structure of the quilombo? Not far from Recife, Olinda and Goiana, the province's major urban centers, the quilombolas could not isolate themselves completely from the land of the white man. It is, indeed, difficult to understand their survival without reference to the political divisions between elites in 1817, 1821–2, 1824, 1831, and during the Cabanada, between 1832 and 1835, which led the state to scale back on its repressive efforts against the rebels of Catucá. Thus, the quilombo grew in moments of elite division and was fiercely combated when the elite was united. The quilombo, therefore, followed the logic of guerrilla warfare. It would utilize the divisions between its adversaries for its own benefit, and in the cooperation of the dispossessed rural population, it found the foundation of its existence as a focal point of resistance. In this context, the cabanos on the other side of the province were the quilombolas' indirect allies.

Because of its tumultuous seigneurial politics between 1817 and 1824, by the mid–1820s the quilombo had achieved an elevated level of efficiency. This is indicated not only by the Government Council's fear of an invasion of Recife, but also by the fact that tillage, huts, and even houses were found in the middle of the wilderness. Another important piece of data in this vein is the large number of soldiers injured in traps or by caltrop (*estrepes*) that required a great deal of work and dexterity to be constructed with efficiency.

The quilombo languished under the pressure of increased repression. Nevertheless, the quilombolas were able to benefit from social divisions and political chaos, from 1817 to the end of the Cabanada, using the time to elaborate their survival strategies. As always, the weakest were the ones most impacted by the urban and rural violence of the 1820s and 1830s. Poverty quickly became a significant unifier between men of divergent racial backgrounds. Blacks and pardos, the freed and the free, were found among the rebels. Robberies and commerce functioned interdependently, with other social outcasts from the white world, such as the gypsy Genoino Dantas, serving as intermediaries.

The last major leader, João Batista, did not have an African name. By then, the quilombo had diversified. If Catucá had, in fact, originated in the flight of malungus, other captives and oppressed people in general later joined forces with the original malungos. Despite the African character of the quilombo, it ceased being an attempt at reproducing African societies and became an American phenomenon, a hybrid, a line of combat against the *status quo* that involved people of diverse ethnic provenance and life stories. Palmares was an attempt to establish an alternative society. Catucá also attempted this ideal, but its precarious position compelled its inhabitants to survive on robbery, hunting, and subsistence agriculture, and there were even those who sought to integrate themselves into the towns of the interior or the parishes beyond the Recife region, as if they were free men.

If we also take into account the mobility of the group commanded by João Pataca and his presence in the towns and slave quarters of the plantations, we can make other inferences. The first is that even with the passage of time and the diversification of the quilombo, the recurrence of *batuques* reveals that religion and festivities continued to comprise part of the cultural references of the quilombolas and a fundamental connection between quilombo fugitives and the non-white, free, freed and even enslaved population of the area. A second inference is that in particular moments, the whites were not strong or numerous enough to defeat the quilombo; from this reality sprung a *modus vivendi* that allowed Pataca to exercise, if not by law, then by practice, the office of justice of peace. This had enormous symbolic value, because it represented the exercise of white authority by a quilombola.

Nevertheless, the conditions of the quilombo's existence as a more or less stable society in the Recife-Olinda area were dictated by the relative impermeability of the forest and disunity among elites. The deforestation brought about by the German colonists made life difficult for the mulunguinhos. The Cabanada (1832–1835) gave them new impetus. Although a completely sedentary community was no longer possible, as has already been stated, during the rainy season, quilombolas would establish "pure palmares." The fact that João Batista's son also became a leader indicates a measure of stability in the command hierarchy: a son succeeding a father.

Upon escaping, it was common for slaves to seek out people of the same ethnic provenance. The common experience of enslavement in the Americas led, however, to the construction of a new identity in the Americas, forging new social bonds that made possible the union of people of diverse origins. Hence, more or less independent groups formed in the wilderness, acting in concert whenever possible. The authorities' mention of the existence of various quilombola groups, the so-called "gangs" in the words of the master class, reveals the existence of these diverse groups, united in the common cause of resistance.

After the Cabanada, elites would no longer struggle against one another until the middle of the following decade, when the Praieira broke out in 1848. The forest would then serve as a hiding place for Borges da Fonseca, the most radical liberal of that rebellion. For that reason, he chose to name his pamphlet of insurrection, the so-called "November Revolution," *O Catucá*. The great irony of this story is that some of the Praieiros who hid in the Catucá had previously attacked the quilombolas, as was the case with the masters of Mussupinho and Araripe plantations.

Zumbi, leader of Palmares, is to this day the name of a location in Recife through which Caxanga Avenue passes. At the end of the nineteenth century, Pereira da Costa observed that Malunguinho and Catucá were names of two locations in the Afogados suburb of Recife. Malunguinho, however, entered into popular culture as a part of the cult of Sacred Jurema, in which it appears as Exu, Master, or Caboclo—which is unique, and is worshiped in areas around greater Recife and Goiana. Many tables of Jurema can be found in the Recife-Olinda area, particularly in the areas near the old quilombo. Only now, the streams that still exist have turned into ditches and small, sickly currents. The police still persecute the enemies of order, who insist on occupying lands that are not theirs.

Haitian maroon leader Makandal became an important component of Vodun in his country, ascending to the pantheon of divinities, perhaps the highest honor that a people can confer on one of its heroes.[84] The religious group of Jurema in Brazil has existed since at least the sixteenth century, when it was a indigenous religion and not the multicultural American melting pot that it is today.[85] In the case of Afro-Brazilian religions, it is plausible to imagine the appearance of a figure that evokes the common condition of being a malungo that unites all captives. Nevertheless, Malunguinho, possessing the "inho" of the Jurema practitioners is clearly a Brazilian divinity and not only a part of the African heritage. The connection between the divinity and the warrior of Catucá is evidenced in another aspect of Jurema that harkens explicitly to the old weapon: the *estrepe*, those pointed sticks that were driven into the ground, placed inside of traps or left alone, as a means of stopping cavalry advances. According to the documentation, many of the soldiers were caught on these devices while chasing the quilombolas. Malunguinho of Jurema, endowed with the power to remove estrepes from the ground is, therefore, the symbolic recreation of the same Malunguinho of Catucá: the real king of Pernambuco's wilderness.

17

QUILOMBOS IN THE PROVINCE OF MARANHÃO, BRAZIL[1]

MATTHIAS RÖHRIG ASSUNÇÃO

In the Brazilian province of Maranhão, large numbers of enslaved workers did live near frontier areas covered by rainforests. The result was an extraordinary increase of maroon groups, or *quilombos*, in this region during the nineteenth century. At the same time, the Revolutions in the Atlantic World led to political instability in the province and created new opportunities for slave revolt. The Atlantic Revolutions also led to the growing politicization of the popular classes, who were influenced by a liberal patriotic discourse. The radicalization of popular movements during the First Brazilian Empire (1822–31) led to a broad alliance of free and enslaved groups through which the quilombo acquired new dimensions. The subsequent political stability achieved by the Second Empire (1840–89) did not prevent large quilombos from surviving in Maranhão until the eve of Abolition.

In this chapter, I combine a chronological and thematic approach to an examination of maroon groups of the slave society in Maranhão, Brazil in the nineteenth century. Beginning with a brief analysis of some relevant aspects of slave society in Maranhão, I then propose a typology of the maroon groups and discuss the more general problem of the (in)efficiency of the State's response. Four case studies are then discussed in greater detail, which help to highlight some of the unique characteristics of the maroons in Maranhão, such as the participation of quilombos in wider political movements, the importance of the gold mining economy, and the intimate relationship between some sectors of society and the maroons, or quilombolas. The first case study concerns a colonial quilombo that was destroyed in 1811. Subsequently, I analyze the role of the maroon communities during the Balaiada Insurrection (1838–1841), which allows for a deeper investigation into the issue of the possible alliance between free and enslaved rebels. The third case study looks at the quilombo known as São Benedito do Céu, which was responsible for the famous invasion of *fazendas* (large plantations or estates) and a town in 1867. This last example is of a *quilombo* that, when the conditions were favorable, took a very offensive stance to the point of claiming the slaves' freedom. Finally, I look at the case of two quilombos subsisting at the end of the 1870s, when the institution of slavery was already in decline.

Maranhão could be considered a late slave society. Despite the introduction of some African slaves in the seventeenth century, it was only in the final quarter of the eighteenth century that the region began to show all the characteristics of fully developed chattel slavery. The importation of twelve thousand slaves during the time of the Companhia do Comércio do Grão Pará e Maranhão (1755–1777) set in motion intensive human trafficking, culminating between 1812–20, in the importation of 41 thousand "pieces." As a result, on the eve of Independence, Maranhão had the largest proportion of slaves (55 percent) in the entire Brazilian Empire. Initially, the slaves were concentrated on the cotton and rice plantations, and later on those producing sugar, which were situated in the valleys of the rivers Itapecuru, Mearim and Pindaré, and in the western lowlands. Conversely, Maranhão did not manage to attract a significant number of European immigrants. Consequently, the white population, or those considered white, was always small: in 1821, they comprised less than 15 percent of the population.

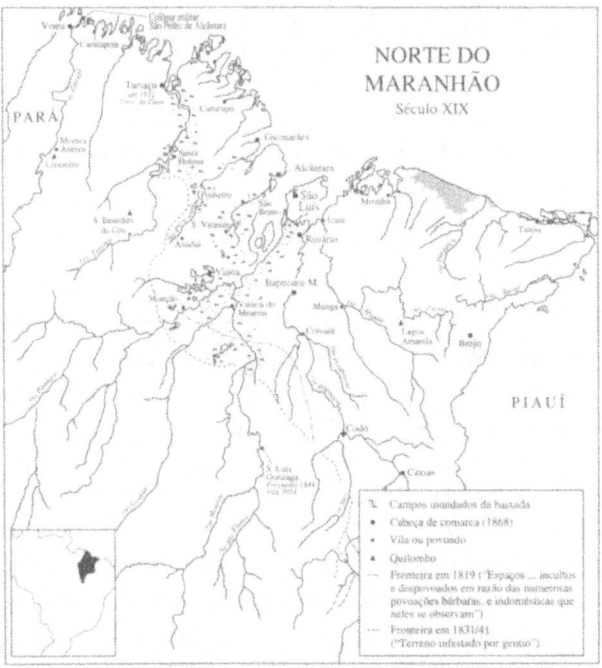

North of Maranhão in the nineteenth century.

In contrast to the sugar-producing Northeast, where the Zona da Mata (area covered with rainforest) is confined to a relatively narrow coastal strip, Maranhão had abundant forested areas with many rivers and streams across almost all of the northern part of its territory. For a long time this led to dispersed settlement in the region and favored the establishment of quilombos along the headwaters of rivers, in areas not occupied by plantations. Furthermore, a large part of the rainforests in the center of the province was completely beyond state control. It was a real frontier, beyond which deserters, quilombolas, and other fugitives could feel relatively safe. Frontiers of this type existed in many other parts of Brazil. But what distinguishes Maranhão is that the area occupied by slave plantations directly bordered the frontier, so that the two were often overlapping. In general, during the nineteenth century, there was no intermediate zone populated by poor free people, who had the role of "exploring" the land, of forming an "expansion front" that preceded the "pioneer front" of the plantations.[2]

Complaints by plantation owners from Itapecuru, Mearim and Viana were as common against quilombolas, as against the "gentio" (gentiles, or rather Indians) who still lived in the nearby forest. The formation of peasant "fronts" that advanced beyond the frontier is a more recent phenomenon, of which the quilombolas could be fairly considered the precursors.

Maroons in Maranhão: An Endemic Phenomenon

In existence since the beginning of the eighteenth century, the quilombos in Maranhão were a phenomenon endemic to slave society, especially after the large-scale introduction of slaves in the final quarter of that century. Further research in Portuguese archives is needed to prove their existence between the 1780s and 1800s. For the nineteenth century, however, their occurrence is well documented in the newspapers, the correspondence of the military, police and judicial authorities, and in the reports by provincial presidents. From this evidence, it can be said that in Maranhão few slave plantations were not surrounded by quilombos. It is difficult to establish just how many there were because the quilombos were hidden social formations and practically the only details we have were provided by those responsible for wiping them out. In many cases, we do not even know the origin of the quilombo in question, nor the number of people who lived there. Often the reports simply mention their destruction without providing further details.

More common are reports of runaway slaves, which are similar to those in other parts of the Empire. These reports include the name of the slave and a description of the distinguishing features by which he or she could be recognized. Sometimes they mention where the slave was heading, generally towards an area of the interior. However, not all the escapees sought refuge in existing quilombos or founded new ones. Some, especially those with lighter skin, tried to pass for freed slaves, like the mulatto Alexandre, who managed to enlist as a soldier in Turiaçu until his master discovered him.[3] Others, in a similar way to the lone *cimarrón* Esteban Montejo, in Cuba, managed to lead a more or less isolated existence. The "crioulo Miguel" escaped from São Luís for nearly two years and "it is said that he is sheltered deep in the forest opposite Itapecuru-Mirim."[4] This slave, according to the provincial government's definition, did not yet merit the name quilombola: "Anyone is considered to be a maroon as soon as he is found deep in the forest, near or far from any settlement, and if he lives together with two or more slaves in a house or hut."[5]

Reports frequently mention small communities of slaves who hid in the forests next to *fazenda*s and which could be considered a first type of quilombo. An example is "the *quilombo* of escaped Negroes next to the *fazenda* 'Tamatatuba' that belongs to the Carmelites" in Alcântara, against which the prior of that order had asked the authorities to take steps since the beginning of 1837.[6] References to these small quilombos occur immediately before and after Independence, and even up until the 1840s, in all the districts and parishes with a large concentration of fazendas and slaves, such as Alcântara, Viana, Vitória do Mearim, Itapecuru-Mirim, Rosário, and Manga do Iguará.

The second type of quilombo comprises those groups that were located further away from the fazendas, and managed to establish a more permanent subsistence economy, and eventually to combine this with selling some of their food surpluses. As Brandão describes in 1865:

> They are afraid of clearing a large area that exceeded their needs because the smoke which rises into the atmosphere would give them away to the whites, who in their murderous hatred neither discriminate by sex nor age. The *Calhambolas* [a synonym for *quilombolas* or maroons] are well aware of this, and consequently restrict themselves to small plantations of corn, rice and manioc; however, some of these republics, which are further away, and which comprise a substantial number of Negroes, grow cotton which they then sell at the house of some *fazendeiro* in exchange for rifles and other arms, cloth etc.[....][7]

These larger quilombos existed mainly in the extended rainforests in the frontier areas. The third and final type was the quilombo that combined subsistence agriculture with gold prospecting. Gold prospecting made possible the greater acquisition of goods and participation in wider trade networks, as we will see in the case of the quilombos of Turiaçu.

The quilombos in Maranhão managed to survive thanks to the region's geography and to the relative weakness and inefficiency of the repressive state apparatus in place during much of the Empire. First, there were never enough forces to police such a vast area. In 1810 the soldiers of the *Primeira Linha* (regular army) comprised only two infantry regiments with a total of 2,134 men. This situation changed little with Independence. Furthermore, the largest contingent of the regular army always remained in the capital. The militias of the *Segunda Linha* were, in theory, more numerous, although ill equipped and unreliable.

In contrast with Southeast Brazil, the Maranhão provincial government only really managed to introduce national guards in the capital. In the interior, attempts to establish these forces, at least during the 1830s, ended in failure, due to the lack of support by the small and even medium-scale landowners. As late as 1868, the provincial president admitted that: "I cannot, however, hide the fact that, either because of bad organization and objectives, or the laziness of its commanders, or because of the aversion of the population, the National Guard has not matched up to the purpose for which it was created."[8]

The third possibility was the use of individuals specialized in the capture of runaway slaves, called *capitães-do-mato*, or the creation of a special police force. Capitães-do-mato had existed in Maranhão since the colonial period, but owing to their nomadic way of life, their low social origins and their relative autonomy, they were always viewed with suspicion by the ruling classes.[9]

Therefore, the lack of adequate policing was the main reason for the increase in the number of quilombos. At least, this was the view of local authorities and *fazendeiros* (owners of large rural estates), who continually asked for reinforcements and petitioned the government. The question, especially after Independence, was who would track down the quilombolas and who was going to foot the bill. The government expected the fazendeiros to contribute, since they constituted the main interested party, although this payment was not always forthcoming. Thus, in 1837 the justice of the peace in Urubu (later the municipality of Codó) wrote to the provincial president:

> Today I received a petition from José Tavares da Silva, Paulo Nunes Cascaes and Raimundo Gabriel Viana, asking me to take steps against a *quilombo* which is said to exist within this town's district [...] The petitioners, Your Lordship, are not committing themselves to pay for the costs necessary for food and war supplies, and I have made up my mind that I should not pay for it myself, [....][10]

This is why he asked the government to take measures. However, the highest authority in the province, especially during the most difficult years following Independence, generally put the ball back in local authorities' court. In 1832 President Araújo Viana approved the measures taken by the justice of peace in the parish of São Bento to launch a voluntary subscription among the landowners in order to try to form "a forest division (Esquadro do Mato) permanently engaged in the pursuit of runaway slaves, of which there are plenty in that parish."[11] He also tried to encourage the judges in other parishes to adopt the same strategy.[12]

In 1835, the situation was again critical in some local boroughs, if we believe the version given by the local councils—which might have overstated the case to obtain funds from the government. The councillors of Rosário explained:

> Throughout this municipality there is not a single force to assist the police in carrying out their duties, and from there stems the wandering of vagrants and criminals, each of whom in turn goes around causing bodily harm one minute and committing murders the next without the territorial authorities being able to strike them with the sword of justice [...] The same happens with the slaves, among which there are a large number of clandestine deserters, and even some living in *quilombos* in parts of the Municipality, and the Justices of Peace are unable to disperse or capture them because, besides having no Force other than the National Guard, unfortunately there are no weapons with which to patrol [....][13]

Councillors from other boroughs complained along the same lines.[14] For these reasons, a rural police force was created in 1835.[15] In each district, a contingent of three to ten men was assigned to help the justice of the peace to maintain order. In order to supplement their meager wage of 6$000 réis, it was specifically stipulated that they could catch runaway slaves in exchange for rewards of 2$000, 5$000 or 10$000 réis per captured slave in the town, outside of the town, or in the quilombo, respectively. Since the municipalities did not manage to shoulder the cost, from 1837 onwards the provincial government had to assume funding of this body. In that year, they guaranteed the wages of 312 police officers, including both soldiers and commanders of the detachments. These contingents—whose names changed, for political reasons, to rural guards—were the main forces responsible for capturing runaway slaves.[16] However, when confronted by the larger quilombos, these forces were also inadequate. Only when the situation seemed to reach crisis point, with public safety seriously under threat, did the government decide to take more drastic measures, such as sending contingents from the regular army to the area.

For use against the quilombos, the general the government first recommended the existing forces in the municipality, that is, the soldiers of the Segunda Linha, the capitães-do-mato, the National Guard then, after 1835, the rural police and, if available, the perennially reduced detachment of the Primeira Linha. However, it did recognize the inappropriateness of using the Segunda Linha and the National Guard for such a task.[17] The failure of the raids was thus due to the soldiers' lack of preparation and to the "bad commandership" of the inexperienced soldiers, or, as we will see in the case of the late quilombos, to the misunderstandings between the commanders of the various forces.[18]

Another reason for the frequent failures in destroying the quilombos was the rainy season, from December to May (the "winter"), which restricted the movement of troops and the cooperation between free slaves and *mocambeiros*. The justice of the peace of the second district of Munim in 1837 reported that

> having carried out Your Excellency's decision regarding a petition by Nicolao José Teixeira and having requisitioned the Justices of Peace of this municipality, they helped me with their detachments, and set off to destroy the *quilombo*s, but since the weather is not good due to the river floods, they could not march to the *Mocambos* [another synonym for *quilombos*] and only caught four blacks who were walking around the *Fazenda* belonging to the plaintiff who petitioned Your Excellency. They had been given refuge by neighboring planters from the same *fazenda*.[19]

There were a number of reasons why planters sheltered runaway slaves. In some cases, the latter worked for the former. The employment of mocambeiros by fazendeiros for agricultural work might seem absurd at first from the point of view of the strict logic of slave society, but it is mentioned in several sources.[20]

Unfortunately, despite the many references to quilombos, in general they do not provide a very precise idea of their internal organization and life, preferring instead to purely military details. The best-documented case from the colonial period concerns a quilombo in the district of Guimarães. Its history, I hope, might be able to shed some light on this type of mocambo in constant conflict with colonial society. This quilombo was founded in 1811 after a slave uprising on a fazenda that belonged to Captain Antônio José Correia. According to evidence provided by his widow, this was a gradual process, since

> the *fazenda* of the deceased Antônio José Correia had rebelled a long time ago [...] and some of the runaway slaves were in surrounding *mocambos* with many other runaways and criminals from where they set out to rob and damage the *fazenda*s referred to [of colonel Luiz Antônio Sarmento da Maia and the aforementioned Antônio José Correia], especially the cattle estates which, being very productive, each year had their herds reduced considerably. In vain we tried to break up that band of miscreant criminal thieves and catch the runaway slaves because we did not know where the *Mocambo* was and because they were warned by neighboring *fazenda*s. Now we have discovered that the aforementioned Antônio José Correia carried out a raid

in order to catch his slaves, but he was killed unfortunately without accomplishing his aim.²¹

After Correia's assassination, the situation clearly became untenable for the region's white masters, to the extent that Correia's widow, as well as the widow of Colonel Sarmento de Maia, the owner of neighboring fazendas, was obliged to move with her family to Alcântara. The mocambeiros apparently had a field day, increasing the number of raids on farms in the area and living off the cattle they took. The provincial government decided to intervene and in August of 1811, they sent a corps of one hundred soldiers to the town of Guimarães.²² Since all the slaves on the region's fazendas were suspected of supporting the mocambeiros, the government did not hesitate in recommending to the captain in command that he use torture as a means of extorting information:

> We have word that the slaves on the cattle estates circumjacent to the *Mocambo* communicate with them and that they help each other. Investigate this seriously and with caution, using among other means, moderate coercion in order to make the slaves confess what they know regarding this matter.²³

Faced with massive military presence some of the quilombolas apparently decided to change headquarters and move to the neighboring district of Alcântara.²⁴ Another group, led by the *cafuz* Rumualdo, slave of the widow Maria Quitéria de Araújo, and a runaway for two years, returned to the region after being spotted in another district.²⁵ He was part of a group of "five blacks, armed with cutlasses and rifles" who travelled from fazenda to fazenda, claiming to be freedmen (*forros*) enlisted in bringing down a mocambo! They asked for information, warm clothing and provisions, which they obtained easily because of the fear they inspired. Three of them (Florêncio, Romualdo, and Raimundo) were finally recognized by several people as the runaway slaves responsible for the death of Captain Correia. According to one witness, Romualdo "pronounced in public that he would not stay away until he had killed the widow's son and son-in-law."²⁶ Perhaps that is why they returned to the fazenda belonging to Maria Quitéria de Araújo, Romualdo's owner, where they stayed the night. According to another informant, a plantation owner, her neighbor, "heard him say how he had shot and killed Senhor Correia and the others and that his aim was to kill the women and small children and finish off the Correia Race [...]."²⁷ But when they learned that the owner had fled to Alcântara with her brother-in-law, Lieutenant-colonel José Teodoro Correia, and that there was a group of soldiers in Guimarães, they decided to "take shelter in the Mocambo of João Congo which is very big."

The government, putting together the information that it had received from the local authorities and from several other individuals, concluded that in addition to the mocambo of João Congo there were various other small groups "which in many places are stable or itinerant," forcing the captain of the detachment to take strong measures. The troop's attacks must have been partly successful since, on the 21 of September, a group of 22 adult slaves comprising twelve women and ten men as well as a few children, were sent to the capital. Some of those on the list were in fact slaves of the deceased Antônio José Correia. However, there are also reports that the "real murderers" had moved to the district of Viana.[28] These references to the communication between the small quilombos near to fazendas and those that were more remote would seem to suggest the existence of networks of mocambos or, as one source suggests, "partial" and "general" quilombos, the first type of quilombo functioning as an outpost of the latter.[29]

In the military excursions, the free black population suffered all kinds of humiliation as is clear from the report by a second lieutenant, who handed over half a dozen prisoners "all of them vagrants and criminals such as are found in this district, the majority of them only free for a month and, although they do not want to confess whether they are *Mocambeiros* or not, I am handing them over because at best they encourage the planters' slaves to go with them, as many have done [...]."[30] The case of this quilombo, which still dates back to the colonial period, is interesting for a number of reasons which recur time and again throughout the nineteenth century: the transition from slave insubordination to the formation of quilombos, the cooperation between quilombos in the rainforest and slaves on the fazendas, and also with the free population, as well as the settling of accounts between slaves and their masters.

Maroons and Popular Insurrection

The war of Independence in Maranhão heralded a period of political instability that lasted until the 1840s. During the years 1822–4, 1831–2, and 1838–40 there were several rebellions, seditions, and other armed movements, resulting from the struggle for power between various elite groups within the province, and from the intervention of the central government. To an increasing degree these struggles involved the poor free population, stirring up the conflicts still further, which in turn facilitated the escape of slaves and the formation of quilombos. Furthermore, the ideological aspect of the conflict between Portuguese and Brazilians, and between conservatives and liberals, as well as reports, however vague, of the large-scale Revolutions in the Atlantic world, could not fail to affect the slaves. As a result, the Independence period in Maranhão also saw plots by slaves and free men, field hands and artisans to obtain freedom. At no point were the enslaved exempt from the revolutionary ideas of their time, which they combined with their previous experience and ideas.

The outbreak of the Balaiada, the biggest ever civil war in Maranhão, between 1838 and 1841, was due as much to the struggle between liberals and conservatives as to the growing rebellion of the colored population against the arbitrary acts of the elite. After 1838 economic exploitation by merchants speculating in manioc flour, or by fazendeiros who retained the monopoly on the sale of fresh meat, was coupled with massive recruitment of poor men to serve in the Imperial troops in other provinces. The growing resistance to recruitment finally caused the province to ignite.

The historiography generally holds that the Balaiada began with an attack on the prison in the town of Manga, on the 13 of December 1838, during which the cowboy Raimundo Gomes and nine companions freed several men held there for recruitment. Gomes complained to the authorities, demanding an end to arbitrary acts and from that point on became one of the rebellion's most important leaders. In truth, during the month of November under similar circumstances, Manoel Francisco dos Anjos Ferreira, nicknamed the Balaio, had already freed his son, who had likewise been recruited.[31] And it was during the same month in 1838 that the situation became highly critical for the masters of slaves in the Itapecuru valley. The situation was so serious that the president of the province felt obliged to report to the police chief (*prefeito*) of the Itapecuru district:

> This Presidency is aware from several petitions by planters in this district that in its territory runaway slaves roam and commit countless disturbances, robberies and murders, together with the criminals who in more isolated areas seek refuge from the police; it befalls you to pursue, disperse and apprehend such people, gathering for this purpose *Capitães-de-Mato* and people used to hunting down *quilombos*, each of whom will receive two hundred *réis* per day [....][32]

Furthermore, he recommended that the mocambeiros were disbanded before the beginning of the rainy season.

A letter from the police chief of Codó provides details about the start of the conflict with the mocambeiros. The slave Benedito, who belonged to Colonel Manuel Telles da Silva Lobo, and who was accompanying another slave, was murdered in broad daylight. In pursuit, the justice of the peace in the district sent a small force of fourteen men, which was defeated by the slaves.

> With that they entered dona Estifânia's house and together with some of her slaves they killed the white overseer José Maria Soares, and Manuel Francisco, a white man; the innocent family of Soares escaped thanks to Divine Providence. They then went on to the *Fazendas* belonging to the Salles orphans, ran and shot at the overseers and took possession of the excellent weapons that all those *fazendas* had, and of the ammunition there was. Afterwards they threatened the neighboring planters and disarmed every man they met on the roads, taking cotton from other people's fields to sell, and trading with Joaquim José Prego, Clemente Duarte Monteiro, Antônio Gonçalves dos Santos and a certain Antônio Busca in Coroatá, and other traffickers, who had supplied them with weapons, sabres, gunpowder, lead shot and bullets, so it is said; [....][33]

This letter insisted that the whole episode could "lead to such grave consequences as a widespread insurrection, which is the main aim of these troublemakers, for which they have sent messengers to all the *fazendas*." Another letter dated 28 November 1838, from three citizens (in charge of the persecution) to the police chief, shows that "Dona Estifânia's slaves are in league with the *mocambeiros*, all of them on guard so that when the soldiers arrive they can open fire from behind." They recommended disarming all the fazendas of the area. They went in at the end of November, and were rewarded with partial success, according to the police chief's report:

> [...] having sent a dispatch of sixty six select men to attack the São Fernando *mocambo*, unfortunately they only found settlements in four different places near to one another, each place with fourteen huts, two fields, and one to burn, saying that they have been dispersed into groups of sixteen, twelve, eight, and six, and that they have moved beyond the river in search of a *mocambo* near to the Souza *fazendas* [....][34]

The report even mentioned that a slave had confessed that the "Negroes" on the fazendas in the district of Caixas "had been in contact with one another, and with many other *mocambos* spread throughout the Province as far as Turi," which fuelled the authorities' fear of a "general insurrection" by the enslaved. After this initial success, the onset of the rainy season apparently prevented the total destruction of the mocambeiros. With the rain there also came a shortage of supplies for the troops, and the deputy policy chief (*subprefeito*) in Codó felt obliged to write to the provincial president concerning the "great lack of [manioc] flour and meat to feed the troops engaged in the pursuit of slaves settled in *quilombo*s," provisions which were sent to him immediately.³⁵

It can therefore be concluded the war between the quilombolas and slave society had already started when the Balaiada broke out.³⁶ The problem is that during 1839 these quilombos are hardly mentioned. In the report sent to the provincial assembly in May that year, the provincial president Sousa e Mello simply noted that

> With the aforementioned force [of regular soldiers] having been diverted to another area, new *quilombo*s developed again: I am told, however [...] that the deputy police chief of the municipality of Codó, in accordance with the wealthy *Fazendeiros*, dispersed these gatherings with a great many deaths and injuries, having employed *homens de mato*, better than the regular troops, to penetrate the *mocambos* and capture runaway slaves.³⁷

It is difficult to establish a direct link between the quilombos of Codó and the quilombolas who fought in the Balaiada, led by Cosme Bento das Chagas. This is because only one year later, in November 1839, again at the beginning of the rainy season—and precisely when the governmental troops suffered numerous defeats such as the taking of Caxias by the rebels in August and Icatu in December—Cosme began the insurrection simultaneously in several fazendas in the municipality of Itapecuru-Mirim. This insurrection was described by the same Sousa e Mello in the following way:

> [...] from the middle to the end of November there was a small uprising of slaves in the district of Itapecuru and in the neighborhood of Rosário, which led to the abandonment of the *fazenda*s, and the suggestions of a slave named Cosme, who had escaped from this city's jail, and who took advantage of the opportunity to incite the slaves of some twenty small estates to escape from their masters' authority, take up arms and declare themselves free.³⁸

He tried to convince the central government in Rio de Janeiro that all the necessary measures had been taken and, for political reasons, he played down the seriousness of the revolt.

> I therefore think that of the 400 slaves gathered at the time many have been dispersed; in accordance with the Commander of the Forces I will pursue them tirelessly [...] I should however explain to your Excellency that this

group instils less fear that at first it should, because most of the individuals are unarmed, some have bows and arrows, and a few better weapons, yet in a poor state: but what is terrible is the infectiousness of this bad example among other slaves and the union of [enslaved] insurgents and [free] rebels, and this is what I will endeavour to prevent at all cost.

However, with the planters having fled their fazendas, the slaves were able to form quilombos much more easily.[39]

According to all the sources, Cosme, taking advantage of the prevailing anarchy, managed to gather up to three thousand slaves. He set up his base at the fazenda Lagoa Amarela, near to Rio Preto, a tributary of the Munim River. This fazenda belonged to Ricardo Nava, killed by the quilombolas after being made to sign a letter granting freedom to his two hundred slaves. Undoubtedly, this slave's boldness, not only in promising freedom but also in actually extorting letters granting freedom or signing them in his own hand, encouraged slaves already anxious for freedom to join him and his group. From the lists of imprisoned quilombolas we know that most of them were slaves from fazendas of the Itapecuru valley. What we do not know is how many were already quilombolas in the forests of Codó before joining Cosme's group. It is also difficult to assess, because it is never clearly defined in the sources, to what degree they stopped being quilombolas in the strict sense of the word, in order to become insurgents, or whether they used the quilombo's organizational structure as a means to a different aim.

Undoubtedly, Cosme's personality was crucial in shaping the aims of his group. Unfortunately, we know very little about this figure, who deserves to be considered the Zumbi of Maranhão. It is thought that he was born in Sobral, in the province of Ceará and that he was more or less forty at the time. In 1830, he was already a freedman and was later imprisoned for murder in the district of Itapecuru-Mirim. Having been sent to jail in São Luís, he managed to escape and return to the shores of the Itapecuru. As a literate person, his belief in the importance of literacy was so great that, in the middle of the war, he set up a primary school in Lagoa Amarela.[40] He certainly was an impressive leader. Renowned for being a sorcerer (*feiticeiro*), he did not hesitate to use the adornments of the Catholic Church in processions that he organized.[41] Even official historians such as Ribeiro do Amaral acknowledged his bravery, as in the combat that took place in December 1839 in the forest near to Gaiola (Itapecuru-Mirim), when the quilombola leader was wounded: "In this last round of fire, the criminal Negro Cosme's leg was pierced by a bullet in response to which, at the head of more than a hundred of his followers, with admirable fury and audacity, he threw himself at 30 of our soldiers [...]."[42] The most remarkable aspect of his personality was his political vision of an alliance with the *balaio* rebels. Cosme proclaimed himself not only "Guardian and Emperor of Freedom," but also "Defender of the Bem-te-vis,"[43] and several letters testify to his offers to join forces with rebel leaders.[44]

A more difficult problem to assess is the rebels' position with regard to slavery. Maria Januária Vilela Santos, author of the most important study on this subject, rightly emphasizes the Bem-te-vis' silence with regard to slavery.[45] The rebels' proclamations re-appropriated many elements of the discourse used by the "exalted" liberals, such as anti-Portuguese sentiments and the struggle against the arbitrary acts suffered by colored people. Nevertheless, they did not demand freedom for slaves. In practice, however, many rebel groups were strengthened by runaway slaves and vice versa. However, although some rebels undeniably discriminated against slaves, it is difficult to generalize. Raimundo Gomes himself offered a passionate defence of the equality between races.[46] Although Gomes was classed as a *cabra*, which in Maranhão was a term used to describe a dark-skinned *mulatto* (who today would be considered black), in terms of color very little separated him in fact from the enslaved blacks. I am also not convinced that the term *povo de cor* (colored people), often used by rebels in contrast to "whites" and "Portuguese," did not exclude the black or the slave, as Vilela Santos maintains. On the other hand, during the rise of the revolt, the balaio leaders ignored the rebel slaves. During its initial phase, Cosme's slave revolt really seemed to be a "separate chapter," in the words of Astolfo Serra.

However, in 1840, with the arrival in Maranhão of Luís Alves de Lima, the future Duke of Caxias, who brought with him money and a strong contingent of soldiers, the revolt entered a new phase, characterized by the dispersion of large rebel groups. The balaio leaders, pursued everywhere by the governmental troops, had to choose: either to give themselves up, and take advantage of the amnesty decreed by the imperial government, or to try to attract a new sector of the population, the slaves, in order to continue fighting. Joining forces with Cosme's quilombolas meant becoming even more radical. According to Luís Alves de Lima, from the middle of 1840 Cosme became "the important figure who the fazendeiros fear most, because he leads 2000 slaves who he had incited to revolt [...]."[47] Thus, Raimundo Gomes, whose troops were disbanded and whose offer of negotiation was turned down in July 1840,

> [...] escaped without weapons or possessions or proper clothes and went to offer himself to the Negro Cosme, who reduced him to being a gunpowder maker and who has him under guard; perhaps Raimundo Gomes does not give himself up because he recognizes that his behaviour is sufficiently criminal to be unworthy of pardon.[48]

This letter suggests that Raimundo Gomes simply became the quilombolas' prisoner. Other sources, however, suggest a different situation, showing that, together with Cosme, Gomes attempted to organize a large-scale slave insurrection.[49] Even after abandoning Cosme's group, Raimundo Gomes continued to attract both enslaved and free people, managing to unite for a short time a group largely composed of runaway slaves in Miritiba (today the municipality of Humberto de Campos).[50]

Governor and Commander-in-chief Alves de Lima's strategy was twofold. On one hand, he planned direct attacks on the rebels and on the largest quilombo in Maranhão's history. On the other, he aimed to prevent at all cost the alliance of free rebels and slaves and that of different groups of slaves. Thus, he wrote that he had "sought, by means of spies, to sow discord amongst them [Cosme's blacks]."[51] This does not appear to have been very successful since, in another letter, he acknowledged that Cosme "has absolute authority" over the quilombolas.[52] He was more successful in convincing the rebel leader Pedrosa to change sides and attack the maroons, which contributed to the successful attack of Lagoa Amarela:

> Today I can assert to Your Excellency that the Negroes settled in *quilombo*s at Lagoa Amarela under the command of the criminal Cosme numbered more than two thousand, and were attacked simultaneously at several places [...] The attack was carried out according to my orders, and after several hours of firing the blacks dispersed, leaving eleven dead, 52 captured, four women, four children, one free rebel, 21 horses, eleven mares, 19 yokes, five saddles, some ruined weapons, gunpowder, lead, two bells, a new damascus altar cloth etc. [...] Our exploratory sorties could not proceed for lack of supplies, and for four days the soldiers ate wild fruits; the rebels taught the blacks to set fire to houses and barns [*paióis*] while fleeing so that our troops could not find resources in these deserts [sic]. Francisco Ferreira Pedrosa, leader of 1,700 rebels, who were gathered in a place named Bela Água, now obey my orders: having known for more than two months that he wanted to give himself up, and fearing that he would not be pardoned, I let him know, via a messenger, that I would accept him on the condition that first he did me some service in payment for having raised weapons against the Government, that he defeat the blacks, and that he give himself up afterwards with

all his people. Indeed, he decided to do what I had ordered, many blacks pursued in Lagoa Amarela fled to Bela Água, and 140 were taken prisoner by the people of the aforementioned Pedrosa who, with our forces, continues to pursue them, and it is to be believed that once this work is done he will lay down his weapons as promised.[53]

Cosme tried to reorganize his quilombo in a place called Guadalupe, between Lagoa Amarela and the town of Brejo. But by this time the strategy of the future Duke of Caxias was already working. Several rebel leaders decided to accept the conditions imposed by the provincial government, that is, they would only benefit from the amnesty offered by the Emperor if first they helped to capture the runaway slaves. The objective was not only to hasten the end of the revolt, but also to incite lasting hatred between the enslaved and poor freemen in Maranhão, as the man who entered official history as the "peacemaker" of the province himself states:

> As one of the aims, to which I have given particular attention, to avoid slave uprisings, is to stir up hatred between slaves and these people [the rebel groups of Pio and Tempestade], I sent those rebels to attack Cosme's new *quilombo*, which they did, sending me the captured slaves and, as well as these, many others have been sent in, taken prisoner by Pedrosa.[54]

Thus, many quilombolas were caught in the crossfire from governmental troops and from the ex-rebels, who knew the area very well. The area where quilombos had been active so far now became unfavourable for them. It might be assumed that Cosme chose Lagoa Amarela, a fazenda far from the frontier and from the rainforests of Codó because it was a good place in the context of the revolt: the balaio activities had been largely focusing on this area between the rivers Itapecuru and Parnaíba, an area where a greater number of poor, free people lived. In fact, the quilombola leader, witnessing the constant dispersal of his group, had tried to cross the river Itapecuru, with the aim of fleeing beyond the agrarian frontier with the remainder of his followers. Unfortunately, during this attempt, in February 1841, he was surrounded and had to witness the massacre of the majority of the 200 enslaved rebels who were still with him. Taken prisoner, he was sentenced to death and executed in September 1842.[55]

An Abolitionist Quilombo

Cosme's quilombo is impressive for its size and the fear that he managed to instil in slave owners, which was possible only because of the exceptional circumstances of the Balaiada. The large quilombos in Turiaçu, however, managed to survive for much longer, each one comprising between two and six hundred people in the nineteenth century. Their outstanding dimensions can be explained by their location beyond the frontier, similar to that of the quilombos in the rainforests of Codó and Mearim. Another factor that contributed to their growth was that, in general, their economy was more diverse. As well as hunting, fishing, harvesting, and subsistence agriculture, they reared cattle and sold tobacco and cotton. And, above all, they prospected for gold in the region of the Maracassumé and Gurupi rivers.[56] The mining created a gold-trading network and led to even greater communication with free people. It was not simply occasional barter with a few people also living on the periphery of slave society, but regular trade with small peddlers, fazendeiros and even merchants from coastal towns such as Santa Helena, Carutapera, and Turiaçu. It is therefore no exaggeration to state that a section of the population and even of the elite was interested in maintaining peaceful relations with the gold mining quilombolas—thus hindering any repressive actions. The provincial authorities were often aware of this collusion and never missed an opportunity to denounce it. On several occasions free people were arrested and cross-examined, which clearly demonstrates the involvement of persons of a certain social prestige.[57]

The first report of quilombos in Turiaçu dates back to the year 1702.[58] At the end of the colonial period, in 1811, the attacks on the quilombos in Guimarães mentioned at the beginning took place, during which reference was made to the large quilombo under the leadership of João Congo. The exact location of this quilombo is unclear, but it must also have been in this area, in the rainforests beyond the frontier. Soon after Independence, complaints began to reappear about "large *quilombos*" that had formed in the valley of the river Turiaçu.[59] As this municipality belonged to Pará until 1852, it was always necessary to co-ordinate any action with the authorities of that province, which did not help matters. In 1834, the provincial president of Maranhão acknowledged the seriousness of the situation for "the inhabitants of the town of Turiaçu and its district," where

> large *Quilombos* of Black Slaves [have formed] from runaways who have come here from all around and who, like insurgents, commit horrible and unheard-of crimes, going around in guerrilla bands each of more than fifty blacks, carrying out robberies and committing murders [...].[60]

The two provinces agreed to finance the dispatch of troops. The attack was partially successful, since they managed to find the quilombo Maracassumé and to apprehend a certain number of runaway slaves, the others having been "dispersed."[61] A little prematurely, the provincial president announced the "extinction" of the quilombos in Turiaçu[62] when, in reality, a few years later there were fresh complaints about maroons in the area. During the presidency of Eduardo Olímpio Machado, in 1853, there was a renewed and serious attempt to put at end to the quilombos in Turiaçu. One troop, arriving from São Luís managed to defeat the maroons of the Maracassumé mines and the group of Cruz Santo, killing twenty mocambeiros and taking 46 prisoners. Thirty slaves gave themselves up to their masters "voluntarily."[63] Again the authorities declared the end of quilombos in Turiaçu, which, this time, was not accepted by the liberal opposition press who pointed out that only a few runaway slaves had been captured.[64] News about the Maracassumé mines, however, attracted the attention of several groups interested in extracting gold. After two completely unsuccessful attempts to settle Chinese and Portuguese colonists in the area, an English firm, the Montes Áureos Gold Mining Company, leased the region of Montes Áureos for seven years, even going as far as transporting costly English machinery to the area. For reasons still unclear, the contract was not renewed, and the quilombolas regained control of the area.[65] This control was so strong that the large quilombos of the 1860s and 1870s, which we will look at below, were able to use gold mining as the main basis of their economy.

The second occasion in the history of Maranhão on which the quilombos managed to cause real panic among the region's ruling elite occurred in July 1867 in Viana.[66] As was the case with the Balaiada, it was the large-scale recruitment of the free population that created the right conditions for slave rebellion. The Empire needed more and more soldiers because of the Paraguayan War (1864–70). All the provinces were obliged to contribute soldiers, whether new recruits or battalions that had already been formed in the National Guard of the province. The result of this *pega*, as the recruitment in Maranhão was commonly called, poor free men of serving age disappeared. Many were in fact recruited. From the municipality of Curupuru alone, up until 1867 more than two hundred men had already been sent to war.[67] The others tried to hide in the forests, where they remained for months or even years. The result was that the slave system lost the intermediary groups that were so important to its survival. Only the masters and their overseers remained facing huge numbers of enslaved workers. With the local police forces drastically reduced, the slaves began to show clear signs of unrest. And the mocambeiros became increasingly daring, as the authorities lamented. They asked for assistance, such as the suspension of the recruitment of rural guards into the army

> in view of the boldness [the runaway slaves] continue to demonstrate, because they are not punished, using the most public roads, recruiting slaves on the *fazenda*s and in the fields, and even taking those who resisted by force [....][68]

Furthermore, the reports about the war were themselves accompanied by rumours about the imminent abolition of slavery.

This favorable context meant that the maroons of the quilombo of São Benedito do Céu felt strong enough to carry out their audacious plan of action. Four hundred men took part, leaving only women, children, and elderly men in the quilombo.[69] First, on 8 July 1867, the quilombolas invaded the Fazenda Santa Bárbara. After raiding it, they occupied the Timbó sugar mill, demanding weapons and ammunition. That same day they invaded the town of Vila Nova de Anadia, where they stole goods from the stores. They spent the night on the Fazenda São José and returned on July 10 to the Fazenda Santa Bárbara. There they forced the administrator to write a letter to the authorities, demanding "freedom for the slaves," and explaining that

> [...] as our desire is to be equal to everyone and to do harm to no-one, we await this freedom in Santo Inácio and if it does not arrive by the fifteenth of the coming month we will have no choice but to take up arms and go there ourselves, and Your Lordships can be sure that we have 1,000 firearms and all of the gentiles' [Indian] bows and arrows for defending ourselves and our freedom [....][70]

On July 10, a troop of 120 men arrived, who managed to move the mocambeiros from the fazenda. However, the latter occupied the surrounding rainforests. Only on July 12, when more reinforcements arrived, were the maroons finally forced to withdraw, with several of them taken prisoner.

What could have led the quilombolas to commit such a bold act? Cross-examinations of the prisoners provide some answers, although it is necessary to treat this kind of information with some caution. With the raid, the maroons sought to equip themselves with ammunition and arms, food, horses and even clothing, as in the attack on the stores in Anadia shows. According to one statement, at that time there was widespread hunger in the quilombo. Another stressed that the indigenous population had threatened the maroons.[71] What is interesting is that they did not attack just any fazenda, but those where some of the quilombolas had come from. Undoubtedly, knowledge of the area helped guarantee the attack's success. It was also easier to gain the support of slaves from a fazenda where friendship ties existed. But on this point the sources differ. The maroon Vicente stated that "all the slaves belonging to the *Fazenda*s Santa Bárbara, Timbó, and Santo Inácio all conspired to escape to the *mocambo*,"[72] which is confirmed by his friend Vicente who asserted that "they had already agreed with the slaves of Santa Bárbara, Timbó, and Santo Inácio, to all meet and steal the gunpowder and lead shot that they found [...]."[73] The quilombola told how "they did not agree; however, they made no opposition to the runaways."[74] It is very likely that at least some of the slaves in the aforementioned fazendas knew about the imminent attack. In any case, once the assault began, the slaves on the fazendas joined forces with the quilombolas. The event had a strong impact on the region's slave owners as in the case of the Timbó sugar plantation, whose owner, recounting the punches, pushes and bashes he received, stated that his own slaves took part in the attack and "they did it, not because the invaders forced them to, but of their own free will."[75]

Personal revenge certainly also played a part in the decision to attack fazendas belonging to former masters. The maroon Martiniano told how they caught the administrator of the Fazenda Santa Bárbara, explaining that it was "the runaways Cosme, Gregorio, and Florêncio, slaves from that very *fazenda*, who caught, tied and beat him and placed him in irons."[76] In a total inversion of power, some member of the group, as in the above example, constantly threatened the life of white masters under the control of quilombolas. And it was not necessarily only slave against master. In Timbó, the free man Joaquim Calisto, a member of the quilombola forces, "wanted to knife the master João, to which some objected saying that they only wanted gunpowder and weapons [...]."[77]

It remains clear, however, that the maroon leaders, such as Daniel and Bruno, at least, had plans that went far beyond these acts of revenge or isolated raids. And the message got through. News of the attack on the three fazendas and the small town of Anadia, together with the mocambeiros' ultimatum, spread "real terror" throughout the *baixada* as this lowland area is known in Maranhão. In the neighborhood of São Vicente Ferrer, for example, the police chief had great difficulty in preventing the whole population from leaving town. Authorities in other municipalities in the area reported similar problems.[78] This panic was noticed by the slaves. As Mundinha Araújo noted according to reports sent to the president, since the uprising, slaves from several parts of the Province have become rebellious, showing themselves to be insolent and slow in their work, as if waiting for the outcome in Viana in order to swell the rebels' ranks, like in the time of the Balaiada.[79]

This was another of the elite's greatest fears: that the slaves would again join forces with the poor free population who had escaped recruitment, leading, as it had done 29 years previously, to a large-scale uprising.[80]

Faced with this situation, it can be said that the provincial President Menezes Dória kept a cool head. He sent troops to Viana and ordered the attack on the quilombo São Benedito. By means of the official newspaper *O Publicador Maranhense*, he spread news that the situation was under control. At the same time, he tried not to ignore alarming reports that arrived from all over. At the end of June, he sent a detailed questionnaire to each town council, asking for precise information about the municipality's slave population, the number, name and precise location of the quilombos, their economy, their trade links, and the state of their weapons. The councils had to provide specific facts before they received any support from the provincial government.

At the same time, the president tried to control the slave rebellion on the fazendas. In exemplary fashion, the police chief from Guimarães went in person to organize the disarmament of slaves on the fazendas belonging to the Baron of Bagé who, according to the police chief himself

> have for many years been managed by administrators who more or less compromise with the slaves out of fear of being murdered, which has happened, and in order to guarantee their survival in view of the profits they make, because mass flight is the fastest means the slaves have when they intend to distance themselves from any administrator; the *fazenda*s are close to one another—the slaves shelter one another and any inquiry one makes about them is risky, because of the resistance already put in practice more than once, and because of the large number of slaves present in any one of the establishments [....][81]

The chief ended up ordering several slaves to be punished and seized a total of 42 firearms and 4 spears.

The attack on the quilombos on July 17, just ten days after the invasion of the fazendas, was less successful. The expedition comprised three delegations from neighboring municipalities—Viana, São Vicente Ferrer and São Bento. With the help of quilombolas taken prisoner on the 10th July attack to serve as guides, they managed to reach the quilombo São Benedito, where they only found one man, who was killed, and a child of two years. The lack of supplies and of co-ordination, as well as disagreements between commanders of the three forces, forced the soldiers to withdraw without having captured the quilombolas. The quilombo's eighty houses were set on fire, but not even the fields apparently were burnt. The destruction was so minimal that soon afterwards the mocambeiros had already returned to the location, and were again producing manioc flour.

For this reason, the provincial president ordered another raid with 120 men, led by a major. The expedition left São Bento on August 27 and arrived two weeks later. It was attacked by the quilombolas and there were losses on both sides. Not even this expedition, however, managed to capture a significant number of maroons and they had to beat a retreat three days later due to a lack of supplies. The situation reached a deadlock. The mocambeiros, who were defeated when they left their forests, never again carried out similar actions, as the provincial government liked to boast. Nevertheless, the raid did not manage to eradicate the quilombos from the area either. The official historiography, due to its need to give the episode a happy conclusion, maintains that the survivors from the São Benedito quilombo were "attacked and completely destroyed by a group of wild Indians" on the shores of the river Gurupi. Mundinha Araújo has shown that this is an incomplete version of the facts, since reports about the quilombolas from São Benedito do Céu appeared in later years. She also demonstrated that some of the leaders, such as Daniel, were found ten years later in another quilombo.[82] However, from then on the relationship with the quilombolas changed—the whites were no longer terrified of a slave insurrection. And, on the part of the quilombolas, there was an awareness that they were just a small group, with insufficient means to face slave society.

Late Quilombos

Several factors contributed to this change. The end of the transatlantic trade and the selling of slaves to the coffee producing southern provinces of the Empire had already changed Maranhão's demography. At this time, slaves constituted only a minority of the population. It could be argued that they still represented a significant minority: many municipalities still had thousands of slaves. However, the end of slavery was undoubtedly approaching. Even if some masters wanted to keep their slaves at all cost, at least after the introduction of the Law of the Free Womb (Lei do Ventre Livre, 1871) few doubted that the days of slavery were numbered.

Another important reason were the changes in relations with the free worker. After the complete failure to attract foreign colonists, the regional elites "discovered" the Brazilian colonist as an alternative in order to make up for the "lack of hands" for agricultural work.[83] It was therefore no coincidence that, from the 1870s, contingents of colonists started to arrive from northeastern Brazil. In fact, the emigration of people from Ceará to the province was an old phenomenon. However, this had occurred in a spontaneous way, via Piauí, through a process of gradual occupation of areas not taken up by fazendas, and only in the oldest areas of colonization in eastern Maranhão. With the drought in the Northeast in 1877, however, the provincial government had great quantities at their disposal in the capital, many of which were sent straight from Ceará. The government settled these groups in strategic places on the frontier, sometimes taking advantage of deforested areas or fields belonging to quilombolas, as in the case of the Colônia Prado, established on the site of the quilombo Limoeiro. Consequently, as Alfredo Wagner has already suggested, from the 1870s or, more precisely, 1877, the houses and fields belonging to the quilombos were no longer systematically destroyed. They represented labour invested and substantial improvements over an uncleared rainforest, that were as attractive as the labour of the quilombolas who the provincial government sought to return to their former owners. "From something to be destroyed the *quilombo*s became important spoils of war, where soldiers were sent in order to watch over and protect these precious spoils."[84]

On the other hand, insofar as the abolitionist ideals started to spread within the Empire, some members of the provincial elite no longer viewed attacks on quilombos as the simple persecution of criminals, in which the summary execution of those who resisted was seen as natural and just. Instead, they preferred the raids to be viewed as attempts to convince culturally inferior beings to return to the heart of civilization. The image of a raid to hunt slaves settled in quilombos could only be seen as anachronistic after the Law of the Free Womb. If on the one hand freedom was being "given" to the children of enslaved women, how was it possible on the other hand to capture children, the offspring of runaways, many of whom had in fact been born free in the forests?[85] During the presidency of Francisco de Sá and Benevides there were therefore two attempts to attract maroon groups by "persuasive means," the first being successful and the second a failure, which is why this policy was soon abandoned.[86]

The first expedition focused on the quilombo São Sebastião, in the valley of the river Turiaçu, in November 1876. The soldiers, led by major Honorato Cândido Ferreira Caldas, managed to make contact, through local guides, with the maroon group led by Daniel, the same leader of the invasion of Viana in 1867. The major guaranteed "for my part there was no hostile intent against him [Daniel] and his companions, on the contrary, I thought of giving them all kinds of benefits within my reach."[87] He convinced Daniel to enter into negotiations:

> Thus I made them see the advantage of abandoning the depths of the forest and leaving that wild existence, especially now that, according to what they tell me, on top of the hardships they suffered, they lived in fear of the Indians who had already attacked and killed many of their companions; I explained to them the advantages of the law of 28 of September 1871, the indispensable condition of registration for the right to slave ownership, the ease with which a hardworking and industrious slave could gain his freedom nowadays, and finally the big difference in treatment that awaits them between coming with me voluntarily and being caught sooner or later.[88]

The leader agreed to hand himself over in principle but requested a month to gather his people who had spread throughout the forest due to the arrival of the soldiers. Major Caldas, through a mixture of promises and threats, managed to take a quarter of the troops to the mocambo, where he intended to establish an educational mission in order to convince those who were frightened of the soldiers' good intentions. He respected the freedom of those who stayed in the mocambo and even allowed trade between soldiers and quilombolas. Despite resistance by some quilombolas, the expedition thus managed to take 114 quilombolas peacefully to the town of Pinheiro six weeks later. However, it is worth highlighting the fact that the support of Daniel, the leader, was undoubtedly encouraged by the fact that the major had promised freedom for both him and his family.[89]

Encouraged by this successful outcome, president Sá e Benavides soon recommended to the director of the military colony at Gurupi, João Manuel da Cunha, that he raid the mocambos of Montes Áureos "preferably using persuasive means."[90] By the end of 1877, he had already sent eighty soldiers to reinforce the troops there, and continued to recommend to the director

> that he employ all of his troops in order to achieve, through persuasive means, the desired outcome, using force only very cautiously, and preventing excesses by the soldiers, and by laying hands on weapons only in self defence in the event of resistance[91]

Cunha, following the footprints of *calhambola* lookouts, managed to enter the quilombo by surprise in January 1878. However, despite the surprise, he did not manage to capture the quilombolas because, according to Cunha, there were not enough troops to surround the quilombo. The maroons escaped into the forest, leaving behind them only a few old men. Using one of these as an intermediary, Cunha entered into negotiations with the leader, Estevão, who he made "see the disadvantage of staying in the mocambo and the advantages that they could gain from leaving."[92] Estevão apparently agreed to give his people up, but in fact he disappeared with them into the forest and the expedition was forced to return due to lack of supplies, taking with them only sixteen captured quilombolas.

The failure of this expedition led to reciprocal accusations among the participants. The leader Cunha accused the Captain Freire of not having carried out his orders and of having aspired to be the leader of the expedition. He also accused him of having behaved in the old way, that is, sacking and conquering, when the aim was to employ "persuasive means." He further denounced the captain for stealing the maroons' gold. Captain Freire, for his part, accused the director of the military colony of old-style cooperation with the quilombolas, giving this as the reason why he had not ordered the fields at Limoeiro to be destroyed. Unfortunately for Cunha, President Sá e Benevides' successor was more inclined to believe the second version. Cunha was dismissed from his post as director of the military colony and Freire was appointed commander of a new raid against the quilombolas of Montes Áureos. The second expedition (March to April 1878) set up headquarters in the former quilombo of Limoeiro and from there it pursued the maroons, who had divided into several groups. Using captured quilombolas as guides, the soldiers managed to defeat three of these groups and to capture 78, among them the leader Estevão. Even though the soldiers knew that they had only managed to capture a fraction of the region's maroons, they decided to withdraw. The operation was considered a success.

These three expeditions are important insofar as they have left us precious sources of information on three quilombos, which constitute almost ethnographic documents. They are, for example, the only known sources from Maranhão to try to reproduce the direct speech of free maroon leaders, when until this point, we have, at best, cross-examinations. Even Captain Freire himself revealed his ethnographic interest. When his observation of Estevão's "festival of the medicine men" (*festa dos pajés*) was interrupted, he relates how "unfortunately it was not possible to hear what happened next, because a soldier, on seeing Estevão, shouted enthusiastically There is Estevão!".⁹³ The negotiations created complex situations, in which the soldiers' power was not absolute, but in which it was important to understand the contradictions among maroons. In summary, the negotiations resulted in closer links with the quilombolas and contributed to a better understanding of maroon society. This is reflected in observations made in the reports, above all those regarding the quilombolas' culture, their religious practices, and their political organization.

Thus we have a detailed description of the quilombo São Sebastião, which was located

> [...] in the center (which was also the highest point) of an attractive circular open area, approximately one thousand braças⁹⁴ in diameter, that ends in fields which surrounded the whole space. Here follows a description of what was there: 58 houses, with straw roofs and walls of mud, the majority with wooden doors and windows. Two of them called Saints' Houses (*Casas de Santo*), clearly distinguished by the crosses erected in front, three were for making flour with the appropriate ovens, one was used as a store and had a threshing floor, in another they kept the clay still, and the others were—the *quilombolas* houses—each so asymmetrical that there were only two slightly regular streets—the upper and the lower one—that were separated from each other by the churchyard of the old chapel; two mills for pressing sugar cane, worked by hand, a large banana plantation and several fruit trees, many tobacco plantations in the yards, as well as pineapples, quite a lot of manioc, cotton, and a nice big stock of chickens and ducks, together with the advantageous situation that a branch of the Japenicana (called the Igarapé de Casa), a river that has never dried up, flows at the foot of the *quilombo*.⁹⁵

The above paragraph describes a fairly diverse economy, including crops that could eventually be commercialized and livestock, features which to this day remain characteristic of rural culture in Maranhão.

Limoeiro was very similar in its spatial organization:

> [...] it has 91 houses, each with three, four, or five blacks with their wives and children, and there are two more houses reserved for prayer, which they call *casas de santos*; one with images of Saints and the other where we found richly adorned wooden figures, bottle gourds with dried herbs and a lot of stones which in ancient times the Indians used as axes, and which the majority of *mocambeiros* worship with an invocation to Santa Bárbara. However, this is nothing else but a medicine man's house. The number of fields in the

mocambo is extraordinarily high and it would take more than a month to destroy them all.[96]

If we assume that in each house there lived six to eight people, Limoeiro would have had between 546 and 728 inhabitants, which gives us an idea of the demographic importance of the large quilombos in the Turi area. The existence of the *casas de santo*, the worship of Santa Bárbara (who corresponds to the *vodun* Sobo in Maranhão's *tambor de mina* religion), São Benedito,[97] and other saints, as well as the reference to the "dance of the drum,"[98] seem to indicate that, far from isolated religious practices, the quilombolas practiced a syncretic religion common to the region's entire black and mestizo Brazilian population. The qualification *pajé* is not necessarily proof of indigenous influence, since the term, extremely pejorative in the language of the elite at that time, was used for any non-Catholic manifestation that was considered "witchcraft."

The relationship between religious power and political power is, however, unclear. In the quilombo Limoeiro, the figure who captain Freire called a pajé is different to the leader Estevão, but the latter apparently used religion to expel members from the quilombo and he sentenced to death two women accused of being "witches." In São Sebastião, the priest was a mulatto called Feliciano, who does not seem to have held a position as one of the leaders.

The use of the word *rei* (king) to describe the maroon leaders has led to the idea that their power was almost absolute. The information contained in these reports, however, suggests something more like a consensual leader, who constantly had to reaffirm his leadership. In São Sebastião, for example, news of Caldas' interview with Daniel and the latter's message that "those who agreed with him should wait for him in the *mocambo*" caused "almost everyone to get annoyed and many quickly left [...]." According to major Caldas, Daniel himself had told him that

> we are indeed very unhappy with the situation [of the *mocambo*] because of the gentiles [Indians], and four years ago when they attacked us for the first time and caused great destruction, I proposed that we go and hand ourselves over to the Imperial government, so that we could be free of those damned people. But some thought the opposite and so time has passed without the situation being resolved, also because everyone is very scared of being returned to their masters' authority because of the bad treatment they have received from them.[99]

What we glimpse in the above passage is almost a grassroots democracy, in which the leader cannot impose his will if the majority is against it.[100] It could therefore be concluded that Daniel, seeing that he could not manage to convince the other quilombolas, sought the whites' help in order to impose his desire to leave the forest and give themselves up. By taking the soldiers into the quilombo he would not meet with further opposition. This is confirmed by the fact that schisms soon appeared within the quilombo, initially led first by lieutenant (*contracapitão*) Sotero (who withdrew before the arrival of the troops, with twenty or so mocambeiros) and later by Lieutenant Ernesto. The latter, however, was disarmed and, together with his dissident companions, taken prisoner.

We find the same power structure, with lieutenants (*contracapitães*) or subcommanders (*subchefes*), in the quilombo Limoeiro. According to some sources, the leader Estevão came to control several inter-linked mocambos. In any case, after the first expedition, the group subdivided in order to escape persecution. As with the maroon group of São Sebastião, it seems that a large number of maroons opposed Estevão's negotiations with the soldiers, "saying that it was betrayal."[101] Only in the case of Estevão were there no significant differences of opinion because he probably used negotiation merely as a tactic to deceive the soldiers,[102] and he did not delude himself by promises of freedom also made to him with the explicit authorization of the provincial government.[103] The case of Estevão is even more complex. According to several sources, he was responsible for seventeen deaths within his own quilombo. Accounts from oral memory collected by David Cleary suggest that power could have unbalanced him to the point of "becoming wicked to the others."[104] One could speculate that these deaths point to a much more absolute power than that of leaders such as Daniel.

Based on the material available so far in relation to quilombos in Maranhão, several conclusions are possible. Maroon communities existed in Maranhão as in any other part of Brazil. Four factors, however, contributed to their exceptional frequency, size and longevity during the nineteenth century. These were the high proportion of slaves in relation to the free population in the north of the province, the existence of abundant rainforests, with many rivers and streams, the existence of a frontier, that is, a vast area not controlled by the State, next to the plantation areas, and the political instability during the years 1820–41.

The period up to 1850 was therefore especially favorable for the formation of quilombos in all areas of the province that had a significant number of slaves. However, with the stabilization of the political situation, the consequent development of the state apparatus, and the increasing density of settlement in older areas of colonization, it seems that after the mid-century quilombos only managed to establish themselves with the same ease in areas that could still be considered frontiers: that is the entire strip of land that stretches from the river Gurupi to the left side of the river Itapecuru (see map). It is significant, for example, that in all the documents catalogued by the Projeto Vida de Negro there is only one case of a quilombo after 1845 in eastern Maranhão.[105]

The frontier situation facilitated the survival of many maroon groups, above all in the rainforests between the river Turi and the river Gurupi, and in those of the Codó and Mearim valleys. In these areas, large quilombos of between two and seven hundred people managed to survive for decades, defying periodic persecutions. The reasons for this success are not solely due to thefavorable ecological conditions, but also to the fact that, far from being isolated communities, the quilombos were part of a complex communication network with the slave society, that provided them with material goods and information about raids. They were in permanent contact with slaves on the fazendas. In some cases, they even went as far as to work for fazendeiros in need of labor. They exchanged or sold produce from their fields (tobacco and cotton) to the free population. The quilombos in the Turiaçu/Gurupi area managed, through gold mining, to involve an important sector of the free population in the gold trade. Therefore, we should not view the quilombos as absolute enemies of Brazilian slave society, but imagine a middle ground that permitted various kinds of relationships.

It would seem also that the maroon groups communicated with one another, exchanging information and eventually planning joint action. This, at least, was slave society's elite constant fear until the 1870s. However, we lack facts in order to assess the extent of this communication. Even more problematic were relations with the indigenous groups. On one hand, some sources suggest peaceful relations.[106] However, it is not surprising that, with the advance of the frontier, indigenous groups who felt that their land was being encroached upon identified the quilombolas as their enemies. This appears to have been the case in the 1870s in the Turi/Gurupi region, as the problems of Limoeiro and São Sebastião maroons bear witness.

In general, the raids on quilombos ended in failure or, at best, in partial victories. These failures were in part caused by the lack of preparation on the part of the troops, their heterogeneity and, consequently, the conflicts between subcommanders. Another ever-present problem was the troops' supplies once in the forest. Many had to return due to lack of resources.

Thus, an initial success—the discovery of a maroon group—came to little because the quilombolas divided into various subgroups and established new mocambos as soon as the troops had left. This kind of problem was only overcome with improvements in the transport system, the advance of the frontier, and the creation of military colonies, such as the one at Gurupi, which could serve as bases.

Although it is necessary to highlight the ambiguities in the relations between the quilombolas and slave society, we should not lose sight of the fundamental antagonisms between the two. Of particular interest is the dynamic between the quilombo and the "insubordination" of slaves on the fazendas. The latter gave rise to the former, as can be seen in the case of the quilombo of Guimarães in 1811, or of Codó in 1838, and in the case of the leader Estevão, who fled to the forest after having murdered his overseer.[107] But the quilombo itself also led to insubordination on the fazendas, which is clear in the case of events relating to Viana or the Balaiada. Thus, the masters' fear of another "Haiti" should not be seen as unjustified paranoia, but as having a very real basis. Many were frightened of facing their former slaves as maroons, ready to settle accounts. Perhaps due to the high mortality of slaves, Maranhão had a reputation as a slave hell, where slaves from other provinces were sent as punishment. For this reason, it also became a hell for the masters, above all those who lived in the middle of a large number of enslaved workers, isolated in the forests. It is therefore not surprising that some masters and administrators entered into agreements with slaves and mocambeiros, agreements that did not always follow the orthodox ideology of slave society.

Another factor that contributed to the relative weakness of the ruling class was the distance that separated the rich from the free poor population. The elite could only count on a very small number of whites who identified with the Portuguese, but these were living mainly in the cities and ports such as São Luís. The vast majority of the free, poor population was of black, indigenous or Northeastern (that is, also mixed) ancestry. While one part was integrated into the slave economy and was prepared to defend the system, another significant segment tried to survive on the periphery of the fazendas. The lack of support for the Imperial state is testified by people's refusal to serve in its troops. The arbitrary actions to which they were subjected, such as the draft, resulted for many in experiences similar to those of the maroons, such as living hidden in the forests. For this marginalized population, always treated with suspicion and frequently persecuted, cooperation with the quilombolas was not seen as extraordinary. When in need, they even sought shelter amongst them. This happened so often that the sources frequently mention the existence of "criminals" or deserters in the midst of maroons, who even trained them in handling firearms. In fact, for the majority of the quilombos about which we have more detailed information, the reports mention that they sheltered free people. The latter could eventually assume some kind of leadership role, as may be the case of Joaquim Calisto in the quilombo São Benedito.[108] Therefore, it is not surprising that the alliance between free and enslaved people became an issue in the Balaiada, since it had always existed on a small scale in the quilombos themselves. The outbreak of the Balaiada, as we have seen, merely took the co-operation between free and enslaved rebels to new levels, without, however, managing to convince the majority of poor free men.

Finally, several aspects remain unclear in relation to the quilombola leadership. We could speculate that the large colonial quilombos were led by Africans, such as João Congo, in contrast to the later quilombos, which in general were led by "Creole" blacks, that is, those born in Brazil and therefore more integrated into the incipient syncretic Afro-Brazilian culture. But is it possible to believe that Cosme's power was "absolute," like his greatest enemy the Duke of Caxias wrote? In the absence of new sources and evidence, the leaders of the large quilombos in Maranhão, such as Cosme, Daniel and Estevão, for a long time yet, will remain enigmatic characters who continue to stir our imagination.

18

"I WAS BORN IN THE FOREST; I'VE NEVER HAD AN OWNER": HISTORY AND MEMORY OF THE MOCAMBO COMMUNITIES IN THE LOW AMAZON RAINFOREST[1]

EURÍPEDES A. FUNES

It may seem strange to many to speak of black slavery in the Amazon, even more when referring to the *mocambo* settlements established there throughout the entire nineteenth century. The aim of this chapter is to touch on the subject of the maroon societies, especially those settled in the lower Amazon region, whose presence was established among the many rural black communities now located by the rivers and lakes of the area. The history of these societies is very much alive in the memory of the *quilombolas*' descendants, grandchildren and great-grandchildren, who have inhabited the forest for a long time and turned it into their space of freedom.[2] Arrested in Belém along with one hundred and thirty five quilombolas from Curuá, Maria Candida was subjected to an inquiry on 28 March 1876, and when asked about who her owner was, she answered: "I've never had an owner as I was born in the forest." Many of her peers answered that they had no owner or they did not know who their owner was supposed to be because they were born in the Curuá forest.[3]

In the history narrated by these *mocambeiros* (descendants of *mocambo communities*, interchangeably called *quilombolas* and *mocambeiros*) lies the Pacoval roots, a black community located by the right bank of Curuá River in the city of Alenquer, in the Western Pará, a region also known as the Lower Amazon rainforest (see Map).[4] This history is present in the memory of the elders, who are great narrators of their ancestors' saga. This allows us to rescue a past not always revealed in written documents—a memory that is a reference of both ancestry and identity. The community of Pacoval, its cultural expressions, its daily routine and lifestyle, reveal its origins, which are better expressed not only by the skin color of its people, but above all by the elders' memory and remembrances of the histories told by their grandparents, which always take us to another past: that of the quilombo communities. The grandparents' history is a lived history. These aspects clearly reveal that not all of these societies formed by fugitive black slaves disappeared to the point of extinction of their respective quilombos, as is suggested, in analysis using the binary logic of formation/destruction, by several other historiographical studies about these groupings.[5]

Map of Amazonas.

I aim thus to understand the historical process of the slave resistance and the constitution of the quilombos as a counterpoint to the slaveholding society and as a permanent presence in the contemporary black communities, which is a theme not much addressed by historians. This work uses both oral memory and written documents to address the history of those who "not only represented troubles for the government," but were also agents of a historical process marked by the resistance and formation of an alternative social space to the enslaver's world, where being free was the greatest experience.[6] By relying on both oral and written sources, the major concern is to present complementary aspects, rather than replacement aspects.[7] It is not about, as told by Jan Vansina,

> the prima donna and her substitute in the opera: when the star cannot sing, the substitute comes; when the writing fails, tradition goes on stage... the oral sources correct the other views as well as the other views correct them.[8]

In this way, we avoid treating the experiences narrated by a community as the single organizing principle of its history, which may lead to a romanticized view of the historical process, magically turning the oppressed one into the only individual. Nor is it about bringing back the "voice of the defeated" and thereafter build new mythologies, but is about realizing that

> the acknowledgment of the right to the past is intricately connected to the present meaning of citizenship generalization by a society that has avoided so far to bring out the conflict and creativity as criteria for the awareness of a common past.[9]

In this context, memory constitutes an element significantly important to the reconstitution of the historical process. In the remaining mocambo communities this memory is more alive among the elders, mocambeiro's grandchildren and great-grandchildren, who are the guardians of the histories their ancestors have told them. It is to them that one turns to enlarge the horizons of the research about these social organizations. One of the basic criteria used to choose the interlocutors is that they are quilombolas' descendants and keepers of a memory which expresses collective remembrances although they are narrated individually.

Raimunda Santana de Assis (as known as Mrs. Dica), 90 years old, granddaughter of mocambeiros Maria Miquelina and Manoel Dionísio, or just Dionísio, who raised her; José Santa Rita, dead at 70 on April 1992, grandson of Manoel Rodrigues de Oliveira Martins, aka Alexandre—"because of Africa's Alexandria"; and Raimundo da Silva Cardoso, aka Donga, 89 years old, grandson of mocambeiro Benedito. Raimunda and Santa Rita, from Pacoval, and Donga, from Trombetas, among other narrators, contributed in a fundamental way with their testimonies for us to reach the past of the several quilombo communities, which were formed by the rivers, Curuá/Cuminá-Panema, Cuminá/Paru do Oeste or Erepecuru, Trombetas, Mamiá, Maicuru, and lakes around the area.[10]

When questioned about their ancestors, the answer obtained immediately is that "they were smart people, they were people from Africa," according to Santa Rita. According to Dica,

> they came from Africa, a nation of people who know everything. The Portuguese started to take their children while they were gathering whistling duck's nests in the field. They were brought to Belém to work, from there to Santarém then to Curuá village. After leaving that place too, they went up the Curuá River looking for better conditions.

This statement is practically a synthesis of the trajectory of many black slaves that, after escaping from slavery, searched for the "fierce waters" of the Amazon River's left-bank tributaries, where they formed the several mocambos existing there throughout the nineteenth century, which continue in the black communities today established by the "calm waters" of the same rivers.

Slavery in the Amazon was not as pronounced, in quantitative terms, as in the mining, sugar and coffee areas.[11] However, even though they shared the work with native people, black people constituted a significant portion of the workforce, especially in agriculture, household services and urban activities. The presence of a slave workforce in the lower Amazon rainforest became more permanent from the second half of the eighteenth century, through government incentives by way of the trading company Grão-Pará and Maranhão, which established a direct relationship between the African ports and the northern part of Brazil. It was there that black people were utilized in the cocoa plantations, up until the mid nineteenth century, subsequently in agriculture, especially in livestock farming. Throughout this period, slavery was also confirmed in household activities. Gradually, the African joined the daily life of Amazonian society.

Based on public archives and parish records collected in Santarém, Alenquer and Óbidos, the majority of the identified African slaves came from southwestern and central Africa, predominantly from the Angola "nation," Congo, Cassange, Beijogo, Guiné, Benguela, and in smaller proportion those from Mina and Mozambique, among others.[12] In a new region, in a habitat predominantly characterized by rain forest, water and long distances, the African slave continuously found means to overcome adversities and adjust to the new society, making his daily life and his social conditions more bearable. From *post-mortem* inventories, it is possible to see that slave groups of that region were not so large. In the 270 consulted inventories, only three masters owned more than fifty slaves, including the Baron of Santarém, the majority of plantations holding 1–5 slaves totaling 128 slaves, and an additional 80 owners holding groups of 6–10 slaves.

The assessment of the goods listed in these documents shows that most of the rural properties in the lower Amazon rainforest were lacking masonry structures. The roofs of the houses were made of thatch and they were generally built from wood, adobe or wattle-and-daub. None of the inventories mentions fortified *senzalas* or slave houses. Most of the slave houses were built from palm thatch, which were not worth enough to be included among the properties. The long distances between properties, difficulty of communication and the low number of slaves in the groups helped to develop a closer master-slave relationship, and the slaves knew how to make use of these conditions. Many of the smaller slave groups were composed of slave family members. There are few inventories where mother and sons are not listed together as it is common to find masters owning two or even three generations of the same family in their properties. Raising a family was the first way that the slave found to lighten his burden in his social universe, since "within the precarious agreement the slaves could get from their owners, marrying meant gaining more control over the living space."[13] A family was the place where the authority was mostly independent of the presence of the slaveowner.

These spaces of autonomy were also sought in leisure moments, when different cultural elements were blended. Making use of religious festivals, enslaved persons used to worship their saints, sing and dance, which generated outrage among priests and "members of society." This is what happened with the Vicar of Itaituba, who asked for measures against the "state of demoralization which has reached the bad, stupid and scandalous habit of panhandling while dressed ridiculously as what they claim to be Saint Anthony, Saint Stephen, especially at the big lake where not a day goes by without hearing drumbeats or revelry songs."[14] In the villages, Sundays and holy days were days of "*pagodes*," "*sambas*," "black parties," and attending the "African casino." The complaints about these leisure moments did not deter them. According to the "the prestigious people of the place," there were moments when the

> slaveowner pays the cost and the public morality suffers. The slave who goes to such *pagodes*, without a penny to his name, does anything, even raiding his master's coffers, to meet the demands their ever-increasing enthusiasm.[15]

In face of this, people requested that the Santarém police chief "forbid access to the Africa casino to those slaves who do not bring written permission from their slaveowners."[16] There certainly was a place where black people, enslaved or freed, were masters of themselves.

On the one hand, these aspects do not indicate in any way that enslaved persons tacitly accepted their social condition or that the slaveowners were explicitly, or even implicitly benevolent, on the other hand. Class struggle does not cease to exist. There are many ways to fight it and it is in their daily lives that slaves created their negation of slavery.[17] Documented sources have demonstrated that the slave as an individual, albeit limited by a social law, could find a space to negotiate and speak up as an historical agent, living in a social environment to which his master belonged. He had complaints about the fate imposed on him and for this reason he was always searching for ways to overcome it, as "it is within these micropolitics that the slave tries to make a living and therefore history."[18] And why do they run away? It would be enough to say: because they are slaves. But there are a number of reasons arising from this condition, leading the captives to take flight.

Searching for Fierce Waters

According to an article published in the *Baixo Amazonas* newspaper, on 8 January 1876, the act of fleeing was an "intuitive fact," motivated by "seduction." Slaves

> do not run away because their owners mistreat them with cruel punishments, nor because inhumane slaveowners subject them to workloads that go beyond their strength. The slave was treated like a family member. However, they flee enticed by seduction, by the traffickers who incite them to leave the company of their owners and live freely in the forest searching for drugs, which they sell to satisfy the greed of these traffickers, who enter the Trombetas and Curuá rivers to collect chestnuts, oil and sarsaparilla. The escape of these slaves did not happen because of their masters' abuse, only because of the seduction.

By observing the content of the slaves' testimonials, we can see that this "seduction" was not the main reason for their flight. Intolerance, cruelty and the breaking of agreements by the masters led the captives to respond with one of the mostly common forms of resistance: flight. The black man João Pedro, when asked about the reasons for the flight of his companions Mandu Molato, Preto João Pachury and José Cuiabá, answered that they escaped because they heard that the new manager of their former owner's properties would "put a spell on them spreading salt on their doorstep and would not give them Sundays and holy days so that they could not raise any money."[19] The harsh treatment by the slaveowners remains in the descendant's memory and is always emphasized when they talk about the flight of their ancestors: "I met old black men and women who had their hands wrapped with cloth due to burns their work caused them; the whites also had the habit to put candles on the slaves' hands in order to illuminate their dining room."[20]

Maria Margarida Pereira Macambira, whose many slaves were "hidden in the *quilombos* of Curiá and Trombetas rivers,"[21] is personified as a symbol of evil, becoming a part of the descendants' imaginary: "sometimes, when mothers are being cruel to their children we say: you're acting like Macambira, since you are killing your children."[22] According to Santa Rita, the mocambeiros

> used to tell stories of what happened to them while serving Maria Macambira, stories about the time when they ate in troughs, as if they were pigs. When a slave misunderstood some order, she ordered them to be whipped, they really took a beating. When the slaves slept for too long, they would cut the strings of their hammocks and they fell on the floor and had to get up to work [...] Everything there was ridiculous domination, to which they were not accustomed, they were obligated to get used to it though, because they came from Africa. Then there was the time when they decided to run away. It was painful, we find it painful what they told us, how they were treated.[23]

Certainly, the "seduction" to go to the forest and be free was not only the appeal of the "seductive traffickers." The image of this lady, who is violent and undoubtedly has a strong personality, is linked to the most significant moments of the history of these mocambeiros, as can be inferred from the words used by those who tell these stories, who, when questioned about who enslaved their ancestors, quickly answered: "Maria Macambira, a wicked woman." The escapes of individual slaves who belonged to this owner and her heirs, including the Baron of Santarém, constitute an origin myth of a considerable portion of the quilombolas who live by the Trombetas river and in particular of those who live by the Curuá river, especially those who later formed the Pacoval.

The individual or collective escape usually occurred at the time of feasts and, more specifically, during the rainy season, from December to June.

> It is troublesome and truly threatening the conditions in which we see the right to property of this district in relation to slaves, [...] a batch of slaves leave their masters to seek refuge in the superb *quilombos* that surround us. Every day there are numerous slave flights registered and occasionally a batch of ten, twelve, twenty and even thirty slaves [...]such as those flights that occurred on the nights of December 28 last year and on the 3 day this month [...] From January to May, the period when the Amazon river rises, is also when the slaves consider an appropriate time to run away. At this time of year the traffic, which is completely fluvial, makes them able to navigate through shortcuts they know or by which they are conducted, without the fear of getting caught.[24]

The season of festivals, the rainy season, and the chestnut season were the times to escape. The slaves took to the river at night, in canoes, and found hidden gaps to break through narrow channels moving from lake to lake. They crossed over from one arm of the river to another through the *paranás* (a *paraná* is a channel between two rivers), entering the Amazon river, going up to the riverhead of its left-bank tributaries, where they would establish themselves high above the first rapids and waterfalls, the "fierce waters."

Mocambos are not known to exist alongside the Tapajós river, right-bank tributary of the Amazon river, perhaps because this river was under greater control of the authorities. It was one of the access routes to the province of Mato Grosso and, in order to reach the first waterfalls, the runaways would have to pass through the villages of Aveiro, Boim, and Itaituba and the Mundurukus settlement, from these there was always heavy recruitment to fight against quilombos. According to mocambeiro Benedito, who tried to take some companions with him, he "had to cross the bamboo thicket, passing by a stream, spending three days to get to the *mocambo*."[25] Knowing the environment became essential for the success of the escapes. In the rainy season, grasses grow on the lakeshores and form earthen dams which obstruct the streams that connect the lakes to each other and to the rivers, hindering the passage and camouflaging the waterway. Established above the falls and rapids, the quilombolas interposed natural obstacles between them and their pursuers. Overcoming them required being a good rower with ability to avoid rocks. In turn, the paths through the forest shortened the distances relative to winding rivers. One had to be an expert to know all of these paths.

According to Santa Rita, when the slaves left Santarém heading to the higher Curuá river dale,

They wanted to follow their people who had already fled to the Trombetas river. They thought that if they went up the river then Maria Macambeira would already be suspicious and would go looking for them. So they decided to go down the Amazon river in order to seek a place where they would not be persecuted, because she would chase them. Then they went to Monte Alegre to hunt by hiding themselves, but since there was not shelter for them out there, since their pursuers were still close behind, they decided to leave Monte Alegre by land and search for their destination so that they could follow their companions who had gone to Trombetas river. That is how they told the story. So they crossed the Maicuru river, but their pursuers were still close behind; then they crossed the Curuá river, but as it is a very dry river at summertime with few fish to feed them, they crossed it to see if they could find out where the fellow fugitives were. They were not able to reach the others, though. So they traversed the Curuá river until they reached the Cuminá river. They went up the river looking for a better place to camp, somewhere they could build their housing. They got there and came upon a huge waterfall [...] Then they crossed along a large flat rock above the waterfall where they spent the night and left a mark there in the road, and they named the waterfall Tracajá.[26]

Reaching their companions, seeking a safe place out of the reach of their pursuers, where it would be easy to gather food in the wilderness, were elements also present in the plans of the black runaways who headed to Trombetas River, not "Trombetas City" as written by Klein.[27]

According to Donga, "it was after they escaped from their masters that they built their village farther inside the Turuna and Ipoana River waterfalls. Maravilha was the first village; after they were attacked the second village was formed by the Turuna River, then they went to Ipoana River, where their pursuers could no longer reach them."[28] "When I was little I got to see from above the waterfall the thin *capoeira*,[29] avocado and orange groves, settlements built by the old black runaways," says Dico about the old mocambo locations by the Trombetas river.[30]

Several paths led to the upper courses of the rivers.[31] After travelling for days through rivers and forests, Blacks could truly break free from their enslaved condition upon reaching the "fierce waters," where "they lived at the center because they wanted to, but the camp and the yard were located on the banks of the bay."[32] The mocambo was the camp and the yard, the place where the slaves could assume their condition of freedmen. Free, he tried to integrate with the environment, with the other culture that there was there—the indigenous culture—to restructure his socioeconomic life and establish bonds with the external world.

Living in the Mocambo

"They arrived there, and started setting up their camp"; "they built villages;" and "they built houses and then came back to pick up their families." The narrators always repeat these phrases when they refer to the moment when the quilombolas found the ideal space to establish themselves. After getting over the initial difficulties, they settled down in navigable passages, above the waterfalls, areas where they could plant and nature was bountiful. "There they are, various palm trees proving that the land is excellent and showing that black people were skilled in choosing the place to be their refuge," wrote Gastão Cruls talking about the old place of the Lauthério mocambeiro, in Erepecuru.[33] The same place was visited by my father Nicoino, in 1877, when he traveled for the first time to that river.[34] The mocambo Maravilha, in return, "was settled on both the edges of Trombetas where it is most narrow. The position could not be more comfortable or well chosen: it is the most strategic point. In the entire village I counted 36 houses built of stucco and covered by straw with doors made of palm leaves," the type of construction still normal in this region.[35] It is necessary to call attention to the fact that the quilombos did not locate only at the margins of the main rivers. In the instances where they established themselves below the waterfalls, they aimed for the headwaters between two islands, as was the case of the mocambos of Inferno, Cipoteua and Caxange, in the narrow riverbanks of Inferno and Mamia, both tributaries of Curuá River.

It is also valid to highlight that the mocambeiros' houses were not necessarily clustered together; they could be spread out in a relatively close space in order to guarantee both security and unity for the group. This is made clear on the statement made by the Franciscan Carmello Mazzarino, who spent ten days, in 1868, among the quilombolas of Trombetas: "there I found about 130 people, besides the Indians who are among the black people, all of whom are divided among many places and in each place I found a beautiful little chapel where they practice some religious acts."[36] Religiosity today is still very strong among the black communities, being Catholicism, at least apparently, the only religion allowed and practiced. Apparently, blessings, practices of ritual faith healing and shamanism, folk medicine ("witchcraft"), and prayers for the souls of the dead are all part of a cultural universe characterized by religious syncretism, which is a strong mark of the identity of these communities, as well as the mocambeiros.

Their sense of devotion is emphasized in relation to their saints, whose images were sculpted from the core of palm tree trunks. Images that chocked Otille Codreau, on his passage through Pacoval in the end of the 1900s, in which he saw some degree of sacrilege, considering them grotesque and deformed:

> Each one has a name: this one is Saint John, that one is Saint Peter, Saint Benedict and there in the company of Saint Luzia, were Saint Rosa, Saint Sebastian and even a black Saint Mary. I wanted to make them destroy all those horrors, completely lacking in artistic expression, and to them they ascribe the grandiose name of saints. These statues are just reflections of their culture, debased to the lowest degree on the social scale.[37]

The feasts in honor of the saints, whose religious acts were conducted by the mocambos's "vicars and church clerks," were also part of the life of the quilombolas, parties where it was hard to distinguish between sacred and profane acts. They were moments of faith and leisure when they danced the *auiê*—nowadays the *marambiré* among people living in Pacoval—drank and made love. According to O. Codreau, after the "*pagodes*" took place in Balcão das Pedras, "the girls and young women spent the next nine months being bothered."[38] A new family was created or an existing family grew. The family institution was the base of the social organization of the mocambos and a guarantee of their reproduction. The escape of entire slave families was frequent, for example Honorato, Mathias Afonso's slave, who, on the night of 4 January 1876, ran away from the "coastal ranch of the Amazon river, taking a mule that weighed about fifty *arrobas* (about 750 kilos) and was followed by a woman, Domingas, a Tupí indigenous woman who often changed her name, and two little children."[39] Others that fled were Severino, a sixteen year old mulatto, and Bento, an eleven year old black child, both children of the black woman Maria Severina, all slaves of José Joaquim Pereira Macambira. Other families formed from the union between mocambeiros and the indigenous population, with whom they shared the same space. The monk Mazzarino performed, in 1867, eighteen weddings in the quilombo he visited in high Trombetas. In reality, what must have happened was the legitimation in the eyes of the Church, of the unions of couples that, consensually, have already been sharing the same house for a long time. This is a common relationship even now among the people who live in Pacoval, where among the 115 families that exist there nearly 50 percent of the couples "are together," in other words, they did not formalize their unions before the law.

The official records indicate the presence of a considerable number of children who were born in quilombos. These observations serve as examples: of the 74 quilombolas arrested in the mocambos of Inferno, Cipoteua and Caxange in Curuá river in 1813, seventeen had their affiliation identified.⁴⁰ Among the 135 mocambeiros of Curuá taken as prisoners to Belém, in the end of March 1876, 39 percent were less than ten years old.⁴¹ The mocambos from the region were increasing because of the natural reproduction of their population and the arrival of the new fugitives from slavery, by their own initiative or encouraged by the quilombolas, when they visited the villages.

> Every year from May to June, the period when the *quilombolas* come down to sell their products and get ammunition and supplies, [...] it is exactly in this time that the escapes of our slaves multiply because it is the most opportune time on account of of the facility that the flooding rivers gives them.⁴²

According to João B. Rodrigues, "it is substantial the number of these scoundrels, more than 1,000, taking into account their offspring that are born and raised there [...] I gather this just from the families I have been with. Africans living today are rare, there are 75 fugitives just in the district of Óbidos, 44 men and 31 women."⁴³

View of Pacoval (Photo: Funes).

Marambiré: dancing the "Ambirá" (Photo: Funes).

Everyday scene (Photo: Funes).

The existence of these quilombos over such a long period, with a significant number of people, implied the presence of a power and leadership structure, which was able to guarantee some unity, in order to coordinate the resistance and assure the reproduction of these societies. The first document that allows for a reading of this structure, in the mocambos of the region, comes from 1813. This document is a report about the arrest of quilombolas from Inferno, Cipoteua and Caxange, in the Curuá river. On the list of the arrested mocambeiros appear the following: João Caxange, head of the mocambo; Sebastião, the head and rebuilder of the mocambo; Manoel, the pastor of the mocambo; Ana Joaquina, the queen of the mocambo; Silvestre, the auditor of the mocambo; Caetano, church clerk. These last two died in combat.[44]

According to Barbosa Rodrigues, when the troops attacked these quilombos, "they saw through the forest, a military force and a black man, still young, who was going to be punished. Next to him there was a black African, down at his feet they saw a black woman fall, crying her eyes out begging for mercy for her son. He responded with the air of a soveriegn 'the king's words cannot be taken back.'"[45] It is interesting to note three points: First, the power of rule in the Africans' hands, there was also one of the quilombos with the name of an African "nation," Caxange, the same as Cassange; second, the "monarchical" way of governing; and, third, the existence of their own justice system. It is also important to highlight figures of the pastor, the church clerk and the auditor, that possibly the administrative structure of these mocambos did not have these definitions, but doubtless performed activities pertinent to their positions, similar to other societies, including African ones. There is some kind of continuity of the African organization and adaptation of American administrative structures. According to Tavares Bastos, black people from Trombetas lived

> under a despotic and elective government, in effect, they nominated their governor, and they say that the deputies and sub-deputies are also elected. They imitate the designation of their authorities the names they knew from the settlements.[46]

In 1875, Barbosa Rodrigues, in order to verify the information given from Bastos in 1866, recalled that when he questioned the quilombolas of Tapagem near the Trombetas river, many of whom had been living there for more than thirty years, whether or not this type of government existed, they answered

> seeking freedom, they did not subject themselves to any power, that each one rules his own family, and since the benefit was common, they lived in total union, and up until the present time there has not been one case of homicide.[47]

Considering that in the beginning of the nineteenth century there was a significant number of Africans in the mocambo, they searched for models of a power structures in their origins. Later, when the presence of local born blacks had increased, the power structure was not broken. The idea of "court," and of "despotic" governments might have disappeared, but not the authority, the chiefs, the heads of the mocambos, leaderships that consisted mostly of the elders of the quilombos. A power which until nowadays is remembered by the old ones who do not see the "respect from the young ones" anymore. The authority of an elder represented that of a father.

"Bicho Do Mato" (Forest Beast)—Survival and Sympathy

In the Amazon, the relationship between quilombola and environment was essential not only for the escape, but, mainly, for the survival and reproduction of the quilombos as a social organization different from the slave order. Busy with agricultural problems and house services, the slave, up until that point, saw a new reality right in front of him, in which, besides agriculture, he would need to hunt, fish and gather wood to guarantee survival.

According to Santa Rita, the mocambeiros who arrived in Curuá and Cuminá "were there for a long time, eating the *babaçu* (palm fruit flour made into a dough) that they called *nhamundá*. They lived like *bichos do mato* (forest beasts)."[48] From this statement, we can see evidence for the change in diet, including new food items that were not part of their regular diet. The food taken from the forest identified them as animals and the "savages" that shared the same space. The expression "*bicho do mato*" is quite symbolic, a pejorative way to refer to an indigenous person, also meaning one who belongs in the tropical forest or a child of the forest.

This "maternal relation" is felt even now in the speech of the older ones, as in the words of Rafael Printz Viana, who lives in the community of Abui, in the upper Trombetas river, for whom

> the forest is, as we say in this song—our mother waterfall—thus we also call our mother forest, our mother because you could say it is from her that we take everything, from health to [...] What I mean is, our mother forest is life.[49]

Medicines for diarrhea, headaches, and antivenom formulas for snakebites and medicines for other ailments are extracted from the forest, which serves as a large pharmaceutical laboratory, and has always been well used by these communities. It was from the living together in and with the forest, by seeing what happens there, observing animals bitten by snakes ingesting several species of leaves, that the mocambeiro discovered an antidote, used even today. "The antidote," whose formula is kept in secret and passed from generation to generation by the Assis family, became an element of identity and power in Pacoval.

In the rivers and lakes they searched, and still search, for fish, the everyday food. They salt cured large quantities to eat in the periods that fish was scarce. They incorporated turtle and turtle eggs into their cuisine. According to J. Maximiniano de Souza, from mocambo Maravilha,

> you can see the Icamiaba mountain covered in grass, black Benedito said that grass is full of sweet potatoes, that it grows there spontaneously and from it they they feed the *mocambeiros* and the savages, it is also said that on this mountain, at a certain time of the year, they lead a big hunt for mountain pig, which they sun dried to provide food for the *mocambo*.[50]

The basic economic activities of these quilombo societies were wood extraction, agriculture and, to a smaller degree, trading. The region where they settled, was, and still is, a unique grove of chestnut trees that extends from the East Paru river to the Trombetas river. In both the past and even today, the harvesting of chestnuts has constituted the natural source of income for the communities. Beside this they extracted sarsaparilla and *copaíba* oil and produced *uixi-pacu* and *piquiá* oils, used in lighting. As in other regions, they also developed agriculture of subsistence in the fields, made in small clearings opened inside the forest, where they planted vegetables and, especially, tobacco and manioc, a species of cassava good for producing flour, a basic food for the mocambeiros. According to Donga, his grandmother used to tell him that when black people ran away from captivity they

> did not take any amount of manioc. Those *caboclas*, big mulattas when they were preparing to run away, they went to the field and gathered the seeds of manioc, tobacco, all the types of plants, watermelon, *maxixe* (a squash-like fruit) and they put them in their hair [...] when they got there, they started planting, and when the others arrived, they already had enough to live on.[51]

In contrast to what was verified in other cases, the quilombos from Curuá, Cuminá and Trombetas rivers were located far away from the big urban centers and did not develop a "parasitic economy," characterized by assaulting and stealing.[52] The big complaint, on the part of the owners, was not against these practices, but in relation to the loss caused by the frequent escape of the slaves, because the mocambeiros convinced the slaves to run away.

Even developing an economy mainly based on subsistence, the quilombos produced more than they needed and so it was commercialized through street venders or sold directly in the city to the "right people." Through commercial relations, the mocambeiros got into the business model of "Aviator" merchandising.[53] They were inserted into the local environment and took on economic importance in the supplies to the regional market, as producers of agricultural goods and lumber. "When you want tobacco, they ask right away: do you want it from the *mocambo*? It is the best one."[54] In this process of insertion, there was a tacit complicity. From one side, the quilombola, when he decides who is the "right person" with whom to conduct business, he was able to get all the products that he needed and even expanded his range of information about what was happening in the city, being able to be aware of the punitive raids before they happened. On the other side, there were the street venders and the merchants of the city interested in maintaining a clientele that could guarantee them a profit; so they passed information on to the mocambeiros, hid them when they came to the village and omitted information about the location of the mocambos.[55] The link with the urban centers, by trading, was part of a network, woven by the mocambeiros, that surpassed the bond with the indigenous people and the "bush negroes" from Dutch Guiana, also in addition to linking the various mocambos of the region.

The white man increased his occupation of the area to such a degree that it forced the indigenous population to retreat further into remote areas, especially those who had escaped the actions of the missions. Once there, freed from the effects of civilization, they were able to maintain their identity and rebuild their territorial presence. It would be these remote regions that would also be occupied by black people escaping from slavery. The encounter between these "two pariahs of society" was marked by moments of conflict and alliance.

> The conviviality of the *quilombolas* appears to have been easier with the Caxuana and Tirió groups. On the other hand, more direct conflicts happened with the Kahyanas, who occupied the middle and upper Trombeta, in the first half of the nineteenth century, motivated mainly by the theft of women. According to a statement by piadze (shaman) caxuana, Tonhirama, as told to Protásio Frikel, black people from *mocambo* Maravilha attacked the village and stole their women.[56]

The indigenous people, on the other hand, got their revenge, provoking retaliation on the part of quilombolas and, thus, "the Kahyanas became afraid of the the *mocambeiros* and resolved the situation quickly. They gathered all the most essential things and left for the headwaters of Trombetas, where their relatives were."⁵⁷ This historical experience of the contact and social interaction with several ethnic indigenous groups resulted in the incorporation of elements of material and symbolic culture, mainly from the Caxuanas of the upper Trombetas and Erepecuru. One concrete example of this phenomenon of sociocultural interaction is the presence (emergence) in the black communities' imaginary of the "myth of the big snake."⁵⁸

The mocambeiros, upon taking possession of the means of resistance available to the indigenous population, renewed their capacity to overcome new challenges. Together with the natives, they learned the secrets of the forest, became familiar with the footpaths through the forest and kept in touch with the quilombolas from Suriname. Even if the communication among the mocambeiros from the upper rivers of the region and the forest "negroes" was infrequent, and the commercial connection among them done through groups of indigenous people that could come and go on both of the boundaries, especially the Xarumas and the Xiriôs, the Dutch colony and the condition of black people there were not unknown. The Brazilian quilombolas knew that, except for the general fields and the Tumucumaque mountain range, slavery did not exist anymore, especially after the decade of 1860. Miss Dica uncovered an aspect previously unknown when she affirmed that her ancestors, because of being persecuted by punitive expeditions, built a second campsite in the upper Cuminá river and that they "stayed there to be near the bay's shore, it was not far from the city of Holanda, they knew where it was but they did not go there because it was not possible."⁵⁹ If the mocambeiros from Cuminá-Panema did not go, the ones from Trombetas "opened a connection with the north and the Dutch colony because of commerce, and so these people rise up little by little and the communication increases more and more; not just black people but many Indians too."⁶⁰ P. Frikel claims, based on indigenous information, that "annually the Dyuka [Djuka] made commercial trips to Tiriô villages [...] the main mutual exchange items were hunting dogs and strong arrows from the Indians, and red cloth, beadwork and iron instruments from the black people."⁶¹

In 1858, the Óbidos deputy already alerted the provincial authorities about the risks associated with the proximity to Dutch Guiana. He said:

> The dangers that surround us are innumerous because, apart from the *mocambos* from Trombetas and some smaller ones [...] there are the Indians on this side of the Tremubitaque mountain range and on the other side of the same mountain range there are three independent republics of black people that undoubtedly must communicate with the people from here using In-

dians as intermediaries [...] From this city to Paramaribo, on the edge of Suriname, there are only 140 leagues of 18 degrees [...] The republics that I told you of before were recognized by the Dutch in 1809 and they exist along the Maroni river, another on the upper Saramaca, and other on the upper Cotica. All of them, consequently, less than 100 leagues from this city. Our farming has been weakened because of the numerous runaways that occur every day and if no action is taken certainly very soon we will be without any slaves.[62]

Having as a basis these distances, the quilombolas from Trombetas were approximately fifty to sixty leagues from the three main groups of "bush negroes":

> Aucan, Saramaccam and Moesinga or Matracone, which by the way has its own known subdivisions among the tribal people themselves, although they were rarely recognized by the others. Thus, by the Aucans general title, black people from Bonni, Paramaccan and Poregoedos are included; the Luango people belonged to Saramaccans and the Koffys to the Moesingas.[63]

The possibility of relocating to that colony, where slavery had already been abolished, was not rejected by the quilombolas on the Brazilian side; they used it as a way to put pressure on the government to recognize their condition of being free people. According to Friar Mazzarino, the mocambeiros from Trombetas suggested to the government of the province conditions for representing themselves, while keeping their freedom.

> The aforementioned black people really want to build a village and each one would pay his respective owner the amount of 300$000 réis to secure their freedom, over a four year term; older ones, however, would require a shorter term [...] They also wish, for a term of six years, to be exempt of any imposition or recruitment for civil or military duties. Lastly, they want to be ruled by a missionary exempt from any civil authority. If any one of the mentioned conditions is not met, they do not want to leave, for the reason that when the Paraguay war is over if the government does not free them they have decided to relocate to the Dutch colony.[64]

The attention is drawn to the fact that "black people" moving to villages also interested this religious man, because it would ease the missionary action with the indigenous population. On the other hand, it must be noted that the mocambeiros' command of what was happening on a larger scale, and the fact that they knew how to use that knowledge, as in the case of the war against Paraguay and the link that was made between this and the abolition of slavery, allowed them to negotiate their freedom from an advantageous position.

The communication among quilombolas happen even to this day in "Brazilian Guiana," as the region between the Tumucumaque mountain range and the Amazon river is known, making possible a strengthening of the mechanisms for information and resistance. Making themselves known to each other these various mocambos enabled an increased mobility, particularly during moments of attack. This happened with the black man Athanásio, who went to Trombetas with his companions after the destruction of his quilombo in Curuá in 1813;[65] and with Basílio Antônio, who was in Maravilha but after "his *mocambo* was destroyed by the government's troop in 1855, he went to another *mocambo* named Tururu, above Maravilha," where he was arrested in a river island of Alenquer, a distant place from this last quilombo.[66] The web of solidarity and interests, woven little by little by the mocambeiros, allowed the quilombos from the Lower Amazon to survive for the entire period of slavery.

Destroyed, Not Defeated: The Resistence of "Mocambolas"

The quilombos represented a constant threat to slave society. They were seen as a "plague," a "long-standing wound"; and they caused losses to the owners' pockets, because part of their property was escaping to the forests, reducing the workforce and resulting in a visibly ruined economy. It was up to the State to put an end to these slave refuges, reestablishing order and the peace. From the decade of 1860 on, there has been no news about any expedition that has come into the Trombetas to attack the mocambos who lived there. As for Cuminá and Erepecuru, there is never any mention in the documents of the destruction of their quilombos. Up until the decade of the 1870s, the mocambeiros from Curuá knew about the punitive attacks more often, probably because they were closer to the urban centers. We will see how the mocambos from this river were persecuted and repressed. The presence of quilombos in Curuá dates from of the middle of the eighteenth century, creating concerns for the colonial government to the point that, in 1799, it was recommended that in the punitive expeditions "there should be good guides and complete secrecy in order that the plans remain firm."[67] For an entire decade the authorities had no success in the fights against the mocambos from Curuá. In 1807, there was a special investigation against them in which, doubtless, the government's recommendations were not followed, since nothing was accomplished because of the lack of guides. And the "*mocambeiros* got more insolent and decided to move out as soon as possible. From that point forward it has never been known where they established the new mocambo."⁶⁸

The first positive result obtained by the military forces occurred in 1813, when they destroyed the quilombos in Inferno, Cipoteua and Caxange, by an expedition that lasted three months, with a body of 375 troops—almost 500 according to the commander —, among them twenty Mundurucu indigenous people, more than two hundred cartridges and ammunition to last a month.⁶⁹ Seventy four quilombolas were arrested, among them men, women, children and an an indigenous woman. Eight mocambeiros died and seventeen managed to escape. The *"quilombos* are destroyed, everything reduced to dust and all the seeds were thrown into the river."⁷⁰ Before the return to Santarém, the commander of the expedition, Manoel Joaquim Bentes, sent correspondence to the military command, asking for permission to land in front of the church Nossa Senhora da Conceição, to whom he wanted to offer the appropriate thanks

> because of so many admirable benefits, it is enough to say that with nearly 500 people and so much shooting not even one person was in danger [...] I told them to ask to the priest and to you, sir, I also ask, to be ready to conduct a mass to the Blessed Mother, I promised her that as soon as we arrive the whole troupe would attend mass, and after that we would march with the prisoners to the barracks, sir, and from there determine what your good sir deems to be the best option. ⁷¹

It was a victory party. The campaign to annihilate these quilombos faced many difficulties:

> Passing through creeks in waist-high water, they crossed steep mountains, rocky roads, and stone quarries. The result was that and the troops as well as the Indians arrived at the port nearly destroyed, where the distribution of flags was determined, but all of them were damaged [...] they spent four or five days like this, never able to discover anything. However the leader of the Mundurucu men went out and spent three days, and fortunately found by tracking, the place where they used to collect black people for their *mocambo*s. It was not easy, so much so that no other troop felt excited about destroying once and for all these awful *mocambos* that they could get, because, just marching they spent eight days to reach the first *mocambo* and another two to get to the last one [...] it can be called terrible, after all, the name of this place is Inferno.⁷²

The arrested mocambeiros were given to their owners. According to the military commander of Santarém, Manoel da Costa Vidal, many of the ones who managed to get away from the surrounding quilombos came to look for godfathers to present to their owners, they "did nothing, these three ran away, and no punishment has been given." And, depending on the treatment at the hand of the owners

> These that cost us tremendous labor, in no time at all they will have formed another *mocambo*, because they are already masters of the forests. Maybe it is worse now than how it has been. These are my feelings and what the experience over here has shown me.[73]

The prediction came true. The quilombos could be destroyed, the quilombolas could not. Just like trees which have their trunks cut off, but, still keep their roots, grow up and blossom again, or just as seeds taken by the birds and rivers are born in other places, having the same quality, the mocambos were born and reborn with the same ideal of freedom in other parts of the forests. For many years, the mocambos from Curuá were repeatedly attacked but were not seriously damaged. Most of the punitive expeditions were defeated more times than they reached success. Failures imposed by bureaucratic impediments, lack of guides, problems of natural causes like droughts or rains, the lack of will of the local authorities, especially the ones connected to the trading and dealing with quilombolas, and the fact of these people knew, in advance, about the campaigns that were being organized against them and moved themselves to other places. In July of 1849, in Santarém,

> there were two raids with 75 in line police officers and 33 Mundurucu Indians working as guides and experts. In the first one the slaves, sensing it, moved to the upper part of Curuá and the raid totally failed; in the second raid, the commander fell sick during the march, and his second in command led the maneuver to establish a perimeter around the *mocambo,* but it was executed so badly that almost all of the black people managed to escape. Only 11 were captured, but after this many slaves came to present themselves to their owners.[74]

In 1863, Curuá was the target of a new campaign, organized by the police deputy of Santarém José Pereira Macambira, Maria Macambira's husband, who did not succeed because "of the difficulties and natural obstacles that the campaign encountered." [75] Worth noting is the fact that the quilombolas "sensed" the expeditions, which has always been done using information from some ally. In this specific case, it is interesting to mention the devotion of these groups; they attributed power of the saints as very important factors for helping fight against the ones who were pursuing them. According to José Santa Rita, every time that Saint Antônio turned his back, it was a signal that an attack on the mocambo was about to happen. The story told by Miss Dica is illustrative. She heard it from her grandmother, and probably was referring to the 1863 expedition:

> It was in the morning, they went there, he was standing exactly where they were coming. Then they said: look the back of Higino, Saint Antônio, let's see how he is, he is giving a signal, let's go with the old woman, an old woman who couldn't see anymore but she knows everything, because in Africa they knew many good prayers, she made her prayers and everything goes right. Then old Higino said: look, let's get out of here, because they are coming after us, they're really coming. Then they had no doubts, they went to harvest in another place, they harvested everything, set everything on fire, and made tents and moved out of there. They had already built houses, ruffled the harvest there, made the flour, and then after five days, they finished bringing all of their belongings. Then, when that day finally came, and there was nothing left there, they were close, Maria Macambira with a man from the village, her two children, a grandson and some other people [...] but they found nothing.
>
> In the swamp, with all that water coming through, one person who was not with their party died, they were washed downstream, they were flooded, Macambira's son drowned and others died of malaria, all of them [...] Then this woman came again, when they got there to Benfica [the first waterfall of Curuá] the rain started pouring so much that she could not pass through and even almost flooded [...] Time was passing by, then quite calmly, the old father said: you know what, let's go and turn ourselves in to the government, it is the right thing to do. Take a look, they harvested the farm, made flour, sugar, harvest the coffee and took everything with them.

This was a big defeat of the quilombolas of Curuá, in 1876. They were arrested by Martinho Beato, by the order of the Justice of Alenquer, according to Santa Rica.

Luiz de Oliveira Martins, was a police deputy of Alenquer, had a house of trade on one of the river islands and for certainly maintained commercial relations with the mocambeiros. Or rather, he continued doing it when they established themselves in Pacoval, after coming back from

Belém where they were taken as prisoners.⁷⁶ In accordance with the Ministry of Justice, the president of the province affirmed that,

> not wanting to undertake force in an unproductive way, after several months, taken certain measures and using persuasive means, thanks to the intelligent execution of the plan given by the police deputy of Alenquer, major Luiz de Oliveira Martins, I was able to destroy the famous *mocambo* from Curuá in Alenquer, well known as the Inferno *mocambo*, and as a result there are 135 black people in this capital whose legal status is being verified.⁷⁷

Certainly one of the "persuasive" means used had to do with the argument that they, the quilombolas, did not need to remain as refugees, because by reason of them not being registered according to the law of 1872, they would be considered free. They were advised then to present themselves to the provincial authorities, doing it with the deputy of Alenquer, who probably offered to be their godfather.

Here we observe the statement of Manoel da Cruz, seventy years old, coming from the Coast of Africa, one of the arrested quilombolas that had already been freed by the heirs of Maria M. Pereira Macambira. He was asked

> what was the name of your owner he said that she was called Maria Majesty the Emperor, who he trusts and who will give him his freedom and to Margarida Pereira. Stated that he went to the authorities of his own volition, because he did not want to live in the woods anymore and he wanted to be of service to his majesty the Emperor in whom he trusts will give his freedom and that of his companions and relatives who advised to come with him.⁷⁸

It is interesting to observe that on 6 April 1876, D. Pedro II passed by Belém because of his trip to the United States. The *Diário de Belém* of 28 March 1876 had as opening news "*Quilombo* do Inferno," informed the arrival of major Martins, who brought with him and also presented to the president of the province

> the chief or head of the inhabitants from that *quilombo*, where there are hundreds of runaway slaves and deserters, asking for your intercession for them to be declared free slaves and the deserters forgiven, to finally restore them into the society.
>
> We do not know the point to which the abovementioned fact is correct, as we do not know if this is something the presidency will be able to do [...] what we do know is that it is necessary extinguish that *quilombo* either by

persuasive means or conciliatory means, or by force, because the *quilombo* Inferno has been, for a long time, a state within another state and constitutes a terror to the inhabitants of the surrounding areas.

In the very same day, the mocambeiros from Curuá made the news in *Jornal de Belém*, which announced their arrival by the ship Óbidos and complimented the deputy because of the success of the expedition: "without using force and with almost no money spent. The honorable deputy baptized approximately 115 of that number of black people, including men and children." In the course of 1876 and 1877, the quilombolas of Curuá were consistently on the pages of the newspapers from Belém, because after taking on their cause, they were more in opposition against provincial government more than just for reasons of abolition, as was the case of *Diário de Belém*, always pointing out loopholes in the law.

It was under the law that 115 mocambeiros, from the 135 taken to the capital, were classified in three orders: the unregistered, the freeborn and the ones in dispute. By order of the judge (according to article 6, paragraph 4 of law number 2040, dated 28 September 1871, and paragraph 4, from article 75, of the regulation expedited by decree number 5315 dated 13 November 1872) 28 quilombolas, and 35 free minors were declared free, because they were born after the Lei do Ventre Livre (Free Womb Law).[79] The others, even the ones that in the interview indicated they did not have owners, were held prisoner, for the reason that their alleged owners claimed a dispute, especially the baron of Santarém and other heirs of Maria Macabira. The disputed quilombolas, and even some considered free, were distributed among particular owners, some paid a deposit to the State, by way of trustee, of 10$000, and others paid nothing. n the first case, Roberto Heskth received three; Firmo Dória, three; Camilo Home, one; Cypriano de Melo, one, and Manoel de Barros Rodrigues, one. On the second modality, Major Chaves obtained one; Solicitor Rosa, one, and Mr. Affonso Moagim and Frederico Rhossard, 34.[80] This attitude generated criticism from the newspapers *Província do Pará* and *Diário de Belém* not because of the fact that the mocambeiros were given in exchange for a deposit, but because of the uneven manner in which they were distributed, generating an editorial dispute with Diário do Grão-Pará, where Rhossard had connections.

In the hands of the trustees, the quilombolas were effectively sent back to slavery, including the ones that had never lived as slaves, having been born in the mocambos. Something that they clearly did not accept. Miss.

Dica points this out, remembering the time when her ancestors were held captive in Belém:

> They left to look for jobs, but lots of them did not do well, they got sick. Then one day they got angry, they came from Rossá [Rhossard]. They came, arrived and told the government that they had decided to leave, that they were working, and that the payment they got was not enough even for the food. If they wanted them to work, they should earn enough for eating.[81]

With this episode, once again the quilombolas, imprisoned again, garnered attention in the newspapers' pages. The *Diário of Belém* of 25 March 1877 reported the state of abandon and violence against the mocambeiros locked in the jail, and added

> that Dr. Meira Vasconcellos interrogated the blacks and heard from them the determinant reason, of not submitting themselves to being a deposit at the Rhossard facility, whose supervisor forced them to work, without providing any clothes and giving them no more than one meal every 24 hours. This fact was confirmed by the unanimous statement of all the unfortunate people from Curuá, made to Mr. Meira Vasconcellos, in the presence of the chief of police and the public prosecutor, and yet did not result in any measures taken by those in power.[82]

Once more, deprivation, violence and the desire to be free motivated these black people to revive their time as mocambeiros. However, in these moments they also searched for legal avenues, hoping that justice would be done and they would be able to obtain, once and for all, their freedom. Actually, the "*mocambolas,*" as they had been described several times by the newspapers, faced not only the cunning of the slaveowners, but also the bureaucracy, the obstacle of the law and the unwillingness to fulfill the law. On 8 March 1877, referring to the slaves

> arrested in *quilombo* Curuá, Alenquer neighborhood, abandoned by their owners and judged free by the judge of orphans of the capital, the Ministry of Agriculture would communicate to the president of the province: 1st, I call free the slaves abandoned by their owners in accordance with article 6, paragraph 1, of the law of 28 September 1871, for a period of five years, subject to inspection by the government, being obligated to control their services, under penalty of being restrained should they live like vagabonds, working in public establishments, a constraint that will cease should they a labor contract, as determined by the referenced 6 article, 5 paragraph, and article 79 of the regulation issued by decree number 5315 of 13 November

1872; 2, I declare as free the mothers of children, who should accompany them, who should immediately be subject to the legislation in accordance with the doctrine of the 1 article, 4 paragraph, of the law that guarantees to the slave mother, that obtains freedom, the right to take with her any children under eight years old.[83]

Because of this ministerial determination and, probably, because of the reports about the conditions of quilombolas, on 28 March 1877, exactly one year after their arrival in Belém, the mocambeiros of Curuá got an important victory in justice against their alleged owners. The judge Meira Vasconcellos, "by given sentence in the question brought by slaveowners Baron of Santarem, José Joaquim Pereira Macambira and Mathias Afonso da Silva, as heirs of the deceased Mrs. Maria Margarida Pereira, against 62 quilombolas of Curuá, declared them free and ordered them to be released from the prison where they were being held."[84] The *Diário de Belém* newspaper did not lose the opportunity to pick on its enemies, comparing them to the mocambeiros:

> Whatever may be the resource that could possibly lodge an appeal, it does not and even cannot have a suspensory effect. Therefore they restored those unfortunate people to freedom, empowered by the presidency, and if they want, they may have passage to Alenquer and let the ones that do not want to return, have the resource of gbeing able to earn their daily bread with the strength God gave us.
>
> We live in a free country, where men dispense custodianship, and because they were black ones from Curuá ignorant of the fact that they needed a guardian and a deposit, there are so many around walking around in the same situation [...] and act, however. Like agents of the public power.[85]

It was the beginning of the return to Curuá.

Victims of arbitrariness, some quilombolas were still kept on the property of Rhossard, in the district of Muaná, in the island of Marajó, until September 1877, when they were helped by an adversary of the already mentioned owner and managed to runaway to Belém. In the escape, the boat where they were sailing was attacked by the police of Mauá and employees of the Carmo's mill. They brutally beat the mocambeiro Severino, Maria dos Anjos's husband, who, guided by other ones, made a petition against Frederico Rhossard. Her partners and she were coming to the capital in order to "get from the president a license for everyone to live in a place named Curuá."[86] Coming back to Curuá, to the rivers and to the forest that for a long time served them as a shelter and a support, where lots of these mocambeiros had been born, represented reconquering their own space, rebuilding their territoriality. On 18 October 1877, Maria dos Anjos and her partners Manuel Assunção, Maria José, Maria Bárbara, Evaristo, José Bicho and Maria Miquelina (Dica's grandmother) were among the passengers of the ship Inca, coming back to Alenquer. With no doubts, they joined with those who had stayed in the woods of the Curuá river, building a new black community, the Pacoval. The mocambeiros' Pacoval, of the "antidote," of marambiré, rose to the category of settlement in 1901, when they had as "governor" Alexandre, Santa Rita's grandfather.[87]

After reestablishing themselves in Curuá, at the end of the decade of 1870, they took back the lifestyle that the mocambos lived, as much from a sociocultural point of view as an economic one. Side by side the subsistence agriculture, they practiced, chestnut picking and the production of the flour, the basis of the community's economy, whose production was commercialized with street venders and dealers from Alenquer, among them Major Luiz de Oliveira Martins, what granted them a standard of life marked by simplicity.

In the view of O. Codreau, it was a way of life that was close to bestial, unrelated to the *Modus Vivendi* of civilized people:

> In Pacoval's population, the primitive *mocambeiros*, the ones who had abandoned their owners, disappeared; their children and grandchildren and even worse, not only these descendants from the *mocambeiros* inherited from their parents all the bad features [...] they returned to the savage state, to barbarism [...] In their constitution there is a mark of degeneration; they are not as strong or as big as the old slaves. This is understandable because a slave was precious to his owner, it was a market value. It was in the owner's best interest not to ruin his slave, so he treated him well. Now there are no more owners and he prefers living very badly, not working. His ideal is idleness, which, allied to the taste for *tafiá* [brandy, in the creole language], we have then the main causes of his degeneration: laziness and ignorance.[88]

The story of Codreau about this black community reveals a strong prejudice, characteristic of the anthropologic orthodoxy of the second half of the nineteenth century, having as suppositions the polygyny and the belief in the superiority of the white race. The effect, according to K. Thomas, "was to push black people very close to the level of the new belief in the animal capacity created for animals."[89]

Probably madam Codreau, in 1900, listened to the same response give to the mocambeiros of Trombetas to Barbosa Rodrigues, in 1875, who said:

> I saw the love of freedom personified there. Two black people, two brothers, Antônio and Miguel, walking skeletons, with white hair showing their age of more than seventy years old, naked, working but not being able to, being in danger when crossing waterfalls, always restless, choosing an unfortunate life he enjoys with tranquility and rest rather than feeling they have to earn power from under the owner. Advising them to come back to their families that they abandoned, that they would be guaranteed their freedom, they answered to me we prefer the life of a free animal to the well-being of a life in captivity.[90]

One feeling present in the mocambos of Curuá and from all the lower Amazon, today present in their descendants who form the black communities of the region, that maintain this absolute sense of freedom, making the past of their grandparents a utopia, is well expressed in the words of Maria Francisca, who lives in Trombetas. She says:

> what I lament and what I feel is seeing our table taken by others and we stay there just looking, hungry and we cannot eat. I am very sorry about that. In my grandparents time, when I was growing up, all this here was free, we have no worries: ah! We have no food, we fish, get a turtle and then we eat...nowadays, we miss that. If we get a turtle, we have to hide to eat, otherwise we can be arrested, we try to survive, here in our land, I miss a lot our freedom time, the time that has gone by.

New realities, new confrontation, new ways of fight. That is history.

19

APPENDIX

The Map of Buraco do Tatu
(The Armadillo Hole)

JOÃO JOSÉ REIS

The first news on the Buraco do Tatu *quilombo* date from 1743. Twenty years after, an attack by a troop of two hundred men, among them indigenous persons, led by Joaquim da Costa Cardozo, resulted in the death of four men and the imprisonment of sixty one *quilombolas* punished by different penalties: whipping, forced labor, fire branding with the letter F as in *fugido* (escaped), deportation and return to slavery.[1]

The blueprint published here is a facsimile from the original kept at the Historical Ultramarine Archive created by Isabel Sangareau da Fonseca in 1948 as part of the collection of the Bahia's State Public Archive. This blueprint constitutes one of the few known cartographic representations of quilombos in Brazil. Another two blueprints of quilombos in Minas Gerais are published in this edition as illustrations in the chapter by Laura de Mello e Souza.[2]

The blueprint of Buraco do Tatu represents not only a physical description of a quilombo—with its houses, street plans, vegetable gardens, brooks, vegetation, defense system and other aspects—it also includes a rare representation of human figures of quilombolas, although this is symptomatic only of quilombolas killed by invaders.[3] Its explanatory caption at once identifies each sector of the blueprint and explains explicitly or in a concealed way the action of the quilombolas and the troops on that day of 1763. Such caption could actually be understood as a narrative of the final moments of Buraco do Tatu. Its transcription follows below:

> Blueprint of the *quilombo* known as Buraco do Tatu at Itapoã coast that on 2 September 1763 was attacked by Major-Captain of the Conquest of the *Gentio Bárbaro* [Foreign Savage], Joaquim da Costa Cardozo. Letter A: a fake road covered by stakes that shows the entrance. Letter D: trenches hidden under stakes. C: planks used as footbridges that could be lifted or lowered used during the day and taken away at night. N: house of the warden in

charge of the footbridges. E: a fountain. T: a Black woman who was washing and screaming killed herself with a rifle. P: a Black man whose legs were broken by a grenade and killed himself. G: a Black man who was able to shoot and was killed. R: a very old Black woman known as a sorcerer who killed herself. Z: the captain's house. B: the village houses of the people. L: stake trench, with stakes as high as a man's chest to as low as a palm. Q: the passion fruit arbor. F: the vegetable gardens. I: the swamp around the *quilombo* deep enough to submerge a man. O: the small footbridge that made way to the small Quilombo. S: the small Quilombo. X: the houses. V: the stake houses. M: footbridge to cross to the ocean. Here the term footbridge is used with the same meaning as a rafter crossing the swamp and the ditches, these ditches were around five palms wide equipped inside with pointy sticks.

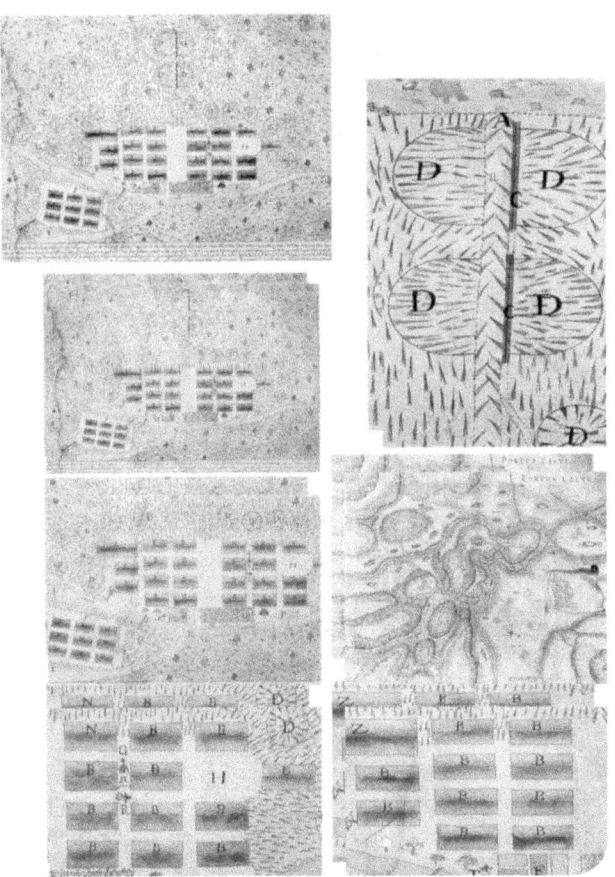

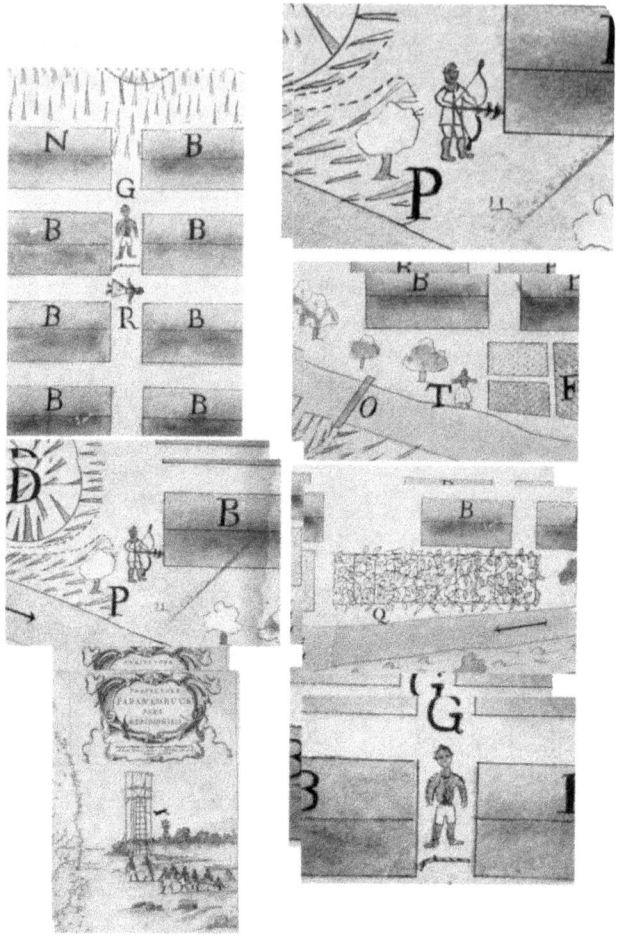

A curiosity of this caption is that the letters that guide the reader do not follow an alphabetic order different, for instance, as that done by the map drawer of the quilombos of Minas Gerais in which the captions follow a strict numeric order. Other captions of the time in maps and blueprints were also conventionally ordered either by numbers or letters.[4] This implies that the map drawer of the Buraco do Tatu did not follow the custom; he did not want to classify just places and actions. He wanted to tell a story rather than offer a dry register.[5] Observe for instance the scattering of human figures in alphabetic order: G, P, R, and T. Observe that when writing the captions he unites them to point out a human drama: the resistance and death of the four persons symbolizing the destruction of that community. The original scattering in the drawing might mean an endeavor to establish a chronological order in the events —each quilombola had died in different moments of the invasion— unlike the caption that would be a more thematic representation, more "interpretative."

It becomes evident the drawer's choice to register in his map solely the world of the enemy, in this case the defeated. Its world remains hidden. He did not bother to register, for instance, the position of the assault troop, although in the caption this is mentioned as an agent of action that resulted in the death of four quilombolas and the caption title itself highlights the attack and its commander.

The quilombolas are predominant in all iconographic representations and in the narrative, either individually —as when the dead quilombolas are brought out or the houses of the leader and the watchman— or collectively, for instance, when the caption refers to the houses of the quilombola "People." There we find quilombolas building houses, planting vegetables, organizing themselves politically and above all establishing a magnificent defense system that enables them to travel safely through a maze of stakes and ditches.[6]

Map and caption give us a vivid impression of a community of runaways intelligently organized, efficient, well protected and dangerous to the slavocratic order. The military engineering, the symmetry of the houses, the capacity to produce food products, the political leadership, the religious authority, the resistance to the attack witness the presence of a superior enemy. Facing the aftermath of the action of the capitães-do-mato troops, the author of the blueprint wanted to celebrate a superior victory as well.

These comments do not exhaust the possibilities of interpretation of this extraordinary document, of the circumstances and the process of its production. They are presented here as matter of introduction for the maps we reproduce and as suggestion for documents of this kind to be more deeply explored as a communicative effort about what those who produced such documents saw, lived and most importantly about how they represented, both in iconography and verbally, the world of the others, in this case the world of the quilombolas of Buraco do Tatu. From the perspective of the quilombolas, as stated before, the enemy-drawer makes us see clearer their capacity for social, economic and military organization and how they made use of a territory under pressure.

NOTES

INTRODUCTION

1. See John Monteiro, *Negros da Terra* (São Paulo: Companhia das Letras, 1994).
2. On Suriname, see various works by Richard Price, among which the following stands out: *First-time* (Baltimore: Johns Hopkins University Press, 1983) and *Alabi's World* (Baltimore: Johns Hopkins U. Press, 1990); on Jamaica, Mavis Campbell, *The Maroons of Jamaica, 1655-1796* (Trenton: Africa World Press, 1990) and various articles by Barbara Kopytoff, "The Early Political Development of Jamaican Maroon Societies," *The William & Mary Quarterly* 35, no. 2 (1978): 287-307; "The Development of Jamaican Maroon Ethnicity," *Caribbean Quarterly* 22 (1976): 33-50; "Colonial Treaty as Sacred Charter," *Ethnohistory* 26 (1979): 45-64; "Jamaican Maroon Political Organization: The Effects of the Treaties," *Social and Economic Studies* 25 (1976): 87-105. About quilombos in various regions of the Americas, see the following collected volume by Richard Price, which, although somewhat outdated, still remains useful, *Maroon Societies* (Baltimore: Johns Hopkins University Press, 1979). The same author updated the historiographical discussion in "Resistance to Slavery in the Americas: Maroon and their Communities," *The Indian Historical Review* 15, nos. 1-2 (1988-9): 71-95.
3. It is not always possible to trace the origin of these groupings back to the slavery period. On these communities, see Eliane Cantarino O'Dwyer, ed., *Terra de Quilombos* (Rio de Janeiro: Associação Brasileira de Antropologia, 1995) and José Jorge de Carvalho, ed., *O Quilombo do Rio das Ras* (Salvador: EDUFBA/CEAO, 1996).
4. [Translator's note:] "Quilombo dos Palmares" was not only the largest quilombo in colonial Brazil, but also the one that managed to resist the longest, thus becoming emblematic of slave resistance.
5. See an evaluation of the historiography on slavery of this period in Luís Carlos Lopes, *O Espeiho e a Imagem: O Escravo na Historiografia Brasileira (1808-1920)* (Rio de Janeiro: Achiame, 1987), *passim*.
6. Raimundo Nina Rodrigues, *Os Africanos no Brasil*, 5 ed. (São Paulo: Editora Nacional, 1977), Chapter 3; Arthur Ramos, *O Negro Brasileiro* (Rio de Janeiro: Civilização Brasileira, 1935); *A Aculturação Negra no Brasil* (São Paulo: Nacional, 1942); Edison Carneiro, *O Quilombo de Palmares*, 4th ed. (São Paulo: Nacional, 1988), the edition of which includes an article, "Sin-

gularidades dos quilombos," pp. 13-25, first published in 1953, in which Carneiro emphasizes the relation among quilombos and the surrounding society. Also, in the "Apresentação" (Presentation) to this edition, Waldir Freitas Oliveria discusses the evolution of Palmarian studies; Roger Bastide, *As Americas Negras* (São Paulo: Difel/Edusp, 1974), esp. Chapter 3; R. K. Kent, "Palmares: An African State in Brazil," *Journal o f African History* 6, no. 2 (1965): 161-75; Eugene Genovese, *From Rebellion to Revolution* (New York: Vintage, 1979), Chapter 2.

7. Pay special attention to the classic work by Melville J. Herskovits, *The Myth of the Negro Past* (Boston: Beacon Press, 1958 [1941]), which remains a source of inspiration, similarly to the collected volume by Joseph E. Holloway, ed., *Africanisms in American Culture* (Bloomington: Indiana University Press, 1990).

8. The inspiration is already present in the classical essay by Sidney Mintz and Richard Price, *An Anthropological Approach to the Afro-American Culture* (Philadelphia: Institute for the Study of Human Issues, 1976), which, nonetheless, defines a rapid Afro-American process of cultural formation that cannot be generalized. In a recent article, analyzing the African institution of the *kilombo*, which inspired the Palmarians to organize themselves, Kabengele Munanga suggests that the Brazilian quilombo would be a "copy" of the African, but then he vehemently clarifies his point about the adaptation that has possibly taken place in Brazil, from which we conclude that there was no copying as such. See K. Munanga, "Origem e Histórico do Quilombo na África," *Revista USP* 28 (1995-6): 63.

9. On Palmares and the Black Movement in the 1920s and 1930s, George Reid Andrews, *Blacks in São Paulo, Brazil, 1888-1988* (Madison: Wisconsin University Press, 1991): 145-8. Aderbal Jurema wrote *Insurreições Negras no Brasil* (Recife: Editora Mozart, 1935). On the communist connections of Edison Carneiro, including his persecution after the movement of 1935, see Waldir F. Oliveira and Vivaldo da C. Lima, *Cartas de Edison Carneiro e Arthur Ramos* (São Paulo: Corrupio, 1987): 79, 83, 91-93 *et passim*; and Deoscoredes M. dos Santos, *Axé Opô Afonjá* (Rio de Janeiro: Institute Brasileiro de Estudos Afro-Asiáticos, 1962) 23 (this reference was brought to us by Vivaldo da Costa Lima).

10. Clóvis Moura, *Rebeliões da Senzala* (São Paulo: Edições Zumbi, 1959 [there is a more recent, revised and expanded edition of this work published by Mercado Aberto, Porto Alegre, 1988]); Clóvis Moura, *Quilombos, Resistência ao Escravismo*, Série Princípios (São Paulo, Ática, 1993. Also see Luiz Luna, *O negro na luta contra a Escravidão* (Rio de Janeiro: Leitura, 1968); Décio Freitas, *Palmares, a Guerra dos Escravos*, 5th ed. (Porto Alegre: Mercado

Aberto, 1984 [revised and expanded edition from the Spanish original published in 1971 and in Portuguese in 1973]). Among the "left" bibliography on Palmares is the work published in the magazine *Anhembi* in 1956, and the recently re-edited work of surrealist and Trotskyist, Benjamin Peret, *O Quilombo dos Palmares: Crônica da "República dos escravos," Brasil 1640-1695* (Lisboa: Fenda, 1988). In a book format, the most recent Marxist interpretation of Palmares comes from Ivan Alves Filho, *Memorial dos Palmares* (Rio de Janeiro: Xenon, 1988). An analysis of the so-called "Paulista school" does not fit here. On this topic, see, among others, Richard Graham, *Escravidão, Reforma e Imperialismo* (São Paulo: Perspectiva, 1979), Chapter 1. Within this "school," the exception is the work of historian Emilia Viotti da Costa, *Da Senzala à Colônia* (São Paulo: Difel, 1966), which presents a more complex perspective on the relations produced by slavery while paying close attention to the discussion on slave rebellions. A pointed critique of the objectification of slaves comes from Sidney Chalhoub, *Visões da liberdade* (São Paulo: Companhia das Letras, 1990): 35-43 *et passim*.

11. See, for instance, Carlos Magno Guimarães and Ana Lucia Lanna, "Arqueologia de quilombos em Minas Gerais," *Pesquisas: Antropologia* 31 (1980): 147-64.

12. In eighteenth century Maranhão, it only took two runaway slaves sheltered in the forest to determine the formation of a new quilombo, as we learned in Matthias Rohrig Assunção's chapter and in what follows it.

13. See, for instance, among already available studies, Julio Pinto Vallejos, "Slave Control and Slave Resistance in Colonial Minas Gerais, 1700-1750," *Journal of Latin American Studies* 17 (1985): 1-34; Katheleen Higgins, "Masters and Slaves in a Mining Society: A Study of Eighteenth Century Sabará, Minas Gerais," *Slavery and Abolition* 11, no. 1 (1990): 58-73; Carlos Magno Guimarães, *Uma Negação da Ordem Escravista: Quilombos em Minas Gerais no Século XVIII* (São Paulo: Icone, 1988): 46-53. And on mining quilombos in Maranhão, Mundinha Araújo, *Insurreição de Escravos em Viana, 1867* (São Luís: Sioge, 1994), 71.

14. Guimarães, *Uma Negação da Ordem Escravista*.

15. See João J. Reis, "'Nos achamos em campo a tratar da Liberdade': Quilombos e Revoltas Escravas no Brasil," *Revista USP* 28 (1995-6): 32-3.

16. [Translator's note:] *Calhambolas* was a term attributed to runaway slaves that remained nomadic.

17. [Translator's note:] *Mestre de campo* was a military rank that is currently equivalent to colonel.

18. [Translator's note:] *Caboclo* is an ethnically mixed person, born of white and indigenous parents.

19. For a more detailed discussion see Flávio Gomes, *Histórias de Quilombolas, Rio de Janeiro* (Arquivo Nacional, 1995).
20. On these quilombos, see Mary Karasch, *Slave life in Rio de Janeiro, 1808-1850* (Princeton: Princeton University Press, 1988), 311-5. In nineteenth century Brazil, "crioulo" was a denomination for a black slave born there.
21. [Translator's note:] The term *pardo* was attributed to those with darker skin, of mixed race.
22. [Translator's note:] *Coiteiros* were those who gave shelter or protected wrongdoers.
23. [Translator's note:] *Crioulo* in colonial Brazil was a term attributed to a black person born in Brazil. In other Lusophone colonies it meant a descendant of European born in the Americas. In contemporary Brazil the term has a generally derogatory connotation and can be attributed to either blacks or mulattos.
24. [Translator's note:] *Cearense* is someone who is from the state of Ceará.
25. Barbara J. Fields, *Slavery and Freedom on the Middle Ground: Maryland during the Nineteenth Century* (New Haven: Yale University Press, 1985), 193.

I

1. Acknowledgments: We owe thanks to the following colleagues: Scott Allen, Célia Marinho Azevedo, Fernando Brittez, Lourdes Dominguez, Joseph Miller, James Cameron Monroe, Charles E. Orser, Jr. João Reis, Michael Rowlands, Michael Shanks, Siân Jones, Deborah M. Pearsall, John Thornton, and Andrés Zarankin. The ideas expressed here are our own, for which we alone are therefore responsible. We must also mention the institutional support from the National Science Foundation, Ford Foundation, the National Endowment for the Humanities, The World Archaeological Congress, Brazilian National Research Council (CNPq), São Paulo State Research Foundation (FAPESP) and the University of Campinas (Department of Historya and NEPAM).
2. J. Thornton, *Africa and Africans in the Making of the Atlantic World* (Cambridge: Cambridge University Press, 1992), 125.
3. J. Thornton, "Early Kongo-Portuguese Relations: A New Interpretation," *History in Africa* 8 (1981): 183-202.
4. J. C. Miller, *Kings and Kinsmen - Early Mbundu States in Angola* (Oxford: Clarendon Press, 1976), 182.
5. J. C. Miller, "A Marginal Institution of the Margin of the Atlantic System: The Portuguese Southern Atlantic Slave Trade in the 18th Century," in

Slavery and the Rise of the Atlantic System, ed. B. L. Solow (Cambridge: Cambridge University Press, 1991), 123-4.
6. P. Curtin, *The Rise and Fall of the Plantation Complex - Essay in Atlantic History* (Cambridge: Cambridge University Press, 1990), 37.
7. J. Thornton, "Legitimacy and Political Power: Queen Njinga 1624-1663," *Journal of African History* 32 (1991): 29.
8. Miller, *Kings and Kinsmen*.
9. J. Thornton, "The Art of War in Angola, 1575-1680," *Comparative Studies in Society and History* 30 (1988): 361.
10. Ibid., 377.
11. Curtin, *The Rise and Fall of the Plantation Complex*, 203.
12. Cited in C. Barleus, *História dos Feitos Recentemente Practicados durante Oito Anos no Brasil* (Itatiaia: Belo Horizonte, 1994), 252; Charles E. Orser Jr., "Toward a Global Historical Archaeology: An Example from Brazil," *Transforming Anthropology* 14, no. 1 (1994): 14.
13. P. P. A. Funari, "Maroon, Race and Gender: Palmares Material Culture and Social Relations in a Runaway Settlement," in *Historical Archaeology: Back from the Edge*, eds. P. P. A. Funari, M. Hall, and S. Jones (London: Routledge, 1999), 308-327.
14. Ibid.
15. See R. K. Kent, "Palmares: An African State in Brazil," in *Maroon Societies*, ed. R. Price (Baltimore: John Hopkins University Press, 1979), 180.
16. T. K. M. Buakasa, "Croyances et connaissances," in *Racines Bantu*, ed. Théophile Obenga and Simão Souindoula (Libreville, 1991), 165-187.
17. J. M. Price, "Credit in the Slave Trade and Plantation Economies," in *Slavery and the Rise of the Atlantic System*, ed. B. L. Solow (Cambridge: Cambridge University Press, 1991), 293-340, 298.
18. F. J. Turner, *The Frontier in American History* (New York: Henry Holt and Co., 1920).
19. A. Pollini and P. P. A. Funari, "Greek perpections of Frontier in Magna Graecia: Literature and Archaeology in Dialogue," *Studia Historica* 23 (2005), 331-344.
20. S. Turner and R. Young, "Concealed Communities: The people at the Margins," *International Journal of Historical Archaeology* 11, no. 4 (2007), 300.
21. I. Kopytoff and S. Miers, eds., *Slavery in Africa: Historical and Anthropological Perspectives* (Madison: University of Wisconsin Press, 1977), 3-81.
22. H. O. Kiriama, "The Iron-using Communities in Kenya," in *The Archaeology of Africa*, eds. T. Shaw, P. Sinclair, B. Andah, and A. Okpoko (London: Routledge, 1993), 497.

23. J. C. Miller, "Retention, Reinvention, and Remembering: Restoring Identities through Enslavement in Africa and under Slavery in Brazil," in *Enslaving Connections: Changing Cultures of Africa and Brazil during the Era of Slavery*, eds. J. C. Curto and P. E. Lovejoy (New York: Humanity Books, 2004), 93.
24. L. Mott, "Era Zumbi homossexual?" *EAVirtual* 3 (2005), 85-88.
25. A Horning, (2007) "Materiality and Mutable Landscapes: Rethinking Seasonality and Marginality in Rural Ireland," *International Journal of Historical Archaeology*, 11, no. 4 (2007), 358-378.
26. C. E. Orser Jr., "The Material Implications of Colonialism in Early Nineteenth-Century Ireland," in *Was Ireland a Colony? Economics, Politics and Culture in Nineteenth-Century Ireland*, ed. T. McDonough (Dublin: Irish Academy, 2005), 66-86.
27. Arthur Ramos, *As Culturas Negras no Novo Mundo* (São Paulo: Editora Nacional, 1946); Edison Carneiro, *O quilombo de Palmares* (São Paulo: Editora Nacional, 1958).
28. Clóvis Moura, ed., *Rebeliões da Senzala—Quilombos, Insurreições, Guerrilhas* (São Paulo: Zumbi, 1959); Décio Freitas, *Palmares—A Guerra dos Escravos* (Rio de Janeiro: Graal, 1978).
29. Clóvis Moura, *Sociologia do Negro Brasileiro* (São Paulo: Ática, 1988), 174-177.
30. Freitas, *Palmares*, 42.
31. Ibid., 45.
32. Ibid., 36.
33. Abidas A. Nascimento, *O Quilombismo* (Petrópolis: Editora Vozes, 1980).
34. Ibid., 46.
35. Ibid., 47.
36. Célia Marinho Azevedo, "A Nova História Intelectual de Dominick La Capra e a Noção de Raça" in *Narrar o Passado, Repensar a História*, eds. M Rago and R Gimenez (Campinas: Editora IFCH, 2000), 123-134.
37. S. J. Allen, "A 'Cultural Mosaic' at Palmares? Grappling with the Historical Archaeology of a Seventeenth—Century Brazilian Quilombo," in *Cultura Material e Arqueologia Histórica*, ed. P. P. A. Funari (Campinas: Unicamp/IFCH, 1998), 141-178.
38. M. Rowlands, "Black Identity and Sense of Past in Brazilian National Culture," in *Historical Archaeology—Back from the Edge*, eds. P. P. A. Funari, M. Hall, and S. Jones (London: Routledge, 1999), 336.
39. C. E. Orser Jr., *A Historical Archaeology of the Modern World* (New York: Plenum Press, 1996), 55.
40. P. P. A. Funari, "The Archaeological Study of the African Diáspora in Brazil: Some Ethnic Issues," in *African Re-Genesis, Confronting Social Issues in the*

Diaspora, eds. J. B. Haviser, and K. C. MacDonald (London: UCL Press, 2006), 184-190.
41. P. P. A. Funari and F Brittez, eds., *Arqueologia Histórica em América Latina. Temas y Discusiones Recientes* (Mar del Prata: Suárez/Unicamp, 2006).
42. Jean-Godefroy Bidima, *La Philosophie Negro-Africaine* (Paris: Presses Universitaires de France, 1995), 3-5.
43. Gilberto Freire, *The Masters and the Slaves* (New York: Alfred Knopf, 1946); Fernando Ortiz, *Cuban Counterpoint* (Durham: Duke University, 1995).
44. See Overview in P. P. A. Funari and L. Dominguez, "Esclavitud y Arqueologia de la Resistência em Cuba y Brasil," *Revista do Museu de Arqueologia e Etnologia* 14 (2004): 209-223.
45. For example, see Funari and Brittez, *Arqueologia Histórica em América Latina*.
46. J. J. Reis, "Quilombos e Revoltas Escravas no Brasil (Maroons and Slave Rebellions in Brazil)," *Revista USP* 28 (1996), 17.
47. Funari, "The Archaeological Study of the African Diáspora in Brazil."
48. Roberto DaMatta, "Nepotismo e jeitinho brasileiro (Nepotism and the Brazilian way)," *Jornal da Tarde, Caderno de Sábado 7 September* (São Paulo: Brasil) 4, no. 5 (1991), 399.
49. P. P. A. Funari and A. V. Carvalho, *Palmares, Ontem e Hoje* (Rio de Janeiro: Zahar, 2005).
50. C. A. Campos, *Zumbi, Tiradentes* (São Paulo: Perspectiva/Edusp, 1998).
51. P. M. Leite, "No túnel da História," *Veja*, January 31, 1996, 103.
52. A. C. Roosevelt, *The Moundbuilders of the Amazon* (San Diego: Academic Press, 1991).

2

1. The initial presentation took place at a conference, "Palmares: 300 Anos," held in São Paulo in November 1994, and the resulting paper was published in Portuguese as "Palmares como poderia ter sido," in *Liberdade por um fio: Historia dos quilombos no Brasil*, eds. João José Reis and Flávio dos Santos Gomes (São Paulo: Companhia das Letras, 1996), 52-59. This revised and expanded version of that Portuguese paper was published in English in 2003 as "Refiguring Palmares," *Tipiti* 1, no. 2, 211-219.
2. Raymundo Nina Rodrigues, *Os Africanos no Brasil*, 2 ed. (São Paulo: Biblioteca Pedagogica Brasileira, 1936).
3. Arthur Ramos, *O Negro Brasileiro* (Rio de Janeiro: Civilização Brasileira, 1935).
4. Ernesto Ennis, *As Guerras nos Palmares* (São Paulo: Editora Nacional, 1938).

5. Edison Carneiro, *Guerra de los Palmares* (Mexico: Fondo de Cultura Economica, 1946).
6. M. M. de Freitas, *Reino Negro de Palmares* (Rio de Janeiro: Ministério da Guerra, 1954).
7. R. K. Kent, "Palmares: An African State in Brazil." *Journal of African History* 6 (1965), 161-175.
8. Clóvis Moura, *Rebeliões da Senzala: Quilombos, Insurreições, Guerrilhas* (Rio de Janeiro: Conquista, 1972).
9. Décio Freitas, *Palmares: A Guerra dos Escravos* (Porto Alegre: Movimento, 1973).
10. See Pedro Paulo de Abreu Funari, "A Arqueologia de Palmares: Sua Contribução para o Conhecimento da História da Cultura Afro-Americana," in *Liberdade por um Fio: Historia dos Quilombos no Brasil*, eds., João José Reis and Flávio dos Santos Gomes (São Paulo: Companhia das Letras, 1996), 26-51.
11. I also write, unabashedly, from the perspective of an ethnographic historian—a perspective developed by a generation of anthropologists, like myself trained in the 1960s—Greg Dening, Renato Rosaldo, David William Cohen, and others (see Richard Price, "Invitation to Historians: Practices of Historical Narrative," *Rethinking History* 5, no. 3 (2001), 357-365).
12. The English word "maroon," like the French and Dutch *marron*, derives from Spanish *cimarrón*—itself based on an Arawakan (Taino) root. See José Juan Arrom, "Cimarrón: apuntes sobre sus primeras documentaciones y su probable origen," in Manuel A. García Arévalo, *Cimarrón* (Santo Domingo: Fundación García Arévalo, 1986), 13-30. *Cimarrón* originally referred to domestic cattle that had taken to the hills in Hispaniola, and soon after to Indian slaves who had escaped from the Spaniards as well. By the end of the 1530s, it was already being used primarily to refer to African American runaways, and the word had taken on strong connotations of "fierceness," of being "wild" and "unbroken." My comparative perspective on maroon societies in the Americas was first spelled out in Price, *Maroon Societies: Rebel Slave Communities in the Americas* (New York: Doubleday/Anchor, 1973).
13. In 2010, the Saamaka People decided that the spelling of their name should be changed from "Saramaka"—which had been the conventional spelling—to "Saamaka," which conforms to their own pronunciation.
14. Richard Price, *To Slay the Hydra: Dutch Colonial Perspectives on the Saramaka Wars* (Ann Arbor: Karoma, 1983).
15. Price, *First-Time: The Historical Vision of an African American People* (Baltimore: Johns Hopkins University Press, 1983); *Alabi's World* (Baltimore: Johns Hopkins University Press, 1990); *Travels with Tooy: History, Memory,*

and the African American Imagination (Chicago: University of Chicago Press, 2008).
16. For details, see Price, *Alabi's World.*
17. Recent evidence from Cuba suggests that the idea that Cuban Maroon communities conducted raids, including rape and vandalism, in order to terrorize the planter population, does not match the historical evidence. See Gabino Corzo La Rosa, *Runaway Slave Communities in Cuba: Resistance and Repression* (Chapel Hill: University of North Carolina Press, 2003). This fits my general impressions from elsewhere in the Americas as well.
18. Caneiro, *Guerra de los Palmares,* 40.
19. Nelson Nadotti and Carlos Diegues, *Quilombo* (Rio de Janeiro: Achiamé, 1984), 169-171.
20. Richard Price and Sally Price, *Les Marrons* (Châteauneuf-le-Rouge: Vents d'ailleurs 2003).
21. See, for example, Richard Price, "Scrapping Maroon History: Brazil's Promise, Suriname's Shame," *New West Indian Guide* 72 (1998), 233-255.
22. Price, *Rainforest Warriors: Human Rights on Trial* (Philadelphia: University of Pennsylvania Press, 2011).
23. Price, *Peuple Saramaka contre État du Suriname: combat pour la forêt et les droits de l'homme* (Paris: Karthala, 2012).
24. See, for example, Freitas, *Palmares,* 46.

3

1. Jean Delumeau, *História do medo no Ocidente (1300-1800)* (São Paulo: Companhia das Letras, 1989), 198.
2. Robert Slenes, "Malungu, Ngoma vem!": África coberta e redescoberta no Brasil," *Revista USP* 12 (dez.-jan.-fev. 1991/1992).
3. *Santidade* was the name that Jesuits gave, first of all, to a certain Tupinambá ritual (*caraimonhang*), in which special shamans called *caraíbas* came into contact with dead ancestors, by becoming incarnated in them sometimes, and urged the group to war and search the "land without evil," a sort of paradise on heroic Tupi mythology. Although Jesuits regarded sanctity of caraíbas as false, the name was eventually spread among settlers, and then designating not only the ritual but also the movements derived from it, like wars, migration and indigenous uprisings in the seventeenth century.
4. Ronaldo Vainfas, *A heresia dos índios—catolicismo e rebeldia no Brasil colonial* (São Paulo: Companhia das Letras, 1995).
5. Editor's note: James H. Sweet cites a use of the word *"Santidade"* to be a word synonymous with *mocambo* or *quilombo*, meaning a hideout for run-

away slaves. He indicates that while the first communities of this sort were composed largely of indigenous people, and that it was African slaves joining the indigenous resistance, later it was African marooned slave colonies that were joined by indigenous runaways. James Sweet, "African Identity and Slave Resistance in the Portuguese Atlantic," in *The Atlantic World and Virginia, 1550–1624*, ed. Peter C. Mancall (Chapel Hill: University of North Carolina Press, 2007), 240.

6. For a more accurate etymological discussion, see Stuart Schwartz, "Mocambos, quilombos e Palmares," *Estudos Econômicos*, 17 (1987), 83-6.
7. Décio Freitas, *Palmares—a guerra dos escravos*, 2a. edição (Rio de Janeiro: Graal, 1978).
8. See Freitas, *Palmares*, 110-1.
9. "Carta de el-rey a Gaspar de Souza" (Lisboa, 19 de janeiro de 1613). Library of Itamaraty, Rio de Janeiro, ff. 218-218v.
10. Richard Price, "Les sociétés d'esclaves marrons" in *Esclave, facteur de production—l'économie politique de l'esclavage*, ed. S. Mintz (Paris: Bordas, 1981), 87-118.
11. Freitas, *Palmares*, 129-30.
12. Stuart Schwartz, *Segredos internos—engenhos e escravos na sociedade colonial* (São Paulo: Companhia das Letras, 1988), 40-73.
13. Antônio Vieira, "Sermão XXVII" (Bahia, anos 1680) in *Padre Antônio Vieira*, ed. Hemani Cidade (Lisboa, 1940), vol. III, 111.
14. Vieira, " Sermão XIV. Na Bahia, à irmandade dos pretos de um engenho em dia de São João Evangelista, no ano de 1633," 30-1.
15. Antônio Vieira, *Sermões, vol. 7* (Lisboa: Officina de Miguel Deslandes, 1679-1689), 402-3.
16. Jean Delumeau, *Le péché et la peur—la culpabilization en Occident* (Paris: Fayard, 1983), 513.
17. Actually, Benci, based on a disciple of Aristotle, highlighted three things concerning slaves: work, bread and food. See T. Wiedmann, *Greek and Roman slavery* (Baltimore: Johns Hopkins University Press, 1981), 186.
18. Jorge Benci, *A economia cristã dos senhores no governo dos escravos (1705)* (São Paulo: Grijalbo, 1977), 49.
19. Ronaldo Vainfas, *Ideologia e escravidão—os letrados e a sociedade escravista no Brasil colonial* (Petrópolis: Vozes, 1986).
20. Andre JoãoAntonil, *Cultura e opulência do Brasil por suas drogas e minas (1711)*, 2a. edição (São Paulo: Melhoramentos/INL, 1976), 91.
21. Ibid., 92
22. See João Lúcio de Azevedo, *História de Antônio Vieira* (Lisboa: Livraria Clássica Editora, 1920), 2: 372.

4

1. The research on legislative sources, which partially subsidized the preparation of this article is part of a larger project funded by CNPq. I appreciate the comments and suggestions made by Sidney Chalhoub and João José Reis on the first version of this article. [Translator's note:] *Capitães do mato* (sing. *capitão do mato*) were a kind of police force in plantation Brazil. Their main role was to "hunt" enslaved Africans. Martins Pena's play "O terrível capitão do mato" (1845) has been translated by Sarah J. Townsend as "Fearsome Slave Catcher."
2. It is evident that there are previous partial documents about Palmares, and in a certain way every narrative implies an interrogation of the past and in this sense, a historical attitude. However, leaving aside the differences between the history "Brazil" or "Portuguese America," after Frei Vicente do Salvador, Rocha Pita was the one who took upon himself the task of writing a *history*. About this author and his work see Jose Honorio Rodrigues, *História da história do Brasil—historiografia colonial* (São Paulo: Melhoramentos/INL, 1979), 494-503.
3. Cf. Sebastião da Rocha Pita, *Historia da América portuguesa (1724)* (São Paulo: Edusp/Itatiaia, 1976), 213-9.
4. Ibid., 214.
5. Ibid., 216-9.
6. These reports were recently issued by Leonardo Dantas Silva, ed., *Alguns documentos para a história da escravidão* (Recife: Fundaj/Massangana, 1988), 17-25, 27-44, respectively.
7. The text of Rocha Pita is virtually reproduced by Loreto Couto (1757) and Southey (1817), serving as an important documentary source for several other authors. The suicide of Zumbi is also stated by Lindley (1805), Oliveira Martins (1876), Rodrigues (1905) and more recently, by M. M. de Freitas (1954). See also Domingos Loreto Couto, "Desagravos do Brasil e "glórias de Pernambuco," *Anais da Biblioteca Nacional*, 25 (1903), 187-94; Thomas Lindley, *Narrativa de uma Viagem ao Brasil* (São Paulo: Nacional, 1969), 128-33; Robert Southey, *Historia do Brasil*, 4a ed. (São Paulo: Melhoramentos, 1977), vol. III, 19-23; Oliveira Martins, *O Brasil e as Colônias Portuguesas* (Lisboa: Guimarães, 1953), 63-5; Nina Rodrigues, *Os Africanos no Brasil*, 5a ed. (São Paulo: Nacional, 1977), 71-93; M. M. de Freitas, *Reino Negro de Palmares* (Rio de Janeiro: Biblioteca do Exército, 1954), vol. 2, 769.
8. It is, no doubt, an absolutely natural procedure in the case of a member of the Royal Academy of Portuguese History and the Brazilian Academy of the Forgotten that, in Varnhagen's criticism, wanted to be the Brazilian Tito

Livio. See also; Francisco Adolfo Varnhagen, *Historia do Brasil*, 7a ed, (São Paulo: Melhoramentos, 1962), vol. iv, 40.

9. See, as an example of the abduction of the Sabine, the roughness of the original republic *(sic)* of Palmares and the reference to Spartacus, Decio Freitas, *Palmares. A guerra dos escravos*, 2a ed. (Rio de Janeiro: Graal, 1978), 37, 41, 124, respectively.

10. José Honorio Rodrigues does not censor himself in commenting on the *Historia da America portuguesa* and ends up stating that its author "is anti-indian, anti-black, pro-slavery, anti-Jewish, anti-paulista, anti-Brazil, pro-Portugal [...]The Dutch attacks are not against the Brazilians, but against Portugal, as their America is Portuguese, and not Brazilian." See also Rodrigues, *Historia da historia do Brasil*, 498.

11. Rocha Pita gets to the point of insinuating that the "glorious and so useful end [that] had the war [...] against the blacks of Palmares" was one of the factors taken into account so that the governor of Pernambuco subsequently obtained the "superior placement of Viceroy of India." The same reference is also made by Loreto Couto. See also Pita, *Historia da America portuguesa*, 219 and Couto, "Desagravos do Brasil," 194.

12. All expressions in quotation marks belong to Pita's *Historia da America Portuguesa*, especially, 216-9.

13. See Carta do Governador Fernão de Souza Coutinho from 1 June 1671 about the "increase in the *mocambos* of the upheaved blacks that gave support to Palmares," Ernesto Ennes, *As Guerras nos Palmares* (Sao Paulo: Nacional, 1938), 134.

14. Agostinho Perdigão Malheiro, *A Escravidão no Brasil. Ensaio Histórico, Jurídico, Social*, 3a ed. (Petrópolis: Vozes/INL, 1976), vol. II, 34, note 67.

15. For further details on this question see my *Campos da Violencia* (Rio de Janeiro: Paz e Terra, 1986), especially, 296-8.

16. Both in *Ordenações manuelinas* as in *Filipinas,* the penalty for those who hid fugitive slaves was banishment. Note that neither of the determinations, however, concerned the escape of slaves in the colony, since the exile was to the island of São Tome, in the case of *Ordenanças manuelinas,* and for Brazil in the *Filipinas*. There are, however, other posterior determinations with specific penalties for settlers from Brazil that committed this crime. See "Dos que ajudam a fugir, ou encobrem os cativos que fogem," *Ordenanças do senhor rey d. Manoel (1521)*, Coimbra, Real Imprensa da Universidade, 1797, livro v, titulo LXXVII, pp. 234-5 and "Dos que dão ajuda aos escravos cativos para fugirem ou os encobrem," *Código Philippino ou Ordenações e Leis do Reino de Portugal... (1603)* (Ed. Candido Mendes de Almeida), 14ª ed., Rio de Janeiro, Typ. do Instituto Philomathico, 1870, livro v, título LXIII,

p. 1212. For measures related to Brazil, see, for exemple, "Carta régia de 3 de novembro de 1696 para o governador do Rio de Janeiro," *Arquivo Nacional (RJ)*. These values are applied in the case of black slaves, for "white slaves [Arabs] or Indian" the "finder's fee" was a thousand *réis*. Whoever exceeded the period of fifteen days at the delivery of the runaway became to be considered a thief subject to penalties relating. The determination also authorized that judges could torture a fugitive summarily, with up to forty lashes, to know who was his master. See "Da pena, que haverão os que acham escravos, aves, ou outras coisas e as não entregam a seus donos nem as apregoam," *Código Philippino*, livro v, titulo LXII, 1210-2., cod. 952, vol. VIII, fl. 60.

17. These values are applied in the case of black slaves, for "white slaves [Arabs] or Indian" the "finder's fee" was a thousand *réis*. Whoever exceeded the period of fifteen days at the delivery of the runaway became to be considered a thief subject to penalties relating. The determination also authorized that judges could torture a fugitive summarily, with up to forty lashes, to know who was his master. See "Da pena, que haverão os que acham escravos, aves, ou outras coisas e as não entregam a seus donos nem as apregoam," *Código Philippino*, livro v, titulo LXII, 1210-2.

18. See "Dos quadrilheiros," *Código Philippino*, livro I, titulo LXXIII, 166-8. Candido Mendes de Almeida notes that the creation of these officers goes back to Don Fernando I; the legislation which served as the basis for this title, however, dates from 1570.

19. See Lopes Gonçalves, "Instituições do Rio de Janeiro colonial, os quadrilheiros," *Revista do Instituto Histórico e Geográfico Brasileiro*, 205 (1949), 401-11. Vide também Mello Barreto Filho e Hermeto Lima, *Historia da Polícia do Rio de Janeiro* (Rio de Janeiro: Ed. A Noite,1939), 27-33; Lara, *Campos da Violencia*, 39-41.

20. The literature about it is extremely scarce, but we should emphasize the analytical effort of José Alípio Goulart, *Da fuga ao Suicídio* (Rio de Janeiro: Conquista, 1972), especially, 69-103. See also Mario Baldo, *O Capitão-do-mato*, Masters dissertation (Curitiba: Universidade Federal do Paraná, 1980); Carlos Magno Guimarães, *Uma Negação da Ordem Escravista* (São Paulo: Ícone, 1988), especially, 63-99.

21. On this point, see, for example, Freitas, *Palmares*, 76-7 and Goulart, *Da fuga*, 96.

22. See "Relação das guerras feitas aos Palmares de Pernambuco no tempo do Governador Dom Pedro de Almeida de 1675 a 1678," Silva (org.), *Alguns documentos*, 27-44, and Pedro Paulino da Fonseca, "Memória dos feitos que se deram durante os primeiros anos de guerra com os negros *quilombolas* dos Palmares, seu destroço e paz aceita em junho de 1678," ibid, 45-64.

23. For a detailed and critical analysis of these expeditions, see Ennes, *As guerras nos Palmares*; Edison Cameiro, *O quilombo dos Palmares, 1630-1695* (Sao Paulo: Brasiliense, 1947); Freitas, *Palmares*; Ivan Alves Filho, *Memorial dos Palmares* (Rio de Janeiro: Xenon, 1988).
24. Commentators considered that expeditions of 1676-8 were the major responsible for the defeat of Palmares, and not the army headed by Domingos Jorge Velho described by Rocha Pita. See also Alfredo Brandão, "Os negros na historia de Alagoas," *Estudos Afro-Brasileiros*, 1 (ed. fac-símile) (Recife: Fundaj/Massangana, 1988),. 60-77. I do not intend to go further on this controversy, nor wrangling over the number of soldiers or dates; what matters is that the joining of forces was and continued to be the primary expedient to end such big and strong quilombos.
25. See "Condições ajustadas com o governador dos paulistas Domingos Jorge Velho em 14 de agosto de 1693 para conquistar os negros de Palmares," in *Alguns documentos*, ed. Silva , 65-9; "Carta do governador de Pernambuco Caetano de Melo e Castro de 18 de fevereiro de 1694 sobre a gloriosa restauração dos Palmares" (from where the quote came from); "Carta de Caetano de Melo e Castro de 4 de agosto de 1694 em que da noticia do feliz sucesso que teve nos Palmares," see also Ennes, *As guerras nos Palmares*, 194-9. The problems faced by people from São Paulo to obtain money, land and other compensations for victory are analyzed by Ennes and Cameiro, *O quilombo dos Palmares*.
26. "Relação das guerras feitas aos Palmares de Pernambuco no tempo do Governador dom Pedro de Almeida de 1675 a 1678," in *Alguns documentos*, ed., Silva , 27.
27. Compare, "Relação das guerras," 41-4 and da Fonseca, "Memória dos feitos," 64.
28. "Consulta do Conselho Ultramarino de 8 de agosto de 1685, em que o governador João da Cunha Sotto-Mayor dá conta das pazes que pedem os negros dos Palmares," See also Ennes, *As guerras nos Palmares*, 143-5.
29. "Alvará de 10 de março de 1682," *Código philippino,* livro iv, aditamentos, 1045-7. Freitas did a beautiful analysis of this "alvará," situating it in the context of post-failure promoted peace by Pedro de Almeida. See Freitas, *Palmares,* 134-9 and also Alves Filho, *Memorial*, 99-103.
30. In 1671, Fernão de Souza Coutinho, stating that Pernambuco was so dangerous with Palmares as it had been with the Dutch, justified it by saying that "the residents in their own homes and plantations have the enemies that can defeat them." In 1687, a letter from Pernambuco, to present some "remedies to the damage of gentile Palmares," pondered that "our army, who can tame the pride of Holland [...] has no effect achieved against these bar-

barians." Caetano Melo e Castro, in 1694, when informing the king about the "happy victory" over Palmares, added that it "was not evaluated as less than the expulsion of the Dutch [...]." See also Ennes, *As guerras nos Palmares,* 134, 161, 194.

31. Lindley, in 1805, under the impact of "the last events of Sao Domingos," commenting on the exceptional number of imported blacks that had been added to the existing slaves in Brazil, noted that such disproportion had not endangered the "public tranquility" because the Portuguese settlers had received a "terrible lesson" with Palmares and, since then, had adopted "superficial humanity" in the conduct related to their slaves. Compare Lindley, *Narrativa de uma viagem ao Brasil,* 128.

32. "Let there be whips, let there be chains and shackle, all the time and with rules and due restraint, and you will see how in a short period of time a rebellion of the slaves is suppressed, for the arrests and beatings, more than any other kind of punishment, kills their pride and break their sense of achievement." Compare, Jorge Benci (SJ), *Economia cristã dos senhores no governo dos escravos (1705)* (Sao Paulo: Grijalbo, 1977), 126 and 165. Regarding this issue, see my *Campos da violencia, passim.*

33. Kent states that such measures were abandoned in the beginning of the Napoleonic wars, what would have contributed for the beginning of the revolts in Bahia after 1807. Compare R. K. Kent, "Palmares: an African State in Brazil," *Journal of African History,* 6: 2 (1965), 175.

34. "Carta do governador do Rio de Janeiro de 5 de julho de 1726," *Documentos Interessantes para a Historia e Costumes de Sao Paulo,* 50 (1929), 60-1, and "Parecer do Conselho Ultramarino de 18 de setembro de 1728," *Documentos Históricos,* 94 (1951), 28-30. The question is present also in manifestation of the Bahia government advising against an agreement with the King of Dahomey, among other reasons, for not being "appropriate that this captaincy join one large number of slaves of a single nation, what could easily result in pernicious consequences." "Carta de Fernando Jose de Portugal a Luis Pinto de Sousa, de 21 de outubro de 1795," *Revista do Instituto Histórico e Geográfico Brasileiro,* 59 (1896), 413-6.

35. The bond between Palmares and the creation of posts of Capitão-do-mato, besides being present in the correspondence of the Governors of Minas Gerais, is quickly set out by Kent, "Palmares: an African State," 175, and also A. J. R. Russell-Wood, *The Black Man in Slavery and Freedom in Colonial Brazil* (New York: St. Martin's Press, 1982), 126.

36. In 1625, in Rio de Janeiro, besides a punitive expedition against the *quilombos,* a reward of 6000 was set for slave caught "close to Serra dos Orgãos" and "half the value of the slave" for those who were caught beyond that, as tells

Vivaldo Coaracy, stating that this is the date of the "institution of Capitães-do-mato in Rio de Janeiro." See Vivaldo Coaracy, *O Rio de Janeiro no século XVII* (Rio de Janeiro: Jose Olympio, 1965), 65-6 and also 158. See also Luiz Luna, *O negro na luta contra a escravidão, 2nd ed.* (Rio de Janeiro: Catedra/INL, 1976), 131-8. S. B. Schwartz mentions a solicitation from 1612 for the nomination of a "field captain" to each parish of Pernambuco. Alípio Goulart republishes an act of the Count of Atouguia from 1656 appointing a capitão-do-mato to the village of Cairu and refers to the creation of a position in Cachoeira, in the hinterlands of Bahia, June 1672; in Sao Paulo, there are mentions dating from the second half of the seventeenth century. See Goulart, *Da fuga,* 79-80 and 279, and S. B. Schwartz, "*Mocambos, quilombos* e Palmares: a resistencia escrava no Brasil colonial," *Estudos Econômicos,* 17, número especial (1978), 67.

37. Moraes says "captains of entries" or "do-mato" designated "those who catch and arrest runaway or marooned slaves." See Antonio de Moraes Silva, *Diccionário de língua portuguesa* (facsímile da 2a ed.) (Rio de Janeiro: Off. da S. A. Litho-Typographia Fluminense, 1922), vol. 1, 342. Raphael Bluteau, in his *Vocabulário portuguez e latino* (Coimbra: Collegio das Artes da Companhia de Jesus, 1712), 2, 126-127, does not mention such these terms.

38. The information comes from a letter of Don Fernando Jose de Portugal, on 30 April 1788, which states that the real estate was not burdened with these posts "because of a statute given to the assault captains on January 28, 1676." See also Goulart, *Da fuga,* 79.

39. Since the end of the sixteenth century, the term *capitão* was used to designate the commander of a *Bandeira* (or company) of ordinances, but in legal documents pertaining to 1570, 1574, 1709, 1749 and 1758 the attribution to hunt runaway slaves is not included. Guimaraes, examining documents of Minas Gerais in the period of 1710-1798, verifies the existence of a military hierarchy between what he calls generally "men of the woods" (*Homens-do-mato*), without it meaning any integration of those with the troops paid by the Crown. However, in describing the militias and relying on Vilhena, Caio Prado Junior mentions the existence of "independent companies with special missions": in Bahia there were "a group [and] two companies of assault captains" that, in peacetime, hunt runaway slaves and criminals. See Graça Salgado (coord.), *Fiscais e meirinhos. A administração no Brasil colonial* (Rio de Janeiro: Nova Fronteira, 1985), 166, 231, 313 e 404-5; Guimaraes, *Uma negação,* 23 and 107; Caio Prado Junior, *Formação do Brasil contemporâneo,* 15a ed. (Sao Paulo: Brasiliense, 1977), 312.

40. This patent letter reproduced by João Francisco Dias Cabral, "Narração de alguns sucessos relativos à guerra dos Palmares de 1668 a 1680," *Revista do Instituto Arqueológico e Geográfico Alagoano*, 7 (dez. 1875), 184-5.
41. Compare "Cartas regias de 19 e 21 de novembro de 1696," *Arquivo Histórico Ultramarino*, cod. 246, fls. 24 e 26.
42. See "Provisão de 26 de novembro de 1714," *Arquivo Histórico Ultramarino*, cod. 247, fls. I -IV.
43. Southey associates the creation of the post in 1724 to the discovery of a planned rebellion to a Holy Tuesday in Minas Gerais: "in consequence of discovery, many blacks fled to the dense forest, fearing that the same evil already experienced in the province of Pernambuco, have instituted the so-called *capitães-do-mato*." Malheiro simply mentions the "Statute of 1724." Varnhagen associates the creation of the captain-major position in the villages, at the beginning of the eighteenth century, to the institution of the captains of the woods in 1722. Schwartz states that "the statute of the capitães-do-mato was published in 1715 and republished in 1722. The version that remained into force was that of December 17, 1724." See Southey, Historia do Brasil, vol. III, 144-5; Malheiro, *A escravidão no Brasil*, vol. I, p. 50 e vol. II, 35; Varnhagen, *Historia do Brasil*, vol. III, 334. Schwartz, "*Mocambos, quilombos* e Palmares," 78.
44. Goulart mentions a statute from the 12th of June, 1701 allegedly made in Vila Rica by Gomes Freire de Andrade. Given the fact that Gomes Freire was sent to Brazil only in 1733, that date is a mistake, probably motivated by the bad transcription made at *Documentos Interessantes*, xiv (1895), 255-6, which he utilizes as source to republish the document; there, the "gang of 1701" appears in a sequence of copies made by the Count of Valadares to be sent to the Governor of São Paulo. All of it leads us to believe that the correct date of this statute is the 12th of June, 1741. See Goulart, *Da fuga*, 79-80 and 281-2.
45. The path here, was initially suggested to me by Southey (*Historia do Brasil*, vol. III, 144-5) and confirmed by later reading the correspondence of the Count of Assumar. Schwartz's article "*Mocambos, Quilombos* e Palmares" is also suggestive in this sense, as it treats both of Palmares and *Mocambos* from Bahia and Minas.
46. "Statuteo para os capitães-do-mato de 4 de fevereiro de 1715," see Guimaraes, *Uma negação*, 129.
47. The procedure of using fixed landmarks to stipulate the "finder's fee" had already appeared in 1680, when the town council of the village of Santa Maria Madalena determined that the "capitão-mor-de-campo" of Alagoas would receive 2000 *réis* to bring back slaves to the villagers, 4000 *réis* if they

were too far from the village, 8,000 for "beyond the limits of Pernambuco," 10,000 for "those from Bahia" and 12,000 *réis* "being from the Palmares woods." This is also present in "Statuteo de Capitão-do-mato de 12 de abril de 1794," passed by the town council of Rio de Janeiro, which discriminates the value of finder's fee based on the distance between the parishes. See Cabral, *Livro de registros de provisões e registros do Senado da Câmara, 1793-1796*, Arquivo Geral da Cidade do Rio de Janeiro, cod. 16-2-23, fl. 106, respectively.

48. "Aditamento de 7 de março de 1716," see Ibid, 130.
49. "Bando de 20 de dezembro de 1717" and "Ordem de 15 de janeiro de 1718," *Revista do Arquivo Publico Mineiro*, xxiv n° 2 (1933), 442–445.
50. "Carta de 13 de julho de 1718," *Revista do Arquivo Publico Mineiro*, III (1898), 251-2.
51. See "Provisão de 12 de janeiro de 1719," *Documentos Interessantes*, xxv (1895), 246-7.
52. "Carta de 20 de abril de 1719," *Revista do Arquivo Publico Mineiro*, III (1898), 263-6.
53. See "Cartas, ordens, despachos e bandos do governo de Minas Gerais, 1717-1721," *Revista do Arquivo Publico Mineiro*, XXIV n. 2 (1933), especially, 459-602.
54. See also among others "Carta de lo de junho de 1719 para o governador da Bahia" and "Bandos de 21 de novembro de 1719," *Revista do Arquivo Publico Mineiro*, XXIV n 2 (1933), 562 e 600-2. It is not shown that those measures have been compiled.
55. "Rules of the captains of the woods promulgated by Dom Lourenço de Almeida, Governor of Minas Gerais, on December 17, 1722, in the village of Ribeirão do Carmo," *Revista do Arquivo Público Mineiro*, II (1897), 389-91.
56. In this case, the statute specifies, the arrest could only be executed by solicitation of the slaveholder or if it was a slave belonging to another district.
57. In 1703, one Alvará determined that before incarcerating the "runaway blacks," diligences provided by ordinances should be enforced to verify whether they were free or slaves. Being free, they should be released at once. In the slave's case, if one could not discover who their owner was, even after issuing edicts, he should sell the slave in public space, discount the expenditures with his apprehension, upkeeping and finder's fee and the rest should go to the general treasurer of the State. See "Alvará de 5 de maio de 1703," *Documentos Históricos*, 32 (1936), 445-7.
58. The Governor of Minas seemed to follow, here, previous royal orders addressed to the Governor of Rio de Janeiro, which indicated that the captains-of-field and members of their escorts should not be prosecuted for the

"accidental deaths or those born of resistance" which might have happened during the attacks on the quilombos. These measures were necessary because if the captains were condemned by the killings, it could be provided "the occasion for such blacks to do in this province [of Rio de Janeiro] what they did in Palmares of Pernambuco." See "Carta regia de 24 de setembro de 1699, dirigida ao governador do Rio de Janeiro," *Coleção das ordens regias mais necessárias ou curiosas que se achavam dispersas e em confusão na Secretaria do Governo do Rio de Janeiro reduzidas a sua ordem natural de 1597 a 1779*, Biblioteca Nacional do Rio de Janeiro, Seção de Manuscritos, cod. 3, 4, 1, vol. I, n. 59.

59. This text published by *Arquivo Público Mineiro*, II (1897), 389-91, transcribes this paragraph with the respective note on the margin saying that this "chapter" had been excluded. In the *Documentos Interessantes*, xiv (1895), 247-50, the same document is transcribed, but based on copies sent by Valadares to the Governor of São Paulo in 1769, in which the paragraph does not appear, indicating the effective exclusion.

60. Clearly, this was not a regular motion to the point that we can take in 1722 as a fixed chronological marker. Besides all the controversy about dates that permeates the scarce bibliography on the subject, just remember the previous statute from 1676 and attempts such as the Council of Vila Rica in registering capitains of the woods active in that region in 1713 (See Goulart, *Da fuga*, 72). In 1715 the Marquis of Angeja gave specific instructions to a *capitão-mor-de-entradas* from Bahia, which contained several elements present in the general regulations, as authorization to kill and injure, the differential payment made for the arrests according to the distance, as well as the taxation of the "quintos reais." See *Documentos Históricos*, 54 (1941), 17-8.

61. As it can be seen in the documentation, such problems stemmed not only from attitudes or practices of the Capitães-do-mato in relation to the fugitives, but could ensue, many times, from the masters and other military officials in contact with them. Sometimes the Capitães-do-mato delivered the slaves directly to the masters, getting paid with higher amounts than the ones normally paid when the slaves were put in jail; other times, it was the opposite, with the slaveholders refusing to pay the right "salaries" owned to the Capitães-do-mato etc.

62. The documentation of the Council of Campos dos Goitacases from the middle of the eighteenth century presents a large amount of references to doubts regarding the types of salary payment of the Capitães-do-mato. We also have found criminal processes and other documents from the end of the eighteenth century mentioning cases of arrests and processes of Capitães-do-

mato arrested or prosecuted for murdering people from the quilombos. See also in my work *Campos da violencia,* especially 297-301.

63. See "Carta do conde de Sarzedas aos oficiais da Câmara de São Paulo, de 23 de junho de 1733," *Revista do Arquivo Municipal de Sao Paulo,* XLIX (1938), 119.

64. "Statuteo para os capitães-do-mato de 20 de julho de 1733," *Revista do Arquivo Municipal de Sao Paulo,* XLIX (1938), 119-22.

65. In Bahia, for example, the Council began to regulate the question through a by-law from 1727. In Minas, however, the highest patents continued to be granted only by the governor, while the positions of soldiers and airmen were provided by senior officers. See Goulart, *Da fuga,* 96, and Guimaraes, *Uma negação,* 67.

66. For those interested in more details, see my *Campos da violencia,* chapter XII. The most curious may even see specific tables about it (relation XI from annex II), that are part of the thesis, with the same title, defended at University of São Paulo, in 1986.

67. In the case of Rio de Janeiro, the hierarchy between the patents seems to accompany the range of the jurisdiction granted to each position, being the capitão-do-mato linked to the parishes and the capitão-mor-de-entradas nominated for the "extramural" region or various "parishes of the city and its suburbs. *Livro de registros de provisões e registros do Senado da Câmara, 1793-1796* and *Livro de registros de provisões e registros do Senado da Câmara, 1796-1801,* Arquivo Geral da Cidade do Rio de Janeiro, cod. 16-2-23 and 16-2-22, respectively.

68. For a more detailed analysis of the relation between colonial and metropolitan dominance, as well as the different levels of repression to the fugitives and member of quilombos, see my *Campos da violencia,* 30-41 and 308-14.

69. "Alvará em forma de lei de 3 de março de 1741," *Colleçao cronológica de leis extravagantes, posteriores a nova compilação das Ordenações do Reino* (Coimbra: Real Imprensa da Universidade, 1819), vol. III, 476.

70. "Provisão de 6 de março de 1741," Biblioteca Nacional de Lisboa—Serão de Reservados, *Legislação sem cota.* Perhaps the text of this provision, which mentions a statute of 1724, is the source of the confusion of Southey and Malheiro, and also of Schwartz, regarding the date of the statute of the capitães-do-mato. Schwartz ("*Mocambos, quilombos* e Palmares," 78) is based in sources from the Arquivo Nacional da Torre do Tombo (Mss. do Brasil, 28, 307-309v) to date the definitive statute of the capitães-do-mato in 1724, which may indicate that I might be wrong.

71. This is actually the same Statute from 1722, whose third paragraph provided as follows: "Those blacks who are arrested in *quilombos* distant from settle-

ments, and that are formed with more than four individuals, settled with ranches and large pestles, the fee paid for those blacks will be twenty eights of gold." See *Documentos Interessantes*, XIV (1895), 248.

72. This is the already mentioned Carta Regia from September 24, 1699. In 1731, the "many and continuous offenses" committed in Minas by "bastards, carijós, mulattos and blacks," led the king to grant also to the governor and the hearing officers of that province the power of death penalty for slaves who killed their masters.

73. "Bandos de 12 e 14 de junho de 1741," *Documentos Interessantes*, xiv (1895), 255-7, the first published also by Goulart, *Da fuga*, 281-2, but in both places erroneously with the date of 1701.

74. It is interesting to notice that the minimum of five fugitives and the dwelling be in a "depopulated" place, characteristics present in the provision of March 6, 1741, are not mentioned in the gang of Gomes Freire from June 12 of that same year, which simply commands to meet the statute with regard to the *quilombo* "even though [...] they have not built ranches or pestles (food mills)." Being away from the centers of settlement, however, seems to have been an important characteristic, to the point that Moraes translates the term "*quilombo*" by "home located in the woods or wilderness, where calhambolas or runaway slaves live." See Moraes Silva, *Diccionario*, vol. 2, 542.

75. The fugitives arrested in "*quilombos* in this city [Sao Paulo]" worth 8 thousand *réis*, but those captured in *quilombos* "at a greater distance" could yield more, according to the arbitration based on leagues travelled from prison. See "Statuteo de 20 de Julho de 1733," *Revista do Arquivo Municipal*, XLIX (1938), 120.

76. See also "Acórdão da Câmara da Vila de Sao Salvador dos Campos dos Goitacases de 4 de Setembro de 1757," *Copia das posturas da Câmara de Campos dos Goitacases*, Biblioteca Nacional do Rio de Janeiro, cod. 3,3,2, doc. n. 393.

77. See *Documentos Interessantes*, xiv (1895), 245-56. See also the allegations of the Governor Dom José de Portugal, in a letter dated from April 30, 1788, in which he stood for the continuity of the positions of Capitão-do-mato, created by the provision of November 26, 1714: besides arresting the fugitives, "the farm spends nothing with them," as the masters of the fugitives "satisfy the due diligence." Eduardo de Castro e Almeida, "Inventario dos documentos relativos ao Brasil existentes no Archivo da Marinha e Ultramar de Lisboa," *Anais da Biblioteca Nacional*, 34 (1912), 82.

78. "Decisão n. 18, guerra," *Collecção das Leis do Brasil* (Rio de Janeiro: Imprensa Nacional, 1809), 20. It is interesting to notice that the recommendation from the Count of Linhares regarding the choice of "black and brown men"

in the companies of "Capitães-do-mato, it seems to consolidate previous practices of incorporating free colored men in these activities.

79. In 1841, in Pará, the Capitães-do-mato were even exempt from military service. See Goulart, *Da fuga*, 71.
80. What does not necessarily mean that the specific literature about Palmares is extensive. From the third and last revised edition of Freita's *Palmares. A guerra dos escravos,* in 1981, by the way, few have bothered to conduct a specific study about the quilombos of Serra da Barriga. The most recent work that I know of is the work by de Alves Filho, *Memorial dos Palmares.*
81. Although the term "republic," initially used by Rocha Pita, is the most common to characterize Palmares, some as Aires de Casal, qualify as monarchical the governance regime of the Serra da Barriga *mocambos*. See Manuel Aires de Casal, *Corografia brasílica, ou relação historico-geografica do reino do Brasil (1817)* (Belo Horizonte: Itatiaia/Edusp, 1976), 256.
82. On the ethnic origins of blacks of Palmares, see Rodriges, *Os africanos no Brasil,* 77-8 and 88-93; Kent, "Palmares: An African State," and also Schwartz, "*Mocambos, Quilombos* e Palmares," 81-6. Freitas vehemently challenges the existence of slavery among them, see *Palmares,* 38.
83. In 1669, the regal instructions for the new governor of Pernambuco clearly consisted in recommendations to extinguish Palmares at any cost. See Freitas, *Palmares,* 92.
84. The description is made by Freitas, 97.
85. "Carta do governador de Pernambuco Caetano de Melo e Castro de 18 de fevereiro de 1694 sobre a gloriosa restauração dos Palmares," see also Ennes, *As guerras nos Palmares,* 194.
86. "Termo de vereação e resolução que se tomou sobre se fazerem luminárias pela restauração de Palmares de 25 de fevereiro de 1694," see Pedro Tomas Pedreira, "Os *quilombos* dos Palmares e o Senado da Câmara da Cidade do Salvador," *Mensario do Arquivo Nacional,* XI, n. 3 (1980), 16.
87. Desembargador Rodrigo de Souza da Silva Pontes—"Quais os meios de que se deve lançar mão para obter o maior numero possível de documentos relativos a historia e geografia do Brasil," *Revista do Instituto Histórico e Geográfico Brasileiro,* 3 (1841), 151-4. See also Norberto de Souza's intervention in "Ata da 233a sessão do dia 22 de agosto de 1851," *Revistav do Instituto Histórico e Geográfico Brasileiro,* 14 (1851), 490-2.
88. See Martins, *O Brasil e as colônias portuguesas,* 64, and Nina Rodrigues, "A Tróia negra. Erros e lacunas da historia de Palmares," *Diário da Bahia* (20, 22 e 23 de agosto de 1905), later reproduced in *Os Africanos no Brasil,* Chapter III.

89. See Pedro Calmon, *Historia do Brasil* (Sao Paulo: Nacional, 1941), vol. II, 412, n. 3.
90. Joaquim Nabuco, *A Escravidão* (ed. compilada do original manuscrito por Jose Antonio Gonçalves de Mello) (Recife: Fundação Joaquim Nabuco/Ed. Massangana, 1988), 106-9.
91. The poem "Saudação a Palmares" wasn't published before his death but it was later included in the collection *Os escravos*. See also this very interesting article of Dale T. Graden, "Historia e motivo em 'Saudação a Palmares' de Antonio Frederico de Castro Alves (1870)," *Estudos Afro-Asiáticos*, 25 (dez. 1993), 189-205.
92. It was after the creation of the United Black Movement Against Racial Discrimination (MNU), in 1978, that the 20th of November, anniversary of Zumbi's death, was chosen as the "National Day of Black Consciousness."
93. The petition was published in the newspaper *O Paiz* (October 26, 1887). See Evaristo de Moraes, *A campanha abolicionista (1879-1888)*, 2ª ed. (Brasília: Ed. Universidade de Brasilia, 1986), 251-4.

5

1. I am thankful to CNPq for the research and post-doctoral fellowships that allowed the collection of this material in archives in Portugal. I am also grateful to Professors Beatriz Gois Dantas, Cândido da Costa e Silva, Jocélio Teles dos Santos, João Jose Reis, Maria Lúcia Mott, Marcelo Ferreira de Cerqueira, and Waldeloir Rego for their insightful comments and bibliographic recommendations that greatly enriched this essay.
2. Frei Agostinho da Conceição, "Sermão do glorioso lusitano santo Antônio, pregado no seu convento e mesmo dia na cidade do Rio de Janeiro a 13 de julho de 1674" (Lisbon: Oficina Antônio Rois d'Abreu, 1675); frei Antonio do Rosário, *Sorte de santo Antônio* (Lisbon: M. Manescal, 1701).
3. Padre Fernando Lopes, *Santo Antônio de Lisboa, Doutor Evangélico* (Braga: Editora Boletim Mensal, 1946). According to Amadeu Amaral, "the popular saints are mirrors of the living soul of the communities and none of the saints was more complete than Saint Anthony," in *Tradições populares* (Sao Paulo: Hucitec, 1976), 364; Gastão Bettencourt, *Os três santos de junho no folclore brasileiro* (Rio de Janeiro: 1947). Pedro Calmon, "Santo Antônio de Lisboa, de Pádua e do mundo," oração proferida no Real Gabinete Português de Leitura, Rio de Janeiro, no 750 aniversário da morte do santo (Salvador: Museu de Arte da Bahia, 2 edição, 1995).
4. Padre Antônio Vieira, *Sermões* (Porto: Lello e Irmãos Editores, 1959); Amaral, 350, refers, without elaborating, to the function of this saint as capitão-

do-mato during slavery in Brazil. Quirino Ribeiro Jr. "Investigação sobre o culto de Santo Antônio," *Revista Sociologia* (SP), volume III, março (1941), 21.

5. Armando Mattos, *Santo Antônio de Lisboa na tradição popular* (Porto: Livraria Civilização, 1937), 18. According to this author, 57 hospices and holy houses had Saint Anthony as their patron in Portugal from the fifteenth century to the eighteenth century; there were three hundred statues of him in the churches of the Patriarchate of Lisbon in 1742. Compare, frei João de Santo Antonio, *Oratórios de santo Antônio* (Lisboa, 1742). Also in the early years of Brazil, Saint Anthony always was the most revered saint. It was the name most commonly attributed to the boys in baptism and the most repeated name day in the national toponymy: only in Minas Gerais are there 118 towns, villages and cities dedicated to the saint of Lisbon, followed by Saint Sebastian, with 88 locations and Santana, with 56. Waldemar Almeida Barbosa, *Dicionário histórico-geográfico de Minas Gerais* (Belo Horizonte: Editôra Saterb, 1971).

6. Miguel Lopez Ferreira, *Epítome da vida, ações e milagres do glorioso padre santo Antônio de Lisboa* (Lisboa: Oficina Ferreiriana, 1732); padre José Pereira Baião, *Epítome crono-genealógico e crítico da vida, virtudes e milagres do prodigioso português santo Antônio de Lisboa* (Lisboa: Oficina de Antônio de Souza Silva, 1735); frei Miguel Pacheco, *Epítome de la vida, acciones y milagros de santo Antônio natural de Lisboa* (Madri: Julian Paredes, 1646) (edição portuguesa: Lisboa, Henrique Valente Oliveira, 1658); George Cardoso, *Agiológio lusitano dos santos e varões ilustres em virtude do reino de Portugal e suas conquistas* (Lisbon: Oficina Antonio Graensbeeck de Mello, 1966).

7. P. M. Henscheinio et *alii*, *Acta sanctorum, [Junii]* (Paris: Victorem Palme, 1867), 237 e ss.; Donald Attwater, *The Penguin Dictionary of Saints* (England: Penguin, 1965); David H. Farmer, *The Oxford dictionary of saints* (New York: Oxford University Press, 1987).

8. *Folha de S. Paulo*, 12 abr. 1993, "Amazônia ganha fragmento de santo Antônio." Even today, over 5,000 letters from devotees asking favors or recognizing miracles delivered by the Saint Anthony intercession reach the basilica of Padua daily.

9. Vieira, *Sermões*, 32.

10. Ibid., 122.

11. Padre João B. Castro, *Mapa de Portugal* (Lisboa, 1863), 253; frei Francisco de Monte Alverne, *Obras oratórias, panegírico de santo Antônio* (Rio de Janeiro: Garnier, s. d.).

12. Frei Isidoro Obrien, OFM, *Santo Antônio de Lisboa* (Coimbra: Editora Coimbra, 1946), 186.

13. Vieira, *Sermões*, 283.
14. Abreu, p. 235 e ss. Although Saint Anthony is par excellence the heavenly "finder," other saints also performed this function. In Bahia of the seventeenth century, thanks to the intercession of the venerable sister Vitória da Encarnação, from the convent of Santa Clara do Desterro, several devotees were able to recover lost objects. Compare d. Sebastião Monteiro da Vide, *História da vida e morte de Madre Victoria da Encarnação* (Roma: Estamparia de Joam Francisco Chracas, 1720).
15. Henscheinio, 249, *"fugitivus servus Perpiniani sistitur."*
16. Ibid., 252.
17. Ibid., 249, *"mancipium fugitivum reducitur."*
18. Farmer, *The Oxford Dictionary of Saints*, 23.
19. Despite having infidels and heretics as the main enemies of the faith, Jews also appear in the biography of this saint and in the popular imagination as the personification of evil, "My Holy Father Anthony, my saint of God, at the night of your name, Jews were burned," recalls this quatrain which probably refers to the massacre of New Christians occurred in 1506, during the reign of Don Manuel; cf. Armando Mattos, 109.
20. Henscheinio, *Acta sanctorum, [Junii,]* 252.
21. Abreu, 91.
22. Padre At, *História de santo Antônio* (Bahia: Tipografia de S. Francisco, 1913), 410.
23. Vieira, *Sermões*, 76.
24. Amaral, *Tradições Populares*, 23.
25. Afrânio Peixoto, *Breviário da Bahia* (Rio de Janeiro: Agir, 1946), 52.
26. Frei Antônio de Santa Maria Jaboatão, OFM, *Novo orbe seráfico* (1761) (Recife: Assembleia Legislativa, 1980), vol. II, 345; *Sermão de santo Antônio em dia do Corpo de Deus no convento de Recife* (Lisbon: Oficina de Pedro Ferreira, 1751).
27. Ibid., 374.
28. In the village of Lagos (Algarve), only in 1668 saint Anthony enlisted as a private in the 2nd Regiment of Infantry, being Our Lady the guarantor. He was promoted to captain in 1683, captain in 1771, major six years later, and lieutenant general in 1780. See Manoel Bernardes Branco, *Santo Antônio de Lisboa, taumaturgo e oficial do exército português* (Lisboa, 1887). Also in Mozambique, the Saint from Lisbon enlisted as captain of the Corps of Marines, becoming ensign in the deployment of the Portuguese India.
29. Luís Henrique Dias Tavares, *História da Bahia* (Salvador: Centro Editorial e Didático da UFBA, 1974), 131.
30. Vieira, *Sermões*, 32.

31. José Carlos Macedo Soares, *Santo Antônio de Lisboa, militar no Brasil* (Rio de Janeiro: José Olympio, 1942).
32. "Linguagem e tradição popular da vila de Serpa" (Festas de santo Antônio), *Revista Lusitana*, vol. IV, (1938), 110.
33. Caio C. Boschi, *Os leigos e o poder* (Sao Paulo: Ática, 1986), 187; Macedo Soares, *Santo Antônio de Lisboa*, 133; Mário Souto Maior, "Minha continência a santo Antônio," *O puxa-saco* (Recife: CEPE, 1973), 77-80. In the village of Igaraçu, rather than the military, Saint Anthony was promoted to council member, with a stipend of 27$000 per year.
34. Macedo Soares, *Santo Antônio de Lisboa*, 18.
35. Frei Pedro Sinzig, O *taumaturgo santo Antônio na história, na lenda e na arte* (Petrópolis: Centro da Boa Imprensa, 1922); frei Basílio Rower, *Convento de santo Antônio do Rio de Janeiro* (Petrópolis: Vozes, 1937); frei Albano Marciniszyn, "Convento de santo Antônio do Rio de Janeiro," *Vida Franciscana*, n 48, ano LIII (1982), 36.
36. "Linguagem e tradição popular da vila de Serpa," 110. Despite the use of the myth of Saint Anthony in the affirmation of Lusitanity against the usurper of Castile, the Prototype of Portugal did not fail to show up grateful for the lavished honors the Spanish offered in 1731, when during the invasion of Oran (Algeria) the commander Mondemar put on the head of the saint his feather hat and admiral insignia, encircling the saint's waist with his sword and putting on the saint's hand the command baton. Chronicles tell that before the arrival of the fleet, a Franciscan friar dressed as an admiral threatened the complete destruction of the infidel city if it did not surrender unconditionally to the Christians. The news of this miracle circulated in Catholic countries, even in distant Germany and Bavaria, where Saint Anthony is represented with arms of an admiral in several churches. See also Macedo Soares, *Santo Antônio de Lisboa*, 110.
37. Vieira, *Sermões*, 76. If in the Christian theological casuistry, especially during the four centuries in which the Catholic Church blessed the black slavery, it was a duty of justice to return the runaway slave to their owners, at the time of the Old Testament (around the year 1000 BC) the current ethics considered it a virtue and duty of the fair to shelter the fugitive slave who asked for protection. Here are the words of Deuteronomy: "Do not deliver to his master the fugitive slave who take refuge in your home. He'll be with you in your land, in the place you have chosen, in one of your cities, where you see fit and do not molest him" (23, 15). As for the use of violence in the tract of captives, Christians strictly followed in the New World the teachings of the Old Testament. "For the slave, bread, punishment and work. The slave only works when is corrected and he only aspires to rest. Loose his hand, and he

will seek freedom. The yoke and the thong do bend the stiffest neck. Continuous work makes the slave docile. For the evil slave, torture and chains. Send him to work so that he is not idle, for idleness teaches a lot of malice. Occupies him at work, for that is what suits him. If he does not obey, subdue him with shackles" (*Eclesiástico*, 33, 25-30). See also Cehila, *Escravidão negra e história da Igreja na América Latina e no Caribe* (Petrópolis: Vozes, 1987).

38. Macedo Soares, *Santo Antônio de Lisboa*, 113. The use by devotees of Minas Gerais of the archaic "Ethiopian" instead of "black" or "slave" perhaps intended to revive in the queen's mind the old memory of the infidels in the land of Prestes João, a mix of savages and infidels.
39. Stuart Schwartz, "Mocambos, quilombos e Palmares: a resistência escrava no Brasil colonial," *Estudos Econômicos*, 17 (1987), 61-89.
40. Jose Alípio Goulart, *Da fuga ao suicídio* (Rio de Janeiro: Conquista/MEC, 1972), 69.
41. *Livro das confissões e reconciliações que se fizeram na visitação do santo Ofício do Salvador da Bahia de Todos os Santos no ano de 1618, apud Anais do Museu Paulista,* tomo XVII (São Paulo, 1963), 429.
42. M. M. Freitas, *O reino negro de Palmares* (Rio de Janeiro: Biblioteca do Exército, 1954), 428.
43. F. A. Pereira da Costa, *Folk-lore pernambucano* (Recife: Arquivo Público Estadual, 1974), 153.
44. Jaboatão, *Novo orbe seráfico,* n. 546.
45. Luiz Mott, *A inquisição em Sergipe* (Aracaju: Fundesc, 1989), 65.
46. Frei Hugo Fragoso, OFM, the kind historian of the convent of São Francisco de Salvador, demonstrates based on Saint Anthony's sermons "the relationship of the Franciscan minorismo with the lowest of society," where the poor get their livelihood with sweat and blood, their poverty resulting from plundering by the rich. Despite the "preferential option for the poor" by the thaumaturge, it is undeniable that, even if he was well-intentioned, in returning runaway slaves to their rightful owners, Saint Anthony acted against the freedom of the poorest of the poor during the slavery in Brazil. ("O minorismo franciscano," s. d., mimeo).
47. Arquivo Nacional da Torre do Tombo, Inquisição de Lisboa, processo n. 886, 22 fev. 1592.
48. *Primeira visitação do Santo Ofício às partes do Brasil, denunciações da Bahia (1591-1592)* (Rio de Janeiro: F. Briguiet, 1935), 350, 351, 544; see also Laura de Mello e Souza, *O Diabo e a Terra de Santa Cruz* (S. Paulo: Companhia das Letras, 1986), 120.

49. Arquivo Nacional da Torre do Tombo, Inquisição de Lisboa, processo de Ana Martins, sentença de 1694; See also Armando Mattos, *Santo Antônio de Lisboa na tradição popular* (Livraria Civilização: Porto, 1937), 49.
50. Arquivo Nacional da Torre do Tombo, Inquisição de Lisboa, caderno do promotor nº 126, fl. 211, Serinhaém, 6 jan. (1762). Besides these three prayers to Saint Anthony, other residents of the same village were accused of using unorthodox rituals, but here they were on the side of the most oppressed, "João Telles, slave of the Captain General João Salvador, besides wizard, gave scapular to a freed slave female to soften her masters;" Simão Angola, slave on the plantation of Cabo, "made prayers and enchantments to tame the heart of the white"; João Vieira Pax, from the plantation of Cavalcanti, "heals screwworm with prayer to Saint Anthony," and Inácia Pereira, brown freed slave, "knows a prayer to soften her master."
51. Mello Moraes Filho, *Os ciganos no Brasil e cancioneiro dos cigano,* (São Paulo: Itatiaia, 1981), 49; Luiz Mott, *Sergipe del Rey: população, economia e sociedade,* (Aracaju: Fundesc, 1986).
52. João da Silva Campos, *Tempo antigo* (Salvador: Secretaria de Educação e Saúde, 1942), 112.
53. Jaboatão, *Novo orbe seráfico,* 347.
54. Luiz Mott, *Rosa Egipcíaca: uma santa africana no Brasil* (Rio de Janeiro: Bertrand Brasil, 1993), 235.
55. Mary Karasch, *Slave life in Rio de Janeiro, 1808-1850* (Princeton: Princeton University Press, 1987), 277, n. 70. According to this author, Anthony of Padua was one of the most powerful saints in the pantheon of the faithful in Rio de Janeiro, in the first half of the nineteenth century, and included among his duties was the return of fugitive slaves to their owners.
56. Thomas Ewbank, *Life in Brazil* (New York: Harper & Brother, 1856), 339 and ss.
57. Richard Burton, *Viagens aos planaltos do Brasil* (Sao Paulo: Nacional, 1983), vol. 1, 122. At this time, according to this author, Saint Anthony was remembered in Minas Gerais mainly as a matchmaker saint.
58. Arquivo Nacional da Torre do Tombo, Inquisição de Lisboa, caderno do promotor n 130, 18 dez. 1777.
59. Arquivo Nacional da Torre do Tombo, Inquisição de Lisboa, caderno do promotor n 134, 28 mar. 1799.
60. Arquivo Nacional da Torre do Tombo, Inquisição de Lisboa, processo n 252, in Luiz Mott, "O calundu angola de Luzia Pinta: Sabará, 1739," *Revista do Instituto de Artes e Cultura,* Ufop, n. 1, dezembro (1994), 79.
61. Arquivo Nacional da Torre do Tombo, Inquisição de Lisboa, processo n. 1551, in Luiz Mott, *Escravidão, homossexualidade e demonologia* (São Paulo:

Ícone, 1988), 90-1. About the association of Saint Anthony with different orishas, see Roger Bastide, *Les Amériques noires* (Paris: Payot, 1967); Dílson Bento, *Malungo: decodificação da umbanda* (Rio de Janeiro: Civilização Brasileira, 1979); Hagamenon O. Guimarães, *Sincretismo santológico* (Aracaju: Secretaria de Educação e Cultura, 1978).

62. Mott, *Rosa Egipcíaca*, 106.
63. Stanley Stein, *Vassouras: A Brazilian coffee county, 1850-1890* (New York: Atheneum, 1974), 202.
64. Eduardo Etzel, *Imagens religiosas de São Paulo* (São Paulo, 1971); A. C. Lemos, "A imaginária dos escravos de S. Paulo," in *A mão afro-brasileira: significado da contribuição artística e histórica*, ed., Emanuel Araújo (Brasília, 1988), 192-7.
65. Robert Slenes, "Malungu, ngoma vem!: Africa encoberta e descoberta no Brasil," *Revista da USP,* n. 12 (1991-1992), 48-67.
66. Arquivo Nacional da Torre do Tombo, Inquisição de Lisboa, caderno do promotor n. 129, 24 mai. 1770.
67. Arquivo Nacional da Torre do Tombo, Inquisição de Lisboa, caderno do promotor n. 128, Sabará, 1762.
68. O. Cacciatore, *Dicionário de cultos afro-brasileiros* (Rio de Janeiro: Forense Universitária, 1977), 48.
69. Goulart, *Da fuga ao suicídio*, 83.

6

1. Carlos Magno Guimarães, *Uma negação da ordem escravista: quilombos em Minas Gerais no século XVIII* (Belo Horizonte, 1983), 145-7, ex. mimeo. If we believe in the data from *Códice Costa Matoso*, the slave population grew until 1738 when it reached the figure of 101,607 individuals. Decreasing from then on, it fell to 88,286 in 1749. In 1786, this population had already recovered and reached 174,135 individuals. See Maurício Goulart, *A escravidão africana no Brasil: das origens à extinção do tráfico* (São Paulo: Alpha-Omega, 1975), 141, 144.
2. Carlos M. Guimarães and Liana M. Reis, "Agricultura e escravidão em Minas Gerais (1700/1750)," in *Revista do Departamento de História,* 2 (1986), 7-36.
3. For more information about the demographic in Minas Gerais, see, among others: Francisco Vidal Luna, *Minas Gerais: escravos e senhores* (São Paulo: IPE/USP, 1981); Irací del Nero da Costa, *Vila Rica: população* (1719-1826) (São Paulo: IPE/USP, 1979); Maurício Goulart, *A escravidão africana no Brasil.*

4. This collection is deposited at Seção Colonial do Arquivo Público Mineiro and is composed of a set of hundreds of manuscripts that originated in the city councils and in Secretaria de Governo das Minas Gerais. These documents will be identified by the acronym SCAPM, followed by the number of the codex and the respective page.
5. On the absence of slaves in the quilombos of Minas Gerais, see Carlos Magno Guimarães, *Uma negação da ordem*, 58-9.
6. See Carlos Magno Guimarães *et alii*, "O quilombo do Ambrósio: lenda, documentos e arqueologia," *Estudos Ibero-Americanos*, XVI: 1-2 (1990), 161-74.
7. On this see Carlos Magno Guimarães, "Quilombos e brecha camponesa," *Revista do Departamento de História*, 8 (1989), 28-37.
8. About this see Guimarães, *Uma negação da ordem*, 101-4.
9. The posts were *soldado-do-mato, cabo-do-mato, capitão-do-mato, sargento-mor-do-mato*, and *capitão-mor-do-mato. Homens-do-mato* was the generic name of these professionals, as opposed to quilombolas, who were called *negros-do-mato*.
10. See Guimarães, *Uma negação da ordem*, 119-25.
11. Norberto Bobbio, Nicola Matteucci and Gianfranco Pasquino, *Dicionário de Política* (Brasília: Ed. UNB, 1992), 954-62.
12. Vladimir I. Lenine, "Uma grande iniciativa," *Obras escolhidas*, 3 (São Paulo: Alfa-Omega, 1980), 150.
13. According to Marx, "the struggle of class against class is a political struggle." Karl Marx, *Miséria da filosofia* (São Paulo: Grijalbo, 1976), 164.
14. SCAPM, códice 29, document n. 129; emphasis added.
15. SCAPM, códice 56, fl. 102v to 103v; emphasis added.
16. SCAPM, códice 67, fl. 26; emphasis added.
17. SCAPM, códice 84, fl. 108v and 109; emphasis added.
18. SCAPM, códice 45, fl. 64v and 65; emphasis added.
19. SCAPM, códice 60, fl. 118v to 119v; emphasis added.
20. Compulsory enlistment of individuals of a certain quality and condition.
21. SCAPM, códice 159, fl. 94 and v; emphasis added.
22. SCAPM, códice 165, fl. 33 and códice 143, fl. 207; v.
23. SCAPM, códice 165, fl. 42.
24. SCAPM, códice 215, fl. 2 to 3v; emphasis added.
25. SCAPM, códice 09, fl. 10v.
26. SCAPM, códice 21, fl. 89 and v.
27. SCAPM, códice 27, fl. 114.
28. SCAPM, códice 49, fl. 69v to 71.
29. SCAPM, códice 34, fl. 20 and v; SCAPM, códice 114, fl. 167 and v; SCAPM, códice 217, fl. 130.

30. SCAPM, códice 123, fl. 103 and v.
31. SCAPM, códice 165, fl. 127 v.
32. SCAPM, códice 199, fl. 13; emphasis added.
33. SCAPM, códice 260, fl. 16v and 17; emphasis added.
34. SCAPM, códice 260, fl. 44v and 45.
35. Guimarães, *Uma negação da ordem*, 119-25.
36. See Charles Boxer, *A Idade de Ouro do Brasil* (São Paulo: Nacional, 1969), 190-1; Octavio Ianni, *As metamorfoses do escravo* (São Paulo: Difel, 1962), 61, 146; Suely R. R. Queiroz, *Escravidão negra em São Paulo* (Rio de Janeiro: José Olympio, 1977), 53.
37. Francisco Vidal Luna, *Minas Gerais: escravos e senhores* (São Paulo: IPE/USP, 1981).
38. SCAPM, códice 04, fl. 740-8.
39. SCAPM, códice 35, documento 110.
40. SCAPM, códice 44, fl. 129v and 130.
41. SCAPM, códice 59, fl. 2.
42. Ibid., fl. 11v.
43. SCAPM, códice 50, fl. 90 to 96v.
44. SCAPM, códice 224, fl. 215-7v.
45. Other information, but of generic character, is in note n. 33.
46. SCAPM, códice 123, fl. 130v.
47. SCAPM, códice 130, fl. 50 and v.
48. SCAPM, códice 171, fl. 8v and 9.
49. SCAPM, códice, fl. 7v and 8.
50. SCAPM, códice 231, fl. 41 and v.
51. SCAPM, códice 260, fl. 16v and 17.
52. The idea that the slave was unable to organize movements or commit acts of a political character can be found, among others, in: Clóvis Moura, *Rebeliões da senzala* (Rio de Janeiro: Conquista, 1972), 21; Octavio Ianni, *As metamorfoses do escravo* (São Paulo: Difel, 1962), 234; Fernando Henrique Cardoso, *Capitalismo e escravidão no Brasil meridional* (Rio de Janeiro: Paz e Terra, 1977), 217-8.
53. SCAPM, códice 02, fl. 160v and 161. This document is also registered to fl. 167 and v and fl. 171v and 172.
54. SCAPM, códice 11, fl. 170 v and 171.
55. It is more likely that the cut was the "Achilles heel" and not an artery, as the document says. According to Assumar, his inspiration was the legislation of Mississippi and Louisiana, but the legislation of Jamaica also should be noted, all of which have proposed drastic measures to punish fugitives. One of these measures was to cut one leg of a repeat fugitive slave and adapt a wood-

en leg to replace it. About this see: SCAPM, códice 4, fl. 556-557 and also Charles Boxer, *A Idade de Ouro do Brasil*, 158-9 and 350 (notes 22 and 23 of Chapter VII); Waldemar de Almeida Barbosa, *Negros e quilombos em Minas Gerais* (Belo Horizonte: s. n., 1972).

56. Here, they are understood generically as residents of Minas Gerais.
57. Quoted by Laura de Mello e Souza, "Os ricos, os pobres e a revolta nas Minas do século XVIII (1707-1789)," in: *Análise & Conjuntura*, 4, 2-3 (1989), 32.
58. This separation was another of the consequences of the rebellion of Felipe dos Santos.
59. SCAPM, códice 32, fl. 93v and 94.
60. SCAPM, códice 02, fl. 171v. Marginal note.
61. See Guimarães, *Uma negação da ordem*, 181-2.
62. SCAPM, códice 84, fl. 108v e 109.
63. Ibid.

7

1. Joaquim José Lisboa, *Descrição curiosa das principaes produçoes, Rios, e animaes do Brazil principalmente da Capiania de Minas Gerais* (Lisboa: Impressão Regia, 1806). Also published in the *Revista do Archivo Publico Mineiro* (*RAPM*) XIV (1910), 551-575.
2. Julio Pinto Vallejos points out that, contrary to the opinions of some historians, slaves did indeed exercise significant power in shaping the nature of the environment in which they lived. "Slave Control and Slave Resistance in Colonial Minas Gerais, 1700-1750," *Journal of Latin American Studies* 17, 1(May 1985), 4-5. In this regard, Vallejos is critical of the position taken by Waldemar de Almeida Barbosa, *Negros e quilombos em Minas Gerais* (Belo Horizonte: n.p., 1972). This is an issue which has occupied a significant place in the historiography of North American slavery. See, for example, Eugene D. Genovese, *Roll Jordan Roll: The World the Slaves Made* (New York: Pantheon Books, 1974).
3. The term calhambola was used in Minas Gerais to refer both to members of quilombos and to runaway slaves regardless of whether they met the legal criteria of membership in quilombos. The latter use of the word is made explicit in a council edict of 1764 wherein the council referred to "thefts which the runaway Negroes commonly called calhambolas make...." Edict da Câmara, Cód. 80 (Série Câmara Municipal de Ouro Preto, APM [herein after CMOP]), fl. 109v.

4. This is the approach of Carlos Magno Guimarães in *Uma negação da ordem escravista: Quilombos em Minas Gerais no século XVIII* (São Paulo: Ícone, 1988). I would like to thank João José Reis for having brought to my attention this richly documented work.
5. President Fernando Henrique Cardoso, in an interview, restated this perception: "There is no purely racial violence in Brazil. But slavery left its marks in the shaping of our society and has caused descendants of slaves to be among the poor segments of the Brazilian people." James F. Hoge, Jr., "Fulfilling Brazil's Promise: A Conversation with President Cardoso," *Foreign Affairs* 74, 4 (July/August 1995), 70.
6. Compromisso dos pretos devotos de Nossa Senhora do Rozario da freguezia da Itaberaba onde he Padroeyro Santo Antonio, Arquivo da Curia de Mariana (ACM) (1743), Chapter 8.
7. The Conde do Assumar, a very effective governor and a man concerned with the issue of race and slavery, unsuccessfully sought a different solution. Noting the large numbers of African-born slaves, the Conde do Assumar in 1719 proposed that the seminaries teach African languages. This would be a way of more effectively catechizing the slaves. From his perspective, it was imperative that the king act to ensure that slaves received religious instruction because royal sovereignty was based upon the king's promise to spread the faith and evangelize the heathens. Thus, wrote Assumar, because the Portuguese brought the slaves to Brazil, they were responsible for educating them about religion. And to do so effectively required using their language rather than Portuguese or Latin. Governador Assumar to Rei, 4 October 1917, Cód. 4(SG), fl. 713
8. An important bibliography is available on the black brotherhood in colonial Brazil. Among these are Manoel S. Cardozo, "The Lay Brotherhoods of Colonial Bahia," *Catholic Historical Review* 33 (April, 1947-January, 1948), 12-30; A.J.R. Russell-Wood, "Black and Mulatto Brotherhoods in Colonial Brazil: A Study in Collective Behavior," *Hispanic American Historical Review* 54:4 (November 1974), 567-602; Julita Scarano, "Black Brotherhoods: Integration or Contradiction?" *Luso-Brazilian Review* 16:1 (Summer 1979), 1-17; Patricia Mulvey, "Slave Confraternities in Brazil: Their Role in Colonial Society," *The Americas* 39:1 (July, 1982), 39-68, and Fritz Teixeira Salles, *Associações religiosas no ciclo de ouro*, Estudos No. 1. (Belo Horizonte: Universidade Federal de Minas Gerais, 1963).
9. See Sylvio de Vasconcellos, *Mineiridade: ensaio de caracterização* (Belo Horizonte: Imprensa Oficial, 1968) and *Vila Rica: formação e desenvolvimento-residências* (Rio de Janeiro: Instituto Nacional de Livro, 1956) for an earlier elaboration of this interpretation.

10. Fray Agostinho de Santa Maria, *Santuario Mariano, e historica das Imagens Milagrosas de Nossa Senhora, e das milogrosamento apparecidas, que se venerão em todo o Bispado do Rio de Janeiro & Mina, & em todas as Ilhas do Oceano,....* 10 vols. (Lisboa Occidental: Na officina de Antonio Pedrozo Gabrao, 1707-1723), 244.
11. Will of Joana Carvalho de Araújo, March 16, 1782, cód. 332, auto no. 6995; Arquivo do Serviço do Patrimonio Histórico e Artístico Nacional in Ouro Preto (ASPHANOP). Teresa Barbosa de Araújo noted that she was a member of the brotherhood of Nossa Senhora do Rosário and mentioned the fact of "having been a queen." Will, July 17, 1775, cód. 97, no. 1259 (AS-PHANOP). In the years 1761 to 1766, 555 people were elected to serve in various positions on the governing board, other than kings and queens. Of these 245 (44.1 percent) were slaves, 161 (29 percent) were freedmen, and 149 (26.9 percent) were freemen. 80.9 percent of elected males were slaves or freedmen the corresponding figure for women was 65.4 percent.
12. Representação que expozerão os Vigarios Collados das Igrejas, undated, Arquivo Histórico Ultramarino, Lisboa (AHU), Minas Gerais, 21 May 1795, cax 140 doc 24.
13. Governor Assumar to King, October 4, 1917, Cód. 4(Série Secretaria do Governo, Arquivo Público Mineiro[SG]), fl. 713.
14. Visitation of São José Bautista, September 25, 1749, Cód. 73(Série Delegacia Fiscal, APM [DF]), fl. 6.
15. Visitation of São José Bautista, 25 September 1749, Cód. 73(DF), fl. 8.
16. Representação dos Vigarios Collados das Igrejas, undated, AHU, Minas Gerais, May 21 1795, cax 140 doc 24.
17. Carta do Conde do Assumar, September 23, 1719, *RAPM* XXIV (1933), 582-583.
18. Because the Portuguese rolls of the confessed, *rois de confessados*, list those present and often provide information about individuals who happened to be absent, Portuguese historians have often used them as substitutes for census tracts. These have proved particularly useful in examining immigration and demographic issues.
19. Rol das pessoas que não satisfazerão, AHU, Minas Gerais, June 4 1780, cax 117 doc 95.
20. *Constituiçõens primeyras do Arcebispado da Bahia feytas e ordenadas pelo Senhor Sebastiao Moneyro da Vide, arcebispo do dito arcebispado Propostas e aceytas em o synodo diocensano que o dito senhor celebrou* (Lisboa: M. Rodrigues, 1765). Originally published in 1720: titulo 71.
21. Capitulos de visita, ACM, Carrancos, Rio das Mortes, fl. 66v.
22. Ibid, fl. 66v.

23. Visitation to Itatiaia, November 25-30, 1733, Cód. 14(ACM), fl. 44v.
24. The explanation may lie more with slave ownership patterns than with opposition to marriage by masters. In Minas Gerais, slaves rarely married someone having a different owner. Thus the concern with slaves marrying appears to be related to property rights issues rather than opposition to marriage. Slaves on large estates often married at high rates. For the slave the result was the same regardless of explanation. But the difference is important in understanding the social and moral paradigms in place at the time.
25. At the same time, the urban context permitted slaves greater freedom of movement and the greater possibility for the transmission of African culture. In this regard, see João José Reis and Eduardo Silva, *Negociação e conflito: a resistência negra no Brasil escravista* (São Paulo: Companhia das Letras, 1989).
26. Ordem do Governador aos Vigarios da Vara de Sabará, Vila Rica, e Mariana. November 26, 1719, Cód. 11(SG), fl. 171v.
27. Ibid, Cód. 11(SG), fl. 172.
28. Carta do Goverador de Almeida ao Vigário de Sabará, December 26, 1719, Cód. 11(SG), fl. 184.
29. Regimento, September 14, 1719, Cód. 6(CMOP), fl. 17v.
30. Ordem do Governador Conde de Assumar, May 20, 1720, Cód. 11(SG), fl. 288v.
31. Ordem do Governador, July 2, 1714, Cód. 9(SG), fl. 29v.
32. Vallejos, "Slavery in Minas Gerais," 23. For 1728 see Report of Overseas Council, September 18, 1728, in *Documentos históricos*, 94, 28-29.
33. Waldemar de Almeida Barbosa, in a valuable examination of slavery in Minas Gerais, by focusing on the documentation of the Secretaria do Governo (the governor's correspondence), is able to provide an analysis of the quilombos during the eighteenth century. The list of quilombo activity that he provides is impressively long. But because it is the captaincy-level correspondence that is the major source of the list, Barbosa is unable to pick up the innumerable smaller quilombos with which the bulk of the population had to deal and which are the focus of this study. *Negros e quilombos em Minas Gerais*, 55-77.
34. Charles R. Boxer, *The Golden Age of Brazil 1695-1750* (Berkeley: University of California Press, 1962), 342.
35. Mappa geral dos Fogos....1767, AHU, Minas Gerais, Cax. 1700-1768.
36. APM, Planilha 20364.
37. A quilombo was defined in the Regimento de Capitão do Mato of 1722 as "where are found more than four... negroes with farms, peloins, and the means to sustain themselves..." Regimento de Capitão do Mato, December 17, 1722, and registered February 22, 1749, Cód. 57, fl. 24. In 1741,

the requirement that there be Ranchos and piloins appears to have been dropped. Bando do Governador, July 12, 1741, Cód. 43(CMOP, fl. 80v. The definition came to be: "Any dwelling with at least five Negro runaways in an unpopulated location." Bando de Governador, June 14, 1741, Cód. 43(CMOP), fl. 82v.

38. Carta ao Sua Mag.e, frota de 1719, Cód. 19(CMOP), fl. 3.
39. Ibid.
40. Ibid.
41. Order do Governor Albuquerque ao capitão mor de Ribeirão, January 21, 1711, Cód. 7(SG), fl. 50v.
42. Carta do Governador Conde de Assumar ao Rei, July 13 1718, Cód. 4(SG), fl. 555.
43. Carta do Governador Conde de Assumar ao Capitao Mor Pascoal da Silva Guimarães, October 31, 1719, Cód. 11(SG), fl. 163.
44. Carta do Governador Conde de Assumar ao Ouvidor de Ouro Preto, October 31, 1719, Cód. 11(SG), fl. 163v,
45. Patente de Francisco Gonçalves Leça, February 25, 1711, Cód. 7(SG), fl. 73. It is interesting to note that in the neighboring mining zone of Goiás, the word pombeiro was used to describe armed men used against Indians. Ordem do Governador Rodrigo Cezar de Menezes, January 3, 1727, *DI,* XIII (1895), 105-106. The word was also used in Africa to refer to slave catchers.
46. *RAPM,* II, 2(April to June, 1897), 389-190. A statute was issued for Goiás on March 30, 1727, *DI,* XIII(1895), 117-119.
47. Regimento do Capitão mor Andre Vellozo, July 1, 1733, Cód. 7(CMOP), fl. 168.
48. Regimento de hum sumario de Capitollos que leverão os Almotaceis, July 8, 1733, Cód. 6(CMOP), fl. 171.
49. In the captaincy de São Paulo, the situation had gotten so desperate that the governor issued orders permitting anyone to kill a calhambola or an Indian who posed a threat: "the said Justices were not to hold them criminal for the death or use of arms…." Bando do Governor Luiz Mascarenhas, December 23, 1747, *DI,* 22 (XXII), 198-199.
50. Alvará, March 3 de 1741, in José Pedro Xavier da Veiga. *Ephemerides mineiras, 1664-1897,* 4 vols. Ouro Preto: Imprensa Official do Estado de Minas Gerais, 1897, I, 275. Original in Cód. 43(CMOP), fls. 85v-86.
51. Termo de Ajuste entre a Câmara e o Capitao major do Mato Francisco de Mattos, March 1, 1735, Cód. 35(CMOP), fl. 5v.
52. Câmara, Informação, December 17, 1735, Cód. 35(CMOP), fl. 65.

53. Patente de Dionizio Marques Pinto, August 4, 1734, Cód. 15 (SG), fls. 135v; Câmara e Homens Bons, January 30, 1735, Cód. 28(CMOP), fls. 153-157v.
54. Carta da Câmara ao Rei, May 14, 1735, Cód. 9 (CMOP), fls. 54v - 55. Examples of the instructions to those charged with collecting the tax, *finta*, are found in the codex, fls. 1 - 4v. By Royal Order, the council was ordered to stop the finta and to repay the taxes which had been collected. The council was told that it had exceeded its authority.
55. Termo de Ajuste entre a Câmara e o Capitao major do Mato Francisco de Mattos, March 1, 1735, Cód. 35(CMOP), fls. 5-7v.
56. Ibid, fl. 5v.
57. Dizem os moradores, October 14, 1739, Cód. 32(CMOP), fl. 223.
58. Instrucções, undated, May 1739, Cód. 32(CMOP), fls. 210-212.
59. Carta da Câmara, May 7, 1740, Cód. 43CMOP), fl. 7v.
60. Representatção dos moradores, May 25, 1743, Cód. 50(CMOPo, fls. 68-68v.
61. Representação, s.d. [October 1748], Cód. 54(CMOP), fl. 119v.
62. Cartas da Câmara, October 12 and 13, 1748, Cód. 54(CMOP), fls. 114v-115 e 116v-118.
63. Cartas aos comandantes das ordenanças de São Bartolomeu, Casa Branca, Congonhas, Itatiaia, Ouro Branco, e Cachoeira, entre outros. December 15, 1748, Cód. 54 (CMOP), fls. 130-137v; Apelo do ouvidor de Ouro Preto em Auto de Correição, June 11, 1749, Cód. 22(CMOP), fl. 106.
64. Carta da Câmara, June 12, 1784, Cód. 112 (CMOP), fl. 84.
65. "Carta da Camara," June 16, 1762, cod. 77 (CMOP), fl. 182; "Carta de patente," Francisco Alexandrino, 31 ago. 1763, cod. 78 (CMOP), fls. 194-195.
66. Representação dos moradores, September 18, 1762, Cód. 77(CMOP), fls. 196-197v.
67. Ordem dada ao Capitão mor, March 13 de March, 1764, Cód. 130(SG), fls. 101v-102v.
68. Carta da câmara, June 12, 1784, Cód. 112(CMOP), fl. 84.
69. "Lista de todas as pessoas que forao prezas...." em M. Rodrigues Lapa, *As cartas chilenas* (Rio de Janeiro: Instituto Nacional do Livro, 1958), 294-295. The great majority of those arrested were Africans. People were arrested for all sorts of crimes including "terrible habits" so that it is impossible to determine how many were really calhambolas.
70. Câmara municipal, January 24, 1798, Cód. 47(CMOP), fl. 123.
71. Quoted in Afonso de A. Taunay, *História geral das bandeiras paulistas*. 11 vols. (São Paulo: Imprensa Oficial do Estado, 1924-1950), 190.

72. Carta de Gomes Freire de Andrada, June 16, 1746, *RAPM*, VIII (1903), 619.
73. Ordem da Câmara, May 6, 1747, Cód. 3(SG), fl. 88v.
74. Carta da Câmara, April 3, 1756, Cód. 65(CVMOP), fl. 236v. Letter published in its entirety in Veiga, *Ephemerides mineiras*, II, 77-80.
75. Ibid., 80-82.
76. Representação, April 28, 1756, Cód. 65(CMOP), fls. 239v-241.
77. Câmara Editais, May 5, 1756 and May 15, 1756, Cód. 65(CMOP), fls. 243v-245 and 255-255v.
78. Regimento do Governador, March 24, 1719, Cód. 6(CMOP), fl. 13. Even royal orders on the subject were issued. E.g., Royal Order, January 24, 1756, Cód. 65(CMOP), fls. 264v-265.
79. "And only those slaves who accompany their Master can use the said Arms or if they go on some endeavor … such that the Master gives them a written note containing a description of the Arms being carried…." Editais, October 26, 1748, Cód. 54(CMOP), fl. 123v. It is interesting to note that similar edicts for the mining zone of Goiás did not permit slaves to carry weapons in the service or presence of their masters. Bando do Governador Rodrigo Cezar de Menezes, 14 de decembro de 1727, *DI*, XIII(1895), 130-131.
80. Moreover, the work slaves did certainly gave them access to tools which could serve as weapons. One official, in a inspection in 1745 noted: "I have learned that the cause for most of the disorders among the said negroes comes from their carrying ropes, knives, and other arms despite the provisions which have been taken…." Auto de Correição, April 2, 1745, Cód. 22(CMOP), fl. 96.
81. Edital, October 26, 1748, Cód. 54(CMOP), fls. 122v-123. This clearly implies that slaves had access to firearms.
82. This was a general problem, of course, throughout Minas Gerais. But the same relationships were reported for the gold mining zones of Goiás. Regimento do Governador Rodrigo Cezar de Menezes, January 1, 1727, *DI* (1895), 103-104. "I have been made aware that in these Mines there are negroes running from their Masters who cannot regain them because some residents invite them into their homes and farms from which considerable damage occurs."
83. Câmara Edital, March 14, 1735, Cód. 32(CMOP), fl. 17.
84. Acordão da câmara, February 3, 1714, "Atas da Câmara Municipal de Vila Rica," *RAPM*, XXV, II (July 1937), 3-166.
85. Edital, February 22, 1741, Cód. 43(CMOP), fl. 35v.
86. Representação dos Mineiros, April 29, 1754, Cód. 63(CMOP), fl. 174.
87. Carta de Gomes Freire de Andrada, June 21, 1737, Cód. 55(SG), fl. 455.

88. Carta de Gomes Freire de Andrada, June 6, 1737, Cód. 55(SG), fl. 393.
89. Petition of Captain Nicolão de Freitas Pacheco, August 19, 1733, Maço Avulso No. 173, APM.
90. Carta de José Antonio Freire de Andrada, July 12, 1760, Cód. 130(SG), fl. 6.
91. Lista de Devasas, Cód. 19(CMOP), fl. 110v.
92. Barbosa, *Negros e quilombos*, 74-75.

8

1. "Consulta do Conselho Ultramarino a S.M. no ano de 1732, feita pelo Conselheiro Antonio Rodrigues da Costa," *Revista do Instituto Histórico e Geográfico Brasileiro* VII (498).
2. "Ordem Régia ao governador e Capitão-General da Capitania da Bahia sobre a necessidade de se congregarem em uma povoação civil todos os vadios e facinorosos que viviam perturbando a ordem pública e tranquilidade dos habitantes das comarcas e mais pormenores a este respeito. Ajuda, 22 de Julho de 1766," Biblioteca Nacional do Rio de Janeiro, Seção de Manuscritos, II-33, 25, 32; See also, Sérgio Buarque de Holanda, *Monções* (São Paulo: Brasiliense, 1990), 68 and 242-3; Arquivo Público Mineiro, Seção Colonial, códice 163, 48v and following.
3. "Do Mestre-de-Campo Inácio Correia Pamplona sobre a Expedição do Campo Grande, Cuieté, e Abaeté termo de Paracatu—De todos os sujeitos, que escreveram sobre esta matéria," Biblioteca Nacional do Rio de Janeiro, Seção de Manuscritos, 18, 2, 6.
4. "Livro Segundo das Cartas que o Ilmo. e Exmo. Sr. D. Antonio de Noronha Capitão General da Capitania de Minas Gerais escreveu durante o seu Governo que teve princípio em 28 de maio de 1776 [sic]," Biblioteca Nacional do Rio de Janeiro, Seção de Manuscritos, 2, 2, 24. "Registro de cartas, ordens e circulares do Governador a autoridades da Capitania e respectivas respostas—1775-1776," Arquivo Público Mineiro, Seção Colonial, códice 207.
5. "Representa hum vassalo amante da patria [...]," Arquivo Público Mineiro, Seção Colonial, códice 218, 191-3.
6. "Do Mestre-de-Campo Inácio Correia Pamplona [...]," 25.
7. Ibid., 108.
8. Ibid., 205.
9. Ibid., 75.
10. "First they would beat the war drums so the blacks would flee, in order that their lives would suffer no danger, as they feared" (ibid., 76).

11. Ibid., 79.
12. Ibid., 25.
13. Ibid., 41.
14. "For Portugal, overseas possessions have always been the dungeon of her delinquents." See A. de Souza Silva Costa Lobo, *História da sociedade em Portugal no século XV* (Lisbon, 1904), 49.
15. "Do Mestre-de-Campo Inácio Correia Pamplona [...]," Ibid., 271-2.
16. Ibid., 294.
17. "Memória do que deve observar na derrota, que tem de seguir o capitão Antonio Cardoso de Souza, para a conquista do gentio, a que vai destinado, e do que há de praticar nesta importante diligência," Biblioteca Nacional do Rio de Janeiro, Seção Manuscritos, 18, 2 6, 1417-20.
18. "Livro segundo das cartas que Ilmo. e Exmo. Sr. D. Antonio de Noronha [...]," 102v.
19. Ibid., 13v.
20. "Edital de D. Antonio de Noronha sobre negros para lutar contra quilombos," Vila Rica, May 15, 1777, Biblioteca Nacional do Rio de Janeiro, 123-4.
21. Ibid., 336.
22. "Carta ao Vice-Rei," Vila Rica, November 19, 1776, Biblioteca Nacional do Rio de Janeiro, 52-3.
23. "Plano secreto para a nova conquista do Cuieté," September 8, 1779, Biblioteca Nacional do Rio de Janeiro, 40-1v.
24. "Para o Capitão-Mor José Alves Maciel," Vila Rica, July 1, 1776, Arquivo Público Mineiro, Seção Colonial, códice 207, 112v.
25. "O livro da Capa Verde—a vida no Distrito Diamantino no período da Real Extração," Júnia Ferreira Furtado, Master's thesis, Universidade de São Paulo (1991), 221.
26. Arquivo Público Mineiro, Seção Colonial, CMC, códice 7, 8-9v.
27. See *Desclassificados do ouro—a pobreza mineira do século XVIII*, Laura de Mello e Souza (Rio de Janeiro: Graal, 1982), 86-90.
28. Arquivo Público Mineiro, Seção Colonial, códice 218, 191-3.
29. Ibid.
30. Michel Foucault, *Surveiller et punir* (Paris: Gallimard, 1975), chapter 1.

9

1. The process of reconstituting the occupation of the Mato Grosso territory was compiled from the following sources: Filippe José Nogueira Coelho, "Memórias chronologicas da capitania de Mato-Grosso" in *Revista do Instituto Histórico e Geográfico Brasileiro*, Rio de Janeiro (2 trimestre 1850),

137-99; Luís D'Alincourt, "Rezultado dos trabalhos e indagações statisticas da provincia de Mato Grosso" in *Anais da Biblioteca Nacional*, vol. 8, 69-171; Barão de Melgaço, "Apontamentos cronológicos da provincia de Mato Grosso" in *Revista do Instituto Histórico e Geográfico Brasileiro*, vol. 205 (out/dez 1949), 207-385; Joseph Barboza de Sá, *Relaçaó das povoaçoens do Cuyaba e Mato Grosso de seos principios the os prezentes tempos* (1775) Cuiabá: Edições UFMT/SEC, 1975); e a partir da seguinte bibliografia: Virgílo Correa Filho, *História de Mato Grosso*, 2nd ed, Rio de Janeiro, 1969; Alcir Lenharo, *Crise e mudança da frente oeste de colonização* (Cuiabá: Edição do UFMT, 1982); Rubens de Mendonça, *História de Mato Grosso* (Cuiabá: Edição do Autor, 1967); Luiza Rios Ricci Volpato, *A conquista da terra no universo da pobreza: a formaçao da fronteira oeste do Brasil* (São Paulo: Hucitec, Brasília, INL, 1987).

2. Sá, *Relaçaó das povoaçoens*, 18.
3. Correa Filho, *História de Mato Grosso*, 459.
4. Volpato, *A conquista da terra*, pp. 85 et seq.; on the subject, see also Maria Thereza Schoerer Petrone, *A lavoura canavieira em São Paulo* (São Paulo: Difel, 1968), 11; Heloisa Liberalli Belloto, *Autoridade e conflito no Brasil colonial: o governo do Morgado de Mateus* (São Paulo: Conselho Estadual de Artes e Ciências Humanas,1979), 29.
5. Volpato, *A conquista da terra*, Chapter 3.
6. Hercules Florence, *Viagem fluvial do Tietê ao Amazonas* (São Paulo: Cultrix, Edusp, 1977), 180 et seq.; Virgílio Correa Filho, *Fazendas de gado no pantanal mato-grossense* (Rio de Janeiro: Ministerio da Agricultura, 1955), 19.
7. Sá, *Relaçao das povoaçoens*, 25.
8. Lenharo, *Crise e mudança na frente oeste de colonização*, Chapter 3; Volpato, *A conquista da terra*, 93.
9. D'Alincourt, "Rezultado dos trabalhos e indagações statisticas," 60 - 68.
10. Sobre o assunto ver Carlos Rosa, *O processo da independência em Mato Grosso e a hegemonia cuiabana* (Cuiabá: SMEC, 1976).
11. Luiza Rios Ricci Volpato, *Cativos do sertão: vida cotidiana e escravidao em Cuiaba, 1850-1888* (São Paulo: Marco Zero; Cuiabá: Editora da UFMT, 1993), 42.
12. Data regarding the population of Cuiabá in 1862 was extracted from the "Relatorio apresentado à Assembléa Legislativa Provincial de Mato Grosso pelo exm° conselheiro Herculanno Ferreira Penna em 3 de maio de 1862" (Cuiabá: Typ. do Mato Grosso, 1864), 35.
13. Volpato, *Cativos do sertão*, 110, esp. note 7.
14. Ibid., 135.
15. Volpato, *A conquista da terra*, 69, esp. 73.

16. Dealing specifically with slavery, see Lúcia Helena Gaeta Aleixo, *Mato Grosso: trabalho escravo e trabalho livre (1850-1888)* (Brasília: Ministério da Fazenda, Dept° Adm/Div. Documentação, 1984); Volpato, *Cativos do sertão*.
17. Sá, *Relaçaó das povoaçoens*, 21.
18. Ibid., 30.
19. Ibid., 36.
20. Correa Filho, *História do Mato Grosso*, 385.
21. Sá, *Relaçaó das povoaçoens*, 37.
22. Coelho, "Memórias chronologicas da capitania de Mato Grosso," 182; Barao de Melgago, "Apontamentos cronológicos da província de Mato Grosso,"266 et seq.; João Domas Filho, *A escravidão no Brasil* (Rio de Janeiro: Civilização Brasileira, 1939), 113; João Severiano da Fonseca, *Viagem ao redor do Brasil* (Rio de Janeiro: Typografia de Pinheiro e Co., 1880-1881), 73; E. Roquete Pinto, *Rondônia*, 5 ed, (São Paulo: Nacional, 1950), 33; Visconde de Taunay, *A cidade do ouro e das ruínas* (1891), 2 ed (São Paulo: Melhoramentos, 1923), 149; and, in more recent texts, see Elizabeth M adureiraide Siqueira et al., *Oprocesso historico de Mato Grosso*, 3 ed. (Cuiabá: Guaicurus, 1990), 131; Maria de Lourdes Bandeira, *Território negro em espaço branco*, 118; Volpato, *Cativos do sertão*, 184.
23. Coelho, "Memórias chronologicas da capitania de Mato-Grosso," 182.
24. Ibid., 182.
25. Ofício de João d'Albuquerque de Mello Pereira e Caceres a Luiz Pinto de Sousa Coutinho, Vila Bela, 30 dez. 1779, cited in Roquete Pinto, *Rondônia*, 33.
26. "Diario da dilligencia que por ordem do illustrissimo e excellentisssimo João d'Albuquerque de Mello Pereira e Caceres, governador e capitão general da capitania de Mato-Grosso, se fez no anno de 1795, a fim de se distruirem varios quilombos, e buscar alguns logares em que houvesse ouro," cited in Roquete Pinto, *Rondônia*, 36.
27. Ibid., 41.
28. Ibid., 42.
29. "[…] from these slaves only six were presently found alive, these were the rulers, priests, doctors, parents and grandparents of the little people of the current Quilombo," Ibid., 41.
30. Lenharo, *Crise e mudança na frente oeste de colonização,* Chapter 2; Volpato, *A conquista da terra*, 54, esp., 63.
31. On the disputes between the Captain-General and the Chamber of Senate of Cuiabá, see Universidade Federal de Mato Grosso (UFMT)/Núcleo de Documentação e Informação Historica Regional (NDIHR), *Anais do Senado da Câmara de Cuiabá*, f. 79 v; Volpato, *A conquista da terra*, 136.

32. "Diario da diligencia que por ordem do illustrisssimo e excellentissimo senhor," cited in Roquete Pinto, *Rondônia*, 43.
33. Ibid., 43. Similar efforts had been undertaken successfully by João de Albuquerque's predecessor, his brother Luís de Albuquerque de Melo Pereira e Cáceres, who in 1778 founded Vila Maria (now the city of Cáceres) on the banks of the Paraguay River, a few dozen indigenous persons escaped from the mission of Chiquitos. On the subject see, Barão de Melgaço, "Apontamentos cronológicos da província de Mato Grosso," 278; Volpato, *A conquista da terra*, 45.
34. "Discurso que recitou o exrn° snr. doutor Estevão Ribeiro Resende presidente desta provincia na occasião da abertura da Assembléa Legislativa Provincial em 1° de março de 1840," s.n.t., 33.
35. "Relatorio apresentado a Assembléa Legislativa Provincial pelo presidente da provincia de Mato Grosso o excm° e escm° snr. conselheiro Herculanno Ferreira Penna em 3 de maio de 1863" (Cuiabá: Typ. Mato Grosso, 1864), 29.
36. Volpato, *Cativos do sertão*, 60.
37. Arquivo Publico do Estado de Mato Grosso (APEMT). The information cited was extracted from a mutilated document, containing no more concerning date or recipient or signature. This is a report of a military mission. Caixa 1865 G.
38. APEMT, document fragment; report of a military mission. Caixa 1865 G.
39. Ibid.
40. APEMT, "Ofício do chefe de polícia Firmo José de Matos ao presidente da província Dr. José V. de Couto Magalhães," Cuiabá, 27 jul. 1867, caixa 1867 B.
41. Dalísia Elizabeth Martins Dolles, *As comunicações fluviais pelo Tocantins e Araguaia no século XIX* (Goiânia: Oriente, 1973), Chapter 4, esp. 91.
42. Eugene Genovese draws attention to the fact that the quilombos almost never reached sufficiency in manufacturing, becoming dependent on foreign exchanges for obtaining cloth, agricultural implements and especially firearms. Eugene D. Genovese, *Da rebelião à revolução*, trad. Carlos Eugênio Moura (São Paulo: Global, 1983), 64.
43. "Relatório apresentado á Assembléa Legislativa Provincial pelo excm° snr. Tenente coronel Francisco Cardozo Junior em 20 de agosto de 1871" (Cuiabá: Typ. Sousa Neves e Cia, s.d.), 12.
44. APEMT, "Ofício do chefe de polícia Firmo José de Matos ao presidente da província Dr. José V. de Couto Magalhães," Cuiabá, 6 jul. 1867, caixa 1867 B.

45. APEMT, "Ofício do vigário da freguesia da chapada dos Guimarães padre Joaquim de Sousa Caldas ao subdelegado do distrito tenente-coronel João José de Siqueira," freguesia da Chapada, 23 mai. 1868, caixa 1868 B.
46. In June 1867, Brazilian army troops had retaken the city of Corumbá and the southern Mato Grosso province. Even so, communication through the Silver River remained compromised.
47. APEMT, "Carta de Antônio Bruno Borges ao presidente da província Dr. José V. de Couto Magalhães," Rio da Casca, 2 jan. 1868, caixa 1868 C. Data on the *quilombo* of Manso River was extracted from information contained in the aforementioned letter.
48. In 1867, the soldiers that were returning from the campaign of retaking the southern part of the province entered Cuiabá contaminated by the smallpox virus. The disease spread easily between people, causing an estimated 50 percent decrease in the population: Volpato, *Cativos do sertão*, 75.
49. "Relatório apresentado á Assembléa Legislativa Provincial de Mato Grosso em 4 de outubro de 1872, pelo exm° snr. presidente da província o tenente-coronel Dr. Francisco José Cardozo Junior" (Rio de Janeiro: Typ. do Apóstolo, 1873), 18.
50. APEMT, "Ofício do chefe de polícia Ernesto Júlio Bandeira de Meio ao presidente da província Dr. Francisco José Cardozo Junior," Cuiabá, 18 nov. 1871, caixa 1871 E; "Relatório apresentado pelo capitão Luciano Pereira de Sousa ao chefe de polícia Ernesto Júlio Bandeira de Meio," Cuiabá, 13 dez. 1871, caixa 1871 E.
51. APEMT, "Ofício do chefe de polícia Ernesto Júlio Bandeira de Meio ao presidente da província Dr. Francisco José Cardozo Junior," Cuiabá, 18 nov. 1871, caixa 1871 E; "Relatório de Francisco José Cardozo Junior, 1872," 20, 22.
52. APEMT, "Relatório apresentado pelo capitão Luciano Pereira de Sousa," 13 dez. 1871, caixa 1871 E.

10

1. Gilka V. F. de Salles, *Economia e Escravidão na Capitania de Goiás* (Goiânia: Centro Editorial e Gráfica da UFG, 1992), 227. See also Luiz Palacin, *Goiás 1722-1822: Estrutura e Conjuntura numa Capitania de Minas*, 2 ed. (Goiânia: Oriente, 1976), 117; and Martiniano J. Silva, *Sombra dos Quilombos: Introdução ao Estudo do Negro em Goiás* (Goiânia: Ed. Barão de Itararé e Editora Cultura Goiânia, 1974), 44.
2. In the eighteenth century, the captaincy of Goiás was much larger than the modern state of Goiás, and its boundaries were ill defined. It was then

900,000 km; today, the modern state of Goiás is only 353,000 km, and Tocantins is 289,000 km. "Throughout its history, Goiás lost cerca 258,000 km." Horieste Gomes and Antônio Teixeira Neto, *Geografia:Goiás /Tocantins* (Goiânia: Centro Editorial e Gráfico da UFG, 1993), 57-60. This current essay concerns those quilombos that were in the territory claimed by the governors of Goiás, whose capital was Vila Boa de Goiás. Thus, it will also include some quilombos in the borderlands, especially Mato Grosso and Minas Gerais.

3. Lisbon, Arquivo Histórico do Tribunal de Contas (hereafter AHTC), 4076, Livro de registro das representações da capitania de Goyaz, 9 August 1787, ff. 45-54.

4. Salles, *Economia*, 290.

5. Lisbon, Arquivo Nacional da Torre do Tombo (hereafter ANTT), maço 600, Ministério do Reino, Letra D, Mappa da Companhia de Dragões da Guarnição da Capitania de Goyaz..., Vila Boa, 17 November 1772.

6. Salles, *Economia*, 230. Some of the best information on ethnicity survives in early nineteenth-century tax records for the City of Goiás at the Arquivo do Museu das Bandeiras (hereafter AMB) and some parish registries of the eighteenth century.

7. Dulce Madalena Rios Pedroso, "Avá-Canoeiro: A história do povo invisível—séculos xviii e xix" (Master's thesis, Federal University of Goiás, 1992), 145; and André A. de Toral, "Os índios negros ou os Carijó de Goiás: A História dos Avá-Canoeiro," *Revista de Antropologia*, 27/28 (São Paulo, 1984-1985), 292-293. As Pedroso notes, "thus the theory that the Avá-Canoeiro Indians are the result of the miscegenation between the Carijó and quilombolas has still not completely lost credibility, because, besides the lack of knowledge of the history of the Avá-Canoeiro, there are strong evidences of the occasional crossing among groups of Avá-Canoeiro and blacks in specific localities of the Goiano territory" (136).

8. On arming "half of his blacks" against the Kayapó, see Lisbon, Arquivo Histórico Ultramarino (hereafter AHU), no. 995, caixa 17, Goiás, 1756-1799, Ofício de João Manuel de Mello, Via Boa, 29 May 1760; Palacin, *Goiás*, 117; and regarding *engenhos* (sugar plantations): one with "300 captives" was near the town of São José de Tocantins (Goiânia, Arquivo Histórico Estadual de Goiás, hereafter AHG, Municípios, São José, Relatório da Câmara Municipal da Villa de São José de Tocantins..., Paço da Câmara, 17 February 1849); and another with 200 slaves was property of a "comboeiro de escravos" (slave trader). AHU, caixa 29, Goiás, 1772-1799, "Requerimento de João Dias de Aguiar," 1790-1794.

9. Gomes and Teixeira Neto, *Geografia*, 91-122.

10. Curt Nimuendajú, *The Apinaye,* trans. by Robert H. Lowie and ed. by Robert H. Lowie and John M. Cooper (New York: Humanities Press, 1967), 2.
11. ANTT, maço 500, Ministério do Reino, Negócios do Brasil e Ultramar, 1730-1823, pacote 1772, Villa Bella, Luis Pinto de Souza, "letter to Luiz de Albuquerque de Mello," Villa Bella, 24 December 1772.
12. Salles, *Economia,* 228.
13. Ibid., 290
14. Ibid., 289-290; and Palacin, *Goiás,* 117.
15. Division into colonial comarcas: Luiz Antonio da Silva e Souza, "Memoria sobre O Descobrimento, Governo, População, e Cousas mais Notaveis da Capitania de Goyaz [1812]," *Revista Trimensal de Historia e Geographia ou Jornal do Instituto Historico e Geographico Brazileiro,* no. 16 (4 Trimestre of 1849), 103-104.
16. Nimuendajú, *Apinaye,* 3. On attacks on fugitive slaves by the "gentiles" of the Tocantins River and request for "hum destacamento" at the Rio "as pederneiras," see AHU, no. 995, caixa 17, Goiás, 1756-1799 [1779?].
17. The black community of São Sebastião in the Bico de Papagaio (parrot's beak) "perhaps was" a quilombo. Oral tradition collected by us in the state of Tocantins, July 1994.
18. ANTT, maço 598, Ministério do Reino, Negócios do Ultramar, Letra B, 1753-1763, "letter of José dos Santos Pereira to Rd.o Dr. Pedro Barboza Cannães, Vigario Geral," São Félix, 5 October 1761; and Rio de Janeiro, Instituto Histórico e Geográfico Brasileiro (hereafter IHGB), Arquivo 1.2.7, v. 36; "Ofício of João Manuel de Mello to the Conde d'Oeiras," Vila Boa, 29 May 1760, f. 82.
19. Rosolinda Batista de Abreu Cordeiro, *Arraias: Suas raizes e sua gente* (Goiânia: s.n., 1991).
20. Serra do Mocambo: Lisbon, Biblioteca Nacional, Seção de Reservados, Cod. 568, "Da Viagem que se faz da Cidade de Bellem [sic] do Grão Pará, athe ás ultimas Colonias dos Dominios Portuguezas nos Rios Amazonas, e Negro Pelo Tenente Coronel de Engenharia João Vasco Manoel de Braun," 1782; and IHGB, Arq. 1.2.7, v. 36, "Ofício of João Manuel de Mello to the Conde de Oeiras, Vila Boa, 30 December 1760, f. 113.
21. Affonso de Taunay, citing Cunha Matos, "says that in Natividade there was [at a] certain time more than 40,000 blacks." Silva e Sousa reported that 12,000 blacks worked in 1732 "on the deflection of the Maranhão river." Silva, *Sombra,* 24-25.
22. Pilar: AHG, Municípios, Pilar, caixa 3, "Histórico de Pilar de Goiás," typescript; and Sales, *Economia,* 290.

23. Pedroso, "Avá-Canoeiro," 133-135.
24. Ibid., 136.
25. Muquém: Paulo Bertran, *Memória de Niquelândia* (Brasília: Fundação Nacional Pró-Memória, 1985), 16, 89-92; and AHG, Municípios, São José, Relatório da Câmara Municipal de São José do Tocantins, 20 June 1846.
26. Tesouras: Salles, *Economia,* 289, 291; and Crixás: Palacin, *Goiás,* 117.
27. Salles, *Economia,* 288-289.
28. Waldemar de Almeida Barbosa, *Negros e quilombos em Minas Gerais* (Belo Horizonte: s.n., 1972), 30-39.
29. José Martins Pereira de Alencastre, *Anais da Província de Goiás* (Brasília: Editora Gráfica Ipiranga, Inc., [1863] 1979), 117; and another version is in Mari de Nasaré Baiocchi, *Negros de Cedro* (São Paulo: Editora Ática, 1983), 31.
30. King: Rio de Janeiro, Biblioteca Nacional (hereafter RJBN), seção de manuscritos, 2,3,9, Documentos vários, ff. 79-80; and Carlota: Salles, *Economia,* 290.
31. Santa Luzia, Bonfim, and Santa Cruz: Salles, *Economia,* 286, 290.
32. São Marcos River: Alencastre, *Anais,* 70.
33. Paranaíba River: Barbosa, *Negros e Quilombos,* 48, 51, 67-68. There are two rivers know as the Rio das Velhas: the Araguari or Rio das Velhas, which used to be in the captaincy of Goiás but is now in Minas Gerais, and the Rio das Velhas, which is a tributary of the São Francisco River. Since the governors of Goiás commonly sent expeditions across the Paranaíba River to pursue quilomnbolas, I am assuming the quilombos were located in the region of the Araguari River, especially since Alencastre locates the relatives of Bartolomeu Bueno, who led a bandeira against quilombos, "in the sertão . . . between the Paranaíba, rio das Velhas and Grande River." See Alencastre, *Anais,* 117. Paracatu: Barbosa, *Negros e Quilombos,* 72.
34. Quilombo das cabeceiras do Abaeté: AHU, caixa 29, Goiás, 1772-1799, "letter of Antônio Pinto de Castro to José Rodrigues Freire," Vila Boa, 8 October 1776.
35. Grande River: IHGB, Lata 397, doc. 2, "Redução dos índios da Capitania de Goiás."
36. The above description is based on correspondence of the governors of Goiás and the reports of travelers. See in particular, Auguste de Saint-Hilaire, *Viagem à Província de Goiás,* trans. by Regina Regis Junqueira (Belo Horizonte: Editora Itatiaia, 1975), 76.
37. Palacin, *Goiás,* 120.

38. José Rodrigues Freire: AHU, caixa 29, Goiás, 1772-1799, ff. 157-158; and ANTT, maço 321, Ministério do Reino, Conselho Ultramarino, Consultas, 1781-1792, pacote 1789.
39. Palacin, *Goiás*, 118.
40. RJBN, I-31, 21,9, Goiás (Capitania), "Cópia da Memória oferecida pelo Capitam d'ordenanças Francisco José Pinto de Mangalhens [sic] em 3 de Janeiro de 1813;" with notes dated 1815.
41. IHGB, Arquivo, 1.2.7, v. 36, "Ofício of João Manuel de Mello to Francisco Xavier de Mendonça Furtado," Vila Boa, 30 March 1765, f. 144.
42. *Relação da Conquista do Gentio Xavante, conseguida pelo Ill.mo e Ex.mo Senhor Tristão da Cunha Menezes, Governador, e Capitão General da Capitania de Goiaz*... (Lisbon: Typog. Nunesianna, 1790), 25.
43. Xavante at Carretão: Mary Karasch, "Catequese e Cativeiro: Política indigenista em Goiás, 1780-1889," trans. by Beatriz Perrone-Moisés, in *História dos índios no Brasil*, ed. Manuela Carneiro da Cunha (São Paulo: Companhia das Letras, 1992), 408. The *História dos índios* has additional information on the modern Xavante and other indigenous populations of Goiás.
44. IHGB, Lata 397, doc. 2, "Redução dos índios da Capitania de Goiás"; ibid on island in Grande River; and on fugitives in the Tocantins region: AHU, no. 995, caixa 17, Goiás, 1756-1799 (1779?].
45. Karajá capture: IHGB, Lata 281, pasta 4, doc. 14, Goiás, Documentos originais sobre a navegação e comércio do Pará para Goiás, "Navegação do rio Araguaia," s.d.
46. Carlota: Salles, *Economia*, 290.
47. Pedestres: AMB, 444, Praça de Militares, Pedestres, 1760 to 1783.
48. AHU, caixa 29, Goiás, 1772-1799, Vila Boa, 8 October 1776.
49. Henriques: AHU, caixa 44, Goiás, 1801-1803, "letter of Governador João Manuel de Meneses to D. Rodrigo de Souza Coutinho," Vila Boa, 7 October 1800; AHU, 1001, caixa 2, Goiás, 1734-1832, 1807; and AHG, Documentação Diversa, no. 66, "Relação do Regimento de Infantaria Miliciana de Henriques," 1823-1824; and "Correspondência dirigida do Comandante da Armas—Raymundo José da Cunha Mattos."
50. Palacin, Goiás, 117; AHU, no. 1002, caixa 4, Goiás, 1736-1825, Manuel Joaquim de Aguiar Mourão, 29 September 1800.
51. José Sebastião Pinheiro, "No Vão ... A Solitária Liberdade de Uma Comunidade Negra," *O Popular* (Goiânia), 31 August[1993?]. My thanks to Cleidemar A. Almeida for a zeroxed copy of this newspaper article. See also "Dos quilombos fez-se Kalunga," in *Goianidade,* special edition (Goiânia, December 1992), documentários 12-13. The anthropologist Mari Baiocchi has also studied these quilombos. According to James Brooke, "about 4,000

descendants" [of slaves who fled to the 'rugged hill country above the Bezerra Falls on the Paraná River'] live in 41 villages scattered over 780 square miles." They have been threatened by about 60 mining, ranching, and farming companies that invaded their lands. See James Brooke, "Brazil Seeks to Return Ancestral Lands to Descendants of Runaway Slaves, *The New York Times* 15 August 1993, International, 12.

11

1. Part of it would be the city of Iguaçu in 1833, and part of the municipality of Estrela, in 1846. The region currently comprises the municipalities of Belford Roxo, Duque de Caxias, Nova Iguaçu and São João de Meriti, belonging to the state of Rio de Janeiro. For socio-economic data in the eighteenth century, see "Memórias publicas e econômicas da cidade de São Sebastião do Rio de Janeiro para uso do vice-rey Luiz de Vasconcellos por observação curiosa dos annos de 1779 até o de 1789," *Revista do Instituto Histórico e Geográfico Brasileiro* (RIHGB), tome XLVII (47), 27. I thank João José Reis his comments on an earlier version of this chapter.
2. See "Relação do marquez de Lavradio," RIHGB, tome LXXVI (79), 289-360.
3. Ibid., 320-4 and 326-9.
4. By the way, Waldick Pereira points out that the difference between the number of slaves employed in the mills and devices that appear in the Marquis of Lavradio's data and the total slave population of the region is due to "the fact that in that information is not included the planters of sugarcane farms, which absorbed a large part of that population." See Waldick Pereira, *Cana, Café & Laranja: História econômica de Nova Iguaçu* (Rio de Janeiro, Fundação Getulio Vargas/SEEC, 1977), 25. Analysing the distribution of slaves in mills and distilleries of Rio de Janeiro in the late eighteenth century from the same data of "Relação do marquez do Lavradio," Iraci Costa points out that mill property with the squad size of 21 to forty captives predominates, while the average number of slaves who worked in distilleries is ten captives. See Iraci del Nero Costa, "Nota sobre a posse de escravos nos engenhos e engenhocas fluminenses (1778)," *Revista do Instituto de Estudos Brasileiros*, 28 (1988), 111-3.
5. See Waldick Pereira, *Cana, Café & Laranja.*
6. See José Mattoso Maia Forte, *Memória da fundação de Iguassú* (Rio de Janeiro: Typ. do Jornal do Commércio, 1933), 36.
7. "Relação do marquez do Lavradio," 320, 323 and 330-1.
8. Maia Forte, *Memória*, 64.

9. Ibid, 46.
10. See John Luccock, *Notas sobre o Rio de Janeiro e partes meridionais do Brasil, 1808 - 1818* (São Paulo, Livraria Martins, 1942), cited in Marcia Maria Menendes Motta, "Pelas 'Banda d'Alem' (fronteira fechada e arrendatários-escravistas em uma região policultora—1808- 1888)" (Niterói, dissertation, ICHF/UFF, 1989), 5.
11. See Maia Forte, *Memória*, 56-7.
12. Ibid., 59.
13. See Pereira, *Cana, café & laranga*; Maia Forte, *Memória*; Renato da Silveira Mendes, *Paisagens culturais da baixada Fluminense* (São Paulo, USP, 1950).
14. For the economic and agrarian studies examining the areas of Itaboraí and São Gonçalo, see, respectively, Ana Maria dos Santos, "Vida econômica de Itaboraí no século XIX" (Niterói, dissertation, ICHF/UFF, 1974), and Motta, "Pelas 'Bandas d 'Alem'."
15. See Pereira, *Cana, café & laranga*.
16. See "Relatório do Ministério do Império, 1855-6," 81 (Na Biblioteca Nacional do Rio de Janeiro—BNRJ—rolo microfilmado).
17. Ibid., 28.35-6 and 38. With regard to disease outbreaks and the high mortality rate of captives in slave societies, we can mention the study of Kenneth Kiple. In addressing the cholera epidemics in the Caribbean in the nineteenth century, it highlights the high incidence of death in the black population. In Cuba, for example, 3/4 of the population who had died due to the cholera epidemic was black (about 75 percent of the dead were slaves). This impact of the epidemic on the black masses was due largely to poor sanitary conditions in which this population lived in towns where the black community prevailed over the poor free population, such as in rural areas where the population was predominantly slaves. See Kenneth F. Kiple, "Cholera and race in the Caribbean," *Journal of Latin American Studies* 17, no. 1 (1985), 157-77.
18. Ibid., 30-1.
19. Ibid., 30.
20. See Pereira, *Cana, café & laranga*.
21. If we compare, for example, the Iguaçu data with population data of slave from Vassouras (Parish of Pati de Alferes) we have in 1850 about 75 percent of the population made up of slaves; in 1872, this rate decreases to 56 percent. See Nancy Priscilla Smith Soeiro, "Customary rightholders and Legal Claimants to land in Rio de Janeiro, Brazil, 1870-1890," *The Americas*, XLVIII: 4 (1992), 495, table 2.
22. If we consider the population census of the whole province of Rio de Janeiro in 1872, we have the following data: 37.5 percent of the population was

slaves, while 62.5 percent were free; 38 percent of the free population was nonwhite and 61.25 percent of the entire population (both free and slave) was non-white. [Translator's note: The term "African" could mean an enslaved person born in Africa, or a person of African descent. The term "creole" could mean a person of African descent born in Brazil or a person of mixed race.]

23. The range of one to fourteen years was constituted by 21 percent, 18 percent from 41 to sixty years, 3.5 percent of more than sixty years and about 7.5 percent of slaves who had unknown age.

24. In connection with this process in the neighboring areas of the Iguaçu region, such as Itaboraí and São Gonçalo, see Santos, *Vida econômica*; Motta, "Pelas Bandas d 'Além." Studying the Fluminense region of Capivari, in the nineteenth century, Castro, for example, highlighted the strategies of the poor freemen in food production agriculture in a region not prone to agro-export activities. Such strategies of the poor freemen consisted in both seeking access to land, and the use of small flocks of slaves as hand labor. See Hebe Maria Mattos de Castro, *Ao sul da Historia: Lavradores pobres na crise do trabalho escravo* (São Paulo: Brasiliense, 1987).

25. As for the names given to the quilombos of the Iguaçu region, it is possible to assume that they were related to their geographical locations. The word *Bomba*, of course, meant Machambomba, a locality of the area (including name of a sugarmill in the region from the seventeenth century). *Gabriel* was the name of a local creek, an important tributary of Iguaçu and Sarapuí rivers. Frederico Fernandes, in an article not without interest, analyzes the meanings of the word *machambomba* in the region of Iguaçu and its Bantu African origin. Cf. Frederico Fernandes Pereira, "Maxambomba - A raiz negra e mística de Nova Iguaçu," Correio da Lavoura, Nova Iguaçu, Saturday 9 and Sunday 10 May 1987, 5. In any event, we do not know if the names of quilombos in Brazil were given by their own inhabitants or just were called because of their geographic location and/or names of their leaders. In this regard, for example, to the Jamaican quilombolas, Campbell draws attention to the fact that a quilombo was named *accompon*, which meant in the African language of the Akan ethnic group, big and/or main city (*onyankopon*). See Mavis C. Campbell, "Marronage in Jamaica: its origin in the seventeenth century," in *Comparative Perspectives on Slavery in New World Plantation Societies,* eds., Vera Rubin and Arthur Tudem, vol. 292, (New York, 1977), 392.

26. National Archive (AN), códice 318, 13 Jul. 1808, vol. 1, fls. 9 v.

27. AN, códice 329, December 15 of 1823, volume 5, 127 v.

28. See Mary C. Karasch, *Slave Life in Rio de Janeiro, 1808-1850* (Princeton: Princeton University Press, 1987), 309.
29. AN, IJ6, maço 164, Ofícios de polícia da Corte, "Ofício do chefe de polícia da Corte enviado ao ministro da Justiça," 12 abr. 1825.
30. AN, GIFI, pacote 5 B 377, documentação identificada, "Petição do doutor Jacintho José da Silva Quintão," 29 abr. 1825.
31. Karasch, *Slave life in Rio*, 314.
32. AN, códice 326, "Registro do ofício expedido ao comandante do distrito da freguezia de Santo Antônio de Jacutinga," 12 jun. 1812, vol. 1, fls. 74, "Ofício do intendente de polícia da Corte enviado ao coronel de Inhomerim," 30 dez. 1811, vol. 1, fls. 58v. - 59; "Ofício do intendente de polícia da Corte enviado ao governador das armas," 16 nov. 1812, vol. 1, fls. 92v - 93.
33. AN, códice 403, 16 mar. 1816, vol. 1, fls. 291.
34. AN, códice 327, ""Ofício do intendente de polícia da Corte enviado ao coronel Miguel Antônio Flangini," 8 jul. 1825, vol. 1, fls. 167.
35. AN, códice 359, 3 jan. 1826, fls. 3-4 and 14, 22 nov. 1826, fls. 63; códice 360, 5 jan. 1827 and 11 fev. 1827, fls. 70 and 89; códice 403, 2 fev. 1826 and 6 abr. 1826, p. 25 and 43 and códice 404, 4 jul. 1827, fls. 56, códice 404, 15 jul. 1828, fls. 141, 9 nov. 1829, fls.188.
36. AN, GIFI, pacote 5 B 510, documentação identificada, 3 mar. 1830.
37. AN, códice 331, 31 mai. 1836, fls. 46 v.
38. "Relatório do vice-presidente da província do Rio de Janeiro," in 1837 (Relatórios de presidentes de província (RJ), 1835/1843—rolos microfilmados). See also José Alípio Goulart, *Da fuga ao suicídio (Aspectos da rebeldia dos escravos no Brasil)* (Rio de Janeiro: Conquista, 1972), 231.
39. AN, códice 331, " Ofícios do chefe de polícia da Corte enviados ao juiz de paz da freguezia de N. S. do Pilar," 23 out. 1838 and 11 dez. 1838, fls. 240 v. and 257 v.
40. Jornal do Commércio, 13 nov. 1859, *Gazetilha*, 1.
41. For a comparative view of the communities of runaway slaves across America, see Richard Price (ed.), *Maroon societies: Rebel Slave Communities in the Americas*, 2nd ed (Baltimore: The Johns Hopkins University Press, 1979).
42. AN, IJ1, maço 868, Ofícios de presidentes de província (RJ), "Ofício do delegado de polícia de Iguassu enviado ao chefe de polícia da província" (RJ), 9 dez. 1859.
43. Although too schematic, Décio Freitas produced a classification of Brazilian quilombos from its main economic practices. see Décio Freitas, *O escravismo brasileiro*, 2 ed. (Porto Alegre: Mercado Aberto, 1982), 38-44.
44. See Edison Carneiro, *O Quilombo dos Palmares*, 3 ed. (Rio de Janeiro: Civilização Brasileira, 1966), 28; Carlos Magno Guimaraes, "Os quilombos do

século do ouro (Minas Gerais—século XVIII)," *Estudos Econômicos*, 18 (1988), 15; Waldemar de Almeida Barbosa, *Negros e quilombos em Minas Gerais* (Belo Horizonte, 1972), 67-8.

45. Instituto Histórico e Geográfico de Nova Iguaçu (IHGNI), manuscritos avulsos, tombo número MS 0253, "Ofício do delegado de Iguassu enviado ao chefe de polícia da província (RJ), 17 dez. 1859 and AN, IJI, maço 488, ofícios de presidentes de província (RJ)," "Ofício do presidente da província enviado ao ministro da Justiça," 27 abr. 1876.
46. AN, IJ1, maço 868, ofícios de presidentes de província (RJ), "Ofício do presidente da província (RJ) enviado ao chefe de polícia da província," 10 dez. 1859.
47. See Maia Forte, *Memória*, 64.
48. AN, IJ1, maço 493, ofícios de presidentes de província (RJ), "Despacho da Presidência da província do Rio de Janeiro," 8 jan. 1878.
49. Cf. Maria Odila da Silva, "Nas fímbrias da escravidão urbana: negras de tabuleiro e de ganho," *Estudos Econômicos*, 15 (1985), 167-80.
50. Jornal do Commércio 30 nov. 1859, *Gazetilha*, 1 (emphasis in original).
51. Diário do Rio de Janeiro, 5 jul. 1876, Noticiário, p. 2. In Amsterdam (Netherlands) in the eighteenth century, because of commercial interests and speculative purposes, rumors were spread about the constant threat of attacks by Maroons of Suriname, causing with it a decline in many commodity prices in local markets. See Price (ed.), *Maroon societies*, 14.
52. Stein analyzing the municipality of Vassouras in Rio de Janeiro province in the nineteenth century covers the permanent seizure of state farmers. See Stanley Stein, *Vassouras: um municipio brasileiro do café, 1850-1900* (Rio de Janeiro: Nova Fronteira, 1990), 116-7, 120-1, 178 and 209-10.
53. AN, IJ1, maço 858, ofícios de presidentes de província (RJ), "Petição enviada ao juiz de fora da Vila Real da Praia Grande," 15 mai. 1823.
54. AN, IJ1, maço 164, ofícios de polícia da Corte, portaria expedida pelo chefe de polícia da Corte, 12 abr. 1825.
55. AN, GIFI, pacote 6 D 5, documentação identificada, 18 jun. 1836.
56. In 1835, the imperial authorities were concerned with the formation of secret societies in the Court, consisting of free people of color, freedmen and captives. It was said that, such societies collected contributions to finance the agitators (slaves and freedmen disguised as street vendors) that would propagate subversive doctrines to the slave masses. See Manuela Carneiro da Cunha, *Negros, estrangeiros: Os escravos libertos e sua volta à África* (São Paulo: Brasiliense, 1985), 74. In Cuba, for example, in the first half of the nineteenth century, the colonial authorities saw the free colored population as fundamentally "dangerous." See Robert Paquette, *Sugar is made with blood:*

The conspiracy of la Escalera and the conflict over slavery in Cuba (Middletown: Wesleyan University Press, 1989), esp. Chapter 4.

57. See Arquivo Geral da Cidade do Rio de Janeiro (AGCRJ), "Código de posturas da illustríssima Camara Municipal" (Rio de Janeiro: Typographia Dois de Dezembro, 1854), título sexto, 55 and 57-8.
58. See for example, Eugene Genovese, *Da rebelião a revolução: as revoltas de escravos nas Americas* (São Paulo: Global 1983).
59. Arquivo Público do Rio de Janeiro (JAP), Fundo JP, coleção 191,5 jan. 1836.
60. AN, IJ1, maço 860, ofícios de presidentes de província (RJ), 2 m a i. 1838.
61. AN, IJ1, maço 446, ofícios de presidentes de província (RJ), "Ofício do chefe de polícia da Corte enviado ao presidente da província (RJ)," 17 dez. 1841.
62. AN, IJ1, maço 868, ofícios de presidentes de província (RJ), "Ofício do presidente de provfncia (RJ) enviado ao chefe de polícia da província," 9 dez. 1859.
63. See Maia Forte, *Memória*.
64. JAP, fundo SPP, coleção 165, documento 42, "Livro de declarações de propriedade de escravos detidos na Casa de Detenção (Niterói) por fugidos," 28 dez. 1868, fls. 42 - 42 v.
65. See Luiz Carlos Soares, "Os escravos de ganho no Rio de Janeiro do século XIX," *Revista Brasileira de História*, 8: 16, (1988), 118 - 124.
66. AN, GIFI, pacote 5 B 380, documentação identificada, 21 mai. 1832.
67. See Stanley J. Stein, 178.
68. Diário de Campos, 14 jul. 1876, Noticiário, 3.
69. Jornal do Commércio, 6 jan. 1860, *Gazetilha*, 1.
70. IHGNI, manuscritos avulsos, tombo número MS 0253, 2 jan. 1860.
71. Jornal do Commércio, 28 dez. 1868, Publicações "A Pedido," p. 2 and AN, IJ1, maço 493, ofícios de presidentes de província (RJ), "Ofício do presidente de província (RJ) enviado ao ministro da justiça," 29 dez. 1877.
72. See D. Mateus Rocha, *O mosteiro de São Bento do Rio de Janeiro 1590/1990*, Rio de Janeiro, Studio HMF, 1991, pp. 56-60 and AMSB/RJ, códice 49, fls.71 - 76v.
73. Arquivo do mosteiro de São Bento do Rio de Janeiro (AMSB/RJ), códice 50, 96-7.
74. See Rocha, *O mosterio de São Bento*.
75. Jornal do Commércio, 14 abr. 1868, *Gazetilha*, 1 and Diário do Rio de Janeiro, 5 jul. 1876, Noticiário, 2.
76. IHGNI, manuscrítos avulsos, tombo número MS 0253, "Ofícios do chefe de polícia da província enviados ao presidente da província (RJ)," 14 fev. 1860 and 23 fev. 1860 and AN, IJ1, maço 462, ofícios de presidentes de

província (RJ), "Ofício do chefe de polícia da província enviado ao presidente da província (RJ))," 29 dez. 1877.

77. Rocha, *O mosteiro de São Bento*.

78. The English traveler Henry Koster, who was in Brazil at the beginning of the nineteenth century and was landowner and also owned slaves in Pernambuco, said about the captives of the Benedictines that: "Almost all these works [of slaves] are done at three in the afternoon, making it easier for workers an opportunity to improve their own properties. Saturday of each week belongs to the slaves to provide their own subsistence, apart from Sundays and holy days. Those who are diligent rarely fail to buy their freedom. The monks do not keep any interference regarding plantations given to slaves, and when one of these dies or gets his freedom, they allow him to bequeath his piece of land to any partner of his choice." Henry Koster, *Viagens ao Nordeste do Brasil* (São Paulo: Nacional, 1942), 512.

79. Koster had drawn attention - as we have seen - to the fact that the captivity of the Benedictines worked in the "task system." In this sense, slaves had more free time to devote to their own economy. Johnson, studying the emergence of a black peasantry in the Bahamas during slavery, highlights how the task system where the captives worked favored the development of their own economies. See Howard Johnson, "The emergence of the peasantry in the Bahamas during slavery," *Slavery & Abolition*, 10, no. 2 (1989), 174.

80. AMSB/RJ, códice 65, 1839-1842, pp. 26 v and 138 v, códice 27, 1839-1842, 22.

81. See Sidney W. Mintz, "A note on the definition of peasantries," *Journal of Peasant Studies* 1, no. 1 (1973), 91-106.

82. See Sidney W. Mintz, "Slavery and the rise of peasantries" *Historical Reflections*, 6, no. 1 (1979), 213-53. See also Ciro Flamarion S. Cardoso, *Escravo ou camponês? O protocampesinato negro nas Américas*, São Paulo, Brasiliense, 1987.

83. For an analysis of the possible links between the economic practices of the Maroons and the plantations of slaves in the last decades of slavery in the province of Rio de Janeiro, see Flavio Gomes dos Santos, *Histórias de quilombolas: Mocambos e comunidades de senzalas no Rio de Janeiro—século XIX*, Rio de Janeiro, Imprensa Nacional, 1995.

84. *O Município*, 30 mar. 1879, "Anúncios," 4.

85. See Ira Berlin and Philip D. Morgan (eds.), "The slaves' economy: Independent production by slaves in the America," *Slavery & abolition*, 12, no. 1 (1991), 1-27.

86. See Sidney W. Mintz, "The origins of the Jamaican market system," in *Caribbean Transformations* (Chicago: Aldine Publishing Company, 1974), 180-213.
87. See David Barry Gaspar, "Slavery, amelioration and Sunday markets in Antigua, 1823-1831," *Slavery & Abolition*, 9, no. 1 (1988), 1-28 and Betty Wood, "'White society' and the 'informal' slave economies of lowcountry Georgia, c. 1763-1830," *Slavery & Abolition*, 11, no. 3 (1990), 313-31.
88. View Gomes, *Histórias de quilombolas*, especially chapter III: "Under the black wave: slaves and *quilombolas* promoting their own emancipation in the last decades of slavery."
89. A pioneer and major study of Brazilian quilombos remains Clóvis Moura, *Rebeliões das senzulas: Quilombos, insurreições e guerrilhas* (Rio de Janeiro: Conquista, 1972) (The 1st edition of this work dates from 1959, published by Editora Zumbi.) Some indicative analyses of the threat that the fugitives communities represented to the men in the United States are themselves in John W. Blassingame, *The slave community plantation life in the antebellum South* (New York: Oxford University Press, 1979), 209-10.
90. JAP, fundo PP, coleção 133, "Representação dos fazendeiros de Capivari ao chefe de polícia da província do Rio de Janeiro," 10 fev. 1885, cited in Humberto Fernandes Machado, *Escravos, senhores e café: um estudo sobre a crise da cafeicultura do vale do Paraiba fluminense (1860-1888)*, Niterói, dissertação de mestrado, ICHF/UFF (1983), 233.
91. See Price (ed.), *Maroon societies*, 10-1.
92. For example, we can mention here the following statement from Décio Freitas: "The quilombos bordered the edge of the slave society: geographic marginalization, economic and social. They did not really offer any serious risk to the system; they caused disruption and losses, and certain, however, left it intact. Setting a primary form of struggle and libertation, they showed themselves incapable of subduing and transforming the whole society. It was a repetitive and hopeless struggle." Freitas, *O escravismo*, 45.
93. See Silvia W. de Groot, "Maroon of Surinam: dependence and independence," in Rubin and Tuden (eds.), *Comparative Perspectives*, 455-63. See also from the same author: "The Maroon of Suriname: Agents their own emancipation," in David Richardson, *Abolition and its aftermath: The historical context, 1790-1916* (University of Hull, 1985), 54-79.
94. AN, Athanázio (slave), defendant; processo crime/Corte de Apelação, caixa 3699, número 2,1863, município de Itu, província de São Paulo, "Interrogatório do escravo Athanázio," fls. 70 v. - 72.
95. Arquivo do Cartório do Terceiro Ofício de Campos (ACTOC), processo crime, Sotero, Robem, Jeremias, Valério, Josué e Silla (réus escravos), crime

de homicídio, 1866, freguesia de Santo Antônio de Guarulhos, maço 319, interrogatórios, fls. 15 - 17v.

12

1. [Translator's note] Indigenes of the then province and current Brazil's southernmost state, Rio Grande do Sul.
2. [Translator's note] Highlands in the northeast of the country know as *minas gerais* (general mines), which later became the state of Minas Gerais.
3. See Barbosa Lessa, "O que era o 'Continente," *Continente*, 1: 2 (January, 1989).
4. See Mário Maestri, *O escravo gaúcho: resistência e trabalho*, 2nd ed. (Porto Alegre, UFRGS, 1984).
5. "Mapa do tenente Córdoba," *cited in* Dante de Laytano, *O negro no Rio Grande do Sul* (Porto Alegre: PUC, 1957), 35.
6. Eleutério Camargo, "Quadro estatístico e geográfico." *De província de São Pedro a estado do Rio Grande do Sul.* Census of RS: 1803-1950, 2 ed. (Porto Alegre: FEE, 1986).
7. See Fernando Henrique Cardoso, *Capitalismo e escravidão no Brasil meridional*, 2nd ed. (Rio de Janeiro: Paz e Terra, 1977), 81.
8. See *O Diccionario geographico, histórico e estatístico do estado do Rio Grande do Sul*, by Octavio Augusto de Farias (Porto Alegre, Globo, 1914). It documents a arroyo in the municipality of Jaguarão that was named *Quilombinho*; it also documents places that were called *Quilombo*, such as the municipalities of Soledade, Santo Antônio, São Leopoldo e Herval; arroyos in the municipalities of Antônio, Santa Maria, Rio Pardo, Santa Cruz, Jaguarão, Pelotas, Caí e Conceição do Arroio. It also lends this denomination to an island in the River Guaíba, a village in the municipality of Taquara and a grove in the municipality of Conceição do Arroio.
9. See Laytano, *O negro no Rio Grande do Sul*, 30.
10. Arquivo Histórico (Historical Archive) de Porto Alegre (AHPA). Minutes from Câmara Municipal [City Council] de Porto Alegre (CMPOA). Vereanças, 1766 a 1780. 1.1.1.1., p. 46. We've added punctuation and modernized the language.
11. AHPA. Minutes from CMPA. Vereanças, 1766a 1780. 1.1.1.1., p. 164; copies 1/2, p. 83.
12. AHPA. Minutes from CMPA Vereanças, 1788 a 1794. 1.1.1.3., p. 156 bis.; copies 2/3, p. 214. The "anjinhos" (little angels) were iron rings used to immobilize the fingers of prisoners and runaway slaves.

13. *Annais (Annals) do III Congresso Sul-rio-grandense de História e Geografia*, v. 2 (1940), 203. We did not find records for this in the Minutes from CMPA.
14. AHPA. Minutes from CMPA. Vereanças, 1794a 1804.1.1.1.4., 112 bis; copies 4, 111. On the years following 1794, the Minutes from the Porto Alegre City Council documented the appointment of slave catchers to the parishes of Nossa Senhora dos Anjos da Aldeia, Gravataí, Santo Antônio da Patrulha, Conceição do Arroio, Rio Pardo etc.
15. See note 6.
16. See Anselmo Amaral, *Os campos neutrais*, s.nt.
17. One of the duties assigned to the "juíz de fora" (external judge) was to take charge of procedures against criminals during his term (municipality).
18. Arquivo Histórico (Historical Archive) do Rio Grande do Sul (AHRGS). Grupo documental (Archival group). Justice. Juízo de Fora. Corresp. April 29, 1813. Packet 20. Helga Piccolo (coord.), "Resistencia escrava no Rio Grande do Sul," *Caderno de Estudo* CPGH, UFRGS (1992), 1.
19. Benguela: Africans that came from the port by same name, located in Angola's southern coast.
20. See Arquivo Público (Public Archive) do Estado do Rio Grande do Sul (APERGS) Porto Alegre. Criminal Lawsuits. 1824, no. 179, packet 7, shelf 3; Flávia de Mattos Motta, "Crime e rebeldia escrava no Rio Grande do Sul: 1820-1845," B.A. in History (Porto Alegre: UFRGS, 1985), 3.
21. See AHGR. Correspondence from the presidency of the province [p. p.] with the police sheriff. March 16, 1849. Code A.5.45. HP, 7.
22. See AHRGS. Correspondence from the presidency of the province with the police sheriff, October 9, 1854. Code A.5.46. HP, 12.
23. See Moacyr Flores, "O quilombo da ilha Barba Negra," *Correio do Povo*, Porto Alegre, May 7, 1983.
24. On October 8, 1829, the Porto Alegre City Council, answering Antônio Cândido, gave him permission to continue his employment as a slave catcher in the capital while bound to respond to the justice of peace of the city. Minutes from CMPA. Vereanças, 5.5.1829-30.1.1.1.9, fl. 122.
25. In the original text: "espadas reiúnas e pistolas." We opted for: "espadas, reiúnas e pistolas." Reiúna: riffle.
26. See AHRGS. February 14, 1829. Archival group: diverse requirements, packet 60, 1829. HP, 4.
27. Auguste de Saint-Hilaire, *Viagem ao Rio Grande do Sul, 1820-1821* (São Paulo, Edusp: Belo Horizonte, Itatiaia, 1974), 57.
28. As in other municipalities, in 1861, the municipal positions of Santo Antônio da Patrulha, dictated: "Art. 39—Any slave found armed with knife, dagger, or any other cutting or piercing weapon, or fireweapon […] will be

jailed and his weapon apprehended; in addition to other penalties, he will be jailed for four days." See Eni Barbosa, *O processo legislativo e a escravidão na província do Rio Grande do Sul: fontes* (Porto Alegre: Legislative Assembly of Rio Grande do Sul; CORAG, 1987).

29. AHRGS. Municipal authorities. City Council of Pelotas. 1833.
30. Robert Conrad, *Os últimos anos da escravatura no Brasil,* 1850-1888 (Rio de Janeiro: Civilização Brasileira, 1975), 253.
31. For more on the movement, see João José Reis, *Rebelião escrava no Brasil: a história do levante dos males* (1835) (São Paulo, Brasiliense, 1986).
32. AHRGS. Corresp. of the City Council de Pelotas AP.P.; correspond. expedited, February 27, 1835. 1832-36. Can 126. Packet 103; Public Library of Pelotas (BPP). Minutes from CMP, May 30, 1835, book 4: 1834-44, fl. 58.
33. See Maestri, *O escravo gaúcho.*
34. *Zungu*: From the language Kimbundu: *nzungu*, noise. In the South, *zungu* or *sungu* were used to describe gatherings of slaves, religious temples or urban inhabitations of the African.
35. Testimony gathered in travels to the region in 1979.
36. AHRGS. Correspondence from June 17, 1820 of City Council of Rio Grande to the governor and the general captain of Rio Grande do Sul. Packet 153, can 138, HP, 2.
37. BPP. Minutes from CMP, May 9, 1832. Book 5. 1832-33, fl. 8.
38. Group of residents that are ecclesiastically depended upon a village.
39. BPP. Minutes from CMPA, November 14,1832. Book 5. 1832-33. p. 44; January 11,1833, fl. 53.
40. AHRGS. Correspondence from the presidency of the province; CMP. May 11, 1832. Corresp. expedited. 1832-6. Packet 103. Can 126.
41. AHRGS. Correspondence with the presidency of the province; CMP. August 6, 1832. Corresp. expedited 1832-6. Packet 103. Can 126.
42. AHRGS. CMP, August 28, 1834. Packet 103. Can 126.
43. BPP. Minutes from CMP, October 10, 1835. Book 4. 1834-44,fl. 28.
44. BPP. Minutes from CMP, Dezember 3, 1834. Book 4. 1834-44, fl. 32.
45. BPP. Minutes from CMP. May 30, 1835. Book 4. 1834-44, fl.p. 58.
46. AHRGS. Correspondence with the presidency of the province; CMP. Corresp. expedited. 1832-6.1835. Can 126. Packet 103.
47. BPP. Minutes from CMP. July 9, 1835. Book 4. 1834-1844, fl. 61. Without specifying the sources of data, the magazine *Princesa do Sul* asserted that the presidency had delivered a sum of "2400$000 *réis* to the Council for the persecution and extinction of *quilombos*. This possibly referred to the sum total.

48. See Ana R. Falkembach Simão, "Resistência e acomodação: aspectos da vida servil na cidade de Pelotas, na primeira metade do século XIX" (Master's thesis, Porto Alegre: PUC, 1993), 81.
49. AHRGS. Correspondence with the presidency of the province; corresp. exped., CMP, July 9, 1835. 1832-6. Packet 106. Can 126.
50. See BPP. Minutes from CMP. August 17,1935. Book 4. 1834-44, fl. 69; José Euzébio Assumpção, "Pelotas: escravidão e charqueadas: 1780-1888" (Master's thesis, Porto Alegre: PUC, 1985), 232.
51. Bernardino Rodrigues Barcellos possessed two dried meat farms on the banks of the Arroyo Pelotas. See. Ester J. B. Gutierrez, *Negros, charqueadas & olarias: um estudo sobre o espaço pelotense* (Pelotas: UFPel, 1993), 122.
52. APRGS. Criminal Processes no. 81; packet 3, shelf 36, year 1835. Pelotas, Jury. AP.
53. The commander Boaventura Rodrigues Barcellos's first marriage was with Cecília Rodrigues da Silva and, his second, with Eulália de Azevedo e Souza. He possessed two contiguous dried meat farms at Costa and at Areal, on the left banks of the Arroyo Pelotas, and a great number of captives. See Gutierrez, *Negros, charqueadas & olarias*, 122.
54. Enslaved African societies still utilized symbolic parental names. For example, *pai* (father) and *mãe* (mother) were denominations attributed to all the members of ones parents' generation. Possibly, pai Francisco was a man of a certain age.
55. See Euzébio Assumpção, "Idade, sexo, ocupação e nacionalidade dos escravos charqueadores (1780-1888)." I Simpósio Gaúcho sobre a Escravidão Negra (First Southern Symposium on Black Slavery), *Estudos Ibero-americanos*, vol. xvi, no. 1-2, 37.
56. The *Kikongo* language was spoken in the regions of the ancient kingdom of the Congo, in the north of Angola. The Portuguese established contact with the kingdom at the end of the fifteenth century. See Mario Maestri, *História da África negra pré-colonial* (Porto Alegre: Mercado Aberto, 1988), 72-84.
57. See also: AHRGS. Correspondence with the presidency of the province; Municipal Council of Pelotas, July 9, 1835. Correspond. expedited, 1832-6. Can 126. Packet 103.
58. Ibid.
59. Public Library of Pelotas. Minutes of the City Council of Pelotas, August 13, 1835. Book 4. 1834-44, fl. 67.
60. Boaventura Ignácio Barcellos bought on the 28 of November of 1827, a coastal land between Cascalho and Boa Vista, at the left margins of the Pelotas River.

61. "Antigoalhas de Pelotas." *A Opinião Pública*, November 9,1928, cited in J. E. Assumpção,"Pelotas: escravidão e charqueadas: 1780-1888," 228.
62. See APERGS. Registry of the Jury of Pelotas. 1848-9. Shelf 36, packet 6; Mário Maestri, *Depoimentos de escravos brasileiros* (São Paulo: Ícone, 1988), 65-9.
63. *Mina*: Africans that came from a region under strong commercial influence of Fort of São Jorge da Mina, in the gulf of Guinea.
64. *Cabinda*: Africans that came from the region of Cabinda, located north of the Zaire River, in Central Africa.
65. *Jeje* or *Gêgê*: Africans that came from the regions located between the Gold Coast [Ghana] and the Slave Coast [Benin] in the gulf of Guinea, particularly from the ancient kingdom of Dahomey, current republic of Benin.
66. "Mapa do tenente Cordoba," cited in Laytano, *O negro no Rio Grande do Sul*, 35
67. "Recenseamento de 1814," cited in Antônio Eleutério Camargo, *Quadro estatístico da província de São Pedro do Rio Grande do Sul* (Porto Alegre: Typographia do Jornal do Commercio,1868).
68. Guilhermino Cesar, "Quilombo e sedição de escravos," *Caderno de Sábado*, *Correio do Povo*, March 20, 1976.
69. AHRGS. Documents from the police station of Rio Pardo. Loose documents. 1847. Packet 26.
70. AHRGS. Documents from the police station of Rio Pardo. Loose documents. 1847. Packet 26. In correspondence dated November 8 of the same year, the police sheriff of Rio Pardo declared that the expenses of the three expeditions were as high as 257$000 *réis* and that they had not yet been paid off. Ibid.
71. AHRGS. Correspondence of the presidency of the province with the police chief. March 16, 1849. Code A.5.45.
72. AHRGS. Correspondence of the presidency of the province with the police chief. Document 308 from September 28, 1850. Code A.5.45, fl. 84. HP, 7.
73. AHRGS. Correspondence of the presidency of the province with the police chief. Document 388. October 31, 1850, fl. 96; document unnumbered. October 27, 1851, fl. 146 bis. Code A.5.45. HP, 8.
74. AHRGS. Correspondence of the presidency of the province with the police chief. Document 7. January 17,1853, fl. 73; document no. 17, January 26, 1853. Code A.5.46, fl. 75.
75. AHRGS. Correspondence of the presidency of the province with the police chief. Document no. 51.March 10,1853. Code A.5.46, fl. 82. HP, 8.
76. AHRGS. Correspondence of the presidency of the province with the police chief. April 26, 1853. Document no. 89. Code A.5.46, fl.90.

77. AHRGS. Correspondence of the presidency of the province with the police chief. April 12, 1853. Document no. 80. Code A.5.46, fl. 88.
78. National Archive (AN), series IJ (1) 5 7 9. Correspondence of the presidency of the province with the Minister of Justice. cited in HP, fl. 11.
79. AHRGS. Correspondence of the presidency of the province with the police chief. Document no. 234. September 28,1854. Code A.5.46, fl. 190 bis. HP, 11.
80. AHRGS. Correspondence of the presidency of the province with the police chief. November 18,1854. Document 306, fl. 203. Code A.5.46; October10, 1854. Document 255, fl. 194 bis.
81. Santa Maria was founded in1797, in the geographical center of the current state of Rio Grande do Sul, on the base of the Mountain of São Martinho, in the Central Depression. Its status was changed to parish in 1837 and to village in 1857. In the early 1800s, the city lived off of agriculture and had more than five thousand inhabitants. See Domingos de Araújo e Silva, *Diccionário histórico geographico da província de S. Pedro* [...] (Rio de Janeiro: Eduardo & Henrique Laemmert, 1865).
82. AHRGS. Correspondence of the presidency of the province with the police chief. October 9, 1854. Document no. 255. Code A.5.46, fl. 194 bis.
83. "Cruz Alta. Hamlet located on the left banks of the Jacuí River, between the cities of Rio Pardo and Cachoeira, which are supplied by produce from small farming. [...]. It belongs to the city of Rio Pardo, with which it forms the fourth district." Araújo e Silva, *Diccionario histórico geographico* [...].
84. AHRGS. Correspondence of the presidency of the province with the police chief. Code A.5.46, documents 112, March 24, 1855, fls. 2 3 4 e 2 3 4 bis; HP, 12.
85. AHRGS. Correspondence of the presidency of the province with the police chief. December 15, 1855. Document no.293. Code A.5.46.
86. AHRGS. January 25, 1856. Document no. 66. Code 5.47, fl. 23 bis.
87. See Jean Roche, *A colonizão alemã e o Rio Grande do Sul* (Porto Alegre: Globo, s.d.), 109.
88. AHRGS. . Correspondence of the presidency of the province with the police chief. January 28, 1857. Code A.5.47. Confidential document, fl. 135.
89. AHRGS. Correspondence of the presidency of the province with the police chief. February 3, 1857. Code A.5.47. Document 440, fl. 137 bis e 138; February 6, 1857. Code A.5.47. Document 446. p. 138 bis e 139; April 7, 1857. Code A.5.47. Document 57, fl. 159 bis.
90. AHRGS. Correspondence of the presidency of the province with the police chief. June 9,1863. Code A.5.49. Document 213, fl. 240 bis; June 22, 1863. Code A.5.49. Document 233, fl. 243.

91. AHRGS. Police body, packet 3. HP, 31.
92. AN, Correspondence of the presidency of the province of Rio Grande do Sul with Ministers of Justice, series IJ (1) 856. cited in HP, 15.
93. AHRGS. Documental group. Police, packet 12. HP, 16.
94. Porto, *Dicionário enciclopédico do Rio Grande do Sul*, Issue I, vol. I, 21. We did not find references on this quilombo. The city of São João de Montenegro, located at the right bank of the River Caí, was founded in 1850 and became a village in 1873, when the city was separated from Triunfo.
95. Museum of Communication Social Hipólito da Costa (MCSHC). *Mercantil*, no. 254. Porto Alegre, Saturday, November 8, 1879. HP, 18.
96. *A Federação*, Year II, January 12, 1885. *cited in* HP, 19.
97. *A Federação*, Year II, January12, 1885. *cited in* HP, 20.

13

1. This chapter is part of a larger project supported by CNPq. In the data collection, I thank the participation of Vera N. dos Santos Silva and Gabriela D. Marcia de Aguiar (fellows PIBIC/UFBa); and comments from Flávio Gomes and his students (Jailton, Sara, Wlamyra and Zacarias) from the seminar "Slavery and Freedom" that I conduct in the Masters in History of UFBa.
2. A *coiteiro* is someone who shelters or protects "thieves."
3. See Erivaldo Fagundes Neves, *Uma comunidade sertaneja: da sesmaria ao minifúndio (um estudo de história local)* (Salvador: EDUFBa, in the press), Chapter 2; Simeão Ribeiro Pires, *Raízes de Minas Gerais* (Montes Claros: Minas Gráfica Editora, 1979), Chapters 15 and 16; and Waldir Freitas de Oliveira, "Os Saldanha da Gama da Bahia," *Universitas*, 33 (1985).
4. In 1829, a bailiff from Salvador regretted that in that time the slaves were not controlled more severely with an iron fist, as in the time of the Count of Ponte: see João José Reis and Eduardo Silva, *Negociação e conflito: a resistência negra no Brasil escravista* (São Paulo: Companhia das Letras, 1989), 52.
5. "Offício do Governador Conde da Ponte para o Visonde de Anadia [16/6/1807]," *Anais da Biblioteca Nacional do Rio de Janeiro* (herewith ABNRJ), 37 (1918), 460.
6. Arquivo Público do Estado da Bahia (APEBA), Ordens régias, 1798-9, vol. 89, doc. 19.
7. "Descrição de Joaquim Pereira da Costa ao príncipe regente nosso senhor" (Lisboa, 1/5/1800), Biblioteca Nacional, 1-31, 30, 83; "Conde da Ponte para o visconde de Anadia," 16/6/1807, 460. About the traffic in Bahia at the

time, Herbert Klein, "A demografia do tráfico atlântico de escravos para o Brasil," *Estudos Econômicos*, 17 (1987), 133.

8. About quilombos during the government of the count of Ponte, I am writing a text, "*Quilombos baianos* no século XIX." Several authors have already studied the Bahian slave revolts, including myself: João J. Reis, "Recôncavo rebelde: revoltas escravas nos engenhos baianos," *Afro-Asia*, 15 (1992), 100-26 (about the revolts during the time of Ponte, 103-5); Ibid, *Rebelião escrava no Brasil: a história do levante dos malês* (1835) (São Paulo: Brasiliense, 1986); among others. For a discussion on the history of the Bahia revolts, see my "Um balanço dos estudos sobre as revoltas escravas da Bahia," in *Escravidão e invenção da liberdade,* ed. Reis (São Paulo: Brasiliense, 1988), 87-140.

9. *Oitizeiro* or oiti: "tree from the rosette family (*Moquilea tomentosa*)," common in the Northeast, which gives a fleshy yellow fruit, with "intense aroma and flavor" (*Novo dicionário Aurélio*). The quilombo of Oitizeiro is not totally unknown to historians, but if I'm not mistaken it was never studied with greater detail. Among the authors that mention him, Pedro Tomás Pedreira, "Os *quilombos* baianos," *Revista Brasileira de Geografia* (1962), 88 (but this author erroneously localizes the Oitizeiro in Minas do Rio de Contas, city of Chapada Diamantina); João da Silva Campos, *Crônica da capitania de São Jorge dos Ilhéus* (Rio de Janeiro: Ministério da Educação e Cultura/Conselho Federal de Cultura), 1981, 190; Stuart Schwartz, *Sugar Plantations in the Formation of Brazilian Society. Bahia, 1550-1835* (Cambridge: Cambridge University Press, 1985), 479-80; Judith Allen, "The Indians of Pedra Branca" (unpublished text), 11-2.

10. Balthasar da Silva Lisboa, "Memória sobre a comarca de Ilhéus [1802]," ABNRJ, 37 (1915), 13.

11. Luís dos Santos Vilhena, *A Bahia no século XVIII* (Salvador: Itapuã, 1969), II, 505.

12. Lisboa, "Memória," 13; "Carta muito interessante do advogado da Bahia, José da Silva Lisboa, para o dr. Domingos Vandelli [18/10/1781]," ABNRJ, 32 (1910), 503. See also, Campos, *Crônica*, 105, 138, 162, 175.

13. About pressures and reactions related to the colonial policy for internal supply farming, see Thales de Azevedo, *Povoamento da cidade do Salvador* (Salvador: Itapuã, 1969), 277 and segs.; Campos, *Crônica*, 170. Citação de Manoel Ferreira da Camara, "Carta II," in *Cartas econômico-políticas sobre a agricultura e comércio da Bahia,* ed. João Rodrigues de Brito (Salvador: APEBa, 1985), 102. Judge Brito also wrote: "They force the Farmer to occupy along with the petty cassava plantation, which goes with any quality of land, the rare and precious clods of black clay, to which the nature gave

the privilege of producing very good sugar and other high value crops." (Ibid, 16). About the supply of Salvador city, in addition to Azevedo's book above mentioned, see Kátia M. de Queirós Mattoso, *Bahia: a cidade do Salvador e seu mercado no século XIX* (São Paulo: Hucitec, 1978), 253-60. About the economic expansion in Bahia during this period, see also Schwartz' studies, *Sugar Plantations*, Ch. 15 and 16; F. W. O. Morton, "The Conservative Revolution of Independence: Economy, Society and Politics in Bahia, 1790-1840" (PhD thesis, Oxford University, 1974), Ch. I; and B. J. Barickman, "The Slave Economy of Nineteenth-Century Bahia: Export Agriculture and Local Market in the Recôncavo, 1780-1860" (PhD thesis, University of Illinois, 1991).

14. Johan Baptist von Spix and Carl Frederich von Martius, *Viagem pelo Brasil*, 1817-1820 (Belo Horizonte e São Paulo: Itatiaia e Edusp, 1981), II, 190.

15. About native groups in the region, see Lisboa, "Memória," and especially Luiz Mott, "Os índios do sul da Bahia: população, economia e sociedade," *Cultura*, 1, no. 1 (1988), 93-120. In an unpublished passage from his memoirs, quoted by Silva Campos, *Crônica*, 171, Balthasar da Silva Lisboa writes about São Jorge dos Ilhéus, the next village at the south of Barra: "hunting, fishing, cassava farming, is his most noble job".

16. APEBa, Ordens régias, 1696-97, vol. 4, doc. 50; APEBa, Portarias, 1693-1711, vol. 460, fl. 101;APEBa, Ordens régias, 1722-23,vol. 17, doc. 6. About quilombos in the area, including some of the ones mentioned here, see also Campos, *Crônica*, 125-6; Schwartz, *Sugar Plantations*, 470; Ibid, *Slaves, Peasants, and Rebels: Reconsidering Brazilian Slavery* (Urbana: University of Illinois Press, 1992), 106-7. Notícias de "haverem nos ditos caminhos [de Ilhéus] negros fugidos" em APEBa, Ordens régias, 1806, vol. 101, doc. 114.

17. Campos, *Crônica*, p. 172.

18. F. W. O. Morton, "The Military and Society in Bahia, 1800-1821," *Journal of Latin American Studies*, 1, no. 2 (1975), 266.

19. APEBa, Cartas do governo, 1805-07, vol. 161, fls. 79,91v-92.

20. Schwartz, *Sugar Plantations*, 471; *Slaves, Peasants, and Rebels*, 110.

21. Vilhena, *Bahia*, I, 246.

22. "Carta do conde da Ponte ao visconde de Anadia," 30/8/1806, APEBa, Cartas do governo, 1805-06, vol. 143, fls. 120-123.

23. See the correspondence from Sá Bittencourt to the count in APEBa, Cartas ao governo, pack 208,210 e 211. The count passed the information to Lisbon: for example, APEBa, Cartas do governo (1806-07), vol. 144, fl. 116v-117. About pataxó resistance in the second half of the eighteenth century, see Mott, "Os índios do sul da Bahia," 114. Another good example

of indigenous insubordination in the region is registered in correspondence from 1807, from the chief captain, ordinary judges and other Santarém village authorities, realizing that the indigenous people (probably Paiaiás) of the local "mission" had almost all "deserted," over the ultimate five years, to settle with their families in "Whites' farms" and mainly in the villages of Nova de Valença and Jequié. APEBa, Cartas ao governo, pack 212.

24. The Count wrote to the metropolis: "the Conquest Troop of the gentile Bárbaro da Pedra Branca [...] is employed to carry out patrols of the roads and the Gold records Detachments, and *lastly* the Entrance of the runaway negroes' Quilombos, [...] as now I practiced it in the entrance, which I told to do in Rio de Contas" [My emphasis]. This letter is from August 29, 1806: APEBa, Ordens régias, vol. 101, doc. 109. About the Pedra Branca Indians in the colonial period, see Maria Hilda B. Paraíso, "Os Kiriri sapuyá de Pedra Branca," *Centro de Estudos Baianos*, 112 (Salvador, CEB/UFBa, 1985), 13-25, and Allen, "The Indians of Pedra Branca," 1-12.

25. The documents to which I'm refering are the "Rezumo das despezas que por Ordem do Doutor Dezembargador Ouvidor Geral e Corregedor desta Comarca Domingos Ferreira Maciel se fizerão com os soldados índios da Pedra Branca etc," and its thirteen annexes, in APEBa, Colônia. Índios, 1758-1807, pack 603. See also the letter from the ombudsman of Ilhéus region, Domingos Ferreira Maciel, to the count of Ponte, 15/11/1806, APEBa, Cartas ao governo, 1803-06, pack 206. A letter from count of Ponte to the Sergeant Major Commander of Pedra Branca troop, dated June 19, 1806, reveals that at that date the expedition had already left for rio de Contas: APEBa, Cartas do governo, 1805-07, vol. 161, fl. 111.

26. Letter from Domingos Maciel to the count of Ponte, 7/3/1807, APEBa, Cartas ao governo, 1803-06, pack 206.

27. See witness No. 21 testimony in "Translado da Devassa que por Ordem do Ilmo. e Exmo. Snr. Conde da Ponte, Governador e Capitão General da Capitania procedeo o Dr. Dezembargador Ouvidor Geral da Comarca Domingos Ferreira Maciel contra os que acoitão, e tem refugiado no Oitizeiro negros fugidos," APEBa, Quilombos, 1806, pack 572-2.

28. "Cartas de Domingos Maciel ao conde da Ponte," 15/11/1806 and 7/3/1807.

29. Ibid. (letter from 15/11/1806).

30. Ibid. "Carta do Conde da Ponte ao Sargento-mor Comandante das Companhias da Conquista da Pedra Branca," 29/11/1806 and "Carta do Conde da Ponte ao Ouvidor Domingos Maciel," 4/1/1806, APEBa, Cartas do governo, 1805-07, vol. 161, fls. 223v e 225.

31. "Maciel para o conde da Ponte," 7/3/1807. "Carta do ouvidor Domingos Maciel para o governador Francisco da Cunha Menezes," 14/12/1803, APEBa, Cartas ao governo, 1803-06, pack 206 (a copy of this latter document was kindly given to me by Richard Graham).
32. See "Rezumo das despezas," document No.13 annexed there.
33. Ibid.
34. The captain was to write (including at night, with the help of candles), which caused expenses with "paper notebooks" and "lights to illuminate."
35. Passages from Ponte quoted in "Copia do offício do illmo. e exmo. snr. conde da Ponte, governador e capitão general da capitania sobre os quilombos do Oitizeiro," parto of the inquest. See note 21.
36. Pedreira, "Os quilombos baianos," 79.
37. "Corpo de Delicto," in "Translado da Devassa".
38. "Offício do Conde da Ponte para o visconde de Anadia [7/4/1807]," 451. When the count wrote these lines he already knew the Oitizeiro dimensions through the reading of the inquest. He also used, in a sly way, the information about the cassava farming that he found there to oversize the *quilombo*, which, he wrote, was "already with fields and plantations" (ibid).
39. Only two farmers from Oitizeiro were not indicted, Félix José, who didn't run away during the robbery; and Félix Rodrigues Fragozo, which, despite having fields in Oitizeiro, had moved away to Maraú at the time of the robbery. "Cartas do ouvidor Domingos Maciel para o conde da Ponte," both from 30/1/1807 in response to the complaint from both farmers to the governor. APEBa, Cartas ao governo, pack 212.
40. The controversy over whether Palmares assigned temporary forms of bonded labor to slaves kidnapped by palmarinos does not interest me, an aspect definitely not solved yet but generally denied by the most recent historiography. See Décio Freitas, *Palmares. A guerra dos escravos*, 5a ed. (Porto Alegre: Mercado Aberto, 1984), 37; Ivan Alves Filho, *Memorial dos Palmares* (Rio de Janeiro, Xenon, 1988), 189-90.
41. Silvia H. Lara, *Campos da violência: escravos e senhores na capitania do Rio de Janeiro*, 1750-1808 (São Paulo: Paz e Terra, 1988), 158,163, 244-455 (quoted case), 263. Also on lords exchange: José Roberto Góes, *O cativeiro imperfeito: um estudo sobre a escravidão no Rio de Janeiro da primeira metade do século XIX* (Vitória: Governo do Estado do Espírito Santo, 1993), 152-5; Maria Helena P. T. Machado, *Crime e escravidão: trabalho, luta e resistência nas lavouras paulistas*, 1830-1888 (São Paulo: Brasiliense, 1987), 115, 116. About the legislation concerning freedom actions at the end of the Colony and during the Empire, Keila Grinberg, *Liberata, a lei da ambiguidade: as ações de liberdade da corte do Rio de Janeiro no século XIX* (Rio de Janeiro:

Relume Dumará, 1994). Runing away to exchange lords was not a Brazilian peculiarity. See, for example, Anthony McFarlane, "*Cimarrones* and Palenques: Runaway and Resistance in Colonial Colombia," *Slavery and Abolition*, 6, no. 3 (1985), 136-7,142; Daniel Meaders, *Dead or Alive: Fugitive Slaves and White Indentured Servants Before 1830* (New York: Garland, 1993), 127-8; Gerald W. Mullin, *Flight and Rebellion: Slave Resistance in Eighteenth-Century Virginia* (Oxford: Oxford University Press, 1972), 113. Caribbean examples of slaves who, without escape, sought to manage their sales: Emilia Viotti da Costa, *Crowns of Glory, Tears of Blood: The Demerara Slave Rebellion of 1832* (New York: Oxford University Press, 1994), 203; Michael Mullin, *Africa in America: Slave Acculturation and Resistance in the American South and the British Caribbean*, 1736-1831 (Urbana: University of Illinois Press, 1992), 164. The arrangements could vary within the slavery. The regent Diogo Feijó granted to his rented slaves, in his will, the ability to define to whom they would be rented: Magda Maria de O. Ricci, "'Nas fronteiras da independência': um estudo sobre os significados da liberdade na região de Itu (17791822)" (master's speech, Unicamp, 1993), 155. Lord exchange in Africa: Martin A. Klein, "Servitude Among the Wolof and Sereer of Senegambia," in *Slavery in Africa*, eds. S. Miers and I. Kopytoff (Madison: The University of Wisconsin Press, 1977), 347-8.

42. Reis e Silva, *Negociação e conflito*, 63-6.
43. About slaves letting themselves be stolen as resistance strategy, see the pioneering article in Brazil on the subject, by Marcus J. M. de Carvalho, "Quem furta mais e esconde: o roubo de escravos em Pernambuco," *Estudos Econômicos*, 17 (1987), 89-110. Also, a dazzling escape and theft in Itu (São Paulo), 1821, in which the free man pretends to be the master of the slave who escapes, is narrated by Ricci, "Nas fronteiras da independência," 199-200.
44. In this regard see Sidney Chalhoub, *Visões da liberdade: uma história das últimas décadas da escravidão na corte* (São Paulo: Companhia das Letras, 1990), esp. Ch. 1.
45. *Correio Mercantil*, 8/8/1839 (from the Nacional Libary collection). Caetité case is registered in APEBa, "Livro de notas do tabelião," pack SJR/25/12, fl. 152v (a copy of this document was kindly given to me by Erivaldo Fagundes Neves).
46. I do not rule out the possibility that, in many cases, the master forced the slave to look for another owner, in which cases the sale actually mattered to the master. It does not seem to be what was happening in Oitizeiro.
47. Dialogue here with Chalhoub, *Visões da liberdade*.

48. "Translado do Inventário, Avaliaçoens e sequestro dos bens que se acharão no Oitizeiro [20/10/1806]," APEBa, "*Quilombos*," 1806, pack 572-2.
49. Slaves price at the time in Kátia M. de Queirós Mattoso, Être esclave au Brésil XVIe-XIXe siècle (Paris: Hachette, 1979), 108.
50. The former owners of Oitizeiro's lands claimed, on this occasion, that Balthasar da Rocha still had not paid the transaction, the land was mortgaged, and because of that, they asked to gain ownership of the land. The ombudsman Maciel took the opportunity to argue (successfully) to the Count of Ponte that the sale of seized property proceeds should be used primarily to pay debts incurred with the assault troops maintenance, and not paying off debts of the coiteiros from Oitizeiro with their creditors. See letter from the ombudsman Maciel to the count of Ponte, 18/2/1807, APEBa, Cartas ao governo, 1807, pack 212.
51. The calculation of the cova and bushel relationship is based on Barickman, "The Slave Economy," 450-5, which found a variation of twenty to forty bushels of flour for every thousand covas. I opted for an intermediate figure, thirty bushels / thousand covas. One bushel is equivalent to approximately 36,27 liters. In the region of Rio de Contas, however, the flour price calculation is based on the document "Rezumo das despezas que [...] se fizerão com os soldados índios da Pedra Branca," mentioned here several times.
52. "Relação dos bens que forão aprehendidos no Quilombo do Oitizeiro e margem do rio das [ras.] e já estão arrematados e vendidos," in "Rezumo das despezas" Document No.14 annexed there; "Carta do ouvidor Maciel para o conde da Ponte," 7/3/1807. In this letter the ombudsman complained that some of the goods found in Oitizeiro, including cassava, had been "misled" before and after making its inventory. The cassava of Félix José, who lived "near the port" of Oitizeiro (who didn't run away with the other residents) and Félix Fragozo (who had fields but didn't live there anymore) were inventoried but not taken to auction, and should therefore be included in that 14 percent difference. See Maciel's letter just shortly referred and also his letters that were referred in note 38. It was usual that, with the repression of colonial quilombo, the expenses would end up relapsing on owners and local authorities. By the end of the operation against Oitizeiro, was due money to several merchants, farmers, regional authorities, which were being paid as the seized goods were being sold. As their value would probably exceed the expenses by a little in the end, it proceeds to say that the government would end the diligence with a positive financial balance.
53. Felippe Vieira, coiteiro and the largest producer in Oitizeiro, was married to a cousin of the Rocha brothers.
54. Schwartz, *Slaves, Peasants, and Rebels*, 82.

55. "Carta muito interessante," 501.
56. Barickman, "The Slave Economy," chaps. 3 and 4; B. J. Barickman, "A Bit of Land, Which they Call *Roça*': Slave Provision Grounds in the Bahian Recôncavo, 1780-1860," *Hispanic American Historical Review*, 74, no.4 (1994), 653 (quote, in which there is some ambiguity in considering the fields "restricted but still significant"). The term "peasant gap" refers to a space within the "slavery" where a production with many features of the peasant economy is dominant. About the subject see, among other works of Ciro F. Cardoso, *Escravo ou camponês? O protocampesinato negro nas Américas* (São Paulo: Brasiliense, 1987). See also Reis and Silva, *Negociação e conflito*, Ch. 2, written by E. Silva; Schwartz, *Slaves, Peasants, and Rebels*, 49-50, 82-4. The literature on *provision grounds* in the Americas, especially in Caribbean, is wide. See, in addition to Cardoso's book already mentioned, recent issue addressing the subject in the journal *Slavery & Abolition*, 12, no. 1 (1991). Especially useful are the prospects of Sidney Mintz, *Caribbean Transformations* (Baltimore: Johns Hopkins University Press, 1974), Ch. 5, 6,7 about Jamaica; and Dale W. Tomich, *Slavery in the Circuit of Sugar: Martinique and the World Economy, 1830-1849* (Baltimore: Johns Hopkins University Press, 1990), Ch. 8 about Martinique. The access to subsistence plots is one of the main axes of comparative discussion about resistance in the USA and Caribbean in Mullin, *Africa in America*, esp. Ch. 6
57. This document was firstly published and discussed by Stuart B. Schwartz, "Resistance and Accomodation in Eighteenth-Century Brazil: The Slaves' View of Slavery," *Hispanic American Historical Review*, 57, no. 1 (1977), 69-81. In Brazil, it was published several times, including Reis and Silva, *Negociação e conflito*, 123-4.
58. Spix and Martius, *Viagem*, II, 179.
59. Some of these characteristics pointed out for the first half of the eighteenth century by Schwartz, *Slaves, Peasants, and Rebels*, 106-7.
60. A similar situation in South Carolina (USA), second half of the eighteenth century, is discussed in Meaders, *Dead or Alive*, 149, 154-5.
61. Quoted by Flávio dos Santos Gomes, "Histórias de quilombolas: mocambos e comunidades de senzalas no Rio de Janeiro—século XIX," master's thesis, Unicamp (1992), 419. In another passage from this 1854 document produced by farmers from fearful Brooms of slave rebellion, it reads that they should "allow that [their] slaves have fields and connect to the ground by love from the property" (Ibid., 418).
62. Paid manumission were a more common phenomenon in urban centers, made easier by the gain system, which placed the slaves in the heart of the market economy that the towns had become. About urban slavery, gain sys-

tem, manumission and freed in Salvador, see, among others, Maria Inês Cortes de Oliveira, *Os libertos: seu mundo e os outros* (São Paulo: Corrupio, 1988); Maria José Andrade, *A mão-de-obra escrava em Salvador*, 1811-1860, São Paulo, Corrupio, 1988 (by carelessness from the editor, the indicated period in the title of the book is not correct, because it should indicate 1888 instead of 1860); Kátia M. de Queirós Mattoso, "A propósito de cartas de alforria," *Anais de História*, 4 (1972), 23-52; Stuart Schwartz, "The Manummission of Slaves in Colonial Brazil: Bahia, 1684-1745," *Hispanic American Historical Review*, 54 (1974), 603-35; Cecília Moreira Soares, "A mulher negra na Bahia no século XIX" (master's thesis, UFBa 1994), esp. Ch. II and III.

63. Cúria de Salvador file, *Devassa nas Freguesias das Comarcas do Sul da Bahia no Ano de 1813* (not cataloged) fls. 8, 9v, 20. I thank Luiz Mott for placing at my disposal his notes from this document.

64. Tomich, *Slavery in the Circuit of Sugar*, 260. It's worth the full quote: "To the master, the gardens were a way of ensuring cheap labor. To the slaves, it was a way of developing an autonomous lifestyle. Based on these conflicting perspectives a fight developed over the conditions of material and social reproduction, in which the slaves were able to appropriate aspects of these activities and develops them around their own interests and needs."

65. Mullin, *Africa in America*, comparing the relationship with the master in the USA—where the master provided the subsistence to the slaves and the fields system was restricted—with those in the Caribbean (especially Jamaica)—where the fields were fundamentals for the subsistence of the slaves—you can conclude that in the second scenario the slaves developed a much more autonomous culture and more persistent endurance.

66. Gomes, "Histórias de *quilombolas*," 49-51, 85-9.

67. In a previous work, I suggest that it's possible to find similarities between quilombo economy and forms of peasant production: João Reis, "Resistência escrava em Ilhéus: um documento inédito," *Anais do APEBa*, 44 (1979), 290-1. See also the suggestive article by Carlos Magno Guimarães, "Quilombo e brecha camponesa—Minas Gerais (seculo XVIII)," *Revista do Departamento de História* [da UFMG], 8 (1989), 28-37.

68. Lara, *Campos da violência*, 246, suggests the expression (which is wisely accompanied by a question mark) to fugitives who start to serve coiteiros as if they were masters.

1. Autos sobre o levantamento de negros projectado na Bahia (1814), Arquivo Nacional da Torre do Tombo, Lisbon (ANTT), Casa Forte, 78, no.11. The plot is mentioned in both Décio Freitas, *Insurreições escravas* (Porto Alegre: Editora Movimento, 1976) and Clóvis Moura, *Rebeliões da senzala: Quilombos insurreições guerrilhas*, 3rd. ed. (São Paulo: Livraria Editora Ciências Humanas, 1981). The two accounts are very similar, although neither author cites the source of the description. They are probably based on the brief description in Pierre Verger, *Fluxo e refluxo do tráfico de escravos entre o Golfo do Benin e a Bahia de Todos os Santos* (São Paulo: Editora Corrupio, 1987), 331.
2. João José Reis, "Um balanço dos estudos sobre as revoltas escravas da Bahia," in *Escravidão e invenção da liberdade*, ed. João José Reis (São Paulo: Brasiliense, 1988), 87-142, provides a review of the literature. The Atlantic Revolutions theme is developed by Eugene D. Genovese, *From Rebellion to Revolution* (Baton Rouge: Louisiana State University Press, 1979). I have noted the difference between slaves and freed people in Brazil in Stuart B. Schwartz, *Sugar Plantations in the Formation of Brazilian Society: Bahia, 1550-1835* (Cambridge: Cambridge University Press, 1985), 468-88. Reis makes an error when he claims that slaves in Rio were arrested in 1805 for wearing cameos with the image of Dessalines. The document in question states that those arrested were not slaves but freedmen (*cabras e crioulos forros*) in the militia. See João José Reis, *Slave Rebellion in Brazil* (Baltimore: Johns Hopkins University Press, 1993), 48; cf. Luiz Roberto de Barros Mott, "A escravatura: A propósito de uma representação a El Rei sobre a escravatura no Brasil," *Revista do Instituto de Estudos Brasileiros* 14 (1973): 127-36.
3. Arquivo Histórico Ultramarino, Lisbon (AHU), Bahia, doc. 29,773. In 1803, 6,437 Africans landed at Salvador, 2,180 or one-third of whom came from Angola. See Arquivo Publico Municipal do Salvador, Visitas das embarcações vindas d'Africa, 1802-29, vol. 182.1.
4. Felipe Nery to Antonio Estes da Costa (Pernambuco, August 22, 1812) stated, "Minas were the best here." Biblioteca Nacional, Lisbon (BNL), Fundo Geral, box 224, nos. 31-33.
5. See the discussion in Reis, *Slave Rebellion*, 5-7. A more extensive discussion with excellent figures for 1808 is provided by Katia M. de Queirós Mattoso, *Bahia, século XIX: Uma província no Império* (Rio de Janeiro: Nova Fronteira, 1992), 82-87. For the mid-nineteenth century, see Anna Amélia Vieira Nascimento, *Dez freguesias da cidade do Salvador* (Salvador: FCBa, 1986).
6. Maria José de Souza Andrade, *A mão de obra escrava em Salvador, 1811-1860* (São Paulo: Editoria Corrupio, 1988). In a sample of 2,461 urban slaves,

1,456 (59 percent) were listed as young (*moço*) or still young (*ainda moço*). Children made up only 17.5 percent (431). New writings on African ethnicity in Brazil are found in "Rethinking the African Diaspora: The Making of the Black Atlantic World in the Bight of Benin and Brazil," ed. Kristin Mann and Edna G. Bay, special issue, *Slavery and Abolition* 22, no. 1 (2001). Mann and Bay also available in book form.

7. Citizens of Bahia to the king (1814), printed in Carlos B. Ott, *Formação e evolução étnica da cidade do Salvador*, 2 vols. (Salvador: Manu, 1957), 2, 103-9. There is a translation in English in Robert E. Conrad, *Children of God's Fire: A Documentary History of Black Slavery in Brazil* (Princeton: Princeton University Press, 1983), 401-6.
8. See my fuller discussion in Schwartz, *Sugar Plantations*, 474-75.
9. Petition of Manoel de Araújo e Góes (July 19, 1792), AHU, doc. 24.600.
10. All six of the Nagô runaways being held in jail in 1831 were described as either *boçal* (unacculturated) or not knowing their master's name. See "Relação dos escravos fugidos," Arquivo Público da Bahia (APB), Presidência da Província, folder 2270 (1831); Barbara Marie-Charlotte Wanda Lasocki, "A Profile of Bahia 1820-1826 as seen by Jacques Guinebaud, French Consul General" (M.A. thesis, University of California, Los Angeles, 1967), 21.
11. Diz Severino Pereira (1798), APB, Ordens Régias 86, 242-45.
12. Ibid. A description of the destruction of these two *quilombos* and the flight of the survivors to yet another settlement is found in a letter of the governor, Fernando José de Portugal, to Rodrigo de Sousa Coutinho (Bahia, April 6, 1797), in Ignacio Accioli de Cerqueira e Silva, *Memórias históricas e políticas da Província da Bahia*, 6 vols. (Bahia: Braz do Amaral, 1925), 3:227.
13. For a view of such a network developed by another quilombo, see Stuart B. Schwartz, *Slaves, Peasants, and Rebels: Reconsidering Brazilian Slavery* (Urbana: University of Illinois Press, 1992), 103-36.
14. For example, see the petition of Francisco Xavier Soares Bandeira, capitão de entradas e assaltos, freguesia de Nossa Senhora de Oliveira, Santo Amaro, who listed his efforts in an attack on "a great quilombo of rebellious slaves in the forests of the town of Cachoeira." APB, Cartas ao Governo 218 (Bahia, September 2, 1809).
15. Reis, *Slave Rebellion*, 41.
16. On this repression see Luiz Mott, "Acontundá: Raízes setecentistas do sincretismo religioso afro-brasileiro," *Anais do Museu Paulista* 31 (1986): 124-47; João José Reis, "Magia Jeje na Bahia: A invasão do calundu do Pasto de Cachoeira, 1785," *Revista brasileira de história* 8 (1988): 57-82.
17. Reis, *Slave Rebellion*, 55-56.

18. The classic works on African "nations" in Brazil are now outdated but still useful. See Nina Rodrigues, *Os Africanos no Brasil*, 5th ed. (São Paulo: Homero Pires, 1977); Artur Ramos, *As culturas negras no novo mundo* (Rio de Janeiro: Civilização Brasileira, 1938)
19. On the Gege see Reis, "Magia Jeje," 68-69.
20. The most complete treatment of the "nations" is Mary Karash, *Slave Life in Rio de Janeiro, 1808-1850* (Princeton: Princeton University Press, 1987), 3-28.
21. Rodrigues, *Os Africanos*, 109.
22. See Mervyn Hiskett, *The Sword of Truth: The Life and Times of Shehu Usuman dan Fodio* (New York: Oxford University Press, 1973); M. G. Smith, "The Jihad of Shehu Dan Fodio: Some Problems," in *Islam in Tropical Africa*, ed. I. M. Lewis (London: Oxford University Press, 1966), 408-19. See Paul E. Lovejoy, "Background to Rebellion: The Origins of Muslim Slaves in Bahia," *Slavery and Abolition*, 15, no. 2 (1994): 150-80.
23. Robert S. Smith, *Kingdoms of the Yoruba*, 3rd ed. (Madison: University of Wisconsin Press, 1988), 125-40.
24. Johann von Spix and Karl von Martius, *Viagem pelo Brasil*, 3 vols. (São Paulo, 1961), 2:171-72. Francis de Castelnau, *Renseignements sur l'Afrique centrale et sur une nation d'hommes a queue que s'y trouveraient d'apres le rapport de negres du Soudan. esclaves à Bahia* (Paris: P. Bertrand, 1851), 8, cited in Verger, *Fluxo e refluxo*, 331.
25. Lovejoy, "Background," 160-65.
26. Verger, *Fluxo e refluxo*, 332.
27. Untitled MS volume, Instituto Histórico e Geográfico Brasileiro (IGHB), box 399, doc. 2, 287-88. This is a curious volume on rebellions and civil disturbances in Bahia. It includes a long chapter entitled "Relação da Francezia formada pelos omens pardos da cidade da Bahia no anno de 1798." See the account by the governor in Count of Ponte to Viscount of Anadia (Bahia, July 16, 1807), in Accioli, *Memórias*, 3:228-30.
28. Count of Ponte to Fernando José de Portugal (Bahia, May 17, 1808), Arquivo Nacional, Rio de Janeiro (ANRJ), I-JJ-317, fols. 205-6. The appended *orden regia* (October 6, 1807) speaks of the "sedição projetada pelos negros aussás."
29. Count of Ponte to Viscount of Anadia (Bahia, July 16, 1807), Accioli, *Memórias*, 3:228-29.
30. Viscount of Anadia to Count of Ponte (Mafra, June 27, 1807), Biblioteca Nacional, Rio de Janeiro (BNRJ), I-31-27, 1.
31. Joaquim Ignacio da Costa, juiz ordinário de Maragogipe to governor (January 31, 1809), APB, Cartas ao Governador 216.

32. Schwartz, *Sugar Plantations,* 482-83; Reis, *Slave Rebellion,* 48-49, provides details. A long letter from the Bahian merchants to the crown reporting the events of February 1814 and suggesting preventative measures is published in Ott, *Formação e evolução étnica da cidade do Salvador,* 2:103-8. It appears in an English translation, which contains a number of errors, in Conrad, *Children of God's Fire,* 401-6. See also BNRJ, II—34, 6, 57.
33. Schwartz, *Sugar Plantations,* 483. See also João José Reis, "Recôncavo rebelde: Revoltas escravas nos engenhos Baianos," *Afro-Asia* 15 (April 1992): 105-7.
34. I have written about the divergence of opinion and actions of the Count of Ponte and the Count of Arcos in Schwartz, *Sugar Plantations,* 484-85. See also Reis, *Slave Rebellion,* 49-51.
35. See Count of Aguiar (Rio de Janeiro, January 16, 1811), in Accioli, *Memórias,* 3:231.
36. Pinto de Madureira was a rising legal star in the captaincy. Member of an important planter family, he eventually became a judge of the Supreme Court (Casa da Suplicação) in Rio de Janeiro. His sister owned Engenho Aramaré in the Recôncavo. See Antonio D'Oliveira Pinto da França, *Cartas baianas, 1821-24: Subsídios para o estudo dos problemas da opção na independencia brasileira* (São Paulo: Companhia Editora Nacional, 1980).
37. The designation "Guruman" is probably the people called by the Portuguese "Galinhas," and sometimes referred to as Gurunxi. They were also Muslims and were closely associated with the Hausa. Like them, they were thought to be rebellious and unsubmissive slaves. See Ramos, *As culturas,* 216.
38. The Bahian census of 1808 listed 5,663 Indians living as part of colonial society. See Mattoso, *Bahia,* 82.
39. João Maciel da Costa, *Memória sobre a necessidade de abolir a introdução dos escravos africanos no Brasil* (Coimbra, 1821), 21.
40. John Luccock, *Notes on Rio de Janeiro and the Southern Paris of Brazil: Taken during a Residence of Ten Years in That Country from 1808 to 1818* (London: Samuel Leigh, 1820).
41. Abelardo Duarte, *Folclore negros nas Alagoas* (Maceió: DAC, 1974), 221-37, provides the text of other shouts and songs used by *ganhadores do canto* in various Brazilian cities.
42. Spix and Martius, *Viagem pelo Brasil,* 2:172. In 1837 it was estimated that the daily wage for a working slave was 320 réis which, with eighty-one Sundays and saints' days removed, came to 90,880 réis. Food costs for maintaining the slave was 160 réis per day, or 58,400 réis a year, to which 7,480 réis for clothing and health care had to be added. This left a profit to the owner of 25,000 réis, but this did not take into account days missed for ill-

ness, punishment, running away, etc. Since a working unskilled slave cost about 400 réis and the minimum rate of interest was 6 percent, an owner could just about break even. See the discussion in Federico Leopoldo C. Burlamaqui, *Memória analytica acêrca do commercio d'escravos e acêrca da escravidão domestica* (Rio de Janeiro, 1837).

43. On cooperation between the two groups, see Leila Mezan Algranti, *O feitor ausente: Estudos sobre a escravidão no Rio de Janeiro, 1808-1822* (Petrópolis: Vozes, 1988), 121-31.
44. João José Reis, "A greve negra de 1857 na Bahia," *Revista da USP* 18 (1993): 8-29.
45. Citizens of Bahia to king (1814), 104.
46. In later testimony by the slave João Aussá, he stated that he had been told that the cantos of other nations, with the exception of the Geges, had also been involved. "Autos sobre o levantamento," 19.
47. *Malungo* was a term of fictive kinship generally applied to another African who had come to Brazil in the same slave ship. The term eventually came to mean simply a friend.
48. "Os signaes que tem destinado para o levante sao huns buzios dos quaes já estão prevenidos e com bastante porção," ANTT, Casa Forte, folder 78, no. 11, p. 5.
49. On the destruction of the candomblé of Assu, see João José Reis and Eduardo Silva, *Negociação e conflicto* (São Paulo, 1989), 32-61.
50. The local magistrate of Maragogipe complained in 1809 that the slave owners gave too much liberty to slaves by allowing batuques that scandalized religion, the state, and public order (APB, Cartas ao Governo 216). The Count of Arcos, governor of Bahia, believed that the best guarantee of tranquility in Brazil's cities was the disunity of the Africans, which was promoted by the batuques. Slave owners denounced his policy as dangerous and wrong. For a partial defense of Arcos, see Marquês de Aguiar to Count of Arcos (Rio de Janeiro, June 6, 1814), BNRJ, II-33, 24, 29. On the election of "kings," see Elizabeth Kiddy, "Who Is the King of the Kongo? A New Look at African and Afro-Brazilian Kings in Brazil," in *Central Africans and Cultural Transformations in the American Diaspora*, ed. Linda M. Heywood (Cambridge: Cambridge University Press, 2002), 153-82.
51. Reis, "A greve negra," 17-29.
52. Luiz Antonio da Fonseca Machado ao Governador (Sergipe de El-Rey, September 1, 1815), APB, Cartas ao Governo 229.
53. Luis Mott, "Violência e repressão em Sergipe: Noticia das revoltas escravas século XIX," *Mensário do Arquivo Nacional* 11, no. 5 (1980): 13.

54. Arquivo Nacional da Torre do Tombo, Lisbon, Casa Forte, 78, no. 11. Throughout the Americas, the most common records we have of slave resistance and revolt come from the judicial proceedings that were used to investigate and punish those responsible. The testimony in such trials, whether given by slave owners, by slaves who had refused to join the movement, or by the rebels them- selves, was often self-interested and must be read with caution, but often this information is all that remains of revolts, and especially of revolts that were planned and never realized. In this case, the slave owner Manuel José Teixeira recounts in detail for the ouvidor geral do crime, the senior judge on criminal matters, what he supposedly learned from his Hausa slave. The testimony seems to have the ring of truth because of the details it provides about ethnic rivalries among the slaves, the organizations of the cantos, or urban work groups, and the plans to link the movement to the quilombos, or escaped slave communities on the periphery of Salvador.

15

1. The author thanks CNPq, for supporting this research, and Hildo Leal da Rosa for the collaboration in collecting the Jurema verses contained in this text.
2. On this subject see: Roberto Motta, *Jurema* (Recife: Massangana, 1988); Clélia Moreira Pinto, "Saravá Jurema sagrada: as várias faces de um culto mediúnico" (Recife master's thesis, UFPE, 1995).
3. Arquivo Público de Pernambuco (from this point forward, APE), anexo 1, plantas 1232, 1233, and 1236 (1806), and 1215, 1216, 1220, and 1237 (1836).
4. Gilberto Freyre, *Casa Grande e Senzala* (Rio de Janeiro: José Olympio, 1980), 452, n. 103.
5. Peter Eisenberg, *Modernização sem mudança* (Rio de Janeiro: Paz e Terra, 1988), appendix 3, 262-3. On the rivers of sugar: Manuel Correia de Andrade, *Geografia de Pernambuco* (Recife: UFPE, 1963).
6. Henry Koster, *Viagens ao Nordeste do Brasil* (Recife: Secretaria de Educação, 1978), 66-8.
7. José Camilo de Melo, "Quilombos em Pernambuco," *Revista do Arquivo Público*, 33-4 (1977-8), 22-3.
8. APE, assuntos militares 3, 6/7/1823, 31/7/1823.
9. Franciso A. Pereira da Costa, *Anais Pernambucanos*, 10 vols. (Recife: Fundarpe 1983-5), vol. 9, 47, 286; *Typhis Pernambucano* (Recife), 1/7/1824.
10. APE, assuntos militares 3, 9/4/1824.

11. "Correspondência Oficial," *Diario do Governo de Pernambuco* (Recife), 4/6/1825. Unfortunately, I was unable to find the document describing this operation, but I have an interesting story that is loosely related. In the early 1980s when I was conducting research for my master's thesis in the Arquivo Público de Pernambuco, an elderly archivist told me that during the military dictatorship a government official who had done much research at the archive was invited to give a lecture in honor of Lima e Silva, Duke of Caxias, son of the other Lima e Silva mentioned in this text, that, before becoming regent, commanded an operated against the Catucá *quilombo*. By chance, right before his lecture, the invited speaker was reading documents in the archive when he stumbled upon an especially long document that contained the signature of the elder Lima e Silva. He did not have time to read the document, but brought it with him to the ceremony. At the end of the speech, he announced the discovery he had made to those present, and that he would read the document to them, even though he had not yet read the contents himself. There was a moment of pure excitement in the audience, which enthusiastically applauded the opportunity to relive a piece of the adventures of the great Lima e Silva, almost 150 years later. As he read the document, he quickly created great unease in the audience. The document spoke of the brutal hunting of fugitive slaves, with reports of deaths and captures. The speaker, fearing that the document had been taken as a veiled critique of the military regime, quickly abandoned the document and changed the subject… And the episode entered into the elderly archivist's collection of anecdotes. Prior, I believe that he had no familiarity with the quilombo of Catucá—I am just now making this connection.
12. APE, assuntos militares 4, 31/1/1826.
13. APE, polícia militar 1, 26/1/1826, 24/2/1826.
14. APE, atas do Conselho do Governo de Pernambuco 2, 8/5/1826.
15. APE, atas do Conselho do Governo de Pernambuco 2, 29/1/1827. This refers to the uprising of August 1826. See João José Reis, *Rebelião Escrava no Brasil: A história do levante dos Malês (1835)* (Sao Paulo: Brasiliense, 1986), 73-4.
16. Few episodes so succinctly reveal how information is transmitted in a resistance movement as these verses that are sung in the streets of Recife during the popular protests of 1823: "I imitate Christophe/the immortal Haitian/Eia! Imitate, my people/Oh, my sovereign people!"
17. APE, atas do Conselho de Governo de Pernambuco 2, 29/1/1827.
18. Torre de Tombo, Lisbon: Ministério dos Negócios Estrangeiros, Pernambuco, caixa 1, 17/12/1835. *A quotidiana fidedigna* (Recife), 18/12/1835.
19. APE, juizes de paz 1, 24/7/1829.

20. APE, policia civil 2, 18/9/1835. Torre do Tombo, Lisbon: Ministerio dos Negocios Estrangeiros, Pernambuco, caixa 1, 17/12/1835. *A quotidiana fidedigna* (Recife), 18/12/1835.
21. APE, "Oficio reservado de Chichorro da Gama a J.J. Luiz de Souza," 28/8/1845.
22. APE, atas do Conselho de Governo de Pernambuco 2, 29/1/1827.
23. Koster, *Viagens ao Nordeste do Brasil*, 413; L.F. de Tollenare, *Notas dominicais* (Salvador: Progresso, 1956), 143. On the subject, see also the commentary of Luís da Câmara Cascudo, in Koster, 417, note 18; Roger Bastide, *The African religions of Brazil* (London and Baltimore: Johns Hopkins University Press, 1978), 85; Robert W. Slenes, "Malungu, ngoma vem: Africa coberta e descoberta do Brasil," *Revista USP* (dec./feb., 1991-2), 12: 48-67. The bond formed between those who came to the Americas on the same ship also had great importance in other regions. Michael Craton, *Testing the chains* (Ithaca and London: Cornell University Press, 1982), 49
24. Documents in Leonardo Dantas Silva (eds.), *Alguns documentos para a história da escravidão* (Recife: Massangana, 1988), 76-91. Publish originally in 1948-9, this important work presents some documents that discuss the Catucá, which contain some truncated names and words. The bulk of these documents have been lost, but it is possible to make up for some of this when cross-referencing with some of the documents available in Pernambucan archives and discussed in this text. For this reason, it is likely that "Matunguinho" or "Mabenguinho" are the result of an erroneous transcription of the name Malunguinho (Ibid. docs. 88, 90).
25. Some travelers confirmed that the captives coming from the coast of Gabon were very "intolerant" of slavery and were inclined to commit suicide. Mary Karasch, *Slave Life in Rio de Janeiro, 1808-1850* (Princeton: Princeton University Press, 1987), 18.
26. E.C. Lopes, *A escravatura, subsidies para a sua história* (Lisbon: Arquivo Geral das Colônias, 1944), 141; David Elits, "The nineteenth century transatlantic slave trade: an annual time series of imports into the Americas broken down by region," *Hispanic American Historical Review*, 67, no. 1 (1987), 114-15; Joseph Miller, "The numbers, origins, and destinations of slaves in the eighteenth century Angolan slave trade," in *The Atlantic slave trade: effects on economies, societies and peoples in Africa, the Americas and Europe*, eds., J.I. Inikori and S.L. Engerman (Durham and London: Duke University Press, 1992), 91-2.
27. In the aforementioned 1829 operation, at least three not yet acculturated slaves were captured in the *quilombo*. Two did not know the name of their master or where they lived (Dantas Silva, *Alguns Documentos*, 79). Another,

captured later, spoke no Portuguese or an African language that authorities were familiar with (APE, informações 3, 9/10/1829).

28. Sérgio Buarque de Holanda, *Raízes do Brasil* (Rio de Janeiro: José Olympio, 1978), 108-9.
29. APE, policia civil 2, 18/9/1835.
30. "Correspondencia Oficial," 8/11/1828 in Pereira da Costa, *Anais* vol. 9, pp. 284-6; *Diario de Pernambuco* (Recife), 24/12/1828; APE, juízes de paz 10, 11/9/1828, 17/9/1828.
31. APE, juízes de paz 1, 4/7/1829.
32. Suely Robles Reis de Queiroz, *Escravidão Negra em São Paulo, um estudo das tensões provocadas pelo escravismo no século XIX* (Rio de Janeiro: Jose Olympio, 1977), 144; Stuart Schwartz, "The Mocambo: Slave Resistance in Colonial Bahia," in *Maroon Societies: Rebel Slave Communities in the Americas*, ed., Richard Price (Baltimore: Johns Hopkins University Press, 1979), 219; Richard Price, "Introduction," Ibid., 13; Bastide, *The African religions of Brazil*, 90-6; Karasch, *Slave Life*, 113; Katia Mattoso, *Ser escravo no Brasil* (São Paulo: Brasiliense, 1982), 161-3.
33. "Correspondência Oficial," 24/2/1829 in *Diário de Pernambuco* (Recife), 28/2/1829.
34. APE, assuntos militares 4, 18/6/1830.
35. The population of Pernambuco perceived this fragility in 1828 and 1851. In both occasions, many churches and government buildings were invaded by the rural population due to rumors that the government planned to enslave "men of color." This was how subordinate groups interpreted the announcement, in 1828, of the end of the slave trade in three years, and the 1850 Eusebio Queiroz law. Marcus Carvalho, "Hegemony and rebellion in Pernambuco (Brazil), 1821-1835" (Universidade de Illinois, Urbana Champaign, Doctoral Dissertation, 1989), 111-3.
36. Correspondência Oficial, 24/2/1829 in *Diário de Pernambuco* (Recife) 28/2/1829.
37. Ibid.
38. "General Antero José Ferreira de Brito ao presidente da provincia," 8/11/1828, in Pereira da Costa, *Anais*, vol. 9, 284-6.
39. *Diário de Pernambuco* (Recife), 24/12/1828.
40. On the importance of the cult of the warrior, Saint Anthony, and its importance for slave resistance: Slenes "Malungu, ngoma vem," 64-5.
41. APE, Juizes de paz 1, 29/6/829, 4/7/1829.
42. APE, assuntos militares 4, 23/11/1830.

43. Arquivo Nacional do Rio de Janeiro (from this point forward, ANRJ), Ministério de Justiça, IJ1820, 26/7/1830. *Diário de Pernambuco* (Recife), 26/2/1829. APE, juizes de paz 2, 11/6/1830.
44. See e.g.: APE, polícia military 1, 26/7/1830.
45. "Sailors and the whitewashed/all of you are finished/Because only the black and pardo/will inhabit Brazil." In Bahia the term "whitewashed" had a different connotation. João José Reis and Eduardo Silva, *Negociação e conflito: a resistência negra no Brasil escravista* (São Paulo: Companhia das Letras, 1989), 85.
46. APE, juízes de paz 8, 7/2/1835.
47. APE, juízes de paz 8, 19/7/1835.
48. "Correspondência oficial," 24/2/1829 in *Diario de Pernambuco* (Recife), 28/2/1829.
49. ANRJ, Ministério do Exército IG1 64, 27/3/1829.
50. Documents in Dantas Silva, *Alguns documentos*, 88-9.
51. APE, juízes de paz 1, 29/6/1829.
52. APE, juízes de paz 1, 4/7/1829.
53. APE, juízes de paz 1, 29/6/1829.
54. APE, juízes de paz 1, 29/6/1829, 4/7/1829.
55. Documents in Dantas Silva, *Alguns documentos*, 73-5.
56. Ibid., 76-92.
57. Ibid., 88.
58. Carvalho, "Hegemony and Rebellion," Chapter 4.
59. APE, assuntos militares 4, 2/6/1830, 5/6/1830, 17/6/1830, 18/6/1830; s.d.: "Amador Queiroz para Franciso Antônio de Souza Leão."
60. APE, assuntos militares 4, 18/6/1830.
61. APE, assuntos militares 4, 29/9/1830.
62. APE, assuntos militares 4, 23/11/1830.
63. APE, polícia militar 1, 5/1/1829; assuntos militares 4, 2/7/1830, 10/10/1830.
64. APE atas do Conselho de Governo de Pernambuco 2, 8/5/1826.
65. APE, atas do Conselho de Governo de Pernambuco 2, 8/5/1826, 29/1/1827. Instituto Arqueológico, Histórico e Geográfico Pernambuco, "Fala de Tomás Xavier Garcia de Almeida ao Conselho de Governo," 1/12/1829.
66. APE, correspondência da Corte 32, 14/12/1829. "Correspondência official," 1/12/1831, in *Diário de Pernambuco* (Recife), 12/5/1831, Ibid., 16/12/1829.
67. APE, correspondência da Corte 2, 14/12/1829. Instituto Arqueológico, Histórico e Geográfico Pernambuco, estante A, gaveta 12, 1/12/1829. ANRJ, Ministério do Império IJJ9 249, 14/12/1829.
68. APE, correspondência da Corte 2, 26/9/1830.

69. APE, polícia civil 18, 2/1/1848. *Diário da Administração Pública de Pernambuco* (Recife), 20/12/1833, Pereira da Costa, *Anais*, vol. 9, 313-6.
70. Carvalho, "Hegemony and rebellion," Chapter 5.
71. APE, juízes de paz 3, 9/1/1831.
72. APE, juízes de paz 5, 22/10/1832.
73. APE, juízes de paz 5, 14/11/1832.
74. APE, juízes de paz 5, 23/11/1832.
75. APE, juízes de paz 3, 3/5/1832, 7/5/1832; juízes de paz 5, 22/10/1832.
76. APE, juízes de paz 8, 30/1/1835, 7/2/1835.
77. APE, juízes de paz 8, 5/2/1835, 7/2/1835; policia civil 2, 18/9/1835.
78. APE, juízes de paz 8, 20/2/1835, 28/4/1835, 30/4/1835, 4/5/1835.
79. APE, juízes de paz 8, 5/5/1835.
80. APE, juízes de paz 8, 14/5/1835, 19/7/1835.
81. APE, juízes de paz 8, 14/7/1835, 24/7/1835, 17/8/1835; polícia civil 2, 2/8/1835.
82. ANRJ, Ministério do Império IJJ9 251, 12/9/1835. APE, polícia civil 2, 18/9/1835, 14/10/1835. Torre do Tombo, Lisboa: Ministério dos Negócios Estrangeiros, Pernambuco, Caixa 1, 17/12/1835. A quotidiana fidedigna (Recife), 18/12/1835.
83. Pereira da Costa, *Anais* vol. 9, 288.
84. Carolyn Fick, *The Making of Haiti: The Saint Domingue Revolution from Below* (Knoxville: University of Tennessee Press, 1990), 59.
85. Roberto Matta, "Indo-Afro-European syncretic cults in Brazil: their economic and social roots," *Cahiers du Bresil Contemporain*, 5 (1988), 34.

16

1. I would like to thank Mundinha Araújo and Manoel de Jesus Barros Martins at the Arquivo Público do Estado do Maranhão, for help in locating some sources on quilombos from the 1870s. I am also grateful to Ivan Costa and to the Projeto Vida de Negro of the Sociedade Maranhense de Defesa dos Direitos Humanos, for allowing me access to the project's reports. This article is a translation of "Quilombos maranhenses," originally published in: João Jose Reis and Flávio dos Santos Gomes (eds.), *Liberdade por um fio: História dos quilombos no Brasil* (São Paulo: Companhia das Letras, 1996), 433-466. The translation was made by Joanne Harwood (University of Essex) and revised by the author.
2. [Translator's note] The Brazilian author José de Souza Martins distinguished two types of frontier: the peasant frontier or "expansion front," which occupied territory based on subsistence agriculture and the marketing of eventual

supplies, and the "pioneer front," which introduced capitalist relations of production.
3. Publicador Oficial, São Luís, 11/3/1837, p. 4010. For the similar case of the slave Ilário de Caxias, see Publicador Oficial, São Luís, 19/4/1837, p. 4033.
4. See Miguel Barnet's classic account, *Bibliografía de un cimarrón* (Havana: Instituto de Etnología e Folclore, 1966).
5. O Farol, São Luís, December (1832), 1512.
6. Art. 12, lei provincial no. 236, from 20/8/1847.
7. Publicador Oficial, São Luís, 26/12/1838, 4491 and 15/3/1837, 4041.
8. F. A. Brandão Júnior, *A escravatura no Brasil precedida d'um artigo sobre a agricultura e colonização no Maranhão* (Brussels: Thiry-Vern Buggenhoudt, 1865), 76-77.
9. Relatorio com que o exmo. sr. dr. Antônio E. de Mello passou a administração desta província ao exmo. sr. Vice-President dr. Manoel Jansen Ferreira, no día 5/5/1868 (São Luís: Imperial e Constitucional, 1868), 12.
10. Several capitães-de-mato were exceptionally brutal, such as the notorious João Bunda, who was responsible for the murder of Portuguese during the War of Independence. The activities of capitães-de-mato were again regulated through the lei provincial no. 236, in 1847, which stipulated that there could not be more than five soldiers under their command and that the latter had to be chosen by justices of the peace.
11. Oficios dos juizes de paz to presidente da província, 1837. Letter of 17/8/1837, Arquivo do Estado do Maranhão, São Luís. (From now on the abbreviation ARQ.MA will be used)
12. Publicador Oficial, São Luís, 27/10/1831, 24, 26.
13. "Carta ao juiz de paz suplente de Guimarães," Publicador Oficial, São Luís, 5/12/1832.
14. Ofícios das câmaras municipais to presidente da província, 1835, ARQ.MA. Letter of 11/7/1835.
15. See, for example, the letter by councillors from Itapecuru-Mirim, desperate at the lack of measures taken by the provincial government. Id., Câmara do Itapecuru-Mirim, letter of 20/11/1835.
16. Lei provincial no. 5.
17. Lei provincial no. 98 from 1840.
18. See the letter from the juízes de paz to the presidente provincial, juízes de paz, ARQ.MA, 17/8/1837.
19. See the complaint from the juízes de paz from Itapecuru-Mirim to the presidente provincial, juízes de paz, 1830, ARQ.MA, letter of 10/10/1830. [Translator's note: Fazenda here also has the meaning of rural neighborhood.]

20. Juízes de paz, 1837, ARQ.MA. Letter of 1/4/1837. Brandão, *A escravatura*, p. 89, writes, for example: "These men [the calhambolas] are not enemies of work, as the whites claim, and in many cases they are employed by fazendeiros (as we know those who do this) on their plantations, [...]."
21. "Carta de José Teodoro de Azevedo Coutinho, de Alcântara a Junta do Governo do Maranhão." Documento no. 19, in Ofícios, requerimentos e representações, existentes na Secretaria do Governo Maranhense, que tratavam das incursões do gentio e mocambo de escravos nas capitanias do Maranhão e Piauí, 1810-1811. This collection comprises a series of 54 documents from the Biblioteca Nacional, Rio de Janeiro (reference: I-4,4,102). From now on reference to this collection will be made using the abbreviation: Mocambo de escravos, 1811.
22. "Carta do bispo Luis de Brito Homem e do intendente da Marinha Felipe de Barros e Vasconcelos, de 10/8/1811." Doc. no. 21, Mocambo de escravos, 1811.
23. "Carta de 10/8/1811." Doc. no. 20, Mocambo de escravos, 1811. In doc. 21, they still recommend: "...carrying out the capture and necessary inquiries, not refraining, if necessary from using force against individuals from that group of slaves in the event of finding evidence of criminal links...."
24. At least this is what the judge in Vila de Alcântara reported. "Carta de Alexandre de Araújo Souza, de 1/19/1811." Doc. no. 24, Mocambo de escravos, 1811.
25. A person of black and indigenous ancestry.
26. "Carta de Leandro José Ribeiro, de 30/8/1811." Doc. no. 25, Mocambo de escravos, 1811.
27. "Carta de João de Carvalho Santo, de 31/8/1811." Doc. no. 26, Mocambo de escravos, 1811.
28. "Carta do comandante da Vila de Alcântara, of 21/9/1811." Doc. no. 39, Mocambo de escravos, 1811.
29. 'There are general and partial quilombos that relate to one another and in times of need provide mutual assistance, [...].' Letter from the justice of the peace in Cururupu, of 18/5/1834," ARQ.MA, cited in "Terras de Preto: quebrando o mito do isolamento. Levantamento preliminar da situação atual das chamadas "Terras de preto" localizadas no estado do Maranhão" (São Luís, Projeto Vida de Negro da Sociedade Maranhense de Defesa dos Direitos Humanos, 1989), 128, ficha no. 21.
30. "Carta do alferes José A. da Costa Ferreira, de 17/9/1811." Doc. no. 41, Mocambo de escravos, 1811.
31. For the details of this episode, see Matthias Röhrig Assunção, *Pflanzer, Sklaven und Kleinbauern in der brasilianischen Provinz Maranhão 1800-1850*

(Frankfurt: Vervuert, 1993), 365 and following. [Translator's note: Balaio means woven basket commonly used by peasants in Maranhão.]

32. "Carta deVicente Camargo a Joaquim José Gonçalves, prefeito da comarca de Itapecuru, de 17/11/1838." Publicador Oficial, São Luís, 1/12/1838, 4467.
33. "Carta de Raymundo Alves da Cruz, subprefeito interino de Codó, a Camargo, de 29/11/1838." Prefeitos de diferentes comarcas ao presidente da província, 1838. ARQ.MA.
34. "Cópia do ofício do subprefeito interino de Codó, Raymundo Alves da Cruz, de 30/11/1838, a Francisco dos Chagas, subprefeito de Caxias." Anexa a uma carta do mesmo ao presidente da província, do 12/12/1838. Prefeitos [...], 1838. ARQ.MA.
35. "Carta de 18/12/1838," reproduced in the Publicador Oficial, São Luís,19/12/1838, 4491.
36. This fact was pointed out by Astolfo Serra, who, however, does not provide further details. See *A Balaiada* (Rio de Janeiro: Bedeschi, 1946), 218-9.
37. See "Discurso que recitou o exmo. snr. Manoel Felisardo de Sousa e Mello [...]," [São Luís] Maranhão: I. J. Ferreira, 1839), 4.
38. "Carta de 11/12/1839." In Correspondência com a Corte do presidente Manoel Felisardo de Sousa e Mello, pacote 1, caixa 741, document from the Seção de Arquivos Particulares, Arquivo Nacional, Rio de Janeiro (from now on AN).
39. "Carta do prefeito de Itapecuru-Mirim, of 18/11/1839." Prefietos ao presidente da província, 1839, ARQ.MA.
40. This fact was even acknowledged by Luís Alves de Lima. See the latter's letter to Francisco de Paula Cavalcante e Albuquerque, of 1/9/1840. Correspondência com vários ministérios, códice 927, vol. 1, carta no. 14, AN, Rio de Janeiro. See also Domingos José Gonçalves de Magalhães, "Memória histórica e documentada da revolução da província do Maranhão desde 1839 até 1840," Revista do Instituto Histórico e Geográfico Brasileiro, 11 (1848), 332-3.
41. This fact is taken from several reports and in particular seems to have inspired the rejection of the quilombola leader by the ruling Catholics. See the legal proceedings relating to Cosme in Maria Januária Vilela Santos, *A balaiada e a insurreição de escravos no Maranhão* (São Paulo: Ática, 1983), particularly 118-9.
42. Apontamentos para a história da revolução da Balaiada na província do Maranhão ([São Luís do] Maranhão: Tip. Teixeira, 1900), vol. 2, 135.
43. "Tutor e Imperador da Liberadade," "Defensor dos Bem-te-vis." The bem-te-vi bird was the symbol of the liberal party in Maranhão and was adopted

by the rebels, who went on to call themselves bem-ti-vis, while balaio was initially a pejorative term used by their legalist opponents.

44. See, for example, the two letters reproduced in Santos, *A Balaiada*, 111. According to Domingo José Gonçalves de Magalhães, secretary to Luís Alves de Lima, who reproduced the aforementionned letter by Caxias almost literally. Cosme also called himself "Guardian and Emperor of Bem-ti-vi freedom." See "Memória histórica," 332.
45. Santos, *A Balaiada*, 87-93.
46. For more details see Matthias Röhrig Assunção, "Popular culture and regional society in 19th century Maranhão," *Bulletin of Latin American Research*, no. 14, 3 (September, 1995), 265-86.
47. "Carta a Francisco de Paula Cavalcanti de Albuquerque, of 1/9/1840." Correspondência do duque de Caxias com vários ministérios, 1840-1, carta 14, vol. 1, cod. 927, AN.
48. Ibid.
49. Luís Alves de Lima wrote: "[...] Raimundo Gomes, desperate, handed himself over to Cosme, with the aim of leading the slaves, and of inciting the fazendas of Codó, and those surrounding Itapecuru, where he could group ten thousand troops in less than eight days." "Carta a Antônio Carlos Ribeiro d'Andrada Machado e Silva, of 22/10/1840," coleção Caxias, c. 808, doc. no. 18, AN. Cosme himself stated in the cross examination that he had tried to raise the troops by order of Raimundo Gomes (clearly an attempt to be judged as a rebel and not as a rebellious slave).
50. In August 1840 rebel freedmen messengers were caught in the district of Alcântara, trying to attract slaves. See the letter from Luís Alves de Lima, of 7/8/1840, coleção Caxias, doc. 9, c. 808, AN. See also Santos, *A Balaiada*, 94.
51. "Carta a Francisco de Paula Cavalcanti de Albuquerque, of 1/9/1840." Correspondência do duque de Caxias, carta 14, vol. 1, cod. 927. AN.
52. "Carta a Francisco de Paula Cavalcanti, of 23/9/1840." Correspondência do duque de Caxias, carta 15, AN.
53. Ibid.
54. "Carta de Luís Alves a Francisco de Paula Cavalcanti de Albuquerque, de 3/12/1840." Correspondência do duque de Caxias, carta no. 18. AN.
55. See Santos, *A Balaiada*, 100-2. See also the court proceedings in the appendices of Santos' book.
56. There is evidence for the practise of gold prospecting for all the large quilombos in the area, such as that of São Benedito do Céu, Limoeiro, and São Sebastião. The only exception appears to be the quilombo of Santa Cruz, which was strictly agricultural. See "Relatório do presidente da província do Maranhão, doutor Eduardo Olímpio Machado, na abertura da

Assambléia Legislativa Provincial, no dia 1 de November 1853" ([São Luís] Maranhão: Imperial e Constitucional, 1853), 7-8.

57. See, for example, the "Interrogatório sobre o envolvimento do major Antônio Fabricio com os escravos mocambeiros do Maracussumé." Documento avulso, ARQ.MA. Also, "Relatório," 1853, 7-8, and Maria Raymunda Araújo, ed., *A invasão do quilombo Limoeiro 1878* (São Luís: Arquivo Público do Estado do Maranhão, 1992), particularly 59-64.
58. "Livro grosso do Maranhão," Anais da Biblioteca Nacional, 66 (1948), 212-3.
59. "Carta do comandante de Guimarães, de 13/10/1828." Ofícios de comandantes gerais de várias vilas ao presidente da província," 1838. ARQ.MA.
60. "Carta de Raimundo Felipe Lobato, vice-presidente, ao presidente de Pará, de 21/5/1834." Publicador Oficial (São Luís), 28/5/1834, 1091.
61. See the two letters from the juízes de paz de Turiaçu ao vice-presidente de Maranhão, de 9/6 e de 15/10/1834. In "Terras de Preto," fichas no. 19 and 27, 128, 130.
62. "Carta de 20/10/1834." Correspondência com o Ministério da Justiça. IJ1 745, AN. This letter mentions 21 captured mocambeiros.
63. For further details see "Report by the provincial president, 1853," pp. 7-8, and David Cleary, *Garimpagem na Amazônia: uma abordagem antropológica*, Rio de Janeiro, Gráfica da UFRJ, 1992, 30-5.
64. See Cleary, *Garimpagem*, 35.
65. Ibid., 35-7.
66. All the information regarding this episode comes from the detailed study carried out by Mundinha Araújo, *Insurreição de escravos em Viana, 1867* (São Luís: Sioge, 1994).
67. Araújo, *Insurreição* , 23.
68. Ibid., 25.
69. The testimonies differ considerably regarding the number of maroons who actually took part in the attack. The criminal proceedings against the slave Martiniano only mention two hundred (Ibid., 203) while others talk of four or five hundred (Ibid., p. 39) or even more.
70. Ibid., 33-4.
71. Ibid., 174 and 175.
72. Ibid,, 158.
73. Ibid., 170.
74. Ibid., 171.
75. Ibid., 154.
76. Ibid., 159. My emphasis. Furthermore, this administrator was held responsible for the inquiry into the mocambo (161).

77. Ibid., 156.
78. Ibid., 99, 110, 120.
79. Ibid., 82-3.
80. Ibid., see the documents reproduced on 85, 90.
81. Ibid., 93-4.
82. Ibid., 132-41.
83. For further details regarding this matter, see Alfredo Wagner de Almeida, *A ideologia da decadência. Leitura antropológica a uma história da agricultura no Maranhão* (São Luís: Ipes, 1983), 165-72.
84. Wagner, Ideologia, 183-7.
85. With regard to this matter see the indignation of Brandão, an abolitionist and son of fazendeiros in Codó, *A escravatura no Brasil*, 86-7.
86. The reports of these expeditions are 1) "Relatório apresentado ao comendador doutor Francisco Maria Correia de Sá e Benevides, presidente da província do Maranhão, pelo major Honorato Cândido Ferreira Caldas, em 13 de janeiro de 1877, dando conta dos resultados conseguidos pela expedição destinada a destruir o quilombo de Turi." Documentos avulsos, ARQ. MA. This report was published by the Diário do Maranhão, São Luís, on the 14, 16, 17 and 18/1/1877, with a brief introduction praising the major's action and deploring the destruction of the quilombo's fields. 2) "Relatório de João Manuel da Cunha sobre a primeira invasão do quilombo Limoeiro, 24 January 1878"; and 3) "Relatório do capitão Feliciano Xavier Freire Júnior sobre a primeira invasão do quilombo Limoeiro," both reproduced in Maria Raymunda Araújo, ed., *A invasão do quilombo Limoeiro*.
87. "Relatório do major Caldas," fl. 4 v.
88. Ibid., fl. 6-6 v.
89. According to Mundinha Araújo who is developing further research on this matter, many quilombolas died soon after going to prison, due to the dire conditions prevailing there. The others ended up being returned to their masters, including the children. Daniel apparently was granted freedom but was taken to court for insurrection and murder. He died in the capital's jail in 1884, where he was serving a life sentence with labour.
90. "Carta de 31/3/1877"; *A invasão do quilombo Limoeiro*, 13.
91. Ibid., 20.
92. Ibid., 25
93. Ibid., 55. Grifos do pesquisador.
94. One braça equals 2.2 metres.
95. "Relatório do major Caldas," fl. 10 v. - 11. See also Diário do Maranhão, 16/1/1877.
96. A invasão do quilombo Limoeiro, 28.

Assambléia Legislativa Provincial, no dia 1 de November 1853" ([São Luís] Maranhão: Imperial e Constitucional, 1853), 7-8.

57. See, for example, the "Interrogatório sobre o envolvimento do major Antônio Fabricio com os escravos mocambeiros do Maracussumé." Documento avulso, ARQ.MA. Also, "Relatório," 1853, 7-8, and Maria Raymunda Araújo, ed., *A invasão do quilombo Limoeiro 1878* (São Luís: Arquivo Público do Estado do Maranhão, 1992), particularly 59-64.
58. "Livro grosso do Maranhão," Anais da Biblioteca Nacional, 66 (1948), 212-3.
59. "Carta do comandante de Guimarães, de 13/10/1828." Ofícios de comandantes gerais de várias vilas ao presidente da província," 1838. ARQ.MA.
60. "Carta de Raimundo Felipe Lobato, vice-presidente, ao presidente de Pará, de 21/5/1834." Publicador Oficial (São Luís), 28/5/1834, 1091.
61. See the two letters from the juízes de paz de Turiaçu ao vice-presidente de Maranhão, de 9/6 e de 15/10/1834. In "Terras de Preto," fichas no. 19 and 27, 128, 130.
62. "Carta de 20/10/1834." Correspondência com o Ministério da Justiça. IJ1 745, AN. This letter mentions 21 captured mocambeiros.
63. For further details see "Report by the provincial president, 1853," pp. 7-8, and David Cleary, *Garimpagem na Amazônia: uma abordagem antropológica*, Rio de Janeiro, Gráfica da UFRJ, 1992, 30-5.
64. See Cleary, *Garimpagem*, 35.
65. Ibid., 35-7.
66. All the information regarding this episode comes from the detailed study carried out by Mundinha Araújo, *Insurreição de escravos em Viana, 1867* (São Luís: Sioge, 1994).
67. Araújo, *Insurreição* , 23.
68. Ibid., 25.
69. The testimonies differ considerably regarding the number of maroons who actually took part in the attack. The criminal proceedings against the slave Martiniano only mention two hundred (Ibid., 203) while others talk of four or five hundred (Ibid., p. 39) or even more.
70. Ibid., 33-4.
71. Ibid., 174 and 175.
72. Ibid,, 158.
73. Ibid., 170.
74. Ibid., 171.
75. Ibid., 154.
76. Ibid., 159. My emphasis. Furthermore, this administrator was held responsible for the inquiry into the mocambo (161).

77. Ibid., 156.
78. Ibid., 99, 110, 120.
79. Ibid., 82-3.
80. Ibid., see the documents reproduced on 85, 90.
81. Ibid., 93-4.
82. Ibid., 132-41.
83. For further details regarding this matter, see Alfredo Wagner de Almeida, *A ideologia da decadência. Leitura antropológica a uma história da agricultura no Maranhão* (São Luís: Ipes, 1983), 165-72.
84. Wagner, Ideologia, 183-7.
85. With regard to this matter see the indignation of Brandão, an abolitionist and son of fazendeiros in Codó, *A escravatura no Brasil*, 86-7.
86. The reports of these expeditions are 1) "Relatório apresentado ao comendador doutor Francisco Maria Correia de Sá e Benevides, presidente da província do Maranhão, pelo major Honorato Cândido Ferreira Caldas, em 13 de janeiro de 1877, dando conta dos resultados conseguidos pela expedição destinada a destruir o quilombo de Turi." Documentos avulsos, ARQ. MA. This report was published by the Diário do Maranhão, São Luís, on the 14, 16, 17 and 18/1/1877, with a brief introduction praising the major's action and deploring the destruction of the quilombo's fields. 2) "Relatório de João Manuel da Cunha sobre a primeira invasão do quilombo Limoeiro, 24 January 1878"; and 3) "Relatório do capitão Feliciano Xavier Freire Júnior sobre a primeira invasão do quilombo Limoeiro," both reproduced in Maria Raymunda Araújo, ed., *A invasão do quilombo Limoeiro*.
87. "Relatório do major Caldas," fl. 4 v.
88. Ibid., fl. 6-6 v.
89. According to Mundinha Araújo who is developing further research on this matter, many quilombolas died soon after going to prison, due to the dire conditions prevailing there. The others ended up being returned to their masters, including the children. Daniel apparently was granted freedom but was taken to court for insurrection and murder. He died in the capital's jail in 1884, where he was serving a life sentence with labour.
90. "Carta de 31/3/1877"; *A invasão do quilombo Limoeiro*, 13.
91. Ibid., 20.
92. Ibid., 25
93. Ibid., 55. Grifos do pesquisador.
94. One braça equals 2.2 metres.
95. "Relatório do major Caldas," fl. 10 v. - 11. See also Diário do Maranhão, 16/1/1877.
96. A invasão do quilombo Limoeiro, 28.

97. "Relatório do major Caldas," fl. 14.
98. Ibid., fl. 14 v.
99. Ibid., fl. 6 v. (my emphasis).
100. Later on the opposition of the vast majority of quilombos to giving themselves in again becomes clear: "Two of them answered that they would do whatever he [Daniel] wanted and the others remained silent" (Ibid, fl. 7 v.).
101. *A invasão do quilombo Limoeiro*, 15.
102. This is according to the statement made by a maroon taken prisoner later on (*A invasão do quilombo Limoeiro*, 52).
103. *A invasão do quilombo Limoeiro*, 17.
104. Cited in Cleary, *Garimpagem*, 41-2.
105. See "Terras de preto; quebrando o mito do isolamento. Levantamento preliminar da situação atual das chamadas Terras de Preto localizadas no estado do Maranhão" (São Luís: Projeto Vida de Negro da Sociedade Maranhense de Defesa dos Direitos Humanos, 1989), 122-39, mimeo.
106. See Brandão, *A escravatura*, 78; Nunes Pereira, *A casa das Minas. Cultos dos voduns jeje no Maranhão*, 2nd ed. (Petrópolis: Vozes, 1979), 54; "Letter from José Feliciano B. de Mendonça to the provincial president Costa Pinto of 31/10/1831." Letters from the Capitães Mores de Ordenança, 1828 (sic), ARQ. MA.
107. *A invasão do quilombo Limoeiro*, 38.
108. However, slave society tended to attribute a leadership role automatically to any free man living among runaway slaves, as happened in his case. In fact, it seems that he had been in the quilombo for only two months before the invasion of the fazendas in 1867.

17

1. *Mocambo* is a community formed by slaves who ran away from their masters. Also called a *quilombo*.
2. A deeper discussion about the questions raised here constituted a significant part of my doctorate's thesis, in process of writing with the History Department of USP.
3. Public file from Pará State (APEP)—police staff—series of question files, 1876. Question files made to fourteen *quilombolas* of Curuá. Inbox documents. The references used here cannot check with the actual ones from the APEP, because at the moment all the documents from the twentieth century had not been organized yet, being found only in boxes and packages, just with indications of dates and organ which they belonged to and, in some cases, the series.

4. About Pacoval there are two monographic papers; Aldrim M. Figueiredo, *O negro na fala do branco: o discurso de madame Codreau sobre os mocambeiros do rio Curuá* (Belém: UFPA, mimeographed, 1989); Ligya Conceição L. Teixeira. *O negro no folclore paraense* (Belém: Secult/FCPTN, 1989).
5. See Carlos M. Guimarães, *A negação da ordem escravista—quilombos em Minas Gerais no século XVIII* (São Paulo: Ícone, 1988); Stuart Schwartz, "Mocambos, quilombos e Palmares: a resistência escrava no Brasil colonial," Estudos Econômicos, 17 (1987), 61-88, One of the most recent papers about quilombos, and that is out of this kind of approach, it is of Flávio dos Santos Gomes, *História de quilombolas: mocambos e comunidades de senzalas no Rio de Janeiro—século XIX*. (Campinas, Master's dissertation, 1992).
6. E. P. Thompsom quoted by Jim Sharpe, "A história vista de baixo," in *A escrita da história,* ed., Peter Burke (São Paulo: Ed. Unesp, 1992), 60.
7. Oral sources: memory, life stories, chants, legends, "tales." Written sources: registered documentation, parochial, official acts, statements of travelers and newspapers.
8. Jan Vansina quoted by Gwyn Prins, "História oral," in *A escrita da história*, 166.
9. Maria Célia Paoli, "Memória, história e cidadania: o direito ao passado," in Cultural Secretary of the municipality/Historical heritage department, *O direito a memória—patrimônio histórico e cidadania* (São Paulo: DPH, 1991), 27.
10. Interviews have been carried out with remainders of quilombolas from black communities of the rivers Curuá, Trombetas, Erepecuru, in the period from 1990 to 1994, in a total of 35 interviewers. I had the collaborations of Aldrim Figueiredo, who passed to me an interview done with Mrs. Dica, in 1988, and Idaliana Marinho, interview carried out with Donga, Santa Rita e Dico, in 1988.
11. For more information about slavery in Pará, see the excellent work of Vicente Salles, *O negro no Pará* (Rio de Janeiro/Belém: FGV/UFPA, 1971).
12. It had been researched in the documents: registers from seventeenth and nineteenth centuries, in the register offices of Santarém, from the nineteenth century in the register offices of Alenquer, Curuá and Óbidos; parochial around Alenquer, Óbidos and jurisdiction of Santarém.
13. Robert Slenes, "Na senzala uma flor: a esperança e as recordações na formação da família escrava" (Campinhas: preliminary version, copies, 1989), 7.
14. Newspaper *Baixo Amazonas*, 26/2/1881. This newspaper was published in Santarém. Many of its news were transcribed by Mr. João dos Santos and kept in his privet file.

15. Ibid., 16/2/1876.
16. Ibid., 10/10/1874.
17. About the relationship owner and slave, see, among others, Eugene D. Genovese, *A terra prometida: o mundo que os escravos criaram* (Rio de Janeiro: Paz e Terra, 1988); João J. Reis and Eduardo Silva, *Negociação e conflito: a resistência negra no Brasil escravista* (São Paulo: Companhia das Letras, 1989); Sidney Chalhoub, *Visões da liberdade: uma história das últimas décadas da escravidão na corte* (São Paulo: Companhia das Letras, 1990); Silvia H. Lara, *Campos da violência: escravos e senhores na capitania do Rio de Janeiro 1750-1808* (Rio de Janeiro: Paz e Terra, 1988); Maria Helena P. T. Machado, *Crime e escravidão* (São Paulo: Brasiliense, 1987).
18. Reis and Silva, Ibid., 21.
19. Register office of the 1 office of Santarém, "Autos de interrogação aos escravos dos falecidos Joaquim Jose Arrelias e José Policarpio Gonçalves," 12/7/1842.
20. Interview with Raimundo Vieira dos Santos (Dico), published in *Folha do Norte* on 3/1/1981.
21. APEP, Police Secretary of Pará Province, offices series "Carta de José Joaquim Pereira Macambira ao chefe de polícia," 17/12/1870. The sender was Maria Margarida P. Macambira's son.
22. Interview with Donga, July 1993.
23. Interview of Santa Rita, February of 1992.
24. Newspaper *Baixo Amazonas*, 8/1/1876.
25. APEP, correspondences of many with the government, 1804-1846. "Auto de interrogatório do escravo Luiz, pertencente a João Inácio Rabello," 6/2/1811.
26. Interview of Donga, July 1993.
27. "In the city Trombetas, northeast of Manaus, the slave leader cafuz (Anastácio) created in 1820, the quilombo of Pará." Herbert S. Klein, *A escravidão africana: América Latina e Caribe* (São Paulo: Brasiliense, 1981), 220-1. Other mistakes: 1—the river Trombetas is in Pará state; 2—in it there was not only one quilombo, but tens of it, spread along the regions of the low Amazonas, low Tocantins, of Salgado, Marajó and Amapá.
28. Interview of Donga, July 1993.
29. Secondary vegetation in a clearing, brushwood, or a defensive ditch.
30. Interview of Dico, January 1981.
31. Rosa Acevedo and Edna de Castro, *Negros do Trombetas guardiães de matas e rios* (Belém: UFPA, 1993), 30, 31. These authors let us understand that there was only one way of safe escape to the slaves to the low Amazonas; it was by Alenquer and Curuá rivers. The documents have shown that, either

32. Intervies of Dica, February 1993.
33. Gastão Cruls, *A Amazônia que eu vi* (Óbidos-Tumucumaque, Rio de Janeiro: Typographia do Annuario do Brasil, 1930), 61.
34. Father Nicolino José R. de Sousa., *Diário das tres viagens ao Cuminá, 1877, 1878, 1882* (Rio de Janeiro: Imprensa Nacional, 1946).
35. João Maximiniano de Sousa, "Uma viagem ao rio Trombetas" in newspaper *Baixo Amazonas*, of 25/10/1875. The author commanded an expedition to the mocambos of this river in 1855.
36. APEP, Found Secretary of the province presidence, series of several offices 1860-1869, box 242, "Office of friar Carmello Mazzarino to the president of the province," 15/1/1868.
37. Ottile Codreau, *Voyage au Rio Curuá* (Paris: A. Lahure Imprimeiur Editeures, 1903), 18.
38. Ottile Codreau, *Voyage au Rio Curuá* (Paris: A. Lahure Imprimeiur Editeures, 1901), 22. Barracão das Pedras is a kind of grout, that is located on the edge of the Erepecuru river, right below the first rapid, place where the quilombolas got together to rest, in their trips, and make parties.
39. Newspaper *Baixo Amazonas*, 15/1/1876.
40. APEP, Code 782. Correspondence of the military commanders of Santarém with several. "Ofício de Manoel Joaquim Bentes," 14/2/1813.
41. *Jornal do Pará*, 21/09/1876.
42. APEP, Secretary of Justice, "Ofício do delegado de polícia de Óbidos a Secretaria de Justiça Pública da Província," 15/1/1854.
43. João Barbosa Rodrigues, *Exploração e estudo do valle do Amazonas* (Rio de Janeiro: Typografia Nacional, 1875), 28.
44. APEP, code 782, "Ofício of Manuel J. Bentes," 14/2/1813.
45. Rodrigues, *Exploração do valle do Amazonas*, 24 and 25.
46. A. C. Tavares Bastos, *O valle do Amazonas* (São Paulo: Nacional col. Brasiliana, vol. 106, 1966), 201.
47. Barbosa Rodrigues, *Exploração e estudo do valle do Amazonas*, 26.
48. Interview of Santa Rita, February 1992.
49. Interview of Rafael Printz Viana, July 1991.
50. Sousa, "Uma viagem ao rio Trombetas" (1875).
51. Interview with Donga, July 1993.
52. Guimarães, *A negação da ordem escravista*, p. 43, and Schwartz, "Mocambos, quilombos e Palmares," 67.
53. Aviator merchandising—a system of trading that implies a direct exchange of products. The "aviator" (merchant) supplies to the supplier goods and in-

struments of labor; in exchange he receives agricultural produce from the "agent."

54. Rodrigues, *Exploração e estudo do valle do Amazonas*, 27.
55. José Alípio Goulart, *O regatão—mascate fluvial do Amazonas* (Rio de Janeiro: Conquista, 1968).
56. Here I followed denominations used by Protásio Frikel in his papers about the native nations of that region: *Dez anos de aculturação Tiriyó—mudanças e problemas*, 1960-1970, Belém, Paraense Museum Emilio Goeldi (MPEG), separate publication, n.16, 1971; "Os últimos Káhyana," *Revista do Instituto de Estudos Brasileiros*, n. 1, 1966; *Os Kaxúana—notas etno-históricas*, Belém, MPEG, separated publications n. 14, 1970; Protásio Frikel and Roberto Cortez, Elementos demográficos do alto Parú de Oeste, Tumucumaque Brasileiro—Índios Ewarhoyána, Kaxúyana e Tiriyó (Belém: MPEG, separated publishing, n.19, 1972).
57. Frikel, "Tradições histórico-lendárias dos Kachuyana and Kahyana," In *Revista do Museu Paulista*, vol. IX, (1955), 229.
58. This is a myth that origins from the firsts Kaxúyana, who survived after Purá and Murá, "two cultural heroes" from this tribe killed Marmaru-imó, the big snake, who lived in the bottom of the river. See Frinkel, *Os Kaxúana—notas etno-históricas*, 9-20.
59. Dica's Interview, February 1992.
60. APEP, Fund of the Secretary if the Province Presidence, series of several offices, "Ofício do frei Carmelo Mazarino," 1868.
61. Frinkel, *Dez anos de aculturação Tiriyó*, 10.
62. APEP, fund of the Secretary of Justice, ""Ofício do delegado de polícia de Óbidos, enviado ao chefe de polícia da província," 9/2/1858.
63. W. G. Palgrave, *Dutch Guiana* (London: Macmillan and Co, 1875), 162-163. About the saramaka communities of quilombolas of Suriname, see Richard Price, *First-time historical vision of an Afro American people* (Baltimore: The Johns Hopkins University Press, 1983).
64. APEP, fund Secretary of the Province President, several offices: "Ofício do frei Camelo de Mazzarino," 1868.
65. Barbosa Rodrigues, *Exploração e estudo do valle do Amazonas*, 25.
66. Register Office of the 2 office of Santarém. "Autos cíveis de arrecadação do escravo Basílio Antônio," 10/9/1867.
67. APEP, Fund of correspondence of several people with the province government, 1809-1819. "Ofício da Câmara de Alenquer," 29/4/1811.
68. Ibid.
69. APEP, Code 782, "Ofício do comandante militar de Santarém, Manoel da Costa Vidal," 25/2/1813.

70. Ibid.
71. Ibid., "Ofício do comandante da expedição Manoel Joaquim Bentes," 14/2/1813.
72. Ibid., "Ofício de Manoel da Costa Vidal," 25/2/1813.
73. Ibid., my emphasis.
74. Speech of Jerônimo Francisco Coelho, president of the Gram Pará province to the Provincial Legislative Assembly, on the opening of the 2nd ordinary session of the 6th legislature, 1/10/1849.
75. Register office of the 2 office of Santarém. "Autos cíveis de libello e justificação de domínio," 21/11/1877. José Joaquim was a witness of the author against the accused Maria Olimpia and her brothers. They were children of the mocambeira Margarida, dead in mocambo of Curuá.
76. Register Office of 2 office of Alenquer. "Inventário de Luiz de Oliveira Martins," 8/2/1888. On the list of debtors names of several people who lives in Pacoval appeared, among them some of the mocambeiros who were taken to Belém in 1876.
77. National file—IJ. 1—214—Office of the province president of Pará to the Justice Ministery. 28/3/1876.
78. APEP, police staff, series of acts of questions, 1876. "Auto de perguntas feito a Manuel da Cruz," 28/3/1876.
79. AN. Office of 24/10/1876.
80. Newspaper *Província do Pará*, 31/5/1876
81. I must highlight that this interview with Mirs. Dica has been carried out before the beginning of the research in Belém's files. She talked about the "getaway of the Rossá" and in that moment I wondered what this meant. Researching in the newspapers of Belém, of 1876, I got the answer when I found out that the mocambeiros of Curuá were given as deposits to Frederico Rhossard, the Rossá one. The oral sources, as Vansina says, cannot substitute the written ones, and the other way round: they complete each other.
82. Newspaper *Diário de Belém*, 25/3/1877.
83. Ibid., 6/4/1877.
84. Newspaper *Província do Pará*, 28/3/1877.
85. Newspaper *Província de Belém*, 28/3/1877.
86. APEP, Found Plice Secretary of the Province, Acts Series. "Autos crimes de inquéritos," 24/9/1877.
87. Pará Government, Law n. 751 of 25/2/1901
88. Codreau, *Voyage au Rio Curuá*, 17.
89. Keith Thomas, *O homem e o mundo natural* (São Paulo, Companhia das Letras, 1989), 163.

90. Rodrigues, *Exploração e estudo do valle do Amazonas*, 20, my emphasis.

18

1. For more information on this quilombo, see Stuart Schwartz, "Mocambos, quilombos e Palmares: a resistência escrava no Brasil colonial," *Estudos Econômicos*, 17 (1987), 71-6, in which this blueprint is also published, on this subject see also, Flávio dos Santos Gomes, "Um recôncavo, dois sertões e vários mocambos: quilombolas na capitania da Bahia, 1808-1824," *Cadernos de História Social*, 2 (1996).
2. On these blueprints of Minas Gerais, see Flávio dos Santos Gomes, "Seguindo o mapa das minas: plantas e quilombos mineiros setecentistas," *Estudos Afro-Asiáticos*, 29 (1996), 113-42.
3. There is an imaginary representation from the 1700s of Palmares originally published in the famous work by Barléus, which is reproduced in this volume.
4. See for instance, Luís dos Santos Vilhena, *A Bahia do século XVIII* (Salvador: Itapuã, 1969), vol. 1, *passim*.
5. Schwartz, "Mocambos," 72-6, has made an ethnographic analysis of this blueprint based on other manuscripts on the repression to *quilombos*.
6. [In the Portuguese original version of this text, Reis uses the term *fojos* for ditches. He explains it as follows:] According to the Moraes's dictionary, *fojo* is "A deep hole that has its opening camouflaged with foliage or subtle trellis and a layer of earth spread in a manner that it would come down with the weight of an animal that crossed it: it is used to trap wolves, and other beasts or prey." The Caldas Aulete's dictionary gives the military definition of the term that seems more appropriate: "Deep and narrow hole that goes down, full of pointy stakes disguised by foliage, reed, earth, etc., meant to capture the enemy."

www.ingramcontent.com/pod-product-compliance
Lightning Source LLC
Chambersburg PA
CBHW071723080526
44588CB00013B/1879